STUDIES IN EVANGELICAL HISTORY AND THOUGHT

Spirituality in Adversity

English Nonconformity in a Period of Repression, 1660–1689

STUDIES IN EVANGELICAL HISTORY AND THOUGHT

Series Editors

David Bebbington, Professor of History, University of Stirling, Stirling, Scotland, UK

John H.Y. Briggs, Senior Research Fellow in Ecclesiastical History and Director of the Centre for Baptist History and Heritage, Regent's Park College, Oxford, UK

Timothy Larsen, McManis Professor Christian Thought, Wheaton College, Illinois, USA

Mark A. Noll, McAnaney Professor of History, University of Notre Dame, Notre Dame, Indiana, USA

Ian M. Randall, Director of Research, Spurgeon's College, London, UK, and Senior Research Fellow, International Baptist Theological Seminary, Prague, Czech Republic
Series Consultants

A full listing of titles in this series appears at the end of this book

STUDIES IN EVANGELICAL HISTORY AND THOUGHT

Spirituality in Adversity

English Nonconformity in a Period of Repression, 1660–1689

Raymond Brown

Copyright © Raymond Brown 2012

First published 2012 by Paternoster

Paternoster is an imprint of Authentic Media
52 Presley Way, Crownhill, Milton Keynes, Bucks, MK8 0ES

www.authenticmedia.co.uk
Authentic Media is a division of Koorong UK, a company limited by guarantee

09 08 07 06 05 04 03   8 7 6 5 4 3 2 1

The right of Raymond Brown to be identified as the Author of this Work
has been asserted by him in accordance with the Copyright, Designs
and Patents Act 1988.

All rights reserved. No part of this publication may be reproduced, stored in a retrieval system, or transmitted, in any form or by any means, electronic, mechanical, photocopying, recording or otherwise, without the prior permission of the publisher or a license permitting restricted copying. In the UK such licenses are issued by the Copyright Licensing Agency, 90 Tottenham Court Road, London W1P 9HE.

British Library Cataloguing in Publication Data
A catalogue record for this book is available from the British Library

ISBN 978–1–84227–7850

Typeset by Tim Grass
Printed and bound in Great Britain
for Paternoster
by Lightning Source, Milton Keynes, UK

Series Preface

The Evangelical movement has been marked by its union of four emphases: on the Bible, on the cross of Christ, on conversion as the entry to the Christian life and on the responsibility of the believer to be active. The present series is designed to publish scholarly studies of any aspect of this movement in Britain or overseas. Its volumes include social analysis as well as exploration of Evangelical ideas. The books in the series consider aspects of the movement shaped by the Evangelical Revival of the eighteenth century, when the impetus to mission began to turn the popular Protestantism of the British Isles and North America into a global phenomenon. The series aims to reap some of the rich harvest of academic research about those who, over the centuries, have believed that they had a gospel to tell to the nations.

In piam memoriam
Geoffrey Fillingham Nuttall
(1911–2007)

Contents

Preface
Abbreviations

Part I: Encountering Adversity

Chapter 1 This Great Eclipse	3
A Precarious Future	3
'As if ... naturally dead'	6
A 'Seditious' People	10
But why?	13
Undeterred	17
Brief Respite	26
Renewed Oppression	29
Changing Times	36

Part II: Responding to Adversity

Chapter 2 When Grace Grows Best	47
'I see grace groweth best in winter'	47
The Mystery of Suffering	48
The Inevitability of Suffering	49
The Value of Suffering	53
Suffering as a Penal Visitation	53
Suffering as an Authenticating Experience	56
Suffering as a Corrective Exercise	60
Suffering as a Didactic Process	61
The Lessons of Suffering	62
Visible Lectures	62

Frost in Winter	63
Like the Plough	64
Pruning Superfluous Sprigs	65
What matters most	65
Would you change places?	67
It proved well	67
Still learning	67
The Privilege of Suffering	68
The Benefits of Suffering	71
Not building on Quicksand	72
Even without Candles	72
Better than Silk and Velvet	73
Money lodged ahead	74
'great lumpish Shoes'	76
Never more endeared	78
What Neighbours see	79
So much Mercy	80
The 'perfect work'	81
Truth did not change	85
No rusty Armour	86
'like children's tops'	87
Swift in their Run	88
'even venture all'	88

Part III: Resources in Adversity

Chapter 3 Dependent on God — 93

Confidence in God	94
Acknowledging God's Sovereignty	95
Proving God's Faithfulness	98
Trusting God's Providence	101
Enjoying God's Presence	105
Appropriating God's Power	107
Affirming God's Holiness	109
Witnessing God's Justice	110
Exalting God's Love	113
Communion with God	115
Confessing Human Need	115

Receiving Divine Resources	122
CONVICTIONS	122
MENTORS	124
PRIORITIES	126
'Open ye doore to God in ye morneinge'	126
More than lip-labour	129
Want of Mercy	132
Some Occasion ... for Gratitude	132
Not hedgehogs	133
Dialogues between us and him	134
DIFFICULTIES	135
Their Bewilderment	136
Their Frustration	138
Their Disappointment	142
Chapter 4 Identified with Christ	**145**
Looking to Christ	146
Convinced of his Love	146
Submissive to his Authority	148
Inspired by his Example	157
Sustained by his Prayers	163
Living for Christ	168
An Incomparable Relationship	169
A Privileged Obligation	172
BEARING THE REPROACH OF CHRIST	172
CARRYING THE CROSS OF CHRIST	174
FOLLOWING THE EXAMPLE OF CHRIST	179
SHARING THE SUFFERINGS OF CHRIST	182
Chapter 5 Equipped by the Spirit	**190**
The Holy Spirit in the Incomparable Word	191
Memorization	193
Illumination	194
Meditation	201
AN APPOINTED TIME	206
AN APPROPRIATE PLACE	208
A PREPARED MIND	208
THE WIDER CANVAS	209
The Holy Spirit and the Dependent Believer	215

Importance	219
Benefits	220
Availability	221
Evidence	222

Part IV: Partnership in Adversity

Chapter 6 Adoring God	**227**
Corporate Worship	228
Sacramental Observance: 'Visible Signs'	231
Baptism	233
INFANT BAPTISM	234
Its Covenant Foundation	234
Its Ecclesiological Significance	236
Its Pastoral Context	238
Its Continuing Efficacy	239
BELIEVERS' BAPTISM	243
An Exemplary Model	244
An Authenticating Seal	246
A Distinguishing Badge	249
A Privileged Token	250
The Lord's Supper	252
ITS UNIFYING VALUE	254
ITS ETHICAL IMPORTANCE	255
ITS CONFIRMATORY NATURE	257
ITS STRENGTHENING POTENTIAL	259
ITS ESCHATOLOGICAL DECLARATION	262
Family Devotion	262
Chapter 7 Sharing Truth	**270**
Teaching by Catechism	270
Learning by Repetition	274
Chapter 8 Maintaining Integrity	**283**
Neglect	283
Priorities	286
Biblical Authority	286
Social Responsibility	287

Spiritual Ideals	289
Practice	291
Offences	292
Cost	297
Restoration	298
Chapter 9 Serving Others	301
Contributors	303
Educators	305
Messengers	312
Preaching	312
Testimony	317
Literature	319
Letters	321
Carers	323
Postscript	**334**
Select Bibliography	**339**
General Index	**362**

PREFACE

Persecution on an unprecedented scale is a disturbing feature of twenty-first century world Christianity. Over 250 million contemporary Christians experience some form of repression. In at least twelve countries it is dangerous to be a believer and in many others Christian activity is viewed with deep suspicion, scrupulously monitored and vigorously restricted. Oppressive regimes have robbed loyal and patriotic people of basic human rights. In this modern global scenario it must surely be relevant for Christians to consider how persecuted believers in earlier times not only developed imaginative survival mechanisms but turned fierce adversity to enriching gain.

Countless twenty-first century Christians experience more ferocious opposition than the people we shall meet in these pages. But whether modern suffering takes the form of political repression, social ostracism, economic deprivation, physical abuse, imprisonment or execution, it must surely be important to discern how other believers coped with similar pressures and hazards when the onslaught was particularly fierce.

The Christians whose story is traced in these chapters were deeply persuaded about their distinctive beliefs and, sadly, not all of them related well to those who thought differently. But the age was not the same as ours, and their greatly valued truths had been dearly bought. It was not a time to surrender lightly convictions that had been treasured in their families for decades. Our more relaxed approach to (in our view) *marginal* differences can make us hastily judgemental about the seemingly intractable stance of earlier generations. But their circumstances were different and they are not to be judged by vacillating twenty-first century norms. For the sympathetic reader, these seventeenth-century people are not distant ancestors we have left behind in an irrelevant past, but valued partners who have gone ahead and continue to speak.

We begin by recalling the political and ecclesiastical scene in England in 1660, with an uncrowned king returning from exile. An attempt at an acceptable religious settlement achieved little, and ushered in almost thirty years of repression. It was feared that without firm control the country might slide once more into fatal disruption. Religion was widely viewed as the social cohesive which held the nation together and those who would not conform to enforced patterns of liturgical worship were regarded not only as dangerously schismatic, deliberately tearing the fabric of the national Church, but also, however unjustly, as potential insurrectionists and likely disturbers of the country's peace.

The book goes on to show how Protestant 'Dissenters' or 'Nonconformists' (the terms are used interchangeably) responded to the hostile legislation. The oppression, neither consistently enforced nor uniform in its application or intensity, was frequently controlled by highly variable local circumstances. Avaricious informers in one locality might be contrasted with tolerant constables and benign magistrates elsewhere. But, wherever the location, Dissenters were under suspicion, huge numbers suffered from exorbitant fines (or the 'distraint' of their essential goods in lieu of payment), arrest and imprisonment; others suffered transportation. Few Nonconformist households escaped hardship in one form or another. All were under threat of persecution, even in contexts where the legislation was not implemented. It was still illegal to welcome more than five visitors to family worship, even if the household was undisturbed. Most Nonconformists knew of harassment in other communities. The continuing threat was intimidating, and clouded the life of many a Dissenter.

The second main section explores how the brutal challenge of repression helped them to define, express and apply their theology of suffering. We are not interpreting their *distinctive* contribution to the themes of suffering and spirituality. They were grateful debtors as well as imaginative contributors, and derived help from a variety of published works, especially the considerable advice-literature of their immediate Puritan forefathers. These earlier writers were not detached theorists; many had also experienced political and ecclesiastical opposition in their own time. Moreover, for many Nonconformists, suffering had been a bitter experience in the lives of their parents and grandparents. They were sustained by truths and stories learnt from childhood, as well as books written by their contemporaries; by a message that encouraged their survival, enabling them to make creative use of potentially destructive experiences.

Succeeding chapters explore the Trinitarian resources which supported them, turning finally from a largely personal spirituality to the corporate values they shared and experienced. We examine the help they received from their fellow-Christians, inspiring their worship, teaching, discipline and service.

In interpreting the Dissenters' experience I have endeavoured, wherever possible, to note the rich contribution of people other than ministers and preachers. The pulpit naturally played a huge part in the story, but ordinary members of these congregations also had good things to share, and often committed their experience to writing. Their letters, journals, commonplace books and diaries are an immensely valuable resource, as are corporately owned Church Books, which preserved the records of local congregations and were sometimes kept by lay members. All these, as well as voluminous devotional books and printed sermons, and the more formal theological publications of the period, provide the primary source materials for a study of this kind.

In quoting from these sources I have not modernized their wayward spelling, punctuation or occasionally bizarre capitalization, preferring to reproduce what they wrote exactly as it is preserved, including their repeated use of *then* instead of *than*.

In pursuing a project of this kind, one becomes increasingly indebted to others. The help I have received from gifted scholars will be partly evident from my footnotes and bibliography, but I wish also to acknowledge all that I owe to one of the most distinguished among them who is no longer with us, Geoffrey F. Nuttall. His enriching friendship over many years and his vast knowledge of church history, always generously shared, was of immense help to me both as a teacher and writer.

I am additionally indebted to Dr David Wykes, the Director, and the staff of Dr Williams's Library, London. I am grateful for the services of the Bodleian Library, Oxford; the British Library, Congregational Library, Evangelical Library and Society of Friends' Library, London; and, most especially, the patient staff of Cambridge University Library's Rare Books Room. At different times, a writer with limited word-processing ability has greatly appreciated the skills of Peter Jamieson, Geoff Barnard, John Whitmore and, not least, my son David. I have especially appreciated the editorial gifts of Dr Tim Grass. Authors gladly acknowledge all they owe to those who mean most to them, and I am no exception. Without my wife, Christine, the research would never have been attempted, let alone continued; nor would it have been made more widely available in this form. I am grateful for her constant encouragement, practical help with this project, and infinitely more.

RAYMOND BROWN

Abbreviations

Account	Edmund Calamy [1671–1732], *An Account of the Ministers ... who were Ejected or Silenced after the Restoration in 1660* (2nd ed.), London, 1713
BDBR	R.L. Greaves and R. Zaller (eds), *Dictionary of British Radicals in the Seventeenth Century* (3 vols), Brighton, 1982–4
BL	British Library, London
Bodl.	Bodleian Library, Oxford
BQ	*Baptist Quarterly*
ChH	*Church History*
CR	A.G. Matthews, *Calamy Revised, being a revision of Edmund Calamy's Account of the Ministers and others Ejected and Silenced, 1660–2*, Oxford, 1934
Continuation	Edmund Calamy [1671–1732], *A Continuation of the Account of the Ministers ... Ejected* (2 vols), London, 1727
CSPD	*Calendar of State Papers, Domestic Series*
DWL	Dr Williams's Library, London
EB	Roger Morrice, *The Entring Book of Roger Morrice, 1677–1691* (ed. Mark Goldie et al., 7 vols), Woodbridge, 2007–9
EHD	Andrew Browning (ed.), *English Historical Documents*, VIII, *1660–1714*, London, 1966
GA	John Bunyan, *Grace Abounding to the Chief of Sinners, with 'A Relation of my Imprisonment'* (ed. Roger Sharrock), Oxford, 1962
GLT	G. Lyon Turner (ed.), *Original Records of Early Nonconformity under Persecution and Indulgence* (3 vols), London, 1911
HistJ	*Historical Journal*
HMC	Historical Manuscripts Commission
HMSO	Her Majesty's Stationery Office
JEH	*Journal of Ecclesiastical History*
JFHS	*Journal of the Friends' Historical Society*
JHC	*Journal of the House of Commons*
JHL	*Journal of the House of Lords*
JURCHS	*Journal of the United Reformed Church History Society*
MW	*Miscellaneous Works of John Bunyan* (gen. ed. Roger Sharrock, 13

	vols), Oxford, 1976–94
n.s.	new series
o.s.	old series
P&P	*Past and Present*
RCHM	Royal Commission on Historical Manuscripts
SCH	Studies in Church History
TBHS	*Transactions of the Baptist Historical Society*
TRHS	*Transactions of the Royal Historical Society*
TCHS	*Transactions of the Congregational Historical Society*

The place of publication for all items cited in footnotes is London unless otherwise stated.

Part I

Encountering Adversity

Chapter 1

'This great eclipse'

'The Lord alone knows what the effects of this Great Eclipse will be.'[1]

'This eclipse of the gospel may tend to the furtherance of the gospel'.[2]

A Precarious Future

In May 1660, the exiled Charles II returned to England. Respecting the fact that there were 'differences of opinion in matters of religion', he had promised 'a liberty to tender consciences'.[3] Initially, things looked hopeful for Presbyterians, and some acknowledged leaders were offered bishoprics,[4] but there were ominous signs that other non-Anglicans might not be accommodated.

Quakers, no strangers to persecution, were particularly vulnerable.[5] Concerned about illegal proceedings against them as well as the preservation of their 'testimony', they kept careful records[6] of local hostility.[7] A Yorkshire

---

[1] Joseph Moore, in *England's Remembrancer, Being a Collection of Farewel Sermons Preached by Divers nonconformists in the Country* (1663), 423–24.
[2] *Oliver Heywood, His Autobiography, Diaries, Anecdotes and Event Books* (ed. J. Horsfall Turner, 4 vols; Brighouse and Bingley, 1882–5), I, 182.
[3] For the Declaration of Breda, see *JHL*, XI, 7–8, in *EHD*, VIII, 57–8.
[4] Edward Reynolds accepted Norwich but Richard Baxter declined Hereford and Edmund Calamy declined Lichfield and Coventry. Baxter thought it possible that invitations might be 'but a temporary means to draw us on till we came up to all the Diocesans desired': Matthew Sylvester (ed.), *Reliquiae Baxterianae* (1696), I, ii, §119. Jean Gailhard believed the offered preferments were a 'bribe': *The Controversie between Episcopacy and Presbytery Stated and Discussed* (1660), 5. Also in the autumn of 1660, deaneries were offered to other Presbyterian leaders, Rochester to Thomas Manton, Lichfield to William Bates, and York to Edward Bowles, but all three declined: Sylvester (ed.), *Reliquiae*, I, ii, §127.
[5] Joseph Besse, *A Collection of the Sufferings of the People called Quakers*, 2 vols (1753), I, 1–2. Besse's 'Introduction' describes 'the principal Points wherein their conscientious Nonconformity' made Friends 'obnoxious to the Penalties of the Law'; cf. Barry Reay, 'Popular Hostility towards Quakers in Mid-Seventeenth-Century England', *Social History* 5 (1980), 387–407.
[6] *A Collection of the ... Epistles of George Fox* (1698), 108–9 (Letter 140, 1657).
[7] For example, of Daniel Baker, a disabled Shrewsbury Quaker who 'proclaimed the Testimony of Truth' in the streets, 'the People sorely abusing him ... through a Multitude of Sufferings': Besse, *Sufferings*, I, 741; 'Great Book of Sufferings' 2, Salop, 6 [Library of the Society of Friends, London], quoted in John Miller, ' "A Suffering

Friend, George Hartus, died in prison and within weeks his widow was arrested, taken 'out of her Bed when sick, and carried away thirty Miles to Prison, from her ten fatherless Children'.[8] Cruelty and abuse of this kind was meticulously documented.

Staunch churchmen, incensed that in many parishes their episcopally ordained clergy had earlier been sequestered[9] and replaced by Presbyterians or Independents, speedily set to work to dislodge such Puritan ministers, enabling their congregations to return to familiar Prayer Book worship.[10] Cockermouth Independents recorded that in 1660 'the afflictions of the Church' began to 'tumble in upon them heaps upon heaps'. An earlier entry in their church book referred to Cromwell, their 'Lord Protector', as 'that eminent servant of the Lord, and nursing father of the Churches'.[11] Such loyalties placed these congregations under immediate suspicion.

At this time John Bunyan was arrested in a Bedfordshire village,[12] having contravened Elizabethan legislation that prohibited attendance at unlawful conventicles.[13] His subsequent imprisonment robbed him of his freedom for the next twelve years. Thousands more were to experience similar severity.[14]

People": English Quakers and their Neighbours, c.1650 – c.1700', *P&P* no. 188 (2005), 82. For Shrewsbury Dissenters, see Janice V. Cox, *The People of God: Shrewsbury Dissenters, 1660–1699*, 2 vols (Shropshire Record Series 9–10; Keele, 2006–2007).

[8] Besse, *Sufferings*, II, 100.

[9] The 1660 Act for Settling Ministers (*Statutes of the Realm*, V, 242–46) gave sequestered clergy the right to return to ministry in their former parishes. Under these provisions, Baxter's predecessor at Kidderminster replaced him; there were almost 300 others in the same situation; cf. I.M. Green, *The Re-Establishment of the Church of England* (Oxford, 1978), 37–49; J.H. Pruett, *The Parish Clergy under the Later Stuarts: The Leicestershire Experience* (Urbana, IL, 1978), 10–19; R. Clark, 'Why was Re-Establishment of the Church of England Possible? Derbyshire: A Provincial Perspective', *Midland History* 8 (1983), 96–97.

[10] *The Autobiography of Symon Patrick* (Oxford, 1839), 37–8; *JHL*, XI, 50; BL, Add. MS 19526, H. Gregory, 'Travels of King Charles II, 1640–60', I, fol.41: 'those who were Episcopalians read the Comon prayers ... at his M[aje]sties first returne, or before'. At Samuel Pepys's London church, his minister 'did begin to nibble at the Common Prayer ... But the people have been so little used to it that they did not tell what to answer': *The Diary of Samuel Pepys* (ed. R. Latham and W. Matthews, 11 vols; 1971–1983), I, 282.

[11] London, Congregational Library, MS. I.i.4, Cockermouth Independent Church Book (transcribed by P.H. Davidson, 1848), 33.

[12] Opening the meeting, Bunyan prayed, and had not even begun to preach when the local constable arrived: John Bunyan, *A Relation of the Imprisonment of Mr. John Bunyan*, with *Grace Abounding to the Chief of Sinners* (ed. Roger Sharrock; Oxford, 1962), 105.

[13] 'An Act to Retain the Queen Majesty's Subjects in Their Due Obedience' (35 Eliz. I.c.1), *Statutes of the Realm*, IV, Part II, 841–43.

[14] In the month prior to Bunyan's arrest, John Howe was accused in Torrington of seditious preaching because of two sermons in which he warned his people concerning the possible reintroduction of ceremonies unpalatable to Puritans: Edmund Calamy, in

Like other Puritan preachers, Bunyan had served in Cromwell's army. Due to 'threatened mischief', ex-Cromwellian soldiers were not to come within twenty miles of London for several weeks before the coronation, 'some such having held seditious meetings'.[15] Conversely, former cavaliers were viewed as unfailing supporters of both Charles and his bishops.[16] Conventicles were places where 'poison' was distilled 'into the hearts of the simple and weak',[17] and 'most of the nation are so weary of former wars that they will undergo anything' rather than 'engage in new troubles'.[18]

Widespread rumours of subversive plots were starkly materialized early in 1661 when Thomas Venner led a Fifth Monarchist uprising in the capital.[19] From his Swan Alley Independent meeting-house[20] he encouraged his followers to fight government forces in the city's streets. Based on Danielic predictions (Dan. 2:44), Fifth Monarchy teaching was a form of millenarian belief which became popular during the Civil Wars.[21] Venner's 'wicked and mad pranke ... against the governement',[22] a localized skirmish, was speedily quelled but, fearing its repetition in the provinces, the king strictly prohibited all meetings of 'Anabaptists, Quakers and Fifth Monarchists'.

Large numbers of innocent Quakers were speedily imprisoned, suspected of disloyalty because of their refusal to take oaths. Reporting on their

---

The Works of John Howe (ed. Edmund Calamy, 2 vols; 1724), I, 9–10. For the detailed 'Information and depositions' regarding these accusations, see BL, Add. MS 11342, fols 15–16; for this reference I am indebted to Martin Sutherland, *Peace, Toleration and Decay: The Ecclesiology of Later Stuart Dissent* (Carlisle, 2003), 46.

[15] *CSPD* 1660–61, 567–68. Bishop Cosin was troubled about those who had 'served as souldiers, or officers against the king, under the command of the late Parliament': *Correspondence of John Cosin, Bishop of Durham* (Surtees Society, 55; Durham, 1870), II, 108, letter of 15 July 1664. Cf. HMC, *Calendar of the Manuscripts of the Marquess of Ormonde*, n.s., III (RCHM, 36; 1904), 306: in 1670, there was 'not one Roundhead' among the 300 horsemen with the Duke of Ormonde.

[16] Barely six months after the king's return, when stability was but momentarily threatened, Dorset 'mustered a troop' of 240 'voluntier Horse ... most of them Commission'd Officers under the late King ... faithful to his Majesty, and well-affected to Episcopal Government': *The Kingdome's Intelligencer*, no. 14 (1–8 April 1661), 1.

[17] *CSPD* 1665–66, 548.

[18] Gailhard, *Controversie*, 2.

[19] B.S. Capp, *The Fifth Monarchy Men: A Study in Seventeenth-Century English Millenarianism* (1972), 199–200; P.G. Rogers, *The Fifth Monarchy Men* (Oxford, 1966), 112–22; R.L. Greaves, *Deliver us from Evil: The Radical Underground in Britain 1660–63* (Oxford, 1986), 50–65; *BDBR*, III, 268–70.

[20] 'that old nest of sedition': *Mercurius Publicus*, no. 1 (3–10 January 1661), 12.

[21] Its militant followers maintained that the 'Saints' must assume control of civil power by force and 'take up arms for King Jesus' as an essential prelude to Christ's return. At his execution, the regicide Major-General Thomas Harrison was reputed to have said that he would shortly return 'at the right hand of Christ to judge them that now had judged him': Pepys, *Diary* (ed. Latham and Matthews), I, 265; cf. *BDBR*, II, 61–65.

[22] *The Life of Adam Martindale* (ed R. Parkinson; Chetham Society, 4, Manchester, 1845), 143.

imprisonment, Francis Howgill knew of '500 in London' and 'neere 4,000 in the Nation'. Disturbed about the prisoners' grim conditions and their 'grievous usage',[23] Margaret Fell had more than one interview with the king[24] but, despite representations, many Friends became desperately sick in prison, some dying there. Many congregations frequently changed their rendezvous, meeting 'in parts and parcels here and there ... because of the great violence' of their oppressors.[25]

'As if ... naturally dead'

Charles II was favourably disposed towards Dissenters but they knew that toleration for them might eventually include the nation's other 'nonconformists', the Catholics. Anti-popery was endemic in England, constantly sustained by John Foxe's popular *Acts and Monuments*; even the illiterate were persuaded by its vivid woodcuts of the Smithfield fires. But whatever the king's religious preferences a new Parliament had a determined strategy: any dissent, Protestant or Catholic, was not to be tolerated.[26]

A series of measures (later known as the Clarendon Code) were brought before Parliament to secure the Anglican monopoly on public worship, marking the beginning of 'the most sustained persecution in English history, and, as it was wholly unsuccessful in its aim, the last'.[27] This 'fearsome apparatus of persecution'[28] was introduced by the 1661 Corporation Act. Those holding municipal office were required to receive the Anglican 'sacrament of the Lord's Supper' within one year; regularly thereafter to swear oaths of allegiance to the

---

[23] *CSPD* 1660–1, 533, March 16, 1661; Norman Penney (ed.), *Extracts from State Papers relating to Friends 1654–1672* (1913), 129.

[24] *George Fox: The Journal*, ed. Nigel Smith (Harmondsworth, 1998), 286, 294, 297; cf. *A Journal, or Historical Account of the life, travels, sufferings, Christian experiences and labour of love in the work of the ministry of ... George Fox* (ed. Thomas Ellwood, 2 vols; 1694–8), I, vii–viii; also *A Brief Collection of Remarkable Passages ... relating to ... Margaret Fell* (1710), 17–40, for her visits to Court and contacts by letter; ibid. 202–10, for 'A Declaration ... from the People of God called Quakers ... June, 1660'.

[25] Cockermouth Independent Church Book, 39. Axminster Independents also met 'sometimes in one obscure place, sometimes in another, in woods and solitary corners': *Axminster Ecclesiastica 1660–1698* (ed. K.W.H. Howard; Sheffield, 1976), 19. For the similar practice of Cranbrook Baptists, see Penney (ed.), *Extracts*, 147–48.

[26] The conciliatory Convention Parliament, which recalled the king in 1660, was replaced in May 1661 by the 'Cavalier' Parliament, its elections following Venner's rising in London. With a dread of political instability, the majority of its members were fearful of 'seditious' Dissent. Presbyterian members were fewer in number than in the Convention Parliament. Its initial task, the public burning of the Solemn League and Covenant (on which the voting was 228 to 103), indicated its aversion to Nonconformity.

[27] N.H. Keeble, *The Restoration: England in the 1660s* (Oxford, 2002), 141.

[28] Michael Mullett (ed.), *Early Lancaster Friends* (Occasional Paper, University of Lancaster Centre for North West Regional Studies; Lancaster, 1978), 12.

royal supremacy and of non-resistance; and to formally renounce the Solemn League and Covenant. Particularly objectionable to Anglicans, the Covenant was a 1643 agreement between the Scots and the English Parliament guaranteeing Presbyterian church government and worship for Scotland, and promising the reformation of the 'Doctrine, Worship, Discipline and Government' of the English Church. To renounce the Covenant was to reject the notion that the Restoration Church needed reformation.[29]

Royal Commissioners, appointed to ensure that the provisions of the Corporation Act were meticulously observed, were primarily drawn from the country gentry, who were mostly firm royalists and episcopalians. With bitter memories of civil war, most of these men resented Nonconformity's influence in the towns, many of which had parliamentary seats. The Corporation Act immediately robbed Dissenters of influence in civic affairs. Two additional measures, passed in the following year, were to have further serious consequences for them.

With the 1662 Quaker Act, Parliament attacked the Dissenting group least likely to engage in revolutionary activity, the Society of Friends. Oaths (offensive to Friends) were demanded and Quakers were denied the opportunity of meeting in a group of five or more, even for their customary 'silent' worship. First- and second-time offenders were to be fined or imprisoned, and any guilty of a third offence transported. The bill received royal assent in May 1662, and the next four months initiated a period of grim suffering for London Friends.[30] Many hundreds passed the long hot summer in crowded, unhygienic prisons. Families became destitute, and thirty London Quakers offered themselves as substitutes in place of the most needy.[31] Some died in prison, men such as

---

[29] Solemn League and Covenant, in *The Confession of Faith and the Larger and Shorter Cathechisme ... Assembly of Divines at Westminster* (1651); text also in J.P. Kenyon (ed.), *The Stuart Constitution 1603–1688: Documents and Commentary* (2nd ed.; Cambridge, 1986), 239–42. Those who signed the Covenant were committed to the 'Reformation of Religion in Doctrine, Worship, Discipline and Government'. Although opposed to episcopacy, the Covenant aimed 'mutually to preserve the Rights and Privileges of the Parliament', and signatories affirmed their loyalty to the monarchy ('to preserve and defend the King's Majestie's Person and Authority'); it insisted 'that we have no thoughts or intentions to diminish his Majestie's just power and greatnesse'. See Jeremy Goring, 'Some Neglected Aspects of the Great Ejection of 1662', *Transactions of the Unitarian Historical Society* 13 (1963), 3–6.

[30] See Besse, *Sufferings*, I, 368–92, for a letter written three months before Burroughs's death, in which he describes the sufferings of Quakers in four London prisons, with 'near a Hundred in one Room ... among the Felons'; cf. also J. Smith, *A Descriptive Catalogue of Friends' Books*, II, 662–63; Norman Penney (ed.), *The First Publishers of Truth* (1907), 159–61; *The History of the Life of Thomas Ellwood ...* (ed. S. Graveson; 1906), 126–74; *The Christian Progress of ... George Whitehead* (1725), 271–74.

[31] The Quaker practice of offering themselves as substitute prisoners predates the Restoration, cf. Fox, *Epistles*, 80 (Letter 93, 1655): 'lay down and offer up your lives for one another'. In April 1659, Friends presented to Parliament *A Declaration of the present sufferings of above 140 Persons ... (Who are now in Prison,) called Quakers,*

Edward Burroughs, the young Bristol Quaker who, hearing of the persecution, travelled to London to 'suffer amongst Friends in that place' and was soon in the company of about 250 fellow Quaker prisoners and (he observed) 'many Baptists'.[32] '[S]hut up among the Felons ... and for want of Prison-room' many 'sickned, and dyed'.[33] Ambrose Rigge was kept a 'close Prisoner ... above Ten Years, under many Sore Abuses ... from several Cruel Goalers'. During his imprisonment his goods were distrained, 'leaving us not a Bed to lie upon, nor any other Necessarys to assist us in Prison'.[34]

The Act of Uniformity[35] passed in May 1662 with a very small majority deprived Nonconformist ministers of their work in parish churches and in university teaching posts. During the Interregnum, such ministers had been entrusted with preaching and pastoral care in parishes and during their incumbency corporate worship had ignored the Prayer Book. Large numbers of these 'intruders' had not received episcopal ordination and the act required all clergy to have been ordained by a bishop, each giving 'unfeigned assent and consent' publicly to the revised Book of Common Prayer, abjuring the Solemn League and Covenant to their congregations, subscribing to the Thirty-Nine Articles, and affirming that they would not campaign for any change either in Church or state.

---

with a briefe accompt of about 1900 more, being but a part of many more that have suffered within these six years last past ... Together with the number of 21 Persons who were imprisoned and persecuted until Death, its signatories expressing their willingness to be imprisoned in the place of fellow Quakers. It was speedily followed by a deputation of over 160 Friends to Westminster Hall bearing a petition repeating their desire to 'offer up our bodies ... to go in their places, in love to our brethren'. The deputation was firmly instructed to leave London immediately and 'submit themselves to the laws of this nation': *Mercurius Politicus*, no. 563 (21–28 April 1659), 374; *Diary of Thomas Burton* (ed. J.T. Rutt; 1828), IV, 440–45. Besse, *Sufferings*, I, iv–vi, reproduces 'a Printed Paper submitted to Parliament ... wherein they make an offer of their own Bodies, Person for Person, to lie in Prison insted of such of their Brethren as ... might be in Danger of their Lives'. In *A Narrative of the Sufferings of J[ohn] P[errot] in the City of Rome* (1661), 10, Perrot says that Charles Bayly arrrived in Rome during his imprisonment and 'offered his life to ransome me'.

[32] Besse, *Sufferings*, I, 389–90. William C. Braithwaite, *The Second Period of Quakerism* (1919), 26, had access to an earlier text of Burroughs's letter which included the reference to Baptist prisoners.

[33] F[rancis].. H[owgill].. *A Testimony concerning the Life, Death, Trials, Travels and Labours of Edward Burroughs ... who dyed a Prisoner in 1662* (1663), 12. Cambridgeshire Quakers, imprisoned 'for Absence from the National Worship', were 'kept five Days and five Nights without any Bed to lie on, though one of them had a young Child sucking at her Breast': Besse, *Sufferings*, I, 91.

[34] Ambrose Rigge, *Constancy in the Truth Commended ... True Account of the Life and Sufferings ... of Ambrose Rigge* (1710), 18–19. Rigge says that if a local official gave them 'but a little liberty ... .once in a twelve month, to go to visit our Families', persecuting citizens 'campaigned 'to have the Sherriff fined' for his leniency.

[35] *Statutes of the Realm*, V, 364–70; *EHD*, VIII, 377–82.

Any parish minister not prepared to submit publicly to these demands by 24 August 1662 was to be ejected from his living. The choice of date was cruel, only four weeks before Michaelmas, when clergymen received a half-yearly payment of tithes for their support,[36] 'ingenious malice'[37] which denied ejected ministers income that would have maintained their families until they obtained alternative employment. Another objection to the 24 August date for compliance was that the revised Prayer Book was not published until 6 August and three weeks later copies had still not reached some counties.[38] Many 'well affected to the church ... made a conscience of subscribing to a book that they had not seen' and 'left their benefices on that very account'.[39]

Although the majority dutifully subscribed, the stringent legislation robbed the Restoration Church of a fifth of its clergy. Over two thousand parish ministers and university teachers who could not conscientiously conform were required to abandon their livings or posts. Men with a high sense of vocation who had given faithful and effective service in their parishes and in the universities became 'non-conformists'. Independents, Baptists and Quakers had no difficulty with the designation. Few of them had any desire to be part of an episcopal national church with a rigidly enforced liturgy, but negotiations since the king's return had encouraged the Presbyterians to believe in that possibility.

Philip Henry's birthday fell on 24 August; he believed it to be 'the saddest day to England since ... the death of King Edward 6'.[40] In 1663 he wrote: 'This day thirty two yeares I was born, this day twelve-month I dyed, that fatal day to ye Godly painful Minist[e]rs of England amongst whom I am not worthy to be

---

[36] A House of Lords amendment to extend the date to Michaelmas was rejected by the Lower House: John Miller, *After the Civil Wars: English Politics and Government in the Reign of Charles II* (Harlow, 1999), 179.

[37] Henry Rogers, *The Life and Character of John Howe* (1863), 100.

[38] John Quick protested that the book did not reach the West of England until 'full five months after this Act came in force'. If compelled to give 'unfeigned Assent and consent', 'With what honesty or conscience could we doe it?': DWL, MS 38.34–35, John Quick, 'Icones Sacrae Anglicanae, or Lives and Deaths of Several Eminent Divines' (undated transcript), II, 528.

[39] G. Burnet, *History of My Own Time* (ed. M.J. Routh, 6 vols; Oxford, 1823), I, 318. They included conscientious ministers who were not likely to become Dissenters, such as Richard Kidder, later bishop of Bath and Wells. During the Cromwellian period, as a committed episcopalian Kidder had loyally obeyed 'orders from a Bishop at a time when it was dangerous to receive them'. But in August 1662 he was required 'to subscribe to a book that I never saw, and could not tell what it contained ... though I used all possible meanes to procure it yet I was not able to get a sight of it ... Some few of my neighbours were in the same condition. They lost their livings as I did'. Kidder was without a living for two years: *The Life of Richard Kidder, D.D., Bishop of Bath and Wells: Written by Himself* (ed. A.E. Robinson; Somerset Record Society, 37; 1924), 10–11.

[40] Transcript of Philip Henry's 1662 Diary, possibly by Thomas Stedman, in the possession of Mr John Warburton Lee of Broad Oak, Whitchurch, Shropshire, entry for 24 August 1662.

numbred.'[41] References to the minister's 'death' were not exaggerated language; phrases such as 'as though the person ... so offending or neglecting were dead' recur five times throughout the act. Many of the ministers struck this sombre note in farewell sermons on the Sunday preceding their ejectment.[42] The printing of these sermons[43] and those preached in London in the early 1660s and published as the *Morning Exercises at Cripplegate* provided valuable ongoing publicity for Nonconformists in the opening decade of the Restoration.

Although legally silenced, the majority of the ejected ministers continued to grasp opportunities for preaching and pastoral care. A Chester Presbyterian, William Cook, was imprisoned for 'repeating [a sermon] in his House, where many people were present'. A preacher silenced in one place might become eloquent in another. Cook 'chose ye common Prison' as his new pulpit, 'where hee hath liberty to preach every day to ye Prisoners'.[44]

Church members suffered as well as ministers. Quakers were particularly vulnerable; huge numbers of innocent people, including many women and children, were cruelly treated.[45] By the close of 1662, '289 Anabaptists and others' were imprisoned in Newgate, having been 'taken at unlawful meetings'.[46]

A 'Seditious' People

In October 1663 Henry noted in his diary that there were 'reports of a Plot' and that two of his friends had been 'secur'd'. Within a few days he too was

---

[41] *Diaries and Letters of Philip Henry 1631–1696* (ed. M.H. Lee; 1882), 145.

[42] *A Collection of Farewell Sermons of divers London and Country Ministers in Three Volumns* (1663), III, 152. Leaving his London parish after sixteen years, Thomas Watson said that as he and his colleagues would 'be laid down shortly as if we were naturally dead', he wanted to 'leave some Legacies with you before I go hence': Thomas Watson, *A Pastors Love ... in a Farewel Sermon* (1662), 7. Cf. Daniel Bull's farewell statement that he was 'now dying in this congregation': in *A Compleat Collection of Farewel[l] Sermons* (1663), [unpaginated].

[43] David Appleby, *Black Bartholomew's Day: Preaching, Polemic and Restoration Nonconformity* (Manchester, 2007).

[44] Henry, *Diaries* (ed. Lee), 157. Henry noted that his friend's 'chamber is cal'd ye Freeman's chamber'.

[45] An intercepted letter from a London Friend to Margaret Fell in November 1662 told of '23 of them' in a Southwark prison '*wth* sicknesse and high feever' who 'Lye in the saddest condition ... some of them soe weake that they [look] like every moment when they should dep[ar]te'. The correspondent told her that the authorities 'tooke severall to prison out of the streetes': one of them was brought before a City Alderman who 'beate him sorely and lugged him by the haire out of one roome into the other': Penney (ed.), *Extracts*, 153–54.

[46] *CSPD 1662–63*, 604–605 (28 December 1662); cf. *The Diary of Bulstrode Whitelocke* (ed. Ruth Spalding; Records of Social and Economic History, n.s. 13; Oxford, 1990), 655.

ordered to appear with others before a local official.[47] Rumour or reality, threats of plots and revolts intensified anxiety in a climate of insecurity and fear.[48] Meeting places were raided and Dissenters' homes placed under observation. When Henry Newcome attended a 'private day' with 'a great many' others, a local spy had been 'set to watch'.[49] Newcome was later accused of conducting 'repetitions' (repeating a recent sermon) in his family.[50]

In this context of suspicion and accusation, Parliament modernized a frequently neglected Elizabethan statute that demanded regular attendance at the parish church and prohibited private meetings, issuing its harsh Conventicle Act in 1664.[51] Its rigorous provisions were designed to inflict maximum damage on Dissenting churches, who 'at their Meetings contrive insurrections'. Numbers at family worship were to be limited; members of a household could only be increased by a maximum of four additional visitors over the age of sixteen. Penalties were severe. Offenders were either to pay a £5 fine[52] or suffer three months' imprisonment, the fine and prison sentence doubled for anyone guilty of a second offence. Third-time offenders were fined £100 or 'transported to any of his Majesty's foreign plantations' (excluding Virginia and New England) for seven years, their goods being sold to pay for transportation. Householders permitting Dissenters to meet in their fields, outhouses or barns suffered the same penalties as conventiclers. Parliament and

---

[47] Even a Nonconformist as reluctant as Henry did not escape suspicion. Although he might profess that 'the lord knowes I know noth[ing] of any such thing', he was imprisoned for a few days. 'Tis ye first time I was ever a Prisoner, but perhaps may not bee ye last', an accurate prediction: Henry, *Diaries* (ed. Lee), 148–49.

[48] For plots in the north of England in 1662–64, see Ronald Hutton, *The Restoration: A Political and Religious History of England and Wales, 1658–1667* (Oxford, 1985), 204–207; and in greater detail S.J. Chadwick, 'The Farnley Wood Plot', in *Miscellanea*, Thoresby Society Publications, 15 (1905–1909), 122–26; A. Hopper, 'The Farnley Wood Plot and the Memory of the Civil Wars in Yorkshire', *HistJ* 45 (2002), 281–303; F. Nicholson, 'The Kaber Rigg Plot', *Transactions of the Cumberland and Westmorland Antiquarian and Archaeological Society* n.s. 11 (1911), 212–32; H. Gee, 'A Durham and Newcastle Plot', *Archaeologia Aeliana* 3rd ser. 14 (1917), 145–56; idem, 'The Derwentdale Plot, 1663', *TRHS* 3rd ser. 11 (1917), 127–40; C.E. Whiting, 'The Great Plot of 1663', *Durham University Journal* 22 (1920), 155–67; J. Walker, 'The Yorkshire Plot, 1663', *Yorkshire Archaeological Journal* 31 (1932–34), 348–59. Although small-scale, these activities were widely reported as justification for the 1664 Conventicle Act.

[49] Newcome hoped that whatever the outcome it would be spiritually beneficial: *Diary of Henry Newcome, 1661–1663* (ed. T. Heywood; Chetham Society, 18; Manchester, 1849), 107.

[50] Ibid. 126.

[51] Pepys's cousin, a barrister and Member of Parliament, called it a 'devilish ... severe act ... beyond all moderation': Pepys, *Diary* (ed. Latham and Matthews), IV, 159–60.

[52] Most would be in no position to produce this large amount of money, and household goods and furniture were then taken away ('distrained') in lieu of fines, and sold locally. £5 was half a year's salary for some of the Restoration Church's lower-paid clergy; indeed, some only received £6 or £7 for the entire year: Pruett, *Parish Clergy*, 82.

the bishops realized that many Dissenters had sympathetic friends among those expected to enforce the law, so penalties were imposed on any official who turned a blind eye to local Nonconformity or any gaoler allowing temporary freedom to a prisoner.[53]

The harassment, arrest and imprisonment of Dissenters that had taken place sporadically since 1660 was with this new legislation increased with a severity hitherto unknown in English religious life. Well-known preachers were particularly vulnerable; an informer might come in the guise of a seeking enquirer.[54]

The new archbishop of Canterbury, Gilbert Sheldon, regarded Protestant Dissent as a dangerous 'disease' to be eradicated by the 'resolute execution of the law'. People who would not 'be governed as men by reason and persuasion, should be governed as beasts by power of force'.[55] The effects of the act were immediate and frequently violent. At one 'great conventicle', constables 'broke open the doors' and 'took 60 men and as many women', among them '11 ministers living in or near Taunton'. But the arrest of the eleven did little to deter Somerset Dissenters, for there were 'as many more who preach up and down'.[56] Meetings in large homes frequently attracted substantial numbers, all contrary to the law, and the authorities were often aggressive in gaining access to an offender's property.[57] Those unable to pay fines were imprisoned. In London, a Quaker correspondent reported that 'Newgate is so full that they have an infectious malignant fever amongst them which sends many to their long home'.[58]

The Broadmead (Bristol) congregation's minister, Thomas Ewins, had been in prison for almost a year when this 'Act of Banishment' was passed. Once the

---

[53] 'An Act to prevent and suppress Seditious Conventicles' (1664): *Statutes of the Realm*, V, 516–20.

[54] An elderly 'Gentlewoman with her Sons and Daughter' made three unsuccessful attempts to hear Baxter preach to his 'Family'. He later 'had secret intelligence from one that was nigh her, that she came with a heart exceeding full of Malice ... to do me what Mischief she could by Accusation': Sylvester (ed.), *Reliquiae*, I, ii, §441.

[55] Bodl., Carte MS 45, fol.151, Sheldon to the Duke of Ormonde, 1663. Sheldon's hostility was evident during his London episcopate: cf. Paul Seaward, 'Gilbert Sheldon, the London Vestries, and the Defence of the Church', in Tim Harris, Paul Seaward and Mark Goldie (eds), *The Politics of Religion in Restoration England* (Oxford, 1990), 49–73. The Great Yarmouth Independent Church Book has this entry for 1 June 1663: 'Shelton became Archbishop of Canterbury a sad day for the nonconformity': DWL, Harmer MS 76.2, Great Yarmouth Independent Church Book, 1642–1813 (transcribed 1848), fol.118v.

[56] *CSPD* 1664–65, 476.

[57] Ibid. 461.

[58] Ibid. 20. Kelly Grovier says that 'the mingled stench of disease and faeces and the cacophonous din of wailing and screeching in the maze of unventilated wards was unutterably horrifying': *The Gaol: The Story of Newgate, London's most notorious Prison* (2008), 94–95; cf. A.G. Matthews, 'A Censored Letter', *TCHS* 9 (1924–6), 262–83, at 266, for an ejected minister's account of London prisons in 1663.

new legislation came into force, some of his church members were also gaoled. Constantly 'followed and hunted with Officers and *Serjeants*', they were 'assaulted ... many a time by men, but Saved by God'.[59] Threat of transportation was a serious deterrent,[60] though not every captain was willing to cooperate.[61] The Quaker leader, George Fox, knew that 'some masters [of ships would not carry them but] set them ashore again'.[62]

Dissenters whose offences did not warrant transportation nevertheless had little respite from local harassment. After 'two Years and an Half Confinement', Thomas Richardson, a Cambridgeshire Quaker, 'above sixty Years of Age', died in prison 'through want of Firing ... and lodging on Straw in Winter Time'.[63] Prisons 'have been made my home a great part of my time', said George Fox,[64] the conditions generally appalling.[65] The number of arrests escalated. In London alone, during an eighteenth-month period from 1664-5 there were over nine hundred convictions.[66]

But why?

The motivation for the repression is highly complex and defies simple explanation. The scene was not remotely static and over three decades, the Dissenters' most strident opponents were at different times drawn from diverse groups, according to varying political, ecclesiastical, social and local factors. The king was no lover of persecution and had little direct part in it until the closing years of his reign. He might well have done more to make life easier for loyal Nonconformist subjects although, as well they knew, Charles and his court were preoccupied with pleasure.[67]

---

[59] *The Records of a Church of Christ in Bristol, 1640–1687* (ed. Roger Hayden; Bristol Record Society, 27; Bristol, 1974), 118–20.
[60] Sir Roger Bradshaigh, a zealous opponent of Nonconformity in Lancashire, believed that the prospect of transportation would quickly reduce their numbers: *CSPD* 1664–65, 485.
[61] Penney (ed.), *Extracts*, 22, 230–1; Braithwaite, *Second Period*, 46. In 1664, the captain of 'the Anne of London' refused to carry Quaker prisoners, fearing 'the Hand of the Lord' was against him and protesting that such an action was illegal: Besse, *Sufferings*, I, 246–47, cf. 51.
[62] *Journal of George Fox* (ed. John L. Nickalls; Cambridge, 1975), 493.
[63] Besse, *Sufferings*, I, 92.
[64] Fox, *Epistles*, 341 (Letter 308, 1674).
[65] In a Lancaster Castle 'tower room', Fox says it 'rained in also upon my bed: and the smoke [from other rooms] was so thick as I could hardly see a candle sometimes and ... so starved with cold and rain that my body was almost numbed and ... swelled with the cold: Fox, *Journal* (ed. Smith), 347.
[66] *Middlesex County Records* (ed. J.C. Jeaffreson; Middlesex County Records Society, o.s.; 1974), III (1625–67), 342.
[67] Hutton, *Restoration*, 185–90; Tim Harris, *London Crowds in the Reign of Charles II: Propaganda and Politics from the Restoration until the Exclusion Crisis* (Cambridge, 1987), 78–80. For satire on the court's debauchery, cf. court lampoons such as 'The

Although the legislation became known as the 'Clarendon Code', this was merely a convenient tag. Edward Hyde, Earl of Clarendon, was Charles's First Minister when the punitive measures went through Parliament; no lover of Dissenters, Clarendon shared the general fear of rebellion but can hardly be accused of being the leading advocate of an oppressive coercion strategy. On returning to England with the king, he was eager for a peaceful religious settlement and had little personal desire to enforce uniformity by means of repressive acts of Parliament.

As to the bishops, some were more tolerant than others, but few were without prejudice. Several had suffered hardship under Cromwell, either during a self-imposed impecunious European exile or by enforced quiescence at home. When the inflexible Sheldon[68] became archbishop in 1663, the Act of Uniformity was already on the Statute Book, having been passed the previous year, but once non-conforming ministers had been ejected he campaigned to have their work outside the parish churches inhibited by the Conventicle Act (1664).

The archbishop implemented this policy of enforced conformity by maximizing his considerable influence among parliamentarians, especially in the Upper House. Some Members of Parliament in both houses were committed Dissenters, and others were openly sympathetic to the Nonconformist cause. On specific occasions these men campaigned for changes in the harsh penal laws,[69] and at times came close to success.[70] Bishop John Hacket of Lichfield recognized that parliamentary success in opposing Nonconformity owed a great deal to the 'great prudence & indefatigable industrie' of his archbishop. Sheldon had employed considerable 'dexteritie'[71] in identifying, informing and manipulating his political allies, to the detriment of many thousands of peace-loving Dissenters.

History of Insipids' (1674) and 'A Dialogue Between the Two Horses' (1676): G. de F. Lord et al., (eds.), *Poems on Affairs of State: Augustan Satirical Verse, 1660–1714*, 7 vols (New Haven, CT, 1963–75), I, 243–45, 274–83. See also Harold Love, *English Clandestine Satire, 1660–1702* (Oxford, 2004), ch.4; Conal Condren and A.D. Cousins (eds), *The Political Identity of Andrew Marvell* (Aldershot, 1990); *Memoirs of Sir John Reresby* (ed. Andrew Browning; Glasgow, 1936), 259: the king at Newmarket 'lett himselfe down from Majesty'.

[68] For Sheldon's influence in the strenuous opposition to Dissent, see John Spurr, *The Restoration Church of England, 1646–1689* (New Haven, CT, 1991), 47–51.

[69] D.R. Lacey, *Dissent and Parliamentary Politics in England, 1661–1689* (New Brunswick, NJ, 1969); A. Swatland, *The House of Lords in the Reign of Charles II* (Cambridge, 1996), 173–99.

[70] Such as measures for comprehension, eagerly desired by most Presbyterians, and some form of toleration, which would have satisfied their fellow Dissenters.

[71] Bodl. MS Tanner 45, fol.278, cf. 288: 'which makes the presbyterians rather rage *then* be humbled, who are in our parts'; Spurr, *Restoration Church*, 50.

As for local gentry, especially those in Parliament, some responsibility for the harsh legislation may be laid at their door,[72] though many were guiltless.[73] They were influential, many shouldering multiple governmental, legal and social responsibilities, serving as Members of Parliament and with additional authority as justices of the peace and as members of grand juries, some as lieutenants or deputies in their localities.[74] Some active royalists among them[75] had suffered socially and economically[76] during the past two decades,[77] and regarded Nonconformists as potential rebels who must be actively repressed in order to prevent the horrors of another civil war.[78]

The punitive legislation cannot be blamed on a triple alliance of bishops, parliamentarians and gentry, for the ranks of all three were sharply divided, and the scenario changed over time. Several bishops, for example, realized that a persecuting regime was socially divisive and religiously untenable, and could not hope to be effective. The nobility was not without its Presbyterian sympathizers.[79] Members of Parliament had divided loyalties, and as the years went by many local gentry came increasingly to realize that their Nonconformist neighbours were totally loyal to king and country, and that repressive measures had only succeeded in fragmenting society.[80] In time, large numbers of gentry who served as justices turned a blind eye to the activities of local conventiclers, refusing to regard peaceable neighbours as a threat to national stability. But, given these necessary qualifications, at varying times and in different geographical locations influential politicians, determined ecclesiastics and forceful magistrates played some part in making life difficult for Dissenters for almost thirty years. In times of hardship, Dissenters turned to

---

[72] 'Lay intolerance, the joint product of experience and indoctrination, was the decisive factor in restoring the Church of England to its old form and its old ascendancy': R.A. Beddard, 'The Restoration Church', in J.R. Jones (ed.), *The Restored Monarchy* (1979), 155–75, at 165; cf. ibid. 157 for examples of nobility who provided homes for sequestered clergy during the Interregnum.
[73] Paul Seaward, *The Cavalier Parliament and the Reconstruction of the Old Regime, 1661–1667* (Cambridge, 1989), 60–61.
[74] Green, *Re-Establishment*, 198–99. Nine Kent Members of Parliament and approximately a third of the county's justices were established tenants on church lands.
[75] Almost half the members of the 'Cavalier Parliament' in the spring of 1661 had been financially penalized for their royalism in the 1650s, or were the sons of such: Hutton, *Restoration*, 152. See also B.D. Henning, *The House of Commons 1660–1690* (3 vols; 1983), I, 32–33, for evidence that the 'Cavalier Parliament' deserved its name.
[76] Seaward, *Cavalier Parliament*, 326–27.
[77] Ibid. 62–67.
[78] Lord Fanshaw spoke for many parliamentary colleagues when he said that the 'villanies' that 'these men' committed 'when they had the power in their hands is most notorious ... let the laws be put in execution against them and they will soon be brought under': *The Diary of John Milward* (ed. C. Robbins; Cambridge, 1938), 221.
[79] The lord of the manor in Benenden, Kent, for example, was one of the parish's staunch Presbyterians: Green, *Re-Establishment*, 196.
[80] Seaward, *Cavalier Parliament*, 60–61.

Foxe's book, if only to remind each other that the persecution might be infinitely worse. In reality, however, far more innocent Protestants died in squalid prisons in the reign of Charles II than at the stake under Mary.[81] Additionally, under Charles thousands were robbed of goods, money, livelihood, security, freedom and health, which cannot be said for life under the Catholic queen.

Given that total submission to the law regarding enforced public worship would have freed them from all oppression, why were Dissenters, in different degrees, so implacable in their refusal to conform to parliamentary legislation? They did not speak with one voice when presenting an apologia for non-compliance. On numerous issues there was a world of difference between Presbyterians and Independents, Baptists and Quakers, and they were far from silent about their disagreements. But the basic matter on which they all agreed was that they prized their own[82] religious liberty and found it impossible to submit to the element of compulsion in such treasured realms as personal faith, doctrinal conviction and corporate worship.

Legally, they were compelled to attend the parish church's services of worship for Morning or Evening Prayer.[83] They did not always do so, but there were penalties for non-attendance and many thousands were repeatedly fined. Legislation robbed them of the freedom to worship as their understanding of Scripture and conscience dictated. Those persuaded that they were called by God to preach and exercise pastoral care as ministers had to be episcopally ordained; no other form of ordination was acceptable. The tithe system demanded that they pay for the upkeep of their parish church and the maintenance of its ministry, whether or not they belonged to its congregation. It was mandatory for them to have their children baptized in the parish churches but many had conscientious reasons for not wishing to do so.

Milton had expressed his distaste that such 'prelaticall tradition' crowded 'free consciences and Christian liberties into [the] canons and precepts of

---

[81] Cf. Tim Harris, *Restoration: Charles II and his Kingdom 1660–1685* (2005), 423–25. Referring to Charles II in the next century, Wesley wrote: 'Bloody Queen Mary was a lamb, a mere dove in comparison of him': *The Works of John Wesley*, 22, *Journals and Diaries, Vol. V (1765–1775)* (ed. W.R. Ward and R.P. Heitzenrater; Nashville, TN, 1993), 118 (11 January 1768).

[82] An important qualification as Dissenters were not always tolerant of views other than their own; for example, few would have supported religious freedom for Catholics, and most Presbyterians, Independents and Baptists were fiercely intolerant of Quakers.

[83] When Charles II returned, Nonconformists had been free from this demand for ten years. Compulsory attendance at the parish church (1 Eliz. and 23 Eliz.) had been revoked under pressure from the Cromwellian army, though against Presbyterian wishes. People were expected to meet regularly at 'some publique place where the Service and Worship of God is exercised', but without penalties for non-compliance: cf. C.H. Firth and R.S. Rait (eds), *Acts and Ordinances of the Interregnum, 1642–1660* (3 vols; 1911), II, 423–24.

men'.[84] It was this policy of penal coercion that was intolerable during three decades of intermittent hardship and adversity. The persecution was not remotely uniform throughout the country,[85] and in many locations there were extended periods of respite, but the legislation's 'formidable legal arsenal' made a potential 'Puritan holocaust'[86] a grim reality in many towns, cities and villages. But we must return to the narrative.

Undeterred

Despite recurrent persecution, many Nonconformist churches continued to thrive, displaced ministers preaching to scattered congregations.[87] With their ejected ministers' encouragement and example, most Presbyterians dutifully attended the parish churches, still hopeful that, given time, their views might be reconsidered and accommodated, supplementing compulsory attendance with the preaching and pastoral care of their ejected ministers, either in homes[88] or at equally illegal conventicles.

A striking early feature of Nonconformist life was the steady growth of networks of supportive relationships and the cultivation of wider contacts with believers throughout the immediate area and beyond.[89] In this respect, Nonconformity was indebted to leaders and members willing to travel. Itinerant preachers traversed considerable distances throughout a region, bringing a sense of dynamic cohesion to otherwise scattered groups. Men such as Thomas Collier, Thomas Grantham, Matthew Clarke, Oliver Heywood, Francis Holcroft, Henry Maurice, William Mitchell and his cousin David Crosley exercised vital ministries in bringing life and hope to remote families and widely dispersed (and often small) groups, as well as to more substantial communities.[90]

---

[84] *Areopagitica* (1644), in *The Complete Prose Works of John Milton* (gen. ed. Don M. Wolfe, 8 vols; New Haven, CT, 1953–82), II, 554, 560. The Dissenters' quest for freedom was sometimes derided by ardent conformists such as George Vernon, who referred to John Owen's 'great Diana, Liberty of Conscience': *Letter to a Friend* (1670), 34.
[85] A. Fletcher, 'The Enforcement of the Conventicle Acts, 1664–1679', in W.J. Sheils (ed.), *Persecution and Toleration* (SCH 21; Oxford, 1984), 235–46.
[86] Mark Goldie, 'The Search for Religious Liberty, 1640–1690', in J. Morrill (ed.), *The Oxford Illustrated History of Tudor and Stuart Britain* (Oxford, 1996), 293–309, at 300.
[87] See, e.g., R.H. Evans, 'Nonconformists in Leicestershire in 1669', *Transactions of the Leicestershire Archaeological and Historical Society* 25 (1949), 98–143.
[88] e.g. Philip Henry in May 1665: 'Friends flock in to us on Sabbath-Evenings ... lord enable, and spin out this thred of opportunity, if it please thee!': *Diaries* (ed. Lee), 199.
[89] For inter-congregational and regional relationships among Baptists in this period, see Raymond Brown, 'Baptist *Relating and Resourcing* in Difficult Times: A Historical Perspective', in P.J. Lalleman (ed.), *Challenging to Change – Dialogues with a Radical Baptist Theologian: Essays presented to Nigel G. Wright* (2009), 11–24.
[90] See GLT, III, 294–98, for a detailed account of Holcroft's widespread itinerancy.

Although many of the ejected ministers did not travel as widely as the itinerants, they regularly visited Nonconformists in a local circuit,[91] serving the needs of scattered groups in nearby towns and remote villages, creating a sense of solidarity among people isolated by restrictive legislation. London ministers[92] also recognized the importance of visiting the provinces, sharing news of Nonconformist life in the metropolis and beyond.

Dissenters' meetings continued to be raided, but Nonconformists often discovered unknown friends among local officials. When Owen Stockton preached in his house, 'word was brought to him, that the Mayor and Aldermen' were about to come. The constable sent to disband the meeting told Stockton that he had sometimes listened to his preaching, 'so that instead of doing him any hurt he gave glory to God' who had 'inclined him to be a Hearer himself'.[93] Reporting to government in 1665, a Canterbury correspondent wrote that 'nothing was prosecuted last session against Quakers, nonconformists, nor the rest of that diabolical rabble', because 'most of the grand jury' were also 'fanatics'.[94]

During the summer of 1665, when London was stricken by the devastating plague, many parish clergy fled the city,[95] leaving Nonconformist ministers to serve its highly vulnerable citizens. Several ejected ministers returned to their former pulpits,[96] much to the annoyance of Archbishop Sheldon and Humphrey Henchman, bishop of London, who had both remained in London. Parliament moved to the relative safety of Oxford and in October 1665 chose an inopportune moment to introduce a further measure against Dissenters. The devastating naval victories of the Dutch[97] might have suggested a policy of internal reconciliation rather than further repression,[98] but the majority of

---

[91] In 1669 Matthew Clarke was reported as preaching in more than 14 different Leicestershire parishes, and his colleague John Shuttlewood in 9 parishes. In the diocese of Bath and Wells, John Galpin preached regularly in 15 local parishes: GLT, III, 78; cf. 86, 287.

[92] Matthew Mead, 'an ejected Minister from Stepney, near London', appears to have preached regularly at Sibbeston, Leicestershire: Evans, 'Leicestershire 1669', 128.

[93] Samuel Clarke, *Lives of Sundry Eminent Persons in this Later Age* (1683), 194–95.

[94] CSPD 1665–6, 42.

[95] *An Historical Narrative of the Great Plague at London, 1665* (1769), 321, mentions the clerical deserters but also the 'great number of learned, able, and pious divines of the establishment clergy who stayed'. Henchman told absent clergy to return or forfeit their livings: Henry Ellis, *Original Letters illustrative of English History*, Second Series, IV (1969), 26–27.

[96] CSPD 1664–65, 524. Lord Arlington warned Henchman of possible 'disorders' if ejected ministers were allowed to return to vacant pulpits.

[97] Henry, *Diaries* (ed. Lee), 200–201 (9 June 1665): 'The Dutch appear'd ... assaulted the isle of Shepey, burnt & sunk several of our best Ships ... which caused great distraction in & about London, men's hearts generally fayling them through fear'.

[98] Though Dissenters were suspected of sympathy with the Dutch, and of hopes that Holland would help them in altering the form of government in England: CSPD 1665–66, Preface, xxv, Summary of letter from Court to Lord Lieutenants (15 July 1666),

parliamentarians, encouraged by the intimidating Sheldon and his episcopal bench, supported additional legislation 'for suppressing unconforming Ministers'.

This was specifically aimed at men who had remained in or near the parishes they had previously served, or were preaching in those localities. Not having 'declared their unfeigned assent and consent' to the Book of Common Prayer, their itinerancy must be curtailed. Sheldon was irritated that there was widespread 'tendernesse for such ill men', who 'have their Emissaryes over all the three Nations & abroad in Holland among our Enemies'. He affirmed that: 'What the Government is in England is well knowne, It is Monarchy in the State and Episcopy in the Church, and the thing promised in the [new] Oath is not to alter the Government in either.'[99] Crown and mitre were inseparable; criticism of the bishops meant disloyalty to the king.

In this context, the Five Mile Act[100] came on to the Statute Book. Unless prepared to take the necessary oaths, a Nonconformist minister was not permitted to live or visit within five miles of any city, town or parliamentary borough, or anywhere else he had previously lived and served. The same prohibition applied to those teaching in schools. The 'Oxford Oath' required the minister to swear that he would not give his support to any project suggesting alteration in Church or state, an impossible demand for those committed to the ideal of reformation. The penalty was a £40 fine,[101] for most of them far more than a year's salary, with the possibility of an additional six months' imprisonment. Informers were to receive one third of the fine.

---

concerning 'disaffected persons within our own kingdoms' planning 'distractions and insurrections here at home'.

[99] Caroline Robbins, 'The Oxford Session of the Long Parliament of Charles II', *Bulletin of the Institute of Historical Research* 21 (1948), 214–24 (quotation at 222), citing Bodl., MS Carte 80, fol.757v. The suggestion that Sheldon may have drafted the bill (Victor D. Sutch, *Gilbert Sheldon, Architect of Anglican Survival 1640–75* [The Hague, 1973], 146) is contested by R.A. Beddard, 'Sheldon and Anglican Recovery', *HistJ* 19 (1976), 1005–17, at 1013.

[100] *Statutes of the Realm*, V, 575; *EHD*, VIII, 382–4.

[101] This was a crippling amount of money for a minister to pay, and most had little option but to choose imprisonment rather than immediate payment or loss of essential goods and furniture. The salary of many Nonconformist ministers supported by congregations of 200–300 was £10–£30 p.a.: cf. Alexander Gordon (ed.), *Freedom after Ejection: A Review (1690–92) of Presbyterian and Congregational Nonconformity in England and Wales* (Manchester, 1917), esp. 7–10, 18, 22, 79, 83, 84, 89. Older ministers of outstanding quality who had held their churches together during difficult times, such as George Larkham, William Bagshawe and Matthew Clarke, were receiving sums of £7–£12 p.a.: ibid. 21, 26, 76. Anthony Sleigh had 'continued among his people' in the Keswick area since the Restoration, 'under many hardships, fineings, imprisonments, exiles' but 'all his people can doe will not amount to above' £5 p.a.: ibid. 22. What was described as a 'competent maintenance' by many churches was £30–40 p.a.: ibid. 100, but note: 'has many children and its hard with him though 30 l pr anum'.

The oath requirement provoked vigorous discussion among ministers. Henry Newcome's circle of friends had 'many serious bouts of canvassing this business, both by word and writing', knowing that '[m]any ministers in Yorkshire and London' had taken the oath,[102] as did almost half of the ejected ministers in Devon. Acknowledged leaders such as William Bates, John Howe, Thomas Jacombe and Matthew Poole[103] believed it right to do so, though sometimes, along with the requisite oath, they submitted a written statement explaining how they interpreted it. Some endeavoured to offer a substitute declaration but soon discovered that finely phrased alternatives were unacceptable.[104] Those unable to take the oath had to uproot their families and move, leaving friends who over the years had given them financial, practical and spiritual support. Oliver Heywood recalled its introduction as 'a day of great scattering, hundreds of ministers being … banished … and this day I come out of Yorkshire to Denton to live in exile'. A change of residence did nothing to inhibit his vigorous itinerancy, but he thought of those who paid a higher price: 'O the teares that have been shed for breaking familys, and separating husbands, wives, parents and children, pastors and people.'[105]

Despite the legislation, Nonconformist pastors continued to grasp whatever opportunities arose for ministry, and most Dissenting congregations invented new survival mechanisms, often maintaining strong numbers. In 1667, General Baptists in Dover had 242 members drawn from a wide area of East Kent.[106] East Anglia also had some good congregations. When William Bridge returned to Yarmouth to preach to local Independents, the people gathered 'in such numbers that by 7 a.m. there is no room to be got'; Nonconformists also met 'in other parts of the town in great numbers'.[107] In 1667, as the three-year period set for the 1664 Conventicle Act drew to its close, some Nonconformists entertained the hope of better things.[108]

London Dissenters were relatively undisturbed in the late 1660s. Baxter recalled that ministers 'who had ventured to keep open Meetings in their houses, and preached to great Numbers, contrary to the Law, were by the King's favour connived at; So that the people went openly to hear them without

---

[102] Newcome, *Autobiography* (ed. Parkinson), I, 154–55.

[103] Sylvester (ed.), *Reliquiae*, III, 13, §21. For Howe, cf. Rogers, *Howe*, 118–20; Frank Bate, *The Declaration of Indulgence, 1672: A Study in the Rise of Organised Dissent* (Liverpool, 1908), 50–51.

[104] J. Simmons, 'Some Letters from Bishop Ward of Exeter, 1663–1667', *Devon and Cornwall Notes and Queries* 21 (1940–1), 359–61.

[105] Heywood, *Autobiography* (ed. Turner), I, 201; cf. Henry, *Diaries* (ed. Lee), 185, citing Psa. 56: 8.

[106] Anon., 'Baptists in East Kent', *BQ* 2 (1924–5), 90–92, 137–41, 180–8, at 137–8.

[107] *CSPD* 1667–8, 277.

[108] *CSPD* 1667, 454. Some Norfolk magistrates were adopting a more tolerant policy because it was widely believed that there was 'a bill to be brought into the House for granting liberty of conscience to nonconformists': *CSPD* 1667, 336.

fear'.[109] Freedom in London encouraged provincial colleagues to greater boldness. Endeavouring to justify a more tolerant approach to Weymouth Dissenters, a local correspondent said that 'he understood that nonconformists met in London unsuppressed by King, Council or city officers', which evinced Clarendon's tart reply that if Londoners 'be rogues, must we be rogues too?'[110] Nonconformists in the capital made the most of their relative liberty. Informers notified the Lord Mayor that one Sunday as many as 12,000 people gathered at 'the several meeting places' in the city 'contrary to the act'.[111]

Dissenters entertained hopes of favourable changes in the legislation,[112] dreams largely without substance.[113] Sheldon's bishops were told to apply the full rigours of the law 'against these disorderly meetings'.[114] Imprisoned in Cambridge, Francis Holcroft warned his optimistic London colleagues of 'False Mistaken Prophets that say, the bitterness of death ... is over'. Referring to the slaying of the two witnesses (Rev. 11), a favourite passage in their martyrological hermeneutic, Holcroft observed that after five years' persecution, 'I think we hardly judge the Witnesses are yet risen'.[115]

---

[109] Sylvester (ed.), *Reliquiae*, III, 22, §57. Pepys heard that 'the nonconformists are mighty high, and their meetings frequented and connived at': Pepys, *Diary* (ed. Latham and Matthews), VIII, 584 (21 December 1667).

[110] *CSPD* 1665–66, 182–83; cf. D.L. Wykes, 'The Church and Early Dissent: The 1669 Return of the Nonconformist Conventicles for the Archdeaconry of Northampton', *Northamptonshire Past and Present* 8 (1991–92), 197–209, at 204–205; GLT, I, 51 ('he was not sorry for *carying* that Conventicle, saying the King gave them liberty'), cf. ibid. 54, 137, 141, 143, 144. When Sheldon asked the St Asaph diocese 'upon what hopes' the conventiclers 'looked for impunity', one considered response was that they 'build their Impunity upon ye Example of London & other places': GLT, III, 72; I, 4.

[111] *The Parliamentary Diary of Sir Edward Dering 1670–1673* (ed. B.D. Henning; New Haven, CT, 1940), 6.

[112] Pepys, *Diary* (ed. Latham and Matthews), VIII, 584 (21 December 1667); cf. *CSPD* 1667, 457. In September 1667, Chester Presbyterians were 'big with expectation that their ... factious ministers should be tolerated to prate in public'; Portsmouth 'fanatics begin to be very confident of a toleration of their principles, and ... their hope is much on the Parliament': *CSPD* 1667, 552.

[113] See Harris, *London Crowds*, 86, for the Dissenters' optimism.

[114] D. Wilkins, *Concilia Magnae Britanniae et Hiberniae*, 4 vols (1737), IV, 588.

[115] F[rancis]. H[olcroft]., *A Word to the Saints from the Watch Tower* (1668), 4, 20, quoting Rev. 11: 3–11. Nonconformist expositors frequently related this passage to their ministers' experience of persecution ('slain') and hope of the predicted 'resurrection'. Benjamin Keach, for example, maintained that the slaying of the two witnesses referred to the sufferings of God's servants across the centuries, including those in England after 1660, some by literal death as 'that godly Woman and Martyr Mrs. Gaunt', but others by 'spiritual' death, in the ejectment of 'many good Protestants, and the taking away of Charters of Cities and Coroporations, silencing worthy Ministers': *AntiChrist Stormed: or, Mystery Babylon the great Whore ... the present Church of Rome* (1689), 145–46. In the same year, Keach published *Distressed Zion Relieved*, whose subtitle referred to *those renowned worthies that fell in England by Popish rage and cruelty ... 1680 to 1688*. For Holcroft, see G.F. Nuttall, 'From Holcroft to Hussey: Cambridge

Sheldon was not alone in his desire to check the resurgence of Nonconformist witness,[116] and was passionate in seeking the speedy renewal of the Conventicle Act, hopefully with more stringent provisions. To this end he ordered his bishops to conduct a thorough enquiry in each diocese to determine precise numbers of Dissenting worshippers and ascertain as much additional information as possible about their teachers, the social composition of the congregations, frequency of meetings, and the reasons for their continuing Dissent.[117] He was reasonably convinced that 'within a few months' they would see 'the seduced people returning from their seditious and selfserving teachers to the unity of the Church',[118] but such optimism was unrealistic. Given the limitations of such records and the likelihood that Nonconformist numbers would hardly be exaggerated, the accumulated data provides a valuable account of Dissenting life in the late 1660s.[119] Earlier legislation had not dampened Nonconformist enthusiasm. The bishop of Gloucester was 'very much perplexed at the many impudent Conventicles in every part of this Countie, & the numbers that openly appear at them, & justify theire meetings to my face'.[120] He had rebuked the local justices for their failure to deal with the Nonconformist 'Disease' which 'is growne to[o] impudent. I have been told to my face in open Court, yt they doe meet and will meet'. The 'illegall meetings'

Nonconformity, 1660–1710', *JURCHS* 1/9 (1977), 241–58, repr. in idem, *Studies in English Dissent* (Weston Rhyn, 2002), 161–80.

[116] Many Members of Parliament were equally hostile to conciliatory measures, urging the king to 'enforce Obedience to the Laws in Force ... according to the Act of Uniformity': *JHC*, IX, 44.

[117] Sheldon was concerned that Nonconformist statistics were inflated, asking 'whether ye same persons do not meet at severall Conventicles, w[hi]ch may make them seem more numerous than indeed they are': BL, Add. MS 34769, fol.70 (Sheldon to Compton, bishop of London, 8 June 1669). Two days later Compton sent a copy of Sheldon's letter to his fellow bishops: ibid., fol.70v. Cf. Wilkins, *Concilia*, IV, 588, Postscript.

[118] Wilkins, *Concilia*, IV, 590.

[119] See David Wykes, 'The 1669 Return of the Nonconformist Conventicles', in K.M. Thompson (ed.), *Short Guides to Records: Second Series, Guides 25–48* (1994), 50–54 (Guide 33) for the origin, location, format, content, value, limitations and uses of the return. Cf. Evans, 'Leicestershire 1669'.

[120] Bodl., MS Add. c.302, fol.71r (William [Nicholson], bishop of Gloucester, to Sheldon, 22 September 1666). For this reference I am indebted to David Wykes, 'They "assemble in greater numbers and [with] more dareing then formerly": The Bishop of Gloucester and Nonconformity in the late 1660s', *Southern History* 17 (1995), 24–39.

were in places 'knowne and frequented' by the justices.[121] In other counties, magistrates were equally sympathetic to Nonconformity.[122]

Illegal meetings continued to attract large numbers. The vicar of Bath reported that the clergyman of a nearby village could only muster two or three for Morning Prayer, 'when at the same time 500 are met in a barn in the town', brazenly equipped 'with seats for the convenience of speaking and hearing'. The disheartened parish minister had tried to attract Nonconformists, 'preaching constantly twice a day to suit their humour ... and ... never uses a note nor writes so much as a word', but with little success.[123]

In 1670, armed with fresh information about Nonconformity's persistent growth, Sheldon pressed for the passing of the Second Conventicle Act,[124] a ruthless measure designed to inflict maximum damage on the Dissenting cause and bring recalcitrant parishioners back to the Restoration Church. Many parliamentarians were unhappy about its vindictive provisions and voiced their reluctance to place it on the Statute Book but, though opposed by some bishops,[125] it secured a majority vote in both Houses,[126] becoming what Andrew Marvell memorably described as 'the Quintessence of arbitrary Malice'.[127]

The fines imposed on those attending a conventicle were not as severe as under the 1664 Act but the penalties for preachers were heavy, £20 for a first offence, to be doubled for a second. If he managed to escape or was unable to pay, the fine was levied on the congregation. Offenders unable to pay had their goods distrained and sold. Conventiclers could be arrested on the order of a single justice of the peace, whereas the first Act had required the compliance of two. More affluent members of a congregation would be required to pay the fines of the poorer worshippers. Householders allowing Dissenters to meet on their premises would be fined £20, and local officials would be penalized if they failed to take action against known Dissenters. Informers were to be

---

[121] Letter of William [Nicholson], bishop of Gloucester, 'To the hands of the Right Wor[shipfu]ll his Ma[jes]ties Justices of the peace now mett at Gloucester', 2 October 1666, in S. Graveson, 'In the year of the Great Fire', *Friends Quarterly Examiner* 78 (1944), 243–45.

[122] The bishop of Exeter complained that at least 14 of Devon's Justices of the Peace were 'arrant Presbyterians', some of them 'as dangerous as any men within my Diocese': Bodl., MS Add c.305, fol.142 (Bishop Seth Ward to Sheldon, 19 December 1663); cf. fol.148 (16 January 1663/4): 'had I not had a parccell of corrupt Justices' and 'so many naughty men in Authority to shelter' Nonconformists; also fol.144.

[123] *CSPD* 1667, 455.

[124] *Statutes of the Realm*, V, 648–51; *EHD*, VIII, 384–86. The Act began by asserting that 'many at their Meetings contrive Insurrections (as late experience hath *shewen*)'.

[125] Philip Henry recorded in his diary: 'Dr. Reynolds, Bp of Norwich being sick sent his reasons agt it, manag'd by Dr. Wilkins Bp of Chester, Dr. Cosins also of Durham against it & Dr. Rainbow of Carlisle': *Diaries* (ed. Lee), 220.

[126] Bate, *Indulgence*, 64–67.

[127] Marvell to William Popple, 21 March 1670: H.M. Margoliouth (ed.), *The Poems and Letters of Andrew Marvell* (2 vols; 3rd ed.; Oxford, 1971), II, 314.

rewarded with a third of each fine and if an accused person's appeal to sessions proved unsuccessful he would incur treble costs. Justices of the peace and constables (not informers) had authority to break into houses. Any magistrate not enforcing the law was required to pay £100, half of which went to the informer.[128] Spying on neighbours became a lucrative pastime.[129]

The king endeavoured unsuccessfully to claim his power of dispensation in the case of approved individuals, though his initiatives may not have been entirely altruistic. While parliamentarians were framing measures to curb Dissenters, Charles was engaged in secret negotiations with his cousin, the King of France, discussions known only to two or three senior ministers. In this 'Secret Treaty of Dover',[130] Charles promised, in return for financial support, to be Catholic France's ally in a future war against the Protestant Dutch. When both monarchs agreed on the timing of the conflict, Charles was to receive military and naval support. Also, at an appropriate time he would announce that he was 'convinced of the truth of the Catholic religion'. When the king expressed hopes of religious liberty, Dissenters had every right to suspect his motives.

The promulgation of the new Conventicle Act gave rise to widespread persecution. On the Sunday before the new legislation came into effect, Bartholomew Ashwood reminded his Axminster members that the early Christians 'took joyfully' the spoiling of their goods, assured of an infinitely 'better and enduring substance' in heaven.[131] It was said that under current legislation it was virtually impossible to arrest a Dissenter and not convict him of some crime or other.[132] In the summer of 1670, Cockermouth Independents hoped to avoid the prospective informer by meeting at 6 a.m: 'Lord, think on thy people in evil times'.[133]

Where local officials harboured personal animosities, there was inevitable injustice. Without a warrant, a bailiff and a constable arrived at Oliver

---

[128] Writing on 10 May 1670, the day 'ye new Act of restraynt' came into force, Philip Henry recorded in detail its wide-ranging provisions, noting how meticulously everything was 'construed ag[ains]t ye offender', a 'contrivance yt some can but admire, but hee that sits in heaven laughs & even this shall bee for our good': *Diaries* (ed. Lee), 226.

[129] In *The Life and Death of Mr. Badman* (ed. J.F. Forrest and Roger Sharrock; Oxford, 1988), 81, John Bunyan graphically portrays the informer as one who 'would watch a nights, climb Trees, and range the Woods a days ... to find out the Meeters'.

[130] *EHD*, VIII, 863–67.

[131] *Ecclesiastica* (ed. Howard), 37, quoting Heb. 10: 34.

[132] Officially excommunicated, Oliver Heywood was not allowed into his parish church, but its churchwarden demanded 'four shillings' for his 'absence from church four sabboths'. He was fined if he did not attend the church and forbidden entrance if he did: *Autobiography* (ed. Turner), I, 190.

[133] In 1671 they agreed that, to be safe, 'all are to be in [their meeting place] before sunrising because of the difficulty of the day': Cockermouth Independent Church Book, 62–63, 71.

Heywood's home with a cart and took his goods and 'caryed them quite away'.[134] In London, Thomas Manton was arrested for preaching in Covent Garden. He could have been charged under the Conventicle Act, but it was thought best to accuse him of contravening the Five Mile Act, giving him a six-month prison sentence.[135] Bristol's Dissenters were forcefully opposed by the co-ordinated activities of an antagonistic mayor and a determined bishop, Gilbert Ironsides, who recruited informers to spy on four consecutive Sundays. The Mayor supervised forced entry into a meeting-house, took names of those attending and convicted some under the Act, but 'seeing they could not make us refraine our Meeting', sent a team to fix locks to its doors. The congregation 'were faine to meet in ye Lanes and highways for severall months' until the appointment of a new Mayor who 'did winke at our thus meeting'. Yet despite the fierce disruption and the death of their courageous pastor, Thomas Ewins, the church was encouraged by the reception of new members.[136]

The financial incentives for informers meant that private houses, as well as more public meeting places, were carefully watched. Local officers came to the house of a Bedfordshire Quaker, 'broke open his Doors, and took away Timber, Malt, Oats and other Things to the value of 70*l* [£70]'. Yet 'he continued stedfast, in permitting religious Meetings at his House, till by repeated Seizures he was so impoverished that, having nothing to satisfy the Fines, he was committed to Prison ... yet his Heart and House continued open to his Friends, who held their religious Meetings there as before'.[137]

In some localities, the application of the law was painfully vindictive, especially the practice of removing working tools, robbing Dissenters of opportunities to earn. A wheelwright's tools were taken, 'not for want of other Goods, but on purpose to disable him from working for his Livelihood. From a poor lame Maid, a Baptist, who earned her Bread by spinning and teaching Children, they took, by the Justice's Order, her spinning Wheel.' The local justice of the peace 'also forbad the Neighbours to send her their Children' for teaching.[138]

Undeterred by the Second Conventicle Act, many continued their ministry. Timothy Root was arrested while preaching, imprisoned in York Castle and

---

[134] Heywood, *Autobiography* (ed. Turner), I, 279 (16 June 1671).
[135] William Harris, 'Memoirs of the Life and Character of Thomas Manton', in Thomas Manton, *Works* (1870; repr. Edinburgh, 1993), I, xix. Manton was vehemently opposed to taking the so-called 'Oxford Oath'.
[136] *Broadmead Records* (ed. Hayden), 128.
[137] Besse, *Sufferings*, I, 8. Also in Bedfordshire, 'a poor widow ... suffered Distress of the few houshold Goods she had among which, having boiled Milk in a Skillet for two sick Children, the Informers threw away the poor Babes Sustenance, and made Prize of the Skillet'.
[138] Ibid., I, 10. When this disabled woman 'had no goods left to distrain' the local justice 'threatned to send her to Bridewell. He not only caused the Goods of several poor People to be taken away, but threatned to punish their Neighbours for relieving them.'

with 'double yrons laid on him' was 'put into the low jayl among 12 thieves'. Officers took '4 or 500 names of people' in his congregation and, under the terms of the new Act, each was made to 'pay 5s a peece'.[139] John Hickes incurred the king's displeasure when discovered to be the anonymous author of an account of Devon Nonconformists who had suffered under the new Act.[140] Subsequently pardoned, he continued to make mention of their sufferings and in a later publication exposed the 'boundless Avarice and unlimited Malice of many Justices of the Peace' and of the 'beggarly Informers, encouraged by them'. His travels in the West Country made him personally aware of the untold hardship of many of 'his Majesties peaceable Subjects'.[141]

Quakers suffered more than most. In the capital, their meeting-houses were razed to the ground.[142] At London's Horsleydown, all the furniture was carried away for sale, then the building itself totally destroyed. Friends met among the rubble, constantly harassed by soldiers who brutally attacked them. Assaulted in the streets, kind neighbours sheltered them in their own homes, in order 'to save their Lives'.[143]

Brief Respite

As the persecution continued, the king received several deputations and told one group of Nonconformist ministers that 'as hee would not willingly bee p[er]secuted hims[elf] for his own Religion, so neither did hee like to p[er]secute others for theirs'.[144] He was not alone in recognizing what Philip

---

[139] Heywood, *Autobiography* (ed. Turner), I, 272; see BL, Stowe MS 755, fol.29, for a manuscript account of Timothy Root's 'inlargement' at York. In 1685 Root conformed, to the great bewilderment of his ministerial colleagues and the distress of his family: cf. *Continuation*, II, 959–60.

[140] [John Hickes], *A True and Faithful Narrative of the Unjust and Illegal Sufferings of Many Christians, injuriously and injudiciously call'd FANATICKS ... in the County of Devon since the 10th of May, 1670* (1671).

[141] 'Some of you have had your standing Corn, some your dwelling Houses, your Work Tools, your Wearing Apparrel; yea your very food seized and destrain'd ... your Houses rifled and emptied of all ... leaving you neither Bed, Stool, Chair, Pot, Pan or Spoon'. In order to meet fines, their goods were sold at prices well below their value, 'as Cows and Bullocks for 2s.6d and Sheep for 12d, 6d. and 4d a piece': John Hickes, *A Discourse of the Excellency of the Heavenly Substance*, 1673, Dedicatory Epistle, [unpaginated]. Accused of involvement in Monmouth's rebellion, Hickes was executed in 1685: cf. [John Tutchin], *A New Martyrology* (1693), 481–504. For a detailed study of Hickes, see GLT, III, 579–618; cf. *BDBR*, II, 86–87.

[142] Besse, *Sufferings*, I, 428–9.

[143] Ibid. 694–98 reprints *The Cry of Innocent Blood ... being a short relation of the Barbarous Cruelties inflicted lately upon ... Quakers at the Meeting in Horslydown* (1670).

[144] Henry, *Diaries* (ed. Lee), 243: 'November 9, [1671] london Min[iste]rs with ye King, Dr. [Samuel] Annesley, Mr.[Thomas] Watson, Mr [William] Whitaker & ye two

Henry described as 'the ineffectualness of rigor for divers yeares'.[145] Personally unhappy about repressive measures, Charles took a constitutionally irregular step in March 1672 when he published a Declaration of Indulgence.[146] Claiming unique power in church matters, he suspended the Penal Laws against all Dissenters, Nonconformist and Catholic alike. The timing of the Declaration is significant, promulgated just two days before declaring war on the country's commercial rivals, the Dutch,[147] as agreed in his secret Treaty of Dover.

In his fateful decision to ignore Parliament, Charles entertained high hopes of enlisting the loyal support of both Nonconformists and Catholics. Protestant Dissenters were permitted to meet in appropriately licensed meeting places, served by teachers with licences of approval by royal authority. Charles knew that the nation would not tolerate total freedom for Catholics, but they were now allowed to meet in homes, as they had done for decades.

Philip Henry noted the mixed reception accorded to the Declaration.[148] After over ten years' repression, large numbers of Dissenters breathed a sigh of relief, and applied for the required licences, though not all were happy in doing so. Many were troubled about its unconstitutional nature, as it gave the king 'a power above the lawes'.[149] If he could annul disagreeable legislation, he might later do the same with laws Dissenters wished to uphold. They feared absolutism in the monarchy; that was how Catholic France was ruled. Perhaps freedom for 'Papists' was the subtle beginning of Catholic domination.[150] Some feared the mechanics of registration; hitherto unavailable details concerning the locations of Nonconformist meeting-places would become government property and the authorities would have the names and occupations of every registered preacher at their fingertips. Should the Declaration be withdrawn, as within a year it was, such information could prove severely detrimental to continuing Dissent.[151]

Vincents [Nathanael and Thomas], to w[ho]m hee said, hee was sensible of their straits & would endeavour their enlargm[en]t.'

[145] Ibid. 249.

[146] *EHD*, VIII, 287–88; Bate, *Indulgence*.

[147] Justifying his Declaration to the House of Commons, the king said that by it he was 'securing Peace at Home, when I had war abroad': *JHC*, IX, 252.

[148] It was a 'thing diversly resented, as men's Interest leades them, the Conformists generally displeas'd at it, the Presb[yterians] glad, the Indep[endents] very glad, the Papists triumph', Henry, *Diaries* (ed. Lee), 250, cf. Heywood, *Autobiography* (ed. Turner), I, 289.

[149] Henry, *Diaries* (ed. Lee), 253.

[150] It was a needless fear. Catholics represented less than 2% of the population and, London apart, were located mainly in rural areas, known and respected by their neighbours as being largely free from strident political or religious ambitions.

[151] Henry, *Diaries* (ed. Lee), 262. The Declaration might be a subtle device to gather more precise information for the later implementation of heavy penalties. Others, remembering the Huguenots, feared everything might end 'in a Massacre, it being now known where such people may be mett with, as if they all had but one neck': ibid. 253.

The Indulgence seriously divided Presbyterians. Many, with little encouragement, still dreamt of comprehension within the Restoration Church.[152] This was, however, a vain hope.[153] The bishops had no intention of recognizing the validity of their ordination, and were irritated by their imperious notion that unpalatable Prayer Book obligations such as the use of the surplice, the sign of the cross in baptism or compulsory kneeling at the sacrament might become optional. The Declaration of Indulgence forced the Presbyterians to recognize, however painfully, that applications for licences made them into a tolerated sect or 'denomination' outside the Established Church.

Many of the older Presbyterians, such as Baxter, Manton and Bates, with nostalgic memories of 'reformed' parishes during the Interregnum, refused to sacrifice the hope of comprehension. Most younger ministers, conditioned by twelve years of repression, loss of freedom and the curtailment of their ministry, followed the lead given by the more realistic Vincent Alsop, Samuel Annesley, James Janeway and Thomas Watson.[154] Such men had no serious objection to being identified with 'separatist' Independents and Baptists who, supremely content with the prospect of toleration, had no desire to belong to a restrictive national Church. A rift in the Presbyterian ranks was evident, even to an unsympathetic outsider.[155] With the exception of all Quakers and some Baptists, Dissenters applied for licences in large numbers. Those who did not claimed that it was not the king's prerogative (or anybody else's) either to grant or withhold a basic human right.

The treasured freedom was short-lived. Bishops, politicians and gentry alike clamoured for the speedy abrogation of the Indulgence. In some parishes, clergy reported decreased congregations.[156] The bishops lamented to the king

---

[152] The 'allowing of separate places' might serve 'to overthrow our parish-order'. 'We are put hereby ... into a trilemma, either to turn independents in practice, or to strike in with the conformists, or to sit down in former silence and sufferings': Matthew Henry, *The Life of ... Philip Henry, corrected and enlarged by J.B. Williams* (1825; facsimile reprint in *The Lives of Philip and Matthew Henry*, Edinburgh, 1974), 128–29.

[153] At least eight different bills for comprehension were brought forward for Parliament's consideration between 1667 and 1689, but all failed: cf. Roger Thomas, 'Comprehension and Indulgence', in Nuttall and Chadwick (eds), *Uniformity*, 191–253; *EB*, I, 238–46; W.G. Simon, 'Comprehension in the Age of Charles II', *ChH* 31 (1962), 440–48.

[154] R.A. Beddard, 'Vincent Alsop and the Emancipation of Restoration Dissent', *JEH* 24 (1973), 161–84, at 166: 'These men came to regard the Great Ejectment as a parting of the ways, a winnowing of the wholesome corn from the irredeemable chaff'.

[155] Sir Joseph Williamson, then clerk of the Privy Council, and no lover of Dissenters, cynically described the older Presbyterians as staid 'Dons', their younger colleagues as venturesome 'Ducklings': *CSPD* 1671–72, 28.

[156] Spurr, *Restoration Church*, 63; cf. *CSPD* 1672, 589: The Bishop of Lincoln was grieved that 'the orthodox clergy are out of heart. Shall nothing be done to support them against the Presbyterians, who grow and multiply faster than the other'? In 1676, the

that 'defections are frequently made ... to the pernicious and destructive novelties' of Dissent,[157] and local squires observed that 'our episcopal congregations look very thin'.[158] Sir John Reresby described Charles's Declaration as 'the greatest blowe that was ever given, since the King's restoration, to the Church of England'. Given this taste of freedom, 'all the lawes' on the Statute Book would never bring Dissenters 'back to due conformaty'.[159] He was not far wrong.

Renewed Oppression

In 1673, conflict with the Dutch again went badly; Charles, desperately short of funds, was compelled to recall Parliament after a gap of almost two years. The first item on the parliamentary agenda was his unacceptable use of the prerogative granting freedom of worship to Dissenters. His financial difficulties were soon rectified but, despite the king's announcement that he was 'resolved to stick'[160] to his fated Indulgence Declaration, the House asserted that 'penal statutes, in Matters Ecclesiastical, cannot be suspended, but by an Act of Parliament', and firmly insisted on its withdrawal.[161] Nonconformity's opponents were delighted.[162]

Technically invalid, the 1672 licences were not recalled by the king for a further two years,[163] but their effective life was only eleven months from their issue.[164] With their withdrawal, Dissenters in several parts of the country suffered renewed persecution.[165] Motivated by the prospect of additional

---

archdeacon of Canterbury reported that 'many left the Church upon the late Indulgence, who did before frequent it': Thomas Richards, 'The Religious Census of 1676', in Supplement to *The Transactions of the Honourable Society of Cymmrodorion* (1925–26), 2–3, citing Lambeth Palace Library, MS 639, fol.168b.
[157] *CSPD* 1673–75, 549.
[158] *CSPD* 1672–73, 300.
[159] Reresby, *Memoirs* (ed. Browning), 84–85.
[160] *JHC*, IX, 246.
[161] Ibid. 252.
[162] 'It was entertained with great joy in the town, with bells and bonfires', said Henry Newcome, 'under the notion of the King and Parliament being agreed, but they expressed much joy and scorn over us': *Autobiography* (ed. Parkinson), II, 204.
[163] Heywood, *Autobiography* (ed. Turner), I, 303.
[164] On an April Sunday in 1673, Philip Henry writes, 'One Sabb[ath] more', and the following Sunday, during their worship, it was 'given out to be ye last Sabb[ath]' they could meet: Shrewsbury School Library, MS James XXVIII, Philip Henry, Diary, 6 and 13 April 1673.
[165] The harassment of Dissenters was neither uniform nor consistent. In 1674, troubled because 'scandalous meetings' had been 'suffered to grow', and many people were 'dayly seduced away from the Church', Durham's archdeacon wrote to the King's Secretary asking whether 'the late Act against Conventicles' ought to be put 'in execution'. He had encountered resistance to his efforts, it being widely held that 'his Majestie at this presentt would not have it soe'. Seeking confirmation of the king's

income, local spies were eager to discover new meeting places and offending preachers.[166]

A further restrictive measure was then introduced, the Test Act (1673).[167] Primarily directed against Catholics, with its required declaration against transubstantiation, it also debarred Protestant Dissenters from local and national government posts and military office by demanding that, in addition to taking the Oaths of Supremacy and Allegiance, an office holder must 'receive the Lord's Supper according to the usage of the Church of England'. James, Charles's brother and successor to the Crown, had been a secret Catholic. Unable to receive Anglican communion, he resigned from the office of Lord High Admiral, clearly declaring his allegiance. Fierce anti-Catholic feeling was further increased that year when the widowed James,[168] now forty, married the fifteen-year-old Catholic princess Mary of Modena, earning a belated protest from Parliament. Pope-burning processions and the lighting of bonfires in London expressed further disapproval of the Duke of York's Catholicism and marriage, and also of the king's foreign policy, sentiments not remotely confined to Dissent[169] but shared more widely in the Restoration Church and beyond it. The country was unhappy about England's alliance with Catholic France, especially after additional French conquests in Europe. From this time, national opposition to 'popery'[170] became even more volatile, resulting in a vigorous campaign to prevent James from succeeding to the throne.

---

wishes, he received Charles's curt reply that 'laws were made to be observed': *The Remains of Denis Granville, Dean and Archdeacon of Durham* (Surtees Society 47; 1865), 13–14.

[166] Owen Stockton's notes of a sermon to Ipswich Dissenters in June 1675 state that the meeting was 'molested by informers': DWL, MS 28.31.3, Sermon on Gen. 32: 1. In the same year, Amersham General Baptists reported John Griffith's arrest and imprisonment because he 'refused to fforbeare to preach at the Command of the Mare [Mayor]': *The Church Books of Ford or Cuddington and Amersham Baptist Churches* (ed. W.T. Whitley; 1912), 204.

[167] *Statutes of the Realm*, V, 782–85.

[168] His first wife, Anne Hyde (mother of the princesses Mary and Anne, who became the country's next two queens), was raised in a firmly Protestant home but became a Catholic at the close of her life.

[169] Harris, *London Crowds*, 93. Generally well-behaved occasions, London's pope-burning ceremonies continued to attract huge crowds, an estimated 200,000 in 1679, (ibid. 104), an expression of popular hostility to 'popery'. For increased animosity at the time of the 'Popish Plot', see Sheila Williams, 'The Pope-Burning Processions of 1679, 1680 and 1681', *Journal of the Warburg and Courtauld Institutes* 21 (1958), 104–18; O.W. Furley, 'The Pope-Burning Processions of the Late Seventeenth Century', *History* 44 (1959), 16–23.

[170] Of James, Duke of York, it was written: 'If e'er he be King, I know Britain's doom; / We must all to the stake, or be converts to Rome': 'A Dialogue between the Two Horses', in G. de F. Lord et al., *Poems on Affairs of State: Augustan Satirical Verse, 1660–1714*, 7 vols (New Haven, CT, 1963–75), I, 281.

For several years, the 'exclusion' issue dominated the political and religious agenda. On this matter, at least, Anglicans and Nonconformists shared a common fear: the distinct possibility of a Catholic monarch and the threat of enforced allegiance to the Catholic faith. In 1676, disturbed about the potential dangers from Catholicism and the robust continuance of Protestant Dissent, the ageing Sheldon asked Henry Compton, bishop of London, to enlist the help of the bishops in collecting precise information concerning the strength of Nonconformity in the English parishes. In addition to general population details, local clergy were to ascertain the number of 'popish recusants', and 'other dissenters' who 'either obstinately refuse, or wholly absent themselves from the communion of the Church of England'. With little justification, the elderly archbishop believed that by the orderly collection of these statistics 'their suppression will be a work very practicable'.[171] No provision was made in the documentation for the 'highly porous'[172] boundary between Dissent and conformity, typified by the substantial number of parishioners with declared Presbyterian convictions who regularly worshipped at the local church but supplemented their spiritual diet at a local conventicle. As regular attenders at their parish church, such 'non-conforming' conformists were never numbered with Dissenters but that, at heart, is what they were. The census figures suggest that less than 5% of the population were Protestant Dissenters and less than 1% were known Catholics.[173]

There was little abatement in the harassment of Dissenters. In the year of the Compton Census, 'it pleased the King importunately to Command and Urge the Judges and London-Justices, to put the Laws against nonconformists in Execution'.[174] Searches were made for unlicensed pamphlets.[175] In the capital, magistrates prohibited the use of some halls where Dissenters met.[176] Its Lord Mayor, Sir Joseph Sheldon, was the archbishop's 'near Kinsman', and several London ministers were arrested and sent 'to the Common Goals [sic] for Six Months ... for not taking the Oath, and dwelling within five miles'. When one was arrested during a Sunday service, his congregation rose up *en masse*, following their minister to the justice's house and on to the jail, 'to shew their

---

[171] Wilkins, *Concilia*, IV, 598 (Sheldon to Henry Compton).
[172] *EB*, I, 22.
[173] For the difficulty of discerning the precise number of Dissenters, cf. Anne Whiteman with Mary Clapinson (eds), *The Compton Census of 1676: A Critical Edition* (Oxford, 1986), lxxvii–lxxix.
[174] Sylvester (ed.), *Reliquiae*, III, §328, 176.
[175] *CSPD* 1676–77, 51. These included *A Letter from a Person of Quality*; *Two Seasonable Discourses*; and *The Naked Truth*, whose authors were to be taken into custody.
[176] BL Stowe MS 209, Essex Papers, January–June 1676, fol.237v, 13 May 1676: 'ye Citty halls they had hired are shut up'. The closure of city halls occurred again in 1683: cf. *EB*, II, 341–42 [P.351].

Affections'.[177] Yet even in vulnerable localities the persecution was sporadic rather than persistent. In the same month as the arrest of the city's Dissenting ministers, provincial Baptist leaders were looking forward to joining their London colleagues for an assembly.[178] They had hopes of sharing news of the churches, compiling a confession of faith and discussing their future, including 'a plan for ... providing an orderly standing ministry in the church'.[179]

The forbidding phantom of Catholic domination gained firmer substance in 1678–9 as a result of the so-called 'Popish Plot'. An unscrupulous agitator, Titus Oates, swore that he had evidence of a Jesuit conspiracy to murder the king, set London ablaze and (with French help) massacre English Protestants, establishing Catholicism as England's exclusive religion.[180] Within days, news of the supposed plot spread quickly throughout the country, making it difficult to separate truth from speculation.[181] Thousands feared that the royal household's Catholic convictions would eventually change the nation's religious allegiance. Prior to the Plot, in January 1678, Cockermouth Independents set aside a day to pray at their minister's home 'in respect to the state of the nation full of favour with reference to Popery', their emotions expressed in the preachers' choice of text: Psalm 68: 1: 'Let God arise, let his enemies be scattered'.[182] Neurotic anxiety continued to take hold of communities in different parts of the country.[183]

During the Exclusion crisis, loosely defined groups emerged either supporting or opposing the exclusion of James from the succession. Their divergent political activities marked the hazy beginnings of what eventually

---

[177] Sylvester (ed.), *Reliquiae*, III, §327–8, 176.

[178] Oxford, Regent's Park College, Angus Library, Porton (with Broughton) Baptist Church Book, 24: the entry for '24th day of ye first month 1675/6', responding to a letter 'from ye Churches meeting at London' (dated 2 October 1675) planning to meet 'the first Wednesday in May next'.

[179] Baptist historian Joseph Ivimey thought it probable that in the event 'the severity of persecution against the nonconformists prevented their meeting': *A History of the English Baptists*, 4 vols (1811–30), I, 416. But by some means or other, representatives from 'London and the country' found an opportunity at that time to compile a Particular Baptist Confession of Faith (1677, later republished, and more widely circulated in 1689), modelled on the Savoy Declaration, itself dependent in many places on the Westminster Confession, showing in a time of persecution 'how much they had in common with the Congregationalists and the Presbyterians': B.R. White, *The English Baptists of the Seventeenth Century* (1983), 117.

[180] John Kenyon, *The Popish Plot* (1972). For contemporary accounts, see *EB*, II, 1–30 [P8–36] for Roger Morrice's abstract of Titus Oates, *A True Narrative of the Horrid Plot and Conspiracy of the Popish Party* (1679); Narcissus Luttrell, *A Brief Historical Relation of State Affairs from September 1678 to April 1714*, 6 vols (Oxford, 1857), I, 1–39.

[181] Newcome, *Autobiography* (ed. Parkinson), II, 227–28.

[182] Cockermouth Independent Church Book, 133.

[183] In this context, Oliver Heywood produced forty reasons why thinking people should be afraid of Catholicism: *Autobiography* (ed. Turner), II, 216–20: 26 January 1680/81.

emerged as the Whig and Tory parties. Whigs campaigned for exclusion, fearing that a future Catholic king might rob them of civil and political liberties, ideals treasured by Dissenters. With their allegiance to 'Church and King', Tories supported James and regarded Dissenters as anti-monarchist traitors, though it was not the king Dissenters opposed but his declared Catholicism. Though committed to religious tolerance, the Dissenters' Whig sympathizers in Parliament were powerless to help. Thanks to generous French subsidies, the financially independent king never called another Parliament during his reign.

Indignant that Dissenters had pressed for the exclusion of a Catholic monarch, Charles was determined that the restriction of their liberties should continue. A displeased king, a bench of resolute bishops, and many of the country's gentry became increasingly hostile to Nonconformist worshippers, whether in meeting-houses or family homes. Offenders were to be punished both for frequenting local conventicles and for not attending parish churches.

In the more intense period of persecution of the 1680s, London and the provinces were equally affected. London meeting-houses were raided and huge fines levied on their ministers.[184] Many of them 'were thrown into Common Goals [sic]; their Meetings ... were everywhere suppress'd; they chose in some Places to meet in the Night in small Numbers'.[185] John Howe told his congregation that ministers like himself were seldom able to walk the streets without fear of assault.[186] Howe found it difficult not to criticize the hostility of Restoration churchmen.[187] His own congregation was raided during one of his sermons, the preacher fined £40 (his second offence) and several of his people committed to prison. Barely six months later, Howe was again accused of holding a conventicle. News of London's troublesome events soon reached the provinces.[188] Thomas Jolly recorded not only 'the imprisonment of brother [Charles] Sagar', one of his members, in Lancaster jail (where Jolly was soon to join him) but further London news such as 'the taking away of the citty's

---

[184] *CSPD* 1680–81, 613; cf. Samuel Annesley's fines in 1682–83: *Middlesex County Records* (ed. Jeaffrreson), IV, 182, 224–25, 302.

[185] W. Tong, *Some Memoirs of the Life and Death of ... John Shower* (1716), 50.

[186] Rogers, *Howe*, 225. Edmund Calamy said that his father (1634–85) 'was never cast in prison, but often had warrants out against him, and was forced to disguise himself, and skulk in private holes and corners, and frequently change his lodgings': *An Historical Account of my own Life* (ed. J.T. Rutt, 2 vols; 1829), I, 88. For another London minister's use of disguise in 1683, see Ralph Thoresby, *Letters of Eminent Men, addressed to Ralph Thoresby* (2 vols; 1832), I, 22.

[187] John Howe, 'The Case of the Protestant Dissenters Represented and Argued', in Rogers, *Howe*, 247–59.

[188] Oliver Heywood heard in Yorkshire that 'Never were meetings so universally broken' as in London: *Autobiography* (ed. Turner), II, 223.

charter'.[189] Such royal interference in local government did not augur well for London Dissenters who had greatly enjoyed earlier periods of relative freedom.

Persecution was widespread.[190] Dissenters 'in all citys, towns, [and] countreys' were under stress and their ministers 'driven into corners'.[191] Writing to Quakers overseas, Fox described England's 'great Persecution', with between 'Thirteen and Fourteen Hundred in Prison … Besides the great Spoil and Havoc … made of Friends Goods … And we are kept out of our Meetings in Streets and Highways … beaten, and abused.'[192] The 'houses and shops' of Axminster Independents 'were rifled, their goods and cattle violently taken away and sold at a small price',[193] yet even on 'a very rainy day' many of their members continued to meet 'in the open air, exposed to the violence of the weather'.[194] Adverse physical conditions were no deterrent to Dissenters.[195] They took heart that, throughout the country, there were local justices and constables with no desire to molest them,[196] although official sympathizers became the target of specific opposition.[197]

Dissenters were not helped by the active participation of some of them in what became known as the Rye House Plot. In the summer of 1683 a group were said to have planned to assassinate the king and his brother at Hoddesdon, where the road narrowed near the Rye House (home of Richard Rumbold, an ex-Cromwellian soldier). The royal party was expected to pass this point on returning from the races, but a fire at Newmarket caused Charles and James to return earlier than anticipated. Several prominent Whigs and some

---

[189] *The Note Book of the Rev. Thomas Jolly 1671–1693* (ed. H. Fishwick; Chetham Society, n.s. 33; Manchester, 1895), 53, 138; for the loss of the charter, see Gary S. De Krey, *London and the Restoration, 1659–1683* (Cambridge, 2005), 382–86.

[190] See Edward Pearse, *The Conformist's Fourth Plea for the nonconformists* (1683), for the persecution of Dissenting ministers in the provinces, e.g. ibid. 83 (Thomas Browning in Northamptonshire).

[191] Heywood, *Autobiography* (ed. Turner), II, 223; cf. *EB*, II, 361 [P363], where Morrice records that 'the severities are great in many places in the Countrey'.

[192] Fox, *Epistles*, 490 (Letter 386, 1683); cf. ibid. 493 (Letter 388, 1683), to Friends in North Africa: 'I think you have more Liberty to meet there than we have here, for they … cast us into Prisons, and spoil our Goods.'

[193] *Ecclesiastica* (ed. Howard), 80; cf. Paul Seaward, *The Restoration, 1660–1688* (Basingstoke, 1991), 120, for similar oppression elsewhere. For arrests in Hampshire in 1683, see Andrew M. Coleby, *Central Government and the Localities: Hampshire, 1649–1689* (Cambridge, 1987), 200–202.

[194] *Ecclesiastica* (ed. Howard), 88.

[195] In the winter of 1683, 'being a hard frost, and Snow on ye Ground', Bristol believers 'met in ye Wood, and though we stood in ye Snow, ye Sun Shone upon us, and We were in peace': *Broadmead Records* (ed. Hayden), 257.

[196] When Thomas Jolly was arrested for 'the officers managed the business with much tenderness': Jolly, *Note Book* (ed. Fishwick), 39.

[197] At Pontefract in 1682 some Justices 'exercised great rigour and severity' on local officers 'for not giving in the names of Conventiclers' and 'imprisoned 7 constables', and fined several more: Heywood, *Autobiography* (ed. Turner), II, 287.

Nonconformists were accused of conspiracy; Rumbold and two other former soldiers were Baptists.[198] Unreliable informers fabricated evidence, elements of truth were wildly distorted, and executions followed. It was claimed that James Scott, Duke of Monmouth, the king's illegitimate son by Lucy Walter, was involved in the conspiracy, though he insisted that he was 'not conscious of any designe'[199] against the king's life.[200] Thousands preferred a Protestant successor but few would stoop to murder. Some Dissenters had made no secret of their conviction that Charles's illegitimate (but unashamedly Protestant) son should become the country's next king, and in some parts of the country he had been widely acclaimed as a preferred successor. Accused of subversive activities, Monmouth was exiled, as he had been a few years previously; his suspected involvement in plotting did little to increase his popularity or that of the Whigs who supported him. Many Nonconformists took every opportunity to distance themselves from such damaging intrigue, but their activities were more intensely scrutinized and, as news of the plot, embellished with attendant rumours, spread around the country, their sufferings increased.[201]

During the intensified persecution, Bunyan wrote his *Seasonable Counsel*, an exposition of the Petrine injunction that sufferers should 'commit themselves to their faithful Creator' and continue to do good (1 Peter 4: 19). Its welcome publication brought rich encouragement to Dissenters with its appropriate blend of comprehensive biblical teaching, historical illustration (mainly from Foxe), pastoral counsel and practical application. Affirming Nonconformist loyalty to king and country, Bunyan recognized that he was writing in hard times when suspicion and false accusation were rife, and innocent Dissenters were at the mercy of avaricious informers. He urged his readers to be careful in everyday conversation; hostile listeners were ready to misquote the most innocent remark. 'I have heard of an *Inn-keeper* here in England, whose sign was the *Crown*'; when this 'merry-man' was 'jovial among his Guests', he playfully pointed to his son, saying, 'This Boy is heir to

---

[198] Writing to the Earl of Arran on 7 July 1683, the Duke of Ormonde maintained that 'Anabaptists or Independents' were among the conspirators: HMC, *Calendar of the Manuscripts of the Marquess of Ormonde*, n.s., VII (RCHM, 36; 1912), 65.

[199] *EB*, II, 430 [P406].

[200] Initially Monmouth denied complicity in the Rye House plot. Later, under pressure, he confessed, and then recanted: John Miller, *James II: A Study in Kingship* (1989), 116; on Monmouth's opposition to assassination, see De Krey, *London and the Restoration*, 360.

[201] Orders were published in Cheshire churches 'to present all that come not to church & to the Sacr[amen]t if above 16' and, aware of 'Restraynts in all places', Philip Henry says that he, his wife 'and many more' were 'presented at Flint for not coming to the Sacram[en]t': *Diaries* (ed. Lee), 319, 321. Henry knew that harassment reached far beyond Cheshire: 'Tidings of great trouble to Min[iste]rs & people both at *london* & elsewhere, how long lord!': ibid. 320. Between 1680 and 1684 the rate of convictions in Norfolk more than trebled: John Miller, *Popery and Politics in England 1660–1688* (Cambridge, 1973), 191.

the *Crown*', a playful comment but with lethal consequences: 'I mistake not the story, *for these words he lost his life*'.[202]

Changing Times

Early in 1685, the nation was shocked to hear of the unexpected death of Charles II.[203] Many were apprehensive about the succession,[204] but James was calmly accepted and in some places the new reign was even greeted with rejoicing.[205] But within months of Charles's death, the Duke of Monmouth returned from exile to enlist popular support for his claim to the crown.[206] News had spread that the dying king had declined Anglican communion and at his special request had been received into the Roman Catholic Church.[207] James, his brother and natural heir, was an avowed Catholic who, during his earlier service as Lord High Commissioner in Scotland, had actively promoted the persecution of the Scottish nonconformists, the Covenanters. Moreover, news from Catholic France of the intense sufferings of the Huguenots did little to encourage the view that English Dissenters had nothing to fear from a new reign.[208] Within three months of Monmouth's short-lived rebellion, Louis XIV had revoked the pro-toleration Edict of Nantes, and the intensified persecution drove half a million French refugees to other lands, large numbers of them to England, all with lurid tales of Catholic repression.

---

[202] Bunyan, *Seasonable Counsel, or Advice to Sufferers* (1684), in *MW*, X, 39.

[203] The king had not been unwell, and was only in his 55th year; cf. BL, MS Add. 29561, fol.55, for a letter to Viscount Hatton dated 7 February 1684/5, referring to the king 'having died yesterday at about noone'. The correspondent reported that 'there are more teares shed' for the dead monarch 'then has been for any King some hundred of yeares: Here are few persons That shew any ioy in their Looks, or pleasantness in their behaviour.'

[204] Recording the death of Charles II, 'to the great griefe of all', a Puritan conforming minister, Isaac Archer, wrote, '[o]ur feares for religion were great': Matthew Storey (ed.), *Two East Anglian Diaries 1641–1729* (Suffolk Records Society, 36; Woodbridge, 1994), 171. Ralph Thoresby said the king's death was 'bewailed with many tears, for the gloomy prospect of popery': *The Diary of Ralph Thoresby* (ed. Joseph Hunter, 2 vols; 1830), I, 180.

[205] Calamy, *Historical Account* (ed. Rutt), I, 116–17; *The Life and Times of Anthony Wood, Antiquary, of Oxford 1635–1695 described by Himself* (ed. Andrew Clarke, 5 vols; Oxford, 1894), III, 129–30.

[206] Another pro-Monmouth rebellion (uncoordinated, though it was meant to be) took place in Scotland, equally unsuccessful, led by Archibald Campbell, Earl of Argyll.

[207] 'With all my heart': John Miller, *Charles II* (1991), 381.

[208] Newsletters circulated information about cruelties in France: HMC, *Fourteenth Report, Vol. III, Appendix II, The Manuscripts of His Grace the Duke of Portland* (RCHM, 29; 1894), 405; cf. also the many references in Morrice's *Entring Book*: *EB*, III, 62–3, 68 ('Every Post brings us an account of further unheard of Cruelties in France'), 73, 124–25, 138–39, 184, 201, 251, 314, 329–30, 388 [P498, 502, 506, 537–38, 546, 575, 588–89, 624, Q20–21, 37, 79].

Things hardly looked well for Dissenters.[209] Unhappily for them, many in the West Country, mainly from society's middle ranks,[210] joined the comparatively meagre numbers of Monmouth's army (three or four thousand at most) as they marched up from the coast, intent on Bristol, enlisting supporters en route, to their sole success, the capture of Taunton. It was a doomed enterprise. In just over three weeks the rising had been quelled, hordes of its supporters arrested and Monmouth executed. Like others who participated in the rising, Dissenters suffered barbaric punishments in the infamous 'Bloody Assizes' conducted by Judge George Jeffreys, whose harrowing cruelties appalled people who had little time for Dissent.[211] In the minds of many, Nonconformity became even more sharply associated with sedition and rebellion,[212] so little was done to ease the continuing repressive measures, now supported by the new king. James said 'he would never give any sort of countenance to dissenters knowing it must needs be faction and not religion, if men could not bee content to meet five besides their own familie'.[213]

One London minister's wife, Mary Franklin, told how her home was searched as they looked for her husband Robert 'at the time when they put several into prisons ... when the troubles were about the Duke of

---

[209] Dissenters were under immediate suspicion. A Sussex Nonconformist diarist reported 'a great many persons imprisoned ... thought best to withdraw myself out of the Towne till the business was over; & not to expose myself to be sent a prisoner to Dovor Castle for nothing; as some others were serv'd, who staid in Towne': *An Astrological Diary of the Seventeenth Century: Samuel Jeake of Rye 1652–1699* (ed. Michael Hunter and Annabel Gregory; Oxford, 1988), 173.

[210] See Peter Earle, *Monmouth's Rebels: The Road to Sedgemoor, 1685* (1977), 196–212, for a detailed analysis of the social composition of Monmouth's army. R. Clifton, *The Last Popular Rebellion: The Western Rising of 1685* (1984), 5–6, 10–11, challenges Earle's view that Monmouth's army was 'made up almost entirely of nonconformists from the great bastions of Dissent in the three counties of Somerset, Devon and Dorset'. For the participation of Axminster Independents, see W.M. Wigfield, '*Ecclesiastica*, The Book of Remembrance', *Somerset Archaeology and Natural History* 119 (1975), 51–55.

[211] Their arrests and punishments are vividly recounted in *The Western Martyrology* (1687), the combined work of Titus Oates ('attempting to resume the public stage': Clifton, *Last Popular Rebellion,* 273); John Dunton, a Whig propagandist; and John Tutchin, a Whig pamphleteer who had had participated in the rising and was imprisoned for seven years. The *Martyrology* presents the story in Foxean terms, clearly identifying the victims with the Marian martyrs.

[212] Many prominent Dissenters openly dissociated themselves from the rebellion. Morrice thought the rising treasonable, consistently describing Monmouth's soldiers as 'Rebells': *EB*, III, 16–20 (P467–70); cf. Clifton, *Last Popular Rebellion*, 272–74.

[213] Henry Ellis, *Original Letters illustrative of English History*, First Series, III (1969), 339; HMC, *XVth Report, Appendix VIII, The Manuscripts of His Grace the Duke of Buccleuch, and Queensberry* (RCHM, 44; 1897), 214–15, for a letter of James, Duke of York, a week before the death of Charles II, saying that the king 'knows ... both the principles and practices of the phanaticks too well ever to give them any indulgence'.

Monmouth'.[214] Nonconformists entirely innocent of the rising came under increasing suspicion. Oliver Heywood spent the whole of James's accession year imprisoned in York Castle,[215] and throughout that time Richard Baxter was subjected to frequent harassment concerning his newly published *Paraphrase of the New Testament*, a devotional aid to family worship. Nonconformity's relentless opponent, Roger L'Estrange, had frequently attacked Baxter across the years,[216] and now claimed that the *Paraphrase* contained eight seditious passages. Almost seventy years of age and far from well, Baxter was frail and vulnerable when brought for trial before the infamous Jeffreys.[217] Not permitted to speak in his own defence, he was imprisoned and would have been confined for the rest of his life, had the new king not intervened at the request of a Catholic nobleman, the Earl of Powys.[218] He was detained 'in pain and languor near two years'[219] though the latter part of his confinement was, according to one visitor (the young Matthew Henry) 'in pretty comfortable circumstances, though a prisoner, in a private house, near the prison, attended by his own man and maid'.[220]

Unlike Baxter, the pastor of the Bristol, Broadmead, congregation did not obtain his release. George Fownes died in Gloucester gaol after being 'kept there for Two years and about 9 months a Prisoner, unjustly and maliciously'. His people had not only been denied his pastoral care but throughout his imprisonment had themselves suffered frequent 'interruption of full Assemblies ... occasion'd by our violent Persecutours'.[221]

---

[214] Anon., 'The Experiences of Mary Franklin', *TCHS* 2 (1905–6), 387–401, at 399.

[215] Heywood, *Autobiography* (ed. Turner), IV, 113–17.

[216] L'Estrange berated Baxter in two works: *A Relapsed Apostate: or Notes upon a Presbyterian pamphlet* [anonymous but by Baxter] *entituled, A Petition for Peace etc.* (1661); *The Casuist Uncas'd in a dialogue betwixt Richard and Baxter, with a Moderator between them, for quietnesse sake* (1680); and on numerous other occasions between 1681 and 1687 in his news-sheet *The Observator*.

[217] See *EB*, III, 10–12 [P464–65], 85–90 [P514–16], for Morrice's account of the charges and trial.

[218] When the book's second edition appeared after Baxter's death, it contained the author's account of the accusation and the unacceptable passages. 'What I said of the murderers of Christ, and the Hypocrite Pharisees, and their sins, the Judge said I meant it of the Church of *England*, though I have written for it, and still communicate with it': *Calendar of the Correspondence of Richard Baxter* (ed. G.F. Nuttall and N.H. Keeble, 2 vols; Oxford, 1991), II, 283.

[219] *Richard Baxter's Penitent Confession and his Necessary Vindication* (1691), 40. Baxter says that he enjoyed 'more quietness in that Confinement than I had done of many years before: Because they had no further to hunt me'.

[220] J.B. Williams, *Memoirs of the Life, Character, and Writings of the Rev. Matthew Henry* (1828; facsimile reprint in *The Lives of Philip and Matthew Henry*, Edinburgh, 1974), 22. For the 1686 persecution of other Dissenters in London, cf. *EB*, III, 183 [P574].

[221] *Broadmead Records* (ed. Hayden), 265–66.

Although such harassment continued in different parts of the country, James's religious priority was to promote Catholicism rather than humiliate Dissenters, but his strident pro-Catholic policies gave rise to increasing concern. Ever impatient, and without Parliament's approval, he enlarged his army (originally enlisted to oppose Monmouth) to twenty thousand men, commissioning almost a hundred Catholic officers, a haughty infringement of the Test Act. The thought of a standing army, never popular, and under such control, chilled the blood of those who feared Catholic dominance. In addition, his soldiers were illegally billeted in private homes and, the year after the rising, in some of London's Nonconformist meeting-houses.[222] Five years earlier, Louis XIV had billeted his troops in Huguenot homes; now England's king was doing the same. These were ominous signs.

When he came to the throne, James had been a convinced Catholic for almost twenty years, during which time he had developed some clear and (he believed) divinely ordained ambitions. James's short reign was a 'disastrous failure'[223] because, in the pursuit of these aims, he refused to consider what was (or was not) politically possible.[224] Markedly impatient, little was allowed to stand in his way, whether the nation's laws, Parliament, government ministers, corporation charters, local gentry, uncooperative bishops, Church or anything else. Sir Matthew Hale, the period's greatest lawyer, exposed and opposed the ruinous notion that 'the Prince is bound to keepe none of the Lawes that he or his Ancesto[rs] have ... *Established*'. How irresponsible to imagine 'that he may repeale them when he sees cause'.[225] But James did exactly that, and was astonished that any should think otherwise.

Determined to introduce committed Catholics into national and local government, the king further insisted that they be appointed to senior Oxford posts reserved for Anglicans, such as the deanery of Christ Church[226] and the presidency of Magdalen College.[227] Such interference did little to retain the

---

[222] Seaward, *Restoration*, 129.
[223] Miller, *James II*, 123.
[224] Morrice noted that on one occasion, when Charles II 'was in a Frank humour', he told Sir Robert Howard that 'his brother the Duke longed impatiently for a Crown, and if he had it he would loose it within 3 yeares': *EB*, IV, 412–13 [Q375].
[225] F. Pollock and W.S. Holdsworth, 'Sir Matthew Hale on Hobbes: An Unpublished MS', *Law Quarterly Review* 37 (1921), 274–303, at 301.
[226] In this controversy, Christ Church was of particular importance, being not only a college chapel but also the Anglican cathedral for the diocese. For these controversial Oxford appointments and the conversion to Catholicism of some Oxford academics, see R.A. Beddard, 'James II and the Catholic Challenge', in Nicholas Tyacke (ed.), *The History of the University of Oxford*, IV, *Seventeenth-Century Oxford* (Oxford, 1997), 907–54. One of these converts, Obadiah Walker, was licensed by James II to produce Catholic propaganda: cf. also J.A. Williams, 'English Catholicism under Charles II: The Legal Position', *Recusant History* 7 (1963–64), 123–43, esp. 129.
[227] A. Macintyre, 'The College, King James II, and the Revolution, 1687–1688', in L. Brockliss, G. Harris and A. Macintyre (eds), *Magdalen College and the Crown: Essays*

confidence of his bishops. Up-to-date news of persecutions in France intensified anti-Catholic polemic,[228] and pulpits provided natural platforms for Protestant anger.[229] Greatly to the annoyance of senior churchmen, James invaded their exclusive domain, the supervision of the clergy, by his surprising 'Directions to Preachers'[230] in which he ordered that their sermons should focus on doctrinal topics rather than polemical ones such as 'popery'. When John Sharp, a prominent London archdeacon, refused to heed his command, James told his bishop to suspend him, but the staunchly Protestant Compton refused to comply.[231] James promptly established a court of Ecclesiastical Commission whose first act was to suspend the bishop, who had earlier displeased the king by his opposition to the appointment of Catholic army officers; as a result Compton had lost his place on the Privy Council.[232] The gap between king and Church was widening and James began to look to Dissenters, Protestant as well as Catholic, for support.

---

for the Tercentenary of the Restoration of the College, 1688 (Oxford, 1988), 31–82. For Morrice on the Magdalen College presidency, see *EB*, IV, 145–50, 164–6 [Q184–87, 197–98].

[228] Morrice associated the spread of Catholicism in England with the continuing persecution of Huguenots, e.g. in December 1686: 'It is credibly reported that a new Mass house is opened in Southwark. Cruelties are constantly renewed in France': *EB*, III, 314 (Q20); cf. R.A. Beddard, 'The Protestant Succession', in idem (ed.), *The Revolutions of 1688* (Oxford, 1991), 1–10.

[229] BL, Add. MS 34508, Mackintosh Collections: Political Correspondence 1685–88, fol.133: '12 Nov, 1686: The Bishop of Durham suspended Dr. Marsh of Newcastle 'for having preached rather Licentious [sermons], contrary to his M[ajesty']s former letters to the archbishops of England'.

[230] Technically a reissue of the 1662 'Directions concerning Preachers' of Charles II, cf. Edward Cardwell (ed.), *Documentary Annals of the Reformed Church of England* (Oxford, 1844), II, 255–59; Luttrell, *Brief Historical Relation*, I, 373. These had warned against preachers who spread 'an evil opinion of their governors', promoting 'disobedience, schism and rebellion'.

[231] Edward Carpenter, *The Protestant Bishop: Being the Life of Henry Compton, Bishop of London* (1956), 82–103. 'The Bishop of London's fame runs high in the vogue of the people. The London pulpits ring strong peals against Popery': Ellis, *Original Letters*, Second Series, IV, 84, cf. 93–94, on 'pulling down popery' in London; T. Sharp, *The Life of John Sharp, Lord Archbishop of York*, 2 vols (1825), I, 69–74; A. Tindal Hart, *The Life and Times of John Sharp, Archbishop of York* (1949), 90–100. Although stridently opposed to 'popery', Sharp was no friend of Protestant Dissenters. Morrice recorded hearing him 'lashing the fanatics or dissenters in my hearing' at Lincoln's Inn, a fortnight 'before he came under the lash himself'; Sharp said later that the Church of England must be defended 'against all its adversaries Whatsoever ... both against Papists and the Reformed Churches': *EB*, III, 191; IV, 171 [P556, shorthand entry; Q203].

[232] Ellis, *Original Letters*, Second Series, IV, 85–86, 96–99; *An Exact Account of the Whole Proceedings against Henry, Lord Bishop of London before the Lord Chancellor* (1688).

Encouraged by an impressive number of Catholic confirmations in the North of England,[233] he mistakenly believed that uninhibited missionary activity would result in rapid conversions[234] and, to make that possible, took steps to secure their freedom from the penal laws. Needing parliamentary approval for the repeal of the Test and Corporation Acts (thus permitting Catholics as well as Dissenters to participate in local and national government) he pursued a policy, initiated by Charles II, of manipulating local government structures with the ultimate aim of securing favourable parliamentary elections. Corporation and borough charters were revoked and reissued, giving more power to central government to make appointments, ensuring that new personnel were sympathetic to James's religious policies. Consequently, large numbers of the country's social hierarchy were deprived of offices that had been in their families for generations. Each Lord Lieutenant was instructed to discover whether his county's proposed justices of the peace would agree to the suspension of the Test Act,[235] which would enable Catholics to become justices or county lieutenants or their deputies. Those who refused to comply with the royal dictates were removed from office, the vacancies created by twelve uncooperative lords lieutenant being filled by Catholics. A high proportion of newly appointed justices of the peace were Catholics. These political ramifications of the king's religious zeal alienated the country's gentry.

Disillusioned with Anglican and Tory lack of support, James repeated in 1687 the action of his brother in issuing a Declaration of Indulgence,[236] again suspending the repressive legislation of the last twenty-five years. Despite its unconstitutional nature, Dissenters initially valued the freedom thus secured,[237] although reservations became evident in their Loyal Addresses.[238] Before long,

---

[233] Michael Mullett, *Catholics in Britain and Ireland, 1558–1829* (Basingstoke, 1989), 79–80; J.A. Hilton, *Catholic Lancashire: From Reformation to Renewal 1559–1991* (Chichester, 1994), 44. Largely through the resolute visitation of a newly appointed vicar apostolic, 20,859 people were confirmed: F.J. Vaughan, 'Bishop Leyburn and his Confirmation Register of 1687', *Northern Catholic History* 12 (1980), 14–18. Morrice reported that the bishop showed the king 'a List of all their names ... and there was much rejoycing amongst the Papists that the true Religion doth so greatly and Wonderfully prevaile': *EB*, IV, 172 [Q203].
[234] James told the papal agent in London, D'Adda, that 'once the laws no longer held people in fear England would be Catholic within two years': Miller, *James II*, 127.
[235] *EB*, IV, 166 [Q198–99].
[236] For the text, see *EHD*, VIII, 395–97.
[237] Presenting one address, Vincent Alsop reminded the king of almost three decades of Nonconformist suffering, contrasting 'the scorching beams of severity, which had almost calcined us to ashes' with the 'coole Breezes of your Ma[jes]ties favour to revive and refresh us'. They appreciated 'the difference betweene the sharp lashes of some of our fellow Subjects, and the healing clemency of our Soveraigne': *EB*, IV, 43 [Q115].
[238] London's three Presbyterian leaders, Richard Baxter, William Bates and John Howe, actively discouraged any address of thanks to the king for the Indulgence. A third of the Loyal Addresses expressing gratitude referred to their expectation of Parliament's approval of the king's action: Seaward, *Restoration*, 131. For example, the 'Address of

Dissenters came to share the fears of their Anglican neighbours when, on issuing a Second Declaration of Indulgence,[239] the king ordered that it be read from all the pulpits in the land.[240] The king was not only dispensing with Parliament but ruling the Church.[241] Seven bishops, including the frail Archbishop Sancroft, refused to instruct their clergy to read the Declaration, not (they insisted) 'from any want of due tenderness to dissenters'[242] but because the Declaration was 'founded upon ... a dispensing power' which had 'often been declared illegal in parliament'. Nonconformists found themselves firmly on the side of the offending bishops,[243] who were imprisoned in the Tower, causing a national scandal.[244] Tried for sedition, they were acquitted, to national rejoicing.[245] The king's manifest lack of wisdom was drawing Church and Dissent closer together.[246]

Then, further to intensify Protestant fears, the queen gave birth to a son and the nation began to envisage an uninterrupted Catholic succession.[247] Many

---

Thanks from the Presbyterians of London, 1687': 'and for declaring your further inclination to engage your two Houses of Parliament in concurrence with you in so excellent a work': *EHD*, VIII, 397–98.

[239] For the text, see ibid. 399–400.

[240] See *EB*, IV, 260–68 [Q255–61], for the clergy's reasons for not reading the king's Declaration. The command that Dissenters also read it publicly was withdrawn: ibid. 279 [Q269].

[241] Equally concerned about the unconstitutional nature of the Indulgence, George Griffith, John Howe and William Bates fully supported the protest of the seven bishops: R.L. Greaves, *Saints and Rebels: Seven Nonconformists in Stuart England* (Macon, GA, 1985), 94.

[242] Calamy commented on Sancroft's reference to Nonconformists: 'I could never hear of any great tenderness of his till then – but better late than never!': *Historical Account* (ed. Rutt), I, 201.

[243] Roger Thomas, 'The Seven Bishops and their Petition, 18 May, 1688': *JEH* 12 (1961), 56–70. Ten Dissenting ministers visited them in the Tower, 'which the king took il[l] and sent for four of them to reprimand them. They answered that they could not but adhear to them as men constant to the Protestant faith': Reresby, *Memoirs* (ed. Browning), 500.

[244] See *EB*, IV, 275–78 [Q266–68], for Morrice's narrative of the bishops' arrest and journey to the Tower, with 'Crouds of people ... generally crying God bless the Bishops'.

[245] Ellis, *Original Letters*, Second Series, IV, 104–10; Luttrell, *Brief Historical Relation*, I, 449: 'great rejoyceings ... in several towns for joy of the bishops acquittall'. For the seven bishops, see J.H. Overton, *The Non-Jurors: Their Lives, Principles and Writings* (1902), 23–83.

[246] Even Sir John Reresby, a fierce opponent of Nonconformity, conceded that 'most men were now convinced that liberty of conscience was a thing of advantage to the nation', if it could be secured 'with due reguard to the rights and privileges of the Church of England': *Memoirs* (ed. Browning), 497.

[247] In Oxford 'Noe Colleges or Halls besides [Christ Church and Magdalen] took any notice of the birth of this prince ... either by bonfier or ringing of bells – knowing full

leading politicians, both Whig and Tory, were persuaded that the crown should go to James's eldest daughter, Mary, a known Protestant who had married William of Orange, a grandson of Charles I. William came to England, ostensibly to guarantee free parliamentary elections and restrain his father-in-law, rather than usurp him,[248] but James panicked and left for France. It was considered that he had abdicated. His daughter Mary, the legitimate heir, did not wish to reign alone and her husband had no intention of becoming a distinguished appendage, so the nation accepted a joint monarchy.

Once satisfied that William and Mary were legitimate rulers,[249] Nonconformists rejoiced in their restored freedom. For many of them, the last decade had been exceptionally painful. Matthew Mead reflected on his life as an Independent minister in Stepney where, in addition to earlier sufferings, in the previous nine years he had encountered 'incessant vexations, by Suits, by Fines, by illegal House-breakings, by Plundering and Spoil, by Imprisonments, Prosecution for Life, by Wandering in a Strange Land'.[250]

It is a mistake to imagine that the accession of William and Mary was welcomed with unanimous acclaim. The exiled king was not without his supporters. By May 1689 England was openly at war with France, with Louis XIV supporting James II, who had soldiers to fight for him in Scotland and also in Ireland, where he had landed in March 1689. That same month, at the Scottish Parliament, the bishop of Glasgow is reputed to have prayed 'for the Restauration of King James', though 'the Auditory' openly denounced him as a 'Traytor' and 'Rebell'.[251] Morrice feared that some 'Toryes' might 'revolt to King James, if he should come with any little Fleete to Sea or Land upon us'. Among those proposed as future justices were 'very many' who opposed King William 'openly and publickly, and many others of them were known to be disaffected to him and to the Common interest of the Kingdome'; William was known to be 'intimidated by the great number of those that lye Cross to him'.[252] Lord Delamere said that Cheshire was 'very much disaffected to King William'

---

well that if he lives he is to be bred up a papist and so consequently the crowne of England and popish religion will never part': *Anthony Wood* (ed. Clarke), III, 268.

[248] Thomas Jolly was not the only bewildered observer. William's 'expedition' was 'strange to us who were altogether unacquainted ... with the grounds of it' but 'wee must needs wish well to ym as protestants': *Note Book* (ed. Fishwick), 91; cf. Thoresby, *Diary* (ed. Hunter), I, 188: 'We were told of an invasion from Holland ... We underlings knew not what to make of these'.

[249] See *EB*, IV, 433–34 [Q391–92], for Morrice's detailed response to the 'Great imputations ... laid upon the dissenters ... that they did not more openly and publickly rise for, and serve the Prince of Orange in this his great attempt for the Redeeming of this Kingdome'.

[250] Matthew Mead, *The Vision of the Wheels* (1689), Ep. Ded. [A3v–A4r]; cf. *EB*, II, 331 [P344]: 'Mr. Meade of Stepneys doores were broke and his Goods distrained on.' When persecution was particularly intense in London, Mead had sought refuge in Holland.

[251] *EB*, V, 60 [Q510].

[252] Ibid. 57, 69 [Q508, 517].

and that he had discovered a list of hundreds who had 'entred into an Association for King James, and several others that have Correspondency with him'.²⁵³ 'Its plain the enemies to King William are very many amongst all ranks of men ... yet [many] openly aver they will never receive King James back again, but King William they would remove and put the Government into other hands, for they are resolved to Confound all rather then Coalesse with the Reformed <interest>²⁵⁴ abrode, which King William alone can be supported by'.²⁵⁵ London theatregoers flocked to see a play that 'made mention of King James's returning to England' and many 'who came ... on that account, clapped their hands, and made a very great noise in the Playhouse, which gave great offence at Court'.²⁵⁶ More seriously, it was 'most credibly' reported to the Privy Council that 'King James has a Council that Sits most nights and dayes in London, to whom he has given full power and authority ... and to Pardon whomsoever they please'.²⁵⁷

But whatever the transitional difficulties, the new reign offered brighter prospects for Protestant Dissenters. The main penal laws against them were suspended, but not the Test and Corporation Acts; as Philip Henry told his son Matthew, 'til the Sacramental Test bee taken off, our Business is not done'.²⁵⁸ That inhibiting 'Business' remained undone for almost a century and a half, but in 1689 the Henry family rejoiced that with other Dissenters they could once again worship without fear. At last their 'silenced' ministers were free to preach whenever and wherever they wished. Over almost three decades Nonconformists had beeen robbed of their religious freedom but there had been inestimable gains, not least in their ability to respond creatively to the experience of suffering.

---

²⁵³ Ibid. 121 [Q561].
²⁵⁴ Interlined text, followed by 'churches' deleted.
²⁵⁵ *EB*, V, 129 [Q568]. A French invasion was thought possible while the king was fighting in Ireland: ibid. 443, 474 [R147, 171]. For Morrice's account of William's victory in July 1690, see ibid. 468–70 [R167–68].
²⁵⁶ Ibid. 290 [R18].
²⁵⁷ Ibid. 293 [R22].
²⁵⁸ Henry, *Diaries* (ed. Lee), 362 (Letter of 1 June 1689).

Part II

Responding to Adversity

Chapter 2

When Grace Grows Best

'I see grace groweth best in winter'[1]

In the closing essay of a fine symposium on rural Dissent, Patrick Collinson, while acknowledging the stimulating and original treatment of the subject by its contributors, observes that the book had said little about 'what they did with their dissent', what they 'preached and heard, how they prayed, how they sang'.[2] Within the limits of its declared theme, this study offers some material towards such an enquiry, particularly regarding the interpretation, development and expression of their personal and corporate spirituality.

The long years of persecution gave Dissenters ample opportunity to reflect theologically on their painful experience. Repressive legislation imposed severe restrictions on their everyday life, involving ministers and members in loss of work, social isolation, family disruption and poverty. Additionally, there were the more predictable adversities – illness, unemployment, domestic tensions and bereavement, especially the distressing loss of children in infancy. One doubts whether so much would have been written on such a theme had it not been for continuing hardship. 'Suffering' is prominent in the titles of many Nonconformist publications during the repression.[3] Whilst Dissenters, like other Christians, were frequently diverted onto marginal themes, continued harassment ensured that their authors did not neglect the exposition of topics of immediate pastoral concern, such as the appropriate Christian response to adversity and hardship. It was natural for them to view life's adversities in the

---

[1] *Letters of Samuel Rutherford* (ed. Andrew A. Bonar; Edinburgh, 1891), 157.
[2] Margaret Spufford (ed.), *The World of Rural Dissenters 1520–1725* (Cambridge, 1995), 390.
[3] E.g. John Bunyan, *Prison-Meditations, Directed to the Heart of Suffering Saints ...* (1663); idem, S*easonable Counsel*, in *MW*, X, 5–104; [Vavasor Powell], *The Sufferer's Catechism* (1664), John Flavel, *Preparation for Sufferings, or The Best Work in the Worst Times* (1682); Nathanael Vincent, *A Covert from the Storm, or The Fearful Encouraged in Times of Suffering* (1671). See also the conformist Edward Polhill, *Armatura Dei ... Preparation for Suffering in an Evil Day* (1682); but especially a Quaker bibliography: Joseph Smith, *Descriptive Catalogue of Friends' Books*, 2 vols (1867), II, 644–83. The entry headed 'Sufferings of Friends for the Testimony of Truth' runs to over forty pages. A more recent Quaker bibliographer states that by 1700 Friends had published 339 items concerning 'Sufferings' or toleration, 'usually combined with appeal for the sufferers': David Runyon, Appendix to Hugh Barbour and A.O. Roberts (ed.), *Early Quaker Writings 1650–1700* (Grand Rapids, MI, 1973), 567–76.

The Mystery of Suffering

In the bewilderment of emotional, spiritual and physical pain they were first to admit that severe suffering defies rational explanation. Frequently penniless and 'reduced ... to a narrow livelihood', the ejected Shropshire minister Thomas Froysell 'had scarce whereon to live, much less ... to give [his] six Children which surviv'd him'. Though refusing to be a 'Complainer of Poverty',[4] he freely acknowledged a natural bewilderment: 'That God should kill his people, and yet love them ... it is a Mystery'. Nevertheless, these believers maintained that all adversity must have some wise and benevolent purpose: 'When God is destroying his Church, he is multiplying his Church ... When a Taylor is ripping the Cloath, and cutting it into shreds and pieces, he is making a comely Garment.'[5] God's dealings with his people were often like a printer 'Composing his sheets, who setteth his letters backwards', but the perplexity is only temporary, for 'in the life to come, we shall fully know the sense of them'.[6] The rational faculties 'will ... say God is destroying, when he is saving' and 'shewing thee the greatest mercy of all'.[7] Suffering believers sometimes fix their eyes 'only in one place', making 'a full stop where God hath not made any'.[8]

It was one of the 'deep Mysteries of Providence' that 'the Church that hath the least of Sin should endure the most of Sufferings'.[9] 'Saints are ships richly laden; therefore will have many Pyrates watching for them'; the 'highest and richest Christian is most eyed, and envyed by the enemies of our salvation'.[10] With his fondness for memorable aphorisms, George Swinnock held that some of 'Gods friends have been ready to question him, when they could not find him ... and reprehend him, because they cannot comprehend him', but 'Human reason is no fit judge of divine actions ... because many of his ways are above our reason'.[11]

---

[4] Richard Steele, 'To the Reader', [unpaginated], in Thomas Froysell, *Sermons concerning Grace and Temptation* (1678); cf. Sylvester (ed.), *Reliquiae*, III, §203, 18.
[5] Froysell, *Sermons*, 11.
[6] George Swinnock, *The Christian-Man's Calling; or a Treatise of making Religion Ones Business* (3 parts; 1668, 1663, 1665), II, 377.
[7] Richard Baxter, *The Saints Everlasting Rest* (1669), 494.
[8] Stephen Charnock, *A Discourse of Divine Providence*, in *The Complete Works of Stephen Charnock* (ed. James M'Cosh; Edinburgh, 1864), I, 10–120, at 112.
[9] Samuel Tomlyns, *The Great Duty of Christians ... Go forth without the Camp* (1682), A2.
[10] Swinnock, *Calling*, II, 350–51.
[11] Ibid. 376.

Baffled by the ruthlessness of their oppressors, persecuted Christians were to take care not to 'censure ... God in his dark providences'. In life's puzzling experiences, 'God seems ... to speak the same language as Christ did to Peter': 'You do not realize now what I am doing, but later you will understand' (Jn 13: 7). As at the foot-washing, 'the instruments are visible, the action sensible, but the inward meaning still lies obscured from our view ... His ways are ... too high for our short measure.'[12]

It was sufficient for these believers to know that God was aware of their pain. After three years' harsh imprisonment in Exeter, Abraham Cheare enjoyed freedom for a few weeks, only to be exiled for his remaining years on Drake's Island in Plymouth Sound. Seriously ill, he wrote to tell his congregation that God's ways were sometimes 'hard to discern', and at times 'he not only tarry long', but can 'even seem to be angry with the Prayers of his People'. In his bewilderment, he said that the Psalmist's assurance 'hath sweetly stayed me ... *put my tears in thy bottle, are they not written in a Book by thee?*'[13] They might not always understand, but they were content that God did, and that one day they would too.

The Inevitability of Suffering

Suffering was not merely inexplicable; it was inescapable. Baxter feared that far 'too little, do many honest Christians think how much of their excellent Obedience' consists in 'Child-like, holy Suffering'.[14] It served to confirm the reality of their faith. Conversely, 'if we our selves have not been partakers of it' we may have 'reason to suspect the truth and sincerity of our profession'.[15] These expositors frequently told their people that 'God had one Son without sin, but no son without sorrow; he had one Son without corruption, but no son without correction.'[16] 'Affliction is the Saints diet-drink ... You may as well separate weight from lead as sufferings from a Saints life'.[17] Until his arrest in 1661, Zachary Crofton preached to one of London's largest congregations. There were times when over two thousand people stood waiting in the street, having failed to get into his 'Tantling meeting-house'.[18] After fifteen months in the Tower, he reminded his contemporaries that the Christian life was 'hard in

---

[12] Charnock, *Providences*, 109–10.
[13] Abraham Cheare, *Words in Season* (1668), 238, quoting Psa. 56: 8.
[14] Richard Baxter, *Dying Thoughts* (1683), 313.
[15] Thomas Gouge, *Joshua's Resolution, or the Private Christian's Duty in Time of Publick Corruption* (1663), 18.
[16] William Dyer, *Christ's Famous Titles or a Believer's Golden Chain* (1670), 110; cf. Swinnock, *Calling*, II, 465: 'God had one Son without sin, but no Son without suffering'; Samuel Clarke, *A General Martyrologie* (1677), A2v; James Birdwood, *Hearts-Ease in Heart Trouble* (1690), 19.
[17] Thomas Watson, *The Fight of Faith Crowned* (1678), 25.
[18] *CSPD* 1660–61, 539, cf. 538.

its passage but happy in its end'. 'He that will wear the Crown of righteousness must run the race of righteousness.'[19]

Vavasor Powell spent all but one of his last ten years in prison. He urged his fellow-Christians not to 'be troubled that the winde now blows in our faces' for 'to live persecuted, and to die Sainted, are commonly inseparable'. A believer 'should never do anything for Christ but he should expect to suffer' for it.[20] They were scarcely 'worthy of the name of Disciples' who gave up 'when once it comes to suffering'.[21] Among Nonconformist ministers, Isaac Ambrose was not alone in quoting the Marian martyr John Bradford to the effect that suffering was 'the ABC of Christianity ... Why do we seek for living comforts where we must expect to die daily?'[22]

Suffering was to be expected because of the teaching of Scripture, the experience of Jesus, the testimony of history and the hostility of contemporaries.

First, every reader of the Bible knew that its best characters had suffered the worst trials. Reminding his contemporaries that the 'Church is Heir to the Cross', the conforming Puritan layman Edward Polhill recalled the grim dimensions of suffering in the Old Testament story. It 'began from the blood of Abel and hath continued ever since. Israel [was] oppressed in Egypt ... vexed in Canaan by the neighbour Nations ... afterwards carried captive to Babylon and at last trod under foot by Antiochus Epiphanes'.[23] George Swinnock recalled Jeremiah's symbolic use of two baskets of figs (Jer. 24): 'One of the sharpest calamities that ever befel Israel, was the Babylonish Captivity, yet even this was in mercy'.[24] The 'good figs' in the prophet's visual aid were the captives. As they made their way to a strange land, onlookers might imagine them to be the 'bad figs' of divine displeasure. But God had sent them to Babylon 'for their good', promising to 'build them and not pull them down'.

In New Testament teaching, it was clearly evident that the 'Tenour of the Gospel Predictions, Precepts, Promises and Threatnings are fitted to a People in

---

[19] Zachary Crofton, *The Hard Way to Heaven* (1662), 1–2, 5.

[20] Vavasor Powell, *The Bird in the Cage chirping Four Distinct Notes to his Consorts Abroad* (2nd ed.; 1662), A3, 14–15. For Powell, see Edward Bagshaw, *The Life and Death of Mr. Vavasor Powell* (1671); and especially R. Tudur Jones, 'The Sufferings of Vavasor', in Mansel John (ed.), *Welsh Baptist Studies* (Cardiff, 1976), 77–91.

[21] Vincent, *Covert from the Storm*, 24.

[22] Isaac Ambrose, *Looking unto Jesus* (1674), 343. The example of John Bradford was regularly used as a model of self-denial and courageous tenacity: e.g. Isaac Ambrose, *Media*, in *Compleat Works* (1674), 147, 154; Edmund Calamy, in *An Exact Collection of Farewel Sermons preached by the Late London-Ministers* (1662), 9, 22.

[23] Polhill, *Armatura Dei*, 4. Although a conformist, Polhill pleaded for an end to the repression of Dissenters. The ejected minister Joseph Moore made similar use of Old Testament examples as he warned his congregation to expect 'and prepare for Troubles ... Wicked Cain killed righteous Abel ... Ishmael persecuted Isaac': in *England's Remembrancer*, 412.

[24] Swinnock, *Calling*, II, 423.

a suffering State'.²⁵ Three days into his imprisonment, Thomas Hardcastle wrote the first of his weekly pastoral letters from a Bristol prison,²⁶ reminding his harassed people that the 'gospel makes ... rather a supposition that we shall be persecuted ... and therefore makes provision, not for our hiding or withdrawing, but for a mouth and wisdom, and says it shall turn to a testimony'. Quoting the Matthean mission address (Mt. 10: 17), he urged them: 'See it and read it: *They will deliver you up &c.*' His people must not be cowards, for 'how shall they meet with you, if you be not found in your duty?'²⁷

Second, the animosity shown towards their sinless Lord during his earthly ministry confirmed that his followers could not hope to avoid persecution. 'Christ left this Lesson with his Disciples when he left the world'.²⁸ 'If the chief Priests and Elders of the Jews accused Christ ... no wonder if those that are chief and great amongst us, accuse poor Christians.'²⁹ As repression began, their preachers frequently recalled the Passion narrative, telling their people: 'If you resolve to follow Christ, you must resolve to bear his Cross after him, as Simon did'.³⁰ All 'Christians must imitate Christ, and suffer with him before they reign with him'.³¹

Third, it had been so throughout all Christian history. Taking leave of his Derbyshire congregation, Joseph Moore reminded them to expect and 'prepare for troubles' because 'Piety hath been persecuted from the beginning of the world'.³² Polhill recalled that the 'Christian Church was first persecuted by the Pagan Emperors, then torn in pieces by Arians and other Hereticks ... Goths and Vandals and at last trod down' by Islamic invaders. 'All along it hath been in a suffering condition.'³³ The 'fathers before us were not slothful ... in serving the Lord', whatever the cost.³⁴ Given the popularity and influence of Foxe's book,³⁵ John Wycliffe³⁶ and the later Marian martyrs³⁷ had an assured

---

²⁵ Sylvester (ed.), *Reliquiae*, I, i, §213, 28 (7).
²⁶ Letters from imprisoned ministers had a richly supportive and didactic precedent. Under sentence of death, the Edwardian reformers expounded spiritual and pastoral themes from their jails: Philip Edgcumbe Hughes, *The Theology of the English Reformers* (1965), 103–18.
²⁷ *Records* (ed. Underhill), 258, quoting Mt. 10: 17–21.
²⁸ Joseph Moore, in *England's Remembrancer*, 412, quoting Jn 16: 2.
²⁹ Ambrose, *Looking*, 360.
³⁰ Moore, in *England's Remembrancer*, 412.
³¹ Sylvester (ed.), *Reliquiae*, I, i, §213, 28 (9).
³² Moore, in *England's Remembrancer*, 412.
³³ Polhill, *Armatura Dei*, 4.
³⁴ John Bunyan, *The Strait Gate or Great Difficulty of going to Heaven* (1676), in *MW*, V, 84.
³⁵ Matthew Newcomen feared that *Acts and Monuments* 'hath formerly been more prized, then of late in England': in *The Second and Last Collection of the Late London Ministers' Farewell Sermons* (1663), 164. But Nonconformist congregations could hardly have forgotten the martyrologist's work, given the frequent quotations and

place in the recital of exemplary forebears, and Samuel Clarke's popular *General Martyrologie* (1640, 1651, 1677) provided further accounts of Christian heroism in dark times.[38] The young Ralph Thoresby, who greatly valued his copy of Clarke's book,[39] recalled hearing his Leeds minister, Thomas Sharp, tell the congregation that because 'it hath been the lot of all the Protestant churches in the nations about us ... why should impenitent England be left unpunished?'[40]

Fourth, Dissenters had little difficulty in accepting the inevitability of suffering while they experienced the undeserved and recurrent hostility of their contemporaries. '[T]hou hast a whole world against thee ... if thou beest a Christian ... The world will seek to keep thee out of heaven, with mocks, flouts, taunts, threatnings, goals, gibbits, halters, burnings, and a thousand deaths'.[41] The Broadmead congregation in Bristol knew that it was not only their minister who would suffer; 'separations and confinements' would be their experience too.[42]

It was particularly difficult when professedly religious people arraigned themselves against them, but Dissenters 'must be self-denying Cross-bearers, even where there are none but formal nominal Christians to be the Cross-makers'.[43] Whatever the source of adversity, believers can anticipate it, for 'a Man is no sooner brought home to God, but he must expect to be hated by the World, assaulted by Satan [and] chastened by the Lord. We shall have Enemies

---

allusions in the preaching of their ministers: cf. Robert Collins, Edmund Calamy and Philip Lamb, in *Compleat Collection*, [unpaginated]. In Bunyan, see *MW*, II, 253; III, 134, 154, 309; VIII, 383–84 (a list of martyrs with precise Foxe references); IX, 345; X, 22, 55, 64; XIII, 497. Bunyan had a three-volume *Acts and Monuments* in his prison cell: Richard L. Greaves, *Glimpses of Glory: John Bunyan and English Dissent* (Stanford, CA, 2002), 604, cf. Thomas S. Freeman, 'A Library in Three Volumes: Foxe's "Book of Martyrs" in the Writings of John Bunyan', *Bunyan Studies* 5 (Autumn 1994) 47–57. Roger Morrice says that by the early 1680s copies of Foxe were 'hard to be got': *EB*, II, 346 (P354); cf. John R. Knott, *Discourses of Martyrdom, 1561–1694* (Cambridge, 1993), 179–215.

[36] 'Wiclliffe saith, that he which leaveth off preaching and hearing of the word of God for fear of excommunication of men ... is already excommunicated of God, and shall in the day of judgment be counted a traitor of Christ': Bunyan, *Relation of my Imprisonment*, in *GA*, 122.

[37] Calamy, in *Exact Collection*, 8.

[38] Clarke's *General Martyrologie* opens with descriptions of Old and New Testament persecutions, before providing narratives of Patristic, early British, Reformation and Marian martyrs. This detailed martyrological sequence is also found in Quaker literature: cf. Rigge, *Constancy in the Truth*, 58–71, 'Against Persecution'.

[39] As did Morrice, who owned its 1677 edition: *EB*, I, 100–1.

[40] Thoresby, *Diary* (ed. Hunter), I, 33.

[41] Bunyan, *Strait Gate*, in *MW*, V, 83–84.

[42] *Records* (ed. Underhill), 261–62.

[43] Sylvester (ed.), *Reliquiae*, I, I, §213, 28.

in our own Houses.'[44] 'Saints must be winnowed, and buffeted, and tryed and tempted ... Christianity is not so easie as many take it to be'.[45] The Lord 'that appointed them to a Crown as to their end, appointed them to the Cross as the way'. The only 'road to Canaan' is through a bleak 'Wilderness'.[46] The experience of suffering confronted them with stark alternatives. As one prisoner put it, 'leave the Cross, loose [sic] the Crown, but bear the Cross, and wear the Crown.'[47]

Bunyan was astonished that Christians should imagine 'that our innocent lives will exempt us from sufferings', and that such 'troubles shall do us ... harm', when without doubt 'God sends them upon us' both 'for our present and future good'.[48] John Corbet insisted that life's adversities must serve some beneficial purpose, for 'if tribulation were not most expedient in this present world, he that is infinitely powerful, wise and good would not appoint it for his dear children'. God 'wishes better to you than you to yourselves'.[49]

The Value of Suffering

Although such suffering was inescapable and, as Vavasor Powell maintained, 'in some sense' a 'necessary ... Condition of Salvation',[50] the most compliant sufferer might question its necessity. In unparalleled anguish, Jesus once asked 'Why ... ?' (Mark 15: 34). Troubled Dissenters frequently sought to explain the purpose of suffering. Perhaps bafflingly to the modern reader, they sometimes held that suffering might be a just punishment. More commonly, they regarded it as a necessary test. They frequently thought of it as a helpful corrective, and invariably believed it was a learning process.

Suffering as a Penal Visitation

Dissenters were often pained that suffering might have been inflicted as divine punishment for negligence, or a specific misdemeanour in their lives. The punitive aspect of suffering loomed large in their thinking, preaching and writing, disturbing pastors and people alike. Jailed for non-attendance at his parish church, the young Julius Saunders was haunted by the thought that the imprisonment was primarily due to his failure to discern God's mind regarding the formation of the Independent church at Bedworth. Quoting the Chronicler's account of the disastrous return of the ark to Jerusalem, he feared that, like

---

[44] Birdwood, *Hearts-Ease*, 24.
[45] Isaac Ambrose, *War with Devils* (1674), 2.
[46] Swinnock, *Calling*, II, 352.
[47] Powell, *Bird*, 50.
[48] Bunyan, *Seasonable Counsel*, in *MW*, X, 6.
[49] *The Remains of ... John Corbet ... from his own Manuscripts* (1684), 262.
[50] Powell, *Bird*, 50.

David, he had not sought God 'after the due order'.⁵¹ When a violent storm damaged the roof of Bulstrode Whitelocke's house, he became anxious that God might be rebuking him for speaking indiscreetly in a 'disturbed passion'.⁵² One Sunday evening, a London Nonconformist minister's four-year-old daughter was injured in a horrific domestic accident that, after several days' intense suffering, claimed the child's life. Her mother, though not remotely responsible, was tormented 'that it was for some great sin that I had committed, it falling on the Lord's day – whether I had kept the Sabbath as I ought'.⁵³

On the Sunday after Samuel Birch was ejected from his Oxfordshire living, he recorded his grief in his prayer journal. 'The Bell calls, but not me; I have now nothing to do, but to look back what I have done amiss, or left undone, whilst I had opportunity of Acting'.⁵⁴ The fear that suffering might be an expression of divine displeasure was deeply embedded in the Puritan conscience. Ministers were particularly vulnerable. Richard Baxter was not alone in his introspective anguish that the ejectment was an act of God's justice 'that so dull a Preacher should be put to silence'. He remembered Melanchthon's saying, that the 'Arrow that woundeth us, was feathered from our own Wings' and, with needless 'Shame and Sorrow', looked back on his 'cold and lifeless Sermons' at Kidderminster.⁵⁵ On the third anniversary of that 'killing day for ... nonconformist ministers', Oliver Heywood invited colleagues to his house 'to lament ... this sad judgment', 'inquire of god [sic] the cause' of such a 'dreadful stroke', and 'the sins provoking to it'.⁵⁶ When Edmund Calamy preached his farewell sermon and, four months later, the sermon for 'which he was committed to Newgate',⁵⁷ he reminded his London congregation on both occasions of John Bradford. That 'blessed Martyr' had prayed: 'Lord, it was my unthankfulness for the Gospel, that brought in Popery in Queen Maries days; and my unfruitfulness under the Gospel, that was the cause of the untimely death of King Edward the Sixth.' Identifying with the martyr's remorse, Calamy shared his bitter conviction with his people that 'it is

---

⁵¹ Warwick, Warwickshire County Record Office, MS CR 802, Bedworth Independent (Old Meeting) Church Book, 1687–1815. For Saunders's two-year imprisonment, see *Warwick County Records: Quarter Sessions Order Book 1682–1690*, VIII (ed. H.C. Johnson; Warwick, 1953), 31, 53, 65; cf. G.F. Nuttall, 'The Beginnings of Old Meeting, Bedworth', *TCHS* 20 (1965–70), 255–64.
⁵² *Diary of Bulstrode Whitelocke* (ed. Spalding), 804 (23 December 1672).
⁵³ Anon., 'Experiences of Mary Franklin', 393.
⁵⁴ G.F. Nuttall, 'A Puritan Prayer-Journal 1651–1663', in *Der Pietismus in Gestalten und Wirkungen: Martin Schmidt zum 65. Geburtstag* (ed. H. Bornkamm, F. Heyer, A. Schindler; Arbeiten zur Geschichte des Pietismus, 14; Bielefeld, 1975), 343–54, at 350.
⁵⁵ Richard Baxter, 'Farewell Sermon' [on Jn 16: 22], in *The Practical Works of Richard Baxter*, 4 vols (1707), IV, 932.
⁵⁶ Heywood, *Autobiography* (ed. Turner), I, 198.
⁵⁷ Edmund Calamy, *Eli Trembling for Fear of the Ark* (1663), title page, in *Exact Collection*.

for thy sin and my sin that the Ark of God is in danger'.[58] Philip Lamb took regretful leave of his Dorset parishioners, pained that he had been robbed of his ministry because of the 'Non-improvement' of the 'rich Priviledges' God had given minister and people in better times.[59]

Dissenters were not alone in attributing life's adversities, natural disasters, poor harvests or plague to divine indignation. Bishop Joseph Hall said such grim happenings indicated that 'God took notice of the notorious sins of a people'. Adverse experiences may be 'examples of his just vengeance'.[60] Preaching after London's Great Fire, the dean of St Paul's (and later archbishop), William Sancroft, said that such disasters were 'products of God's Righteousness upon our Unrighteousness'. It was folly to pin the blame elsewhere, on the 'Dutch or French'; 'Turn your eyes inward into your own Bosoms'. Reflecting on the previous year's plague, which 'cut down almost a hundred thousand', Sancroft warned that the sword of the angel of death could strike again 'unless we prevent it by our speedy Repentance'.[61]

George Swinnock asked sufferers carefully to observe the nature of their affliction, for 'God payeth some in their own coyn.' Was their adversity in any way related to their previous misconduct? 'Sometimes the sin is written in broad letters on the forehead of the punishment ... The Egyptians killed the Jewish children, and God slew their first born.' He asks the searching question: 'Art thou disgraced? Examine thy self, whether thou hast not slandered others ... revealing their faults when thou hast concealed their vertues ... Put the question to thy soul, whether thou hast not to others, occasioned the same suffering.'[62]

It was not only suffering individuals who were disturbed about hypothetical punishment. Sensitivity about corporate deficiencies frequently gave rise to fears that persecution may have been divine chastisement for a local church's spiritual negligence. Richard Alleine was of the view that the 1662 ejectment had robbed many congregations of ministers because they had failed to respond warmly to their message in easier times.[63] The continuing absence of gifted

---

[58] Calamy, in *Exact Collection*, 22.
[59] Philip Lamb, *The Royal Presence, or God's Tabernacle with Men* (1662), sig. A2.
[60] Joseph Hall, *Works* (10 vols; 1863), V, 525.
[61] William Sancroft, *Lex Ignea, or The School of Righteousness, A sermon preached before the King on October 10, 1666, at the Solemn Fast appointed for the late fire in London* (1666), 21–22, 50–51.
[62] Swinnock, *Calling*, II, 400. Thomas Brooks also preached about the possible correlation between present suffering and former offences: *The Privie Key of Heaven* (1665), 'Epistle Dedicatory ... to some afflicted friends', in *Works* (6 vols; Edinburgh; 1980), II, 151.
[63] Richard Alleine, *The Godly Man's Portion and Sanctuary Opened, being the Second Part of Vindiciae Pietatis* (1663), 47–8, a view shared by many others, e.g. John Barrett, who feared that his Nottingham congregation had not been as responsive to his ministry as they might have been, 'so many of you strangers unto Christ, who have heard so much of him, and have been so oft invited, perswaded, and pressed to come in to him':

preachers might put a new value on good biblical exposition.[64] Alleine was not alone in believing that in such bleak circumstances 'empty Pulpits shall preach to them' and '[i]f they have no longer the light with them, their darkness shall instruct them'.[65] Francis Holcroft firmly believed that both he and his scattered Cambridgeshire congregation were at least partly to blame for his imprisonment and their continuing adversities. It was because of 'those worldly Lusts, and Covetings, and ungodliness' that 'our God has thus wasted us'.[66]

Although the Baptist minister Hercules Collins admitted that 'God does not always afflict for sin', he was equally convinced that 'most Affliction is upon that account'.[67] As in biblical times a sovereign God had controlled godless kings, so he could use rapacious informers and heartless persecutors as contemporary agents to 'distress his Church and People for their sins'. They must patiently 'bear the fruits of their own transgressions'.[68] But the punitive dimension was not allowed to dominate their interpretation of suffering. They were persuaded that most experiences of hardship could actively promote the believer's spiritual maturity.

Suffering as an Authenticating Experience

Nonconformist expositors repeatedly emphasized the importance of suffering as a test of reality.[69] 'The fiery furnace wil prove and improve the souls spiritual strength'.[70] 'Afflictions sanctified, are the conspicuous Seal' of the believer's 'Adoption, and Title to Heaven'.[71] Some people who were happy to

---

in *England's Remembrancer*, 49. His friend John Whitlock held that the silencing of Nonconformist preachers was evidence of 'Gods displeasure' at preachers and their congregations: ibid. 42–43. Calamy told his London congregation that for thirty-seven years they had sat under the ministry of faithful preachers but many had become 'Sermon-proof, that know how to sleep and scoff away Sermons': in *Exact Collection*, 13.

[64] 'There is hardly any way to raise the price of the Gospel-Ministry, but by the want of it': Calamy, in *Exact Collection*, 14.

[65] A[lleine]., *Godly Man's Portion*, 49. John Whitlock said that the compulsory silence of the ejected ministers might become 'the most powerful and effectual Sermon' that congregations had ever heard: in *England's Remembrancer*, 42.

[66] H[olcroft]., *Word to the Saints*, 10; cf. *Records* (ed. Underhill), 262–63, 269, 352–53, for similar ideas in the letters of Thomas Hardcastle.

[67] Hercules Collins, *The Scribe instructed ... Kingdom of Heaven*, in *Three Books* (1696), 27.

[68] Bunyan, *Of AntiChrist and his Ruine* (1692), in *MW*, XII, 426–27.

[69] 'You never make Religion your business, till the world see you can let such great things goe, as Life, Estate, Liberty, to keep it ... You never glorifie the truths of God so much by practice, or writing as by suffering for them': Robert Collins, in *Compleat Collection*, [unpaginated].

[70] Oliver Heywood, *Heart-Treasure* (1667), 30.

[71] William Bates, *The Great Duty of Resignation to the Divine Will in Afflictions enforced from the Example of our Suffering Saviour* (1684), 50.

profess faith in congenial circumstances found it difficult to maintain their commitment in adversity. But, in persecuting times, Christ was addressing them directly:

> let me now see ... who it is that will bear the cross for me ... So he asks you in the day of trial, Lovest thou me more than these? ... If you love me more than liberty, you will freely go to prison for me ... Hereby it will be known whether you love Christ indeed, or whether you do but talk of it.[72]

An imprisoned London minister reminded his people that persecution sifted out the genuine from the insincere. If they had merely 'pin'd' their faith 'upon other Mens Sleeves', persecution would soon 'discover [uncover] a zeale without knowledge'; it 'Remaines a duty Zealously to maintain what you have Espous'd', whatever the cost.[73] From his Bristol prison, Thomas Hardcastle also distinguished between genuine and 'counterfeit and common faith' which 'costs but little' and 'will not endure in a time of sharp persecution'.[74] Another imprisoned minister recalled that in Christ's parable 'the stony and thorny ground were not discovered untill time of Temptations ... Copper coin may lie in the bag with gold and silver'. '[T]here is 'never more need then now of ... thorow searching, whether we be in the Faith, and Christ be in us'.[75] Joseph Caryl described suffering as the 'tryal and touchstone of sincerity', bringing professing Christians 'to the furnace, to try whether you be dross or gold'. Life's experiences 'put sincerity to trial', for nothing 'tells us what our state is more plainly than our behaviour' in the time of testing. 'The touchstone is a worthless stone in itself, but it serves to try the gold.'[76]

John Flavel's people had often stood near the Dartmouth quayside and looked at unsteady passengers at the end of a rough passage. 'Thousands ... embark themselves in the profession of religion in a calm, but if the wind riseth, and the sea rageth ... they desire to be landed again as soon as may be;

---

[72] David Clarkson, *Practical Works*, 3 vols (Edinburgh, 1864–5), I, 457–58.
[73] Hercules Collins, *A Voice from the Prison or Meditations on Rev. 3: 11* (1684), 10; cf. *EB*, II, 332 [P344]: in November 1682 'Mr. Collins an Annabaptists goods were distrained ... They broke his doore and entred in at it. There are latent Convictions against most of those that are distrained upon'; considerable sums varying from £100 to £250 were demanded. Collins's meeting-house at Wapping was also raided at this time, its windows smashed and the pulpit and seating destroyed: Ivimey, *English Baptists*, II, 449. Collins would have been a prime target, having just written *Some Reasons for Separation from the Communion of the Church of England and the Unreasonableness of Persecution upon that Account* (1682).
[74] *Records* (ed. Underhill), 298.
[75] Powell, *Bird*, A3v.
[76] Joseph Caryl, *An Exposition with Practical Observations upon ... Job* (12 vols; 1644–66; facsimile ed., Berkley, MI, 2001), I, 135. Thomas Brooks also describes persecution as 'a Christian's touchstone ... that will try what metal men are made of': *Works*, IV, 282.

for they never intended to ride out a storm for Christ.'[77] Vavasor Powell advised those encountering adverse experiences not to be 'slothful in proving' in adversity their 'knowledge of, faith in, love towards, walking after and suffering for Christ'.[78]

'Affliction will search whether thou art sound or no', said George Swinnock.

> The Master, who hath excellent Scholers, desireth that they be examined, and posed throughly, because their profiting doth thereby appear to his praise ... Job and Paul shall be pickt out ... to proclaim to the whole earth, that weak dying man can overcome Hell it self, through the assistance of Heaven ...[79]

In the summer of 1675, when Owen Stockton was preaching at a 'private fast at Ipswich', his people were 'molested by ye informers' but despite the presence of unwelcome visitors the preacher began his exposition by distinguishing between the enemy's plans and God's purposes in persecution. 'Satan's design in raising [troubles] against ye gospel is no cause for [them] to desist from ye wayes of God'. God's design is to prove them, so if they can 'hold [on] in his way' it 'will be a great evidence of our sincerity'.[80]

During the tragic weeks of the London Plague, William Dyer used the narrative of the sacrifice of Isaac (Gen. 22) to illustrate the necessity of testing in a believer's life. In adverse circumstances, God may deprive his people of 'some special necessary mercy, to see ... whether they can live by faith upon the God of mercies when the mercies are gone'.[81]

The Axminster church was not alone in discovering that, in the course of its painful testing, persecution sifted the local congregation. When they were under God's 'winnowing providences ... much chaff was discovered'. Some members 'appeared to be as light grain' and, in time of 'sore staggerings and shakings', many 'good souls, through fear of sufferings', abandoned their allegiance to the local church.[82] Thomas Gouge said that 'the true Reason why, in times of tryall, so many fall off from their profession' is because 'they never knew why they tooke it up ... If men only provide themselves with Summer garments ... can we wonder when the rain beats upon them, if they run into some hole to hide themselves?' It was an 'absolute necessity' that the Church 'be tryed by Afflictions ... as dark nights serve to discover the stars' for, in 'the same Floor, Corn and Chaffe lye mingled together. Affliction is Gods wind,

---

[77] John Flavel, *The Touchstone of Sincerity* ([1679]), in *Works* (6 vols; 1968; first publ. 1820), V, 573.
[78] Powell, *Bird*, A4.
[79] Swinnock, *Calling*, II, 353, 349.
[80] London, DWL, MS 28.31.3, Owen Stockton, Notes of Sermon on Gen.32: 1 [27 June 1675].
[81] William Dyer, *Christ's Voice to London* (1670), 70.
[82] *Ecclesiastica* (ed. Howard), 115.

sent by him on purpose to sever them'.[83] The imprisoned Joseph Alleine feared that he could see 'great tryals coming', times when 'Professors' would 'fall like leaves in the Autumn, unless they be well set[t]led' in their faith.[84] And Swinnock observed: 'Thou couldest hardly have thought thy faith to have been so weak till thou wast like Peter walking in these tempestuous waters, and ready to sink in them'.[85]

Persecution not only distinguished between authentic and counterfeit church members, but also between genuine and time-serving ministers. Alleine urged his Nonconformist colleagues not to forsake their ministry in the interests of personal safety. After the ejectment, some had been reluctant to preach or engage in any form of pastoral ministry, but their fearful silence was only too eloquent in the unbelieving world. Unjust suffering confirmed the reality of the preacher's message.

> Shall We shift off our Work for fear of Persecution? ... Are not these the very things which we have ... preached, and pressed on our People; and shall we make them believe, by our flinching, that these things were not so? ... Are these things true or are they not? If not, why have we taught them? if they be, why do we not live up to them?

Their ejectment had provided a unique opportunity to demonstrate that they were not in ministry for personal gain. Their opponents had dismissed them 'as self-seekers, and such as looked little further than their Maintenance'. Persecution was a time to 'pluck up these prejudices by the roots'. The 'most self-denying services are the best evidences'; 'now is the time for you to settle your selves for ever in the Affections of your People' and, more importantly, whenever 'was there such a time to lay up treasure in Heaven as now'?[86]

---

[83] Thomas Gouge, *Joshua's Resolution*, 5–6: 'There is chaff mixed with the wheat, corruption with their graces; there needs a rough wind to separate them. There is dross in the best metal, there needs a furnace or a fining pot to work it out.' Cf. Clarkson, *Works*, II, 238.

[84] Joseph Alleine, *Christian Letters*, 13 (13 June 1663; published with [Theodosia Alleine], *The Life and Death of ... Joseph Alleine* (1671), but separately paginated). I have provided the letters' dates, whenever stated, as numeration varies slightly in different editions.

[85] Swinnock, *Calling*, II, 393.

[86] Joseph Alleine, *A Call to Archippus, or an Humble and Earnest Motion to some ejected Ministers ... to take heed to their Ministry, That they fulfil it* (1664), 26–27, 18–19. Eleven years after the publication of *A Call to Archippus*, this passage formed an acknowledged extensive quotation in one of Hardcastle's prison letters to his Bristol congregation: *Records* (ed. Underhill), 354. Alleine's life and work were well known, especially in the West Country, largely through his writings and the publication of a popular biography by his wife, Theodosia.

Suffering as a Corrective Exercise

Acknowledging that suffering is a test of faith and an indication of a genuine ministry, Nonconformist preachers also emphasized that adversity may serve a disciplinary function in the life of a believer. 'Corrections are grievous, but ... they purifie and make us gracious'.[87] Stephen Charnock believed that 'God many times saves his people by sufferings ... snuffing the candle makes it burn the clearer'.[88] 'Persecutions are the workmen that will fit you and square you for God's buildings', said Thomas Brooks.[89] Thomas Watson was another London minister with the same message: 'God never stretcheth the strings of his viol, but to make the musick so much sweeter.'[90]

Swinnock multiplied illustrations to emphasize that adversities served to increase grace in the believer's life. 'He sendeth sharp Frosts to kill the weeds of sin'. Dissenters' homes provided conspicuous illustrations. '[S]weet spices the more they are pounded, the more fragrant smell they send forth. The Gold of grace shineth most brightly in the fire'. 'Wisps scowre vessels and make them brighter'.[91]

During a lengthy imprisonment, the General Baptist minister John Griffith was honest enough to acknowledge that, though privileged 'to suffer Bonds' for the sake of his Lord, he found his heart 'not so cleansed and brought to the foot of Christ' as he had hoped. He prayed that it might still please God 'to sancifie these Bonds ... then may I bless the Lord ... that ever I lay in Newgate'.[92]

Adversities might even be a divine protection mechanism, keeping the sufferer further from sin and closer to God. Fierce opposition, 'Sathan's Temptations', may be 'thorns in your wayes, to keep you from straying and running wrong'.[93] God may not be scolding them for the past but refining in the present and equipping for the future.

Reflecting on a lifetime of hardship, James Birdwood feared that at times Christians may be too quick 'to think God hates us, because he corrects us'.[94] Continuing his expositions of Job at the beginning of the persecution period, the London minister Joseph Caryl emphasized that God might be using life's afflictions 'as medicines ... to restore [their] spiritual hearing'. Preoccupied with other things, they may have failed to hear God's urgent message either through 'the voyce of the word' in Scripture or the 'workes of God' in experience. 'When words do not prevail to open the ear, fetters and cords' may more quickly gain our attention. In works of tender mercy God speaks

---

[87] Swinnock, *Calling*, II, 422–23.
[88] Charnock, *Works*, I, 77.
[89] Thomas Brooks, *The Crown and Glory of Christianity* [1662], in *Works*, IV, 281.
[90] Thomas Watson, in *Exact Collection*, 55.
[91] Swinnock, *Calling*, II, 349–50, 398.
[92] John Griffith, *Some Prison Meditations and Experiences* (1663), Epistle Dedicatory. A3 (ii).
[93] Ambrose, *War with Devils*, 2.
[94] Birdwood, *Hearts-Ease*, 30.

'sweetly' but in affliction 'he trumpets to us'. He reminded his people of Augustine's saying that prosperity is 'the gift of God comforting us' while adversity is 'the gift of God admonishing us'.[95] George Hughes believed that God sometimes chastised to 'render sin more odious to his people'. It was a form of spiritual surgery, for God deemed it 'a great mercie to lance that he may not kill'.[96]

Through hardship, many Dissenters came to realize that in adversity God not only uncovered disturbing things about themselves but also revealed inspiring truths about himself. Suffering frequently opened their eyes either to new things about God or to familiar things that they knew intellectually but not experimentally. With memories of rural Wales, Vavasor Powell's numerous imprisonments[97] taught him that affliction 'is the spiritual shepherds hook with which he draws back stragling, straying and out-shipping sheep'.[98]

Encouraging an urban congregation in severe times, David Clarkson shared the same message but with different imagery. 'A judge punishes offenders, because justice must be done ... But a father corrects his child that he may make him better ... not because he would show himself just, but because he is affectionate.' God was their tender and experienced doctor who 'proportions what he administers to the nature of his patient's distemper', those 'ingredients, so much of them, and no more' than were 'sufficient for the cure'.[99] Whatever the hardships, they would ultimately serve a beneficial purpose; 'all his Corrections will be for your good and profit'. Emerging from trouble, the Psalmist could say, '*It is good for me that I have been afflicted*'.[100]

Suffering as a Didactic Process

In expounding the purpose of suffering, these pastors gave special prominence to its teaching potential. God had 'many ways to make his Scholars learn their lessons'.[101] 'In prosperity God speaks ... but we will not hear, but in the time of adversity God opens the ears.'[102] Abraham Cheare referred to his enforced exile on Drake's Island as 'this School of Instruction, unto which he hath sent me'.[103]

---

[95] Caryl, *Job*, XI, 232–3, quoting Augustine, *Enarrationes in Psalmos*; cf. Thomas Manton, *A Practical Exposition of the Lord's Prayer* (1684), 412–13; idem, *A Practical Commentary, or an Exposition ... upon the Epistle of James* (1657), 20–21.
[96] George Hughes, *Dry Rod Blooming and Fruit-Bearing* (1644), 14–15.
[97] With the exception of an eleven-month period of freedom in 1667–8, Powell spent the last full decade of his life in prisons.
[98] Powell, *Bird*, 15–16.
[99] Clarkson, *Works*, II, 188.
[100] Powell, *Bird*, 33.
[101] Swinnock, *Calling*, II, 356; cf. Thomas Jacombe, in *The London-Ministers Legacy to their several congregations, being a Collection of Farewell Sermons* (1662), 82: 'For we are like idle boyes, or bad Schollers, that learn best when the rod is over us.'
[102] Jacombe, in *London-Ministers Legacy*, 82 (sermon defectively paginated).
[103] Cheare, *Words*, 221.

As a London prisoner, Hercules Collins described suffering as the believer's 'School of Affliction': 'something is to be learned there ... not ordinarily learned by other ways'.[104] George Swinnock encouraged Nonconformists to regard afflictions as a servant on a necessary errand, 'a messenger from thy Sovereign, and thy best friend'. They must 'not dismiss him till his business be done, especially pondering that thy God hath sent him for thy profit'.[105]

Suffering believers were not always rapid learners. 'Perhaps we may lie the longer in it, because God's End may not be answered upon us.' Paul was not immediately delivered from his troublesome 'thorn' and 'David lay so long in God's Furnace' in order 'to learn God's Statutes'.[106] The didactic value of suffering became a theme of supreme importance, and to the more detailed aspects of this teaching we now turn.

The Lessons of Suffering

He 'who doth not feel the smart of the rod, will never hear the voice of the rod'.[107] As they reflected on their experience of suffering, a number of lessons became especially prominent in their thinking and teaching.

Visible Lectures

These pastors recognized that spiritual instruction may be more speedily and effectively communicated through adversity. 'Lessons learned in Affliction ... stick most, and stay longest with us', especially when those sufferings 'are more directly for his cause'.[108] Recalling the Johannine Upper Room discourse, Baxter asked, 'When did Christ preach such comforts to his Disciples' as when their hearts were 'sorrowful because of his departure?' He spoke 'Peace' when the doors were bolted for fear of their persecutors. When did Stephen see heaven opened except in the hour of severe trial?[109] In 1684, following years of repeated harassment and adversity, William Jenkyn was arrested at a prayer meeting in his London meeting-house and taken to Newgate prison, where he died three months later. In that jail, he had ample occasion to remember what he had said on the day he took leave of his congregation, that the Church's afflictions were 'not consuming fire, but trying fire'. God taught his servants 'excellent lessons by the light of this fire' and they would not be destroyed

---

[104] Collins, *Scribe Instructed*, 37.
[105] Swinnock, *Calling*, II, 357.
[106] Collins, *Scribe Instructed*, 29, quoting 2 Cor. 12: 7; Psa. 119: 71; cf. Baxter, *Dying Thoughts*, 312–13 (Appendix): 'And it is God's Mercy to some of us to make our sufferings long, that we may have a competent time of learning'.
[107] Swinnock, *Calling*, II, 393, 445.
[108] Powell, *Bird*, 33.
[109] Baxter, *Rest*, 495; cf. Swinnock, *Calling*, II, 360: 'Under a shower of stones about Stevens ears, his eyes saw the best sight that ever was seen, Acts 7: 56.'

'though the fire be never so spreading'. God 'will not suffer this fire to exceed their strength; it shall burn up nothing but their drosse'.[110]

William Greenhill's voluminous exposition of Ezekiel became popular reading for ministers during the persecution. Preached as sermons prior to the Restoration, its message about the prophet's agonizing experience in exile spoke powerfully in print to a generation under severe testing. When 'people are in captivity, a Prophet amongst them will do well'. When his hearers are 'in misery, they see the uncertainty of life, the insufficiency of all creatures ... now is a good season to bring the truths of the eternall God unto them'.[111]

The ejected minister Thomas Case wrote fully about the blessing of adversity. From personal experience, Case maintained that in 'the School of Affliction' Christians 'come to know more of God ... by half a years sufferings, then by many years Sermons'.[112] In adversity people may clearly perceive some biblical truth previously ignored, marginalized or unrecognized by them. Bartholmew Ashwood likened it to a Johannine miracle story, describing 'afflictions' as 'Christ's clay and spittle to open his peoples eyes', enabling them to see human sin, its consequences and its remedy.[113]

Frost in Winter

Trouble might 'unglew' suffering believers from the materialistic values of a godless world.[114] People were more 'ruined by Prosperity' than by trouble.[115] Reminding his Axminster friends of a familiar parable, Bartholomew Ashwood said that the 'Prodigal never thought of returning till all was gone'. In persecution God knocked off 'the golden fetters from their feet, that he may bring their soul out of prison'.[116] Better 'to be preserved in Brine than rot in

---

[110] William Jenkyn, *The Burning yet unconsumed Bush ... Two Farewell Sermons* (1662), 19.

[111] William Greenhill, *An Exposition of the five first Chapters ... of Ezekiel* (1650), 304–305.

[112] Thomas Case, *Correction, Instruction: or a Treatise of Afflictions* (1652), 91. Accused of involvement in Christopher Love's plot against Cromwell, Case was imprisoned for five months, producing reflections that after his release became a book, reprinted in successive years and published again in 1671. Reading these papers, Thomas Manton told Case: 'the Spirit of God went into prison with you', and recalled Tertullian's saying that the martyrs were 'sequestred from the world' to 'converse with God'. Indeed, 'I could even envy your prison-comforts': Case, *Correction*, A2v–A3.

[113] Bartholomew Ashwood, *The Heavenly Trade, or the Best Merchandizing* (1679), 328, an allusion to Jn 9: 6–7.

[114] Collins, *Scribe Instructed*, 29: '[Perhaps] God keeps the Rod upon thy Back because thou art too much glewed to the World'.

[115] Bates, *Great Duty*, 9, cf. 52.

[116] Ashwood, *Heavenly Trade*, 329–30; cf. 329: 'Men come to read their miscarriages best by the fire-light of affliction'.

Honey'.[117] Their expositions frequently used the changing seasons as a telling illustration. Biting winter winds were seldom welcome, but the cold was 'needfull' and was a sign of God's continuing care as well as his unique power. If the weather were 'alwayes warme', it would be 'worse for us'. Life's 'providential changes', when people were 'sometimes under clouds and darkness', were all for their good. It was necessary to have 'chilling times as well as springing times'. A harsh winter served to kill off the weeds, and 'perpetual shining and faire seasons are reserved for Heaven'.[118] Trials functioned as 'Frost did in winter, or Rain in Spring ... The heat of prosperity would have burnt us, if God has not sent this Cloud of affliction to cover us'. Trouble put life in perspective, and alerted sufferers to the supreme value of things money could not buy. Quoting an eighth-century Hebrew prophet, Powell said that adversities might be used to keep Christians from the 'further mischief' they might experience if they continued resolutely to pursue life's transient treasures: '*I will hedge up thy wayes*' with thorns.[119]

Like the Plough

Moreover, adversities challenged human arrogance. 'Times of extremity make us more humble', said Stephen Charnock, 'and humility, like the plough', breaks up the hard ground of human self-reliance. We do not 'censure an artificer for hewing his stones, or beating his iron'. It is by 'his cross providence' that God 'prepares the church for fruitfulness whilst he ploughs it'.[120] William Bridge used an illustration from contemporary writing conventions to drive this point home: 'if ever we be call'd to suffer' we must 'read over our sufferings, and throw dust' upon them. 'As one that hath written a Letter ... will read over the letter, and then he mends it ... and throws dust, dust, dust upon the letter', so we are to 'throw dust, I mean humility' upon our sufferings.[121] According to Collins, life's 'humbling Dispensations' kept these believers 'in lowly frames'.[122] They realized, wrote Nathaniel Vincent, 'how assuredly we should sink, if an arm from Heaven were not stretched forth to sustain us'; 'sufferings being sanctified are hugely efficacious', for 'bearing the yoke will tame' an arrogant or rebellious nature.[123]

---

[117] Collins, *Scribe Instructed*, 14.
[118] Caryl, *Job*, XI, 131, 495–96; cf. Charnock, *Works*, I, 111: 'The seasons of the year ... orderly succeed one another; and the coldness of the winter is but a preparation for a seasonable spring and a summer harvest. We do not unrighteously accuse God of disorder in his common works, why should we do it in his special works of providence?'
[119] Powell, *Bird*, 13–14, quoting Hos. 2: 6.
[120] Charnock, *Works*, I, 106, 11.
[121] William Bridge, *Seasonable Truths in Evil Times* (1668), 48 (Sermon 2).
[122] Collins, *Scribe Instructed*, 26–27.
[123] Vincent, *Covert*, 19.

Pruning Superfluous Sprigs

'Afflictions and persecutions will discover what metal men are made of', said Thomas Brooks, quoting the steadfastness of the three Hebrew patriots during the Babylonian exile. 'They would rather burn than bow [to the king's golden image] ... which was evident proof of their sincerity'. With more than a hint at the contemporary context, Brooks says that Daniel's courageous trio were determined that they 'would be nonconformists' even if 'court, city and country cried up conformity'.[124] Predictably, the Daniel narratives became something of a favourite with Dissenting preachers, especially in the early years of repression.[125]

Bunyan said that we 'are apt to overshoot, in days that are calm, and to think our selves ... more strong' than we are. Adversity can 'cut off those superfluous spriggs of pride and self-conceitedness'. We would 'be overgrown with [the] flesh, if we had not our seasonable Winters'.[126] Charnock believed that suffering thrusts us 'into the secret chamber of our own heart' which, prior to our troubles, we had little intention of visiting 'by a self-examination'.[127] It is in 'the School of Affliction', argued Collins, that the Lord discloses to the soul its own 'Impotency and Insufficiency', and the fact that it cannot 'bear trials honourably, without Divine Grace and Assistance'.[128]

What matters most

When adversity disturbs life's normal routine, it may cause believers to reflect on their priorities and provide opportunity for a serious reappraisal of human values. In hard times, Christians may come to discern afresh the true worth of things. The devil 'can make the truth in thy esteem to be little', and he can also 'make [the] sufferings great and ten times more terrible'. A prison may look 'as black as Hell', and when household goods are forcibly removed in lieu of fines 'the loss of a few Stools and Chairs' seems 'as bad as the loss of so many *baggs*

---

[124] Brooks, *Crown and Glory*, in *Works*, IV, 281–82; cf. Bunyan, *Christian Behaviour* (1663), in *MW*, III, 18: 'Touching mens prosecuting their Zeal for their Worship &c. that they do think right ... Nebuchadnezzar will have his Fiery-Furnace, and Darius his *Lyons-Den* for nonconformists.'

[125] Bunyan, *MW*, I, 258; VIII, 383; Robert Collins, in *Compleat Collection*, [unpaginated]; William Cross, in *England's Remembrancer*, 164; Jacombe, in *Exact Collection*, 77, 79; John Galpin, in *The Third Volum of Farewel Sermons, preached by some London and Country Ministers* (1663), 195; George Swinnock, *The Pastors Farewell and Wish of Welfare for His People* (1662), 51; Matthew Mead, *The Pastors Valediction* (1662), 20: 'Daniel rather chosed to be cast to Lions, then to lose the Peace of his Conscience'; and, among Quakers, Rigge, *Constancy in the Truth*, 61–62.

[126] Bunyan, *Seasonable Counsel*, in *MW*, X, 8–9.

[127] Charnock, *Works*, II, 361.

[128] Collins, *Scribe Instructed*, 30.

of Gold'.[129] Across the centuries, suffering experiences, however harrowing, have been used to help believers realize the superior value of better treasures. Many have come to the clear realization that there are worse things than suffering. They would rather keep their faith than lose their suffering. Holiness was of greater value than happiness. Integrity was better than tranquility.

Nonconformist preachers frequently reminded their congregations to fear sin more than suffering. Benjamin Keach's widely circulated allegory, *The Travels of True Godliness*, did not attain the popularity of *Pilgrim's Progress* but both authors shared the same message. The first of its many editions appeared in shops and bookstalls in 1683, the year of the Rye House Plot. A few Dissenters were clearly implicated[130] in the attempt to assassinate the king and his brother, but suspicion fell upon all Nonconformists, and that was enough to fuel increasing hostility. Many in authority dismissed 'Conventiclers' as 'enemies of the Crown', their seditious meetings a cover for planning dangerous enterprises.[131] It was a time when the 'Trouble, Opposition, Reproaches and Persecutions' mentioned in Keach's sub-title became painfully characteristic of Nonconformist life. The highly coordinated informing activities of London's 'Hilton Gang' made life both difficult and costly for preachers and hearers in the metropolis,[132] and similar harassment was experienced in the provinces. Theirs was a time, as Bunyan said, 'to fight and wrestle in ... a place to be tryed in'.[133]

'Godliness' is personified in Keach's travelogue; he 'will suffer rather than sin'.[134] Whatever the cost, this pilgrim will stand by his resolute choice: 'Lord, rather let me have a good heart than a great estate', for 'though he loves many things besides God, yet he loves nothing above God. The man fears sin more than suffering,'[135] was a popular aphorism, frequently repeated in

---

[129] Bunyan, *MW*, X, 17.
[130] For Nonconformist complicity in the plot, see Greaves, *Glimpses*, 470–76, 489–92; idem, *Secrets of the Kingdom: British Radicals from the Popish Plot to the Revolution of 1688–1689* (Stanford, CA, 1992).
[131] In *The nonconformists Vindication: or, Mr. Furguson's Fault No General Crime* (1683), an anonymous author protested that Dissenters were being widely punished although totally loyal to the king and entirely innocent of any seditious activity.
[132] Nearly 4,000 Dissenters were 'bound over, indicted, or summarily' convicted for attending conventicles in the London area in the 1680s. Many of them 'suffered more than once, so the crude totals are much higher still': Harris, *London Crowds*, 66.
[133] Bunyan, *A Holy Life* (1683), in *MW*, IX, 296.
[134] B[enjamin]. K[each]., *The Travels of True Godliness ... shewing the Troubles, Oppositions, Reproaches, and Persecutions he hath met with in every Age, together with the Danger he seems to be in at this present Time ...* (3rd ed.; 1684), 5; cf. ibid. 45–46, referring to suffering Protestants in France. A companion volume, *The Travels of Ungodliness*, appeared later.
[135] Keach, *Travels of Godliness*, 4–5. For the popularity of Keach's allegories, see Austin Walker, *The Excellent Benjamin Keach* (Dundas, ON, 2004, 167–74.

Nonconformist preaching.[136]

Would you change places?

Adversity confronted the Dissenter with stark alternatives. Bunyan told persecuted Dissenters that it was better to bear pain than inflict it: 'thou art in the fire', whilst the oppressors 'blow the bellows: but wouldest thou change places with them?'[137] Acknowledging that he too would rather be a sufferer than a persecutor, Hardcastle offered another alternative: he would rather be a sufferer than a defector. In the first of many letters from prison, he told Bristol people that he had seen a 'bright side' to his adversity: endurance was better than desertion. It was infinitely preferable to have been forcibly 'driven and pulled from' his work than to be numbered among the faint-hearted who had chosen to 'draw back from it. Let us not be ashamed of the gospel of Christ.'[138]

It proved well

Suffering also taught these Christians to depend entirely upon God. Hardcastle exhorted his Bristol people to 'Fear men less, and trust God more. The more we venture upon him, the better he is.' After spending half a year in gaol, he could testify: 'We have ventured upon six months' cross in his way ... and it proved well'.[139] There had been dark days, but God had been good to him. By contrast, when things went well, believers were in danger of pretentious self-reliance. Powell held that 'Christ puts most of his oyl in Broken Vessels' for 'in broken hearts there is most grace' and there it is 'best kept'.[140]

Still learning

Nonconformist preachers frequently alerted their people to the common and serious danger of emerging from persecution seemingly without gaining anything of spiritual or moral value. It was 'doleful for a man to come out of affliction, as a sheep out of a Ditch, dirty and defiled' but no 'better for [the] affliction'. Worse than not learning anything, some might be so damaged by the experience that they were less committed than before, like a child who was 'more forward when he is corrected for his faults!' Lessons not properly learnt

---

[136] For example, 'Be more afraid of sin then of Suffering': Thomas Watson, in *London-Ministers Legacy*, 33; 'rather choose the greatest affliction than the least sin': broadsheet, *Old Mr. Edmund Calamy's Former and Latter Sayings upon Several Occasions* (1674); 'chuse any suffering, rather than the least sin': Philip Lamb, in *Compleat Collection*, [unpaginated].
[137] Bunyan, *MW*, X, 72.
[138] *Records* (ed. Underhill), 257.
[139] Ibid. 282.
[140] Powell, *Bird*, 74.

might need to be repeated in a different form. 'If the ten plagues do not reform Pharaoh, the red Sea shall ruine him'.[141]

Recovering from a serious illness, John Owen preached a series of sermons on Psalm 130, particularly on verse 1: 'Out of the depths have I cried unto thee, O Lord'. He exhorted his congregation: 'Labour to grow better under all your Afflictions'. God's intention was to use them to enrich believers, not to impoverish or damage them. Owen added to his exhortation the same note of ominous warning. If a specific adversity did not prove beneficial, God might need to inflict another to achieve his purposes. 'He will not cease to thresh and break the bread-corn until it be meet for his use.'[142]

There was something to be gained in the most severe trial. In such troubled times, many were helped by the published letters of Samuel Rutherford, and his memorable sayings found their way into many a Nonconformist sermon. People would have recalled his counsel to a correspondent who had suffered her 'own large share of troubles,' but had so far proved 'an ill scholar'. The 'banished minister' told her of the many things he had gained as 'Christ's prisoner' and it was imperative that she too might benefit from her ordeal. 'Madam, ye must go in at heaven's gates' with 'your book in your hand, still learning'.[143]

The Privilege of Suffering

A dominant theme, constantly recurring in these sources, was that mature Christians come to regard suffering as a unique privilege. Tracing seven stages of Christian experience, Baxter was in no doubt that 'sufferers' enter 'the highest form of the school of Christ'.[144] Brooks considered 'affliction and persecution for holiness' sake' to be the 'greatest and highest honour ... in this world', supporting his conviction with vivid stories of early Christian sufferers and the Marian martyrs, who viewed their sufferings as the highest accolade.[145]

When Mary Franklin wrote about the further imprisonment[146] of her minister husband and the removal of all their possessions in the winter of 1684, she said that she could only look 'upon it as an honour that the Lord should count me worthy to suffer anything for his sake'. She was not theorizing. The persecution had never been worse for London Dissenters. The 'Hilton Gang' had amassed

---

[141] Swinnock, *Calling*, II, 405–407.

[142] John Owen, *A Practical Exposition upon Psalm 130* (1669), 329; also in *Works*, VI, 583.

[143] *Letters of Rutherford* (ed. Bonar), 151.

[144] Baxter held that at the first stage we are primarily 'exercised with fears of hell and God's displeasure', but at the seventh stage the believer is intent on 'following him with our cross and being conformed to him'. God does not usually 'try and exercise his young and weak ones with the trials of the strong ... as he doth the ripe confirmed Christians': Baxter, *The Divine Life* (1664), in *Works* (ed. Orme), XIII, 307–309.

[145] Brooks, *Works*, IV, 292–93.

[146] Franklin had been arrested and imprisoned earlier, in 1682: *EB*, II, 331 [P344].

huge sums of money by informing on them; this highly organized, unscrupulous team of over forty men and women devoted their Sundays to the infiltration of Nonconformist meetings, gathering names of regular worshippers so that they could return with warrants for the arrest of preachers and members of the congregation. Authorized to receive a third of the fines, they spent the rest of the week either collecting the money or distraining goods in the case of Dissenters unable to pay.[147]

Mary Franklin described the Saturday afternoon when the authorities arrested her husband, Robert, for preaching at the Presbyterian meeting in London's Glovers' Hall.[148] An informer entered their home 'in a great fury' with 'his drawn sword in his hand'. Once her husband had been taken to prison, other informers 'returned to our house ... it being 10 of the clock at night'. After eating all their food, 'they went into every room ... and set down the goods, in order to their taking of them away on the Monday'. On the Monday morning, 'they offered me to buy my own goods ... and when they could not prevail for money ... fell into a great rage ... pulling and knocking down the things, and sent for two carts, which they filled that night'. The following morning they returned with yet another cart, and 'took away the rest', leaving not her 'so much as a chair to sit in or a cup to drink' from. Yet Mary Franklin wished to record her sense of deep privilege, that she 'should have the honour to be one of those that should help to fill up the measure of Christ's sufferings'.[149] She would have agreed with Thomas Goodwin that 'to have our graces, especially ... our faith and patience tried ... to the glory of God' was 'the greatest spiritual privilege that can come to us' this side of heaven.[150]

William Dyer's readers hardly needed to be reminded that persecution might be more costly than the deprivation of goods. Dissenters knew of people whose earthly life had ended in gaol. But, said Dyer, the persecutors 'take a life from you which you cannot keep, and bestow a life upon you which you cannot lose'. It is always 'an honour to be dishonoured for Christ'.[151] Hardcastle maintained that 'a season of suffering righteously' is to be 'prized as much or more' than a time of peace. Bearing their present suffering was a token of genuine commitment to Christ that might never come to them again: 'Do we know that God will ever honour us with such an opportunity, if we neglect this

---

[147] Mark Goldie, 'The Hilton Gang and the Purge of London in the 1680's', in *Politics and the Political Imagination in Later Stuart Britain: Essays Presented to Lois Green Schwoerer* (ed. Howard Nenner; Rochester, NY, 1997), 43–73.

[148] Edmund Calamy said that, as a boy, he was present on only two occasions when Nonconformist preachers were disturbed. One was at a meeting 'in Bunhill-fields' conducted by Robert Franklin; the other at William Jenkyn's congregation 'in Jewen-street'. Calamy said that 'in both places' the intruders were 'fierce and noisy, and made great havoc': *Historical Account* (ed. Rutt), I, 89.

[149] 'The Experiences of Mary Franklin', 396–97, quoting Col. 1: 24.

[150] Thomas Goodwin, *Works*, II, 431.

[151] Dyer, *Titles*, 212.

[one]?'[152]

Joseph Alleine used his stark and uncompromising *Call to Archippus* to address fearful ministers who might not be exercising their gifts or grasping new opportunities for service: 'Is it not a really glorious Priviledge to suffer for Christ and a Badg[e] of singular Ho[no]ur?' These diffident preachers must reflect, not on what they might lose but what they would miss: 'What will so much ... further our experiences, help on Mortification, and Inhance our Eternal Glory, as our patient bearing for Christ?'[153] As Abraham Cheare lay dying in Drake's Island prison, he testified: '[m]y God ... hath brought me into bonds' and 'this honour have not all his Saints, though they be a People near unto him'. Those who had been at his bedside remembered that he particularly 'minded that word' in 1 Peter 4: 16, saying 'what a blessed thing it was to suffer as a Christian'. It was 'a rich privilege to 'begin, hold on, hold out, and at last', through death, 'come off [from this world] as a Christian'.[154]

During imprisonment, Bunyan used an Old Testament illustration to indicate that his tribulations had proved to be 'the spoils won in Battel', which he had 'dedicated to maintain the house of God'. He had gained far more than he had lost and 'would not have been without this trial for much'.[155] Many of his contemporaries thought similarly. Lawrence Spooner suffered frequent harassment, the raids of informers and innumerable hardships, including the seizing of his goods and cattle, but talked only of his assets. 'I durst not have exchanged my condition with the greatest men in the world ... what I lost is more than made up'. In the darkest times, he had gained 'so large a crop' of priceless 'experience'.[156]

George Hughes's detailed expositions of Genesis were published by his son Obadiah. Father and son's joint incarceration on Drake's Island had deepened their conviction that the believer's '[a]fflictions and oppressions' might be 'God's legacies sometime to his Church'.[157] The Rothwell minister Thomas Browning testified: 'I tell you ... if you knew what Christ's prisoners ... enjoyed in their Goals [sic], you would not fear their Condition, but long for it.'[158] From prison in Leicester, another Northamptonshire minister, John Maidwell, wrote to his daughter and her husband, saying that although his

---

[152] *Records* (ed. Underhill), 259.
[153] Alleine, *Call to Archippus*, 26.
[154] Cheare, *Words*, 182, 178.
[155] Bunyan, *GA*, §339, citing 1 Chron. 26: 27.
[156] Samuel James, *An Abstract of the Gracious Dealings of God with some Eminent Christians* (4th ed.; 1774), 24, from the manuscript testimony of James's grandfather, Lawrence Spooner.
[157] George Hughes, *An Analytical Exposition of Genesis ... Exodus* (1672), 595. Although imprisoned on the island at the same time, father and son were kept apart.
[158] Matthias Maurice, *Monuments of Mercy* (1729), 53; cf. Edmund Calamy, in *Exact Collection*, 8: 'In Q. Maries days the Martyrs wrote to their Friends out of Prison, If you knew the Comforts we have in prison, you would wish to be with us'.

persecutors had caused him 'much trouble', he was far from lonely, for God had given him 'the company of many of his servants about 40 both ministers and others, so that ... did our enemies know what kindness they have shown in sending us hither, they would soon release us, out of envy for our happiness', for such 'communion with God and his people ... makes our prison a palace to us'.[159] When Keach was in the pillory at Aylesbury, he told his friends not to be fearful about the cost of Christian witness. 'Oh! did you but experience ... the great love of God and the excellencies that are in him, it would make you willing to go through any sufferings for his sake.'[160]

The Benefits of Suffering

Oliver Heywood had no doubt that God would always 'do our soules good by our fears and tears and troubles'.[161] The imprisoned Suffolk minister John Fairfax told his godly father that he hoped the experience would come to 'signifie something' for him, and that his 'holy and wise God' would 'make use of it'. His confinement was continuing, he said, because 'God hath something yet to worke in me before he worke for me' by effecting his release.[162] Eager to help those who had suffered severe family losses during London's plague, Thomas Brooks urged them to 'view the rod on every side. If there be briars on one side, there is rosemary on the other'. The Christian who 'looks on the rosemary side ... will bear up patiently, gallantly and cheerfully'.[163] Not always easy to detect, rich blessing could be hidden in the worst of sorrows. For Owen Stockton, 'All troubles are sanctified to those that are Christ's'.[164]

'Nothing is intolerable that is necessary'.[165] 'The Church grows by tears and withers by smiles'.[166] At the close of his life, the London Baptist leader Hanserd Knollys told his people that after a sixteenth-month imprisonment, he could only bless God 'for Prison mercies'.[167] Nathanael Vincent prayed, 'Thy Prisoner blesses thee that ever he had the honour to be in bonds for thee ... Thy presence is so sweet, that he would go to any place to have more of it.' Since

---

[159] DWL, MS 12.63 (22), Letter from John Maidwell, 6 July 1685.
[160] Thomas Crosby, *The History of the English Baptists* (4 vols, 1738–40), II, 207.
[161] Heywood, *Autobiography* (ed. Turner), I, 188.
[162] Edgar Taylor, *The Suffolk Bartholomeans* (1840), 128.
[163] Brooks, *Privie Key of Heaven*, in *Works*, II, 154. From prison, Hardcastle assured his congregation that our 'Father corrects us lovingly and gently', taking us 'on his knee' to correct us; 'he smiles whilst he is striking': *Records* (ed. Underhill), 269.
[164] Owen Stockton, *Consolation in Life and Death* (1681), 71.
[165] Swinnock, *Calling*, II, 422.
[166] Charnock, *Works*, I, 78.
[167] *The Life and Death of that old Disciple ... Hanserd Knollys, who died in the 93rd year of his age, written with his own hand to the year 1672, and continued in general with an epistle by Mr. William Kiffin* (1692), 45. In 1684, Morrice recorded that Knollys, 'about 84 yeares of age an Anabaptist is now and has been in the new prison about six or eight months': *EB*, II, 467 [P431].

imprisonment, his peace of mind had certainly 'been more perfect'.[168]

Listening to Dissenters' sermons, reading their journals and diaries, and overhearing their conversations in letters, it is possible to be more precise in identifying the specific advantages that came to them through life's trials.

Not building on Quicksand

Life's harrowing experiences demand resources totally beyond mere human powers. William Greenhill gleaned striking narratives from the Old Testament to illustrate the believer's urgent need of divine support. Bereft of other help, Israel's exiled leaders turned instinctively to Ezekiel. Likewise 'Jereboam when his sonne was sick, sends to Ahijah the prophet to know what should become of him', and 'Naaman in his leprosy goeth to the prophet Elisha for helpe'. In extreme trouble, Hezekiah despatched a messenger to Isaiah.[169]

Even unsteady church members who, under pressure, forsook the 'paths ... of his suffering ones' had a silent message for fellow-Christians. While in prison, Abraham Cheare heard discouraging news of those who were 'departing ... from their holy Professions'. As 'stars ... cast down ... from their excellency', they were a constant warning to other believers for on them 'this inscription is manifestly engraven, as a caution to us ... *Lo, this is the man that made not God his confidence*'. They reminded dependent Christians of the 'shortness of self-sufficiency'.[170]

Praying at a Fast Day in a Derbyshire home, one ejected minister confessed their need. 'The distresses of thy people are to quicken them in applying to thee ... farewell worldly confidences ... Let us not think to intrench ourselves in any created security' or 'build our hope on a quicksand'.[171]

Even without Candles

Their greatest discovery in adversity was that God never leaves his people without the specific help they need. Utilizing the well-known Old Testament theophany, Samuel Clarke said that, however fierce the flames, Christ, 'the Angel of the Covenant', was always in the burning bush, 'either to slack the fire, or to strengthen the Bush, and make it incombustible'.[172] Brooks referred to 'the deriding question which persecutors put to the saints in the time of their trial and troubles, *Ubi Deus?* Where is now your God?', to which believers

---

[168] Vincent, *Covert*, A3r.

[169] William Greenhill, *An Exposition continued upon the sixt[h] to ... thirteenth Chapters ... Ezekiel* (1649), 138, citing Ezek. 8: 1; 1 Kings 14: 2–3; 2 Kings 5: 5–9; Isa. 37: 2.

[170] Cheare, *Words*, 239–40.

[171] *Baptist Annual Register (1790–1802)* (4 vols; 1793–1803), III, 331–32 (verbatim record of a prayer by Robert Porter of Pentridge, Derbyshire, 19 June 1672).

[172] Clarke, *General Martyrologie*, A, 'To the Reader', quoting Exod. 3: 2.

'may return a bold and confident answer, *Hic Deus,* Our God is here ... he will never leave us nor forsake us'.[173] God had promised either to 'support them in Trouble, or deliver them out of Trouble'.[174]

Strength and support was guaranteed, but there might well be times when, physically exhausted, emotionally drained or socially isolated, the sufferer was too overwhelmed to identify and appropriate the promised help. Life's '[s]addest providences' and even the 'most terrible things ... often carry a great deal of sweetness and comfort in them', said Robert Seddon in a farewell message to his Derbyshire congregation, although sometimes 'through ignorance and unbelief' Christians 'hardly discern' them. 'We ... too little eye ... the things that are not seen.'[175] John Owen pleaded with his contemporaries not to complain when buffeted by adversity. Although God had 'a cup of Affliction in one hand' he had 'a cup of Consolation in another. And if all [the] Stars withdraw their light ... assure your selves that the Sun is ready to rise.'[176] Baxter expressed it perfectly: 'He is not without light that hath the shining sun, though all his candles be put out. If God be our God, he is our All, and [that] is enough for us'.[177]

Better than Silk and Velvet

Many who trusted God in severe trials and deprivations frequently discovered that initial resentment was gradually replaced by deep contentment. With personal experience of life in Newgate, Hercules Collins defined such trust not as a stoic acceptance of life's circumstances but as the readiness to 'have our Will swallowed up in the Will of God', acknowledging that only 'God seeth [what is] best for us'.[178] In one of Bulstrode Whitelocke's last sermons to his family, he reminded them that when Christians encountered hardship, so much depended on their response to it. In God's sovereignty, 'whatever happens is best – if I make it so'. The most destructive opponent could not take away the best things in life. 'They that have taken away my goods, and have banished me into the woods, cannot hinder the earth from putting forth the flowers, nor the

---

[173] Brooks, *Crown and Glory,* in *Works,* IV, 276, quoting Psa. 42: 10; Heb. 13: 5.
[174] Thomas Watson, *Light in Darkness, or Deliverance proclaimed unto the Church ... in all despondencies and discouragements* (1679), 17.
[175] Robert Seddon, in *England's Remembrancer,* 211.
[176] Owen, *Practical Exposition,* 329; also in *Works,* VI, 583; cf. Jacombe, in *London-Ministers Legacy,* 84: 'when one hand is upon the Saint to afflict, then the other hand is underneath ... to support'; Hercules Collins, *Counsel for the Living ... A Discourse ... Arising from the Deaths of Mr. Fran[cis] Bampfield and Mr. `Zach[ary] Ralphson* (1684), 28: 'God's Providential Dealings with his people in this world are like Chequer-work, there is the dark, as well as the light side of Providence. If we have some peace, we have some trouble'. Both these ministers died in Newgate when Collins was a fellow prisoner.
[177] Baxter, *Divine Life,* in *Works* (ed. Orme), XIII, 320.
[178] Collins, *Scribe Instructed,* 42–3.

trees from yielding their fruit, nor the birds from singing ... No, not me ... At least from being contented.'[179]

Bunyan acknowledged that during his first long imprisonment life had often been difficult, yet despite many 'turnings and goings' he had proved that in life's worst trials believers were often enriched with God's surprising gift of contentment. Later in life, it was this rich quality of contentment that Bunyan identified in the Shepherd's boy in Part II of *Pilgrim's Progress*. With a 'well-favoured Countenance', the lad 'sate by himself' as he sang,

> I am content with what I have,
> Little be it, or much:
> And, Lord, Contentment still I crave,
> because thou savest such.

The Guide testified that this boy in 'very mean Cloaths' lived 'a merrier Life' and with more 'Hearts-ease' than 'he that is clad in Silk and Velvet'.[180]

David Clarkson's London congregation were exposed to frequent harassment but he urged them not 'to murmur ... or to give way to any sallies of impatience', whatever the nature of their troubles. 'Will you not be content the Lord should cure you', trusting his wisdom in choosing the best and most effective method of improving them? 'While you are under afflictions, you are under cure'. Jesus referred to the cup his Father had given him (Jn 18: 11). '[F]lesh and blood' naturally 'shrinks at it. Yet it is a Father that mingled it', and though 'the ingredients be bitter, they are wholesome'. Clarkson pleaded further with his people to respond not only submissively but 'cheerfully' to these purposive afflictions. Though the experience 'be bitter, it is to make me well' and 'since he chastens us for our profit, we ought to be thankful'.[181]

Money lodged ahead

When the persecution was most fierce, God would renew their cheerful contentment by his promised gift of grace. 'He that filed off Peters Chains' would not leave them bereft of help.[182] Strengthened by inexhaustible resources, the persecuted Christian finds that he can 'play the Man in the dark'. 'Thou[gh] he slay me yet will I trust in him, is the Language of that Invincible Grace of God.' In this life, there is an alarming 'sufficiency of evil ... to destroy the best Saint ... were it not for the Grace of God'. But, says Bunyan,

---

[179] Ruth Spalding, *The Improbable Puritan: A Life of Bulstrode Whitlocke 1605–1675* (1975), 253. The quotation is from a lengthy unfoliated manuscript of Whitelocke's sermons: BL, Add. MS 53728.
[180] John Bunyan, *The Pilgrim's Progress* (ed. J.B. Wharey, rev. Roger Sharrock; Oxford, 1960), Part II, 238.
[181] Clarkson, *Works*, II, 239.
[182] William Cross, in *England's Remembrancer*, 164, alluding to Acts 12: 7.

those who receive this grace can cope creatively, 'to manage our selves in doing and suffering according to the will of God'.[183] In 'the cloudy and dark day' of persecution, diffident believers may be haunted by 'the fear of Man, the terrors of a prison, of loss of goods and life'. With such a grim prospect, 'all things look black', and then, without further warning, 'the firey tryal is come' upon them. But, at such a time, they will always 'find Grace to help in time of need'.[184]

Moreover, the dependent believer proves that this assured supply of grace is continually replenished. Bunyan was amazed that some Christians he knew lived like spiritual paupers, continuing to 'walk in their threadbare Jackets, with Hose and Shooes out at Heels' when their Father has promised them fresh resources for every changing situation. He uses a choice illustration from the experience of a youthful seventeenth-century traveller. Knowing that his son is about to embark on a long journey, and alert also to the likely danger of the highway robber, the wealthy father ensures in advance that totally adequate resources are available to him at appointed places en route.[185] Sufficient grace is never lacking but will only be provided when it is necessary. 'Great Men when, and while their Sons are Travailers, appoint that their Bags of Mon[e]y be lodged ready, or conveniently paid in at such and such a place ... so [that] they meet with supplies. Why so are the Sons of the great one'. The God who 'has allotted that we should travail ... at a great distance from our Fathers House ... has appointed that Grace shall be provided for us ... as need requires'. But travellers must ask for what they need; 'my Lord expecteth his Son should acquaint him with the present emptiness of his Purse' so that he may receive 'a supply of Grace'.[186] When their spirits are flagging, dependent believers prove that the 'Reviving Cordial' of grace will not only 'beget life' but 'maintain it'. Grace is God's guaranteed 'Preservative' for the Christian's 'spiritual Health'.[187]

Such grace is promised not simply to enable persecuted believers to absorb their sufferings passively, but also that, despite adversity, they might give themselves energetically to positive good deeds among their neighbours. Bunyan affirmed that 'great Grace is reserved for great service'. However difficult the times, believers shall have 'what shall qualifie and fit' them for whatever assignments God has for them 'in the World'. It may be a challenge they have never attempted before: 'new Work, new Tryals, new Sufferings, or something that will call for the Power and vertue of all the Grace thou shalt

---

[183] Bunyan, *The Saints Privilege and Profit* (1692), in *MW*, XIII, 203, 235, 242.
[184] Ibid. 237.
[185] For late seventeenth-century letters of credit and bills of exchange, see R.D. Richards, *The Early History of Banking in England* (1929), 236–38; cf. Bunyan, *Seasonable Counsel*, in *MW*, X, 24, for reference to provision for the safe deposit of money in view of highwaymen.
[186] Bunyan, *Saints Privilege*, in *MW*, XIII, 244.
[187] Ibid. 184.

have to keep thy Spirit even and thy feet from slipping ... in new Engagements'. New opportunities demand fresh grace, clearly promised, though not to the indolent. Those who glory in the assurance of spiritual resources but fail to use them in the service of others may be neither equipped nor used; 'idleness may turn him that wears a Plush Jacket into Rags. David was once a Man of great Grace, but his sin made the Grace ... shrink up, and dwindle away'.[188]

'great lumpish Shoes'

Furthermore, suffering is often used to loosen the believer's dependence on merely temporal things. God devises ways to 'make this World uneasy to us, or else we may be loth to leave it to go to a better'.[189] Unwelcome events provide Christians with 'a sight of the emptiness of this World, and the fadingness of the best it yields'.[190] 'In trouble', the world's 'emptiness is more easily discerned', said Nathanael Vincent, so 'build not your nest here' for 'the whole Forrest is sold to Death'.[191] Writing from prison, Abraham Cheare warned his people that even if, unlike their pastor, they keep their freedom, they might well lose their possessions. The greedy informer is already poised, ready to plunder their well furnished homes and claim his loot. He already knows where he can get an excellent price for the best chattels, and will be sure to claim his entitled third. So why not surrender such things to God in advance of possible trouble? It is best if 'pleasant pictures, costly coverings and all our delectable things may be so crucified to us and we to them in the love of them, that it may be no hard thing when the Lord calls for them to glorifie him'.[192]

In the persecution many believers had been 'brought off from trusting in the Creature, that is, by Losses, Crosses, Disappointments from Men'.[193] In 1663, when Quakers were experiencing a 'thick Night of Darkness', George Fox urged them not to fret too much about parting with their possessions. In early life he had cared for sheep, and his letters to persecuted colleagues occasionally take up the shepherding theme. 'And fear not the loss of the Fleece, for it will grow again'.[194] Resolute and sustained opposition is 'a Time of Shearing and Clipping'. Persecuted Quakers must be 'dumb before their Shearers' but they are to take heart, for 'he that gave his Back and his Cheek to the Smiters, overcame and reigns'. Such a Lord 'hath a tender Care of his Sheep ... therefore let your Minds be out of all outward things and visibles; and fear not

---

[188] John Bunyan, *The Desire of the Righteous Granted* (1692), in *MW*, XIII, 157–58.
[189] Collins, *Scribe Instructed*, 53.
[190] Bunyan, *Seasonable Counsel*, in *MW*, X, 35.
[191] Vincent, *Covert*, 22.
[192] Cheare, *Words*, 242.
[193] Collins, *Scribe Instructed*, 53.
[194] Fox, *Epistles*, 199 (Letter 227, 1663).

the Fleece, for it will grow again'.[195] Often present when Friends' possessions were distrained, Fox warned others:

> The Lord may try you by Persecution, or spoiling your outward Goods, which he has given you ... And let none sell their Birth-right for a Mess of Pottage ... And let none have their Eyes wander after their carrying away the Fleece, nor look back at Sodom's judgments ... and he can make the Fleece grow again.

With his keen love of the Bible,[196] Fox adds to these two allusions (to Esau and Lot's wife) yet another. With a reproachful glance at well rewarded informers, he recalls that 'Daniel's Windows were open towards outward Jerusalem, in the time of the informers, when he pray'd to his God, as he did before'. Ought not all their 'Windows and Doors be open toward [the] heavenly Jerusalem ... therefore keep your Meetings in the time of Sufferings, as you did before', no more fretful about the consequences than Daniel was.[197]

Believers robbed of valued goods were invited to reflect. 'Possibly, thou didst rely on Creatures. Thy leaning on those staves hath broken them in pieces, which otherwise would have been helpful to thee in thy journey'. God sometimes made 'the creature our Grief that it might not be our God'.[198] They could lose their best possessions, but might be better Christians without them. Nautical imagery seemed appropriate. 'Thy God knoweth how much the vessel of thy soul will carry, and therefore putteth no more goods aboord, lest thou shouldst sink ... as many poor Barks have done out of covetousness'. Some have carelessly taken in 'a greater fraught [freight] then they could safely sale [sail] to Heaven with'.[199] Bunyan's athletic imagery drove the point home. The eager runner was unlikely to make progress 'if he fill his Pockets with Stones ... heavy Garments on his Shoulders, and great lumpish Shoes on his Feet ... If thou intendest to win, thou must Strip' and lay aside such hindrances. 'Thou must, So Run.'[200]

In hazardous times, Nonconformists might sit loose to possessions but be over-dependent on their leaders. In 1664, bereaved Friends lamented the death

---

[195] Ibid. 151, 312 (Letters 194, 1666; 279, 1670); cf. 352 (Letter 314, 1675): 'God can make your Fleece grow again, after the Wolves have torn the Wooll from your Backs'), and 394 (Letter 332, 1676): 'And so never fear the loss of the Fleece, for God can make it grow again, as he did poor Job's'.

[196] The Quakers' earliest historian said that what Fox 'read in the Bible never slip'd out of his remembrance' and 'though the Bible were lost it might be found in the Mouth of George Fox': G. Croese, *General History of the Quakers* (1696), 14; cf. G.F. Nuttall, 'Nothing else would do: Early Friends and the Bible', *Friends Quarterly* 22 (1982), 651–9, repr. in idem, *Early Quaker Studies and the Divine Presence* (Weston Rhyn, 2003), 13–24.

[197] Fox, *Epistles*, 339–40 (Letter 307, 1674).

[198] Swinnock, *Calling*, II, 397.

[199] Ibid. 428.

[200] Bunyan, *The Heavenly Foot-Man* (1671?), in *MW*, V, 154–55.

of John Samm and two other Quakers in Northampton gaol, 'being 12 steps underground'.[201] They were reminded that although there was 'great need, of Valiants in this day', believers must not cling to their intrepid colleagues. God will 'have no Idols', but there was no need for despondency, for 'Neither will he have his work neglected'. He would 'have his Childrens Hearts made loose to all things under the Sun', even exemplary mentors. By 'the Lords taking away of his Servants of late' they might 'come the nearer unto that Teacher ... which cannot be removed into a corner'. Christ alone has a 'Ministry which cannot be taken away'.[202]

Never more endeared

Dissenters had good reason to believe that suffering enriched their corporate solidarity. They were encouraged to 'say, come let us hold together; there's no way in the world to hold on together like suffering'.[203] In trouble they realized how much they meant to each other. Speaking to a group of Ilchester prison friends about to be released, Joseph Alleine urged them not to forget the support they had received in gaol from their fellow prisoners: 'Let the Bonds of your Affliction, strengthen the Bonds of your Affection'. God had sent some ministers to prison that they may 'be more Indeared one to another ... then they were before'.[204]

Fox returned to his shepherding theme when encouraging Friends to support one another in persecution. Sheep will 'set their backs and tails against the storme and tempests and bleat for one another'. If anyone should try to 'part the sheep asunder ... they will run al[l] on heaps again and wil[l] keep together ... And so Christs sheep beareth fruite in the winter storms ... sitting atop of the highest hil[l] and mountain, with their backs against the weather.'[205]

Persecuted Dissenters were scarcely ever without the support of fellow church members. Imprisonment provided opportunities for practical help, beginning with the moment of arrest. When the ejected minister Robert Collins was taken to prison in Exeter, 'more than an Hundred of his Hearers accompany'd him on Horseback' to the local gaol.[206] Like Fox's vulnerable sheep, they knew how supportive it was to keep closely together. God's people were 'never more endeared, than when most persecuted; never more united

---

[201] John Samm, *A Salutation to the Little Flock ... And an exhortation* (1663), 9.
[202] John Crook, *A True and Faithful Testimony concerning John Samm*, in *The Design of Christianity testified in the Books, Epistles and Manuscripts of ... John Crook* (1701), 217–18.
[203] Robert Collins, in *Compleat Collection*, [unpaginated].
[204] [Alleine], *Life*, 71–72.
[205] Anon., 'Manuscript volume in the handwriting of Thomas Thompson (1631–1704) of Skipsea, Yorks', *JFHS* 28 (1931), 50.
[206] *Account*, 252.

than when most scattered'.[207]

What Neighbours see

Suffering also provided these Christians with unique opportunities for witness. Their message 'would get more advantage by the holy, humble sufferings of one gracious Saint meerly for the word of righteousness, then by ten thousand Arguments'.[208] It was said that like 'the Israelites in Egypt', the more Quakers were afflicted, 'the more they multiplied and grew'. 'Religion ... has not a more popular Argument in her Favour, than the Patience and Constancy of her afflicted Confessors.'[209] Brooks reminded his London congregation of the 'ten cruel persecutions' suffered by the early Christians, and Tertullian's witness that 'the oftener they were mown down, the more they grew'. Camomile 'grows and spreads by being trod upon'. Paul's captors might lay 'irons upon his legs' but were powerless to 'lay a law of silence upon his lips'. In a Roman dungeon, the apostle was eloquent, and young 'Onesimus was converted when Paul was a prisoner'.[210]

Joseph Alleine claimed that adversity was a natural occasion for silent preaching. Sufferers could let the world know that 'they could Live comfortably on ... God alone', totally relying on his character and his word, 'his Attributes, and Promises, though they should have nothing else left'.[211] To an imprisoned minister, Alleine wrote: 'I wish your enlargement [freedom] from your bonds' but even more 'your enlargement in them; That your Prison may be but the Lanthorn through which your Graces, Experiences, Communion, and Prison attainments, may shine most brightly to all beholders'.[212] Elsewhere Alleine argued that imprisonment presented a Christian with a unique arena for consistent and persuasive testimony. Nonconformist prisoners were 'Critically observed'. 'The Eyes of God, and Angels are upon you, and the eyes of men are upon you'. They 'should be more Holy than others' because, though robbed of their 'Libertys', they were 'called

---

[207] Flavel, *Preparation*, in *Works*, VI, 11.
[208] Collins, in *Compleat Collection*, [unpaginated]; cf. Matthew Mead, *The Almost Christian Discovered, or the False Professors Tried and Cast* (1662), 44–45: the 'Halcyon-days of the Gospel' may 'provoke Hypocrisie, but the sufferings of Religion prove sincerity'. Many of the ejected ministers emphasized this theme: cf. Richard Baxter, Thomas Lye, Matthew Mead, William Beerman, Daniel Bull and Philip Lamb, in *A Collection of Farewell Sermons of Divers London and Country Ministers in Three Volumns* (1663).
[209] Besse, *Sufferings*, I, iv.
[210] Brooks, *Crown and Glory*, in *Works*, IV, 283–85; cf. Clarke, *General Martyrologie*, A2: 'Like the Camomile, which the more you tread it, the more you spread it. Yea God knoweth that we are best, when we are worst.' Cf. Heywood, *Heart-Treasure*, 32: 'like Spices, the more they are bruised, the better is the savour of their Graces'.
[211] [Alleine], *Life*, 62.
[212] Alleine, *Letters*, 162 (10 January 1664).

forth ... to be the Witness of Christ Jesus'.[213] The witness would be especially impressive if the believer responded positively to life's greatest challenges; a joyful life was a powerful evangelistic persuasive.[214] If we

> ... shew the world no Religion but Sighing, and Complaining, and live a sadder life than they, and yet talk of glad tidings of Christ ... we may talk so long enough, before they believe us, that seem no more to be believers our selves, or before they will leave their fleshly pleasures, for so sad and dreadful a Life as this ...

By contrast, this 'Heavenly, Joyful Life' was 'a ... wonderful help to the Converting of the world'.[215]

At a time when opposition to Dissenters was particularly fierce almost everywhere, Bunyan contrasted believing and non-believing responses to intimidation in four ways. First, the believer will search for some 'good' in his adversity, whereas 'other men can see none' at all. Second, believers will be determined to 'pass by those injuries' that are inflicted upon them, physical, financial or social, when unbelievers might seek revenge. Third, by their resilient response, Christians will show they have 'grace', and are divinely enabled 'to bear what other men are not acquainted with'. Finally, persecuted Christians will readily confess that many of their 'graces are kept alive by those very things that are death to other mens Souls'. Bunyan asks where else 'can the excellency of our Patience ... meekness ... long-suffering ... love, and of our Faith appear, if not under Tryals'?[216] The 'world hath eyes to see what you can do' in trouble, 'as well as ears to hear what you can say. Christians ready 'to follow the Lord through the roughest ways of sufferings', will 'preach the excellency of Christ'.[217]

So much Mercy

Far from complaining, imprisoned Dissenters frequently testified that the restriction of liberty encouraged greater thanksgiving.

> We think we could praise God best, if we wanted nothing; but experience tells us the contrary ... Have not thy own highest Joyes and Praises to God ... been occasioned by thy dangers, or sorrows? ... What glorious Songs of Praise had

---

[213] [Alleine], *Life*, 73.
[214] Flavel held that to see a believer coping creatively with suffering 'would be of more use to ... convince the world, than all the sermons that ever they heard', whereas when they observe that 'prisons and sufferings *affright* and terrify us as much' as unbelievers, Christian witness is marred: *Works*, VI, 20.
[215] [Alleine], *Life*, 12.
[216] Bunyan, *MW*, X, 36.
[217] Flavel, *Preparation*, in *Works*, VI, 20–21.

God from Moses at the Red Sea, and in the Wilderness ... which he should never have had if they had been chusers of their own condition ...[218]

Deprived of privileges they had previously taken for granted, ministers became increasingly grateful for the many other things that had enriched their narrowly confined lives. Reflecting on his prison experience, Alleine could say: 'I see so much Mercy in this very Gaol, that I must be more thankful for this than for my Prosperity. Surely the name of the place is, The Lord is here'.[219]

When the Five Mile Act demanded that Alleine leave his Taunton friends, he reminded them that 'Your Condition is never such but your mercies are infinitely greater ... Elijah was never so happily fed at a full Table as when it was a time of great Famine.' Rather than grieve over an enforced separation, minister and people alike should be overwhelmed with gratitude. Present deprivation cannot rob them of 'mercies past'. Opportunities would hopefully arise for them to meet again, but he told them: 'if I had never hopes to enjoy one day with you more', he was determined that 'the last day should be a day of praise'.[220] From a Bristol gaol, Hardcastle itemized his cause for thanksgiving. He was grateful

> that we are yet alive; that we are not given up to the wills of our enemies, though we have been in their hands; that the Lord has blessed us ... to bear a testimony to his ways and worship; that we have not fallen down ... that the gospel has not lost, but gotten ground by our sufferings ...[221]

The 'perfect work'

Many people who suffered harassment during persecution affirmed that it had served to increase their patience. Bunyan reminded his friends that 'some of the graces of God ... cannot shew themselves ... nor what they can do: but as thou art in a suffering state ... Patience, in persecution, has that to ... shew ... and perform' which 'cannot be ... performed anywhere else', but in the arena of personal or corporate suffering.[222] Powell exhorted his readers to 'be Patient' for, 'of all other Lessons, this is to be exercised in time of Tribulation'. During the long winter, while 'the Husbandman sigheth' because of 'the hard season, the Corn rooteth; and whilst he waiteth, the harvest cometh'.[223]

With a preacher's eye to practical application, George Hughes developed the 'patience' theme as he expounded the Joseph narrative. The cupbearer's forgetfulness of Joseph's help in prison teaches that '[u]nkindness from

---

[218] Baxter, *Rest*, 273.
[219] Alleine, *Letters*, 34–35 (28 September 1663).
[220] Joseph Alleine, *Remaines of that excellent Minister ...* (1674), 99–101.
[221] *Records* (ed. Underhill), 353.
[222] Bunyan, *Seasonable Counsel*, in *MW*, X, 6.
[223] Powell, *Bird*, 43–44.

creatures are but to make his Saints learne more patience toward God.'[224]

Fox taught Quakers the necessity of patience in enduring hardships in the cause of 'Truth'. When attacked or persecuted, they must never strike back, but absorb the hurt, not reacting belligerently, or becoming resentful. 'And Friends, go not into the Aggravating Part to strive with it, lest ye do hurt to your Souls, and run into the same Nature; for Patience must get the Victory ... So let your ... Patience be known to all.' Retaliation multiplied the trouble, 'for that which joins to the Aggravating Part sets up the Aggravating Part, and breeds Confusion'.[225] 'Impatience under affliction, according to Samuel Clarke, made it much more grievous' to endure, like 'a Man in a Feaver, that by tossing and tumbling, exasperates the disease, and encreaseth his own grief'.[226]

A striking example of Nonconformist patience, and of supreme good coming from unwelcome experience, is that of Thomas Goodwin's reaction to the loss of over half his library in London's Great Fire. One of the city's leading Independent ministers, Goodwin was, until the ejectment, President of Magdalen College, Oxford. A distinguished Reformed theologian, biblical expositor and prolific writer, he had acquired an extensive library over the years. As the fire spread rapidly through the city streets and people carried valuable commodities to safety, over half of Goodwin's library was transferred to a 'safer' location. No sooner had his books been moved than the wind suddenly changed direction, quickly engulfing the alternative premises, destroying everything. Booksellers who had rapidly moved their stocks to the safe cellars of St Paul's were to see them totally destroyed when, 'the church itself being on fire, the exceeding weight of the Stones did break into the Vault and let in the Fire'. Baxter saw 'half burnt Leaves of Books' carried by the wind to where he lived at Acton, while 'others found them near Windsor, almost twenty miles distant'.[227] Books were expensive items in the seventeenth century,[228] and Goodwin's lost volumes were particularly valuable, worth over

---

[224] Hughes, *Genesis*, 499.

[225] Fox, *Epistles*, 87 (Letter 109, [c.1656]).

[226] Clarke, *General Martyrologie*, A2v.

[227] Sylvester (ed.), *Reliquiae*, III, §31. Most 'of the Libraries of ministers, Conformable and Nonconformable', in the city were destroyed, along with those of 'many Nonconformists of the Countrey, which had been lately brought up to the City'.

[228] The value of Morrice's library was in the region of £500: *EB*, I, 71. Baxter told a 1673 correspondent that many Nonconformist ministers known to him were 'so poore' that they were not in a position 'to buy many bookes': Baxter, *Calendar* (ed. Nuttall and Keeble), II, 148 (Letter 911). The previous year, an unsympathetic Court correspondent described the limited financial support of a Presbyterian 'Minister (with ten children) [who] hath preacht a week day Lecture to a large congregation within two miles of London, and for a year's pains hath not received above 9 pounds': BL, Stowe MS 186, fols 16r–23v, 'The Present State of Nonconformists'; cf. G. Lyon Turner, 'The Religious Condition of London in 1672 as reported to King and Court', *TCHS* 3 (1907–1908), 192–205, at 198. For the income of Presbyterian and Congregational ministers in this period, see details of both adequate and meagre salaries, by counties, in Gordon,

£500, a considerable sum of money.[229] He treasured his library and, thinking he had possibly loved it too much, began to wonder whether the incident was 'a rebuke of Providence'. Goodwin responded to the loss by exploring the multi-dimensional virtue of patience in an extended exposition of James 1: 4: 'Let patience have her perfect work, that ye may be perfect and entire, wanting nothing.' His highly relevant treatment of the theme took shape as a series of sermons to his congregation, many of whom had also suffered as a result of the Great Fire or in the devastating plague of the previous year. With the alarming news of damage inflicted by Dutch warships on the best of the English fleet in the Medway, many must have wondered whatever would happen next. When published, his book brought immediate support to Nonconformist people in harrowing circumstances, as well as helping a wider reading public.[230]

Goodwin's exposition is a brilliant combination of relevant preaching, exegetical skill and pastoral concern. He defines patience as 'a constant persisting', either 'to do the will of God without fainting' or 'to suffer the will of God with submission, and quietness, and cheerfulness' to the end of our days.[231] Persuaded that there is no superior quality, Goodwin maintains that patience is 'the eminent perfection' of a believer, illustrating his theme from three 'persecution' contexts in the New Testament. From the rich Christology of Hebrews, he recalls that it was uniquely demonstrated in the life of Christ, so that even Jesus, in the unique perfection of his human nature, 'must go to school ... to learn' patience (2: 10; 5: 8–9), becoming a salutary example to Christians living in dark times. In the letter of James, Goodwin observes that the Old Testament prophets' undeterred patience is seen as even more commendable than their compelling preaching (5: 7–8, 10–11). He adds the example of Job, whose evident godliness had gained divine approval: James 'cries him up' not for his sanctity but 'for his suffering'. From Revelation, Goodwin notes that its exiled author identifies himself as a 'companion in tribulation, and in the kingdom and patience of Jesus Christ' (1: 9), putting patience 'into his coat of arms'. The rich 'grace of patience' is 'the highest perfection of a Christian'.[232]

Goodwin also identifies four 'contrary passions' that hinder the development

---

Freedom after Ejection; Geoffrey S. Holmes, *Augustan England: Professions, State and Society 1680–1730* (1982), 111–14.

[229] It is difficult to translate the sum into contemporary values but, in modern terms, his books may have been worth £50,000. Patrick Collinson suggests that to ascertain the approximate value of seventeenth-century figures, the amount might be multiplied by a hundred, cf. 'The Cohabitation of the Faithful with the Unfaithful', in O.P. Grell, J. Israel and N. Tyacke (eds), *From Persecution to Toleration: The Glorious Revolution and Religion in England* (Oxford, 1991), 51–76, at 64.

[230] Thomas Goodwin, *Patience and its Perfect Work under Sudden and Sore Tryals* (1667), in *Works* (12 vols; Edinburgh, 1861), II, 429–67.

[231] Goodwin, *Works*, II, 436.

[232] Ibid. 433–34.

of patience, all strikingly evident in persecution. First, 'inordinate grief' over 'what we have lost, or are like to suffer'; the believer becomes more preoccupied with losses than resources. The second is envy, 'when the loss falls heavy on me, saith the sad heart', whilst appearing to leave other believers in relative comfort. Third, 'inordinate fears', when, despairing, we 'are apt to project a thousand things for the future', such as 'that poverty or beggary will follow'. The final one is discontent, or 'murmuring against God'. Patience is 'perfected' in human life when the Christian seeks God's supernatural help in the subjugation of these damaging preoccupations.[233]

He expounds the ideal of willingly submissive patience by which the believer is gratefully surrendered to God's sovereignty and his love. First, true faith 'brings home' to the human soul 'the dominion of God' over everything we have and are, 'to do what he will with them'. Goodwin believes that 'patience' (*hupomonē*, James 1: 4) here describes endurance under 'afflictions mainly for the gospel', though James 'doth manifestly carry in his eye' other trials, evident from his biblical examples. Although Old Testament prophets suffered from hostile religious contemporaries, Job was not harassed by that particular adversity; in his case, natural disasters wrought havoc on his property, possessions and family. As the tragedy unfolded, Job was totally ignorant 'of that transaction between God and Satan' in which he was a test case. In his distressing experience, he accepted all as from 'the hand of God, though extraordinary'. Acknowledging God's sovereignty, Job recognized that his ways are 'past finding out' and in distress could say: 'He taketh away … and who will say unto him, What doest thou?' (9: 10–12). Reflecting on his personal, and his people's, losses, Goodwin says: 'He took away your goods, and who could hinder him?' Faith 'brings home to the heart a message of a higher sovereignty'. By his undeserved gift of eternal salvation, God has demonstrated that he desires only the best for believers, so will they not also 'give him leave to exercise his dominion' over everything else in their lives, including their 'earthly lumber and … appurtenances'?[234]

The tested believer also knows that, however intense their trials, the Sovereign God is also the Eternal Lover who will not allow anything to damage, let alone destroy, anything of ultimate value in the life of the harassed Christian. 'Faith brings home the love of God', which serves to 'strengthen patience in the greatest distresses'. From the majestic closing verses of Romans 8, Goodwin echoes Paul's radiant certainty in God's incomparable sovereignty ('If God be for us') and Christ's unchanging love ('Who shall separate us?'). It is not only 'that he, loving us, joins his strength to ours to support us', but that the love of God and Christ will always be 'coming in fresh upon our hearts', 'making us 'cleave to God, and so follow him through all weathers and

---

[233] Ibid. 446–49.
[234] Ibid. 440, 437–38, 440–41.

endurances'.[235]

Goodwin insists that the God who asks sufferers to be patient never demands what he cannot supply. When James says, 'If any of you lack wisdom, let him ask of God' (1: 5), Goodwin believes him to be identifying a specific area of immediate need: the wisdom to respond with due patience to life's tempestuous adversities, 'how ... to manage a man's self under trials ... patiently'. Goodwin says that 'Calvin and most others' also identify wisdom here as 'this special grace' of patience in suffering.[236] 'If any man lack' acknowledges human inadequacy in the face of life's trials. Believers are encouraged to 'ask of God' because of a triple promise. As their unique Giver, God is constantly generous ('liberally'), unfailingly compassionate ('upbraideth not', unwearied by frequent asking) and totally reliable ('it *shall* be given him').[237]

Truth did not change

Bunyan confessed that never in all his life had he 'so great an inlet into the Word of God' as in his prison cell. Scriptures he 'saw nothing in before, are made in this place and state to shine upon me'.[238] Drawing perceptively on Ezekiel's exilic ministry, Greenhill said that 'before men are afflicted, and humbled for their sin, they refuse and sleight the Word of God', but 'let his Prophets come and Preach powerfully and terribly unto them ... they mind it not' for 'a heart under affliction ... will give due honour to the Word of God ... Affliction opens mens eyes ... and men come to see their Ingratitude towards God.'[239] When Alleine was released from Ilchester gaol, he wrote to tell an imprisoned colleague that the promises of God had been 'never so sweet in this world' to him 'as in and since' his own imprisonment. Now 'you have a whole showl [shoal] of Promises come in to you which you had not before; I mean, all the promises' to sufferers, to which other believers have 'not so immediate, but only a remoter right, unless in a suffering state'.[240] Hercules Collins quoted a

---

[235] Ibid. 441–43.
[236] Expounding James 1: 5, Calvin said: 'This passage ... uses *wisdom* in the sense of yielding oneself to God in the face of all disaster': *Calvin's Commentaries: A Harmony of the Gospels Matthew, Mark and Luke, Volume III, and the Epistles of James and Jude* (transl. A.W. Morrison; Edinburgh, 1972), 263. Manton also maintained that 'wisdom' here should be considered 'with respect to the Context', that 'there is need of great Wisdom for the right managing of afflictions' in time of trouble': *James*, 33–35.
[237] Goodwin, *Works*, II, 461, 463–67.
[238] Bunyan, *GA*, §321.
[239] Greenhill, *Exposition continued*, 25, cf. 137–38: 'great ones in times of affliction wil[l] seek unto the Prophets ... Afflictions abate the pride of great mens spirits, remove prejudice, awaken conscience, convince of sin'. They remind afflicted people of 'Gods greatnesse and Authority over the highest, the shortness of life' and 'of judgement'. In harrowing circumstances, even 'great ones' will 'be glad to goe to a poor Prophets house, and heare a word from him'.
[240] Alleine, *Letters*, 158, (10 January 1664).

popular Nonconformist aphorism when he claimed that Scripture has 'a Salve for every Sore'[241] but, when all is well in life, believers may not fully appreciate the Bible's incomparable worth. Prior to trouble, the 'Word of God ... is almost ... as a full Table to a full Belly who loathes the Hon[e]y-comb'. Christians 'may preach and hear many a good Sermon and ... many a gracious Promise [may] be mentioned' but when adversity strikes, 'what the Soul hath often read, now he can feel, and experience that it was good' to 'have been afflicted'. In adversity, Christians are 'taught to know the Word more practically, and feel it more powerfully'.[242]

During long hours of imprisonment, many came to appreciate the relevance and reliability of the Bible. Their preachers had often expounded the promises of God, and what was true in brighter days was certainly applicable in darker circumstances. Baxter put it memorably: 'Truth did not change, because I was in a Goal [jail]'.[243] The 'Creature Springs' of this world's resources are 'often empty and dry, but the promises' of God are like deep wells, 'alwaies full'.[244]

No rusty Armour

Suffering also served to develop the believer's spiritual maturity; 'we are afflicted, that we may grow'.[245] 'Grace never rises to so great a height as it does in times of persecution. Suffering times are a Christian's harvest times'. It could bring the best out of a believer. 'Many a man had not been so gracious, if the times had not been so dangerous.'[246] When he had been in Bedford gaol for five years, Bunyan wrote a book in which, at one point, he bared his own soul. Dissenters admired the heroism of their incarcerated leaders but there was nothing romantic about prolonged imprisonment: 'While we are here, we are attended with so many weaknesses and infirmities, that in time the least sin or sickness is too hard for us'. But despite the physical discomfort, material deprivation, emotional isolation and spiritual conflicts, the prisoner still believed that such adversities made the sufferer's heart 'more deep, more experimentall, more knowing, and profound; and so more able to hold, contain, and bear more'.[247]

David Clarkson maintained that no Christian is 'complete unless he have on his whole armour' and suffering demands that we wear it. It 'would lie rusting by us, if we were not roused to the use of it'. Without adversity, the 'soul would

---

[241] Collins, *Scribe Instructed*, 16.
[242] Ibid. 23, 31–32, 37.
[243] Sylvester (ed.), *Reliquiae*, III, §125; cf. Fox, *Epistles*, 199 (Letter 227): 'And never heed the Tempests nor the Storms ... be ... Valiant for the Truth. For the Truth can live in the Goals [Gaols]'.
[244] Robert Asty, *A Treatise of Rejoycing in the Lord Jesus* (1683), 63.
[245] Bunyan, *MW*, X, 72–73.
[246] Brooks, *Works*, IV, 286–87.
[247] Bunyan, *The Resurrection of the Dead* (1665?), in *MW*, III, 222, 239.

grow drowsy, and grace would lose it[s] strength for want of use ... We have no more grace, in effect, than what we use'.[248] Thomas Manton was equally convinced that Christians are allowed to encounter adversity so 'that Grace may not lye sleeping in a dead and unactive Habit, but be drawn out into act and view, for his Glory and Praise'.[249]

'like children's tops'

Suffering can strengthen the Christian's hold on familiar truths. The 'excellency of faith is beclouded, till it be put upon a thorough tryal'.[250] From their earliest days, catechetical instruction at home and then expository preaching had made Dissenters deeply aware of Christian themes, but in persecution conventional teaching was put to the test. It is 'one thing to discourse of a Battel, and another to be engaged in the heat of it'.[251] In severe trouble they progressed from knowing such things intellectually to proving them experientially. 'The most excellent Christian Vertues would be comparatively of little use without hard Trials.'[252] Whatever the hazards, nothing could deprive them of the great realities of their faith. 'O Christian, let persecutors do their worst, they can't reach thy soul, thy God, thy comfort, thy crown'.[253]

Persecution encourages steadfastness and serves to reinforce and buttress the believer's faith. Baxter knew of an 'abundance of Ministers' who had come 'out of long imprisonment' unscathed and undaunted. True, others had deserted the ranks 'in a time of suffering', but history also testified that intense opposition frequently 'inflameth the opposed party into a greater zeal', and 'silencing or imprisonments' did nothing to 'change their judgments' about the things that matter most.[254]

In the course of his Yorkshire itinerancy, Oliver Heywood encouraged scattered Nonconformists to use relative peace to acquire inner resources for future trials. When trouble comes, the 'time of affliction is a spending time' for 'if there be any Grace within, tribulation wil[l] draw it out'.[255] Many oppressors came to recognize that, instead of weakening Dissenters, persecution markedly increased their resilience. One frustrated Member of Parliament observed that they were 'like children's tops; whip them, and they stand up, let them alone

---

[248] Clarkson, *Works*, I, 458.
[249] Thomas Manton, *A Practical Exposition of the Lord's Prayer* (1684), 413–14.
[250] Manton, *James*, 21.
[251] Bates, *Great Duty*, 12.
[252] Ibid. 62–63.
[253] Brooks, *Works*, IV, 266.
[254] Richard Baxter, *An Apology for the nonconformists Ministry* (1681), 195–96.
[255] Heywood, *Heart-Treasure*, 30.

and they fall'.[256] Far from being crushed, their trials rejuvenated them.

Swift in their run

Dissenters discovered that experience of suffering serves to build character. Using Hosea's imagery, Clarkson said that nothing 'will better hinder corruption from taking its course than a hedge of thorns'. Being surrounded with 'peace and plenty in the world' subtly 'cherishes our lusts' and gradually make us less than the people we might otherwise be. But egocentric preoccupations are checked and restrained by adversity; selfishness 'languishes when it is fastened with us to the cross'.[257] Adversity can produce qualities that might lie undiscovered if life were to remain constantly tranquil and untroubled. Recalling the stories of Noah and Lot, Bunyan asked who was 'so holy as they, in the day of their affliction', and, sadly, who was 'so idle as they in the day of their prosperity?' Life's severe trials are 'against the grain of the flesh, but they are not against the graces of the spirit'.[258]

In the closing year of his life, Bartholomew Ashwood prepared for publication his *Heavenly Trade*, which contains many of the insights shared with his Axminster congregation over twenty years. They had experienced considerable hardship, meeting in woods and fields[259] and suffering the imprisonment of their minister. Recalling familiar New Testament teaching (1 Cor. 9: 24–6; Gal.2: 2, 5: 7; Phil. 2: 16; Heb. 12: 1), Ashwood uses athletic imagery to stress that, far from distracting Christians from their commitment, persecution may be an essential part of their training. 'Afflicting Providences are God's dieting his racers, that they may be more long breath'd, and swift in their run towards glory.' The loss of 'worldly treasures' might become 'but the taking off of a heavy cloak-bag from the Shoulders of Sion's Travellers'.[260]

'even venture all'

Ashwood's 'swift ... run' to glory is a reminder of the Dissenters' persuasion

---

[256] A. Grey, *Debates of the House of Commons, 1667–1694* (10 vols, 1763), I, 220 (2 March 1669).
[257] Clarkson, *Works*, I, 459, quoting Hosea 2: 6; cf. Joseph Moore, in *England's Remembrancer*, 412–13: suffering may help a Christian to 'sit loose to every creature'. A submissive believer may 'with ease ... part with that to which he is dead already'.
[258] Bunyan, *Seasonable Counsel*, in *MW*, X, 36.
[259] *Ecclesiastica* (ed. Howard), 21–22, cf. 38–39: 'Sometimes ... they have been constrained to retire into more solitary places, and to change the place of their assembling up and down in woods, in fields, in obscure desert places'. They were often 'constrained to take the solitary night watches' but 'members have been added', even 'in the worst of times'.
[260] Ashwood, *Heavenly Trade*, 330–31.

that adversities will 'endear heaven to us'.[261] Suffering is 'the Saints high-way to Heaven' and, given the assured and imperishable glory of the reward, leaving 'a little worldly dust and dirt' or 'undergoing a few months or years imprisonment' is a mere nothing. Heaven is certainly 'worth the suffering for'.[262] In this world, the godly 'are here in an imperfect state' and God uses adverse experiences in this life 'to train them up' for a more certain future.[263] 'Heaven's Gates ... are wide open to receive' them, and present trouble is but a stepping-stone to promised glory.[264]

Adversity sharpens the vision and points believers to wider and better horizons. John Howe's pastoral experience was that sufferers 'live much upon the borders of eternity'. His ministry in London convinced him that 'those souls' that 'prosper and flourish' are they 'that have so unspeakably more to do with the other world, than with this'. Adversities 'direct our eye forward'.[265] Clarkson makes imaginative use of Old Testament narratives in describing this prospect of a brighter future:

> The ark was more acceptable to Noah's dove, when she found no rest to the soles of her feet on the face of the earth. The thoughts of the promised kingdom were sweeter to David when he was hunted as a partridge upon the mountains. Canaan was more acceptable to the children of Israel when their burdens, oppressions and sufferings increased in Egypt.

How 'sweet the thoughts of approaching glory to those who are here reviled, and abused', whereas 'when all things succeed with us in the world as we desire, heaven is neglected' and 'we are apt to forget that we are pilgrims and strangers' on earth.[266]

Adversities 'make Heaven the sweeter to us', said Bunyan, assuring his suffering contemporaries of infinitely better things ahead. Travelling to Heaven, as those who are 'hard pursued' by 'the persecutor', not only makes 'the safety there' all the more attractive,[267] but adjusts their perspective on the impermanent things of this life. They look on their homes 'as inns and lodgings in a journey' where they 'rest as it were but for a night, and to leave all as it were the next morning'. All the 'occurrences of this life' are but 'the passages of one day, compared with that eternity which is in their eye'.[268] In harrowing

---

[261] Clarkson, *Works*, I, 459.
[262] [Powell], *Sufferer's Catechism*, 25.
[263] Corbet, *Remains*, 257.
[264] Bunyan, *Heavenly Foot-Man*, in *MW*, V, 167.
[265] John Howe, *Satan's Malice in Inflicting, and Christ's Compassion, in Curing Diseases, Funeral Sermon for Mrs. Esther Sampson*, in *The Whole Works of John Howe* (ed. John Hunt, 8 vols; 1810–22), IV, 189–213, at 204.
[266] Clarkson, *Works*, I, 459–60, quoting Gen. 8: 8–9; 1 Sam. 26: 20; Exod. 1: 13–14, 2: 23.
[267] Bunyan, *MW*, X, 73.
[268] Clarkson, *Works*, II, 383.

circumstances, they needed the frequent reminder, 'Keep thine Eye upon the Prize'.[269] They were 'passengers to another world'.[270]

The period was not without ingenious millenarian theorists, weaving complex notions of God's future plans,[271] and some Dissenters were among them; but in the second half of the century it was this more applied, pragmatic eschatology that was given the most prominent place in Nonconformist teaching. Reflecting on heaven was not an exercise in speculative escapism but the incentive for immediate action.

> Sometimes when my base Heart hath been inclining to this World ... the very consideration of the glorious Saints and Angels in Heaven, what they enjoy, and what low thoughts they have of this World altogether, how they would befool me ... and say to my Soul, Come Soul let us not be weary, let us see what this Heaven is' and 'let us even venture all for it ...'[272]

---

[269] Bunyan, *Heavenly Foot-Man*, in *MW*, V, 167.

[270] Baxter, *Christian Directory* (1673), in *Works* (ed. Orme), IV, 95; cf. 200.

[271] Howe warned of the danger of bizarre and unprofitable eschatological speculation. In an Appendix to *Of Thoughtfulness for the Morrow* [1681] he exposed 'the immoderate desire of knowing things to come', believing it unfitting for a Christian to be 'very particular, or confident in our interpretations and expectations upon such occasions' which 'serve us, for no other purpose, than only to gratify our curiosity': *Works* (ed. Hunt), II, 301–69, at 345, 348.

[272] Bunyan, *Heavenly Foot-Man*, in *MW*, V, 168.

Part III

Resources in Adversity

Chapter 3

Dependent on God

Persecuted Dissenters could hardly have emerged from prolonged adversity without reflecting on a wide range of enriching biblical truths. Pastors encouraged their people to believe that, far from damaging them, persecution had the potential to make them both 'more fit for communion with God' and 'more fit for service' to others.[1] Some insights into God's nature and attributes might never be understood and valued except through trials. 'God often brings his People into great Depths ... before Deliverance comes, that ... his glorious Attributes may be more displayed and magnified.' The Church 'must have a Red Sea before them and a potent Army pursuing them. Daniel must be in the Lions Den, and the three Children in the fiery furnace'. These 'are the Times God takes to deliver and save ... so he may have the Glory alone'.[2]

Agnes Beaumont, a member of the Bedford congregation, was severely tested as a young Christian. Fiercely opposed to her Nonconformist allegiance, her angry father locked her out of the family home. Shunned and slandered by her neighbours, she testified to God's kindness. '[T]he more trouble and sorrow I have had ... the more of gods [*sic*] presence I have had'.[3] Her pastor preached that God's 'Wisdom and Power and goodness' can be seen in 'Thunder, and Lightning ... Storms, and darkness ... There is that of God to be seen in such a day as cannot be seen in another'. Then, the frail and vulnerable receive greater strength, for he makes 'Shrubs to stand' whilst 'Cedars ... fall'.[4] The imprisoned John Perrot told his Quaker fellow prisoners that 'now more than ever you know him to be God indeed'. He had proved that to be true during his incarceration in Rome. Never 'had I such sweet union, fellowship and conversation with my Maker and Husband, as I have had in these most extream times of my tryals'.[5] Theirs was an essentially Trinitarian faith, and little was of greater consequence than their perception of the greatness of God, the uniqueness of Christ and the ministry of the Holy Spirit. We turn, then, to look firstly at their deepened appreciation of the nature and attributes of God.

---

[1] Clarkson, *Works*, II, 466.
[2] Collins, *Scribe Instructed*, 28–29.
[3] *The Narrative of the Persecution of Agnes Beaumont in 1674* (ed. G.B. Harrison; n.d.), 3. Throughout the narrative she frequently describes her awareness of God's presence in difficult times; e.g. ibid. 4, 6, 73–75.
[4] Bunyan, *MW*, X, 8.
[5] John Perrot, *The Suffering Seed of Royalty* (1661), 6–7.

Confidence in God

Knowing God better was a paramount concern. When repression began in the early 1660s, Baxter confessed that in his younger days he had 'thought that a Sermon of the Attributes of God and the Joys of Heaven' was not 'the most excellent'. Then, he was tempted to say: 'Every body knoweth ... that God is great and good, and that Heaven is a blessed place'. What he wanted to hear was, 'how I may attain it'.

> And nothing pleased me so well as the Doctrine of Regeneration and the Marks of Sincerity ... but now I had rather read, hear or meditate on God and Heaven than on any other Subject: for I perceive that it is the Object that altereth and elevateth the Mind ... which it most frequently feedeth on ...

He spoke for many. 'Had I all the Riches of the World, how gladly should I give them, for a fuller Knowledge, Belief and Love of God and Everlasting Glory!'[6] In a private journal, Baxter's close friend John Corbet wrote that communion with God was his 'chief joy' and that he 'would not only have God hereafter, but here in this world for my chief good. He is even now better than all the World'. Twelve years later, he had not changed his mind. 'I desire this love not only as ... evidence of my Salvation, but for it self. I had much rather have a heart to love him perfectly, than to have all the Riches, Honours and Pleasures of this World.'[7]

Moreover, deeper knowledge of God was something to be deliberately sought. Christian doctrine was not a coldly detached academic interest; it had supremely practical implications for everyday life. Honest reflection on God's omniscience is 'an effectual means, to keep men from playing the Hypocrite with God'. Similarly, recalling his omnipotence will 'keep us from immoderate fearing or doubting, fainting or sinking, in times of straights and distresses', knowing that he is not only able but eager to help. Convinced of his immutability, believers would be delivered from 'despondency', and from the 'questioning of his love, when he seems to hide his Face'.[8]

Their theology was inseparably related to everyday life. William Perkins had testified to a previous generation that the happiest life 'ariseth from the

---

[6] Sylvester (ed.), *Reliquiae*, I, I,§213, 8, 6.

[7] John Corbet, *Self-Imployment in Secret* (1681), 6, 16. Published a year after Corbet's death, the book contains his dated personal notes concerning 'The State of my Own Soul', material not written with a view to publication: ibid. A2v.

[8] J[ohn]. B[artlet]., *The Practical Christian* (1670), 34–35. Similarly, Thomas Watson taught that meditation on God's omniscience will 'restraine us from sinne. Will the thief steal when the Judge looks on?' It also tests the believer's sincerity: 'If I juggle in my repentance, the God of heaven takes notice.' Watson goes on to emphasize the practical implications of meditation on God's holiness, wisdom, power, mercy and truth: Thomas Watson, *A Christian on the Mount, or a Treatise concerning Meditation* (2nd ed.; 1659), in *Three Treatises* (6th ed.; 1660), 340–41.

knowledge of God'. Theology was 'the science of living blessedly for ever'.[9] From their earliest days, catechisms had encouraged the hope that they might 'enjoy' God[10] not only in a promised heaven but also in this present life. In sharing their experience of God during three decades of intermittent harassment and diverse hardship, a number of key themes attain special prominence.

Acknowledging God's Sovereignty

Naturally baffled about God's purpose in allowing them to suffer repression and deprivation, they frequently returned to the belief that God is in supreme control of his universe and all its events. A broadsheet collection of 'Old Mr. Dod's Sayings' hung in many Nonconformist homes, assuring its readers that 'There can be no Afflictions and Miseries befall us, but by God's Appointment; and cannot hurt us, but must needs do us good, if we be God's children.'[11] When Richard Hollingworth wrote to Henry Vaughan, locked up in Lincoln Castle, he attributed his friend's imprisonment not to the malice of the minister's opponents but to the sovereignty of God. It was in 'his wise [prov]idence' that their 'Good God' had permitted 'his churches enemyes' to deprive them 'of so good a shepheard' as Vaughan, promising that, for the prisoner and all like him, God would certainly 'sweeten yt bitter cup'. He was able to 'mix so much sun[shine]' with those 'great showers of raine' that had fallen upon Vaughan in recent times.[12]

Familiar biblical narratives constantly renewed their confidence in God's sovereign, if occasionally baffling, activity in the life of his people. Writing from prison, Vavasor Powell assured his readers that an incomparably mighty God 'hath his will, and hand in all Actions ... in this World', even in episodes 'most strange and most sinful'. The selling of Joseph as a slave, the persistent hardening of an Egyptian ruler's heart, and the stubborn rejection of the pagan kings, Sihon and Heshbon, were examples of God's decisive, if bewildering, purposes. Maliciously pursued by Saul, David opened his mind to the possibility that the jealous king's hatred might even be part of a greater plan. It could be that 'the Lord' has 'stirred thee up against me'.[13]

Concerned lest some might dismiss these examples as only 'Old-testament proofs' and suggest that 'God dealt at that time in another way, than he doth now in Gospel daies', Powell produced New Testament evidence for God's

---

[9] William Perkins, *A Golden Chaine or the Description of Theologie*, in *Works* (3 vols; Cambridge, 1616–18), I, 11.
[10] The *Westminster Longer Catechism* states: 'Man's chief and highest end is to glorify God and fully to enjoy him for ever.'
[11] Broadsheet, *Old Mr. Dod's Sayings* (1671).
[12] DWL, Baxter Letters, 6.56 (Hollingworth to Vaughan, 1 December 1661). Vaughan, Vicar of Grantham, had been imprisoned on refusing to use the Book of Common Prayer in public worship.
[13] Powell, *Bird*, 3–4, quoting 1 Sam. 26: 19.

sovereignty. Jesus affirmed that Pilate's power had been given 'from above', and the early Christians were convinced that whatever the destructive intentions of Herod and their other opponents, hostile powers could only perform what God had 'determined before to be done'. Powell reminded his harassed readers that their destiny was not in the hands of oppressors, informers or magistrates. Christ alone held the keys to their future.[14] He pressed home the implications and relevance of his biblical examples. 'If your enemies hate you, look upon it as Gods turning their hearts to hate you (as the Egyptians did the Israelites)'. If cursed by their opponents, as Israel's king was by Shimei, they should acknowledge, as David did, the possibility that 'the Lord ... hath bidden him'.[15]

The death of Christ was the most persuasive example of supreme good transcending appalling evil. 'Treachery in Judas, Perjury in the false witnesses, Cruelty in the Judges & souldiers & people – yet all was made subservient to ye good of the Elect'. Philip Henry maintained that the story of the cross will always 'quiet our spirits' concerning all the 'designes of unreasonable and wicked men. God can turn them to another end than that they intend.'[16] Thomas Browning told his Northamptonshire congregation that he did not want to come out of prison 'a Moment before his time'.[17] In 1686, one bewildered West Country congregation acknowledged that the Lord who was 'stirring up' their fierce persecutors was the same God who had recently 'stirred up' their anticipated deliverer, James, Duke of Monmouth, and yet shattered their political dreams.[18] God 'ordereth men sometimes to wonder at events, which at present they do not understand'.[19] Stephen Charnock insisted that undeserved persecution and similar 'dismal afflictions' were part of an inexplicable divine plan. The artist 'first puts on the dusky colours on which he intends to draw the portraiture of some illustrious beauty'. God snuffs the candle to make it 'burn the clearer'. Shipwrecked passengers may come safely ashore on one of its planks; that which was 'the occasion of their loss' becomes 'a means of their safety'.[20]

Persecuted Dissenters treasured three basic convictions concerning God's sovereign purposes in their lives: he knows what is best, does what is right, and gives what is necessary.

God knows what is best. A London minister, with experience of

---

[14] Ibid. 5, quoting Acts 4: 28; Rev.1: 18.
[15] Ibid. 6–7, quoting Psa. 105: 25, 2 Sam. 16: 11.
[16] Cambridge, Cambridge University Library, MS 7338, Philip Henry, Sermon notes on Gen. 45: 8.
[17] Maurice, *Monuments of Mercy*, 52. Cf. Norman Glass, *The Early History of the Independent Church at Rothwell* (1871), 23; for Browning's undated prison letter to the Rothwell church, see Maurice, *Monuments*, 49–54; and for that to the Broughton church, ibid. 54–56.
[18] *Ecclesiastica* (ed. Howard), 77, 93.
[19] Hughes, *Genesis*, 534.
[20] Charnock, *Works*, I, 77.

imprisonment, was persuaded that if 'Satan could not enter a Herd of Swine without Christ's leave, surely he cannot without it disturb one Saint'.[21] Not 'a stroke more shall bee laid' on his children 'but what hee commands himselfe for his childrens good'.[22] From prison, Thomas Hardcastle testified that 'Faith shows a believer that all is for the best which the Lord wills and orders'.[23] God is determined to enrich his children not impoverish them. God 'was saving thee, as well when he crossed thy desires, as when he granted them', said Baxter, 'as well when he broke thy heart, as when he bound it up'.[24] Along with 'dark clouds he intermixes bright Stars'.[25] A preacher who lost two 'tender babes' and wider family members in the Plague testified that the 'same Power that caused your Sun to go down at mid-day, when you least suspected, can also cause it to rise at midnight, when you least hope'.[26]

God does what is right. He will never 'suffer an unrighteous ... act to be done by his own hand'.[27] The devil 'cannot put the least Dram into any temptation, but as it is measured out by the hand of God'.[28] God's plans for his children will never contradict his nature. Even in the immense anguish of the Plague, Samuel Shaw echoed the patriarch's conviction: 'Shall not the Judge of all the Earth do right?'[29]

God gives what is necessary. No hardship would come their way without the resources to make it bearable. From personal experience, a London minister could testify: 'God is as good in Prison as out.'[30] Life's hardships are 'weighed and measured by God himself' who, with the adversity, 'will give ... a proportionable strength'.[31] In his 'strong and powerful love', God will not deny his children 'any thing that is truly good for them ... nor allow them anything that is really hurtful'. In things that concern the 'real and eternal happiness' of their souls, God never gives believers 'what's sweet, but what's meet ... whether they would have it or no'.[32] Nathanael Vincent told his people that when 'we look upon God as Lord, we should never quarrel or murmur at any thing he is pleased to do to us or with us'. When their sovereign God always acts 'wisely, justly, [and] faithfully', how can 'Fretting and Impatience be justified'?[33]

---

[21] Hercules Collins, *Mountains of Brass*, in *Three Books* (1696), 23.
[22] George Hughes, *Dry Rod Blooming and Fruit-Bearing*, 11.
[23] *Records* (ed. Underhill), 276.
[24] Baxter, *Rest*, 32.
[25] Watson, *Light in Darkness*, 18–19.
[26] S[amuel]. S[haw]., *The Voice of one Crying in the Wilderness* (1674), A2r, 67.
[27] Swinnock, *Calling*, II, 448–49.
[28] Ambrose, *War with Devils*, 11.
[29] S[haw]., *Voice Crying*, 49, quoting Gen. 18: 25.
[30] Collins, *Counsel*, 25.
[31] Ambrose, *War with Devils*, 10–11.
[32] S[haw]., *Voice Crying*, 62, 61.
[33] Nathanael Vincent, *The Cure of Distractions in attending upon God in several sermons preached from 1 Cor. 7: 35* (1695), 133–34.

In bewildering times, one of Baxter's Welsh correspondents expressed the robust confidence that 'though the Arke of the Church should be tossed from one extreame to the other, yet when god himself is both Mast[,] stern & Anchor ... It shall at length cast upon Ararat.'[34]

Proving God's Faithfulness

Whatever happened, God would never let them down. This reassuring certainty was demonstrated in Scripture, verified by covenant, confirmed in history and declared in experience.

First, great personalities of Old and New Testament became a constant reminder of unfailing help in clouded days. Narratives describing the hazardous experiences of Job, Joseph and Jeremiah were a particular inspiration. In a persecution context the stories of Job's intense bewilderment, of young Joseph suffering unjustly at the hands of the 'family of faith', and of Jeremiah's pain at the strident opposition of religious and political contemporaries, brought the message of Scripture home with striking relevance.[35] Such characters were not simply to be admired but emulated in their resolute commitment to a faithful God.[36]

Moreover, one particular dimension of biblical teaching provided them with specific assurance of God's faithfulness. Covenant (or Federal) theology was given special prominence in Nonconformity, though Dissenters did not all think alike on it. Most agreed that God's relationship with humanity was initially based on a 'Covenant of Works'. Eternal life was a conditional gift to Adam, dependent on his obedience to God's commands. Knowing that Adam would disobey, God planned a greater 'Covenant of Grace'.[37] Many Dissenters, such as Owen and Bunyan, maintained that this covenant took the form of a unique 'agreement' between the Father and the Son concerning the salvation of all those destined to believe in the work of Christ. Others defined the covenant of grace in terms of a pledge of eternal security for the elect, conditional on their personal appropriation of Christ's work on the cross. Such thinking about the covenant provided a reassuring paradigm of divine faithfulness. God had promised on oath that truly committed believers belonged to him for eternity, whatever the hazards and adversities on the way. One woman who had been a member of Holcroft's congregation during intense persecution said at the close

---

[34] Baxter, *Calendar* (ed. Nuttall and Keeble), II, 13 (Letter 667), quoting Gen. 8: 4.

[35] For example, in the preaching and writing of Hercules Collins: Job (*Scribe Instructed*, 26, 34, 44, 48, 52; *Mountains of Brass*, 23–24); Joseph (*Scribe Instructed*, 36); and Jeremiah (ibid. 62).

[36] Thomas Gouge, *Christian Directions* (1675), 25; exemplary biblical personalities were 'patterns of imitation: For ... to this end are they recorded unto us'.

[37] *A Declaration of the Faith and Order ... [of] the Congregational Churches in England ... at the Savoy, October 12, 1658* (1659), ch.vii, 14; *The Savoy Declaration of Faith and Order, 1658* (ed. A.G. Matthews; 1959), 84–85.

of her life that 'she had not the least concern about future events, for now she believed the decrees of God, and knew that he did all things well'.[38]

Trust in God's covenant faithfulness saw these believers through dark times. The London Baptist leader Benjamin Keach insisted that the covenant which God had made with his people through Christ was 'Established from all Eternity' and 'cannot be Repealed, Altered or Changed', for 'God is thine, and Christ is thine for ever'.[39] In a context of hostility and oppression, Dissenters derived immense comfort from this. During a particularly fierce time of persecution, John Flavel reminded his Dartmouth people of 'the Covenant of grace, in the bosom of which thou art wrapped up'. Whatever the hazards, they were eternally safe because the author of the covenant was 'not a *fickle* creature, but a *faithful* God'. Ruthless enemies might remove their material possessions but their spiritual wealth was totally beyond the reach of the most rapacious aggressor.[40]

Congregations were frequently reminded that, as active partners in this covenant, they must never forget their obligations, but they were also assured that 'what is a condition in one scripture, is a matter of promise in another'.[41] God unfailingly provides whatever he requires. Although Covenant theology placed its major emphasis on God's reliable promise in the agreement, Puritans did not ignore its human dimensions of commitment, responsibility and accountability.

Furthermore, their convictions about the faithfulness of God had been confirmed in history.

> Think much of them that are gone before ... [said Bunyan]. Sometimes, when my base Heart hath been inclining to this World, and to loiter in my Journey towards Heaven, the very consideration of the glorious Saints and Angels in Heaven ... hath caused me to rush forward ... and to say to my Soul, Come Soul, let us not be weary, let us see what this Heaven is ... Surely Abraham, David, Paul and the rest of the Saints of God, were as wise as any are now, and yet they lost all for this Glorious Kingdom.[42]

Dissenters were also enriched by the awareness that, throughout the

---

[38] James, *Abstract*, 80; cf. John Preston: 'Then, if ever thou art in covenant with God, and hast this seale in thy soule, that there is a change wrought in thee ... then thy election is sure, and be sure that God will never alter it, for he is unchangeable': *Life Eternall, or a Treatise of Knowledge of the Divine Essence and Attributes* (1631), 84–85 (Sermon 13, Part II).

[39] Benjamin Keach, *The Everlasting Covenant: A Sweet Cordial for a Drooping Soul, A Sermon preached at the Funeral of Henry Forty ... Abingdon ... wherein the Arguments used to prove the Covenant of Redemption a distinct Covenant form the Covenant of Grace, are Examined, Weighed and found Wanting* (1693), 43.

[40] Flavel, *Preparation*, in *Works*, VI, 80.

[41] Ibid., quoting Jer. 32: 40.

[42] Bunyan, *Heavenly Foot-Man*, in *MW*, V, 168.

centuries, men and women of faith had been supported and strengthened by a faithful and unchanging God. John Foxe's popular *Acts and Monuments* preserved narratives not only of the English Reformers, with their firm convictions about God's faithfulness in persecution, but also stories from the early Christian centuries, describing the heroism of believers who could not be shaken from their confidence. Nonconformists were followers of heroic people; it was a privilege to belong to such company.

Testimonies from more recent oppression frequently emerged in their writing and preaching. When Norwich Independents formed their church in 1642 they declared their ancestry; the church book's opening pages traced their hazardous beginnings during the Laudian oppression. Grieved by the 'silencing of divers godly ministers and the persecuting of godly men and women by Bishop Wren' in 1635-6 'in Norwich, Yarmouth and other places', their fellow believers had sought refuge in Rotterdam. The changed circumstances of the 1640s encouraged their return, for 'the furthering of the light ... in their native Countrey'. Whatever the dangers, they testified to God's faithfulness in bringing them home. They had returned with the blessing of friends in Holland who prayed that 'trueth and peace' might 'be their portion'.[43] Truth they continued to treasure but, in less than twenty years, peace was in short supply. Writing about persecuted Protestants in his own time, Baxter affirmed that 'Our God, our Rule, our Hope, our End and Portion are the same in the Inquisition, Prison and Flames, as in Prosperity. We have a Kingdom that cannot be moved, and Treasure that none' can steal.[44]

This assurance of God's faithfulness was an enriching dimension in the spirituality of their fellow believers, shared in personal experience and applied to their own lives. Mary Churchman recorded her experience of God's faithfulness to her as a young believer. In her late teens she came to personal faith with Nonconformist friends but, when her parents heard of it, was driven from her home with nothing 'except the clothes on my back'. In 'a time of scarcity of provisions', she obtained employment but 'lived chiefly upon barley bread'. Penniless and without change of clothing, she 'was obliged to borrow for necessary change of linen'. Grieved at her banishment, she became seriously ill, and her employer sent to her mother saying that her daughter 'had a great desire to see her'. But Mary's father told the messenger that 'if he did not immediately get out of his yard, he would shoot him dead'. A fortnight later, however, her mother sent her young daughter 'a box of wearing apparel', which Mary received 'with these words on my thoughts ... *For your heavenly father knoweth that ye have need of all these things*' (Mt. 6: 32). Through a long period of emotional stress, material deprivation and physical discomfort,

---

[43] DWL, MS 76.1, 'The Church Book belonging to the Society of Christians who assembly for divine Worship at the Old Meeting, Norwich' (transcript by Joseph Davey, 1848), fols 1–2.
[44] Baxter, *Calendar* (ed. Nuttall and Keeble), II, 12 (Letter 664).

this young believer testified to the faithfulness of God, especially manifest in the spiritual support she received at her Dissenting meeting. 'I lived in this place with difficulty three years, but in all that time never knew what it was to have a barren Sabbath ... I gathered my manna on the Sabbath, and it always tasted sweet and good'. Later, she found more congenial employment in another believer's home, but the house was raided whilst her pastor, Francis Holcroft, was staying there. Holcroft was arrested and imprisoned, and the 'officers ... came and seized a whole house of goods'. It was a time of severe persecution. Locally,

> ... dissenters could have no meetings, but in woods and corners. I myself have seen our companies often alarmed with drums and soldiers; every one was fined five pounds for being in their company ... But the greater the temptation the greater the deliverance ... Blessed be God, satan by his assault only bruised my heel, my head remained whole.

Reflecting later on these experiences, she testified that in their fierce adversity 'God was with us much ... how I do remember ... The Lord was a covert from that storm and tempest, and a strong rock in that day of trouble.'[45]

Mary Churchman's experience of God's faithfulness was enriched by her knowledge of Scripture (remarkable for such a young believer) and the supportive fellowship of her local conventicle. Many of these Nonconformists proved with Bunyan that 'what is from God is fixed, as a nail in a sure place'.[46]

Trusting God's Providence

A new member welcomed among Bury St Edmunds Dissenters 'related God's dealings with her Soull & ye several passages of his Providence'.[47] Such compassionate interventions in their daily lives were distinct 'providences' that must be identified, acknowledged, remembered, recorded and shared.

First, the 'providential' event must be identified. 'The smallest of God's providences should not be past by without observetion',[48] for the 'unobservant temper is displeasing to God'.[49] Once observed, it was important to discern what God may wish to communicate by them: 'every Providence hath a voyce & says something'.[50] The ejected Exeter minister John Bartlet told his people that this discipline would 'make you acknowledge God in all your ways';

---

[45] James, *Abstract*, 72–76.
[46] Bunyan, *Christ a Compleat Saviour* (1692), in *MW*, XIII, 332; cf. Isa. 22: 23.
[47] DWL, Harmer MS 76.4, Whiting Street Congregational Church, Bury St Edmunds, Church Book, 1646–1801 (transcribed 1849), fol.61.
[48] *The Diary of Roger Lowe, of Ashton-in-Makerfield, Lancs 1663–1674* (ed. W.L. Sachse; 1938), 35.
[49] John Flavel, *Divine Conduct, or the Mystery of Providence* [1678], in *Works*, IV, 414.
[50] Henry, *Diaries* (ed. Lee), 354.

without it, many tokens of his kindness might go unnoticed and unappreciated. They should, for example, note his generosity towards them in gifts they receive, regarding donors as sensitive friends who were serving as divine agents. Many ejected ministers suffered extreme financial deprivation and gratefully recalled times when, in their 'wants, and streights', God 'raised up friends' to supply their needs.[51] In September 1660, Henry Newcome lost his post as regular preacher at Manchester's Collegiate Church,[52] and over the next few years was frequently anxious about his slender finances. He noted how richly God had met his needs, as when 'ye Lord' sent him 'seasonably' forty shillings 'from Mr. Birch. Blessed be God.' Later, an identical amount was brought by one of Lady Booth's servants: 'I doe not know yt ever I spake to her in my life, but it pleaseth God to put us into w[ha]t hearts he pleaseth for our present supply'. Such provision continued throughout Newcome's life: 'I was just without money this day, and the Lord sent me in a merciful and unexpected supply'.[53] Nonconformists traced God's providence also in his protection during hazardous journeys, and noted specific help given to themselves and to their friends. Newcome acknowledged 'ye L[or]d's gracious providence tow[ard] Mr. Case in bringinge ym [him] safe up to London', ensuring his 'safety from a gulfe & quicksand in ye way'.[54] These 'providences' must not only be identified but also acknowledged with thanksgiving to the generous God who had given them. This recognition would enlarge their 'hearts in thankfulness for his distinguishing providences', causing them to 'admire, and adore him in them',[55] stimulating praise and calling them to 'a deep ... veneration of God'.[56]

In the pressure of harassed lives, such provision was easily overlooked, so, in moments of reflection, instances should be deliberately recalled. Too many people 'write them in the dust', and they quickly fade 'because they are not written on our hearts'.[57] Joseph Alleine reminded friends imprisoned at Ilchester that, once released, they should often recall God's generosity. 'Keep your Manna in a Golden Pot, and forget not him that hath said so often,

---

[51] B[artlet]., *Practical Christian*, 58.
[52] Robert Halley, *Lancashire: Its Puritanism and Nonconformity* (2nd ed.; Manchester, 1872), 346–48.
[53] Newcome, *Diary* (ed. Heywood), 19 (probably Robert Birch, a Manchester curate: *CR*, 56), 147. For other instances of financial provision experienced by Newcome, see *Autobiography* (ed. Parkinson), 240; *Diary* (ed. Heywood), 103, 150, 155, 180.
[54] Newcome, *Diary* (ed. Heywood), 16. This was probably another ejected Presbyterian minister, Thomas Case, who had earlier served in Lancashire, and made a return journey to the county in the second half of 1661.
[55] B[artlet]., *Practical Christian*, 53.
[56] John Collinges, *Several Discourses concerning the Actual Providence of God* (1678), 171.
[57] John Ryther, *Sea-Dangers and Deliverances Improved*, published with *James Janeway's Legacy to his Friends* (1675), 108, 102.

Remember.'[58] Recalling 'prison mercies' would enable them to face fresh challenges and remind them that, however great the adversity, necessary resources would always be available.

Dissenters were encouraged to put into writing these personal experiences of God's goodness. 'Trust not your slippery memories ... Written memorials secure us against that hazard'.[59] 'It is a thousand pities such choice helps should be lost', said Flavel. 'Keep catalogues of all your remarkable experiences; treasure them up as food to your faith in time to come.' It is a 'singular encouragement' to 'turn over the records of God's dealings with you in years past'.[60] Once released from Chester jail, Adam Martindale listed the seven good things that he had received through his arrest and confinement. 'I think I rather gained then lost by that imprisonment. A mercie ... not usuall with me ... Though malicious enemies reported that I was melancholie, I never had a more cheerful time in all my life'.[61]

Part of the secret was counting the blessings. In his pastoral work, John Owen met many believers who were 'poor in experience' because they 'have no stock'. Although 'they may have had many tokens for good, yet they have forgot them', and 'have not laid up anything for ... a hard time'. On occasions when God was specially kind to them, they should 'set this down for your own use'. It is 'as easy a way to grow rich in spiritual experiences as any I know'.[62]

Believers must not only record these experiences but frequently return to them. John Ryther urged his contemporaries to 'read over your Register, your ancient Records, how good God hath been at such a time', asking themselves, 'why should I despair, and cast off all hope now?'[63] They should have 'frequent recourse to them' when 'new wants, fears, or difficulties arise', so that they would ask themselves: 'Was I never so distressed before?'[64] The discipline of writing out these 'providences' was meant to benefit not just the writer but their family and friends. They might prove 'useful to others when we are gone'. It was a good thing to 'leave these choice legacies' to others.[65]

In dark times, many Christians also took time to record 'providential' events in the lives of others. John Bartlet was not the only preacher to recall the provision made for 'Martyn', an endangered French Protestant compelled to hide suddenly 'in the time of the Parisian massacre'. The vulnerable fugitive 'had a Hen that came constantly' to his hiding place 'every Day, and laid an

---

[58] Alleine, *Letters*, 70.
[59] Flavel, *Mystery of Providence*, in *Works*, IV, 496.
[60] Flavel, *Preparation*, in *Works*, VI, 46.
[61] Martindale, *Life* (ed. Parkinson), 234–35.
[62] *The Works of John Owen* (ed. W.H. Goold; 24 vols; Edinburgh, 1862), IX, 561.
[63] Ryther, *Sea-Dangers*, 123.
[64] Flavel, *Mystery of Providence*, in *Works*, IV, 497.
[65] Ibid. 496.

Egg, by which he was sustained for a Fortnight together'.[66] Personal journals preserved the details of such 'divine interventions' and a number of books detailed particular happenings widely regarded as providential events. Flavel wrote expansively about such experiences in the lives of the many sailors known to him.[67] Other writers published similar narratives,[68] and their popularity was not remotely confined to Dissent.[69]

Unwelcome as it might be, there was much to learn from 'Correcting-providence'. Had believers not been lovingly disciplined, they might have 'gone on still in such and such [an] evil course' and would 'have been as ... earthly and covetous ... as others'. They were 'not to repine at the Rod, but bless God for it'.[70] God could be at work in the occasional rebuke of a friend or neighbour. Newcome wrote that 'When ... Caleb Broadhead said something to me (about a matter, which has always been my trouble), I thought that he needed not to have said it; but the Lord would have him say it, that I might be troubled and humbled.'[71]

Sir Matthew Hale maintained that in his younger days 'the strange providences of God in laming and disabling his horses, and other impediments in a journey towards London, for worldly advantages, on the Lords day ... did convince him ... for ever after to spend that day as he hath since done.'[72] In

---

[66] B[artlet]., *Practical Christian*, 59. The story was also told by Flavel in his *Mystery of Providence*, in *Works*, IV, 355. Similar 'providences' from the time of the Parisian massacre were related by Thomas Brooks: *Works*, IV, 298.

[67] John Flavel, *A Narrative of some late and wonderful Sea Deliverances*, in *Works*, IV, 497–515.

[68] Increase Mather's *An Essay for the Recording of Illustrious Providences* (1684), for example, was exceptionally popular, being reprinted twice in New England in the year of publication, and also that year in London, followed by another edition in 1687. Mather began this work by using an initial collection sent to John Davenport by some of his English friends. Richard Baxter told Mather he was 'so much taken with your history of prodigies', saying that he had additional narratives if Mather wished to make use of them: Baxter, *Calendar* (ed. Nuttall and Keeble), II, 308.

[69] Two Elizabethan Puritan ministers, Thomas Beard and Thomas Taylor, had published *The Theatre of God's Judgments* (1597). Taylor was minister of St Mary Aldermanbury, London, and Beard master of Huntingdon Grammar School, where the young Oliver Cromwell was one of his pupils. William Turner, a Sussex vicar, published *A Compleat History of the Most Remarkable Providences ... in this Present Age* (1697), an anthology complied from both conformist and Nonconformist writers, with examples of courage from Patristic and Reformed sources, including narratives describing the heroism of French Protestants: ch.40, 1–12.

[70] B[artlet]., *Practical Christian*, 61.

[71] Newcome, *Autobiography* (ed. Parkinson), II, 199.

[72] Baxter, *Calendar* (ed. Nuttall and Keeble), II (Letter 939); Baxter, 'To the Reader', in Thomas Gouge, *The Surest and Safest Way of Thriving* (1676), sigs A7v–A8v, repr. in *The Works of Thomas Gouge* (1706), 105–107. In her pre-conversion days, Mary Churchman regularly set her father's 'great dog' to molest 'a godly woman' as she made her way each Sunday to a Dissenters' meeting, 'sometimes half a mile together and with

such 'cross-providences' we may 'quiet our spirits', knowing that in these adversities we may discern that an infinitely wise God 'hath a hand in all'.[73] Grieved at the disastrous outcome of Monmouth's rebellion, Axminster Independents described the failure as an 'amazing providence'. Their pastor, ruling elder and a number of members had publicly identified themselves with the duke's cause, yet their church book honestly records that the rising was used to 'correct the vain confidence' of men. They had been 'looking too much to men and instruments, and not so firmly relying upon the Lord'. Prior to the fateful Battle of Sedgemoor, their pastor and elder, along with others, left Monmouth's army and 'by the good providence of God ... returned home in safety', suitably chastened though not without danger in the months that followed.[74] The bitter experience had some hard lessons, for some experiences of life defy rational explanation. There was little point in punishing themselves about the wisdom of their involvement in the rebels' cause.

Enriching blessings might follow distressing experiences. As the earth needs 'chastening frosts and mellowing snows', so our lives benefit from 'nipping Providences'.[75] Recalling that Joseph's ill-deserving brothers obtained food from Egypt, the imprisoned George Hughes knew that 'Providence, though it orders afflictions, yet ... giveth supplies'.[76]

The identification and recording of 'providences' was not intended to encourage self-gratification; the practice should make their recipient a better person, more alert to the needs of others. 'Search and see, What benefit you have reaped by them', for they provoked some searching questions. Have these 'distinguishing providences' enriched believers in 'thankfulness, serviceableness, and fruitfulness?' When

> God hath done this ... for you above others ... what have you done for Him above others[?] ... Has God's goodness *to* you, wrought more goodness *in* you to others, stirr'd you up to do more good to the Country, Church, State, Place, City, Family, wherein God hath set you?[77]

Enjoying God's Presence

Dissenters were not only provided with well-timed interventions and corrective experiences. In their diaries, journals and correspondence, they repeatedly confirm that in adversity God came to them, and few were more eloquent in

---

the most bitter invectives'. Mary later said that 'such was the preventing providence of God', the dog 'never once fastened upon this gracious person, notwithstanding ... I constantly made it my business to set him upon her': James, *Abstract*, 67–68.
[73] B[artlet]., *Practical Christian*, 35.
[74] *Ecclesiastica* (ed. Howard), 97.
[75] Flavel, *Mystery of Providence*, 261, 263, 252; also idem, *Works*, IV, 493, 487.
[76] Hughes, *Genesis*, 523.
[77] B[artlet]., *Practical Christian*, 64–65.

their testimony to the divine presence than imprisoned believers. The unsanitary conditions of Abraham Cheare's Exeter gaol were not remotely unusual, but God's company transformed prisons into 'the presence-chambers of the great King'.[78] George Swinnock recalled that 'one of the Martyrs' had said, 'I thank my God for this prison ... more then for any Palace; for in it I find my God most sweet to me'.[79] The theme enriched the testimony of Friends. A young Quaker, Joseph Coale, wrote that 'neither Prison-Walls, and Locks, nor the Cruelty of Man' could 'obstruct ... the manifestation of his presence, which ... carries above all Sufferings'. The reality of God's presence made 'Days, and Hours and Years ... pass away as a moment, because of the enjoyment of ... seeing him ... who ... gives strength to bear what he calls to'. Nothing could rob him of the unchanging 'Issues of the Lord's Love' during a six-year incarceration at Reading, where he eventually died in his early thirties.[80] Locked up for three years with mentally sick people in Rome, a fellow Quaker wrote to encourage his London Friends, 'shut up in Dens and Holes, in crouds and clusters' at the time of Venner's rising. For 'though your Dens are noysome, and your Dungeons darkness ... his Presence [is] as the light of the Sun ... What is liberty without God', he asked, 'and What is more pleasant than a Prison with my God?'[81]

From another prison, Bunyan rejoiced that 'their King is at their Whistle' and 'never out of hearing', recalling two familiar Old Testament characters who had suffered at the hands of people who ought to have been their companions, telling illustrations in a time of religious persecution. In the presence of enemies, David was calm 'in the Valley of the shaddows of death', for God was with him. In crisis, Moses would rather have died 'where he stood, then to go one step without his God'. So, 'if he will but go along with us, what need we be afraid of ten thousands that shall set themselves against us'?[82] An imprisoned apostle proved that the 'presence of God' transforms 'the Stocks in to a Musick-School'.[83] Swinnock found inspiration in the Jacob narrative. When the patriarch 'halts through a blow on his thigh, the place is turned into a Peniel, that is, the Face of God. 'Twas an happy sight that was accompanied with a sight of Gods face.'[84]

Joseph's harrowing experience in Egypt repeatedly captured Dissenters' attention. Like them, he suffered at the hands of brothers. Their persecutors professed to be of the same 'family' of faith yet, wherever Joseph went, God was with him. George Hughes, another prisoner, reflected on the experience of Joseph's father, Jacob, exchanging the security of his home in Canaan for an

---

[78] Letter to William Punchard, 17 September, 1662, in Ivimey, *English Baptists*, II, 105.
[79] Swinnock, *Calling*, II, 418.
[80] *Some Account of the Life, Service and Sufferings of ... Joseph Coale* (1706), 146.
[81] John Perrot, *To the Suffering Seed of Royalty* (1661), 6.
[82] Bunyan, *Pilgrim's Progress*, 131–32, recalling Psa.23: 4; Exod. 33: 14–15.
[83] Polhill, *Armatura Dei*, 23, recalling Acts 16: 25.
[84] Swinnock, *Calling*, II, 418.

unknown future in Egypt: 'God carrieth his Church safely where he calls it, even to Egypt' for 'God can make places of exile to be for the greatest increase of the Church ... God's gracious presence with his Church in the worst places, may quiet them against fears.'[85] Edward Polhill reminded his readers that 'Joseph's Prison would have been very dismal, if God had not been there'. In our 'own Creature-weakness', how could they possibly survive adversity 'if the never fainting Creator' were not present to 'strengthen us'?[86] Joseph's experiences took him from a secure home to an undeserved prison, 'where his soul enters into irons', but 'God is with him still, sold with him, enslaved with him, accused with him, imprisoned with him'. Citing the assurance in Isaiah that in all our afflictions God is also afflicted, Hughes emphasized God's determination always to be 'in the same condition with his Joseph'. 'God's Josephs are no losers by being in prison', for his 'gracious presence maketh souls prosperous, where ever they be'.[87] In adversity, God is saying: 'when my people ... suffer great distress for me, then they have my comforting, supporting, imboldning and upholding presence to relieve them'. Joseph's father was in great trouble when he fled from Esau, but 'what a good nights lodging' Jacob had, for, bereft of other help, he was assured of the presence of God. One 'like the Son of God' walked in the fire with Daniel's friends, and Daniel himself 'sat and saw that the hands of Angels were made Muzzels for the Lyons mouths. I say, was it not worth being in the Furnace and in the Den, to see such things as these?'[88]

Thomas Brooks assured his London congregation that suffering believers would never be alone: 'If the bush, the church, be all on a-light fire, the angel of the covenant will be in the midst of it ... God will bear his children company, not only when they are in a delightful paradise, but also when they are in a howling wilderness.'[89]

Appropriating God's Power

God's presence guaranteed his resources. 'Divine help is nearest when a saint's danger is greatest.'[90] In the early 1680s, when the persecution was at its worst, Bunyan wrote his *Seasonable Counsel*, reminding his readers that the 'faithful Creator' who made them knew precisely what was necessary to sustain them. Nothing was impossible for him, and they had no need to fear for their own future or the destiny of God's people, for 'nothing can die under a *Creators* hands ... The cause of God, for which his people suffer, had been dead and buried a thousand years ago, had it not been in the hand of a Creator.' Who

---

[85] Hughes, *Genesis*, 557, 556.
[86] Polhill, *Armatura Dei*, 22.
[87] Hughes, *Genesis*, 491 (quoting Isa. 63: 9), 493, 484.
[88] Bunyan, *MW*, X, 23.
[89] Brooks, *Works*, IV, 276–77.
[90] Ibid. 276.

could have possibly imagined that

> ... the three Children could have lived in a fiery furnace, that Daniel could have been safe among the Lyons, that Jonah could have come home from his Countrey, when he was in the Whales belly, or that our Lord should have risen again from the dead: but what is impossible to a Creator?[91]

The theme of the omnipotent Creator recurs in the teaching of Hercules Collins. He reminds believers 'under pressing Trials'[92] that God delivered 'a Lecture of Creation' to a bewildered sufferer who 'thought to die in his Nest':[93] 'Where were you, Job, when I laid the earth's foundations? ... Who can dispose of his Creatures better than he which gave them a Being'?[94] God knows that 'the Soul cannot go through Trials honourably, without his Spirit to strengthen and comfort',[95] so he never disappoints them. In the midst of severe testing, God imparts superhuman strength. When 'the darkness is greatest, thy troubles at the highest, and thy hopes lowest', God lovingly intervenes.

Drawing on Foxe, Flavel reminded his readers of two courageous young believers during the Marian persecution. 'What a presence of spirit' there was in Thomas Drowry, the 'poor blind boy ... when he was examined by the Chancellor'; and (from early Christian times) how bravely the twelve-year-old Spanish martyr Eulalia 'acted above those years', and with such heroism, inspiring the fearful.[96] Strength is promised. But persecuted Christians only receive divine strength when, dependently, they relinquish their own. 'So long as a man has encouragement elsewhere, he does not encourage himself in the Lord his God.'[97] Father to four children, Bunyan illustrates the truth from family life: 'This is the way that Fathers take to encourage their Children, saying, run, sweet Babe while [until] thou art weary, and then I will take thee up and carry thee'. It is so with Christians who have exhausted all human resources; 'when they are weary, they shall ride'.[98] Christ himself

> ... was deserted in death, much more than many of his People ... and yet he was carried well through all his Darkness and Desertion ... and so died conquering,

---

[91] Bunyan, *MW*, X, 76–77.
[92] Collins, *Mountains of Brass*, 38. In the Epistle Dedicatory, Collins says that *The Scribe Instructed* and *Mountains of Brass*, the first two of his *Three Books*, reflect his experience and teaching 27 years earlier, i.e. in the late 1660s.
[93] Collins, *Scribe Instructed*, 52, 26.
[94] Collins, *Mountains of Brass*, 38.
[95] Collins, *Scribe Instructed*, 26.
[96] Flavel, *Preparation*, in *Works*, VI, 82; cf. John Foxe, *Acts and Monuments* (ed. J. Pratt, 8 vols; [1877]), VI, 654; VIII, 144–45; I, 270–72.
[97] William Bridge, *A Lifting up for the Downcast* (1961; first publ. [1648?]), 32.
[98] Bunyan, *Heavenly Foot-Man*, in *MW*, V, 169.

tho in Darkness, by believing. And thus God can do with thee ... for such as trust in him shall never be confounded.[99]

Affirming God's Holiness

The presence of God was a searching reality as well as a physical support. Genuine love for God 'makes men fear to sin and provoke the eyes of his glory'.[100] Nothing could be hidden from their omniscient God. 'I also sought to hide my self, but I could not; for the Man that sat upon the Cloud, still kept his eye upon me ... the Judge had always his eye upon me, shewing indignation in his countenance.'[101]

A sensitive awareness of the power of sin and its destructive potential was a continuing aspect of their spirituality. To yield to temptation was to sin against God; 'there is no Arrow of Judgment falls down upon us, but what was first [in sinning] shot upwards by us'.[102] William Jenkyn, the London minister, died in prison. His final message reminded his friends of the 'heinousness of sin'. How offensive must it be 'since it can provoke a God of much Mercy to express much severity'.[103]

In the summer of 1661, when Puritan ministers had cause to fear what the future might hold, Philip Henry recorded in his diary: 'I am afraid of nothing but sin'.[104] The imprisoned Joseph Alleine warned his Taunton congregation of the danger of compromise with this malicious opponent. 'God will not smile on that Soul that smiles on Sin ... Other Enemies you must Forgive, and Love' but not spiritual enemies. 'It's dangerous to dispute with Temptations'.[105] Joseph provided a persuasive example of uncompromising holiness of life: 'how shall I do this great evil ... There is nothing more loathsome to an holy soul'.[106] Tempted by his employer's wife, 'Joseph would loose his coat rather than his chastity'. He knew the damaging consequences of transgression. Identifying six aspects of this particular temptation, George Hughes imagined young Joseph addressing the temptress: 'The thing thou movest is a great sin. Adultery [is] against God's command, and [the] Covenant of marriage, against mine own body and thine, against the family of my Lord, and [the] threatenings of God'.[107]

Dissenters knew, however, that all too often sin was not horrific but attractive. Thomas Watson was determined to expose its perilous potential. The

---

[99] Collins, *Scribe Instructed*, 62–63.
[100] Hughes, *Genesis*, 487.
[101] Bunyan, *Pilgrim's Progress*, 37.
[102] Broadsheet, *Mr. Jenkin's Dying Thoughts* (1685).
[103] Ibid.
[104] Henry, *Diaries* (ed. Lee), 90.
[105] Alleine, *Letters*, 23 (31 July 1663).
[106] Flavel, *Touchstone of Sincerity*, in *Works*, V, 55.
[107] Hughes, *Genesis*, 489, 487.

devil 'would paint over sin with the Vermilion colour of Pleasure and Profit, that he may make it look fair. But I shall pull off the Paint from sin that you may see the ugly face of it.' The enormity of sin was a recurrent theme. Compromise with sin is the beginning of sorrows; this ruthless enemy defaces life's choicest gifts, virtues and qualities, dropping its lethal 'poison on our holy things' so that, given the opportunity, it even soils and 'infects our Prayers'.[108]

Witnessing God's Justice

Frequently opposed by disloyal betrayers, avaricious informers, hostile constables, unsympathetic magistrates and, occasionally, heartless soldiers, Dissenters were under no illusion about the final destiny of their oppressors. An omniscient God would not overlook the slightest injustice. Their conviction about God's ultimate judgement on their opponents was undergirded by biblical narrative, historical events and contemporary experience.

With his fine use of familiar biblical illustration, Bunyan gave it memorable expression: 'thou art in the fire, and they blow the bellows: but wouldest thou change places with them?' Their cruelties can only 'better God's people', and 'refine them as silver'; 'all the ways of the persecutor' are under divine control. 'Gods hook is in their nose'.[109] Creatively applying biblical narrative, Bunyan contrasts two New Testament persecutors, contemplating both the downfall of evildoers and the miracle of potential transformation in the life of a vicious enemy. For 'who knows whether it is determined' that their persecutor 'should remain implacable to the end, as Herod, or whether they may thorough [sic] grace obtain repentance for their doings, with Saul'. If the persecuted believer's prayer 'should have a casting hand in the conversion of any of them it would be sweet to thy thoughts, when the scene is over'.[110]

Historical incidents supported their teaching about the awesome judgement of God. 'Persecutors never thrive upon that bloody Trade', said Watson, recalling that the emperor Diocletian had 'rased down the Christians Temples, and burnt their Bibles'. But 'God was avenged on him; he was afterwards stricken with Phrency, and poisoned himself. ... Christ will be too hard for all his Enemies'.[111]

Philip Henry frequently recorded occasions when, in his view, God's judgement was demonstrated in local events. 'The undersherriff the first day of the Assize being a bitter p[er]secutor, was struck with sudden death, drinking in a Tavern.' Later, 'Mr. Bostock ye Prosecutor was bury'd ye first day of ye

---

[108] Thomas Watson, *A Body of Practical Divinity ... Sermons on the Lesser Catechism* (1692), 76.
[109] Bunyan, *Seasonable Counsel*, in *MW*, X, 72–73.
[110] Ibid. 71, citing Acts 12: 21–23; 9: 1–18.
[111] Watson, *Light in Darkness*, 22.

Assize', adding 'Digitus Dei'.[112] Specific events, considered as acts of divine judgement, were often recalled when Nonconformists met. Henry recorded: 'Mr. St[eele] inform'd mee of ye remarkable hand of God' upon a rural dean, who was intent on persecuting a local Dissenter 'and would not bee p[er]swaded to defer it'. But, 'the very night before, hee was struck with a fit of ye Stone', adding another sombre 'Digitus Dei'.[113]

Letters from family or friends contained news of similar happenings in other parts of the country. A Lancashire clergyman 'active in Indicting Mr. Taylor of Bury for a Conventicle before the end of ye Assize was kil[le]d by one Ward then under Cure with him for madness', though the patient was 'in a way of recovery'. Two people who had presented themselves as witnesses in court 'ag[ains]t Mr. Ince of Dunhead in Wilts were suddenly smitten by ye just hand of God, one of them dy'd repenting'.[114]

Richard Conder's narrative of Holcroft's ministry similarly relates specific examples of how 'the lord brought doune' determined opponents of the local church, claiming that these were far from isolated instances of serious trouble that befell those who harassed Dissenters.[115] The reluctant Essex conformist Ralph Josselin wrote of a neighbouring clergyman, 'feirce against all dissenters and very intemperate in his speeches [who] died of a cancer in his mouth', adding, 'thy judgments a great depth.'[116]

Local congregations recorded similar events in church books. Axminster Independents noted that an informer who 'so wickedly devised the overthrow' of their church was 'mortally wounded in a quarrel' with a man 'who had been a confederate with him' in persecuting them. The offender speedily left the area, 'so that both these troublers ... were cut off in one day ... He ordaineth his arrows against the persecutors.'[117] As a congregation they had lost members because of 'that monster of men, that cruel judge', George Jeffreys, in 'the bloody and barbarous assizes' that followed Monmouth's rebellion. Their church book tells of the judge's unsuccessful attempt to flee the country, and his imprisonment and subsequent death, confirming for them the psalmist's warning that 'Bloody and deceitful men shall not live out half their days'.[118]

---

[112] Henry, *Diaries* (ed. Lee), 104–105, 157.

[113] Ibid. 171; similar 'judgements' are noted in Jolly, *Note Book* (ed. Fishwick), 66–67.

[114] Henry, *Diaries* (ed. Lee), 106–107.

[115] H.G. Tibbutt, 'Francis Holcroft', *TCHS* 20 (1965–70), 295–301, at 300–301; cf. the antagonistic justice killed by his own bull: Theophilus Gale, *The Life and Death of Thomas Tregoss* (1671), 16–17.

[116] *The Diary of Ralph Josselin 1616–1683* (ed. Alan Macfarlane; Oxford, 1976), 626.

[117] cf. Watson, *Light in Darkness*, 22: 'God has his Arrow upon the String to shoot at Persecutors, and be assured God never misseth his mark.'

[118] *Ecclesiastica* (ed. Howard), 84 (quoting Psa. 64: 7), cf. 88, 138 (quoting Psa. 55: 23). George Fox also took pains to preserve 'Examples' of divine judgement on cruel oppressors; 'the Lord cut him off soon after', *Journal* (ed. Smith), 353, cf. 286, 291, 342, 362, 363, 364, 407, 413; *The Narrative Papers of George Fox* (ed. H.J. Cadbury; Richmond, IN, 1972), 209–31, esp. 219.

Pained by vindictive oppressors and misapplication of the law, Quakers recorded precise details of local persecutions and, early in their history, began to publish these narratives,[119] initially by counties.[120] Dates and names of both victims and persecutors were provided, so that facts could be verified.

The wider publicity was deliberate. Such pamphlets[121] provided an opportunity for writers to express, on behalf of sufferers, a natural indignation at their physical abuse and material deprivation. They also enabled local readers to appreciate the nature and extent of their neighbours' sufferings, and informed Friends in other localities of the physical and financial needs of colleagues who had been deprived of essentials, such as tools for daily work, and the opportunity to provide for their families. They provided specific imprisonment details so that the victims could be visited with practical necessities and assured that their families would not be neglected. These publications also drew the attention of fair-minded justices and local authorities to the inappropriate behaviour of some of the people deputed to take action on their behalf. Additionally, the booklets frequently contained vivid descriptions of subsequent events in the lives of persecutors, such as those we have seen earlier, all regarded as divine judgement on vindictive oppressors. They were intended as warnings to judges, magistrates, justices, constables, informers and others who might be tempted to join the ranks of the Dissenters' opponents.[122]

For Quakers, as for others, it was of crucial importance that, given this wider publicity, these accounts should be accurate and reliable sources of legal information. Rumour and hearsay were studiously avoided and any factual detail subsequently considered exaggerated, erroneous or suspect was, wherever possible, corrected or expunged.[123]

---

[119] Printed and manuscript collections of such 'judgments' were not peculiar to Puritanism, Nonconformity or this period. The extensive appendix to Foxe's *Actes and Monuments* (1596) describes in vivid detail the 'severe punishment of God upon the persecutors of his people and enemies to his word': *Acts and Monuments* (ed. Pratt), VIII, 628–71; cf. Clarke, *General Martyrologie*, 539–44. For the use of judgement stories in Bunyan and others, see his *Mr. Badman* (ed. Forrest and Sharrock), xix–xxvi; Alexandra Walsham, *Providence in Early Modern England* (Oxford, 1999), 65–115.

[120] E.g. William Dewsbury, *A Discovery of the Ground from whence Persecution did arise, and the Proceedings of those that were Actors in it, in Northamptonshire* (1665); Leonard Fell and William Addamson, *The Persecution of them People, they call Quakers, in several places in Lancashire* (1656); [anon], *The Lamentable Sufferings of the Church of God in Dorsetshire, and the persecution there* (1659).

[121] These publications were occasionally more extensive than a pamphlet, such as the 172-page volume of composite authorship, *The Best Answering to the North, in the fierce Persecution of the Manifestation of the Son of God ... in the County of Cornwall* (1657).

[122] For example, *Journal of George Fox* (ed. Ellwood), 264–65 (The first edition had defective pagination; for this reference, see the *second* p.265 in the book).

[123] E.g. *George Fox's 'Book of Miracles'* (ed. H.J. Cadbury; Cambridge, 1948), 91–93, which discusses two instances of corrections made to accounts of judgements in the first edition of Fox's *Journal*. Derbyshire Friends were unhappy about the details provided of

What was particularly serious about the persecutors' onslaughts was that an attack on believers was regarded as a direct assault on God. Cain 'persecuted his Brother for righteousness sake, and so espoused a quarrel against God'. Anyone who 'persecutes another ... fights against God'.[124] With typical bluntness, Bunyan warned such offenders lest they be committing an unpardonable sin. Deliberately attacking godly people was infinitely worse than using a sword to mutilate a royal portrait. The illustration was apposite: Londoners knew that the Guildhall portrait of James, Duke of York, had been slashed.[125] To persecute believers was to deface their king's image and he would not overlook those who do them harm. How 'contrary do they act to God, whose work it is to cause Darkness and Sorrow to the Righteous'.[126] Baxter noted that God 'will receive none but those that loved his servants ... And if he will say to those that did not entertain them, *Depart from me* ... what will he say to those that hate and persecute them?'[127]

But Dissenters were encouraged to believe that even the most ruthless persecutor might yet come to faith. 'Mercy is God's Darling Attribute', which 'he loves most of all to magnifie', said Thomas Watson. 'Justice is God's strange work [Isa. 38: 21] ... But Mercy is his proper work'. Longing for more peaceful times, and that some of their antagonistic contemporaries might turn to God, Watson pleaded for continuing hope: 'Why may not Mercy give the casting Voice for this Nation?'[128]

Exalting God's Love

It was not difficult for them to believe that God would be merciful to their oppressors, for they too had been rebels. The God who had welcomed them would not reject others, however recalcitrant they might be. The fatherhood of God was a 'favourite and insistent theme' in English Puritanism.[129] Richard

---

the severe 'judgement' on a local named persecutor, suspecting 'the verity of part of the relation and request that it may be left out'. A new page omitting the suspect material was printed and copies sent 'to every county to a couple of discreet faithful Friends to take out the old leaves and put in the new as carefully and neatly as they can'.
[124] Bunyan, *MW*, X, 100.
[125] Bunyan, *An Exposition of the First Ten Chapters of Genesis, and part of the Eleventh*, in *MW*, XII, 252. This work, published posthumously (1692), was probably written shortly after the Guildhall incident: Greaves, *Glimpses*, 462–63. For details of the event, see Luttrell, *Brief Historical Relation*, I, 160. Bunyan would not have made the comment about the unpardonable sin glibly, for he himself had suffered considerable mental distress earlier in life fearing he might possibly have committed it.
[126] Watson, *Light in Darkness*, 21.
[127] Richard Baxter, *The Last Work of a Believer* (1682), 27–28, quoting Mt. 25: 40–41
[128] Watson, *Light in Darkness*, 31–32.
[129] G.F. Nuttall, *The Holy Spirit in Puritan Faith and Experience* (Oxford, 1947), 63; cf. the prayer of the West Country minister George Trosse: 'Lord, let all thy Dealings with

Sibbes claimed: 'the word *Father* is an epitome of the whole gospel ... Thou mayest fall into sin, but God is still thy Father. This relation is everlasting'.[130] The Lancashire Presbyterian, Richard Hollinworth, said that just as 'children cry Dad and Mam', so 'Christ taught us to call God our Father'.[131] Such Puritan writers were the spiritual mentors of late seventeenth-century Dissenters, among whom leaders such as Owen and Watson also gave rich expression to this cardinal theme. God's 'free, undeserved and eternal' love was 'the great discovery of the gospel', and the foundation of the believer's relationship with the Father. Owen recalled that when the disciples were about to be separated from Jesus, he not only told them 'that he would not forget them when bodily he was gone from them', but instructed them to hold on to this declared truth and assurance, 'The Father himself loveth you'.[132] For the original disciples, as for Owen's contemporaries, it was a message for hazardous times.

Watson suggested a variety of reasons why God is 'the best Father' by far. A devoted human father may have undoubtedly good intentions that are not in the best interests of his children, but God is a Father with infinite wisdom, knowing 'the fittest means to bring about his own designs'. The love of many fathers is unquestionable, but God is 'the best Father, because the most loving'. 'If earthly fathers should be ever giving, they would have nothing left to give; but God is ever giving' and, with inexhaustible riches, 'has not the less'.[133] Baxter urged his readers to cultivate 'true believing thoughts of the exceeding infinite love of God'. We should 'always think of God ... as we do of a friend', as one who always loves us, 'even more than we do our selves'.[134] However puzzling and difficult life's circumstances, harassed Dissenters could be assured that God cared for them more, and better, than anybody else, and could always tell 'where the shoe pinches'.[135]

In his infinite kindness and patience, God recognized human frailty and knew that in adversity the best of people can make huge mistakes. 'How much did God wink at in Job, and in Jonah, and in David, in their Distress'.[136] These biblical characters were utterly sincere in their love for God but disappointed him, yet he tenderly allowed for the pressures they were under. He knew their

---

us proceed from Fatherly Love and Covenant Mercy': Isaac Gilling, *Life of Mr. George Trosse* (1715), 132.

[130] Richard Sibbes, *The Christian Work* [1639], in *The Complete Works of Richard Sibbes* (ed. A.B. Grosart, 7 vols; Edinburgh, 1862–4), V, 25.

[131] Richard Hollinworth, *The Holy Ghost on the Bench, or the Spirit at the Bar* (1656), 47.

[132] John Owen, *Of Communion with God the Father, Son and Holy Ghost* (1657), in *Works* (ed. Goold), II, 19–20, quoting Jn 16: 26–27.

[133] Thomas Watson, *The Lord's Prayer* (1960), 3.

[134] Baxter, *Rest*, 690–91.

[135] Cambridge, Cambridge University Library, MS 7338, Philip Henry, Exposition of Gen. 15, 22 August 1658.

[136] Collins, *Scribe Instructed*, 61.

trials and, as Bunyan put it, there is not one tear but 'it is now in the bottle of God'.[137]

Dissenting preachers consistently focused on God's love as 'the attribute that sways all'. 'I will love such a one', declares this compassionate God, 'let his condition be what it will be'. If that believer should fall into sin, 'I will fetch sin out of him again, that I may delight in him'. Should they encounter a seemingly insuperable difficulty in their lives, 'then love sets power on work', for 'mercy, and power, and justice, and wisdom, and all, they all work together in a way of subordination to love'.[138]

Communion with God

However meaningful and inspiring their theological foundations, personal communion with God was vital if Dissenters were to be sustained in dark times and make a spiritual impact in local society. Their conventicles were illegal but their daily conduct was eloquent, and their ministers were persuaded that, if they and their members were to be at their best, it was essential that they spend some time each day with God. Regular prayer was crucial. 'All that comes from God to you, or to you from God, must come in this channel'.[139] Dissenters frequently stressed two important aspects of prayer. First, sin mars communion with God; second, by communing with him on a daily basis, believers receive the necessary resources for daily living in a frequently hostile environment.

These believers found inspiration and comfort in biblical narratives that honestly described the sins, failures, forgiveness and restoration of some of their best characters. Convinced of God's love and of his holiness, acknowledgement of sin was the first step to renewal. To be heedless, apathetic or flippant about moral failure was an offensive affront to God's loving and holy character. It was for this reason that Dissenters considered it important to devote some time each day to the exercise of self-monitoring. We turn now to this important aspect of their personal spirituality.

Confessing Human Need

Books written by Armagh's Calvinist archbishop James Ussher were popular among Dissenters. He taught that prayer's necessary elements should include 'a remembrance of thy life past'. There was always need for the praying believer 'to examine, first our hearts and their affections', then 'our thoughts ... words' and 'actions'.[140] A specific daily time for communion with God should not omit

---

[137] Bunyan, *MW*, III, 237, an allusion to Psalm 56: 8.
[138] Goodwin, *Works*, II, 151–52.
[139] Flavel, *Works*, VI, 65.
[140] James Ussher, *A Method for Meditation* (1651), unpaginated introduction, 'The Contents of the Book'. Self-examination was a crucial aspect of Puritan spirituality; for

a period of honest reflection on the believer's inner life. This was effected with a rigorous self-scrutiny that may sometimes, with introspective souls, have reached unhealthy proportions.[141] Whatever its dangers, Oliver Heywood was persuaded of the crucial role of his soul's 'self-conference'.[142] God 'hath so frequently called upon me to descend into my oune hart, to commune therewith, to search and try my ways, to examine my selfe, to prove my worke' for this 'concernes the weal or woe of my immortal soul to al eternity'.[143] Reflecting on the familiar Daniel narrative, Watson acknowledged that it 'is little pleasure to read the hand-writing on the wall of conscience'. People are 'like tradesmen' in precarious financial circumstances, 'loth to ... cast up their accounts, lest they should find their estates low'. Believers may be equally disinclined to 'look into their guilty heart, lest they should find something there which should affright them'.[144]

The Puritan concern to probe the inner life is characteristic of the period's culture, manifest in the popularity of autobiography; the keeping of diaries, memoirs and spiritual journals; and the recording of 'experience', not only for delivery at a local church as part of an application for membership, but also for personal and sometimes wider use, preserving meaningful events and 'providences'.[145] In 1657, the young Philip Henry wrote:

> This was the first yeare in which I began to keep an Account of my Time in this method ... 'tis a pleasing, profitable, heavenly Art. O Deus, Doce me numerare dies meos. The Day of a Deliverance is to bee remembred, and God takes it ill when wee doe not remember it.[146]

In April 1665, the young ejected minister Owen Stockton began to keep a spiritual diary but was disturbed lest it degenerate into a self-exalting exercise.[147] On its first page he reflects on its appropriateness, asking himself

---

example, 'betook me to privat praier and examenation': *Diary of Lady Margaret Hoby, 1599–1605* (ed. D.M. Meads; 1930), 65.

[141] Young Samuel Jeake 'kept formerly a Catalogue of sins committed by me in order to a deeper humiliation' but, assured of forgiveness, he came to see that it was not appropriate to record 'that which God will remember no more': *Diary of Samuel Jeake* (ed. Hunter and Gregory), 98.

[142] Heywood, *Heart-Treasure*, 25.

[143] Heywood, *Autobiography* (ed. Turner), I, 133.

[144] Thomas Watson, *Heaven taken by Storm* (1669), 58.

[145] E.g. the accounts of Agnes Beaumont's encounter with adversity as a member of Bunyan's Bedford congregation (*Narrative*, ed. Harrison); the experiences of Mary Churchman, one of Francis Holcroft's converts (James, *Abstract*, 67–79); Richard Conder's narrative of family experience during Holcroft's ministry (Tibbutt, 'Holcroft'); and innumerable Quaker 'testimonies'.

[146] Henry, *Diaries* (ed. Lee), 32.

[147] Although he regularly kept such a diary, Heywood also recognized the dangers: *Autobiography*, I, 133.

'whether this recording of experiences of the working and dealings of god [*sic*] with my soul made for ye glory of God'. In his quest, two passages from the Psalms became especially relevant, combining the elements of personal gratitude and encouraging testimony. 'Come and hear, all ye that fear God, and I will declare what he hath done for my soul' and 'One generation shall praise thy works to another, and shall declare thy mighty acts. I will speak of the glorious honour of thy majesty, and of thy wondrous works.'[148]

At such a time their subjective response to objective truth was of immense importance. 'Feelings' and 'experiences' were to be analysed, interpreted, recorded and shared. Bunyan preached what he 'felt, what I smartingly did feel'. In the frequently harrowing account of his quest for assurance, he constantly exposes the intense anguish of an extended search, touching depths of self-despair; his 'poor Soul did groan and tremble to astonishment'.[149] The explorative journey within was an essential, if uncomfortable, spiritual exercise.

In the course of his Taunton ministry, Joseph Alleine was at pains to promote this 'Conscientious, and frequent Performance of ... Self-Examination', crucial for 'the bringing down of Sin' and the 'furtherance of Holiness, both in Heart, and Life', commending it fervently in his preaching; he talked to his people 'in Private about it and got a promise from the most of them, that they would every Night ... spend some time in secret ... to call themselves to an account, how they had carried it that day'.[150] During his Ilchester imprisonment, Alleine wrote to remind them of its importance as a spiritual discipline. He had left them 'some helps for daily examination', specially prepared written material with specific advice about how best to conduct the exercise, lest they 'should grow slack, and slight, and careless' in it. He urged them never to let 'a day pass, but you do solemnly and seriously call your selves to an account [of] what your Carriage hath been to God and men'.[151]

In a series of weekly pastoral letters, the exiled Samuel Wells made an identical appeal to his Banbury congregation. 'Be frequent and serious in the Examination of your own hearts and ways' for, of 'all the duties belonging to a Christian', this practice of daily 'searching or trying ... is one of the most necessary, and yet most neglected'.[152]

In commending the practice, these ministers assert that it has excellent

---

[148] DWL, MS 24.7, Owen Stockton, 'Observations and experiences of gods dealing with my soul and other memorable passages of his providence taken and recorded since April 1st 1665, by Owen Stockton; continued to 24 August 1680', fol.1, quoting Psa. 66: 16; 145: 4–5.
[149] Bunyan, *GA*, §276.
[150] [Alleine], *Life*, 47.
[151] Alleine, *Letters*, 44 (20 October 1663).
[152] Samuel Wells, *A Spiritual Remembrancer ... with 32 Epistolary Discourses ... by their Absent Pastor week after week* (1676), 16, 127.

biblical precedent. Passages of self-deprecation in the Psalms were not written 'from Ostentation and vain Glory', but preserved 'for the instruction of their own, & succeeding Ages'. Those Old Testament saints were being ruthlessly honest about themselves, and such passages represented genuine self-portraiture. John Howe says that we commend a portrait because 'it is like the Face. So have good Men ... not spared to put in the Distempers, and Disaffections of their Spirits ... as great Blemishes ... as a Wart or Mole on the Face'.[153] The psalmist frequent exemplified 'sundry ways of Communing with our own hearts', says Alleine, expounding the theme by focusing on Psalm 4: 4: 'Stand in awe and sin not; communion with your own heart upon your bed, and be still'. This personal conversation with the inner self ('O my soul') provides consolation (Psa. 116: 7), rebuke (Psa. 42: 11, 43: 5), exhortation (Psa. 62: 5), instruction, and the necessary 'Examination ... on which all the rest do depend'. The heart of every woman and man 'is always talking to it self', and those secret, inaudible conversations may expose unworthy ambitions, jealous obsessions, corrupt motives, hidden pride, destructive intentions and other secret preoccupations. Believers 'should often step in and see what it is that they are talking of', to 'see if they are well employed, and if they be not, set them a Task'.[154] The 'task' was to offer a spiritual alternative to unprofitable thinking. Alleine and his Nonconformist contemporaries believed this necessary for five reasons.

First, he reminded his congregation of the prevalence of ignorance about one's self.[155] It is 'so hard' for people admit to their darker, damaging potential; they are 'so generally mistaken' in making a realistic assessment of their strengths and weaknesses, for 'the heart is deep' (Psa. 62: 6). Self-discovery can be a painful experience. Peter genuinely believed he had the moral strength to remain true to Christ in hostile circumstances yet, even with his Master's warning, 'Christ could scarce put him out of this conceit ... And who would have thought there was that swearing, and cursing in his heart as there was? And so of David's Adultery', who would have believed such treachery was possible?[156] Neither King Hezekiah 'nor no body else would have thought that there could have been' such pride 'in his heart' especially after God had been so generous to him.[157] The pastor pleads with his people, 'be not too sure of your own hearts'.[158] A Christian cannot see 'a jot into his own heart, till the

---

[153] John Howe, preface to Corbet, *Self-Imployment*, A2v–A3v.
[154] Alleine, *Remaines*, 5–6.
[155] Richard Baxter, *The Mischiefs of Self-Ignorance* (1662); idem, *The Practical Works of the Rev. Richard Baxter* (ed. W. Orme, 23 vols; 1830), XVI; cf. N.H. Keeble, *Richard Baxter, Puritan Man of Letters* (Oxford, 1982), 133–39; *Narrative Papers of Fox* (ed. Cadbury), 209–31, esp. 219.
[156] Alleine, *Remaines*, 2.
[157] Ibid. 3, citing 2 Chron. 32: 31.
[158] Ibid.

Lord do spring into the soul with a new light, as he did into the Prison'.[159]

Second, Alleine warned of the danger of self-deceit. People treasure 'that good common opinion that men have of their hearts. Though their hearts are full of odious poyson ... yet they cannot see it till God open their eyes by conversion.'[160] In order that 'no man may be a Self-deceiver, let every man be a Self-searcher.' They must not imagine that simply to be of the 'Professing Party', a nominal Christian, 'will serve his turn'.[161] 'Tis easie to mistake Education for Regeneration, and ... Illumination for Conversion, and a partial Reformation and external Obedience, for true Sanctification.'[162] William Dyer issued a similar warning: 'Acquaint your selves with your selves ... A man may be acquainted with the grace of truth, who never knew the truth of grace.'[163] Even when commendable things are done, they may be prompted by impure motives: 'look to the Root, as well as to the Fruit. Eye, not onely your Actions, but your Aims. Remember what a strict and severe Eye you are under.'[164]

Third, Alleine emphasized the necessity of self-discovery. Nothing could be more important than this painful but corrective exposure: 'daily self-examination will make you to live holily and dye comfortably'.[165] Heywood believed it deeply beneficial 'to compare my past and present state ... whether grace be stronger, corruptions weaker, my hart more soft, conscience more tender, wil[l] more bowed, rectifyed, resolved, and my life more reformed'.[166]
Watson maintained that self-scrutiny is an essential aspect of the healing process, describing 'self-searching' as 'heart-anatomy'. A Christian must be like a soul surgeon searching for 'what is flesh, and what is spirit; what is sin, and what is grace ... The eye can see everything but it self. It is easie to spy the faults of others, but hard to find out our own'.[167]

Fourth, Alleine recognized the cost of contrition. God kept the Israelite people forty years in the desert, with many 'sharp tryals', to 'know what was in thine heart'. 'One would have thought they had never been guilty of such horrid unbelief to distrust God, when they did feed upon, and weared miracles. It hath cost them so many sad falls to know them.'[168] Many Dissenters recorded failures in their private journals as a means of alerting themselves to perilous

---

[159] Ibid. 4, an allusion to Acts 12: 7.
[160] Ibid.
[161] Alleine, *Letters*, 78 (16 April 1663); cf. 204 (24 July 1663): 'None so miserable in all the world as an unsound professor of religion now is'. See also Mead, *Almost Christian*, 'To the Reader', [unpaginated].
[162] Alleine, *Letters*, 88 (7 July 1666).
[163] Dyer, *Titles*, 216.
[164] Alleine, *Letters*, 89 (7 July 1666).
[165] Alleine, *Remaines*, A4v (Direction 10).
[166] Heywood, *Autobiography* (ed. Turner), I, 151.
[167] Watson, *Heaven taken by Storm*, 56–57.
[168] Alleine, *Remaines*, 2–3.

areas of temptation.[169] The diaries or spiritual records of Oliver Heywood, Philip Henry, John Corbet, Gervase Disney and the conformist ministers Isaac Archer and Ralph Josselin have numerous examples of personal contrition. Philip Henry's birthday provided a natural occasion for serious reflection. 'This day compleats the thirtieth year of my Age ... no older Alexander was when hee had conquer'd ye great world, & I have not yet conquer'd the little world, myself'. With the increasingly threatening ecclesiastical and political restrictions, he continued, 'so old Christ was w[he]n hee began to preach, & according to ye present face of th[ings] I am now as if I had done preaching' but 'hee can do his work without us'.[170] Out of a sense of painful remorse, Henry frequently noted his deficiencies on a particular day. 'With wife at Shrewsb[ury] where [we were] much made of', both 'among Friends, & Sundays opportunityes [preaching] ... being good, but a barren heart mars all.'[171] '[W]ith wife at Stanwardine – much made of there but little good done, by reason of a vayn, unfixt, unfruitful heart.'[172] Again, 'at home each night this week & last ... time not fil'd up, lord p[ar]don'.[173] Henry confessed he was not always inspired when others prayed: 'mett some Freinds at Mr. Thomas, where we pray'd together, but my heart was out of frame, lord, let not my sin hinder the success of that day'.[174] In the next month, at a similar home meeting, 'my heart much out of frame, cumbred with many th[ings]' but, conscious of his frailty, he rejoiced that the work did not depend on his feelings; 'blessed bee God, wee are under a Coven[an]t of grace'.[175]

Fifth, Alleine believed in the value of self-interrogation. Every Dissenter was not as spiritually sensitive as Philip Henry. Some might set aside some time for self-examination but, hurriedly, fail to identify their errors and end up convinced that on a particular day little had seriously clouded their horizons. Such people were in need of specific help to avoid a cursory and profitless assessment of the day's activities, and Alleine provided the necessary structure to prevent glib evaluations. Given the danger of self-deceit, a casual

---

[169] DWL, MS 90.10, Diary of Sarah Savage, 1688–95 (copied 1812), fol.1 (8 December 1688): 'Saturday night spent a little time in looking over my papers ... finding how it hath formerly been with me. I've just come to fear decay in grace because I do not watch over the motions of my heart so strictly as formerly'; cf. Tom Webster, 'Writing to Redundancy: Approaches to Spiritual Journals and Early Modern Spirituality', *HistJ* 39 (1996), 1–34.

[170] Henry, *Diaries* (ed. Lee), 93 (24 August 1661). By this point some of Henry's colleagues had lost their livings, having been replaced by previously sequestered clergy. Two days earlier, his friend Richard Steele, vicar of Hanmer, had called on him: 'we are in doubt what to doe in poynt of conformity, lord, say unto us, this or that is the way, & wee will walk in it'.

[171] Ibid. 229.
[172] Ibid. 240.
[173] Ibid. 262.
[174] Ibid. 133.
[175] Ibid. 137.

examination of the inner life was unlikely to reach the heart of the problem. The believer might need to be provided with specific, searching questions for him to put to honest use on a daily basis.

Alleine's proposal was that every member of his congregation address 'Several Questions' which he had 'drawn up for them in writing', each supported by biblical references.[176] The interrogations were gathered under five headings: 'For y[ou]r Duties [i.e. spiritual exercises, such as prayer, family worship], Sins, Heart, Table and Calling. The eight questions on 'Duties' included: 'Did God find me upon my bed when he looked for me on my knees', a question supported by the example of morning prayer in the life of both Job (1: 5) and David (Psa. 5: 3). For 'healthy bodies, six or seven hours' sleep is 'enough ... be sure that you do use some Self-denial about your sleep'.[177] A further question, 'Have ... I prayed to no purpose, or suffered wandering thoughts to eat out my duties?', was accompanied by the prophetic exposure of Jeremiah: 'thou art near in their mouth but far in their reins', along with the exacting word of Christ: 'If thy hand or thy foot offend thee, cut them off'. The daily reading of Scripture was also examined ('Have I neglected or been very overly [superficial, cursory] in the reading of God's Word'), and the attention devoted to recent preaching: 'Have I digested the sermon I heard last? Have I repeated it over? And prayed it over?', all corroborated by Mary's example, who 'kept all these things and pondered them in her heart' (Lk. 2: 19, 51).[178] Before retiring to bed, it was important to 'take notes' of their 'hearts all the day & read them over in the evening'. Evening interrogations included the recollection of specific opportunities the day had presented for self-denial, and whether, in contacts with others, they had 'not dropped something of God and left some good savour behind'. Had the day given some occasion for doing something 'more than ordinary for the Church of God'? Examination included further searching questions concerning the believer's eating habits as well as his daily work.[179]

Alleine's prison letters pressed home the necessity of this rigorous enquiry: 'have you not your secret Haunts of evil? ... do you not hide some Iniquitie as a sweet morsel under your Tongue? ... Do you chose Holiness, not out of bare necessity, because You cannot go to Heaven without it, but out of love to it?'[180] Without 'the constant use' of such 'short Questions' there was little hope of significant 'growth in Holiness'.[181]

The exiled Samuel Wells suggested that the basic question should focus on the believer's primary ambition: 'What is [it] that I truly aim at? ... Does my

---

[176] [Alleine], *Life*, 47–51.
[177] Ibid.; Alleine, *Remaines*, 6–7.
[178] [Alleine], *Life*, 48; cf. Alleine, *Remaines*, 8–9.
[179] Alleine, *Remaines*, 1–27, where, in a sermon on Psa.4: 4, Alleine expands on the questions in *Life*, 48–51.
[180] Alleine, *Letters*, 93 (29 June 1666).
[181] Ibid. 114 (undated).

will ... submit to the will of God in all things?' As an aid to memory, he provides them with a simple structure for daily self-interrogation: 'Do I mourn for sin bitterly, give thanks for mercies heartily, pray fervently, Is my eye constantly upon the rule of God's Word?'[182]

Ministers such as Alleine and Watson were convinced that self-examination played a vital role in their people's devotional life, encouraging them to confess their failings, recognize their vulnerability, acknowledge their dependence, refine their ambitions and affirm their ideals. But, however important, self-examination was not allowed to dominate Nonconformist teaching about communion with God, and we turn now to the second aspect of the theme – waiting upon God for daily guidance, support and strength.

Receiving Divine Resources

In persecuting times, when a believer may be 'shut out from Ordinances, his soul may bee satisfied with Marrow and Fatness, when it meditates ... in the night-watches'.[183] In encouraging the practice of daily prayer, Nonconformist preachers affirmed their convictions, valued their mentors, expounded their priorities and confessed their difficulties.

Convictions

Prayer was an obligatory spiritual responsibility as well as an enriching privilege, and was given a threefold importance. It was vital for the believer's personal development, for the glory of God, and a means of helping others.

Personal prayer was 'the pitcher that fetcheth water from the Brook' said Bunyan, 'and for want of water the Garden withers'.[184] It was one of the 'Conduit-pipes whereby the water of life is derived from Christ into the hearts of Christians'.[185] With so many legal prohibitions, moral distractions and spiritual hindrances, daily prayer was their unique opportunity for intimate 'familiarity with God'.[186]

During the early months of his first imprisonment, Bunyan began to prepare a manuscript on this crucial theme. *I will Pray with the Spirit* became typical of his rich devotional writing across the years, skilfully combining biblical teaching, personal experience, pastoral sensitivity, simple and memorable

---

[182] Wells, *Spiritual Remembrancer*, 130–31; cf. Newcome, *Diary* (ed. Heywood), 30, for the '*pretious* use' of the searching questions Henry Newcome used in self-examination.
[183] Heywood, *Heart-Treasure*, 24.
[184] John Bunyan, *A Treatise of the Fear of God* (1679), in *MW*, IX, 5–132, at 120.
[185] Swinnock, *Calling*, I, 96.
[186] The emphasis on tender 'familiarity' is an important aspect of the Puritan doctrine of prayer, cf. Nuttall, *Holy Spirit*, 64; Sibbes, *Works* (ed. Grosart), I, 364; III, 456–57; William Dell, *The Building, Beauty, Teaching and Establishment of the truly Christian and Spiritual Church* (1651), 'To the Reader', [unpaginated]: 'Having obtained this grace from God to be called into some friendship and familiarity with Jesus Christ'.

everyday illustrations, clear homiletical structures (encouraging memorization) and, in this case, a polemical application, with a forthright attack on the Book of Common Prayer. He described 'true Prayer' as a trinitarian relationship with God, 'a sincere, sensible, affectionate pouring out of the heart or soul to God through Christ, in the strength and assistance of the holy Spirit'.[187]

'We seldom read of Gods appearing ... to any of his Prophets or Saints in a throng', said Baxter, 'but frequently when they were alone', claiming patristic support for his teaching.[188] The desire to pray was incontrovertible evidence of authentic spiritual experience: ''tis evermore the companion of true conversion to sett people a praying'.[189]

Howe observed that life's unwelcome experiences, such as illness, bereavement, deprivation and persecution, may become 'a means of the greatest advantage' if they drive a prayerless believer into the presence of a welcoming Father. God says that in trouble some Christians 'will seek me early, from whom, otherwise, I should never hear, it may be, all their life long'. He uses adversities that he may, 'upon any terms, hear from you' and 'when he has got you into a more tractable disposition, there is hope' of transformation.[190]

But seeking God in prayer was not done solely for personal advantage. Primarily it was for God's glory. These ministers had been denied opportunities for public service but, if they and their people wanted to do anything for God, they could do nothing better than pray. They insisted that it was always the highest and best form of service, and that nothing pleased God more than when a believer prayed. Preaching to his London congregation prior to ejectment, William Jenkyn told them that God was 'exceedingly taken' with the praying Christian when lovingly besought for 'Peace and Pardon, Peace of Conscience, Pardon of Sin, Strength against Sin'.[191]

Moreover, Jenkyn emphasized that, although their neighbours might not recognize it, intercessors made an incalculable contribution to the welfare of local society. 'Every Heavenly Prayer ... hath a worth that a carnall eye does not see'. Praying people, uniquely 'useful and beneficiall' in the community, were 'the great common blessings of the world'. Those who were 'pull'd down by the world, are those for whose sake God doth not pull down the world'.[192] George Newton spoke in similar terms. The 'fervent prayers of the meanest Saint are an Incredible defence to any place'.[193] Reminding Taunton people of

---

[187] Bunyan, *I will Pray with the Spirit* (1662/3), in *MW*, II, 235.
[188] Baxter, *Rest*, 715, quoting Cyprian and Chrysostom.
[189] Henry, *Diaries* (ed. Lee), 253 (cf. Acts 9: 11). Bunyan supports this conception of prayer as evidence of genuine conversion, contrasting the 'swarms of our praierless professors': *Strait Gate*, in *MW*, V, 82.
[190] Howe, 'Satan's Malice', in *Works* (ed. Hunt), IV, 203.
[191] Jenkyn, *Bush*, 10.
[192] Ibid. 9.
[193] George Newton, *A Sermon preached at the Funeral of Mr. Joseph Alleine* (1672), 33.

Alleine's work among them, Newton expressed his conviction that there was a special virtue in the intercessions of a 'Praying Minister', who served as a divinely appointed 'protection to the people'. He recalled the distinctive prayer ministry of biblical characters such as Moses, Aaron and Samuel (quoting Psa. 99: 6), convinced that, although 'some private Christians' might well '[e]xcel a holy Minister' in the gift of prayer, God was pleased to have special 'regard to the Intreaties of his faithful Ministers ... his Remembrancers for the good of that people'. Taunton believers were not only bereft of an exemplary leader but an effective intercessor; 'you have lost your covering if a storm of wrath should fall'.[194]

Mentors

Dissenters were indebted, therefore, not only to devoted teachers in the ministry of prayer but also to inspiring examples. Heywood advised his hearers to '[c]onsult with such Christians as converse much with God in a corner, and you shall see their faces shine as Moses' did'.[195] He grieved at the death of his father-in-law, John Angier: 'A praying Moses is gone'.[196] Many ejected ministers used farewell sermons to promise to intercede for their people when no longer able to instruct them. Though 'my lips be sealed up', said Philip Lamb, 'that I may not speak from God to you, yet I shall not cease to speak to God for you, as ever I have done'. Hostile parliamentary legislation could not rob them of that ministry. 'And though I cannot have you in my eye, yet I shall lodge you in my heart', asking 'nothing of you but your Prayers, [and] shall hope to meet you daily at the Throne of Grace'.[197]

Ardent and passionate prayer was what Quakers remembered most about George Fox. William Penn wrote that 'above all' else, Fox 'excelled in prayer'. It was the 'inwardness and weight of his spirit' and 'the reverence and solemnity' with which he approached God which impressed those who heard him pray. People were moved by 'the fewness' and yet the 'fulness of his words', and even those who had only limited contact with him were amazed at how his praying was 'used to reach others with consolation'. Penn thought Fox at prayer the 'most awful, living reverent frame' he had ever seen. Friends all over the country testified that Fox 'knew and lived nearer to the Lord than other men', for those believers that know God 'most, will see most reason to

---

[194] Newton, *Sermon*, 33–35.
[195] Heywood, *Heart-Treasure*, 133; cf. also idem, *Closet Prayer, a Christian Duty* (1671), 38–39, with its references to the prayer ministry of 'the magnanimous Luther'; William Gardner, a 'Martyr in Portugal'; George Wishart, 'one of the holiest men and choicest Reformers Scotland ever had'; and 'the great U[s]sher'.
[196] *Oliver Heywood's Life of John Angier of Denton* (Chetham Society, n.s. 97; Manchester, 1937), 74.
[197] Philip Lamb, in *Compleat Collection*, [unpaginated].

approach him with reverence and fear'.[198]

The example of praying people around them was a rich inspiration to Dissenters,[199] as were the earlier prayers of those that had gone ahead. Old Simeon Ashe was 'universally belov'd', well beyond the ranks of Presbyterians. His funeral took place on the day before the ejectment. No stranger to physical suffering, and often confined to home, he was 'always Chearful', and his London 'House was much frequented'. What colleagues valued far more than his generous hospitality was his 'fluent Elegancy in Prayer'. He had gone 'seasonably to Heaven, at the very Time when he was cast out of the Church' and with his passing church members, colleagues and the City itself 'lost the benefit of his prayers'. With this uppermost in mind, his friend Edmund Calamy spoke of him and all such intercessors as 'the Chariots and horsmen of a Nation', whose earnest secret prayers were the country's 'preservative'. Prayer was a 'Jewel that did beautifie and adorn' Ashe's entire ministry. On their Fast Days, he 'was the Minister that was chosen to conclude with prayer', so that his intercessions were in the minds of everyone as they made their way home. He was 'often in the Mount of God', so his 'Conceived prayers' were not 'vain Tautologies ... some unjustly charge men with', but 'the very breathings of God's Spirit'. In his final hours 'he was able to say, as Dr. Preston did as he lay a dying, "I shall change my place, but not my company" '.[200]

Thomas Vincent was one of the Dissenting ministers who stayed in London during the Great Plague to preach and provide physical and emotional support and essential pastoral care. He grieved that because of the ejectment of ministers and the more recent Five Mile Act, scores of men with great 'gifts of Prayer' had been robbed of their parish ministry. Without their influence, standards had degenerated, inviting God's judgement on a morally degraded court and people. Had any place been favoured with so 'many burning and shining lights'? 'O what prayers have there formerly been in London Pulpits'. How often, in 'confession of sin have they rak'd into the dunghil of a rotten heart', and with what compassion did they 'besiege God as it were' for his merciful forgiveness.[201]

In order to intercede without danger of arrest, many of these ministers and their colleagues prayed throughout the night. Samuel Shaw and his friends met

---

[198] William Penn, Preface to *The Journal of George Fox* (Bicentenary ed., 2 vols; 1891), I, xlvii–xlviii.
[199] Calamy says that, having such 'an admirable Gift in Prayer', the Wiltshire ejected minister Peter Ince, 'a great sufferer for his Nonconformity', was known among his friends as 'Praying Ince': *Account*, 60.
[200] Ibid. 1–2; *Continuation*, I, 1–6; Edmund Calamy, *The Righteous Man's Death Lamented* (1662), at the close of *London Minister's Legacy* [separately paginated], 3, 25–6; Sylvester (ed.), *Reliquiae*, I, ii, §420.
[201] T[homas]. V[incent]., *God's Terrible Voice in the City ... in the History of the two late dreadful Judgments of Plague and Fire in London* (1667), 25–27.

in an appointed home, and were 'fain to steal to the place in the Dark, stop out the Light and stop in the Voice, by cloathing and fast closing the windows, till the first Day break down a Chimney' gave them 'notice to be gone'.[202]

These congregations fervently believed that there was an undeniable correlation between the prayers of ministers and the blessings enjoyed by their people. Thomas Jolly's elderly mother told him of 'a good man, who laboured in the ministry without success' but, distressed at his apparent ineffectiveness, began 'keeping ... secret dayes in an old tree' and 'was much owned [of God] afterwards', to the transformation of his ministry and the great enrichment of his congregation.[203]

Priorities

Dissenters insisted that in their personal devotions, believers should pray regularly, sincerely, penitently, gratefully, compassionately and attentively.

'Open ye doore to God in ye morneinge'

The believer needs to pray with disciplined regularity, an injunction not as simple as it might first appear. Every day, innumerable distracting issues claimed their attention. Although prayer ought to be as natural as a dependent child frequently speaking to a caring father, the analogy frequently broke down. Bunyan was not alone in admitting that he did not always feel like praying. 'For ... when I go to pray, I find it so loth to go to God'. 'Oh the starting-holes ... in the time of Prayer!' and 'how many by-wayes the heart hath, and back-lains, to slip away' from his presence. Agonized in spirit, he had been 'strongly perswaded' to 'seek the Lord no longer'. But, then he remembered 'how large' were God's 'Promises ... to sinners', and that 'it was ... not the full, but the empty' that 'God 'extended his Grace and Mercy unto', and he turned again to prayer.[204]

Separated from his Kettering congregation, John Maidwell urged them: 'Slumber not over secret prayer'.[205] It was one of 'the great distinguishing Duties of an upright Christian', and its neglect was serious: 'May not our Closets ... witness against us?'[206] Painting a memorable word-picture, Bunyan exposes the inconsistency of a prayerless Christian life. Some believers, living in reasonably spacious homes, are pleased to say that they had a secluded room,

---

[202] *Account*, 426–36, at 435. Commenting on Shaw's 'melting Words in Prayer', one of his friends said he had heard him 'for two or three Hours together, pour out Prayer to God without Tautology or vain repetition ... as has dissolved the whole Company into Tears': ibid. 435–36.

[203] Jolly, *Note Book* (ed. Fishwick), 81, cf. 138.

[204] Bunyan, *MW*, II, 256–7, 265–66.

[205] Anon., 'The Prison Letters of Thomas [John] Maidwell', *TCHS* 3 (1907–8), 367–78, at 375.

[206] John Shower, *Serious Reflections on Time and Eternity* (1689), 187–88: 'How seldome are we there? How quickly are we gone? How easily diverted?'

highly convenient for private prayer; but Bunyan asks how frequently it is used. There is an 'iniquity that attends the Closet', when people 'have a Closet to talk of, not to pray in'. Could it speak, the room 'would say, my owner is seldom here upon his knees before the God of Heaven; seldom here humbling himself, for the iniquity of his heart, or to thank God for the mercies of his life'. When the tardy occupant eventually enters the room, he may do so, 'formally, carnally, and without reverence and godly fear', pleading 'for that in his Closet' which 'he cannot abide in his house, nor his life'.[207] Some prayer is crowded out by more attractive priorities, as in the case of those who 'do oftener frequent the Coffee-house than their closet'. People with materialistic ambitions appear to find it easier to rise early in the morning 'to make bargains, than to pray unto God, and begin the day with him'. But he that 'runs from God in the morning, will hardly find him at the close of the day', whereas the woman or man 'that finds God in his closet, will carry the favour of him into his house, his shop' and all the day's opportunities. Secret prayer enriches everything else. Bunyan recalled that when 'Moses had been with God in the Mount, his face shone', and his fellow-Israelites knew it, for 'he brought that glory into the camp'.[208]

Believers genuinely desiring to pray will always find an opportunity to do so. Whenever young Isaac Archer was away from home, or in unsympathetic company, he would 'walke out and pray, or pray in bed, or as I went home next day'.[209] Travelling was often used for quiet prayer. 'To Newport, alone,' wrote Philip Henry, 'but ye lord was with mee & I had often sweet communion with him by the way which is my strength and song.'[210]

People with a wide variety of occupations, many involving strenuous physical activity and frequently hindered by natural tiredness, were urged to give God their best by beginning their days with prayer. 'Open ye doore to God in ye morneinge, yt other th[in]gs come not in & keepe him out all ye day'.[211] They should not let 'worldly business thrust out heavenly duties but perform them in the first place',[212] at the start of every day, remembering that their 'first and last thoughts' in each day are 'of the greatest consequence'.[213]

Nothing, however good, must deflect them from prayer. When Henry Newcome and William Bagshaw met together they recalled the practice of a fellow-Minister that, whatever 'company he was in, w[he]n ye houre of prayer he had set came, he would tell ym he had a friende he must go to, and so ...

---

[207] Bunyan, *A Holy Life*, in *MW*, IX, 324–25.
[208] Ibid. 325–6, quoting Exod. 34: 29–35.
[209] Storey (ed.), *Two Diaries*, 106.
[210] Henry, *Diaries* (ed. Lee), 263.
[211] Newcome, *Diary* (ed. Heywood), 192.
[212] *Association Records of the Particular Baptists of England, Wales and Ireland to 1660*, Part II, *The West Country and Ireland* (ed. B.R. White, Baptist Historical Society; London, n.d.), 86.
[213] Alleine, *Letters*, 57 (14 November 1663).

would be excused'.[214] When persecution increased, prayer with others was an especially valuable means of support; to minimize the possibility of disturbance, night meetings became common. When Thomas Jolly was due to appear at his local assizes, his church gave 'Most of a night' to prayer for their minister and for 'many others in wors[e] condition, that fetters might fall off & prison doors fly open'.[215] Jolly's own practice was to set aside one day in each month when he went away to a quiet place, allocating specific topics for the entire day's prayers.[216]

Crowded homes, the presence of unsympathetic family members or occasional parental hostility meant that Dissenters often found it easier to pray outdoors. George Fox said that rather than 'hear the priest ... I would get into the orchard, or the fields, with my Bible, by myself'.[217] Many, like Bunyan, had 'sighed under every hedge for mercy'.[218] God's presence 'makes a croud, a Church', and revelation of his word 'maketh a closet, or solitary wood or field to be kin to the Angelical Chore [choir]'.[219] Many experienced a heightened sense of the divine presence outdoors in the created world. Sibbes had affirmed that every creature 'hath a beam of God's glory in it' and that the 'whole world is a theatre of the glory of God'.[220] As a young Oxford student, and in later life, Joseph Alleine was pleased 'to spend his most secret Hours' outdoors, 'in the by Places, in the Fields, or Woods'.[221] West Country Baptists were encouraged to remember 'that Isaac went out into the field to pray' and 'our Lord went out into a mountain apart to pray'.[222] Lawrence Spooner 'frequently retired into the fields' in times of increased persecution, where he 'spent a great part of the night in earnest cries'.[223] Prior to becoming a Quaker, young Josiah Langdale would often go with a friend 'on First Day Mornings into the Field, taking a Bible', so that they could read, meditate and pray together, frequently in silence.[224] Roger Lowe, a young Lancashire Dissenter, often prayed outdoors. 'Att night I, being somewhat sad, resorted to Ashton Town Heath, and there

---

[214] Newcome, *Diary* (ed. Heywood), 87.

[215] Jolly, *Note Book* (ed. Fishwick), 68.

[216] Ibid. 1, 2, 3, 5. Entries for most months from 1671–93 are found in the book; for example,'6th m. [1671] was upon the account of my temptation to security and worldlimindedness'; '9th m. was for confirming the covenant twixt God and my soul'; 11th m was to humble myself ... in this heavy stroke, that the lord should take away a son of such pregnant hopes'.

[217] Fox, *Journal* (ed. Smith), 10.

[218] Bunyan, *GA*, Preface, 3.

[219] Richard Baxter, *The Reasons of the Christian Religion* (1667), 458.

[220] Sibbes, *Works* (ed. Grosart), IV, 241, cf. 213.

[221] [Alleine], *Life*, 57.

[222] *Association Records*, II (ed. White), 86.

[223] James, *Abstract*, 10.

[224] London, Library of the Society of Friends, MS Box 10/10, 'Some Account of the Birth, Education and Religious Exercises and Visitations of God to Josiah Langdale' (1673–1725), fol.8.

poured out a prayer to God, being aside of a ditch. ... Som[e] what effected and betooke my selfe soliterily into Townes Feild and there kneeld me downe ... and prayed'.[225] After a day's preaching, the itinerant minister Henry Maurice made it his regular practice to pray 'out in the fields' before going on to the house where he was to spend the night.[226]

More than lip-labour

Sincerity was of infinitely greater importance than specific requests. The praying Christian does not 'wear two vizards ... for it is the heart that God looks at'.[227] For this reason Bunyan dismissed as 'lip-labour' the use of prayers composed by others; it was to ignore Christ's warning about 'vain repetitions'.[228] But Nonconformists did not speak with a single voice on the issue. An undated discussion paper prepared by Philip Henry, on 'Whether a stinted liturgy or set form of Prayer, publique or private bee lawful', outlines many of the arguments used in debating the divisive subject.[229] Most Presbyterians favoured a liturgical form of worship and therefore raised little objection to the use of 'composed' prayers in other contexts.[230] Independents and Baptists were, in the main, opposed to the 'stinted forms' of liturgical worship and to the use of any prepared prayers, believing that only 'conceived' or extempore prayer was appropriate in both public worship and personal devotion.[231]

Bunyan's *I will Pray with the Spirit* is a forceful attack on the Anglican liturgy. Its sharp invective is understandable; the imprisoned author had been indicted for not attending his parish church and was unlikely to appreciate its

---

[225] Lowe, *Diary* (ed. Sachse), 15, 27, cf. 16–17, 53, 58–59.

[226] B. Cottle and M.J. Crossley Evans, 'A Nonconformist Missionary Journey to Lancashire and Cheshire in July, 1672', *Transactions of the Historic Society of Lancashire and Cheshire* 137 (1987), 77–91, at 86–87.

[227] Bunyan, *I will Pray*, in *MW*, II, 237.

[228] In this, Dissenters were following the teaching of some early Puritans: cf. Horton Davies, *The Worship of the English Puritans* (1948), 103–108.

[229] Henry, *Diaries* (ed. Lee), 366–67.

[230] There were exceptions. William Bagshawe records his discomfort with a prescribed liturgy, maintaining that it was not imposed by the apostles, that the Lord's Prayer was not invariably used corporately in the early church, and that church history offered no convincing evidence of uniform liturgical worship. He claimed that some patristic references suggested the use of extempore prayer, and that 'prayers should answer to providences' and have 'a regard to everyone's circumstances', i.e., relate to contemporary issues: cf. his private notebooks, cited in J.M. Brentnall, *William Bagshawe: The Apostle of the Peak* (1970), 37.

[231] Writers as diverse as John Saltmarsh (*Sparkles of Glory*, 1647), Walter Cradock (*Glad Tydings from Heaven*, 1648*)*, George Fox (*Something in Answer to the Old Common Prayer Book*, 1660), Vavasor Powell (*Common Prayer Book No Divine Service*, 1660) and John Owen (*A Discourse Concerning Liturgies and their Imposition*, 1662) were opposed to liturgical prayer: Nuttall, *Holy Spirit*, 66–73; Greaves, *Glimpses*, 154–58.

liturgy. At his trial, he was appalled by the assertion of one of the justices that the Book of Common Prayer 'hath been ever since the Apostles time'. Bunyan's swift response was: 'shew me the place in the epistles, where the Common Prayer-book is written, or one text of Scripture, that commands me to read it, and I will use it'.[232]

Baxter's moderate approach favoured both liturgical and extempore prayer in public worship, and did not deny the usefulness of written prayers in private. His books frequently contained prayers he had composed 'as Spectacles to dark Sights', and 'Sermon Notes to weak Memories', acknowledging that written prayers were 'oft[en] a help' to him, as to others, especially younger Christians, who 'cannot at first pray well (at least before others) without them'. Many mature believers were also pleased to use them, matching 'their Affections to sound words oft repeated'.[233] William Thomas shared Baxter's view that written prayers were 'composed for young Beginners ... to train them ... to go first by a Form, that leaving the form, which was a great help at first, they may go ... without leaning on such Supports'. Thomas recalls that the Marian martyr John Bradford, 'when he was in prison, wrote a prayer for his Mother that she might learn how to pray for him', desiring her 'to say it dayly', and wrote 'another for all her house, to make use of in their Evening Prayer'. Thomas reminded Nonconformists of the many prayers in Scripture, in addition to the Lord's Prayer, encouraging their use by praying believers.[234]

But Bunyan was unconvinced: 'let not thy mouth go any further than thou strivest to draw thine heart along with it'.[235] He had met many, like Justice Keeling, 'so hot for Forms' but 'not the Power of prayer. Scarce one of forty among them, know what it is to ... have communion with the Father through the Son ... but for all their prayers, they still live cursed, drunken, whorish and abominable Lives'. He had little time for those who had their prayers 'at their finger ends ... for such a day, and that twenty years before it comes. One for *Christmass*, another for *Easter*, and six dayes after that ... All which the

---

[232] Bunyan, *Relation of My Imprisonment*, with *GA*, 117.
[233] *An Account of the Reasons*, 19, printed with Richard Baxter, *Catholick Communion Defended against both Extreams* (1684), 19. Baxter's *Account* addressed 'Twelve Arguments said to be Dr. John Owen's, noting Judgment about Communion with Parish Churches'. Dealing with Owen's belief that written prayers' were 'Romish', denying the Spirit's work, Baxter asked: 'Do you think when Calvin formed the Liturgy for Geneva and France, he had so Malignant a Design, as to defeat the Spirit's help? Or do our English Psalms and Tunes quench the Spirit?' He was persuaded that 'that which hurteth some, may be a help to others ... May not a man use the Lord's Prayer by the Sprit's help?'
[234] William Thomas, *A Preservative of Piety* (1662), 'Epistle to the Reader', [unpaginated]. For the prayer Bradford prepared for his mother's use, see Foxe, *Acts and Monuments* (ed. Pratt), VII, 264–66. Thomas also makes marginal reference to [John Philpot], 'A Prayer to be said at the stake by those that God shall count worthy to suffer', ibid., VII, 686.
[235] Bunyan, *I will Pray*, in *MW*, II, 277.

Apostles came short of'.[236]

Those Puritan ministers who conformed in 1662 were frequently embarrassed about using the new liturgy and often preferred 'conceived' prayer. Ralph Josselin was ill at ease on the first Sunday the new Prayer Book was 'laid in the deske' for him. Finding it there the following Sunday he 'used part in the morning, but in the afternoon [it was] taken away'. The next Sunday he comments that the new book was '[b]rought again, but pitcht and abused'.[237] Citing Malachi's injunction about offering God the best, the young ordinand Isaac Archer greatly preferred extempore or 'conceived prayer'. It 'followed my affections, and was the language my wants dictated to mee'. He confessed that he had 'a grudge' when compelled to use the Prayer Book, 'because it affected mee no more'.[238]

Many of these ministers had been greatly influenced at university by the godly lives of Puritan tutors or chaplains, and came to adopt many of their mentors' firmly held convictions. When George Trosse was a student at Oxford, the chaplain of his college, 'a pious and gracious Person, who had an excellent Gift of Prayer', once prayed in chapel 'with the most proper Language ... and ... Elevation of Soul'. But the new master of the college 'unworthily revil'd him, taxing him with Pride and Impudence ... that he thought his own tautological Prayers and crude Notions better than the Common-Prayer', and did this 'before all the Scholars present'. The master brought the Prayer Book 'into the Desk, and there read it' with 'Incredible Swiftness ... running a Race'. Trosse 'was grieved to see a Prayer read, as a School-Boy reads his Lesson, instead of the Pouring out such warm Prayers as we had been accustom'd to'.[239]

The experience of the young Trosse might be placed alongside that of the elderly Bagshawe. During his final illness, a young minister came specially to pray with him. Bagshawe 'joined heartily in every Petition ... blessing God that had help'd' his visitor with 'such apt Expressions', making him 'wonder' that some people were so opposed to 'free (or premeditated) Prayer'. Bagshaw said: 'there is not a Prayer in all their Book wou'd have suited my Present Circumstances so well as this has done'.[240]

Yet even Dissenters who were unhappy about set forms of prayer did not imagine that extempore prayer was free from abuse. In later life Bunyan was painfully aware that some 'conceived' prayer was more notable for its length than for its sincerity. 'To pray by a Book ... is now out of fashion. He is counted no body now that cannot at anytime, at a minutes warning, make a

---

[236] Ibid. 240, 247–48.
[237] Josselin, *Diary* (ed. Macfarlane), 492 (12, 19, 26 October 1662).
[238] Storey (ed.), *Two Diaries*, 100.
[239] *The Life of George Trosse* (ed. A.W. Brink; Montreal, 1974; first publ. 1714), 119–20.
[240] John Ashe, *A Short Account of the Life of the Rev. Mr. William Bagshaw* (1704), 9–10.

Prayer of an half hour long. I am not against Extempore prayer' for 'there are a great many such Prayers made, especially in Pulpits' but, he added sadly, 'without the breathing of the Holy Ghost in them'.[241]

Want of mercy

Genuine sincerity was best expressed in confession of sin. Self-examination made praying believers more sensitive to personal unworthiness, readily acknowledging 'the sin that cleaveth to the best' spiritual 'performances'.[242] The loftiest prayers could degenerate into selfishness, pride and ostentation. There was need of 'a sence of the want of mercy, by reason of the danger of sin ... Prayer bubleth out of the heart when it is over-pressed with grief and bitterness ... and that first from a sence of sin.' Quoting the remorseful King David, Bunyan recalled that it is 'not long discourses, nor eloquent tongues, that are ... pleasing in the ears of the Lord; but a *humble, broken and contrite heart*'. But equally, sin could keep a believer from prayer: 'If I regard iniquity in my heart, the Lord will not hear my Prayer.'[243]

Moreover, prayer exposed sin. The bright light of God's holiness contrasted sharply with human transgression. When Henry Newcome 'prayed in secret', he became aware of his personal failings; in his case, unworthy thoughts 'in ye night' and his reluctance to practice self-denial.[244] On the evening preceding a family day of prayer, John Angier would urge his children and servants 'to search out and confess their sins', and always 'used such means as might by God's help prove effectual for [the] reformation both of himself and his Family'.[245]

Some occasion ... for gratitude

Nonconformists were encouraged to make thanksgiving a dominant feature in their prayers. 'Thankfulness ... proceeds from pure grace', said Thomas Goodwin. 'Self-love makes us more forward to pray than to give thanks, for nature is all of the craving and taking hand'. But '[g]reat blessings that are won with prayer are worn with thankfulness: such a man will not ask [for] new [things], but he will withal give thanks for old'.[246]

Eager not to overlook God's kindness, many Dissenters itemized their reasons for thanksgiving. Saturday evening was a time when Newcome looked back over the preceding days, clearly recording God's 'Mercys ys [this] week'.[247]

---

[241] Bunyan, *A Discourse upon the Pharisee and the Publicane* (1685), in *MW*, X, 129.
[242] Bunyan, *Strait Gate*, in *MW*, V, 122.
[243] Bunyan, *I will Pray*, in *MW*, II, 237–38, 272–73 (cf. Psa. 51: 17; 66: 18).
[244] Newcome, *Diary* (ed. Heywood), 68.
[245] *Life of Angier*, 95.
[246] Goodwin, *Works*, III, 389–90.
[247] E.g. Newcome, *Diary* (ed. Heywood), 55: '1. Prevented passion. 2. Preserved children from hurt at shootinge. 3. Children ill and yet no worse. 4. Ye glorious publicke

Specific days of thanksgiving were kept for a variety of blessings. Heywood and his friends did so for the 'deliverance in child bearing' of five wives in their local congregation.[248] Newcome shared one in special gratitude for a fellow minister's recovery from illness.[249] As Angier 'took more occasions than many others of keeping days of thanksgiving so God gave him still more occasions of thankfulness'. He noticed that 'when a day of thankfulness was appointed, God sent in some fresh matter to increase [their] joy in the Lord'. God so welcomes 'that lovely duty, that he incourageth to it'. In his final illness, Angier said: 'what a mercy is it! my understanding is as good as ever in all my life ... that tho my bones are vexed, my soul is not sore vexed'; and again, 'I bless God I am not afraid of death'.[250] The end of each year provided further opportunity for a thanksgiving day. Aware that he had been specially helped during local persecution, Thomas Jolly invited local ministers to join him in thanksgiving 'under my roof, the church not thinking it convenient [wise] to meet there in the day time'.[251] Even when he lost his eldest son, he 'gott up to keep a day of thanksgiving ... on behalf of my son deceased' and in bereavement listed eight reasons for personal gratitude that God had given him such a fine son.[252]

Not hedgehogs

In any believer's prayer life, self-centred insularity was a lurking danger. Some are 'never moved to pray, but in their own ... distresses'. William Gouge likened them to the loveless priest or preoccupied Levite in the Lucan parable, passing by 'on the other aside'. There is 'no one thing' in the world 'whereby we can be more beneficiall and doe more good to any' than 'in and by Prayer'. To neglect compassionate intercession is both 'plaine inhumanity' and 'plaine Atheism'. It is to 'bewray [betray] too much self-love' and 'too much distrust in God'. When Jesus urged his followers to love their enemies, 'hee addeth, Pray for them'. Love 'is a debt which we owe to our brother' and 'they which neglect it, sinne'.[253] Taking leave of his Buckinghamshire congregation, George

---

respite iust in due time. 5. Kindness of my natural friends to mee. 6. Others' kindness continued'.
[248] Heywood, *Autobiography* (ed. Turner), II, 94.
[249] Newcome, *Autobiography* (ed. Parkinson), I, 180. Local churches also kept Thanksgiving Days for such occasions as their 'Pastor's recovery out of a violent sickness': Cockermouth Independent Church Book, 21.
[250] *Life of Angier*, 74, 114.
[251] Jolly, *Note Book* (ed. Fishwick), 67.
[252] Ibid. 6. His son had been preparing for the ministry, and had been helped spiritually by an excellent tutor; he 'was in some measure kept from the sins of the times or was humbled wherein hee had stepped aside'; his illness 'gave mee and him time to prepare'; he had a safe journey 'going to see' his sick son and bringing him back home; he was sure his son was safe eternally; God had supported him in his great loss, and had greatly helped his distressed wife, especially when Jolly had to be away from home.
[253] William Gouge, *The Whole Armour of God*, in *Works*, I, 182–83.

Swinnock told them that the believer 'who prayeth for himself and not for others, is fitly compared to a Hedghog who laps himself within his own soft down, and turns his brissels to all the world beside'.[254] The 'secret place' and corporate 'fast day' alike must look beyond personal and domestic issues, and must have a window on the outside world. Although it is not their primary aim, intercessors discover that their own lives are enriched when they pray for others. God 'never revealed his love to Moses more than when he prayed most for God's people'.[255] Believers experiencing persecution were always on the hearts of their fellows, especially those suffering imprisonment. Mary Franklin wrote to her minister husband, Robert, when he was in Aylesbury gaol to tell him that his London church members had appointed a day to be 'keept at mr. coopers' to 'seek ye lord [on] thy behalf'.[256]

Corporate prayer had a unifying effect in the life of local churches. Nonconformists of different denominational traditions recognized the benefit of uniting for prayer, especially when local leaders were under arrest. Four congregations in Bristol gathered in 1675 to pray for two of their convicted ministers and two members who had been sent to Westminster for trial. This 'union, and joynt praying together, was Much liked of, by all parties ... driven together by this universall trouble'. They met quarterly for united intercession and on additional 'Occasionall dayes ... as often as need should require', exploring other ways in which they might encourage each other in difficult times.[257]

Praying with compassion reminded Dissenters not to ignore the practical needs of those for whom they were praying. Whenever John Angier had a fast day at his home, 'it was his way to inquire concerning [the] fatherless and Widows, and such as were in [any] necessity' in the local community, 'that something might be sent to them, for whom nothing was provided, as he often said'.[258]

Dialogues between us and him

Preachers frequently emphasized the importance of praying attentively, reminding their hearers that praying people should carefully listen for God's instructions in prayer and deliberately look for specific answers to their prayers.

Prayer was listening as well as asking. Cut off from his Kettering congregation, John Maidwell wrote to tell them to 'mind what God says to you as well as what you say to God'.[259] While praying, they should wait quietly to

---

[254] George Swinnock, *The Pastors Farewell and Wish of Welfare to his People* (1662), 23–24.
[255] Goodwin, *Works*, III, 366.
[256] Anon., 'The Prison Correspondence of an Ejected Minister', *TCHS* 1 (1901–4), 345–52, at 347.
[257] *Broadmead Records* (ed. Hayden), 159–63.
[258] *Life of Angier*, 95, an intended echo of Neh. 8: 10.
[259] Anon., 'Letters of Maidwell', 375.

hear whether God might be reminding them of something he had already said about their needs. Somebody who had 'been long praying against poverty, or the like distress' might discover that in the stillness 'God lets fall this or the like promise into thy heart, *I will never leave thee or forsake thee* ... which quiets and contents thy mind. This is an answer ... observe such answers, for they are precious.'[260] As Bunyan was praying, a word of Scripture would often 'dart' into his mind, meeting some of the need for which he was seeking guidance.[261]

They must also look, paying careful attention to the precise way in which God answered their prayers. Heywood kept a careful record of 'Remarkable Returns of Prayer', which included the period when he was imprisoned in York Castle for almost a whole year. Prevented from exercising his vigorous itinerancy, he could still pray and noted with what frequency, and in what way, his prayers were answered.[262] Our 'speaking to God by prayers, and his speaking to us by answers, is one great part of our walking with God', and praying people should 'compare our prayers and his answers together', for they are 'dialogues between us and him'. When the prayerful Dissenter looks carefully for answers, it will encourage thanksgiving. 'The reason you pray so much, and give thanks so little, is that you observe not God's answers; you do not study them.' Looking for answers will tell them a great deal about themselves. They 'will gain much insight' into their 'own hearts, and ways, and prayers, and ... learn how to judge of them'.[263] It indicates whether they are trusting in God, contented and grateful, or faithless, despondent and disgruntled.

Scrutinizing their prayers may not have been a comfortable exercise, but many proved it a necessary and profitable one. What they asked for exposed their values and priorities.

DIFFICULTIES

Thomas Goodwin wrote *The Return of Prayers* for believers who feared 'that little or nothing comes of all their prayers'.[264] The discipline of prayer was not easy and raised a series of recurrent spiritual and pastoral problems. Three of the most common difficulties were, first, their bewilderment at God's apparent indifference, not answering their prayers in the way they expected; second, their frustration at his possible weariness with them for praying so badly; and, third, their disappointment at his seeming distance or absence when they were

---

[260] Goodwin, *Works*, III, 377, quoting Heb. 13: 5.
[261] Bunyan, *GA*, §204, cf. 270. Cf. the similar experience (and language) of one of his young church members '[t]hat Scripture would often dart into my mind': *Narrative* (ed. Harrison), 8 (quoting Psa. 50: 15); 'Towards night that Scripture would often run in my mind [quoting Job 5: 19] ... And yt was A mighty word to mee [quoting Deut. 33: 27]': ibid. 51, cf. 22, 24, 25, 36, 42.
[262] Heywood, *Autobiography* (ed. Turner), IV, 64–171.
[263] Goodwin, *Works*, III, 362–63.
[264] Ibid. 356.

engaged in the exercise of earnest prayer.

Their Bewilderment

A frequent problem was the perplexity of 'unanswered prayer'. The ejected minister Samuel Birch kept a prayer journal and, prior to the Restoration, recorded a lengthy account of 'the great dissapointments which I have undergone, and the contrary returnes which the Lord hath made to my prayers in 18. months past'.[265] Thomas Goodwin insisted that God always answers prayer but that we are slow to 'spy out', or identify, the answers. God is sometimes 'wronged' by us 'standing ... as debtor' in a petitioner's 'accounts' even though he has been a 'creditor long ago'.[266]

Sometimes God is determined to answer Dissenters' prayers, but not in their lifetime. Stephen prayed for his aggressors, says Goodwin, but did not live to see one of the worst become an incomparably gifted advocate. Paul urged Timothy to pray for kings, that Christians may 'lead a quiet and peaceable life', but such prayers were hardly answered in Nero's reign nor were they 'accomplished till Constantine's time'. Some of the most fervent requests, such as 'the conversion of those thou hadst prayed for', may not be answered until the intercessor is in heaven.[267] Goodwin says that praying people may not see an immediate answer, but the fact that they have prayed what may possibly have been a difficult prayer, such as for ruthless enemies, was likely to result in special blessing upon them. The opponents may not improve but the intercessor might, and that may be the best answer to their prayer. There are other times when, in making a specific request, an earnest yet attentive petitioner may come to discover something new about God. The 'revealing of himself is oftentimes all the answer' God 'intended to such a prayer' so that, instead of 'a particular mercy', the believer might enjoy the increased 'assurance of God's love.'

In times of persecution, Dissenters would have appreciated Goodwin's example of someone who might 'pray against some evil coming upon his church', which God in his sovereign wisdom 'yet intends to bring'. But along with it they are given peace and comfort, the assurance that 'it shall go well with thee, and that thou art greatly beloved of him'; in such times, we are 'to take this for all the answer he means to give'. They might not escape the threatened onslaught, but appropriate resources are not lacking.[268]

God sometimes enables petitioners to realize that they can be the answer to their own prayers, 'to be ... carver' of their own 'mercies'. Or, when the answer is delayed, God may be asking them to think about how the petition was framed. Did they pray submissively, as Christ did in Gethsemane? Did they

---

[265] Nuttall, 'Prayer-Journal', 347.
[266] Goodwin, *Works*, III, 384, 356–57.
[267] Ibid. 365–66, quoting Acts 7: 60; 1 Tim. 2: 2.
[268] Ibid. 370, 378.

'trust God's judgment in the thing', says Goodwin, 'and not thine own'? At times, the specific thing prayed for is denied but the petitioner receives 'some greater and further mercy ... If we had had many of our desires, we had been undone ... so the denial of a godly man's prayer ... is laid as a foundation of a greater mercy.' Sometimes 'the very denial breaks a man's heart, and brings him nearer to God' and 'by the loss of that one thing he learns how to pray better, and so obtain a hundred better things afterward'. Praying people must ask whether 'there be not a ... turning of the thing desired into some other greater blessing ... for God ... doth improve ... and lay out the precious stocks' of our prayers 'to the best advantage'. Goodwin has a helpful illustration: an English tradesman has an overseas agent to whom he 'sends for such and such commodities', supposing them to be the very best for sale in this country. But the agent, 'knowing the state of things and the prices, sends him over, instead of them, such as shall sell better and bring in more profit'. He may be said 'to answer his letters ... better than if he had sent those very commodities he writ for'.[269] God answers their prayers, but not always in the way they expect. Henry said much the same. 'Though the answer be not always in the thing asked, yet it is in something else as good, or better.'[270]

Heywood encouraged his scattered Yorkshire congregations to continue praying even 'if thou gettest little thereby ... yet wait on God still', illustrating his point from the familiar world of local commerce: 'Trades-men will go to Markets and Fairs, and set open their Shop-doors, and Windows, though there be little to be done or gotten many times'. Likewise, 'the Christian [should] keep this market of holie duties' and also 'go upon the Exchange to spie what good bargain he can meet with for his soul ... '[L]earn to maintain commerce with heaven stil[l], lest you lose your custome'.[271]

Bunyan also raised the issue of seemingly 'unanswered' prayer, insisting that 'delayes ... are no tokens of his displeasure' and that God 'may hide his face from his dearest Saints'. He shares his own experience of baffling delays, when he could do little else than 'cleave to him ... though for the present he made no answer'. Believers should remain in total dependence and 'continue, though it be long', trusting with the prophet Habakkuk that in God's time an answer will come.[272]

The reluctant conformist minister Isaac Archer had already lost two young daughters, and pleaded with God to spare the life of his young son. His diary records the parents' bewildered sorrow but persistent faith.

---

[269] Ibid. 383–84, 394–95.
[270] Letter to Henry Ashurst, 15 December 1686, in Henry, *Life*, 163. This letter, concerning Ashurst's prayers for a sick child, is one of a series of monthly letters exchanged between Henry and Ashurst, which offer similar perspectives on 'unanswered' prayer to those of Goodwin.
[271] Heywood, *Heart-Treasure*, 130.
[272] Bunyan, *I will Pray*, in *MW*, II, 265–66, quoting Hab. 2: 3.

We both had a kind of perswasion that he would live with us, because he was obtained by prayer ... But God saw good to take him away ... Thus my confidence was dashed, and God is unaccountable for what he doth ... I reckoned my case like Abraham's, and Hannah's and the Shunamites ... God may answer prayer in anger, and deny in mercy; and I will love God stil[l].[273]

Their Frustration

Lack of concentration and wandering and distracting thoughts presented additional difficulties for these praying people. Ministers were no less vulnerable than their members. Newcome once felt at his 'baselyest' and 'defeated' during 'pretious' family prayers, with intrusive 'thoughts of a balcony betw[een] ye kitchen and parlour window. A th[ing] never thought of at another time.'[274] As a young Cambridge student, Archer wrote for help from his Puritan father, troubled not only 'with vaine thoughts in prayer' but also because he 'would sleep at prayers in my tutour's chamber'. His father's reply attributed such distractions to Satan's work; his son 'must watch ... and that was the way to weaken' the enemy 'and drive thees fowles away which would eat up my sacrifice, as Abraham did'. It was important for him to 'goe on cheerfully', knowing that he 'could not be freed from' such distractions 'in this life, though they should be [his] burden'.[275]

Nathanel Vincent wrote comprehensively about 'distractions', sharing biblical insights as well as personal and pastoral experience. He confessed that a sense of his own 'Wandrings', both in private prayer and in the exercise of his public ministry, had driven him to 'more serious study how to prevent them'.[276] He held that the quality of a believer's devotional life improved every other human activity; 'everything else' in life 'would be done the better'.[277] His leading ideas on 'wandering thoughts' might best be interpreted with the aid of a series of negatives.

First, he urged praying believers not to be surprised by distractions. A sinister enemy was determined to 'step into the Chariot' of their daily prayer life 'and begin to drive it away from God'.[278] There is no one 'this bold Enemy will not set upon, since he tempted Christ himself'; 'no wonder if he perswades

---

[273] Storey (ed.), *Two Diaries*, 159, quoting Gen. 22: 9–14; 1 Sam. 1: 11–12, 27; 2 Kings 4: 8–37.
[274] Newcome, *Diary* (ed. Heywood), 21.
[275] Storey (ed.), *Two Diaries*, 62, quoting Gen. 15: 11. Baxter similarly told his readers that their hearts could 'betray' them in prayer by trivial thoughts. The restless mind 'will be turning aside like a careless servant, to talk with every one that passeth by', but if 'the ravenous fowls of wandering thoughts, do devour the Meditations intended for Heaven', believers were to '[d]rive away these birds of prey ... from thy sacrifice' by 'watchfulness and violence with your own imaginations': Baxter, *Rest*, 772–74.
[276] Nathanael Vincent, *Cure of Distractions in attending upon God in several sermons preached from 1 Cor.7: 35* (1695), 'To the Reader'.
[277] Ibid., Ep. Ded. A3r–A3v.
[278] Ibid. 147

us not to worship God'. In the sanctity of the Upper Room, he 'set upon Judas and entred him, while he was with Christ himself at the Table'. How then can 'you imagine that when you are about to draw nigh to God, Satan will not ... lay baits ... to divert your Minds from the Work of God'.[279]

Second, prayerful believers are not to be daunted by distractions. All is imperfect this side of Heaven. Distracting thoughts are 'a Fault that is most easily incurred', says Vincent.[280] There are 'sinful imperfections ... as well as actings of grace' in our highest and best endeavours.[281] Genuine concern about defective praying is God's choice gift. It is by 'Grace in the Heart, that its Wandrings are perceived', and such imperfections are 'common to all Gracious Souls'. Christians are engaged in warfare, and 'tis part of their Militancy to be conflicting with distracted Thoughts'.[282] Indifference to such hindrances is a symptom of spiritual decadence. The 'less a Saint is troubled at his own Distractions ... God is the more displeased'.[283]

Third, prayerful believers must not be complacent about distractions. Imperfection does not excuse indolence. The quest to pray more acceptably must never be abandoned, and 'acceptable' praying is that which pleases God rather than satisfies the petitioner. Unbelief is an infinitely greater hindrance than the occasional distracting thought, and 'Discontent, and Impatience quite spoils Prayer'. Jonah prayed but was dejected in doing so because God had acted in a way that vexed him. 'How could the Lord be pleased with Jonah's Petition?'[284] 'Uncharitableness' of any kind threatens prayer because it 'imbitters' and has 'a monopoly of the thoughts, and fixes them upon Injuries received', even when they are 'but imaginary injuries ... Perhaps revenge ... is wish'd for, and meditated' upon, even in the place of prayer. When the believer comes to pray, 'there is so much anger ... against Man that God's anger is not feared ... neither is his love valued'.[285] When the minds of believers are seriously focused on prayer, intrusive thoughts will not always be bad. 'If the subtle Serpent cannot divert the Mind ... by bad thoughts, he will endeavour to do it by good ones'. 'A good thought becomes a bad one' when it is 'entertained at a time that is not proper for it'. Such distractions not only 'make us forget what we are doing' but, more seriously, the holy God 'to whom we are speaking'.[286]

Fourth, praying believers should not be deflected by distractions. When the restless mind wanders in prayer, the diversion must be used, not shunned. Whether the alien thought is good or bad, its sudden arrival is revealing. An

---

[279] Ibid. 202–203.
[280] Ibid. 146.
[281] Ibid. 184.
[282] Ibid. 253–54.
[283] Ibid. 186.
[284] Ibid., citing Jonah 4: 2–3.
[285] Ibid. 209.
[286] Ibid. 153.

item has been placed on the mind's priority agenda that might enrich prayer if, instead of being dismissed as an unwelcome intruder, it is treated as a beneficial stimulus, prompting the petitioner to turn the 'distracting' thought into earnest prayer. If the thought is unworthy it should be turned to confession. Distracting thoughts may concern life's immediate needs. The earnest petitioner becomes aware that, far from praying, she is trying to manage domestic finances. These 'Wants' and 'the necessity of having them supplied' are appropriate invasions. Vincent says they must be transformed from distracting anxieties to specific requests, confidently addressed to an 'all-sufficient' God, eager to supply those needs, 'be the Wants never so great and many'. An awareness of other people may steal into 'our Minds when we are before God', and these thoughts can be changed from alien diversions to compassionate intercessions. Vincent recalls that while Paul was praying in a Roman dungeon, young Timothy's needs frequently came into his mind. The imprisoned apostle turned affectionate concern into heartfelt prayer, spanning the continents as he remembered Ephesus, where his vulnerable colleague was coping with the undoubted hazards and rich opportunities of ministry in a pagan environment. Thoughts came flooding in: Timothy's godly inheritance, inevitable trials, undoubted needs and available resources, as well as Paul's natural and repeated desire to see him again (2 Tim. 1: 3-8, cf. 4: 9, 21). Such thoughts had, both 'night and day', become passionate prayers, and 'a matter of thanksgiving' that, separated by distance, the apostle 'was at the Throne of Grace', playing his part as an informed intercessor for a valued successor.[287]

Fifth, praying believers must not feel defeated over distractions. With perceptive sensitivity, Vincent deals at some length with the issue of wandering thoughts in the experience of a Christian prone to depression. 'Melancholy' was one of the prevalent 'Diseases of the Minde' in the period,[288] and many genuine believers were troubled by deep and recurrent despondency. Bunyan seems to have been severely harassed by it at specific times in his life.[289] On a number of occasions Baxter reveals his compassionate concern by writing helpfully about it.[290] Vincent brought to the discussion the pastoral experience

---

[287] Ibid. 181–82.

[288] Robert Burton, *The Anatomy of Melancholy* (1628), Pt I, i.3 (7); cf. Michael Macdonald, *Mystical Bedlam: Madness, Anxiety and Healing in Seventeenth-Century England* (Cambridge, 1981), 150–60.

[289] His spiritual autobiography, *Grace Abounding*, depicts a frequently tortured soul, deeply disturbed about his sins and the need for assurance. On at least one occasion during imprisonment, 'it being my turn to speak', he felt 'empty, spiritless and barren', unable 'to speak among them so much as five words of Truth, with Life and Evidence': *MW*, III, 69. But he did speak, an exposition which was expanded into *The Holy City, or the New Jerusalem* (1665); cf. Greaves, *Glimpses*, 35–41, 51–60, 174–76, 201–202, 232–43, 422–24, 602–603.

[290] Sylvester (ed.), *Reliquiae*, III, §184; Baxter, *Christian Directory*, in *Works* (ed. Orme), III, 218–38; *God's Goodness Vindicated for the help of such (especially in Melancholy) as are tempted to deny it* [1671], ibid., VIII, 509–33; *The Right Method for*

of a lifetime, urging depressed Christians not to give up praying because of distracting thoughts. He extends his practical advice to believers who are unwell or deeply troubled about life's serious problems, encouraging them to pray briefly but frequently. 'It is not length but life ... that God looks at.' Short prayers are best, and they should use their prayer times to 'look unto Jesus', concentrating specifically on the supportive Christ rather than the perceived barrenness of their prayers.[291] A believer suffering from depression should postpone two otherwise helpful spiritual disciplines until the dark clouds begin to lift. The first is meditation, which demands a measure of concentration likely to prove difficult, making 'the Head ... ake' and possibly enveloping the depressed mind in an additional 'mist of Confusion'. The second, self-examination, is more perilous still. In such an exercise, Christians prone to depression will find themselves passing numerous 'Censures and Judgment upon themselves'. The devil will capitalize on gloomy introspection and be extra 'busie about them', insinuating that 'they are Hypocrites and have no Grace, that they are cast away and utterly forsaken by the God of all Grace'.[292] Although they would be wise to avoid these two disciplines, they should continue to pray, even if they feel that 'their performances are but mean and sorry'. Their God is omniscient and compassionate, discerning 'sense in the soul, when perhaps there is hardly any sense in the words', for 'he takes notice of the ... good inclination of the heart towards himself'. When, 'against the Will', their 'Thoughts ... do wander', he will meet them with appropriate resources.[293]

Finally, Vincent pleads with believers troubled by distractions not to be forgetful. Three great Christological themes must fill the horizons of believers whose prayers are marred by wandering thoughts. They must remember Christ's atonement in the past, his intercession in the present and his promise for the future. His atoning death 'made compleat Satisfaction' for 'the sins of their holy things' as well as for all 'their other Iniquities' in life. All 'faulty and imperfect' prayers, though they seem 'nothing but Sin and Distraction', are presented by Christ to the Father, their evident 'defects covered with Christ's Righteousness'. Christ is their present Intercessor. Now in heaven 'he ceases not to intercede for Believers' and, although 'a thousand faults ... be found' in

---

a Settled Peace of Conscience and Spiritual Comfort, ibid., IX, 22–25; *Obedient Patience: Its nature in General and its exercise in Twenty particular cases*, ibid., XI, 450–60; *The Cure of Melancholy and Overmuch Sorrow by Faith and Physic*, ibid., XVII, 235–85; *The Poor Man's Family Book*, ibid., XIX, 416–30. See also the references in Baxter's correspondence: *Calendar* (ed. Nuttall and Keeble); N.H. Keeble (ed.), *A Subject Index to the Calendar of the Correspondence of Richard Baxter, with another Baxter Letter* (DWL Occasional Paper 13; 1994), s.v. 'Melancholy'.

[291] With similar pastoral concern, Baxter advises those suffering from depression to pray briefly: *Christian Directory*, in *Works* (ed. Orme), IV, 311.

[292] Vincent, *Cure*, 192–94.

[293] Ibid. 196.

their best prayers, he 'sees some Fire in the Smoking Flax', even though there might be 'much that is offensive with it ... When a well of Water is muddy at the top', there can be 'purer Water working up from the Spring at the bottom'. God 'will not utterly reject' their prayers, 'when there is a hearty desire to do it well, and an hearty grief 'tis done no better'.[294] Christ's promise is for a better future. In the heaven he has prepared, entered and guaranteed to believers, all 'Distractions and Complaints' in prayer 'will be at a perpetual end'. Then, 'out of Satan's reach', no unworthy thoughts will hinder. 'The Vision of God Face to Face, will fix the Mind and Thoughts upon him eternally' for, 'having once looked on, they will never care to look off [any] more'.[295]

Vincent was at pains to apply these biblical insights by offering practical advice to those longing for uninterrupted communion with God. Let their first waking thoughts in the morning be of God. 'As soon as you are awake, let your Souls work Heaven-ward ... If the Lord has ... the first thoughts and desires, you are likely to be blest with better thoughts and desires afterwards.' Frequent short prayers will 'mightily help to keep a sense of him upon your Hearts' throughout the day. The praying believer's 'Hopes should be high' for 'we are not able to conceive how much he can do for us'. Total dependence is vital, for to be 'very poor in Spirit' is to have a 'pressing sense of ... spiritual Necessities'. When the 'condemned Malefactor ... cries for a pardon' he is not troubled with wandering thoughts; people with 'such a smart feeling of their Needs ... can scarce think of any thing besides'.[296]

Their Disappointment

Another problem commonly acknowledged, especially by ministers, was the lack of any awareness of God's presence. Even when they prayed, God seemed infinitely distant from them. Their sense of disappointment recurs frequently in diaries and spiritual journals. In the summer of 1672, the Independent minister Henry Maurice went on preaching journeys in Lancashire and Cheshire, and during his travels frequently experienced times when his prayer life seemed to be entirely without inspiration. His diary records the despondency.

> I prayed also in the family with some restraint of spirit ... I went to prayer first, having very little sense [of God's presence] ... I repeated in the family & prayed, but very dead and drowsy I was ... I prayed in private after, being dry and hard ... Disorder & discouragement would fayne prevayle upon my spirit this morning ... I prayed in private having little sense or encouragement, yet blessed be the Lord for ever.[297]

---

[294] Ibid. 255–56.
[295] Ibid. 257.
[296] Ibid. 221–22, 225–26, 228.
[297] Cottle and Crossley Evans, 'Nonconformist Missionary Journey', 85–87.

The tireless itinerant, Oliver Heywood frequently commented on occasions when God 'wonderfully inlarged my heart far beyond my expectations',[298] yet, when sharing in a day of thanksgiving for a neighbour 'for God's mercy to him in his deliverance out of prison', he confessed, 'I found my heart in a very dull frame and not so affected as usually I am in those solemne and sweet exercises'.[299] At another time, Heywood was participating in a 'private fast' at Denton Hall, where 'there was a great assembly'. Invited to lead the congregation in prayer, he lacked liberty in doing so, and found himself 'much straitned and found my spirit much out of frame'. His diary entry refers to the 'wisdom and goodness of God' in allowing him to have this experience, possibly God 'withdraws' to keep 'pride from me'.[300] On another occasion, Heywood preached to his people at Coley about the importance of maintaining set times for prayer, 'though your hearts be often out of frame'. Their prayer life must not be dependent on vacillating emotions; they should 'keep canonical hours, (as it were)', however they feel. It is 'the folly of our trifling spirits' to neglect prayer 'when our hearts are not in tune', with the misguided expectation 'that they will be in a better frame another time'. But do they seriously think 'that one sin wil[l] excuse another? or that we shal[l] be better fitted by a present neglect? ... [D]isuse is more likely to 'make us loather to go to God another time'.[301] Had they not found that 'a dead and discouraged entrance' to the place of prayer often 'increased to sweet enlargements'? The caring pastor is importunate: 'O Christians, be sure you be found in prayer though you come hardly to it; and have much ado to keep at it, and have more hazard to get something by it'. There will be a reward: 'one Pisgah-sight of Christ in a promise wil[l] quit the cost, and hazard a thousand fold ... yea for ought I know though you meet not with God as you desire at that time, yet God may own and crown that undertaking as much as the most heart-meeting exercise, because there is most of obedience' in it.[302]

Whether time allocated to petition and intercession was inspiring or not, Nonconformists had no doubt about the necessity and efficacy of prayer. Whatever their future's trials, unhindered access to a God who longed to hear them was a treasure beyond price. As he preached publicly to his City congregation for the last time, Thomas Lye told them that 'when all my strings are broke I have one left, I can pray yet'; and that same path of prayer was also open to his people. However great the hazards, 'as long as thou canst pray, thou wilt never dye'. It was a strengthening word for the tough days ahead. When 'there is no relief on Earth ... pray to Heaven'.[303] Prayer was the best

---

[298] Heywood, *Autobiography* (ed. Turner), I, 190.
[299] Ibid. 227.
[300] Ibid. 189–90.
[301] Heywood, *Heart-Treasure*, 130.
[302] Ibid. 131.
[303] Thomas Lye, *The Fixed Saint, held forth in a Farewell Sermon ... All Hallows, Lumbard Street* (1662), 28–29.

expression of their total dependence upon God. Life's harsh experiences caused many Dissenters to recall Swinnock's aphorism that 'we lye to God in prayer, if we do not rely on him after prayer'.[304] Comparable resources were not to be found elsewhere.

---

[304] Swinnock, *Pastors Farewell*, 24.

Chapter 4

Identified with Christ

Nonconformist spirituality was essentially Christocentric. Nothing in their teaching and experience was of greater importance than the uniqueness of Jesus, 'the exhibiter, revealer and unfolder of all the fulness of the ... attributes of God'.[1] Preachers focused on biblical passages from both Old and New Testaments which exalted the person and work of Christ, frequently devoting series of sermons to expounding his names, titles, person, mission and achievements.[2] One of their great Puritan mentors, Richard Sibbes, maintained that every minister 'should labour ... to be always speaking somewhat about Christ'. In every sermon, he should be the 'theame and marke to ayme at'. The preacher's privileged role is to 'hold up the tapistry' and 'unfold the hidden mysteries of Christ'.[3] Written in the context of suffering, Samuel Rutherford's letters rapidly gained popularity among English Dissenters in the first decade of the Restoration.[4] As an 'exiled prisoner', he marvelled at his 'new-opened treasures in Christ', assuring a correspondent that, for those who maintain a 'neerer' and 'growing communion', there were always fresh 'curtains to be drawn by, in Christ, that we never saw, and new foldings of love in Him'. Rutherford was convinced he would never 'win to the far end of that love, there

---

[1] Asty, *Treatise of Rejoycing*, 31.
[2] For example, Philip Henry's extensive preaching during 1688–89 on 'what Christ is made to believers', later published in *The Miscellaneous Works of Matthew Henry* (1830), 3–115 (separately paginated Appendix); and separately as *Christ all in all* (1863). This was followed by a another series of twenty sermons in 1690 on 'the history of Christ', with a further series on Christology in 1691–92, all briefly described in Henry, *Life*, 402–403 (Appendix XX). see also Dyer, *Titles*, based on the titles in Isa. 9: 6; Ambrose, *Looking to Jesus*; John Owen, *Meditations and Discourses on the Glory of Christ*, in *Works*, I, 274–461.
[3] Ambrose, *Looking to Jesus*, 'To the Reader', [unpaginated], quoting Richard Sibbes, *Bowels Opened ... divers Sermons on the Fourth, Fifth and Sixt[h] Chapters of the Canticles* (1639), 428.
[4] Writing to an imprisoned minister in 1664, Joseph Alleine refers to 'your welcome Jewel in Mr Ruth[erford']s Letters, from which I trust my soul; & others may reap no small benefit': Alleine, *Letters*, 157 (10 January 1664). A publication by another imprisoned minister, Francis Holcroft, refers to 'Holy Mr. Rutherford': *Word to the Saints*, 8; cf. Ashwood, *Heavenly Trade*, 329. See also John Coffey, *Politics, Religion and the British Revolutions: The Mind of Samuel Rutherford* (Cambridge, 1997).

are so many plies in it'.[5] Even when Henry preached on some aspect of practical Christian behaviour, 'he would always have something of Christ in his sermon'. It was 'either his life, as the greatest pattern of the duty, or his love, as the greatest motive to it; or his merit, as making atonement for the neglect of it'.[6]

The theme of towering importance was the crucial necessity, incomparability and unique effectiveness of Christ's sacrificial and saving work. All else was subordinate to that. 'Let thy Study be much exercised about Christ', said Bunyan, 'what he is, what he hath done ... Why he Cried, why he Died ... be much in musing and considering these things'.[7] The cross was 'the standing way-mark, by which all they that go to Glory must pass by'.[8] Dissenters had received this perspective from their Puritan forefathers, but they also knew that the primacy of their soteriology must never be at the cost of minimizing complementary themes of Christian teaching or discounting other aspects of Christian spirituality.

Looking to Christ

The interpretation of four Christological themes was particularly relevant in the development of Nonconformist spirituality during this period of continuing repression and intermittent persecution. Surveying the vast range of biblical teaching they gave special prominence to Christ's unchanging compassion, unique authority, human example and present intercession. The ideal was that every believer might be convinced of his love, submissive to his authority, inspired by his example and sustained by his prayers.

Convinced of his Love

Isaac Ambrose was continually enthralled by 'the glorious shinings of the love of Christ to beleevers'.[9] Their relationship with Christ was characterized by a sense of unpayable debt. However harrowing their own sufferings might be, they knew beyond all else that they were loved. Christ had come to them when they least deserved it, finding them in their sins as foul-smelling 'swine' wallowing 'in the mire'. Overwhelmed by the pungent stench of their iniquity, he 'would fain ... hold his nostrils, yet he would come and wash us'.[10] 'Did you ever hear of a man that took in a beggar from the door to be his heir' or one that

---

[5] *Joshua Redivivus, or Mr. Rutherfoord's Letters* ([Edinburgh], 1664), 28, 31; *Letters of Rutherford* (ed. Bonar), 199, 215.
[6] Henry, *Life*, 138.
[7] Bunyan, *Heavenly Foot-Man*, in *MW*, V, 154.
[8] Bunyan, *MW*, V, 159.
[9] Ambrose, *Looking to Jesus*, A2r (Ep. Ded.).
[10] Alleine, *Remaines*, 206.

'took in his enemy ... and made over all that he hath to him? Thus hath Christ done for us.'[11]

This assured love inspired their gratitude. Just as lovers look gratefully at the choice things given to them as 'tokens of love', so 'if you would be in love with Christ be often looking over the love-tokens of Christ'. These include 'pardon for thy sins' (the guilty offender is 'is a thrice happy man that hath got his pardon'); 'a Patent' [certificate or licence] or 'firm conveyance' to heaven; constantly replenished gifts of faith and love; and the promised indwelling 'compassionate Spirit ... He hath done more for thee in this, than he hath done for all the world beside.'[12]

This assured love guaranteed their comfort. 'It is a Love that heightens under all our sorrows'. The 'greater our troubles are, the more he loves'. Christ 'sees a Believer, it may be, laying under great distresses of body or in great Agonies of spirit', and this 'draws out his love'. Believers may never have 'such discoveries and evidences of the love and kindness of God' as when they are 'in a low condition'.[13]

This assured love diminished their loneliness. In many instances, persecution proved to be an isolating experience. It cut believers off from others, at times physically, by imprisonment or exile; often domestically, through the ostracism of an unsympathetic family; or socially, by legal prohibitions or neighbourhood conventions; but Christ's compassion was changeless. Loving them, he would never leave them. He was not content to be their occasional visitor, but had become a permanent resident in their lives. 'O what love is this', said Alleine, that in 'those hearts that have been stables of unclean lusts ... Christ should take up his abode'.[14] There would certainly be times when they might be denied the immediate awareness of his presence but its guaranteed reality was never in jeopardy. The 'love of your Jesus is so great' that 'he will leap into a furnace to keep you company'.[15]

This assured love undergirded their security. Whatever changes might occur in life's external circumstances, their compassionate Lord would never lose sight of them. Preparation for, and participation in, the Lord's Supper provided them with regular and appropriate occasions for meditation on Christ's costly and incomparable compassion. Joseph Alleine maximized these opportunities, assuring his frequently harassed Taunton people that Christ 'can as soon forget himself as forget us'. At their communion services, Alleine deployed graphic biblical imagery to remind them that the names of Christians are engraved in Christ's heart, recorded in his book, written on his hands and included in his legacy. In the Old Testament's priestly regulations, Aaron's breastplate was

---

[11] Ibid. 197.
[12] Ibid. 209–11.
[13] Asty, *Treatise of Rejoycing*, 27.
[14] Alleine, *Remaines*, 199, quoting Ezek. 36: 25–27.
[15] Asty, *Treatise of Rejoycing*, 29.

'upon his heart' and set there '[f]or a memorial' but, more momentously, Christ 'hath your names there that he might never forget you'.[16] Loving those he has cleansed, believers' names are, 'for remembrance sake, engraven upon his hands' and he has written 'our names down upon his book ... Mark, Christ keeps his book for you, lest you should be forgotten.' In their daily work, men 'keep their books, because they will not let anything be mistaken or forgotten'. A tradesman's journals may be lost or accidentally mislaid, but the names of believers are set down in imperishable records, preserved in heaven.[17] Moreover, when people draw up their wills, they remember especially those they love. When Christ 'made his last Will and Testament' he demonstrated his love by 'putting our names into his will'.[18]

This assured love determined their priorities. He not only put 'his Spirit into our hearts' but also put 'his glory into our hands ... Now then, what a great trust is this'. Everything good in the world 'was made for this end, to promote God's glory'. In the most costly event in world history, Jesus gave his life, and did so that God might be glorified. Believers are best able to exalt that divine glory for they are uniquely indebted to Christ's sacrifice. Glorifying their loving Lord is both their incalculable privilege and awesome responsibility. Surely,

> he loves you well, that trusts his glory with you. Your unworthy walking will more dishonor Christ, than any thing in the world beside. None can honour Christ as you; and none can dishonor him as you ... They that have such a Jewel put into their hands, had need be careful.[19]

Submissive to his Authority

The redemptive work of Christ was unquestionably central in their thinking, and the only appropriate response was total surrender. No genuine Christian 'may pretend to be a rule to himself' and 'act according to the dictates of his own will and pleasure'. The individual's life is under divine ownership. Nobody has 'wisdom enough to direct and govern himself' and the determination to do so 'would be the highest invasion of the divine prerogative that could be imagined ... We may as well pretend to be our own makers as our own guides.'[20]

If Christ was not their Lord, other controlling influences would assume his rightful place, dictate their lifestyle, control their choices and shape their destiny; 'every lust will be a lord'. It is a profound mercy 'to be under government', said Richard Alleine, for '[w]here there's no King' there will be

---

[16] Alleine, *Remaines*, 201, quoting Exod. 28: 29.
[17] Ibid. 206, quoting Isa. 49: 16; Rev. 21: 27.
[18] Ibid. 198.
[19] Ibid. 199–200.
[20] Flavel, *Works*, II, 399.

'as many kings are there are devils and sins'. Their Lord 'comes not to get but to give' but, unwilling to surrender, the non-submissive Christian forgets the generosity of Christ. He complains that 'there's no liberty left me to be miserable' and 'if I will be his' it is on the condition that 'I must be happy'.[21] Yet Christ must be acknowledged not only as Saviour from sin, but as Lord and King in the lives of these believers. This dominant theme was reiterated in a variety of contexts.

First, Christ's lordship was expounded in their preaching. Many of their expositors recognized that, especially in persecution, some believers might be grateful for Christ's saving work, removing their sins and guaranteeing their eternal security, without going on to acknowledge his claim over every part of their lives. David Clarkson was particularly aware of the unbiblical nature of such an attitude to Christ. Some might be presumptuous enough to imagine that they can 'have part of him', but the genuine believer 'cannot endure' that Christ 'should be divided ... he will have him ... as his Lawgiver no less than a Saviour'. Like Thomas, he confesses Christ as 'a Lord to rule him as well as a Jesus to save him ... Pardon will not satisfy him without purity'. The New Testament believer 'would be redeemed not only from hell ... but from that which might give Christ any distaste at present', so that he is 'King in all his royalties ... not only with his crown for glory and happiness, but with his sword and sceptre'. Clarkson knew that in adversity an individual might choose to have as 'much of Jesus as you will, but as little of him as Lord' as possible; or 'if as Lord, yet not really, universally, or solely', preferring to 'pick and choose something in Christ it likes ... and leave the rest'. Such a 'presumer' would 'have Christ's righteousness to satisfy justice, procure him a pardon, and purchase him heaven; but he cares not for Christ's holiness'. Everything is not yet under his rule; some things are 'too difficult, too hazardous' and they encroach 'too much upon their ease, or pleasures, or carnal humours, or worldly interest'. The 'sceptre of Christ' must 'waive [all] that'. The believer who acknowledges Christ's lordship desires to be saved not only from future judgement but also from present allurements. 'He would have him come into his soul with the government upon his shoulders', and 'with his sword ... put to death his dearest corruption'. The surrendered believer 'desires nothing more than to be brought fully and unreservedly under the government of Christ'.[22]

Philip Lamb's final appeal to his people in Bere Regis included the telling reflection that no genuine lover of Christ ever baulked at his lordship. 'Did we honour Jesus Christ as our King, Lord and Lawgiver, we should be more

---

[21] Richard Alleine, *Heaven Opened* (1665), 29–30; cf. Vincent, *Cure*, 130: 'When we look upon God as Lord, we should trust him for deliverance from other Lords ... The Lord can turn the Heart perfectly to hate the sin that was most of all beloved; and the strength of sin is gone once 'tis hated'.

[22] Clarkson, *Works*, I, 103–104. Obadiah Grew reiterated the same message to Coventry Dissenters: 'The true Believer takes Christ for his Lord as well as his Saviour': *Continuation*, II, 852.

careful to remember what he hath spoken to us.' Far more was involved than intellectual assent to a Christological affirmation. The ejected minister appeals to his vulnerable people: 'As your King, let him ... rule over you.' Whatever the future, they were in strong hands. 'If Christ be your King, God will be your Father; God loves to come where Christ has his throne.'[23] Hercules Collins insisted that it is far 'too low for a Christian to say, I must submit', for it is 'the Glory' of a believer 'to chuse the Divine Will'. Egypt's ruler was compelled to submit, 'but it was sore against his Will. A Believer should submit ... out of Choice, not Force', and in that, as in all else, 'Christ is our Pattern'. He 'did sometimes recoil ... under the Sense of approaching Trouble, as good Men sometimes do', but out of love for God he 'was for complying with the Divine Will, tho it was to die'.[24] Preaching as direct as this brought many Dissenters to a place of grateful, willing and joyful surrender.

Second, submission to Christ's lordship was promoted in their literature. The resolute Christian is aware of the cost of discipleship but, as the imprisoned Thomas Hardcastle wrote to his Bristol congregation, all believers 'must follow Christ in the way that he chooses, and not in the way that we choose for ourselves'. Those who go on 'the errands he sends us ... neither lack nor lose anything that is good for us'. In undemanding circumstances, the believer may speak warmly about the qualities of 'faith, and hope, and patience', but when troubles come we 'care not to have occasion to make use of them for ourselves', preferring a life without costly tests.[25] The concept of submission became conspicuous in popular allegory. Bunyan's commitment to the supremacy of Christ's lordship is evident in the use he makes of his names and titles from the beginning of *The Pilgrim's Progress*. Three times in its earliest narrative Christ is described as 'King', and in those opening pages is further identified as the 'Governour of that Countrey, the Lord of the Place whither thou art going', and its 'Law-giver'.[26] When, later in the story, Christian reflects on the hazards of pilgrimage, he sings about his preservation and consequent submission:

> O world of wonders! (I can say no less)
> That I should be preserv'd in that distress
> That I have met with here! O blessed bee
> The hand that from it hath delivered me! ...
> Yea, Snares, and Pits, and Traps, and Nets did lie
> My Path about, that worthless silly I
> Might have been catch't, intangled and cast down:

---

[23] Philip Lamb, in *Compleat Collection*, [unpaginated].
[24] Collins, *Mountains of Brass*, 39–40.
[25] *Records* (ed. Underhill), 261.
[26] Bunyan, *Pilgrim's Progess*, 1–29; cf. G.F. Nuttall, 'The Heart of *The Pilgrim's Progress*', in idem, *Studies in English Dissent* (Weston Rhyn, 2002), 67–79.

But since I live, let JESUS wear the Crown.[27]

In another allegory, the Baptist leader Benjamin Keach asks the enquiring reader whether he has 'received a whole Christ with a whole heart ... not only as a Priest, to die for him, but also as a Prince to rule over him? Doth he obey all God's Precepts, as well as believe all God's Promises?'[28]

Third, Christ's lordship was affirmed in their catechisms. The ejected Presbyterian Thomas Trescot prepared a manuscript catechism to be used as part of his congregation's preparation for communion services in Somerset villages. It illustrates the pattern of teaching adopted by many Nonconformist ministers. Its sixty-one questions were followed by detailed answers, most of which were divided into sub-sections, each supported by biblical references. Among these, Trescot taught that the authenticity of personal faith was known by a series of 'properties and Qualities' which included 'taking [the] whole Christ ... as our prophet', which meant acknowledging 'Christ as Lord as well our o[u]r Saviour'.[29]

In his exposition of the Westminster Shorter Catechism, Thomas Watson paid special attention to the believer's submission to his uniquely authoritative Lord. He contrasted the tyrannical rule of human lords with the beneficent dominion of Christ, who 'rules them with Promises as well as Precepts', so that 'all his Subjects become Volunteers', grateful debtors, more than 'willing to pay their Allegiance to him'. In persecuting times, he both defends and empowers his submissive people. If enemies are successful in eradicating the Church, they must 'first strike through Christ, before they can destroy his Church'. He is the believer's 'King [and] though our Lusts' may be 'too strong for us', they are 'not for Christ to conquer ... Many would have Christ their Saviour, but not their Prince', but those who 'will not have Christ ... to rule them, shall never have his Blood to save them'. In his love, 'he hath honoured you, to make you his Subjects'.[30]

Fourth, Christ's Lordship was confessed in their communities. This was particularly so in the case of Independents and Baptists, whose churches were usually formed on the basis of a covenant signed by all their members.[31] A

---

[27] Bunyan, *Pilgrim's Progress*, 66.
[28] K[each]., *Travels of True Godliness*, 96; cf. idem, *Gospel Mysteries Unveil'd, or the Exposition of all the Parables and many express Similitudes* (1701), Book III, 46: 'you must espouse a whole Christ, not Jesus only, a Saviour, but Christ the Lord; not simply ... as a Priest to Dye for you, but as a King to Rule in you'.
[29] Taunton, Somerset Archaeological and Natural History Society archives, manuscript book of 17th-century sermons, Thomas Trescot, 'A Catechism by way of preparation to ye worthy receiving of ye Sacrament of the Lords Supper', fol.31.
[30] Watson, *Body of Practical Divinity*, 109–11.
[31] Some Independents and Baptists did not approve of church covenants. John Goodwin regarded them as unbiblical, without precedent in New Testament churches and an unhelpful feature of church life: cf. Thomas Goodwin, *Works*, XI, 526–40, for letters exchanged in 1639 between John and Thomas Goodwin. John Rogers did not deny their

striking feature of these church covenants was their affirmation of the lordship of Christ in both the personal and the corporate life of every member. With 'one consent' their members 'first gave themselves to the Lord, and to one another'.[32] These corporate covenants had a rich history. Meeting for worship on the basis of a mutually acceptable covenant was a characteristic of some 'underground' congregations during the Marian persecution,[33] and became a distinctive feature of the illegal Separatist churches during the reign of Elizabeth. In each case, the persecution context was significant: deliberately separating from their parish churches, members gave public expression in these covenants to their total allegiance to Christ rather than to ecclesiastical conventions or political pressures. Covenanting was costly.[34]

This primary allegiance to the lordship or kingship of Christ figured prominently in church covenants, which were usually signed by every incoming member. When Holcroft's scattered church in Cambridgeshire 'multiplied ... and increased', though 'under many afflictions', a new congregation was established at Clavering, near Saffron Walden in Essex. Even in a 'day of Jacobs trouble', they joined together 'in a perpetuall covenant ... in professed

---

usefulness but thought them not 'necessary for all time': Rogers, *Ohel or Bethshemesh ... An Idea of Church Discipline* (1653), 453, 455–57. Hanserd Knollys believed they lacked precise biblical authority, asserting that nothing should be added to the requirement of faith, repentance and baptism. But Benjamin Keach and his son Elias both popularized local church covenants; cf. also G.F. Nuttall, *Visible Saints: The Congregational Way 1640–1660* (Oxford, 1957), 78; [W.T. Whitley], 'Church Covenants', *BQ* 7 (1934–35), 227–34.

[32] *The Minutes of the First Independent Church [now Bunyan Meeting] at Bedford 1656–1766* (ed. H.G. Tibbutt; Bedfordshire Historical Record Society, 55; 1976), 17.

[33] The Marian 'underground' covenants appear to have been primarily negative, emphasizing their separation from the established church rather than their separation to the Lord and each other. At Stoke, Suffolk, 'giving their hands together', they 'concluded by promise one to another, that they would not receive [the sacrament] at all': Foxe, *Acts and Monuments* (ed. Pratt), VIII, 557; cf. B.R. White, *The English Separatist Tradition* (Oxford, 1971), 9. A determination not to participate in the worship of their parish churches also featured in seventeenth-century Independent covenants, e.g. at Bristol: *Broadmead Records* (ed., Hayden), 90; and at Bedford, where they 'imbodied into fellowship', resolutely separate from 'the prellatical superstition', preferring 'the non-conforming men': *Bedford Minutes* (ed. Tibbutt), 15; cf. also John Owen, *Eshcol, A Cluster of the Fruit of Canaan ...* (1647), in which Owen's 'Rules' for 'those who walk in fellowship' include '[s]eparation ... from ... false worship' and 'unwarranted ways of worship': in *Works*, XIII, 67–69.

[34] Reflecting on the familiar threefold office of Christ, one Elizabethan prisoner had criticized conformist worship. 'You preach Christ to be priest and prophet, but you preach him not to be king, neither will you suffer him to reign with the sceptre of his word in his church alone; but the people's canon law and the will of the prince must have the first place, and be preferred before the word and ordinance of Christ': 'An Examination of certain Londoners before the Ecclesiastical Commissioners, 1567', in *The Remains of Archbishop Grindal* (ed. W. Nicholson, Parker Society; Cambridge, 1843), 205; cf. White, *English Separatist Tradition*, 24–25.

subjection to our Lord Jesus our King', testifying to these 'solemn vowes' as 'we lift up our Right hand to heaven to our God'.[35] The Wattisfield, Suffolk, congregation publicly declared the 'Subjection' of their 'Wills to the Will' of their 'Redeemer'.[36] The Independents at Woodbridge in the same county recorded their covenant on 'a Parchment Roll', affirming that 'we give up ourselves ... and all that we have', receiving 'Jesus Christ [as] our King, Priest and Prophet'. They must be obedient to the king's commands, for their covenant included a promise to 'Endeavour to Know ye Scriptures more fully'.[37]

Such promises were frequently made in dark times. The 'menaces of adversaries' could not deter Axminster members from 'voluntarily giving themselves up to the Lord and to each other ... solemnly covenanting ... to walk together in a due and faithful attendance upon the Lord Jesus Christ'.[38] The phraseology of surrender is deliberate: 'giving up ourselves to Him to walk, through the strength of Christ, together'.[39] When, following the 1664 Conventicle Act, local 'persecution waxed hotter', members 'resolved to stand their ground', confessing a higher loyalty. They had unitedly and publicly 'taken the Lord Jesus Christ, Zion's King, for their only Lord and Lawgiver ... notwithstanding the menaces or edicts of men'.[40]

Near-identical wording is used in most of these early covenants. Borrowing familiar Pauline language, they 'first gave themselves to the Lord' (2 Cor. 8: 5) and did so within a congregational setting. The local covenant was no documentary relic; subscription involved personal affirmation in a corporate context, not only initially also but on additional occasions of covenant renewal, when members committed themselves afresh to its exacting obligations.

The practice of Axminster Independents was to read their covenant 'deliberately and distinctly' when 'each and every individual member subscribed', usually by lifting up 'their right hand to heaven in testification of their real assenting to this covenant'. Then they 'subscribed with the hand', either by signing their name or making their mark.[41] Their covenant was reaffirmed in times when they were aware of spiritual decline, on days of

---

[35] Chelmsford, Essex Country Record Office, MS D/NC//35/1, Clavering Church Book, fols 24v–25r ('The Covenant first entred into at Woodhall the 22th day of the twelfth month, 1682/3').
[36] DWL, Harmer MS 76.15, Wattisfield Church Book, 1678–1847 (transcribed 1849), fol.9.
[37] Harmer MS 76.5, Records of the Congregational Church worshipping at the Quay Meeting, Woodbridge, Suffolk, 1651–1851 (undated transcript), fol.1.
[38] *Ecclesiastica* (ed. Howard), 11, 10.
[39] Ibid. 29.
[40] Ibid. 25–26. Nathanael Vincent 'took no notice' of the officers who came to arrest him in 1681, telling them that 'he had a command from the King of Kings to preach in that place': *CSPD* 1680–1, 613.
[41] *Ecclesiastica* (ed. Howard), 31.

humiliation and prayer, and when new members were admitted. It was renewed during the illness of their pastor (reminding them especially of their acknowledged responsibility for the care of each other), and after the painful administration of church discipline.[42] Renewal occurred again following the death of their minister, the members 're-giving up themselves to the Lord and each other afresh', so 'that the bond of union ... might be preserved'. Another occasion for renewal was after a church conference when they discussed (and declared their opposition to) occasional conformity. Additionally, there were times when it was publicly renewed as part of their preparation for the Lord's Supper.[43] Many churches renewed their covenant at a time of 'public calamity',[44] or whenever they welcomed a new minister.[45] On each of these occasions, members made a fresh commitment to Christ as Lord of their lives. Reaffirmations tested the personal allegiance of every individual. At Cockermouth, those present 'one by one, did solemnly renew their Covenant in the Lord'.[46]

Allegiance to Christ was frequently expressed in the familiar terms of his threefold office as prophet, priest and king, titles that were given prominence in the Westminster and other confessions of faith. As prophet, his will must be heard and, as king, obeyed. The kingship of Jesus was particularly meaningful when challenged by ecclesiastical demands and political obligations.[47]

Public confession of the lordship of Christ was frequently reiterated at the

---

[42] Ibid. 54–55; cf. [Thomas Mall], *A True account of What was done by a Church of Christ in Exon (whereof Mr. Lewis Stucley is Pastor) ... when two members thereof were Excommunicated* ([1658]), provides ten 'Reasons why a Church of Christ should then renew their Covenant with God' when a member is 'justly Excommunicated'.

[43] *Ecclesiastica* (ed. Howard), 29–30, 33, 45, 48, 54, 67–68, 123.

[44] As at the time of the 'Popish Plot', when Owen's London congregation used the opportunity for 'the solemn renovation of our covenant with God': *Works*, IX, 496.

[45] Great Yarmouth Independent Church Book, fol.126.

[46] Cockermouth Independent Church Book, 102.

[47] Fifth Monarchist views of a stridently political nature (and not all were political) meant that many preachers thought it prudent to exercise care when expounding a theology of Christ as king. Following Venner's rising with its use of 'King Jesus' phraseology, they were all too aware that confessional affirmations of Christ as 'only King and Lawgiver' were open to serious misrepresentation. An informer might be either ignorant of their Christology or intentionally distort the preacher's message, reporting them as a seditious group openly opposed to the monarchy, espousing republican ambitions. John F. Wilson says that in the 1640s, when preachers referred to Christ as king, 'the effective result was the denigration first of Charles I as the accepted king or ruler within the realm and then of a parliament composed of other than the saints': *Pulpit in Parliament: Puritanism during the English Civil Wars, 1640–48* (Princeton, NJ, 1969), 232; cf. Appleby, *Black Bartholomew*, 108–109, for some occasionally confrontational 'Christ as King' references in the farewell sermons of the ejected ministers, e.g. John Hieron, in *England's Remembrancer*, 122: 'love him as our King, to submit to his Government, to be ruled by his Laws ... to suffer no other Lord besides him, *to have Dominion over us*' [Heiron's italics].

Lord's Supper, especially at the reception of new members. At Bristol, 'when ye Bread and wine lay on ye Table', their minister told them that they must not only acknowledge Jesus as 'theire Priest to make Atonement to save them' but also '*Hearken* to *Christ* as theire teacher, and obey him as theire King'.[48] It was not the conventional phraseology of a risk-free preacher. Hardcastle had spent most of the previous year in prison. In one of his letters, he had expressed his conviction that the 'great gift next to believing on Christ, is suffering for Christ', reminding them of Christ's threefold office, and that in their 'faithful and patient enduring' their king would protect them in 'the hour of temptation'.[49] Newly admitted members, 'standing up ... in ye Midst of ye Congregation', knew that in Bristol such loyalties were constantly put to the test. It was not only that their pastor had been imprisoned: in the month following the new Baptist members' reception, a local Independent meeting was forcefully dispersed after the arrest of several of its people, an intervention demanded by Bristol's bishop, Guy Carleton.[50]

Further opportunities for affirming Christ's lordship were provided by the use of personal covenants, actively encouraged within Presbyterian congregations,[51] though not in them alone. Baxter emphasized that the believer accepts Christ as 'savior & Lord', for 'in both relations will he be received, or not at all. Faith will not only acknowledge[e] his sufferings, and accept of pardon and glory' but will 'acknowledg[e] his Soveraignty, and submit to his Government', entering 'into a cordial Covenant' whereby Christ 'delivereth himself ... to the sinner; and the sinner delivereth up himself to be saved and ruled by Christ'.[52]

The most prominent advocates of personal covenants were the Somerset Presbyterian ministers, father and son-in-law, Richard and Joseph Alleine. A covenant for individual believers was commended in Richard Alleine's *Vindiciae Pietatis*.[53] Widely used and deeply influential, it was frequently

---

[48] *Broadmead Records* (ed. Hayden), 190.
[49] *Records* (ed. Underhill), 278.
[50] *Broadmead Records* (ed. Hayden), 190.
[51] Thomas Doolittle, for example, 'solemnly subscribed a Covenant with his God': Daniel Williams, *Christian Sincerity ... Funeral Sermon ... Thomas Doolittle* (1707), unpaginated conclusion.
[52] Baxter, *Rest*, 141–43.
[53] Baxter identified Joseph Alleine as 'author of that *Synopsis of the Covenant* in *Mr. Richard Alleine's* Book': [Alleine], *Life*, 17. Richard Alleine's *Vindiciae Pietatis* (1660) enjoyed immense popularity, reaching seven editions before the end of the century; cf. Joseph Rogerson, *The Real Christian's Character ... Funeral Sermon for ... Mrs Rebekah Woolley ... of Derby* (Nottingham, 1716), 24: 'There was found amongst her Papers a Form of Covenant, taken out of Mr. Alleyne's Works and sign'd and seal'd by her, Jan.6, 1691'; Joseph Porter, *The Holy Seed, or a Funeral Discourse occasioned by the death of ... Thomas Beard ...* (1711), 36: 'the better to confirm my Soul, I will subscribe Mr. *Allens's* Covenant'. For the continuing use of personal covenants in the

copied and circulated, and sold in an abbreviated form as a large, single-page broadsheet to be displayed in homes as a daily check on Dissenters' spiritual priorities.

They were urged to prepare their own covenant 'in writing, set your hand to it and keep it as a Memorial of that solemn Transaction'. Once again, it anticipated a persecution context: 'And since thou hast told me that I must suffer if I will Reign, I do here Covenant with thee to take my lot as it falls ... and by thy Grace assisting me to run all hazards with thee'. The theme of total submission dominates the personal covenant. 'I do solemnly avouch thee for my Lord and God ... bowing the neck of my soul under the feet of thy most Sacred Majesty'. 'I ... do willingly put my Neck under thy Yoak ... subscribing to all thy Laws'. 'I renounce my own will and take thy will for my Law'. The use of Christological titles is significant, emphasizing both love and loyalty. The intimacy of the believer's relationship with Christ is heightened by the imagery of marriage: 'I do here solemnly joyn my self into a marriage Covenant with him' and 'do take thee for my Head and Husband, for better for worse, for richer for poorer, for all times and conditions, to love, honour and obey thee before all others, and this to death'. The pledge of love is expressed in terms of total submission: 'thou art now become my Covenant-friend and I through thine infinite Grace, am become thy Covenant-servant'.

Believers who entered into these covenants were first to acknowledge that in hard times personal faith might waver as firm commitment was challenged. The covenant included a plea that, whatever life's fluctuating experience, this initial resolution will always be regarded as paramount. Hopefully, no 'unallowed miscarriages' or behaviour 'contrary to the settled bent and resolution', will ever 'make void this Covenant ... And the Covenant which I have made on earth, may it be ratified in Heaven.'[54]

Nonconformist ministers encouraged congregations to use their own copies as a check on daily conduct. Each morning it provided an objective ideal; in the evening it might expose failure, identify areas for improvement, encourage repentance and renewed commitment.

As with corporate covenants adopted by congregations, personal covenants were subject to frequent renewal. Heywood's journals record different occasions when he renewed his 'Solemn Covenant' to be Christ's 'bond servant for ever' and 'wholly the Lords'. It was renewed, for example, on the anniversary of his baptism, 'wherin I was listed to be thy souldier', and again after he 'fell into a course of carelessnes, self-conceitedness' and 'formality' in

---

eighteenth century, see G.F. Nuttall, 'Methodism and the Old Dissent: Some Perspectives', in idem, *Studies in English Dissent*, 265–67.
[54] Joseph Alleine, *Directions for Covenanting with God* (broadsheet, 1674). Oliver Heywood frequently used marriage imagery in the context of personal covenant renewal, grateful that 'it is not every misdemeanour that doth dissolve the marriage-knot': *Autobiography*, I, 317–18.

his prayer life, and as part of his preparation for the Lord's Supper.[55] Similarly, Jolly made use of his monthly 'retireing' days for the renewal of his personal covenant, especially when he felt 'beseiged and buffetted withall' and disappointed that he found such 'lit[t]le encouragement' from colleagues in the ministry.[56] Henry and Stockton[57] were not alone in renewing their covenants at New Year, Henry itemizing specific additional promises.[58] It was of the greatest importance to renew the personal covenant after known failure, conviction of sin and repentance,[59] but times of special thanksgiving were also appropriate for its renewal.[60]

Inspired by his Example

When love and loyalty were put to the test, these believers looked for assurance that their motives, priorities, decisions, and actions were such as would honour their Covenant Friend. In times of potential defection and disloyalty, a perfect role model was essential. Without marginalizing the unique saving work of Christ, preachers frequently reminded their suffering people of his unrivalled example. The priority of his death was not allowed to eclipse the relevance of his life. Dissenters were not likely to forget the stark aphorism of the veteran leader, Edmund Calamy the elder: 'He that will not follow the Example of Christ's Life, shall never be saved by the Merits of his Death.'[61] Christ's sufferings 'were designed not only for our Redemption', said William Bates, 'but for our Instruction and Imitation'.[62] Joseph Alleine reminded fellow ministers that in Petrine Christology these themes are perfectly balanced.

---

[55] Heywood, *Autobiography* (ed. Turner), I, 307–32, cf. III, 214–38. Heywood bought a small book in which 'to write Reflections upon yearly and solemn ingagements to be the Lords'; cf. III, 227: 'providences I met with in AD 1687 and an Acknowledgmt of god therein and a covenant subscribed'.

[56] Jolly, *Note Book* (ed. Fishwick), 87: 'for the confirming of the covenant 'twixt God and my soul'; cf. ibid. 3.

[57] Stockton, 'Observations and experiences', fol.85: 'January 1st, 1673 ... I resolved with myself to engage my heart afresh and to renew my Covenant w[i]th ye Lord ye beginning of this new year to be ye Lords servant'.

[58] Henry, *Diaries* (ed. Lee), 160–61; Henry promises to grasp 'all opportunityes of doing good to souls, not only taking but seeking them', and to be 'less fearful ... When ye flail of Affliction o: lord is upon mee let mee not bee as ye chaff that flyes in the face, but as ye Corn that lyes at thy feet'; cf. ibid. 199: 'Covenants solemnly renewed'.

[59] Swinnock, *Calling*, II, 405.

[60] As, for example, when Henry enjoyed a 'Sweet Sabbath' and noted Amos 3: 3 in his diary, doubtless the text for his sermon ('Can two walk together, except they be agreed'), to which he added: 'lord I am agreed & will walk with thee, covenants renew'd to that purp[ose]. Lord Jesus bee my Surety': Diary of Philip Henry, 23 February 1673 (not included in Lee's edition of Henry's *Diaries*).

[61] *Old Mr. Calamy's Sayings*. The saying is also found in Dyer, *Titles*, 108.

[62] Bates, *Great Duty*, 4; cf. Nathanel Vincent, in *Morning Exercise at Cripplegate* (ed. James Nicholls, 6 vols; 1844, first publ. 1674), IV, 437–51.

'Christ suffered for us, both as our Surety [1 Peter 2: 24; 3: 18] and Pattern [2: 21]'.[63]

Ministers emphasized the theme because they considered themselves under a special obligation to make Christ their pattern, acknowledging with John Owen that 'the exemplary life of a minister' is nothing less than 'the life of Christ in him ... A pastor's life should be vocal; sermons must be practised as well as preached.' Noah's workmen built the ark but perished in the waters. It was a serious warning. 'If a man teach uprightly and walk crookedly, more will fall down in the night of his life than he built in the day of his doctrine.'[64] It is precisely the same appeal as that made earlier by Baxter to fellow ministers in Worcestershire: 'Take heed to yourselves, lest your example contradict your Doctrine ... Lest you unsay with your lives which you say with your tongues, and be the greatest hinderers of the success of your own labours'. The most persuasive message is nullified by inconsistent conduct. 'One proud surly Lordly word, one needless contention, one covetous action may cut the throat of many a Sermon'.[65]

For ministers, the responsibility of following Christ's example was a vocational priority, but members were under an identical obligation. Frequently penalized for preaching at conventicles, James Birdwood recalled that 'Christ's sufferings on Earth were of two kinds ... for Satisfaction for our sins' and also for 'our Imitation ... Shall we think to fare better than him? His sufferings were to teach us to bear ours with Christian Patience, and to sanctify ours'. The sufferings of Christ were not confined to the cross. His entire adult life was 'a Life of Suffering, he knew what Trouble meant ... he knew what it was to lose a Friend; for in his greatest trouble, all his Disciples (whom he calls his Friends) forsook him and fled'.[66] Before leaving, George Thorne urged his Weymouth congregation: 'Let the example of Christ be your pattern' and 'set this copy always before you'. The preacher became specific as he recalled their Lord's example to them in oppression: pleasing the Father, accepting suffering as from from God's hand, giving 'unto Civil Magistrates and Rulers what was their due', forgiving enemies, helping others, bearing witness and glorifying God in everything.[67] William Dyer insisted that believers must 'be as willing to be ruled by Christ' as they 'are willing to be saved by Christ'. For if 'the life of Christ be not your pattern, the death of Christ will never be your portion ... God will suffer no man to wear the livery of Christ upon him, who

---

[63] Alleine, *Call to Archippus*, 26.
[64] Owen, *Eshcol*, in *Works*, XIII, 57.
[65] Richard Baxter, *Gildas Salvianus: The Reformed Pastor* (1656), ch.I, section VIII, 22.
[66] Birdwood, *Hearts-Ease*, 127–28.
[67] George Thorne, *The Saints Great Duty in Times of Dangerous Afflictions, Persecutions and Oppressions* (1664), 49, 51, 53, 56, 57, 58–60. In another farewell sermon, John Barrett said that the 'life of Christ is a Christians Copy ... for us all to write after': in *England's Remembrancer*, 46.

hath not the likeness of Christ within him'.[68] Samuel Tomlyns was of the same mind: 'The Sufferings of Christ were not only expiatory, but exemplary; they did not only serve to appease God, but also to instruct and animate men to tread in his steps'. As '[m]embers of the Church they [too] must look to drink Christ's Cup'.[69]

Imprisoned Friends were not likely to forget the passion narrative, but George Fox reminded them that like Jesus their love 'must bear all things ... So be Meek and Low, then ye follow the example of Christ ... who suffered by the Unjust ... whose Back was struck, Hair pluck'd off, and Face was spit upon, and yet cried, *Father forgive them*'. This, 'in Measure', all 'Followers of the Lamb' must seek earnestly to 'attain to',[70] and not only in prisons but also in their meetings. Leaders must not be like persecutors, who 'strive for Mastery', but like their Lord, who knelt in service. 'Wash one another's Feet, take Christ for your Example that I may hear of no Strife among you', and 'trample all that which is Contrary to God under your Feet'.[71]

In the first year of their marriage, Mary Franklin's husband Robert was arrested and imprisoned thirty miles from their home. She was in the final stages of pregnancy and gave birth to a stillborn child, 'judged by most to be occasioned ... by reason of my husband being so far from me'. Franklin was eventually allowed home but for some time was under house arrest, 'guarded by soldiers ... every Lords day ... by 7 o'clock in the morning, and continued till 7 at night'. Naturally grieved at the loss of their first child, she remembered that her 'blessed Lord ... was our example and pattern' in the 'suffering of affliction' and he had warned that the people of God 'must expect trouble'.[72]

Yet, insisting on the uniqueness and necessity of Christ's saving death, some Dissenters were hesitant about an exemplarist Christology. They were fearful that it might be used to support a doctrine of salvation by works, in which we 'make *our selves* the Saviours, and jostle *Christ* quite *out* of doors.' Among their contemporaries were sincerely religious people, 'trying what they can do for Life' but 'the more they stir the more they sink under the weight of the Burthen that lies upon them'.[73] An exemplarist spirituality had firm biblical authority[74] but in theological debate some Dissenters were reluctant to stress its

---

[68] Dyer, *Titles*, 108–109.
[69] Tomlyns, *Great Duty*, 3.
[70] Fox, *Epistles*, 171 (Letter 208, 'To Friends in the Ministry', 1661).
[71] Ibid. 61 (Letter 64, 1654).
[72] 'The Experiences of Mary Franklin', 391.
[73] John Bunyan, *Of Justification by an Imputed Righteousness* (1692), in *MW*, XII, at 300.
[74] E.g. being sent out into the world in mission as Christ was (Jn 17: 18; 20: 21), giving sacrificially as he gave (2 Cor. 8: 9), living with true humility, like him (Phil. 2: 5–8), learning meekness from him (Mt. 11: 29), being compassionate as he was (Eph. 5: 2), forgiving as God has forgiven us through Christ (Eph. 4: 32), in behaviour 'walking as

leading ideas. In rich and popular devotional works, earlier Anglican theologians of the stature of Jeremy Taylor had portrayed Christ persuasively as 'the Great Exemplar',[75] and exemplarism was vigorously expounded in popular conformist writing of their own time, such as that of Bunyan's *bête noire*, Edward Fowler. This Bedfordshire vicar (later bishop) was, in his opponent's view, of 'Unstable Weathercock Spirit' and could conveniently 'hop' from his earlier 'Presbiterianism, to a Prelatical Mode'.[76] Bunyan became his fierce critic when, in the closing months of his twelve-year sentence, he received a copy of Fowler's *The Design of Christianity*. In little over six weeks, Bunyan produced his brusque reply, peppered throughout with caustic invective. It starkly dismisses the work: 'Your book Sir is begun in Ignorance, mannaged with Errour, and ended in Blasphemy'.[77]

In his book, Fowler had presented Christ's human life as the 'eminent Example of all the parts of vertue', the unrivalled pattern of human 'Freedom, Affability and Courtesie'. Jesus was the perfect gentleman, gifted with the 'greatest Candor and Ingenuity ... most marvellous Gentleness and Meekness ... Deepest Humility ... Greatest Contempt of the World ... most Perfect Contentation [contentment] ... Tenderest Compassion ... Stupendious Patience and Submission' to God, immense 'Confidence and Trust in God' and 'the most Admirable Prudence'.[78] During his short ministry, Jesus 'Preach'd holiness to mens Eyes no less than to their Ears, by giving them the most stupendious Example in his own Person, of all the parts' of authentic Christian living.[79] Fowler described committed believers as those who strive to 'write after that Fair Copy' of 'our Saviour's most Excellent Life'.[80] The key to certainty of salvation is 'making his Life our Pattern'; thus 'we shall assure ourselves that the Design of Christianity is effected in us, and that we are indued with the Power of it'.[81] People who 'sincerely and industriously endeavour to imitate the Holy Jesus in his Spirit and Actions, can never be

---

he walked' (1 Jn 2: 6), being pure as he was (1 Jn 3: 3), and, like him, absorbing bitterness and hatred when made to suffer unjustly (1 Peter 2: 18–21).

[75] Jeremy Taylor, *The Great Exemplar of Sanctity and the Holy Life ... described in the History of the Life and Death of Jesus Christ* (4th ed.; 1667); cf. J. Sears McGee, *The Godly Man in Stuart England 1629–1670* (New Haven, CT, 1976), 107–13, for the *Imitatio Christi* motif in Anglicanism.

[76] Bunyan, *MW*, IV, 83, 101: 'and if time and chance should serve you, backwards and forwards again'. Bunyan was particularly fierce in his criticism, because, brought up in a Puritan home, Fowler had been a Presbyterian minister, and both his father and brother were among the ejected ministers.

[77] John Bunyan, *A Defence of the Doctrine of Justification, by Faith in Jesus Christ* (1671), in *MW*, IV, at 123.

[78] Edward Fowler, *The Design of Christianity* (1671), 36.

[79] Ibid. 39.

[80] Ibid. 296.

[81] Ibid. 281.

ignorant of what it is to be truly Christians; nor can they fail to be so'.[82]

Bunyan was irate that, in the robust presentation of his case, Fowler had written scurrilously about doctrines infinitely precious to the imprisoned preacher. The vicar had asked: 'Is it possible that Faith in Christ's Blood, for the forgiveness of sin, should be the onely act which justifieth a Sinner?'[83] Fowler insisted on the importance of moral effort, albeit divinely enabled, saying that 'the true explication' of the 'Imputation of Christ's Righteousness … consists in dealing with sincerely righteous persons: as if they were perfectly so'. The purpose of the gospel was 'to make us partakers of an Inward and Real Righteousness; and it being but a secondary one that we should be accepted, and rewarded as if we were completely righteous'.[84] Fowler argued that, for some Puritans at least, an exclusive and intense concentration on the imputed righteousness of Christ had issued in moral indifference, a stance that Bunyan would likewise have found both erroneous and offensive.[85] When he read Bunyan's biting response, Fowler's earlier injunction that Christians should 'Practice … that vertue of Meekness, and sedateness of spirit towards injurious persons' must certainly have been put to the test. Fowler deplored the fact that some conformist clergy were guilty of inconsistent behaviour but tilted at Puritan preachers, widely 'admired for their ability in dividing of an hair' and 'Doughty Dexterity in Controversial Squabbles', criticism that Bunyan repeated verbatim in case his readers had not seen Fowler's book. Calvinists were inevitably disturbed by Fowler's criticism of 'such as Preach upon free Grace', especially that of 'laying hold on Christ's Righteousness … and renouncing their own Righteousness', cynically adding, 'which they … have none at all to renounce'.

Bunyan was not alone in his fear that an exemplarist Christology might marginalize the crucial message of salvation by grace alone, promote mere moralism, and even encourage Arminianism by placing an undue emphasis on human effort rather than divine grace.[86] Without necessarily agreeing with every aspect of Fowler's teaching, Richard Baxter produced a less hostile response. He recognized that Fowler's major fear was antinomianism, doctrinal convictions about undeserved grace tenaciously held alongside a blatant disregard of Christian moral responsibility. Baxter recognized that

---

[82] Ibid. 296.
[83] Ibid. 224.
[84] Ibid. 225–26.
[85] Cf. Bunyan, *A Holy Life*, in *MW*, IX, 331: 'though thou art set free from the law as a Covenant for life, yet thou art still under the law to Christ, and it is to be received by thee, as out of his hand'.
[86] For discussion of such issues by these writers and their contemporaries, see Spurr, *Restoration Church*, 296–311. For Bunyan and Fowler, see Isabel Rivers, 'Grace, Holiness, and the Pursuit of Happiness: Bunyan and Restoration Latitudinarianism', in N.H. Keeble (ed.), *John Bunyan: Conventicle and Parnassus, Tercentenary Essays* (Oxford, 1988), 45–69; Greaves, *Glimpses*, 278–86.

antinomianism was the 'Sore' that Fowler's 'Plaster was provided for', and acknowledged 'how much excellent matter' there is in his *Design*, 'which the foresaid [antinomian] persons and diseases need'.[87] Baxter knew that it was not helpful to neglect the unique human example of Jesus. 'Christians must imitate Christ, and suffer with him before they reign with him'.[88] Henry also taught that 'the two great ends' of Christ's Incarnation were that 'by *dying* he might satisfy God's justice for our sins, and so make peace; and that by *living* he may set before us an example'.[89] In a time of repression and persecution, Christians will share their Lord's concern always to please God, his 'contempt of this world' ('riches, honours, pleasures'), his 'charity towards all men' (demonstrated in love for his enemies), and especially 'his carriage under his sufferings ... so submissive'; and 'such should ours be'.[90]

It was an imperative equally endorsed by Flavel, who held that the 'life of Christ is the believer's copy' and, though a Christian 'cannot draw one line or letter' as exact as Christ's copy is, 'yet his eye is still upon it'. No lesser model will do. Most agree that the apostle Paul 'was a great proficient in holiness and obedience', ever 'striving to come up to the top of holiness, yet when he looks up and sees the life of Christ ... so far above him, he reckons himself still but at the foot of the hill ... "Not as though I had already attained ... but I follow after" '.[91] Flavel has a warm pastoral heart and presents his lofty spirituality

---

[87] Richard Baxter, *How far Holinesse is the Design of Christianity ... referring to Mr. Fowlers Treatise on this subject* (1671), 20. The book was written in response to a critic who claimed that Baxter's 'Aphorisms and other Writings have had some hand is breeding such opinions' [as Fowler's]: ibid. 3. In Sylvester (ed.), *Reliquiae*, III, §183, 85, Baxter recalls the controversy over Fowler's *Design*. He had asked Fowler to be patient with his Puritan critics, for Fowler had spoken 'feelingly against those quarrelsome men that are readier to censure than to understand'. Baxter urged him 'to take heed lest their weakness, and censoriousness' should make Fowler 'too angry and impatient with Religious People, as the Prelates are, and so ... favour a looser Party because they are less censorious'. See Hans Boersma, *A Hot Pepper Corn: Richard Baxter's Doctrine of Justification in its Seventeenth-Century Context of Controversy* (Vancouver, BC, 2004), 306–10; Baxter, *Calendar* (ed. Nuttall and Keeble), Letters 847, 854, 857, 862, for the 1671 correspondence between Baxter and Fowler; F.J. Powicke, *Richard Baxter under the Cross* (1927), 53–59. For the later meeting between Baxter and Fowler, cf. *EB*, III, 207–208 [P593]. Morrice knew that in the 1680s Fowler was attacked by his London parishioners because of his irenic approach to Dissenters; cf. Mark Goldie and John Spurr, 'Politics and the Restoration Parish: Edward Fowler and the Struggle for St. Giles, Cripplegate', *English Historical Review* 103 (1994), 572–96.
[88] Sylvester (ed.), *Reliquiae*, I, §213, 28 (9).
[89] Philip Henry, 'What Christ is made to Believers' [Sermon on Jn 13: 15], in *Works of Matthew Henry*, Appendix, 57.
[90] Ibid. 59.
[91] Flavel, *The Fountain of Life* ([1671]) in *Works*, II, 398–401, quoting Phil. 3: 12. Flavel quotes Bernard of Clairvaux's reflection that Christians receive their name from Christ and, 'as they inherit his name, so they should also imitate his holiness'. Flavel

with sensitive compassion, knowing that many who genuinely long to 'follow Christ's example, but ... meeting with strong temptations, are frequently carried aside from the ... designs of their honest, well-meaning hearts'. Their failure brings 'great grief', so he urges them to remember that 'defects in obedience make no flaw' in their justification, which is grounded not on their obedience but upon Christ's. It is better to have treasured an earnest desire for Christlikeness, even if they deem themselves to have failed, than not have sought it at all. The quest may have caused them 'to have a deeper hatred of sin than others have; and to love God with a more fervent love than others do'. A sovereign God can even make 'excellent uses' of 'infirmities and failings', turning them to their 'unexpected advantage'. By 'these defects' he conquers pride, 'beats you off from self-dependence', and makes his promised heaven more attractive. 'O the blessed chymistry of heaven, to extract such mercies out of such miseries!' Despite their failures, the immutable bond of their 'everlasting covenant' with God holds firm and, although their sins grieve him, their sorrow for sin pleases him. Failure will chasten but a generous Lord has promised to sustain them.[92]

Christ was not simply presenting them with a portrait from history of an ideal but tantalizingly unattainable life. Although physically removed now from the arena of this world's pressures, he had once fully experienced them for himself and was actively engaged in a different, unique and vital ministry in heaven. The perfect Pattern was the contemporary Intercessor.

Sustained by his Prayers

The heavenly session of Christ was a prominent feature of Restoration Nonconformist spirituality. He had not simply left these Christians with an example on earth but had taken their humanity to heaven, where he was their compassionate 'Sponsor', the believer's friend at court. Christ 'is not idle now he is in heaven but, as on earth he ever went about doing good, so now ... he spends all his time in heaven in promoting the good of his people'.[93]

Joseph Alleine told his Taunton members that Christ made three farewell love gifts to his people: a permanent sacrament, an imperishable sermon (Jn 14–16) and an empowering prayer (Jn 17). 'Look into his last prayer' and see 'how lovingly doth he carry us in his arms to his Father, when he was going out of the world, begging his Father that he would sanctifie us ... and that he would

---

insisted on its obligatory nature, claiming that every believer is 'bound' to the 'imitation of Christ, under penalty of losing his claim to Christ'.

[92] Flavel, *Works*, II, 417, 419, 420–21. In *The Living Temple*, John Howe portrayed Christ as 'an exemplary Temple, to which all other were to be conformed ... whereby he was also a virtual one, from which life and influence were to be transfused to raise and form all others': *Works* (ed. Hunt), I, 77–458, at 332.

[93] Ambrose, *Looking*, 541.

at length bring us to enjoy his glory.'[94] The memorable intercessions in the garden were perpetually maintained in heaven.

It 'is our common practice', says Ambrose, 'to desire the prayers one of another, but ... who would not have a share in the prayers of Jesus Christ?'[95] In expounding this dimension of New Testament Christology, Ambrose preserves the element of adoring wonder. Christ presents 'our persons in his own person to his Father, so that now God ... must behold the Saints in his Son'. They are 'in near relation to himself', so 'mystically ... when Christ intercedes, he takes our persons, and carries them in unto God the Father in a most unperceivable way to us'. We 'dare not be too inquisitive' about 'a secret not revealed by God'.[96] Other writers point out that it is 'a great priviledg[e]' for us 'to have a Sollicitor there' who is both 'skilful and faithful'.[97] During his earthly ministry, 'Christ 'frequently put forth acts of pity, mercy and succour to those that were in any distress' and he 'retaineth this sympathy and fellow-feeling with us now he is in heaven'. He 'plays the advocate for his suffering people, and feelingly pleads for them'.[98]

In hard times, Dissenters frequently returned to this inspiring New Testament theme. They asked precisely how Christ's intercessions for them were superior to the best prayers of those who treasured them most, and constantly emphasized the uniqueness of his intercessory ministry in heaven.

First, they knew that Christ prayed for them with unique empathy. This theme of total identification brought immense comfort to persecuted believers. Christ was their protomartyr; he too had suffered at the hands of bitter opponents. 'When you suffer, the Lord himself suffers with you', wrote the imprisoned Nathanael Vincent. Christ 'feels the stroak, and is wounded in the wounds of his faithful followers'.[99] 'How feelingly doth he cry out at the hurt of his poor Members on earth', wrote another prisoner, '*Saul, Saul why persecutest thou me?* ... *w*hen we are touched on Earth he feels it in Heaven'. Who else in the world demonstrated 'the reality of his love ... as Christ hath done? ... Who will impoverish himself to enrich his friend?' He 'is gone into heaven, on purpose, there to present you before the Lord, that you may be

---

[94] Alleine, *Remaines*, 208–209
[95] Ambrose, *Looking*, 530.
[96] Ibid. 543.
[97] Birdwood, *Hearts-Ease*, 132, 98.
[98] Brooks, *Works*, V, 194.
[99] Vincent quotes Luther's saying that when any part of a physical body is harmed, 'the sense of pain appears in the head and face ... the whole countenance is alter'd. And in like manner 'tis in the Mystical Body, when any member is wronged': *Covert*, 38. His title page describes its author as 'a Preacher and Prisoner of Jesus Christ ... written during his close confinement, when few could come at him but his God, who yet abundantly made up for the want of other company'. His book is dedicated 'To Him that is Higher than the Highest': ibid. A2r.

always in remembrance before him'.[100]

Ambrose entered feelingly into the anguish of a severely buffeted Christian. ... I am in a suffering condition ... all my friends have dealt treacherously with me ... I stand for Christ but there is none stands by me'. He urged such a believer to 'bear up ... it may be that thou art in want, and so was Christ, he had no house; thou art persecuted, and so was Christ; sin loads thee, and so it did Christ'. A unique Intercessor is praying. 'Is not this enough to cause thy very heart to leap ... ?' If they could hear 'the voice of Jesus' pleading for them, they would 'be cast into an extasie'.[101] 'But I am afraid', says another believer, 'and surely Jesus did not experience fear'. Ambrose insists that he did, and it was a terror infinitely more acute than anything a persecuted believer might dread on earth. In Gethsemane's garden, Jesus 'began to be agonised ... all his powers and passions within him were in conflict ... how suddenly he is struck into a strange fear; never was man so afraid of the torments of hell as Christ (standing in our room) is of his Father's wrath'. The intensity of his 'lethal and deadly' anguish took him to the threshold of the grave. The fear of separation from God far transcends that of opposition from men. However intense the believer's distress, it can never be worse than what Christ experienced in that garden, and because of it he perfectly identifies with the fearful Christian.[102]

Second, they maintained that Christ prayed for them with unique delight. They belonged to him and as their Brother he interceded with immense pleasure. In one of his prison letters, Alleine used a resurrection narrative and a distinctive Matthean parable (Mt. 28: 10; Jn 20: 17; Mt. 25: 40) to remind his congregation that in this life and at death Christ is 'not ashamed to call them Brethren'. Despite the disciples' failure to stand by him in his darkest hour, they were part of his greatly treasured family. 'Even when he was ... risen from the dead ... he own'd poor weak believers for his brethren'. So, 'keep this ... as a Cordial at your heart ... that you have a kinsman, a Brother there, a man like unto your selves'. In life's threatening tumults they could be bold, 'both in ... coming to him' for help, and at his coming to them, at death. 'Let not the Terror he will com[e] *affright* us Christians, for he is our brother ... bone of our bone'. In the future, 'when he ... sits upon the throne of his glory', he will recall what they have done to support those he loved. Then 'he will own the very least, and lowest among poor believers, before all the world' as 'his Brethren'.[103] Bunyan turned to the message of Hebrews to emphasize the same truth. Christ certainly feels for believers because he wore their humanity, but also because they belong to his cherished family. 'As there is a *natural* sympathy in Christ ... so there is a *relative* sympathy', for 'he is become one Brotherhood with us ... So

---

[100] Alleine, *Letters*, 100 (11 August 1665).
[101] Ambrose, *Looking*, 567–68.
[102] Ibid. 379.
[103] Alleine, *Remaines*, 239–40.

then, when Nature and Relation meet, there is a double Obligation.' A man may rush to help someone in need because, as a fellow human being, he is naturally concerned. How much more would he do so for a member of his own family?[104]

Third, they held that Christ prayed for them with unique mercy. Others might forgive a guilty person when they transgress, but patience might be quickly exhausted if precisely the same offence was repeated day after day. Yet their merciful High Priest was constantly absorbing identical personal transgressions. As prophet, Christ had taught these believers how to avoid sin, but they frequently ignored what he had said; yet as their priest, he was continually forgiving. When morally defeated (and the accusing 'Devil is ... exceeding busie', exposing 'these and these sins'), Ambrose urges the guilty Christian not to 'altogether despond'. They must remember that their Priest is 'at God's right hand, and there he sits till all his enemies be made his footstool', and 'are not thy sins his enemies'? Recalling the Johannine High Priestly Prayer (Jn 17), he says that 'one piece' of that prayer' that Christ makes for believers is either to shield them from evil, or keep them in it.[105] In Old Testament times, 'Sacrifice and Intercession' were freely offered to anyone who sinned through ignorance but 'if a man sinned presumptuously [Num. 15: 30]' cleansing was not available. But Christ 'makes Intercession for all sins', and 'every sin though it boyl up to blasphemy (so it be not against the holy Ghost) shall, by vertue of Christ's intercession', be completely and immediately forgiven.[106]

Fourth, they rejoiced that Christ prayed for them with unique compassion. The discouraged saint (as well as the abject sinner) needed an Intercessor. Some were particularly sensitive about their disappointing prayer life, fearing that all their prayers were marred by some 'defect, imperfection, [or] sin'. They prayed so badly that they were in constant 'need of a new prayer, to beg pardon for all the defects' of earlier petitions, and 'then another prayer to heal the flaws of that prayer' and so on. Weighed down with despondency, the treasured opportunity of communion with a God became a depressing litany of human failure. Yet such dejection is only valid 'if there were no intercession of Christ',

---

[104] 'Now both he that sanctifieth (which is Christ) and they who are sanctified (his Saints) are all of one ... as Children of a Father, *for which cause he is not ashamed to call them Brethren* [Heb.2: 11–12] ... So then it is for a Brother ... that he doth make Intercession ... *In all things it behoved him to be made like unto his Brethren, that he might be a mercyful High Priest:* A Brother is born for Adversity' and therefore 'he maketh Intercession for us more affectionately': Bunyan, *The Saints Privilege and Profit*, *MW*, XIII, 227–30.

[105] Ambrose, *Looking*, 567, citing Jn 17: 11–12, 15. From Hebrews, Ambrose focused on Christ's twofold work, 'the one expiatory ... the other presentatory ... the first was performed once for all, the latter is done continually, the first was for the obtaining of redemption, and this latter is for the application of redemption': ibid. 528.

[106] Ibid. 538.

for Christ 'offers up our persons and woodden prayers ... to his Father'. His prayers and those of a Christian are inseparable, for Christ 'so mingles them that they seem but one'.[107] The Christian's finest prayers may be 'sullied' and spoilt with 'offensive corruptions', but 'Christ is there to present all your petitions to God ... to *perfume* them as well as *present* them.'[108] When the believer's prayers seem totally inadequate, Christ 'observes what evil or what failing' is in them, 'and he draws that out and takes it away, before he presents them unto God'.[109] It was not only these believers' prayers that might be defective; so much else in their lives may be far from worthy. They may need 'a great deal of faith, love, heavenly-mindedness, mortification, knowledge'. These are the *hysterēmata*, 'the remains, or things wanting, as the apostle calls them' (1 Thess. 3: 10). So, if it is 'infancy in thy soul', and 'grace be but yet in its weak beginnings ... this may encourage, that by reason of Christ's intercession, it shall live' and grow. 'He is not only the author, but the finisher of it', and he is 'ever begging new and fresh mercies for you in heaven; and will never cease till all your wants be supplied'; this is the assured 'fountain of relief against all your fears'.[110]

Fifth, they maintained that Christ prayed for them with unique wisdom. They offered their prayers with the passionate desire that they might be speedily answered, but so much that they requested might be contrary to God's highest purposes for them. In their ignorance, they fervently pleaded for things that might destroy them. When Christ prayed, he knew exactly what would be of maximum benefit to them and what would certainly not. In expounding this theme, many preachers complemented their portraiture of an omniscient Intercessor with the imagery of Christ as a discerning and tender Physician. Correctly diagnosing the sickness, he not only supervised 'all the Ingredients put into their Potion, but also the weighing to a Grain, every Dose that shall be given'. They were not simply needy patients but 'such extraordinary friends ... his Wife, and Children, his Brethren, Sisters, and Companions'.[111] He alone knew precisely what they needed and would never give less than the best. Reflecting on this compassionate wisdom, Stockton said that at 'the intercession of Christ the nature of troubles and afflictions are changed'. With his touch upon them, 'they are not evils but good things to the People of God'. Along with the psalmist, the most harassed believer may testify: 'It is good for

---

[107] Ibid. 570–71. All that the believer does is less than it might be, but through the intercession of Christ 'the defect' of our prayers 'is covered and removed': ibid. 528.
[108] Flavel, *Fountain of Life*, in *Works*, I, 174, 176.
[109] Asty, *Treatise of Rejoycing*, 53. Asty told his Norwich congregation that Christ 'perfumes' all their 'Spiritual Offerings and presents them to God' as 'acceptable ... notwithstanding the weakness and imperfections in them as they come from us'. The best 'liquor of our spiritual services hath a tang of the vessel through which they pass'.
[110] Flavel, *Works*, I, 175.
[111] Powell, *Bird*, 19.

me that I have been afflicted' (Psa. 119: 71).[112]

Sixth, they rejoiced that Christ prayed for them with unique power. Whatever he desired would never be denied. Those in gaols were 'Prisoners of Hope'. When Christ says, 'Come forth, even a Lazarus shall brake out of a Grave: And if he have the Key of the Grave, surely the Keyes' of other prisons 'are at his command' also.[113] Among the unimaginable resources the Intercessor Christ has at his disposal, is the power either to protect his people from adversity or to uphold them in it.

This unique Intercessor is committed to his people's defence. God 'may not always keep off troubles and afflictions' but, at the intercession of Christ, 'he keeps off the *evil* of trouble', that is, the damage it can inflict spiritually. For example, trouble might 'make us sin against God', or cause us to 'forsake' his ways, or 'fret and curse'. Christ prayed that when adversity came it would not harm them as believers. Moreover, through his intercession, believers are 'upheld under their troubles and kept from fainting'.[114] 'If a flock of sheep have a Lyon for their Captain, they need not fear the Wolf'. Although a Captain 'may give his Soldier armour ... he cannot give him strength', but Christ empowers his dependent people.[115] Whatever the cause, nature, range or intensity of human afflictions, Christ has the ability not only to sustain but also to use adversities so that they become 'advantageous to us' in every possible way. He has the power 'to give what we want', 'to secure us from what we fear', or 'to ease us of what is grievous', transforming the most menacing adversity into an ultimately enriching experience.[116]

Whatever their circumstances, these Christians knew that they were greatly treasured by a High Priest totally aware of the vulnerability of each physical body, who personally 'concerns himself with all its ... alterations'. In John Reeve's words, he both 'makes our Bed' and 'holds our head in our sicknesses'. When this life is drawing to its close, he is there, 'whence it is said, We sleep with Jesus'.[117] This Intercessor's love far transcends the narrow limits of this brief life. It will never end.

Living for Christ

Such immense, unchanging realities demanded a radical response: nothing less than a totally committed life. The greatest perils were an easygoing

---

[112] Stockton, *Consolation*, 68.

[113] Vincent, *Covert*, 71–72.

[114] Stockton, *Consolation*, 67.

[115] Thomas Watson, *The Fight of Faith Crowned ... preached at the Funeral of Mr. Henry Stub[b]s* (1678), 7.

[116] Clarkson, *Works*, III, 87.

[117] John Reeve, *ΜΕΤΑΣΧΗΜΑΤΙΣΜΟΣ, or a Sermon preached ... Funeral of Thomas Brooks* (1680), 8.

nominalism,[118] a reliance on church attendance[119] or a merely notional agreement with basic Christian teaching[120] without an evident and inevitably costly relationship with Christ. Separated from his people, Alleine's prison letters frequently reiterated the warning that mere church attendance or appropriate moral conduct was not nearly enough. There must be a personal, decisive, wholehearted dependence on Christ, and a surrender of the whole life to him. Christian discipleship demanded a transformed lifestyle, initiated by a grateful surrender. Their preachers expounded this commitment to Christ in terms of an incomparable relationship and a privileged obligation.

An Incomparable Relationship

They fervently maintained that the repeated biblical assurance of Christ's love, its certainty, cost and permanence, was fittingly acknowledged only by a believer's loving response. Preachers constantly stressed that Christians can only respond to his loving initiative in their lives. Innumerable Dissenters, however, were intellectually persuaded of the doctrinal truth of Christ's love but burdened with a guilty conscience, and so feared that they might not be included in its wide compass. From Ilchester gaol, Alleine wrote to reassure his people haunted by this common fear: 'How shall I know if I am an Object of Electing Love?' As their minister he has no reason to doubt the reality of their faith, but his compassionate language of assurance might not have appealed to some fellow Calvinists: 'if You have chosen God, he hath certainly chosen You', though his critics might have been reassured by his subsequent sentence. 'You could not have Loved, and have Chosen him, unless he had Loved you first.'[121]

Bunyan was among those tortured souls uncertain of Christ's love for them personally. On a day when his work took him to Bedford, he listened to 'three

---

[118] Those who, according to the Leeds minister Thomas Sharp, think 'that if they go to church for an hower on the Lords day, God is Beholden to them': Leeds, Yorkshire Archaeological Society, MS 21, 'Diary of Ralph Thoresby', fol.135 (2 June 1680). For this reference, not included in Joseph Hunter's 2-vol. 1830 edition of the *Diary*, I am indebted to David L. Wykes, ' "The Sabbaths ... spent before in Idleness and the neglect of the word": the Godly and the Use of Time in their daily Religion', in R.N. Swanson (ed.), *The Use and Abuse of Time in Christian History* (SCH, 37; Woodbridge, 2002), 211–22, at 221.

[119] Bunyan wrote of the cold formality of those 'whose Religion lies in a few of the shells of Religion': *Desire of the Righteous*, in *MW*, XIII, 145. Such people 'retain the name, and *shew* of religion, but are neglecters, as to the power and godly practice of it': *Treatise of the Fear of God*, in *MW*, IX, 27.

[120] Before leaving them, Thomas Lye warned his London congregation of the danger of a merely 'implicite faith' (*Fixed Saint*, 25–26), that accepts the authenticity of teaching simply because the preacher says so; see also William Beerman, in *Compleat Collection*, [sig. Ssv]: 'take all for truth the Minister tells them'.

[121] Alleine, *Letters*, 36 (25 October 1663).

or four poor women' who knew that they were loved, 'sitting at a door in the Sun'. The seemingly incidental detail about the bright sunlight gains particular significance in the developing story. They told 'how God had visited their souls with his love in the Lord Jesus', and they talked 'as if joy did make them speak ... as if they had found a new world'. Reflecting on their artless testimony, it seemed to Bunyan that these new-found friends were 'set on the Sunny side of some high Mountain ... refreshing themselves with the pleasant beams of the Sun', whilst he was 'shivering and shrinking in the cold, afflicted with frost, snow, and dark clouds'. He longed to 'goe even into the very midst of them' and comfort himself 'with the heat of their Sun'. But he was haunted by the same fear that troubled Alleine's friends in Taunton: 'How can you tell you are Elected? and what if you should not? how then?'[122] The thought of not being loved by Christ was a bleak and chilling prospect, as life without sunshine. Election was not a doctrinal enigma that Bunyan might talk over dispassionately with a group of informed people. He was deeply and profoundly disturbed, 'ready to sink ... with faintness in my mind ... many weeks oppressed and cast down ... giving up ... all my hope'. Fearing he 'was not called', he envied the Galilean fishermen, 'as when the Lord said to one, *Follow me*; and to another, *Come after me,* and oh thought I, that he would say so to me too! how gladly would I run after him ... That which made me fear, was this, lest Christ should have no liking to me, for he called *whom he would*', and Bunyan grieved he might not belong to that privileged number. If only he 'had been born *Peter*' or 'been born *John*, or ... heard him when he called them ... but oh I feared he would not call me'. 'In this condition' he 'went a great while,' until an unnamed preacher turned his thoughts to the undistinguishing love of Christ. For 'when comforting time was come, I heard one preach a sermon upon those words in the *Song* [of Solomon 4: 1], Behold *thou are fair, my Love*'. Those two words, 'My Love', were the preacher's 'chief ... subject matter', and what helped Bunyan most was his assurance that Christ loves every individual man or woman, especially when, assailed by doubt, they are 'under temptation and desertion'. Then, 'poor tempted soul', said the preacher, 'when thou art assaulted and afflicted with ... the hidings of Gods face, yet think on these two words, MY LOVE, still'.[123]

> So as I was going home, these words again came into my thoughts ... *Thou art my Love, thou art my Love,* twenty times together; and still as they ran thus in my minde, ... began to make me look up ... Then I began to give place to the Word, which with power, did ... make this joyful sound within my soul ... *Thou art my*

---

[122] Bunyan, *GA*, §§37, 38, 40, 53, 59.
[123] Ibid., §§ 61–62, 72–73, 75, 89–90; cf. Fox, *Journal* (ed. Smith), 44: 'And as I walked towards the gaol, the Word of the Lord came to me, saying: "My love was always to thee, and thou art in my love." And I was ravished with the sense of the love of God'.

Love; and nothing shall separate thee from my Love ... I thought I could have spoken of his Love ... even to the very Crows that sat upon the plow'd lands.[124]

The sermon marked the beginning of his certainty, though not the end of his search. His troubled mind found continuing help, primarily in the promises of the Bible but also, yet again, in the experience of others. To the artless testimony of the Bedford women was added the expository skills of a gifted theologian. A tattered book came into his hands, 'ready to fall piece from piece, if I did but turn it over'. It was Luther's commentary on Galatians, its message so inspiring that, 'before all the books' that he had ever seen, it was the one 'most fit for a wounded Conscience'.[125] In the pages of that sixteenth-century English translation of Luther, Bunyan stumbled on a call to renewed assurance. Its exposition of Galatians 2: 20 came like a shaft of bright sunshine, with its echoes of Paul's radiant certainty: 'the Son of God who loved me and gave himself for me'. Luther had found undeniable assurance through its personal pronouns. 'Read therefore with diligent attention', said the reformer,

> and with great vehemence these words *Me* and *for me* and so practice with thy selfe that thou maist well conceave and print this *Me* in thy heart, and applie it unto thyselfe with a stedfast faith, not doubting but thou art of the number of those to whom this Me belongeth. Also that Christ hath not onely loved Peter and Paule, and given himselfe for them, but that the same grace also which is comprehended in this *Me,* doth as well pertaine and extend unto us as unto them. For as we cannot denie but that we are all sinners ... so we cannot denie but that Christ died for our sinnes yt he might make us righteous.[126]

Though not remotely free from anxious thoughts, the Bible's message and Luther's commentary brought Bunyan to a place of exaltation: 'I loved Christ dearly ... I felt love to him as hot as fire'. Later tormented that he had let Christ down badly, he found comfort in biblical stories of miserable failures who had been mercifully restored. Distressed that he might have 'horribly abused the holy Son of God', he saw that Christ 'was still my friend'. It was as though he was saying: '*I loved thee whilst thou wast committing this sin, I loved thee before, I love thee still, and I will love thee for ever.*' The undeniable fact of Christ's undeterred love was accentuated for him by the rich promise 'in that blessed sixth of *John, And him that comes to me, I will in no wise cast out.* Now I began to consider ... that God had a bigger mouth to speak with, than I had a heart to conceive with'. His harrowing quest had taught him that 'great sins do draw out great grace; and where guilt is most terrible and fierce, there the

---

[124] Ibid., §§91–92.
[125] Ibid., §§129–30.
[126] *A Commentarie of M. Doctor Martin Luther upon the Epistle of S. Paul to the Galathians* (1575), 84.

mercy of God in Christ ... appears most high and mighty'.[127] His personal story, committed to writing during his prison years, was to be greatly used, bringing immense comfort to thousands of others. The compassion of Christ for him had awakened a deep and lasting responsive love, a love that found expression in a lifetime of pastoral ministry, effective preaching and extensive writing.

In the development of Nonconformist spirituality, nothing was of greater importance than love for Christ. Meditations at the Lord's Supper provided Taunton Presbyterians with regular opportunities personally to acknowledge Christ's love for them and publicly confess their love for him. 'Love cannot be satisfied, but by love again. It must be paid in its own coyn'. He deserves their love, for 'when he came, you spit upon him, and refused him, yet he would not be put off from you'.[128] Only a pre-eminent love for Christ could deliver them from an injurious self-love. 'It will make thee ... cease admiring thyself'. For it is only when 'man sets down himself as a Bankrupt' that he can see that 'Christ comes with a full purse, and faith with an empty hand.'[129]

Love for Christ was crucial, not only for their finite life but for their eternal destiny. Baxter was persuaded that, at the end of life, when 'it comes to the trial, the question will not be, who hath Preached most, or heard most, or talked most; but who hath loved most?' In that day 'Christ will not take Sermons, Prayers, Fastings ... instead of love'.[130] Once in heaven, believers will wish they had loved him more on earth. Will they not 'look back upon a life of mercies? doth not kindness melt you? And the Sun-shine of Divine goodness warm your frozen hearts?' Can believers possibly 'over-love him' now?[131]

A Privileged Obligation

Those who profess to love Christ discovered that, like him, they soon encountered hardship. Love for Christ, and his love for them, enabled them to face harsh experiences with resilience and resourcefulness. Loyalty to Christ was a costly allegiance, expressed in daily life as they bore his reproach, carried his cross, followed his example and shared his sufferings.

Bearing the Reproach of Christ

When conventicles were disturbed and the people roughly handled, onlookers often gathered to witness the disorder. Occasionally exposed to ridicule, members might also be 'spoiled [of their goods] ... imprisoned' and 'condemned', 'hooted and pointed at by men'. 'Nothing is more ordinary and

---

[127] Bunyan, *GA*, §§131, 192, 191–92, 215, 249, 252.
[128] Alleine, *Remains*, 213–14.
[129] Ibid. 217–18, 219–20.
[130] Baxter, *Rest*, 601.
[131] Ibid. 33.

common, than that the world should ... brand and black those that will not wear the Livery' of 'its Manners and Examples'. That was what it meant to bear Christ's reproach, for 'we are no worse used and treated than our Lord was'. Shall 'we doat on our Credit' in Christ, said the Hampshire Dissenter Samuel Tomlyns, and yet 'shrink and recoil from sufferings when the Son of God submitted ... to them'? Unbelieving neighbours 'are no better natured' towards Christ 'now he is in his Exaltation' than 'they were in his state of Humiliation'. They continue just 'as ... injurious to his People as they were to him in his own person'.[132] Persecution provided a unique context for identification with Christ: 'Never wonder that thou art hated of men or persecuted of men', for 'if Christ himself were now amongst us ... he would be the most hated man in all the world'.[133]

The implication of such teaching is that in local persecution every genuine believer will readily identify with the reproach of God's people, coming alongside sufferers in their adversities, offering sympathy and support, as did young Jane Keach in 1664. When her husband, Benjamin, was in the pillory at Aylesbury and Winslow, his wife, in her early twenties, stood alongside him and was not silent: there she 'frequently spoke in vindication of her husband, and the principles for which he suffered'.[134] William Jenkyn warned contemporary Christians that to avoid taking their stand with persecuted believers was to go 'the way of the multitude'. Had a desire for social acceptability outweighed their love for Christ? However ruthlessly God's people were despised by the world, they would always be of infinite value to him. 'There is a silent dignity in reproached piety ... As it was with Christ, so it is with the servants of Christ'. A godly woman or man was still holy, 'though never so much disgrast [disgraced] and contemned by men ... Dost thou love Holiness when [it is] compassed about with sufferings and persecution ... the Lord will remember what thou didst for such and such a Servant of his in trouble or distresse'.[135]

---

[132] Tomlyns, *Great Duty*, 4–6, 20.
[133] Ambrose, *Looking*, 404.
[134] Crosby, *English Baptists*, II, 206; cf. Walker, *Keach*, 77–9. In addition to his wife, 'several of his religious friends and acquaintance' accompanied him to this public humiliation: Crosby, *English Baptists*, II, 204. For a detailed account of Keach's arrest and interrogation by magistrates because of the publication of his 'seditious and venomous' book, *The Child's Instructor, or a new and easy Primmer* (1664), see Crosby, *English Baptists*, II, 185–209. Keach maintained that his pillory experience was 'the greatest honour that ever the Lord was pleas'd to confer upon me': Walker, *Keach*, 72; Crosby, *English Baptists*, II, 207. Crosby was well informed, as Keach was his father-in-law.
[135] Jenkyn, *Bush*, 12–14.

Carrying the Cross of Christ

Bearing reproach is passive. It concerns the willing and patient acceptance of vilification and abuse, graciously accepting things the sufferer is powerless to change. Carrying the cross is active; it involves positively, voluntarily and cheerfully responding to the challenge of a difficult and demanding assignment. Bunyan reminded Dissenting sufferers that Bethlehem's innocent infants and, more recently, the French Protestants' children suffered passively; they had no choice in their cruel destiny. But Moses actively chose to suffer affliction with the people of God, and true believers must do the same, 'chuse suffering rather than sin'. When believers 'take up their cross ... an act of the will is intended'.[136]

Quaker leaders constantly reminded Friends that carrying the cross was both a deliberate choice and a daily responsibility. For 'as the receiving of Christ is the means appointed of God to Salvation', so 'bearing thy daily Cross is the only true Testimony of receiving him'.[137] In a letter from Aylesbury gaol, John Crook urged Friends to avoid 'Self-safety' which lures them away from 'the daily Cross', rather to 'love the Cross of Christ ... that all may be Slain and Crucified' that hinders God's people.[138]

William Penn's *No Cross, No Crown* proclaimed the centrality of this truth in Quaker spirituality.[139] His inspiration to write the book in his mid twenties possibly came from his older friend, Thomas Loe, whose persuasive preaching had been instrumental in his 'convincement'. In the closing moments of his life, Loe had taken young William by the hand, saying, 'Dear heart, bear thy cross ... and God will give thee an eternal crown of glory ... There is not another way.'[140] Only a few months later, Penn was incarcerated in the Tower of

---

[136] Bunyan, *MW*, X, 41–43. Bunyan here raises a pastoral concern that troubled many Dissenters, the suffering experienced by innocent children who had to endure deprivation, ostracism, even pain, because of their parents' spiritual allegiance, when the children themselves had no control whatever over the choices made by their elders. An evident lover of children, it was an issue that caused Bunyan immense emotional pain during his own imprisonment. He recalls those such as the 'poor infants that in Ireland, Piedmont, Paris, and other places' endured acute physical suffering, even death. Their 'consent' had not 'been in the suffering, yet they have suffered ... for righteousness', and may 'in some sence be called *Martyrs* of Jesus Christ'. He expands his point in order 'to comfort all those who have had, or yet may have their children thus suffer'. God has his 'Saints small in age as well as in esteem'.
[137] William Penn, *No Cross, No Crown* (1682 ed.), 25 (II, §5). Reference is made in these notes to both the first (1669) and the later (1682) edition. Penn's 1682 chapter and section divisions are provided in brackets for the benefit of readers using later editions.
[138] John Crook, *Design of,* 129.
[139] On its title page, the author is identified as 'An humble Disciple and patient Bearer of the Cross of Jesus'.
[140] Quoted in Braithwaite, *Second Period,* 60–61.

London for publishing an unlicensed book.[141] His immediate response was to use the imprisonment to prepare a new manuscript for the press that appeared in bookshops and on market stalls the following year, equally without licence.[142]

Penn's book was a vigorous challenge to the nominalism of contemporary institutional Christianity. The envisaged reader was the casual enquirer interested in Christianity provided that it did not involve personal sacrifice, 'a Night-walking Nicodemus', willing to meet Christ, but only 'in the dark Customs of the World', that he might 'pass as undiscern'd for fear of bearing the reproachfull Cross'.[143] For Penn, effortless discipleship was a contradiction in terms, a totally unavailable option. He strenuously maintained that there was no more authentic evidence of salvation than cross-bearing, and no more effective act of witness. Although 'the Knowledge and Obedience of the Doctrine of the Cross of Christ' is 'of Infinite moment to the Souls of men', as 'the only Door to true Christianity ... it is so little understood, so much neglected, and what is worse, so bitterly contradicted' by the lifestyle of professing Christians.[144] The way of the cross is 'an Inward submission of the soul to the will of God, as it is manifested by the Light of Christ in the consciences of men, though it be contrary to their own Inclinations'.[145]

Cross-bearing involved a threefold renunciation: of institutional Christianity, contemporary culture and personal self-centredness. Penn's exposure of institutional Christianity traced the Church's gradual decline from the earliest times, how it 'fell from Experience to Tradition, and worship, from power to Form, from life to Letter'.[146] His stark, uncompromising critique of the contemporary church was that 'there seems very little left of Christianity but

---

[141] Occasioned by a public discussion with the London Presbyterian minister Thomas Vincent, Penn's *The Sandy Foundation Shaken* (1668) was a direct attack on aspects of traditional Christian doctrine. Braithwaite admits that in its writing Penn's unquestionable 'zeal outran discretion': *Second Period*, 61.

[142] The 1669 edition was thoroughly revised (not always helpfully, according to Braithwaite, *Second Period*, 62) and greatly enlarged for that of 1682, which was three times as long. Chapters I–VIII and XI–XIII of the 1682 edition contain completely new material. 'An exaggerated impression of Penn's early religious maturity has been caused by the 1682 edn. being used as though it had been composed in 1669': Braithwaite, *Second Period*, 62.

[143] Penn, *No Cross* (1669), 5 (X, §11). This opening sentence of the first edition illustrates its blunt, almost combative, style. This 'Night-walking Nicodemus' sentence is postponed in the more entreating 1682 edition until after over two hundred pages. The first edition plunges immediately into a forceful apologia for the distinctive Quaker lifestyle, dealing initially with 'Sixteen Reasons why Cap-Honour and Titular Respects are neither Honour nor Respects'. The 1682 edition does not concentrate at the beginning on outward conduct but on the necessary inner transformation, moving to an exposure of inner transgressions such as pride, gluttony and avarice, rather than matters of dress and speech.

[144] Penn, *No Cross* (1682), 2–3 (I, §1).

[145] Ibid. 42 (III, §5).

[146] Ibid. 35 (II, §9).

the Name'. Many who belonged to their congregations, of whatever denomination, were little other than 'True Heathens in disguise'.[147] Vibrant worship 'by which the Ancients prayed, wrestled and prevailed with God' had degenerated to a 'dull and insipid Formality'. Physical 'bowings and Cringings, Garments and Furnitures, Perfumes, Voices, and Musicks'[148] had usurped the place of radical discipleship. The way of Christ's cross was not one of ritual ceremonial but of transformed life.

Additionally, bearing the cross demanded the rejection of popular culture and its widely accepted social norms, 'the greatest curiosity and care about visible toyes, for which they never were created'. This included such coveted luxuries as 'curious Trim's, rich and changeable Apparel, nicity of Dress, invention and imitation of Fashions, costly Attirements, mincing Gates [gaits], wanton Looks, Romances, Plays, Treats, Balls, Feasts', preoccupations that would never have 'been in mind if man had staid at home with his Creator'.[149] If such diversions were God's intended lifestyle for a believer, then how should one interpret those biblical exhortations that emphasize the 'need of a daily Cross? a self-denying Life? working out Salvation with fear and trembling? seeking the things that are above? having the Treasure and heart in Heaven?'.[150]

Infinitely more costly is the abandonment of personal self-centredness. Penn believed that many professing Christians took little time to examine their own lives, declining 'to audit Accounts' in their own consciences, 'with Christ thy Light' shining into the dark corners of personal behaviour.[151] The cross is 'that Divine grace and power' which deliberately 'crosseth the carnal wills of men ... and their corrupt affections'. It constantly opposes 'the inordinate and fleshly appetite' of the human mind, 'and so may be justly termed the instrument of mans wholly dying to the world, and being made conformable to the will of God'.[152] Although this 'great Work and Business of the Cross' involves rigorous 'self denial',[153] Penn insists that it is fully attainable for all believers willing to pursue a superior ambition, treasure their unique incentive

---

[147] Ibid. 3–4 (I, §2).

[148] Ibid. 35 (II, §9).

[149] Penn, *No Cross* (1669), 42, ch.III, Reason 8; cf. *No Cross* (1682), XVII, §3. Bunyan was equally critical of the provocative 'Fashions of the times': *The Barren Fig Tree* (1673), in MW, V, 20.

[150] Penn, *No Cross* (1669), 36 (XVI, §1). For Friends, cross-bearing was given essential practical expression in the wholehearted acceptance of a Quaker lifestyle, including the adoption of unadorned clothing, the rejection of conventional flattery, shunning of oath-taking and the like. Concerning Quaker dress, Penn challenges his female readers by asking whether biblical and extra-biblical characters such as 'Eve, Sarah, Susanna, Elizabeth and the Virgin Mary use[d] to Curle, Powder, Pummatum, Patch, Paint, wear false Locks of strange colours ... embroyder'd Pettecoats, Shooes and Slip-slaps, lac'd with Silk or Silver lace, and ruffl'd like Pigeons-feet': ibid. 45 (III, Reason 9).

[151] Penn, *No Cross* (1682), 33 (II, §8).

[152] Ibid. 38–39 (III, §1).

[153] Ibid. 46 (IV, §1).

and claim the promised resources.

The prior ambition that displaces self-love is the overwhelming desire to please God. The mighty conquerors in world history, the great 'Alexanders and Mighty Caesars', sought to please themselves. but in all that Christ did 'he aimed to please his Father'.[154] Believers must do the same.

The inspiring incentive is Christ's exemplary life of self-denial. None 'can be true Disciples, but they that come to bear the Daily Cross, and ... follow the example of the Lord Jesus Christ through his Baptism of Afflictions, Tryals and Temptations'.[155]

> The Son of God is gone before us, and by the bitter cup he drank, and baptism he suffered, has left us an Example ... O come! let us follow him ... the most Victorious Captain of our Salvation! ... 'Tis this most perfect Pattern of self-denial we must follow, if ever we will come to Glory ...[156]

The deliberate and continual abandonment of everything in life contrary 'to the meek and self-denying Life of holy Jesus'[157] is an exacting standard that cannot possibly be achieved by the slender resources of unaided human nature. Daily cross-bearing, this 'great token of Discipleship', though costly, is not an exercise in strenuous self-effort. Those who 'receive Christ in all his Tenders to the Soul' are guaranteed the necessary power, 'that is, an inward force and ability to do whatever he requires: strength to mortifie their Lusts, controle their Affections, resist evil Motions, deny themselves, and overcome the World in its most inticing Appearances'.[158]

Penn was an alert observer of human nature and of the contemporary social scene, as well as being a keen reader with a highly retentive memory. His 'literary masterpiece'[159] is the work of a writer with a logical, analytical, well-stored mind and a refreshingly fine wit. Penn quoted freely from a wide range of authorities, classical,[160] patristic[161] and (to a lesser extent) the Reformers.[162] He produced a major contribution to contemporary devotional literature, with some outstandingly memorable sentences. With its biblical insights, practical

---

[154] Ibid. 47–48 (IV, §5).
[155] Penn, *No Cross* (1669), 39.
[156] Penn, *No Cross* (1682), 46–48 (IV, §§2, 5).
[157] Penn, *No Cross* (1669), 38.
[158] Penn, *No Cross* (1682), 24–25 (II, §5)
[159] R. Newton Flew, *The Idea of Perfection in Christian Theology* (Oxford, 1934), 283.
[160] Most especially Penn, *No Cross* (1682), 376–486 (XIX, §§1–90).
[161] Ibid. 503–11 (XX, §§5–15). For example, writing about the rejection of social conventions such as 'hat-honour' and the use of deferential language, Penn quotes (ibid. 192–93, IX, §39) a letter of Jerome to Celentia, a passage also cited, and similarly, by Robert Barclay, *An Apology for the True Christian Divinity* (1736), 523 (Proposition xv).
[162] See Penn, *No Cross* (1682), 208–209 (X, §10), 267–68 (XIII, §20), for Luther, Erasmus and Tyndale.

application and occasionally trenchant humour,[163] *No Cross, No Crown* is a remarkable combination of historical illustration, literary allusion, social concern,[164] spiritual sensitivity and contemporary relevance.

The theme of daily cross-bearing was not peculiar to Quakerism. Baxter exhorted his readers to 'Live in Communion with a suffering Christ ... Die daily by following Jesus with your Cross'.[165] James Birdwood also insisted that 'Afflictions *from* God, as well as *for* God are part of our Cross which we must take up daily.'[166] The scholarly Theophilus Gale held that the 'noble, great and free' Christian 'is one who can 'bear great crosses with equanimitie and patience'. Such a believer 'follows God in afflictive providences' uncomplainingly, becoming 'a King over his crosses'. That man's 'losses prove his gain, his reproche his glorie, his confinement, his libertie'.[167]

William Dyer said that a sacrificial response to persecution was unlikely in people who had not earlier submitted themselves completely to Christ. They 'that carry not the yoak of Christ upon their necks, will never carry the cross of Christ upon their backs'.[168] During the early weeks of his imprisonment, Joseph Alleine urged his congregation to prepare for suffering. They would never be tested beyond their ability to endure, but must never forget that 'Persecution is one of your Land-marks ... you have learnt nothing that [has] not begun at Christ's Cross'.[169]

---

[163] Penn exposes the miser 'who rarely opens his purse till Quarter-day for fear of losing it', and who 'hungers with Money in his Pocket in a Cook's shop: Yet having made a God of his Gold ... thinks it unnatural to eat what he worships'. Penn claimed to have known some such people who 'when Sick would not spare a Fee to a Doctor ... and so died to save charges: a constancy that canonizes them Martyrs for Money': ibid. 262–63 (XIII, §§15–17).

[164] Note Penn's concern for the poor; for instance, he contrasts extravagant spending on 'superfluous Apparel, foolish may-games, Plays, Dancing-shewes, Taverns, [and] Alehouses' with the urgent need to have 'pale faces ... more commiserated, the grip'd-bellies reliev'd, and naked backs cloath'd ... the famish'd Poor, the distressed Widdow, and helpless Orphant ... provided for': *No Cross* (1669), 60–61 (III, Reasons 12–13); *No Cross* (1682), 367–68 (XVIII, §10).

[165] Baxter, *Last Work*, 'To the Reader', a2v–a3; cf. his *Dying Thoughts*, Appendix, 313: 'Oh how great a part of Christianity is to understand and rightly bear the Cross'; idem, *Works* (ed. Orme), XVIII, 47; Clarke, *General Martyrologie*, Ar., A2: 'whosoever will take Christ truly, must take his Cross as well as his Crown, his Sufferings as well as his Salvation'.

[166] Birdwood, *Heart's-Ease*, 22.

[167] Theophilus Gale, *The Court of the Gentiles*, 5 vols, Part IV (1677), 95 ('Of Reformed Philosophie', Book I, ch.3).

[168] Dyer, *Titles*, 155; a true Christian 'studies more how to adorn the cross, *then* how to avoid the cross'.

[169] Alleine, *Letters*, 9 (28 May 1663).

Following the Example of Christ

In practical terms, this meant following him in willing renunciation. Christ surrendered everything and, in a time of persecution, believers may be called to follow his steps in abandoning their greatest treasures. 'What an honour has he put upon me', said Hardcastle, 'how glorious are these marks of the Lord Jesus'. Recalling Christ's entry into Jerusalem, the imprisoned minister asked:

> Has the Master need of my ass? ... he shall have it with all my heart ... The consideration of Christ's sufferings does wonderfully melt the heart of a true believer, into a rejoicing over his cross, and a readiness and resolution of mind to follow him ... against all opposition ...[170]

For many, it involved the most costly surrender possible, that of home and family life. Following Christ's example was a vital dimension of Bunyan's message to his contemporaries. Nothing must stand in the way. As Christian ran for 'yonder shining light', his wife and children 'began to cry after him to return' but he 'put his fingers in his Ears, and ran on crying, Life, Life, Eternal Life: so he looked not behind him'.[171] This reflected Bunyan's early experience as a believer: following in Christ's steps soon led to imprisonment and deprivation of family life. While in prison, he wrote that he had been helped by Paul's life-threatening experience of persecution in Asia, and the apostle's words about 'the sentence of death' (2 Cor. 1: 9). He said that it was

> by this Scripture I was made to see, that if ever I would suffer rightly, I must first pass a sentence of death upon everything that can properly be called a thing of this life, even to reckon my Self ... Wife ... Children ... health ... enjoyments, and all, as dead to me, and my self as dead to them.

It was the most sacrificial dimension of his commitment, for 'parting with my Wife and poor Children hath oft been to me in this place as the pulling the flesh from my bones'. This was not simply an act of costly self-denial for himself, but one of having to place complete trust in God for their welfare. He might attribute some of the emotional pain to the fact that he was 'somewhat too fond' of them, but it was also because he was naturally haunted by 'the many hardships, miseries and wants that my poor family was like to meet with ... especially my poor blind Child, who lay nearer my heart than all I had besides'. The thought of his ten-year-old daughter sitting in the dark without the caring support of her father was an unrelieved ache. When he considered all that she might suffer, it 'would break my heart to pieces ... I cannot now endure the wind should blow upon thee: but yet ... I must venture you all with God, though it goeth to the quick to leave you'.[172] He treasured his family but, prior

---

[170] *Records* (ed. Underhill), 315, citing Mt. 21: 2–3; Heb. 12: 1–4, 13.
[171] Bunyan, *Pilgrim's Progress*, 10.
[172] Bunyan, *GA*, §§325, 327–28.

to the persecution, had declared in writing his greater loyalty: 'give me Christ on any terms whatsoever he cost: though he cost me friends ... comforts ... all that ever I have ... it will not be kept back ... Father, Mother, Husband, Wife, Land, Livings, nay, life and all shall go, rather then the soul will miss of Christ.'[173]

Bunyan knew that such sacrificial renunciation was not an isolated or rare experience. During persecution, the tension would emerge afresh in the lives of countless Nonconformist families. Writing specifically to help sufferers, he graphically portrayed the temptations that may come from a Dissenter's own family faced with the prospect of the householder's arrest. It was a test of love:

> perhaps the wife of the bosome lies at him, saying, O do not cast thy self away ... what shall I do[?] thou hast said, thou lovest me, now make it manifest by granting this my small request ... Next to this come the Children, all of which are like to come to poverty, to beggery, to be undone for want of wherewithal to feed, and cloath, and provide for them ... Now also come Kindred and Relations ... some chide, some cry, some argue, some threaten, some promise; some flatter ... These are sore temptations ... But God is faithful ... thou shall not have a bigger load, than God will give thee shoulders to bear.[174]

Recognizing the strength of family solidarity, Quaker writers frequently highlighted domestic aspects of the renunciation theme. Rejected by their families, a number of them paid a high price in the initial stages of their Christian experience.[175] John Crook makes precisely the same point as Bunyan when he says that among those things which discourage the potential sufferer is the 'Predominancy of the Affectionate Part ... towards our Relations and Friends; and sometimes in [them] towards us'. There are times when 'it works under Pretence of providing for them', particularly when one can cite biblical authority for this, 'because it is written, *He is worse than an Infidel that provides not for his Family*'. Crook observes that this preoccupation with the family is also seen when 'it is in others towards us', showing itself 'under the colour of Kindness', when friends and family prioritize the family's needs. Crook provides as example the moment in the gospel narrative when, in a storm-tossed boat, Peter calls out: '*Save thy self, Master*', as though his primary concern was for the safety of his Lord, but 'afterward, being under the Passion of Fear ... openly and foully denied his Master'.[176] Both on the lake and in the

---

[173] John Bunyan, *The Doctrine of Law and Grace Unfolded* (1659), in *MW*, II, 144, cf. Thomas Lye's reference to the Marian martyrs' being in danger of recanting on seeing their dependent families: Lye, *Fixed Saint*, 29.

[174] Bunyan, *MW*, X, 89–90.

[175] Rigge, *Constancy in the Truth*, 5–7: 'my Father and Mother stood far from me, and I became as a Stranger to my Mother's Children' but 'the parting ... was little in comparison of that Joy which was set before me'.

[176] Crook, *Design*, 329, citing 1 Tim. 5: 8. For similar treatment of the 'family temptation' theme by a Quaker leader who suffered many years of imprisonment, cf.

garden, Peter's priority was self-preservation, not love for Christ.

Such renunciation did not start with the surrender of family and possessions. Hercules Collins said that Christians must prepare themselves 'to wear the Publick Cross, by wearing it first more privately'. A Christian will never 'be able to part with his Houses, Lands, Liberties ... that cannot first part with a secret lust'.[177] The same thought occurred to Philip Henry but an honest diary entry from 1665 presents the truth as a treasured ideal rather than a present attainment: 'Hee that will suffer hardship when he is called thereunto, must use every day to deny hims[elf] in lesser matters', adding, 'and therein I am wanting'.[178]

These expositors presented a rigorous lifestyle, but they believed with Joseph Caryl that the Spirit's 'chief design' in preserving Job's story was to make it unmistakably clear that 'holy' people can never 'claime priviledge from the cross'.[179] From Ilchester prison, Joseph Alleine urged his people to make this firm commitment unitedly as families. 'Oh! set up God in your Houses'. In persecuting times, they cannot possibly be content 'with a cheap and easie Religion' which costs nothing and yields nothing.[180] Will they not remember their 'Marriage Covenant' with Christ? They took him then, ' "for Richer, for Poorer, for better, for worse". Now prove your love to Christ ... when most slighted ... among men'. Now they could publicly affirm that they had loved 'a naked Christ when there is no hopes of worldly advantage, or promoting of self interest in following him'.[181]

Thousands of Dissenters were given repeated opportunities to follow Christ's example by loving their enemies. This demanding obligation has a prominent place in an exposition of Nonconformist spirituality in dark times. The Quakers had most to say about it,[182] but they were far from being alone.[183]

William Dewsbury's use of the Gen. 22 narrative in his exhortation to 'offer up the dearest Isaac' and to 'trample upon all the fear of Man, and upon all the Representation of hardships, of parting with dear and tender Wife or Loving Husband, or with your dear and tender Children ... and to see their faces no more': Second letter [1664], in W[illiam]. D[ewsbury]., *This for dear Friends in London, and them that are Aboard Ship, in order to Transportation; or else where all abroad* (1664), 6.

[177] Collins, *Voice*, 30.
[178] Henry, *Diaries* (ed. Lee), 167.
[179] Caryl, *Job*, XI, 648.
[180] Alleine, *Letters*, 41 (14 October 1663).
[181] Ibid. 82 (undated).
[182] Isaac Penington, for example, was 'filled with ... love to and prayers for those who had been the means of outwardly afflicting me and others upon the Lord's account': *The Works of Isaac Penington* (1681), I, 406; cf. also Penn's assertion in the unpaginated preface to the *Journal of George Fox* (ed. Ellwood), that Friends 'did not only not show any disposition to Revenge but forgave their cruel Enemies showing Mercy to those that had none for them', for 'they did freely Forgive ... Help and Relieve those that had been Cruel to them'.

Persecution's greatest harm would be to rob them of their love, especially for those people responsible for their suffering.

While in gaol, Baxter reflected that to lose 'one Grain of Love was worse than a long Imprisonment'. Financial deprivation, the confiscation of valued property, or a custodial sentence would only be injurious if it damaged the sufferer, 'seeing we are not near so much hurt by their Severities, as we are by our Sins'.[184] Baxter insisted that if the innocent sufferer would guard against giving way to 'secret wishes of hurt to your adversaries, or to reproachful words against them ... of hurting yourself by passion or sin, because others hurt you by slanders or persecution ... God will keep you from any hurt from enemies'.[185] Love must be expressed in full and free forgiveness of, and heartfelt prayer for, those who had hurt them most.

In 1661, the brisk young Quaker pamphleteer Edward Burrough travelled from Bristol to be alongside London Friends who were being brutally treated.[186] Before long he was in Newgate himself, praying by name for the vengeful civic dignitary who had put him there.[187] Prison officials resolutely ignored the king's command ordering Burrough's release and, in the winter of 1663, he died, urging his fellow-Quakers 'to live in love and peace'.[188] The following year, Esther Biddle wrote from another London gaol to an imprisoned Quaker leader in the North of England. She claimed that Burrough's persecutor, Sir Richard Browne, had ill-treated her also, and 'kicked me till I was sore, and strucke me on the mouth'. She too prayed, 'the Lord forgive him, he knows not what he does'.[189] Christ's prayer for his opponents must be theirs also.

Sharing the Sufferings of Christ

In a context of recurrent hostility, Nonconformist preachers drew rich inspiration from the passion narrative. The Lord's Supper provided ministers with appropriate occasions to view the severity of their own hardships in the light of the courageous response of Jesus to religious opposition, political

---

[183] Bunyan believed that loving and forgiving enemies was uniquely persuasive. Christ's prayer from the Cross, 'Father, forgive them', convinced the centurion that Jesus was a righteous man. He saw 'how Jesus carried it in these his sufferings, as well as to see the execution done': *Seasonable Counsel*, in *MW*, X, 35–36, 102. An entry in John Corbet's personal journal for 1663 says, 'I have no settled Bitterness or Revenge against my Enemies, but I love, pitty and pray for them': *Self-Imployment*, 10.

[184] Sylvester (ed.), *Reliquiae*, III, §125, 3, 2.

[185] Baxter, *Christian Directory*, in *Works* (ed. Orme), II, 125.

[186] London prison conditions at this time were described by an ejected minister: 'Many have dyed in imprisonment & bin even stifled through thronging together, & want of ayre, & necessary helps &c.': *CSPD* 1663–64, 63–65.

[187] H[owgill], *Testimony concerning Edward Burroughs*, 12; Josiah Coale's Testimony, in *The Memorable Works of Edward Burroughs* (1672), [unpaginated].

[188] Burrough was greatly loved by Friends. Over 1,500 people were at his funeral: Penney, *Extracts*, 170. *CSPD* 1663–64, 63–65, doubtless refers to Burrough.

[189] Penney, *Extracts*, 222.

manipulation, emotional sorrow, social rejection and physical onslaught. They took care to highlight the uniqueness of Christ's sufferings as the only means of human redemption; people are not saved by their sufferings, however intense and unjustified, but only by his sacrifice. Yet their costly adversities were to be viewed and endured in the light of his.

In 1682, when persecution of London Dissenters was at its worst, the Presbyterian minister Thomas Doolittle published an extended series of communion expositions, *The Lord's Last Sufferings shewed in the Lord's-Supper*. Doolittle, onetime assistant to Baxter and his continuing friend, was highly regarded as a preacher and author. His earlier book of communion sermons, *A Treatise concerning the Lord's Supper* (1667), had already reached its eleventh edition by 1680, so further reflections were assured of a wide readership. The book could scarcely have been published at a more opportune time. Suffering was a prominent theme in Nonconformist life and thought, and increasing numbers of Huguenot refugees were finding their way to England, with grim stories of barbaric persecution at the hands of France's Catholic authorities.[190]

The harsh legislation of the previous twenty years, as well as earlier Elizabethan legislation,[191] began to be even more rigorously applied and ruthlessly enforced. London meeting-houses were raided, and ministers and members haled before magistrates who often had little desire to punish the offenders. Doolittle himself was convicted of preaching in the autumn of 1682.[192] He was fined £40, a considerable sum.[193] Undeterred, he continued to minister and in the following spring was made to pay an additional £100 for repeatedly preaching during the intervening months. His experience was multiplied throughout London, while the 'Hilton Gang' conducted a widespread and lucrative campaign, raiding conventicles on a regular basis.[194]

---

[190] Horton and Marie-Hélène Davies, *French Huguenots in English-Speaking Lands* (New York and Washington DC, 2000).

[191] A parliamentary measure, aimed at 'uniting His Majesty's Protestant subjects', proposed the repeal of such laws and was brought before the House of Commons. But, realizing that the proposed alternative legislation might prove detrimental to Catholics, Charles II had it discreetly withdrawn and Parliament dissolved, never to meet again during the remaining five years of the king's life. Powerless to act, the House voiced its objection to the king's action by announcing that the Elizabethan legislation they had endeavoured to repeal 'ought not to be enforced against Protestant dissenters'. Such laws were not only 'grievous' to the sufferer, but seriously weakened 'the Protestant interest', encouraged 'Popery' and were 'dangerous to the peace of the kingdom'. Charles had little interest in their dissatisfaction: quotations from Rogers, *Howe*, 193.

[192] For legal action taken against Doolittle and other London ministers, see *EB*, II, 327 [341]; *CSPD* 1680–81, 592, 613; cf. *EB*, I, 498–501 (Appendix 38), for later opposition.

[193] Archbishop Sancroft claimed that he lived on £40 a year: Thomas Bruce [Earl of Ailesbury], *Memoirs of Thomas, Earl of Ailesbury* (2 vols; 1890), I, 155.

[194] Goldie, 'Hilton Gang', 43–73. The gang were ultimately discredited and found guilty of perjury: cf. *EB*, II, 333, 339, 346, 446; III, 249 [P346, 350, 353, 416, 623]; and the

In this context, Doolittle expounded the passion narratives in the Gospels. His primary aim was to provide those present at the Lord's Supper with a 'pattern, or Example' for meditation during communion, so that they might leave the service strengthened in faith and 'more inflamed with Love to and Desires after Christ'. The Gethsemane narrative spoke directly to their vulnerable condition. Those 'whom God loveth most, he might call out to greater exercises by Affliction'.[195] If their sinless Lord experienced such brutal hostility, it was vain for his followers to claim a future without pain. 'God had but one Son without sin, but he had never a one without Scourging'.[196] Jesus used the anticipation of forthcoming suffering to affirm his intimate relationship with God. Christ felt totally deserted, 'yet he did not despair … he still looked upon God as his God and Father'. It was important for suffering believers to learn from Christ's renewal of trust in a compassionate and caring God. 'Thus we … if we be in affliction, should go to God, as to our Father', even 'if we be in desertion', with no sense of the divine presence. The believer could still 'go to him as our God, and trust him and depend upon on him', even when he seemed 'to be most displeased with us, and doth lay his Hand most heavy upon us'.[197]

Christ responded to suffering by increased and intensified prayer. 'Prayer is a sending to Heaven for help when we are ready to faint in our afflictions'. Jesus' prayer expressed his total abandonment to God's unique purpose for the daunting hours ahead. If 'it is for his glory and our good to have affliction removed' then it is appropriate to 'desire it' but, if not, they must submit their 'wills to his and patiently bear it'.[198] Gethsemane is the most persuasive example that God hears, even 'when he doth deny us the thing in kind that we ask for'. Christ prayed 'that the Cup might pass from him', yet, Hebrews says 'that in this thing he was *heard* [Heb. 5: 7],' not ignored, 'for though God did not free him from dying, yet God inabled him to go through it'. Frustrated by his troublesome 'thorn', Paul prayed repeatedly for its removal. The apostle 'was denied the thing that he asked; and yet he was heard, in that God promised assisting sufficient Grace'.[199]

Doolittle acknowledged that in persecution it was wise to take sensible precautions, and there were times when it was right to avoid arrest. During the ministry of Jesus, there were moments 'when they would have laid hands upon him' when he 'did withdraw, and convey himself away from them', for this unique hour had not arrived. Earlier withdrawals were as much part of God's

---

broadsheet, Philoeusebias Misonebulonides, *A Letter to Hilton, the Grand Informer: In Answer to his Several Late Printed Libels* (1682).
[195] Thomas Doolittle, *The Lord's Last Sufferings showed in the Lords-Supper* (1682), 3, 21–2.
[196] Ibid. 294.
[197] Ibid. 56.
[198] Ibid. 59–60.
[199] Ibid. 60.

plan as the moment of willing surrender. Christ here teaches his followers 'that ... in some cases it is lawful to consult our own safety'.[200] At other times, submission to persecutors is the only way for believers to prove their integrity, bear witness, encourage fellow believers and glorify God. In the early 1680s, this was relevant biblical exposition, with fine pastoral sensitivity and immediate practical application to many in that vulnerable London congregation and beyond.

But what of those professing Christians who refused to share his sufferings? The story of Peter's denial exposed a prominent and sensitive theme, the grief of the Dissenter who had deliberately shunned a unique opportunity to suffer for Christ. It was a highly relevant narrative anywhere in the country at that time, but especially in London. Any persecuted believer faced with the prospect of financial deprivation, distraint of goods or lengthy imprisonment with enforced separation from a dependent family, might be tempted to abandon their earlier resolute commitment. In addition to the greatly increased sufferings of the period, the presence of thousands of Huguenot refugees in London and elsewhere alerted Dissenters to the widespread anguish of those among them who, under pressure, had renounced their Calvinistic faith. They found refuge in England, but many had made their dangerous escape heavily burdened with a guilty conscience. Such exiles were the Dissenters' new neighbours. Describing the great 'distresse' of these French refugees, the ejected minister Roger Morrice wrote about 'very many' who had sought refuge in London, 'severall familyes of which are well knowne to mee and others of my acquaintance ... These have left all for Conscience-sake and here many of them have neither acquaintance, habitation, meat nor drink'.[201]

People outside London were equally aware of the atrocities in France.[202] Charles II had given approval in 1681 to the proclamation of a public 'brief', an appeal for financial support for the refugees, and parish clergy were urged to arrange for house-to-house collections.[203] The preaching of appropriate sermons, providing information and urging generosity, was widely encouraged by the publication in 1681 of George Hickes's *The True Notion of Persecution Stated*, and in the following year of Samuel Bolde's *Sermon against*

---

[200] Ibid. 86–87.
[201] *EB*, II, 210–11 [P242].
[202] A 'publique Fast' Sermon (24 April 1678) by Philip Henry shares detailed news of the persecution: Chester, City Record Office, MS D/MH 10. I am indebted to Dr David Wykes for this reference.
[203] E.g. at Earls Colne, Essex, in 1681: Josselin, *Diary* (ed. Macfarlane), 635; cf. Grell, Israel and Tyacke (eds), *From Persecution to Toleration*, 94–5. Further collections were encouraged on later occasions, particularly in the spring of 1688, when the French King had 'set open the prison doores in some Provinces, and given them Liberty to depart out of his Dominions ... naked and almost starved, Some ... released Prisoners came over into England the last Weeke ... all their Estate reall and personall being taken from them': *EB*, IV, 248, 255–56 [Q247, 252].

Persecution.²⁰⁴ A succession of tracts and pamphlets had appeared during the 1670s describing the plight of Protestants, not only in France but also in Germany and Hungary, and private newsletters as well as more public newspapers reported increasing persecution.²⁰⁵ Specific references to cruelty and injustice became widely known, such as the Frenchman 'who was Committed to the Gallys, only for perswading a Person to hear one of the Protestant Ministers preach'. A 'Gentlewoman who was a Protestant being Marryed to a Roman Catholic Gentleman, was ordered to do Penance ... for not coming to Mass ... and afterward to be banished out of the Countrey'. She managed to escape but a local Protestant minister said to have 'vindicate[d] the lawfulness of her Flight' was given her punishment and banished. It was later reported that 'all those who Practice the Law' and 'all manner of Artificers and Tradesmen' were forbidden 'to Exercise their several Imployment ... under the highest Penalties unless they will turn Roman Catholicks'.²⁰⁶

Increasing pressure affected every area of their life: church, home, social relationships, and work; it was almost inevitable that some would conform and publicly disown their Protestant faith. London's Huguenot churches²⁰⁷ made provision for the readmission to membership of distressed exiles who had

---

²⁰⁴ Although both Hickes and Bolde were appalled by the persecution in France, they held divergent views regarding the legislation against English Dissenters, evident from their titles. Hickes, a High Churchman, regarded the 'true notion' of the statutes as the necessary 'punishment' of all opponents of 'true' religion, which should never be described as 'persecution', although this was certainly a fitting term for the French atrocities. Hickes described the sufferings of French Protestants, but they receive only passing mention in Bolde's sermon, which he uses mainly to attack the unjust persecution of English Protestant Dissenters; cf. Mark Goldie, 'The Theory of Religious Intolerance in Restoration England', in Grell, Israel and Tyacke (eds), *From Persecution to Toleration*, 331–68, at 359–62. Deprived in infancy, Bolde had been brought up and educated in the Chester home of an ejected minister, William Cook. This early debt and influence doubtless gave rise to his spirited and occasionally injudicious language, e.g. his reference to this country's persecutors as the 'devil's agents'. On the orders of the bishop of Bristol's court, Bolde's vigorous plea for tolerance led to his imprisonment but he was released on the bishop's unexpected death. William Smythies later published *An Earnest Exhortation to Charity for the Relief of the French Protestants* [1688]. For the encouragement to clergy and people to give generously, see Robin Gwynn, *Huguenot Heritage: The History and Contribution of the Huguenots in Britain* (2nd rev. ed.; Brighton, 2001), 164–65, 168–72, 178. No diocesan was more active in this respect than Henry Compton, bishop of London, who reminded his clergy that 'no case could more deserve your pity' and 'God excuses no man from being good': Gwynn, *Huguenot Heritage*, 165; Carpenter, *Protestant Bishop*, 331.

²⁰⁵ For an introduction to the pamphlet, tract and newspaper coverage in this context, and for much else in the Huguenot story, I am indebted to Gwynn, *Huguenot Heritage*.

²⁰⁶ *Domestick Intelligence, or News from both City and Country*, no. 14 (22 August 1679); no. 16 (29 August 1679).

²⁰⁷ Robin Gwynn, *The Huguenots of London* (Brighton, 1998).

defected, many of whom had done so solely to keep their families together.[208] Morrice heard from his new French neighbours that some had their children 'snatch't from them' and sent to 'popish Nurseryes'.[209] Special services of *reconnaissance* to express penitence and offer readmission were held for large numbers of grieving refugees who stood before the congregation, giving public expression to their remorse.[210] In the year Doolittle's book was published, a widow made *reconnaissance* at the Huguenot church in the City of London 'for her weakness in giving way to the violence used against her and going to *mass*'; another expressed 'her grief at being forced to attend *mass*'.[211] Such services, attended by large congregations, were widely known about in London and provided a sombre local context to any exposition of Peter's denial.

Doolittle analysed Peter's disloyalty, maintaining that his reaction to the unexpected interrogation in the garden exposed some specific weaknesses, especially prevalent in a time of persecution. Peter's initial mistake was that he relied on his own slender and inadequate moral resources, failing to renew his dependence on God. Those were extremely dangerous days, when personal faith was to be severely tried, but Peter did 'not commit himself to God in times of trouble'. The fierce onslaught of persecution in London was a trumpet call to renewed confidence in a sovereign God and total reliance upon him. Fear was the disciple's second failure and Doolittle maintained that Peter's terror was sadly 'inordinate'. He had not been confronted with a threatening public examination 'by a Magistrate sitting in the place of Judicature', but casually challenged by a mere 'Maid that kept the door'.[212] As they sat at the Lord's Table, the London congregation knew that the disciple's cowardly response was in stark contrast to the heroism of some French believers in their own time who had stood firm in the presence of ruthless persecutors. In his popular *Account of the Persecutions*, Jean Claude said that the Huguenots' 'infinite number of Fugitives' had fled to England with nothing but 'Tears and Miseries to bring along with them'.[213] Many certainly had slender material possessions

---

[208] The *dragonnades* obtained forced 'conversions', demanding that the Huguenots attend mass and sign a paper publicly abjuring their 'erroneous' Calvinistic beliefs.

[209] *EB*, II, 210–11 [P242]. In 1681, *Animadversions upon the French King's Declaration* expressed deep concern that Louis XIV had that June encouraged the disintegration of families by publishing a decree promoting the conversion to Catholicism of Protestant children as young of seven.

[210] For the public verbal confession made at these services, see Davies and Davies, *French Huguenots*, 60–61.

[211] *Minutes of the Consistory of the French Church of London, Threadneedle Street, 1679–1692* (ed. Robin D. Gwynn, Huguenot Society of Great Britain and Ireland Quarto Series, 58; 1994), 77, 83.

[212] Doolittle, *Sufferings*, 156.

[213] [Jean Claude], *An Account of the Persecutions and oppressions of the Protestants in France* (1686), 1. Incensed about the publication of Claude's pamphlet, the Catholic James II had it suppressed, publicly burnt (*EB*, III, 117 [P533]), and its English translator, Samuel Rayner, a minor canon of St Paul's, arrested, all of which only served

but they had also come with news of outstanding heroism and loyalty, inspiring stories that found their way into the sermons of many a contemporary English preacher. Not all had disowned their Protestant faith.[214] Claude had concluded his narrative with a testimony that would have challenged any Dissenter in danger of valuing his reputation, property or safety more than his faith. In the multitude of harsh trials, persecuted fellow believers in France had not been 'destitute of Comfort'. Totally loyal to their king and state, they had 'for Twenty years together suffered with exemplary Patience all these furious and dreadful Storms'. Thousands preferred to abandon their homes rather than deny their Lord. They had been given a strength that would not be withheld from their English friends, however fierce the onslaught.[215]

In addition to Peter's concern for his own physical safety, there was a further dimension to his denial, 'a breach of Promise made to Christ himself'. Though warned of defection, he had made a passionate declaration of firm allegiance to Christ, 'that he would dye before he would be offended because of him'. But even under gentle pressure this vehement affirmation proved little more than cheap words. It was a caution to those who had publicly aligned themselves with a Dissenting congregation not to deny in their lives what they had declared with their lips. Peter's self-assured protestation of loyalty taught them never to have 'confidence in our selves' or in earlier spiritual experiences. Although these harassed believers were immensely grateful for 'grace already received', they must not rely on previous blessings. Their trust must be in God alone.[216]

Without a permanent home, Christ had few possessions, and the clothes that belonged to him were removed on his arrest. The preacher knew that people in his congregation, and many others, had suffered the cruel experience of seeing their meagre, often essential, possessions 'distrained' by local officials to cover the cost of fines. Doolittle used the story of the naked Christ to say that 'if we should suffer the loss of outward things, for the sake of Christ, we should take it patiently ... yes joyfully' for so did their Lord and the early Christian believers (Heb. 10: 34). 'What base ingratitude is this in many, that they will rather leave Christ, his ways and worship, than hazard the loss of superfluous

---

to increase sympathy for the victims. Awareness of cruelty to French Protestants was widespread prior to Claude's *Account* and other late seventeenth-century publications. In 1652, Fox and his colleagues in the north of England heard from French people that 'in their nation they used to tie the Protestants to trees and whip them and destroy them': Fox, *Journal* (ed. Smith), 110. News of the appalling Piedmont massacre in 1654 was circulated by Jean-Baptiste Stouppe (then minister of the London Huguenot congregation in Threadneedle Street), *A Collection or Narative sent to ... the Lord Protector ... concerning ... Massacres ... in the Valleys of Piedmont* (1655).

[214] A newsletter of March 1687–8 described contemporary Languedoc Huguenots, who 'notwithstanding all the misery they are put to ... continue firm and will not be deterred from meeting publicly. There are six thousand of them in the wood': HMC, *Fourteenth Report, Portland MSS*, 405.

[215] [Claude], *Account*, 47.

[216] Doolittle, *Sufferings*, 156–58.

enjoyments ... and will flinch and forsake' their faith, 'long before it comes to parting with the clothes upon their backs'. Believers should 'moderate' their affections for the things of this world, for 'if we suffer the spoiling of our Goods for Christ, it is no more than Christ hath suffered for us before'.[217]

Doolittle's exposition addressed crucial pastoral issues concerning believers' anticipation of the next life, particularly how they approached death. From wide experience, he knew that many Christians pass from this life in joyous expectation, but he was equally aware of genuine believers who had experienced heavily clouded days in terminal illness. Christ's total dereliction had been preserved in the Gospels to bring them lasting assurance. Life's approaching end was a time for renewed trust. However bereft, 'remember when you come to dye' that 'he hides not his face from your Souls'. It was only the consciousness of God's presence they had lost, not its reality. And if, at such a time, they were favoured with a sense of God's nearness, they must remember that 'it was not thus with Christ my Lord ... I am comforted because he was forsaken'.[218] His loneliness in suffering assured fretful believers of Christ's immediate presence and their secure destiny.

---

[217] Ibid. 395, 408–409.
[218] Ibid. 368, 425.

Chapter 5

Equipped by the Spirit

The person and work of the Holy Spirit was an important, though rarely dominant, aspect of the theology of Restoration Dissenters.[1] Convinced Trinitarians, for the most part,[2] they emphasized (and in polemical contexts defended) the deity of the Spirit,[3] but their expositions concentrated primarily on his distinctive ministry in the life of believers. Among Nonconformist theologians, John Owen offered the most extensive treatment of the Spirit's person and work in his massive ΠΝΕΥΜΑΤΟΛΟΓΙΑ (1674),[4] and John Goodwin provided a lengthy exposition of the Pauline injunction to 'be filled with the Spirit' (Eph. 5: 18).[5] Additional, and familiar, references to the work of the Spirit are found with some frequency in the sermons and writings of Dissenting preachers. In their interpretation of the Spirit's work, two themes were especially prominent: the Holy Spirit in relation to the incomparable word, and the dependent believer.

---

[1] The work of the Spirit possibly received greater attention immediately prior to the Restoration in response to the different challenges of Quaker and of anti-Trinitarian teaching; cf. Nuttall, *Holy Spirit*; H.J. McLachlan, *Socinianism in Seventeenth-Century England* (Oxford, 1951).

[2] John Biddle, Paul Best and John Knowles each published works denying the deity of the Holy Spirit; such writers had a limited following in seventeenth-century Dissent. See Biddle, *Twelve Arguments against the deity of the Holy Spirit* (1647); idem, *A Twofold Catechism* (1654); *A Short Account of the Life of John Biddle* (1691); Paul Best, *Mysteries Discovered* (1647); and John Owen's expansive response, *Vindiciae Evangelicae* (1655), in *Works*, XII, 3–590.

[3] For example, while staying in London, the young Ralph Thoresby heard a sermon from Samuel Slater junr on Acts 5: 3–4, 'whence he provd the Holy Ghost to be God': Diary of Ralph Thoresby, 2 September 1677. Slater was probably there that Sunday as a visiting preacher during the ministry of Stephen Charnock, whom he would succeed in 1680: Walter Wilson, *The History and Antiquities of Dissenting Churches and Meeting Houses in London* (4 vols; 1808–14), I, 338–42.

[4] John Owen, *Pneumatologia, A Discourse concerning the Holy Spirit* (1674), in *Works*, vols III–IV.

[5] John Goodwin, ΠΛΗΡΩΜΑ ΤΟ ΠΝΕΥΜΑΤΙΚΟΝ, *or A Being Filled with the Holy Spirit* (1670; repr. Edinburgh, 1867).

The Holy Spirit in the Incomparable Word

As with all the Puritans, the Bible was uppermost in Nonconformist spirituality, and regular, frequently systematic, exposition of Scripture was the predominant feature of their corporate life. When the young Agnes Beaumont's father threatened to disinherit her if she continued to attend Bunyan's meetings at Gamlingay, what grieved her most was that if she obeyed her angry father she would 'heare gods word noe more'.[6] The prescribed liturgy was the dominant feature of worship in parish churches, but expository preaching was pre-eminent in Nonconformist worship. Therefore, once their corporate activities became illegal, Bible reading in the home was given enhanced priority, and there is abundant evidence that they grasped every opportunity for increasing their biblical knowledge.

Agnes Beaumont's artless *Narrative* is a striking example of the importance and relevance of Scripture in the life of a young Dissenter. Her story describes the events of a harrowing week in the life of a twenty-two-year-old Bedford church member. In 1674, the times were difficult. Charles II's short-lived Declaration of Indulgence had been withdrawn, and Nonconformist meetings were once again prohibited. It was a severe winter and the uneven Bedfordshire roads were thick with snow. As Bunyan passed through her village on horseback, Agnes begged for a lift to the Gamlingay meeting and (reluctantly) the preacher agreed to take her. At such a time, a well-known leader among local Dissenters could have been arrested and, as a family man, not short of accusers, he hardly wanted to be seen carrying a young unmarried woman.[7] When malicious gossipers told Agnes's widowed father, he locked her out of their Edworth home. At one time, he had attended Bunyan's meetings himself but had not responded to the preacher's evangelistic message, and was now extremely angry that his daughter could be getting a bad name for herself in the surrounding villages. A young lawyer, unsuccessful in his attempts to woo her, was spreading lurid tales among neighbours. Unable to gain access to the home, Agnes spent the cold night in a barn, 'and it was a very darke night ... A Night to be remembered to my lifes End ... It frose vehemently yt night, but I felt noe Cold.' The next morning, she pleaded with her father to allow her indoors, or at least to bring out her Bible and her 'pattings' to protect her feet in the snow. He refused her requests and was adamant; she could return to the family home only on condition that she promise never again to attend a conventicle. She suggested a compromise. Would he let her in if she confined her contacts with Dissenters to Sundays only and promised not to attend midweek meetings? He

---

[6] *Narrative* (ed. Harrison), 44.
[7] In a later edition of *Grace Abounding*, Bunyan defended himself against scurrilous local accusations of immoral behaviour with women. He did not have his '*Misses ... Whores ... Bastards,* yea *two wives at once,* and the like'. Indeed, 'I seldom so much as touch a Womans Hand, for I think these things are not so becoming me': *GA*, §§309, 315.

demanded her total withdrawal from all Dissenting involvement, at least during his lifetime; 'if not I should never have A farthing ... And he held out the key to mee. Said he, "I will never offer it to yow more, and I am resolved yow shall never come within my doore Againe while I live". And I stood Crying by him in the yard.'[8]

The account of her experience over the ensuing days, her reluctant capitulation, immediate remorse, and her father's change of mind, is a moving one. What is important here is its indication that this young believer's faith was informed, inspired, fortified and challenged by Scripture. Her own reading of the Bible, and her pastor's extensive quotations from almost every part of it, had made an indelible impression. 'Soe then I stood at his Chamber Window, pleading and Intreating of him to let me in, beggin and crying. But all in vaine; insteed of letting me in, he bid me begone from the window, or Else he would ... sett me out of the yard.' Her angry father was resolute. He would not open the door. But in that moment a greater dread invaded her sensitive mind: 'Soe then I stood at ye window silent, and that Consideration came into my mind, "How if I should come at last when the doore is shutt and Jesus Christ should say to me, 'Depart from me I know yow not'." '[9] Her reference recalled Bunyan's preaching, possibly at that very period of his ministry.[10]

Agnes's short *Narrative* contains over sixty verses from almost a third of the books of the Bible, the references being almost equally divided between Old and New Testaments. She had been a member of her local church for barely a year but she had been a careful listener and knew her Bible extremely well.

The same can be said of another young Dissenter, Roger Lowe. The *Diary* of this Lancashire apprentice-shopkeeper is full of Scripture. He was not nearly so circumspect in his behaviour as Agnes, and some questionable ale-house companions did little to develop his spirituality, but young Roger knew his Bible, always regretted his lapses and frequently applied the teaching of Scripture to his everyday life.[11]

Dissenters insisted that the Bible must not only be read but also treasured. In the farewell message to his Chesham congregation, William Dyer quoted a popular aphorism, urging them to '[p]rize the Word of God by the worth of it, that you may never come to prize the Word of God by the want of it'. Some Dissenters dreaded that, by one means or another, they might be denied access to their Bibles, and for many prisoners the fear was realized. Meetings were illegal but personal Bible reading was a permissible devotional activity. 'The lesse ... you hear' in public meetings, said Dyer, 'the more doe you read'. In

---

[8] *Narrative* (ed. Harrison), 22–23, 40–41.
[9] Ibid. 20–21.
[10] Bunyan, *MW*, V, 75, 98. *The Strait Gate* was another of Bunyan's greatly expanded sermons. Licensed in November 1675, it may well have been preached initially to his Bedfordshire congregations in the previous year.
[11] Lowe, *Diary* (ed. Sachse), 15, 28, 29, 35, 36, 37, 42, 47, 48, 49, 51, 55, 58, 61, 64, 68–69, 70, 83, 111, 112, 118–19.

their Bibles, 'all sinns are here forbidden, all holiness is here commanded'; in Scripture 'every action and motion' of their lives could be seen 'as a step Heaven-ward' or 'a step Hell-ward'.[12] In examining how the centrality of the Bible was made a reality in daily living, three aspects are especially prominent: memorization, illumination and meditation.

Memorization

A large proportion of Dissenters had known 'the best of Books'[13] from their earliest days. Oliver Heywood's wife was able to read 'the hardest chapter in the bible when she was but foure years of age', and when only six could 'write down passages of the sermon in the chappel'. The Berkshire Quaker Oliver Sansom came from a nominal church background but began reading when he was about six years old and within four months 'could read a Chapter in the Bible pretty readily'.[14] In many families, memorization of Scripture verses was actively encouraged, and in adult life, especially in times of increased persecution, many were fortified by verses learnt by heart. At the ages of ten and nine respectively, Heywood's two 'very towardly' sons, 'plyed their book, read chapters, learned chatichismes, got some chapters and psalmes without book, John repeated the 12th [chapter,] Eliezer the 10th of Revelation'.[15]

The biblical knowledge of Nonconformist people was extraordinary, and their capacity for memorization remarkable.[16] Nathanael Vincent was said to have 'so strong a Memory, that ... when he was but Seven years Old he was wont, for the ease of his tired Father, to repeat his Sermons in the Evenings of the Lord's Day'.[17] In his teenage years, Josiah Langdale was greatly helped by

---

[12] William Dyer, *A Cabinet of Jewels* (1663), 37, 39; cf. Edward Bury, *A Help to Holy Walking, or a Guide to Glory, containing Directions how to worship God, and to walk with him in the whole course of our Lives* (1675), 65. 'If we are kept shorter in respect of Publick means, the greater should be our care to improve all private helps. If we have less ... preaching, the more need to give attendance to Reading': 'Preface to the Reader', *England's Remembrancer* (1663), A2v.

[13] Bunyan, *Pilgrim's Progress*, 29.

[14] Heywood, *Autobiography* (ed. Turner), I, 58; Oliver Sansom, *An Account of Many Remarkable Passages in the Life of ... Oliver Sansom* (1710), 2.

[15] Heywood, *Autobiography* (ed. Turner), I, 234. Both sons would enter the Nonconformist ministry.

[16] In his early twenties, Arise Evans stayed for three months in a Coventry home where there was 'an old Chronicle ... that showed all the passage in Brittain and Ireland from Noahs Floud to William the Conqueror ... a great volume'. He read it whenever he had spare moments during the daytime, 'and bought Candles for the night, so that I got by heart the most material part of it': A[rise]. Evans, *An Echo to the voice from heaven. Or a Narration of the Life, and Manner of the Special Calling and Visions of Arise Evans* (1652), 13.

[17] Nathaniel Taylor, *A Funeral Sermon occasioned by the sudden death of Nathanael Vincent* (1697), 24. One ejected minister, Samuel Birch, said that his daughter Hester, who died when she was seven, 'could repeat without book the Ten Commandments

Thomas Hewson, a thirty-year-old blind thresher. Hewson had 'lost his Sight when about Ten Years of Age; he was never Taught further than the Psalter ... yet this Man taught our Master's Children ... he was a Man of great memory, and of good Understanding'.[18] Robert Pasfield, an 'utterly unlearned' servant in a Puritan household, could neither read nor write but, with a fine gift for memorization, was 'well taught of God' and 'mighty in the Scriptures'. He could easily provide the precise reference for almost any biblical text.[19] Biblical passages had been carefully memorized by an illiterate servant who made application for membership of a Bury St Edmunds Independent church. She shared her spiritual experience with some members who produced it in written form to read to the church meeting, an 'account ... full of Scripture' despite the fact that she 'canot read'.[20] Friends of the Suffolk Independent minister Samuel Fairclough described him as 'a walking Bible'. He rarely used 'any Concordance; for there was not a passage of the whole Scripture almost ... but he would tell you not only the Chapter and Verse, but the place of the page where it was Printed'.[21] When in later life Samuel Angier could no longer read, 'he frequently entertain'd himself with repeating the greatest Part of David's Psalms, and Paul's Epistles'.[22] Determined to prepare himself for every possible hardship, the London Presbyterian minister Thomas Vincent 'had the whole New Testament and Psalms by Heart'. He often said that they who 'took from him his Pulpit and his Cushion, might in time demand his Bible also'.[23] They knew the book well; but more was necessary than the exact repetition of words.

Illumination

Pastorally concerned about the spiritual welfare of London apprentices, Baxter wrote his *Compassionate Counsel for all Young Men*. Hundreds of these youths had come from homes all over the country to work in the metropolis but life was precarious and fraught with serious moral dangers. Even if their masters expected them to attend public worship, mere religion would accomplish little if the Holy Spirit was not actively at work in their lives. Baxter urged them to recognize the essential nature of his ministry of illumination: 'Your souls are

---

Creed &c. many psalmes, part of the gospell, almost ½ of th'assemblyes shorter Catechisme &c. and understood the principles of Religion, and way of salvation by Christ much beyond the usuall capacity of her age': quoted in Nuttall, 'Prayer-Journal', 346.

[18] Langdale, 'Some Account of ... Josiah Langdale', fols 7–8.

[19] William Hinde, *A Faithfull Remonstrance of the Holy Life and Happy Death of John Bruen Esquire of Bruen Stapleford in the County of Chester* (1641), 56–57.

[20] Bury St. Edmunds Congregational Church Book, fol.62.

[21] Clarke, *Lives of Sundry Eminent Persons*, Part I, 164.

[22] *Continuation*, I, 111.

[23] *Account*, 32.

dead to God and Holiness, and your [religious] duties dead, till the Spirit of Christ do quicken them. You are blind to God and mad in sin, till the Spirit illuminate you and give you understanding.' Only the Holy Spirit could 'renew ... hearts, and make them fit to delight in God ... Study therefore obediently these Writings of the Holy Ghost and confidently trust them'. Now that Christ has ascended, the Spirit is his 'Agent on Earth, by whom (in Teachers and Learners) he carrieth on his saving work'.[24] When Christiana's children were catechized, Prudence asked, 'And how doth the Holy Ghost save thee?', to which young James replied, 'By his Illumination ... Renovation, and ... Preservation'.[25] The Independent minister John Evans was separated from his Wrexham congregation, but wrote to urge them to be 'much in searching the scriptures ... and wait for the Spirit's teaching through them ... When you cannot take forth new lessons, learn the old better.'[26]

Preachers insisted that Holy Spirit interprets and applies the biblical message, and relates it to the life of the reader. Obedient practice must follow hard on the heels of scriptural knowledge. 'The Soul of Religion is the practick part',[27] and the essential transition from what believers know to what they do can be effected only by the Holy Spirit. As Anne Bradstreet said to her New England friends: 'Many can speak well but few can do well. We are better scholars in the Theory, then the practique part, but he is a true Christian that is proficient in both.'[28]

Intellectual acquaintance with the text did nothing to guarantee the personal appropriation of its message. The bare words of the Bible, however familiar, could never meet the depths of human need without the work of the Holy Spirit to convince the reader of its truth and apply the word to the individual mind. 'He that would utterly separate the Spirit from the word had as good burn his Bible.'[29] Bunyan had learned the same truth from the Bedford Independent minister, John Gifford, during the early months of his tortuous quest for personal faith. He was urged not to receive 'any truth' merely 'upon trust, as from this or that or another man ... but to cry mightily to God, that he would convince' them of its 'reality ... and set us down therein, by his own Spirit in the holy Word'. Gifford warned his hearers that if they failed to do this and merely imbibed Scripture second-hand, then, 'when temptations come, if strongly, you not having received them with evidence from Heaven, you will find you want that help and strength now to resist, as once you thought you

---

[24] Richard Baxter, *Compassionate Counsel to all Young Men ... especially I, London Apprentices, II Students of Divinity, Physic and Law, III, The Sons of Magistrates and Rich Men* (1681), 106–108.
[25] Bunyan, *Pilgrim's Progress*, 224.
[26] Matthew Henry, *Life of ... Philip Henry*, ed. Williams, 369–70 (Appendix XIV).
[27] Bunyan, *Pilgrim's Progress*, 79.
[28] 'Meditations Divine and Morall', in *The Complete Works of Anne Bradstreet* (ed. J.R. McElrath and Allan P. Robb; Boston, MA, 1981), 195.
[29] Owen, *Works*, III, 192.

had'.[30] Bunyan was not alone in seeking the Spirit's help in obtaining this 'confirmation ... from Heaven' that a particular verse or passage of Scripture was both personally applicable and powerfully effective in his own life. Hardcastle also insisted that, to be effective 'the word of God' must be 'realized and imprinted upon our hearts through the Spirit', and not dependent on 'tradition, custom, example &c'.[31]

As a young man, John Owen discovered that there was a world of difference between knowing the truth and experiencing the power of that truth. Born into a devout Puritan home, he had treasured biblical truth from his earliest days, but gradually realized that he lacked an experiential knowledge of the power of the truth he loved deeply and knew so well intellectually. He came to see that only the Holy Spirit could effect that essential progression from excellent head knowledge to personal experience. Although the words of Scripture were unique, something more was needed if a radical transformation was to take place in his life. It came in 1642 as he sat, 'not yet freed from his melancholy and spiritual troubles', in the London church of St Mary Aldermanbury. He had gone to hear Edmund Calamy, and when it was announced that the celebrated preacher could not be there that day, his cousin urged him to leave along with others. There was plenty of time to go nearby to hear Arthur Jackson at St Michael's, but Owen felt compelled to stay. The 'country minister' deputizing for Calamy preached on Christ's word: 'Why are ye fearful, O ye of little faith?' The biblical text (Mt. 8: 26), totally familiar to Owen, was used by the Spirit 'for the removing of all his doubts'.[32] It addressed his deepest needs and gave him the assurance that he was loved by Christ and truly belonged to him.

The preacher Owen had hoped to hear, Edmund Calamy, knew that there were times when 'a distressed Saint' could turn expectantly to familiar passages of Scripture, only to have 'no comfort in reading them ... But if the Spirit of God did come in, and open his eyes to behold the rich mercies wrapt up in these Promises, and his Interest in them, they would fill him with comfort above

---

[30] Bunyan, *GA*, §117. John Milton exposed those who 'beleeve things' simply because their 'Pastor sayes so, or the [Westminster] Assembly so determine'. He argued that 'Truth is compar'd in Scripture to a streaming fountain; if her waters flow not in a perpetuall progression, they sick'n into a muddy pool of conformity and tradition': *Areopagitica*, in *The Complete Prose Works of John Milton*, II: *1643–1648* (New Haven, CT, 1959), 543.

[31] *Records* (ed. Underhill), 124. James Birdwood had the same message for West Country Dissenters. 'If we read these things and ... do not pray earnestly that the Holy Spirit would bring them home and lay them close to and fix them on our Hearts, they will ... yield us no Comfort': *Heart's-Ease*, 97.

[32] John Asty (ed.), 'Memoirs', in *A Complete Collection of the Sermons of ... John Owen* (1721), iv–v. The story is likely to be reliable as Asty was dependent for biographical information on Owen's close friend, Sir John Hartopp, to whom the book of sermons is dedicated.

expectation.'[33] It was this Spirit-inspired confirmation and personal application of Scripture that the ejected Northamptonshire minister Thomas Browning was seeking when he recorded in his personal journal: 'And yet Christ hath suffered. Ah I want some further worke of God upon my heart about it.' Browning was thoroughly familiar with the biblical text but confessed: 'I do not find the Spirit bringing me words for instruction and strengthening as I desire ... I have them not upon my heart with power and evidence with life and sweetness that I am really strengthened thereby', honestly adding, 'I don't find the reading of the Word so to me as I would have it.'[34]

The Bible was of momentous significance because of its distinctive function: revealing the true self in the immensity of human need, and unveiling Christ in the sufficiency of divine grace. Bunyan portrayed Scripture as the unique 'Looking-glass', 'one of a thousand'. It presents a sinner 'one way, with his own Feature exactly', yet 'turn it but an other way, and it would shew one the very Face ... of the Prince of Pilgrims himself'. Such 'excellency is there in that Glass' that those who 'have a mind to see him' will by 'the very Crown of Thorns' and 'the holes in his Hands', know beyond doubt that they are loved.[35]

Even Scripture that they had not consciously memorized could return vividly to their minds. In Agnes Beaumont's adversity this word was like a skilfully directed arrow: 'still this Scripture would often dart in upon my mind'.[36] During that wintry night in the barn, scriptural phrases came to her with supportive strength: 'that Scripture came with mighty power upon my heart'. Harassed as she was, it penetrated her troubled mind: 'the same Scripture would run throw and throw my heart'. During that long night, 'bewaileing the loss of my fathers love ... that good word darted upon my mind, "The father himselfe loveth yow" '.[37] She may well have heard this from Bunyan in the Bedford Meeting. From personal experience he knew 'how great a task' it was, without the Spirit's help, 'for a poor soul' weighed down by sin 'to say in Faith, but this one word, *Father!*' He could testify but a few years later, 'I myself have often found, that when I can say but this word *Father*, it doth me more good, than when I call him by any other Scripture Name'.[38] Even if Agnes was to lose her own father, another, and better, remained.

When, fearful about her future, she accepted the alluring door-key, and stood inside her home, it was her immediate recollection of Scripture that exposed her

---

[33] Edmund Calamy, *The Godly Man's Ark, or City of Refuge in the Day of his Distress* (6th ed.; 1669), 98–99.
[34] London, Congregational Library, MS I.f.34, Thomas Browning, Autobiography, [unfoliated].
[35] Bunyan, *Pilgrim's Progress*, 287. Bunyan also makes use of the mirror imagery in his *A Book for Boys and Girls, Divine Emblems or Temporal Things Spiritualised*, in *MW*, VI, 250 (Emblem xlviii, 'Upon a Looking-glass').
[36] *Narrative* (ed. Harrison), 24, 36.
[37] Ibid. 25.
[38] Bunyan, *MW*, II, 252; VIII, 247.

frailty:

> And as soone as I got within the doore, that dreadful Scripture came upon my mind, 'They yt deny me before men, them will I deny before my father and ye Angells that are in heaven'; And yt word 'he yt forsaketh not ffather and mother and all yt he hath, is not worthy of me' 'Oh, thought I ... what have I done this night?'[39]

The references to 'father' are especially poignant; yielding to the pressures of a fractious father she had momentarily ignored a greater Father. When Agnes was reconciled to her earthly father, the word was still pursuing her, even anticipating the sad events of the night when her then-penitent father would die at home. 'Towards night that Scripture would often run in my mind ... them words runn through my mind'.[40] Similar expressions, describing biblical verses darting into, and running through, the mind, recur throughout her pastor's *Grace Abounding*, including the same phrase, 'that dreadful Scripture'.[41] She had listened attentively to Bunyan's preaching.

Barely two days after he had received his daughter back into the home, Agnes's father was to be taken seriously ill. 'I was strucke w[i]th A paine at my heart in my sleepe', he said. 'I shall dye presently ... And he sat upright in his bed, Crying out to the Lord for mercy'. He was able to dress, but:

> As he sat by the fyre ... he Changed black in ye face ... And as I stood by him to hold his head, he leant Against me with all his Weight. Oh, this was A very frightfull thing to me indeed! ... if I leave him, he will drop in [the] fier; And if I stand by him, he will dye in my Armes, And noe body neare mee. 'Oh', I cryed out, 'Lord helpe me, what shall I doe?' Them words darted in upon my mind, 'Feare not I am with thee; be not dismaied, I am thy god ... I will up hold thee'.

As she ran to her brother's home for help, the ground thick with snow, her fear of the dark night was natural enough. Yet again, this young believer was sustained by Scripture:

> I was suddainly surprised w[i]th these thoughts, that there was rogues behind mee, that would kill mee. With that I hastily lookt behind mee, and those word[s] dropt upon my mind, 'ye Angels of thee Lord Incampeth round About them that feare him.'[42]

The experience of Agnes Beaumont reveals how firmly rooted in her mind were the words of Scripture. Nonconformist pastors encouraged their people to treasure the Bible's unique message by practising the discipline of reading it

---

[39] *Narrative* (ed. Harrison), 42.
[40] Ibid. 51.
[41] Ibid. 42; cf. Bunyan, *GA*, §230.
[42] *Narrative* (ed. Harrison), 54–60.

every day. Convinced of its unique power of persuasion, many of them could relate stories of people who had experienced conversion through reading the Bible at home. Richard Baxter's father had been brought to personal faith 'by the bare reading of the Scriptures in private, without either Preaching, or Godly Company, or any other Books but the Bible'.[43] Nobody could complain that biblical teaching was above the level of their intellectual ability. God's word in Scripture was purposely written 'in a plain language', said William Thomas, 'that ... no simple man might make this excuse that the Scriptures are hard'. The Bible's message was 'so plain ... that any workman may see the way to Heaven, if he has eyes to see'. He quoted Chrysostom's exposition of the Lucan parable of the rich man and Lazarus, that 'the grace of the Holy Spirit ordained that ... uninstructed and illiterate men' should be among those who composed the biblical books, 'so that the most unlearned of all men, should ... benefit by the reading' of them.[44]

Edward Bury, a friend and near neighbour of Philip Henry, acknowledged that the believer may not always feel like reading his Bible, but 'if difficult duties be neglected, we shall never reach Heaven'. There are problematical passages, to be sure, but 'the most necessary' truths are 'plain and easie'; 'here indeed a Lamb may wade, and an Elephant ... swim'.[45] This is not to infer that the reading of Scripture will always fire the believer's imagination. With refreshing honesty, Bunyan confessed the variability of his own experience.

> I have sometimes seen more in a line of the Bible then I could well tell how to stand under, and yet at another time the whole Bible hath been to my as drie as a stick, or rather, my heart hath been so dead and drie unto it, that I could not conceive the least dram of refreshment, though I have lookt it all over.[46]

Dissenters were encouraged to regard Scripture as a priceless treasure, but to recognize also that they would have limited insight into its unique worth and power unless the Spirit revealed its incomparable value to them. From pastoral experience Owen knew that in times of overwhelming adversity some genuine believers had often gone expectantly 'for water to the well' of Scripture, but were 'not able to draw'. They had turned to biblical promises for refreshment, only to 'find no more savour in them than in the white of an egg'. But when those same promises 'are brought to remembrance by the Spirit the Comforter, who is with them and in them, how full of life and power are they!'[47]

The Spirit's help in applying Scripture to present needs was to be sought on a daily basis. Thomas Froysell recalled that the disciples were baffled about the

---

[43] Sylvester (ed.), *Reliquiae*, I, I, §1.
[44] Thomas, *Preservative*, 'Epistle to the Reader', quoting Chrysostom, *De Lazaro*, Discourse 3.
[45] Bury, *Help*, 66.
[46] Bunyan, *GA*, 102, Conclusion, §4.
[47] Owen, *Works*, XI, 347.

precise meaning of a parable until they urged Christ 'in private to unlock the Cabinet' of his teaching, that he might 'shew them the Jewel, or meaning of it'.[48] To marginalize this daily 'exercise' was to expose oneself to innumerable perils. Alleine's daily self-interrogation included the searching question: 'Have I not neglected or been very overly [superficial] in the reading of God's holy Word?'[49]

In a farewell message to his Somerset church, William Thomas urged them to read and receive the biblical message not only as a jewel to cherish but as essential food to digest for their spiritual sustenance.

> Every man hath (as it were) two men; one inward, the other outward. The inward man is the Soul made after the image of God. The outward man is the Body ... These two men live and subsist by a different nourishment; the body by receiving natural food, the soul by receiving the Word of God.[50]

'If you would maintain a Heavenly Spirit, get all the nourishment you can for it' said the Axminster Independent minister Bartholomew Ashwood.

> The Word and Ordinances are to the inner-man, as nourishing food to the outward, which strengthens the spiritual part, and maintains its vigour and activity ... Your bodies can better want their appointed food, than your souls their daily bread.[51]

Bible reading schemes were suggested to young Dissenters. Nurtured in a Puritan home, Isaac Archer read through his Bible in a year, and continued this practice during his undergraduate years in Cambridge, 'according to Mr. Bifield's directions'. He confessed, however, that he did not derive the benefit he might have done, largely 'for want of due meditation'.[52] The Bible was to be read as God's letter to the people he loved. Friendship 'imposeth upon every man the reading of a friends letter', and 'reading 'the Letters of the highest

---

[48] Thomas Froysell, *Sermons concerning Grace and Temptations* (1678), 6, quoting Mk 4: 10.

[49] Alleine, *Remaines*, 8. For many Independent congregations, the discipline of daily Bible reading was part of the church's covenant obligation. On joining the Woodbridge church, new members pledged themselves to 'Endeavour to know ye Scriptures more fully ... being led by ye Spirit': Records of the Woodbridge Congregational Church, fol.1.

[50] Thomas, *Preservative*, 1. In support, Thomas quotes Augustine's observation in *Ad Fratres in Eremo*, Sermo 56, on 2 Cor. 4: 16.

[51] Ashwood, *Heavenly Trade*, 140–41.

[52] Storey (ed.), *Two Diaries*, 60, referring to Nicholas Byfield, *Directions for the Private Reading of the Scriptures* (1618). Byfield's scheme was to read three to four chapters from the Old Testament, followed by two from the New, each day. His popular *Directions* included an analytical study of every biblical book and suggestions concerning 'things specially to be marked' in the course of daily reading.

God' is 'the highest duty' of every Christian.[53]

Thomas feared that some of his regular churchgoing contemporaries were more committed to habitual attendance at communion than to the regular reading of Scripture, ready 'to receive the Token, that is the Lord's Supper', but 'careless of reading the Letter with which that token is sent'. The sacramental 'Tokens' are 'annexed' to the Scripture, which describes their 'profitable use', and without it 'the Sacrament may be like Judah's pledge, a condemning token' rather than a spiritual blessing.[54]

Many Dissenters with a genuine desire to profit from daily Bible reading were discouraged by a variety of 'distractions'. Nathanael Vincent suggested some practical measures to help those genuinely troubled by the problem, including the recognition of Scripture's 'divine authority', its sufficiency as their essential 'guide ... to everlasting blessedness', and their dependence on the Holy Spirit, 'by whose inspiration' it was given. As they open their Bibles, they should imagine 'the Lord himself just by you, when you read his Word', and anticipate his specific guidance, as if divine instruction 'had dropt from God out of Heaven into your hand', that 'every step' taken in life, might be 'rightly ordered'. It was of immense importance not simply to receive God's word as they read, but to talk to others about it; 'it will fix it in your Thoughts and Hearts better'.[55]

It was not considered sufficient, however, to give themselves to reading Scripture privately or hearing it expounded publicly. It was also of the greatest importance to cultivate the art of meditating upon it. This was spiritual exercise that drove the Word more deeply into their minds.

Meditation

The Puritan tradition emphasized the necessity of both significant involvement in society and disciplined withdrawal from it. Intensely critical of 'Popery', they were not sympathetic to the monastic escape (as they saw it) from the harsh realities of the everyday world.[56] Yet many of their best writers acknowledged a debt to that tradition and admired the spirituality of devout leaders such as Chrysostom, Augustine, Jerome, Bernard of Clairvaux and others, and the margins of many Nonconformist publications are replete with quotations from their writings.[57] Dissenters were united, however, in the

---

[53] Thomas, *Preservative*, 6.
[54] Ibid., referring to the grim narrative in Gen. 38: 17–18, 26.
[55] Vincent, *Cure*, 233–37.
[56] 'I cannot praise a fugitive and cloister'd vertue, unexercis'd & unbreath'd, that never sallies out and sees her adversary, but slinks out of the race, where that immortall garland is to be run for, not without dust and heat': Milton, *Areopagitica*, in *Complete Prose Works*, II, 515.
[57] Nathanael Ranew, *Solitude Improved by Divine Meditation* (1670), A4v: 'The great scholars of the world have not only been great readers but great Students in musing and

resolute conviction that Christian holiness was not to be sought in a monastic retreat but among the daily pressures of home, work, church and local society.

Social involvement was essential but, to be effective, appointed periods away from the world were also vital, so that the believer could spend time with God, and in that daily exercise meditation played a vital role. As Baxter put it: 'Though I would not perswade thee ... to the Hermites Wilderness, nor to the Monks Cell, yet I would advise thee to frequent solitariness.' He honestly admitted that Puritans had 'fled so far from the solitude of supersitition, that we have cast off the solitude of contemplative devotion'.[58] Lovers want to be together, and the believer's love is best expressed in prayerful communion. Preston defined holiness as 'nothing else but ... a keeping of the heart close to God ... and this love makes us doe'.[59]

Many of them were persuaded that regular time for quiet reflection was a physical benefit as well as a spiritual obligation. John Downame had reminded his generation that recreation is 'not onely lawfull, but also profitable and necessary, if wee bee exercised in them according to God's Word'. For the Christian, this life is an arena of conflict, and God knows that 'we could not hold out in our pilgrimage and warfare without some refreshing'. Therefore he has 'graciously allowed us some time ... to take pleasure and delight, that being refreshed, we may more lustily proceed in our journey'. He has not made us 'fit instruments of perpetuall motion' for, just 'as the strings of a Lute let down & remitted, doe sound sweeter when they are raised againe to their full pitch ... so our bodies and minds if they have no remission from our labours, will make but dull musicke'. Downame insists that this is true, 'not onely of our bodies, but also of our minds'; they too 'cannot doe things above their strength',[60] so time for quiet reflection is necessary, mentally as well as physically.

Nonconformists were hardly innovators when it came to expounding the benefit, purpose and pattern of meditation. They drew widely on earlier writers. In the immediate post-Reformation period, some Protestants regarded meditation with suspicion as a primarily Catholic form of devotion. The English medieval mystics such as Julian of Norwich, Richard Rolle, Walter Hilton and the author of *The Cloud of Unknowing* were neglected or marginalized by them, and even summarily dismissed as devotional writers

---

pondering', men such as 'Cyprian, Ambrose, Augustine and other Saints in the succeeding Ages'.

[58] Baxter, *Rest*, 715.

[59] John Preston, *The New Creature, or a Treatise of Sanctification* [published with *The Saints Qualification*] (1634), Sermon I, 319.

[60] John Downame, *A Guide to Godlynesse* (1629), 262–64. The benefit of meditation is not overlooked by Richard Rogers: 'That as men wearied, desire rest; so we ... may *seeke* ease to our *mindes* by meditation': *Seaven Treatises* (1610), 253. When writing about meditation, Baxter also insists on the importance of its contribution to 'a sound and chearfull body': *Rest*, 692–93.

whose message and methods belonged to an unreformed past.[61]

Among seventeenth-century Puritans, however, the meditative tradition found fresh advocates in Richard Greenham[62] and Richard Rogers.[63] Greenham presented meditation as the most appropriate response to preaching, the means by which the hearer can 'digest' the sermon, and apply it by 'the continuall searching of ourselves' in the light of its teaching, endeavouring to 'lay up all [these] things in the treasures of our hearts'.[64] It was, however, the steady stream of writings over the first half of the century by Greenham's friend Joseph Hall that brought the practice of devotional meditation into the lives of members as well as ministers, conformists and Dissenters alike.[65] Given this impetus, Nonconformity produced its own advocates of meditation. Though frequently creative in presentation, their basic ideas were largely dependent on earlier authors. Isaac Ambrose wrote fully and imaginatively on the subject but drew heavily, and without specific acknowledgement, on what Hall and others had written; he also made extensive use of Baxter's comprehensive treatment of the theme in *The Saints' Everlasting Rest.*

In emphasizing its worth, Nonconformist writers held that meditation enhanced the value and effectiveness of every other spiritual discipline. It was the 'duty by which all other duties are improved'.[66] Prayer, Bible reading, attendance at public worship, listening to Christian preaching, participation in the sacraments, keeping the Sabbath, service to others, were all greatly enriched if they became the focus of meditation. A recent interpreter of Puritan spirituality claims that George Swinnock believed meditation occupied a 'place of distinction among the spiritual duties by virtue of the fact that it is practised in conjunction with all of them, and ultimately determines their success'.[67]

---

[61] The fifteenth-century classic, *The Imitation of Christ,* was edited and published by Thomas Rogers, but in a truncated version, its entire 'Book Four', with its concentration on sacramental devotion, omitted.

[62] *The Workes of ... Richard Greenham,* Part II: *Grave Counsels and Godly Observations* (3rd ed.; 1601) is a collection of Greenham's meditations, alphabetically arranged, from 'Admonition' through to 'Zeale' in 75 chapters, and published after his death in 1594 in the hope that they would encourage regular devotional meditation.

[63] Rogers, *Seaven Treatises,* 243–316. Rogers focuses on the necessity of self-examination and the disciplined reading of Scripture, dealing with some of the problems a believer may encounter in doing so.

[64] Greenham, *Grave Counsels,* in *Workes,* 205.

[65] Joseph Hall, *Meditations and Vowes, Divine and Morall* (1605): *Arte of Divine Meditation* (1607); *Holy Observations* (1607); *Occasional Meditations* (1630); *The Remedy of Prophanenesse, or the True Sight and Feare of the Almighty* (1637); *The Breathings of the Devout Soul and Select Thoughts ... A Century of Divine Breathings for a ravished Soule* (1648); *Susurrium cum Deo: or Holy Self-Conferences of the Devout Soul* (1651); *Holy Raptures* (1654).

[66] Baxter, *Rest,* 695.

[67] J. Stephen Yuille, *Puritan Spirituality: The Fear of God in the Affective Theology of George Swinnock* (Milton Keynes, 2007), 190. For a well-documented introduction to

As to the nature of meditation, Baxter described it as 'Preaching to ones self'. It is entering into 'a serious debate' with one's own heart, urging it 'with the most weighty and powerful Arguments' as did the Psalmist: 'Why art thou cast down, O my Soul' (Psa. 42: 11) and 'Bless the Lord, O my soul' (Psa. 103: 1-5). Unhurried meditation provided the opportunity for 'pleading the case with our own Souls', and Baxter repeatedly insisted that such teaching was not remotely innovative.[68] 'The like you may see in the Meditations of Augustine and Bernard'. Here is 'no new path ... but that which the Saints have ever used in their Meditations'. Imaginatively, Baxter suggested that his readers might care to reflect on the pulpit skills of an admired preacher and make him their meditation model, noticing how carefully he instructed, explained, exhorted, issued warm appeals and applied his message. They could not do better than 'set him as a pattern ... for ... imitation' and practice the preacher's art as they addressed themselves in meditation. Baxter applied these familiar preaching categories to the devotional exercise of personal meditation because 'every good Christian is a good Preacher to his own Soul'.

One of the preacher's priorities is 'Explanation', so the believer is encouraged to 'study the difficulties' in the biblical passage chosen for meditation 'till the doctrine is clear'. This should be followed with 'Confirmation', with its unhurried reflection on the way in which those particular verses strengthen personal faith, before moving to 'Information', recalling 'any supportive arguments' from other biblical passages. 'Instruction' is a further aim, for those who meditate must ponder the verses' practical implications, honestly confessing under 'Examination' specific items of failure: 'try thy self' and 'chide thy heart for its Omissions and Commissions'. Accepting the necessity of 'Reproof', those who meditate must 'be willing to discover' [uncover] their personal 'neglect'. 'Application' addresses the issue of how, in specific terms, such errors are to be put right in everyday life. 'Encouragement' is also important, noting the specific support offered by this teaching, closing with special '[t]hanks to God' for everything this self-addressing exercise of the internal 'preacher' has revealed.[69]

No longer able to minister regularly to the same congregation, a significant number of ejected ministers used something similar to this 'homiletical' form of spiritual discipline to preach to themselves and, as a consequence, frequently reflected on the importance of meditation for their people. On a bleak Monday, barely six weeks after 'Black Bartholomew' day, Henry Newcome was naturally missing his warmly appreciative Manchester congregation. Gone were the days when he could reflect prayerfully on what he had preached the

---

Puritan teaching regarding meditation, see Joel R. Beeke, *Puritan Reformed Spirituality* (Grand Rapids, MI, 2004), 73–100.

[68] Such ideas were frequently expressed by Greenham and Rogers when describing the nature of meditation.

[69] Baxter, *Rest*, 744–45.

previous day, and the help it may have brought to specific people whose pastoral needs were known to him. He was first to admit that, in the earlier cultivation of his own devotional life, he had been greatly helped by the discipline of regular sermon preparation. The message had touched his own heart before it reached theirs, and he had derived much personal inspiration while preparing to help others, Now, by contrast with earlier days, it was no longer possible to make the excuse that personal meditation had been crowded out by sermon preparation.

> I desire to make improvement of my present condition for meditation, heretofore w[he]n I offered to meditate I had some sermon to make, & my meditations came out upon ym usually. Now I have yt let [hindrance] taken off. Sure it is yt now I should finde no excuse from yt duty.[70]

When the ejected Essex minister Nathanael Ranew was confined to home at the time of London's Great Plague, he gave himself to a serious study of the theme. He maintained that meditation was the spiritual discipline that supplemented and enhanced two other essential elements in daily communion with God. Meditation enriched Bible reading and stimulated prayer. Ranew insisted that the 'true Christian' must 'grow' all his 'life time' and those who 'meditate most, will grow most' and keep 'growing to the end'.[71]

For the Bible to have a lastingly beneficial effect in daily life, it must be read unhurriedly, slowly imbibing the words of the text, for 'as Meat cannot nourish if not digested, no more will the word till by meditation, thou makest it thy own'.[72] 'It is like the ... digesting power, by helping to concoct spiritual food, and turn it into spiritual nourishment', and this 'is not by head-work, but heart-work, when the will ... resolvedly chuses, and the affections earnestly embrace heavenly things.'[73] In Ranew's exposition, the Christian desiring to meditate 'must act the part of the Exquisite Miner' and 'dig deep' and, unhurriedly, 'dig all over ... and gather up the Riches of it ... as they come to view in the Mines of Spiritual Treasure'. In meditation there must be a 'searching and scanning ... an extension of thoughts, a looking about' for the riches, meaning, implications, consequences and demands of what the Christian is reading. 'Pondering is an expression from Goldsmiths and Tradesmen'. Such men 'desire to know the full weight of a thing', its 'value or worth for their profit and use. Thus the ... Goldsmith weighs his Silver and Gold, the Jeweller weighs his rich Pearls, Rubies and Diamonds'. Those who meditate 'must hold the scales, to weigh, so

---

[70] Newcome, *Diary* (ed. Heywood), 131.
[71] Ranew, *Solitude*, A3v. Many writers use this imagery of meditation as essential sustenance. Baxter says that as in the body 'the stomack must chilifie the food', so 'the understanding must take in Truths, and prepare them for the will, and it must receive them, and commend them to the affections': *Rest*, 698 [paginated incorrectly as 798].
[72] Bury, *Help*, 62.
[73] Ranew, *Solitude*, A3–A3v.

well as we can, these so rich and precious things ... these ... Pearls of Heavenly Treasure ... that unspeakably surmount all other things'.[74]

Baxter urged his readers to anticipate heaven by meditating on the heavenly life, and not 'wilfully resist the Spirit' by ignoring the priority of such a 'revealed duty'. It would lead to 'an increase of all thy graces', enabling them to 'grow beyond the stature of ... Christians' who neglected it, for (although meditation was 'considered to be a Duty by all'), it was constantly 'denied by most'. Those who practised meditation would find it made them infinitely 'more serviceable' in the places where they lived and worked, and enriched beyond measure their 'fellowship with God'.

But these preachers believed that its neglect was widespread. Many people, greatly 'troubled in mind, if they omit but a Sermon, a Fast, or a Prayer in publick or private' were not remotely disturbed if they have 'omitted Meditation ... all their life time'. The neglect was serious because the Holy Spirit used meditation as the divinely appointed means whereby the believer received the realities eloquently described in the pages of Scripture.[75] Nonconformist preachers and writers therefore offered practical guidance to overcome this neglect.

An appointed Time

Believers with a desire and determination to meditate are honouring an appointment made with God. They are saying: 'Lord, I now come purposely to see thee ... to spend some fit portion of time with thee'. 'Every Meditation', says Ranew, 'is giving a fresh visit ... to this best of Friends'.[76] Baxter knows that although 'a stated time' for meditation is desirable, it is not always possible. Many do not have 'their time at command, and therefore cannot set their hours', and 'many are so poor that the necessities of their families will deny them this freedom'. People in these circumstances should 'redeem time as much as they can', given 'the very labours of their callings'. Frequency is of the greatest importance, thus preventing 'a strangeness betwixt thy soul and God ... Seldomness will make thee unfruitful in the work.' The more it is practised, the more it will be valued, and the greater the consequent benefit. 'If thou eat but [one] meal' in 'two or three daies, thou wilt lose thy strength' as quickly as it comes. It is important for every individual to choose the best opportunity for meditation, and that should be 'when their spirits [are] most active and fit for contemplation'. For Baxter, the time 'I have always found fittest for my self is ... the Evening, from Sun-setting to the twilight'.[77]

---

[74] Ibid. 42–43.
[75] Baxter, *Rest*, 694–95.
[76] Ranew, *Solitude*, 67.
[77] Baxter, *Rest*, 703–709; cf. Ambrose, *Compleat Works*, 182, on 'the Nature and Kinds of Meditation': 'No time can be prescribed for all men ... it is enough that we set apart that time wherein we are aptest for that service'.

Dissenters were encouraged to use sermons as useful vehicles for later meditation. It was for this reason that large numbers of them took careful notes during preaching so that they could have the sermon readily available, either for personal meditation or 'repetition' in the company of others. When, in younger life, John Angier went to hear John Rogers preach at Dedham, he made sure that 'after [the] Sermon, when others staid, discoursed, [and] dispatched business, he for his part went home to his chamber'. There, he 'meditated, prayed, work'd the Sermon upon his heart for about an hour, and thereby imprinted it so lastingly upon his memory' that by the 'time the family got home', he was happy to participate in family life.[78] It was an ideal not easily attained. In later life, Philip Henry noted in his diary the saying of 'a Godly Man a Hearer of his' that had greatly 'affected' him: 'I find it easier to go six Miles to hear a Sermon, than to spend one quarter of an Hour in meditating and Praying over it in secret (as I should) when I go Home.'[79]

Edmund Calamy senior, the ejected rector of St Mary Aldermanbury, was convinced that the 'reason why all the Sermons we hear do us no more good, is for want of Divine meditation'. It 'is not the having of meat upon your table will feed you, but you must eat it and not only eat it, but ... digest it'. One sermon well 'meditated upon, is better than twenty Sermons without meditation'. Calamy knew of people who 'hear a Sermon, go away, and never think of it afterwards' and 'never seek by meditation to root' the message in their hearts.[80] Henry Newcome grieved that he had not meditated on a sermon heard a few days earlier, 'and being alone desired to be humbled for my neglect of meditation thro' so much busynes ... And so I had profit from meditateinge on Mr. Jones his sermon ye last Wednesday on Psa. 17: 3'.[81] Again, 'Mr. Johnson ... preached savouryly on Phil. 2: 14 ... I meditated after & had comfort and wee had very sweet repetition.'[82]

Whatever the most appropriate time, solitude was essential, but in homes of modest size, and frequently crowded, this was rarely possible. It was when Newcome visited a hugely spacious home that the need for occasional seclusion swept over him. 'I went to see my Lord Delamere ... and being walking in that great dining room there, I had a very fine solitary hour. I could not but conclude that we lose much by not being alone sometimes, and ... I meditated of this – Who loved me?'[83] Moreover, once alone the exercise must be unhurried, with time for 'viewing and reviewing' and 'bettering of Thoughts'. All too often,

---

[78] *Life of Angier*, 51.
[79] Henry, *Diaries* (ed. Lee), 330.
[80] Edmund Calamy, *The Art of Divine Meditation* (1686), 31–2; cf. James Ussher, *A Method for Meditation* (1651), 49: It is 'required of every man' to take the sermon 'home to himselfe ... as they did in gathering of Manna', for 'every Sermon is but a preparation for meditation'.
[81] Newcome, *Diary* (ed. Heywood), 94.
[82] Ibid. 134.
[83] Newcome, *Autobiography* (ed. Parkinson), I, 138.

'we are too hasty and eager' to bring our devotions to an end. It is not simply 'Digging into the Golden Mine', says Ranew, but '[d]igging long'; this is what 'finds and fetches up the Treasure'.[84]

An appropriate Place

The right place must be found, 'freed from every hindrance'. If a student cannot 'study in a crowd', how much more do believers need to be alone for meditation when they are using 'all the powers of the Soul ... upon an object so far above Nature'. Some appreciated the opportunity of meditating outdoors, as Isaac had done, and Jesus who used 'a solitary Garden' so frequently that Judas knew exactly where to find him. 'Christ had his accustomed place ... and so must we.' Christ meditated in Gethsemane 'on the sufferings that our sins had deserved' but we meditate 'on the glory he hath purchased, that the love of the Father, and the Joy of the Spirit, might enter at our thoughts, and revive our affections, and overflow our souls'.[85] After hearing a disappointing sermon at the start of the day, the young Ralph Thoresby 'retired into the garden' in the evening, where he 'had more satisfaction in half an hour's meditation ... than in all the day besides'.[86] For those who lived with large families, undisturbed meditation in the open countryside gave them a rich sense of the greatness and glory of God. The diary of Roger Lowe has many references to his outdoor meditations. Disappointed about a fragile relationship, he 'went to Towne Heath and meditated upon these words: "It's good to hope and quietly to waite." Observation: that hopeing and waiting for a possible thing is a Christian's duty in time of difficultie'.[87]

During his extensive itinerancy, Oliver Heywood frequently used journeys for meditation. 'I set out towards Craven travelled al alone, but had much of gods presence in meditation ... I rode to Alverthorpe, in the way god helped my heart in admiring his goodness ... God helpt me in meditating of the work of redemption in my journey ... oh it was a Bethel in my journey homewards that day'.[88]

A prepared Mind

Baxter insisted on the importance of preparation. In Eden, 'mans heart had nothing in it that might grieve the Spirit'. Then, it was 'the delightful habitation of his Maker ... There grew no strangeness, till the heart grew sinful, and too loathsome a dungeon for God to delight in'. Yet, through the unique work of Christ, the human heart can still be 'renewed and repaired by the Spirit, and purged of its lusts, and beautified with his Image'. A merciful God 'will yet

---

[84] Ranew, *Solitude*, 45, 47.
[85] Baxter, *Rest*, 714–16.
[86] Thoresby, *Diary* (ed. Hunter), I, 43.
[87] Lowe, *Diary* (ed. Sachse), 64.
[88] Heywood, *Autobiography* (ed. Turner), II, 78, 99, 107, 113.

acknowledge it his own and, Christ will manifest himself unto it, and the Spirit will take it for his Temple and Residence'. The believer's part must include laying aside all distractions 'of thy business ... troubles ... enjoyments ... that may take up any room in thy Soul'. Get it 'as empty as possibly thou canst', that it may be 'filled with God. ... Thrust not Christ into the stable and the manger, as if thou hadst better guests for the chiefest rooms.' As the leprous king Uzziah was speedily removed from the Jerusalem temple, 'thrust these thoughts from the Temple of thy heart, which have the badge of God's Prohibition upon them'. If alien preoccupations can be dismissed, lofty thoughts of God must take their place. Everyone needs 'to have the deepest apprehensions of the presence of God', and his 'incomprehensible Greatness'. 'Suppose thou wert going to such a wrestling as Jacobs, or to see the sight which the three disciples saw' in the Mount of Transfiguration, 'how reverently wouldst thou both approach and behold!' The benefits are incalculable; 'if it do succeed, it will be an admission of thee into the presence of God ... and admit thee in the next room to the Angels themselves, a means to make thee live and die ... joyfully'. He that 'trades at Heaven ... is the only gainer, and he that neglecteth it is the only loser'. How 'seriously should this work be done!'[89]

The wider Canvas

Meditation on the words of Scripture was always given priority but, like many Christians of their time, Dissenters also recognized the value of what earlier writers described as 'occasional meditation'. Although God has spoken primarily in Scripture, he had also communicated his message through creation. The aim of such meditation was to 'spiritualize all outward objects and occurrences ... There is no creature in which there are not manifest footsteps of the power, wisdom, and goodness of God.' The objective was to 'see God in all things, and thereby make some spiritual use, and improvement' of them.[90]

There were times when they focused their spiritual attention specifically on the natural world. The writings of Richard Sibbes were highly popular among Dissenters; he used the opening exaltation of Psalm 19 to suggest that '[e]very creature hath a beame of Gods glory in it', describing the created world as 'a Theatre of the glory of God'. Sibbes held that 'all the spirituall vigour of every thing comes from the holy Spirit', who 'elevates nature above it selfe, and sets a spirituall stampe, and puts divine qualities upon it';[91] for the spiritually

---

[89] Baxter, *Rest*, 716–18.
[90] Thomas Gouge, *The Young Man's Guide thro' the Wilderness of this World to the Heavenly Canaan* (1672), 28. Baxter said that by 'comparing the objects of Sense with the objects of faith' we may the better discern 'the transcendent worth of Glory, by arguing from sensitive delights as from the less to the greater': *Rest*, 753.
[91] Richard Sibbes, *The Excellencie of the Gospell above the Law* (1639), 244, 60. In expounding the glory of God manifest in the world he has created, Sibbes goes on to assert that the majestic splendour of creation is diminished when compared to the glory

sensitive believer, the created world thus becomes vocal. The Welsh Puritan Walter Cradock also encouraged his readers not to neglect God's message in the world around them. It could be discerned there as well as in the pages of their treasured Bibles. 'For the creatures are God's Characters: God hath written his will in his word at large, and hath written a copy of it (as it were) in the creatures, that by one we might be enabled to understand the other.' God has 'so cast things by his creation and providence ... that every thing might resemble heavenly things'. We should all 'learn something from the creatures ... so that they should not be onely for our use', but also that we 'observe their nature, and qualities, and learn somewhat from them'.[92]

Baxter was not always happy about Cradock's views, but they had this love of the natural world in common. In addition to their Bibles, believers must 'learn to open the [volumes of] creatures and ... providence, to read of God and Glory' so that 'we might have a fuller taste of Christ and Heaven in every bit of bread we eat ... than most men have in the use of the Sacrament'. Every 'condition, and creature' provides us with 'advantages to a heavenly life ... if we had but hearts to ... improve them'.[93] 'Meditation hath a large field to walk in, and hath as many objects to work upon, as there are matters, and lines, and words in the Scripture',[94] for '[e]very creature hath the name of God and of our final Rest written upon it'. A devout believer can discern this message as clearly as he can read on a signpost 'the name of the Town or City which it points to'. This 'spiritual use of creatures and providences' is 'Gods great end' in giving them to us, and 'he that overlooks this end, must needs rob God of his chiefest praise'.[95]

Baxter urges believers to use their 'senses' in meditation as well as their reason and 'affections'. 'Compare ... the excellencies of heaven with those glorious works of creation which our eyes do now behold. What a deal of wisdom, and power and goodness' are manifested in them. 'What a deal of the Majesty of the great Creator doth shine in the face of this fabric, the world! ... What rare workmanship' in the creating of the human body and those of animals. 'What excellency in every plant we see ... in the beauty of Flowers! ... What glory is in the least of yonder Stars ... What an inconceivable glory hath the Sun! Why all this is nothing to the glory of Heaven' and, contrasted with the promised glory, it 'is but as the wall of the Palace-yard'.[96]

Reflecting on the glory of the created world, the Oxford Dissenter and

---

of God's mercy and the 'compassion that shines in Christ', for the 'glory of the creature is worth nothing to this': ibid. 244.
[92] Walter Cradock, *Divine Drops Distilled from the Fountain of Holy Scriptures* (1650), 36, 45–6 [45 is numbered 39 in error]. For Cradock, see Geoffrey F. Nuttall, *The Welsh Saints, 1640–1660* (Cardiff, 1957), 18–36.
[93] Baxter, *Rest*, 687–88.
[94] Ibid. 700–701.
[95] Ibid. 686.
[96] Ibid. 756–57.

horticulturalist, Ralph Austen, published a technical work on fruit farming, a *Treatise of Fruit-trees,* which was followed by a series of meditations on *The Spiritual Use of an Orchard* (1653). Its author discerned a distinctive Christian message in the actions of planting, feeding, grafting, protecting (from disease), transplanting, pruning and enjoying fruit trees. For Austen, a 'Garden of Fruit-trees is a Volumne full of good Notions', with teaching of spiritual importance to the alert onlooker. An 'illiterate man may here read distinctly, And the Learned man may find matter enough ... to exercise his Wisdome and Judgement'.[97]

Dissenters who acquired the art of discerning God's message through the created world recorded such lessons in diaries and journals. Baxter's message was identical to that of Thomas Taylor, that '[e]very Creature may be a Preacher to him in whom the spirit first inwardly preacheth',[98] and such messages need to be written down and preserved for later reflection[99] and possibly for the use of others.[100] William Kiffin was among those who recorded their meditations and experiences primarily to edify their children.[101]

Philip Henry often recorded occasions when God spoke to him through family details, everyday happenings and local events. 'The first day of my son John's putting on a coat', which the devoted father turned to a prayer: 'cloth[e] him, lord, with grace, with righteousness, with Christ Jesus'.[102] In March 1661 he was, like others, concerned about the future. It was by no means clear that he and his Presbyterian colleagues would be 'comprehended' within the national

---

[97] Ralph Austen, *The Spiritual Use of an Orchard,* [with *A Treatise of Fruit Trees*] (1653), unpaginated dedication 'To the Reverend Dr, Langley'. For Austen and his leadership in Baptist life in Oxford, see Larry J. Kreitzer, *'Seditious Sectaryes': The Baptist Conventiclers of Oxford 1641–1691* (Bletchley, 2006), 199–243.
[98] Thomas Taylor, *A Man in Christ, to which is added a Treatise, containing Meditations from the Creatures* (1628), 104.
[99] 'For the stricter observing his Conversation', Thomas Doolittle 'kept a Diary that by a review he might gain Experience, and rectifie Mistakes': Williams, *Christian Sincerity*, unpaginated conclusion.
[100] *Memoirs of the Life of ... the Rev. Thomas Halyburton, Professor of Divinity ... at St. Andrews* (3rd ed.; Edinburgh, 1733), 7–8: 'But if I can recount the Lord's gracious Conduct toward me ... in a way of Conviction, Illumination, Conversion, Consolation, and Edification ... and if ever it should fall into the Hands of any other Christian it might ... be not unuseful'; and [Bagshaw], *Vavasor Powell*, 19: 'These few things ... I have set down ... to keep a memorial of the Lords benefits; and to stir up others, into whose hands these few notes may come.'
[101] William Orme (ed.), *Remarkable Passages in the Life of William Kiffin* (1823), 1. Cf. [Henry Newcome], *A Faithful Narrative of the Life and Death of ... John Machin* (1671), 56–57: of his spiritual journal, Machin said, 'The occasion of making and writing this Book, was ... for my Sons sake, and Posterities imitation'; Walter Wood (ed.), *Memoirs of Walter Pringle* (Edinburgh, 1847), 1: 'Since God gave me children, it hath been much upon my mind to record, for their use, the wonderful goodness of God to me ... to stir up and exhort my children ... to lay hold on the offered salvation'.
[102] Henry, *Diaries* (ed. Lee), 90.

church. Would he be allowed to continue as curate at Worthenbury?[103] 'Garden prepar'd. I sow, God knows who may reap; the lord make me wise to sow to the spirit & then of the spirit I shal bee sure to reap life everlasting'. A week later: 'Garden finisht, in time of an eclipse, lord lift up upon mee the light of thy countenance, & let noth[ing] cloud it towards my soul.' He later expressed his longing for 'a Spiritual heart to improve natural objects for heavenly purposes', praying 'lord, work such a heart in mee'.[104] Even his fractious father-in-law's disapproving glance provided a moment for spiritual reflection, and recalled a rich Old Testament benediction; Daniel Matthews had never been happy about the marriage. On a visit to the family home, Katharine Henry observed that her 'father's countenance was less serene yn of late it hath been, whatever is ye matter', her husband noting in his diary, 'lord, lift up ye light of *thy countenance upon us.*' As Christmas approached that year, noticing 'how busy ... people were to praepare their houses for christmas', he longed that 'so & much more busy should I bee to prepare my heart for Xt'. When, three years later, his sisters 'remov'd to Kensington from little Chelsey', he noted that 'here we have no continuing city, but wee seek one to come'.[105]

Bunyan insisted on the primacy of Scripture in meditation, but also encouraged devotional reflection on the created world, believing that 'it is the wisdom of God to speak to us oft-times by Trees, Gold, Silver, Stones, Beasts, Fowls, Fishes, Spiders, Ants, Frogs, Flies, Lice, Dust &c'. If 'we count there is no meaning in them', we are deaf to the 'Voice' of the God who speaks through them.[106] It was natural for him to write in this way when he had encouraged

---

[103] The previous month he had met the dean of Chester. He 'p[er]swaded with me to conform, telling mee, else my preferm[en]t was gone and what? are you wiser then the King & Bishops, but God grant that I may never bee left to consult with flesh and bloud in such matters.'. A few days later, 'Ministers met at Hanmer, to discourse about the lawfulness of re-ordination ... as for mys[el]f I am at present of the mind it ought not to bee, the former being sufficient, lord shew us what thou wouldst have us to doe': ibid. 78.

[104] Ibid. 81, 169. Earlier entries demonstrate that Henry was keenly alert to the spiritual value of occasional meditation. In February 1663, for example, the task of planting 'Ha[w]thorn-sets ... to hedge in ye Ortyard' brought to his mind a familiar Psalm [80: 12–16], which he turned to a prayer: 'lord bee thou a wall of fire round about thy Church, & let not ye wild boar out of ye Forrest devour thy tender plants'. A few weeks later, a 'great Oak' had 'fallen by ye Turf-house ... tis likely scores of yeares growing to that bigness, yet cutt down in a day, though not without much adoe', recalling another Psalm [76: 6, 12]: 'hee slips off ye spirit of Princes, as a man would slip off a flower between his fingers with ease'. A few months later he put on a 'new suit', adding in his diary, 'lord, cloth[e] me with thy Righteousnes[s], which is a comely costly lasting everlasting Garm[en]t'. The next month he recorded that there was a 'great store of Plums about ye house this year, beyond w[ha]t hath been ordinary', praying in Johannine terms, 'lord, make mee as fruitful to thee as ground, trees &c. are to mee, herein would my father bee glorified': ibid. 130, 133, 144, 146, 137.

[105] Ibid. 153, 186.

[106] Bunyan, *Solomon's Temple Spiritualized (*1688), in *MW*, VII, 5–115, at 94.

children to learn from eggs, candles, frogs, snails and sheets of paper.[107] When Bunyan's Prudence catechized her boys, she urged them not only to 'give ear to what good talk' they might 'hear from others' but, also to '[o]bserve also and that with carefulness, what the Heavens and the Earth do teach you'.[108]

Everyday events might convey an arresting spiritual message.[109] Indeed, the New England Puritan Anne Bradstreet maintained that there 'is no object that we see; no action that we doe; no evill that we feele or feare, but we may make some spirituall advantage of all: and he that makes such improvement is wise as well as pious'.[110]

Commonplace events and objects became vehicles for the transmission of spiritual truths. Ambrose was convinced that 'a holy heart' will 'convert and digest' everyday occurrences 'into spiritual and useful thoughts', urging his readers to develop this practice of 'holy, sweet and useful Meditations out of all objects'.[111] Ideally, from life's 'ordinary occurrences and occasions', the sanctified believer should be able to distil 'holy, and sweet, and usefull meditations' out of all 'the things he sees & heares'.[112] Christians ought to 'make a spirituall use of naturall things, and so turne earth (as it were) into heaven'. This world 'is a great library ... wherein we may read and see plainly the attributes of God'. Even 'inanimate creatures have a voyce, and speak loudly to men; our part is to 'learn their language, and hearken to them'.[113]

There are abundant illustrations of the practice, with occasionally bizarre examples. Firmly believing that 'there is nothing that wee can see, which doth not put us in mind of God', Joseph Hall produced a whole series of them. Some 'footsteps of a Deity' may be visible in 'every Ant and Worme in the ground, every Spider in our window'. If we but 'sharpen our eyes, to a spiritual perspicacity', we can always discern something of the 'omnipotence, and infinite *wisdom*' of their Creator'.[114] We should 'suffer no object to crosse us in our way' without putting it to 'some Spirituall use, and application'.[115] 'Every thing that we see, reades us new lectures of Wisdome, and Pietie. It is a shame for a Man to bee ignorant, or Godlesse, under so many Tutors.'[116] Christians might meditate, for example, on their morning act of dressing, on witnessing

---

[107] Bunyan, *Book for Boys and Girls*, in *MW*, VI, 190–269.
[108] Bunyan, *Pilgrim's Progress*, 226.
[109] Diary of Sarah Savage, fols 6–7: 'Tuesday morning An occasional Meditation – the coals coming to the fire with ise on them at first seemed as if they would put out the fire but afterwards made it burn more fiercely. 'Tis often so, that which seemes against me is really for me. Have not afflictions worked for my good?'
[110] Bradstreet, 'Meditations Divine and Morall', 195.
[111] Isaac Ambrose, *Prima, Media and Ultima* (4 parts; 1654), II, 68–69.
[112] Thomas Goodwin, *The Vanity of Thoughts Discovered, with their Danger and Cure* (1643), 12.
[113] Austen, *Spiritual Use of an Orchard*, vi–vii, ix.
[114] Hall, *Remedy of Prophanenesse*, 54–56.
[115] Hall, *Occasional Meditations*, 'Epistle Dedicatorie'.
[116] Ibid., 'The Proeme', [unpaginated].

'an Eclipse of the Sunne' or seeing a 'gliding Starre'. Given unhurried reflection, there are things to be learnt from a carefree robin, a soaring lark, fighting cocks, a barking dog, a dormouse, a wasp sting, gnats in the sun, boys playing, a coin in the bottom of a river and, soberly, 'a Grave digged up'.[117]

Spiritually profitable meditation might focus, for example, '*Upon the sight of a Crow pulling off wooll from the backe of a Sheape*'. Reflecting on such a common rural occurrence, Dissenters would find its message helpful in time of persecution. Bishop Hall was no stranger to opposition and as a convinced Calvinist had encountered considerable hardship during the Laudian period, especially on account of his sympathetic attitude to Puritans. In adverse circumstances, harassed Nonconformists of the next generation would appreciate the relevance of Hall's imaginative reflection. 'How well these Creatures know whom they may be bold with. That Crow durst not doe this to a Wolfe, or Mastive'. Rather, '[m]eekness of spirit commonly drawes on [attracts] injuries. The cruelty of ill natures usually seekes those, not who deserve worst, but who will beare most … Sheepish dispositions are best to others; worst to themselves'. In times of oppression, believers must be 'willing to take injuries' and not be 'guilty of provoking them'. For 'harmlessnesse', said Hall, 'let me goe for a Sheepe, but whoesover will bee tearing my fleece, let him looke to himselfe.'[118]

Focusing in meditation on 'a Crum[b] going the wrong way' suggests that the Hackney Dissenter William Spurstowe was not lacking in ingenuity, but his message about the vulnerability of life was not remotely trivial. A 'mean and contemptible thing' such as a crumb 'hath scarce substance enough to be felt' but in the wrong place at the wrong time it has the power to kill, for 'in the Throat, it is such as can hardly be endured'. 'O, how frail and mutable is the Life of Man', so speedily destroyed, not only 'by Instruments of War and Slaughter', but by a single '*Hair*, a Raisin-Stone, a Feather, a Crum[b], and a thousand such inconsiderable things, which have a power to extinguish Life, but none to preserve it'. What may be casually dismissed as 'small sins' can become 'great dangers to the soul'.[119] Believers were to acquire 'the skill to *spiritualize* all objects, and providences, turning every thing by a Divine Chymistry … into spirit and nourishment', inspiring a deeper awareness of God and of themselves. First, 'to climbe up to a more clear Vision and fervent love of God, and then descending make these a clear Mirrour' in which to see ourselves. Like 'windows', they 'let in that light into the private and dark recesses of the heart' leading, hopefully, to 'a more thorough purgation of it

---

[117] Ibid. 172–74, 7–9, 9–10, 32–34, 87–91, 60–64, 37–59, 146–48, 226–28, 125–27, 99–102, 140–46, 20–22.
[118] Ibid. 72–73.
[119] William Spurstow, *The Spiritual Chymist, or Six Decads of Divine Meditations* (1666), 11.

self.'[120] Spurstow offered meditations on the morning dew, a magnifying glass, a ship's rudder, a moulting peacock, a looking glass, the contrast between a bee hive and wasps nest, even 'a debauched Minister', and many more.

Occasional meditation of this kind was not lacking in critics, and the practice became popular enough to be panned by unsympathetic readers, notably Jonathan Swift in his brief *Meditations upon a Broomstick*.[121] At one time, even Milton treated it disparagingly.[122] Untroubled by such criticism, meditating believers continued to use customary objects and events as instructive 'signposts',[123] directing them to realities beyond themselves. They believed it to be a devotional practice with good biblical precedent as, for example, in the Old Testament's graphic Wisdom literature. Job discerned immense spiritual lessons from the created order. Ecclesiastes drew heavily on creation and material things for its lessons: sun, wind, sea, rivers, wine, laughter, houses, vineyards, eating, drinking, weeping and innumerable others. The moral teaching of Proverbs was illustrated from the behaviour of insects and animals as well as humans (good and bad) in a variety of different poses, traders in sexual favours, traffickers in damaging talk, thieves, drones, lovers of money, flatterers and the rest. Jesus himself was in a rich prophetic and wisdom tradition when he invited reflection on aspects of the natural world and 'in his thoughts translated the book of the creatures, into the book of grace'.[124] Believers with a love for Scripture felt perfectly at home with the idea of meditating on visual objects as well as verbal truths.

The Holy Spirit and the Dependent Believer

In the wide range of their teaching on Christian spirituality, Dissenters

---

[120] Ibid., sig. A3v, 'The Preface to the Reader'.
[121] Embarrassed by repeated requests to read Boyle's *Meditations* in a fashionable household, Swift inserted his parody into Boyle's book and read it seriously to the assembled company: *The Prose Works of Jonathan Swift* (ed. Temple Scott, 12 vols; 1897–1908), I, 331–4; it is included with *A Discourse concerning the Mechanical Operation of the Spirit*, from *A Tale of a Tub* (1704; facsimile repr. Menston, 1970). Cf. J. Middleton Murry, *Jonathan Swift, a Critical Biography* (1954), 112–13.
[122] John Milton, *Animadversions upon the Remonstrants Defence against Smectymnuus*, (1641), 29: lampooning Hall, he refers to 'A Meditation of yours doubtlesse observ'd at Lambeth from one of the Archiepiscopall Kittens'.
[123] U. Milo Kaufmann, *The Pilgrim's Progress and Traditions in Puritan Meditation* (New Haven, CT, 1966), 188.
[124] Goodwin, *Vanity of Thoughts*, 12; cf. ibid: 'So our Saviour Christ ... when he came by a well, hee speakes of the Water of life'. See also Hall, *Occasional Meditations*, 'Epistle Dedicatorie', where he says: 'the Lord of Life himselfe Who upon the drawing of water from the well of Shilo, on the day of the great Hosanna, tooke occasion to speake of those Living waters w[hi]ch should flow from every true beleever'; Austen, *Spiritual Use of an Orchard*, 'Preface to the Reader': 'Our blessed Saviour ... taught much by similitudes'.

particularly emphasized the creativity, sensitivity and crucial necessity of the Holy Spirit's ministry in the life of a believer.

First, they rejoiced in the Spirit's creative originality in the experience of every Christian. He does not choose to deal with every person in exactly the same way. Every believer is dependent on the same biblical message but its truths are not communicated, received, understood, applied or experienced in precisely the same form or manner by all. People have distinctive personalities, possess different intellectual capacities and come from diverse backgrounds. Knowing human dissimilarity, the Spirit deals with each one differently. In younger life, Baxter was troubled that, unlike some of his contemporaries, he had not experienced a sudden conversion. He worried that his 'Grief and Humiliation' over sin 'was no greater, and because I could weep no more for this'. He came to see that not every Christian has a dramatic initial encounter with Christ and that with many the 'soul ... groweth up by degrees'. It was not his 'Nature' to 'weep for other Things' in life, so it was hardly surprising that he would not be as emotionally distressed as others. 'I understood at last that God breaketh not all Mens hearts alike'.[125]

Thomas Goodwin maintained that a believer might know rich things about God that he could not adequately communicate to others, or may only be able to express in a partial or fragmentary form what he knows deeply from experience. He spoke of a man who, admiring an excellent portrait of Queen Elizabeth, said, 'I have one picture of her that I will not sell for all the pictures of her in the world ... I saw her but once ... and the image of her remains still in me; which image he could convey to no man living'.

> [There] are those things in Christ ... which can never be pictured out by words ... Therefore ... if you ask me what it is the saints know, which another man knows not, I answer you fully, he himself cannot tell you, for it is certain, as to that impression which the Holy Ghost leaves upon the heart of a man, that man can never make the like impression on another.

A fellow Christian 'may describe it to you, but he cannot convey the same image and impression upon the heart of any man else'.[126]

Dissenting preachers frequently referred to the sensitivity of the Spirit. Convinced of his personhood, they insisted that he who imparts indescribable joy can be seriously grieved. Emphasizing his immeasurable love, Owen maintained that believers grieve the Spirit when they ignore him. All the Holy Spirit's 'actings towards us and in us are fruits of love' and this 'requires a return of love'. By 'negligence and carelessness', Christians can drift away from their earlier loving obedience and holiness into this sad and serious 'defect of an answerable love'.[127]

---

[125] Sylvester (ed.), *Reliquiae*, I, I, §6, 3–4.
[126] Goodwin, *Works*, IV, 297.
[127] Owen, *Works*, IV, 414.

Ashwood held that the Spirit is most grieved when believers 'abuse' his kindness. From Isaiah 63: 9–10, he recalled how the Israelite people 'rebelled and vexed his holy Spirit', despite God's care for them, and that in 'all their afflictions, he was afflicted'. 'Nothing does more grieve the Spirit of God than the abuse of his kindness ... when the Lord hath been ... bearing with, and carrying of them for a long time; and all this is slighted', when 'the Soul takes no notice of all this grace'. 'Unkindness from those we love' affects us more deeply than 'injuries from strangers or enemies', and 'such are the sins of Believers', said Ashwood; 'they are ... enemies to their own Souls'. The Spirit sees that some believers, 'by their carnal affections, and sensual passions ... do not onely resist him, and frustrate his work in them; but ... lose many a mercy'. Ashwood urges his people 'to be tender of the Spirit' and 'not unkind to his person', that they 'do not undervalue' what he has done for them, nor 'resist' all he still wants to do in them.[128]

'God is angry with wicked men's sins, but he is grieved for yours', as 'when a man's wife that lies at his bosom, or his child, shall wrong him'. Goodwin imagines 'a father that is a magistrate' or 'one that maintains a student in a college'. If he is compelled to punish his charge as an offender, 'he punisheth himself; so must God afflict himself to afflict you. Put not the Lord into these straits if you have any love in you.'[129] Sibbes had put it starkly: 'What greater unkindnesse could there possibly be', even 'treachery, to leave [the] directions of a friend to follow the counsaile of an enemy ... leaving a true guide, and following the Pirate.'[130]

John Howe expounded the same passage in Isaiah 63, warning his London congregation of the danger of 'vexing' the Holy Spirit. The Spirit knew what was best for them and was grieved when they deliberately opposed anything that was for their good. Isaiah described the Israelites' sin as rebellion, implying not an isolated act but 'a continued course of disobedience' throughout their history. Howe believed Christians might best understand the seriousness of 'vexing' if they reflected on the various titles by which the Spirit is described in the Old and New Testaments. The 'Spirit of truth' (Jn 14: 17) is grieved when believers 'have a light esteem' of Scripture, are casual about reading it, marginalize its importance or seem indifferent to its message. The 'Spirit of grace' (Heb. 10: 29) is grieved when they despise or reject the gospel of Christ, and as the 'Spirit of faith' (2 Cor. 4: 1) he is hurt when people continue in 'obstinate unbelief', regarding God's word 'no more than we would regard the word of a child'. The Spirit who inspires genuine contrition and repentance (Zech. 12: 10) is grieved by the 'impenitent hard heart' and, as the 'Spirit of love' (2 Tim. 1: 7), by the life that 'keeps at a distance' from God.

---

[128] Ashwood, *Heavenly Trade*, 137–40.
[129] Goodwin, *Works*, III, 416.
[130] Richard Sibbes, *A Fountain Sealed, or the Duty of the Sealed to the Spirit* (1637), 25–26.

The 'Spirit of power' (2 Tim. 1: 7; Jn 6: 6) is saddened when his help is stubbornly rejected, and the 'Spirit of holiness' (Rom. 1: 4) is hurt when, 'impatient of restraints', believers insist on pursuing their own, frequently damaging, lifestyle. The 'heavenly Spirit' is preparing Christians for the next and better life (2 Cor. 1: 22; 5: 5) and is grieved when they allow themselves to be 'swallowed up' by those 'inclinations and tendencies' which are 'running downwards', while the Spirit of God is aiming 'to lift us up towards God and heaven'. The 'Spirit of prayer' (Zech. 12: 10; Isa. 43: 2) is hurt when people 'who formerly loved prayer, are now grown out of love with it'. 'Animosities among the people of God' are hurtful to the Spirit of unity, who is always encouraging believers to love each other.[131]

In emphasizing the crucial necessity of the Spirit's work in the life of a believer, many preachers turned to the Pauline imperative that believers must be 'filled with the Spirit' (Eph. 5: 18), and discovered its most comprehensive interpretation in the writings of John Goodwin. His series of sermons, *ΠΛΗΡΩΜΑ ΤΟ ΠΝΕΥΜΑΤΙΚΟΝ, or A Being Filled with the Holy Spirit*, first appeared in print in 1670, five years after its author's death. Regarded with suspicion because of his outspoken[132] and suspect political loyalties ('republican'),[133] ecclesiastical commitment ('Independent')[134] and doctrinal convictions (pro-Arminian), Goodwin had been ejected in 1662 from St Sepulchre's, Coleman Street, London. Like Owen, he was a Nonconformist Independent but, decidedly unlike Owen, either sympathetic to, or accused of, Arminian ideas,[135] a theological position unusual among English Puritans.[136]

---

[131] John Howe, Sermon 'On Vexing the Spirit', preached at the Haberdashers' Hall, London, 1 June 1677, in *Works* (ed. Hunt), VI, 239–51, at 241–45.

[132] Unafraid of controversy, John Goodwin was described as 'a Man by himself; was against every Man, and had every Man almost against him. He was very warm and eager – whatsoever he engag'd in ... and with all his Faults must be own'd to have been a considerable Man'. He 'wrote such a number of Controversial Pieces, that it would be no easy thing to reckon them up with any exactness': *Account*, 53; *Continuation*, I, 78; cf. John Coffey, *John Goodwin and the Puritan Revolution* (Woodbridge, 2006).

[133] Goodwin defended the execution of Charles I: *The Obstructors of Justice; or A Defence of the Sentence passed upon the late King ... wherein the Justice and Equity of the said Sentence is demonstratively asserted* (1648). Copies of the book were burnt publicly on Charles II's return but Goodwin escaped further censure. Cf. also his *Anti-Cavalierisme; or Truth pleading as well the Necessity as the Lawfulness of this Present War* (1642); Tai Liu, *Puritan London: A Study of Religion and Society in the City Parishes* (New York, 1986).

[134] John Goodwin, *Os Ossorianum; or, A bone for a Bishop to pick* (1663).

[135] John Goodwin, *Redemption Redeemeed* (1651); *Triumviri; or The Genius, Spirit and Deportment of the Three Men, Mr. Richard Resbury, Mr. John Pawson, and Mr Geo. Kendall, in their Late Writings against the Free Grace of God in the Redemption of the World* (1658). Milton's biographer John Toland described Goodwin as 'the great Spreader of Arminianism': *The Life of John Milton* (1699), 125. However, Goodwin might be more accurately described as 'anti-Predestinarian' (*The Saints Interest in God* (1640), 79–80), and an opponent of limited atonement (*God a Good Master and*

The book carried a warm commendation from Ralph Venning, a fellow Independent, though a convinced Calvinist. Venning said that, although he was 'not ... of the same mind and opinion' as Goodwin 'in some 'controverted points', he had derived immense profit from the manuscript. Venning was aware that in 'his wonted genius' Goodwin tended to 'traverse a great deal of ground' before he reached 'his designed journey's end', but travelling with such a gifted writer and expositor was infinitely worthwhile.[137] Venning knew that, although he differed from Goodwin on important theological issues, Calvinists and Arminians had a great deal in common in their interpretation and pursuit of Christian spirituality. Goodwin maintained that the command to 'be filled with the Spirit' had been 'generally neglected and forgotten' by the majority of his Christian contemporaries, 'their consciences' being 'little better than dead unto it'.[138] Goodwin's extensive treatment of this crucial aspect of the Spirit's work is a major contribution to Nonconformist spirituality during the repression, sufficiently distinctive for us to devote the rest of this chapter to its interpretation. In expounding a wide range of closely related themes, he pays special attention to the importance, benefits, availability, and evidence of the fulness of the Spirit in the life of a believer.

Importance

Goodwin responded to the challenge of studied indifference to, or evasion of, this divine command to be 'filled with the Spirit', by emphasizing its obligatory nature. Presented neither as an invitation nor an appeal, God requires and expects it of those who are committed to him, and he would never 'exhort the saints to impossibilities'.[139]

This further work of the Spirit was a crucial aspect of Christian experience. Without his indwelling fulness, believers are unlikely to reach their spiritual potential.[140] Dependent solely on human ability, they will always 'stumble, and betray the honour of God'.[141] It is every person's 'duty to become a

---

Protector (1640), 118–19), rather than a committed Arminian. In his preaching and writing, he frequently quoted Calvin with warm approval; cf. also E. More, 'John Goodwin and the Origins of the New Arminianism', *Journal of British Studies* 22 (1982–83), 50–70.

[136] For an introduction to some members of Goodwin's London congregation who became General Baptists or Quakers, and to other Nonconformist Arminians, see Geoffrey F. Nuttall, 'John Horne of Lynn', in *Christian Spirituality: Essays in Honour of Gordon Rupp* (ed. Peter Brooks; 1975), 231–47.

[137] Goodwin, *A Being Filled*, 8.
[138] Ibid. 313.
[139] Ibid. 319.
[140] Thomas Ewins also preached about a 'second work' of the Spirit in the life of a believer: [Robert Purnell], *The Church of Christ in Bristol* (1657), 52–54.
[141] Goodwin, *A Being Filled*, 44–45.

benefactor'[142] in society, and those who refuse the Spirit's gift cannot hope to make an effective evangelistic impact on their contemporaries.[143] Most believers live at a lower level of spirituality than God intends. There 'is not one of a thousand that grows up to the ... stature' of the ideal woman or man in Christ. Some believers are 'voluntary dwarfs', content 'not to do more to be saved than is of absolute necessity',[144] but God expects Christians to receive his 'fullest and highest'[145] gifts, both for this life and the next.

Benefits

Following an extended exposition of the Holy Spirit's deity, Goodwin explains why this fulness is 'so greatly desirable'. To be 'filled with the Spirit' promotes holiness, imparts courage, inspires service and effects Christlikeness.

First, emphasizing the Spirit's expulsive and enabling power, Goodwin asserts that his pervading presence 'will leave no place' for damaging lusts 'to play their parts within us'.[146] Using temple imagery from both Testaments, he says that in the 'inner temple of the heart ... there will be such a glory of holiness there' that there will be no room for 'those base companions – unclean, impure, carnal and sensual desires and inclinations' which have 'haunted your souls'. He guards against any suggestion that the Spirit-filled believer is thereby delivered, instantaneously or totally, from conflict with 'contrary lustings'. Goodwin is opposed to 'the perfectionists amongst us'. As long as believers are in this world, the 'flesh will be still interrupting and mingling itself' with their 'actions' but, when 'filled with the Spirit', these alien intruders 'will have no opportunity to magnify themselves' and 'gather strength'. 'Even as Christ coming into the temple drove out those that bought and sold', so 'the Spirit of God ... will chase away ... all that rabble of evil-doers ... unclean lusts and desires'.[147]

Second, this empowering presence guarantees increasing courage in the face of adversity. Believers 'filled with the Spirit' will 'dwell amongst lions, even as Daniel did, without fear or danger of being destroyed and devoured with them', a highly relevant dimension of his teaching in time of persecution. Such 'afflictions, pressures, and trials, which ... grind the faces and break the bones of other men', will not destroy those who are Spirit-filled. Possessing 'prince-like resolutions' of godliness, they 'will not be ... turned out of the way by every gust of temptation'.[148]

Third, this fulness inspires service. Recalling the appointment of deacons in

---

[142] Ibid. 48.
[143] Ibid. 65.
[144] Ibid. 87.
[145] Ibid. 88.
[146] Ibid. 229.
[147] Ibid. 230–32.
[148] Ibid. 233, 5.

Acts 6: 3, Goodwin says that when believers are 'filled with the Spirit', it gives God 'holy pleasure and delight' to 'employ' them in his 'many actions and services'. Such liberated and empowered people 'will be vigorous ... in their work', not distracted 'by every toy or trivial occasion that shall present itself'. People 'do not ... put what they drink into bottles that are smoky', destroying the 'pleasantness of the taste', so God takes no pleasure in 'the management of his affairs' by people not dependent on his Spirit.[149] In church life, 'the most excellent services of God and of men' are less effective than they might be because of a 'natural averseness' to being entirely committed to God's work. 'Your being filled with the Spirit will free you from all [such] encumbrances in the ways of holiness', and any work, 'whether for God or men', will be joyfully undertaken. Stephen's final service for God took place in the most hostile circumstances imaginable, yet 'filled with the Spirit', he stood before his ruthless opponents with the face of an angel.[150]

Fourth, this work of the Spirit makes believers 'like unto Jesus Christ' in 'the advancement of the peace and happiness of the world'. They will 'not so much mind or manage' their own interests in life, but be 'willing to take Christ's design' along with them. 'Filled with the Spirit' they will pray 'more effectually and with greater acceptation',[151] with the deep assurance of a 'better eternity'. They 'who have not some competent anointing' 'hardly hold out in suffering. ... For to be called forth and strengthened by God to suffer for Christ's or the gospel's sake, is a matter of peculiar ... gift from God'.[152]

Availability

God would not have so frequently 'admonished and called upon us'[153] to be filled with the Spirit if it were not possible. Nothing 'can hinder us ... but our voluntary neglect',[154] and prayer 'will fetch ... anything out of the treasury of God'.[155] The believer must come dependently to the promised Giver of this necessary gift. Even to frame the question 'How?' and then to express the desire to be filled, is evidence of the Spirit's initiative. He stimulates the hunger, creates the appetite and provides the food.

Insisting that the Spirit always takes the initiative, Goodwin said that he was present in every human mind long before anyone 'believed ... otherwise there would have been no ... moving unto things either morally or spiritually good'. He does not choose to work 'compulsively' in people's lives, 'but only so as to leave them at liberty', with 'at least a possibility of going their own way'. All

---

[149] Ibid. 243–44.
[150] Ibid. 244–45, quoting Acts 6: 15.
[151] Ibid. 248–49.
[152] Ibid. 251–52.
[153] Ibid. 254.
[154] Ibid. 320.
[155] Ibid. 280.

must understand, however, that they 'could never have called for nor sought for his assistance, did not the Spirit first move them' to do so.[156] The Spirit comes to unbelievers as an occasional and urgent visitor, but to believers as a permanent and resourceful resident, 'when they receive him in a greater measure' than they could possibly have done before.[157]

Goodwin emphasizes both the necessity of seeking and the impossibility of refusal. If believers ask for this gift, it will never be denied to those who 'present themselves ... as weak and impotent',[158] in need of promised resources.[159] Additionally, believers who long to be 'filled' will surrender themselves to the Spirit's direction in their lives, expressing a genuine desire to be 'led by the Spirit' (Rom. 8: 14). 'You know there are some horses will not be led, but a man must pull and haul them after him; but there are other horses that are obedient and tractable in your hand.' Those who long to be 'filled with the Spirit' are unhesitatingly teachable. They 'go along with him ... willing to accept' him as 'their leader and guider', knowing he will only lead to supremely good things, to that which will honour God, exalt Christ, help others and, ultimately, bring nothing but enrichment to themselves.[160]

Evidence

Goodwin goes on to discuss the assurance and evidence of this fulness. In a period when many hesitant believers longed for assurance of salvation and agonized as to whether or not they were numbered among the elect, Goodwin aimed to dispel all doubt about the fulness of the Spirit. He offers a series of searching tests by which the Spirit-filled believer may be identified.

The first test is that of a transformed personality. They possess a 'calm and yielding' character that is 'pure' (James 3: 17), ever striving 'to avoid all pollution with sin'. In their relationships with others, they are 'peaceable', and 'of a yielding and quiet spirit in their own worldly affairs'.[161] Goodwin regrets that 'there is a kind of [aggressive] zeal in a man's secular ... affairs, which is found in too many [professing Christians] which is hardly ... consistent with ... being filled with the Spirit'.[162] By contrast, Spirit-filled believers are not forceful and truculent, 'and yet when occasions require are apt to quit themselves like men of courage and resolution', and all this 'argues that they have a very rich anointing of the Spirit of God'.[163]

Eager obedience is a further 'test', characterized by the desire both to grasp

---

[156] Ibid. 256.
[157] Ibid. 259.
[158] Ibid. 257.
[159] Ibid. 258.
[160] Ibid. 267–68.
[161] Ibid. 291.
[162] Ibid. 293.
[163] Ibid. 291.

Christian teaching intellectually and to practise it in everyday life. For 'alas, there is not one man or woman of many that do live up to their light'. They read the truths on the pages of their Bibles but leave them there. 'Their eyes are generally better than their hearts.'[164] An experienced pastor, Goodwin knows that to live consistently as a Spirit-filled Christian is no easy assignment. 'The commodity indeed is rich, but it is very costly; yet if you would go to the price of it, it is to be had at the hand of Jesus Christ',[165] who both exemplifies (Jn 12: 23–4) and encourages (Jn 12: 25–6) the believer's mortification. Sin must be slain; the lustful eye removed, the greedy hand amputated. The apostle Paul 'could stop the flesh, as it were, with a curb in the midst of its career', like an 'excellently taught' horse, that will stop in the midst of his way with the least check of the bit or bridle'.[166] Such immediately responsive self-control is 'performable only by the Spirit of God' but 'where it is performed ... thoroughly ... it must needs argue a great presence of the Spirit'.[167]

Genuine purity, 'detesting what is sinful and unclean', is further evidence of the Spirit-filled life. He is the Spirit of 'holiness', and every 'agent endeavoureth to make the patient like himself'. A Christian might 'abhor one kind of sin' but 'either practise ... or connive at ... another', this kind of selective holiness hardly proves that a believer 'is filled with the Spirit of God. And thus you have many great pretenders unto holiness'. The Spirit teaches Christians that all sin is offensive to God.[168]

Evidence of Spirit-filled living is also to be found in an ambition for 'the glorifying or manifesting of God' and a 'worthy degree of heavenly-mindedness'. Like a divine ambassador, the Spirit of God came down from heaven 'to negotiate the interest and affairs of his own country' and to transform women and men preoccupied with the things of this world into 'heavenly and spiritual' citizens.[169] People with this radical destiny live with their eye on a better future, ready 'to take up any cross, though never so heavy', particularly in a hostile environment. Even when 'the iniquity of those who persecute' abounds, the Spirit-filled Christian 'will not so much as stoop or step out of the way for it', and 'there cannot be a more promising sign ... of a person being filled with the Spirit of God than this'.[170]

A final test relates to believers' use of the Bible. It is 'the property of the Spirit of God to reveal the mind of God in the Scriptures', and he may choose to 'reveal ... truths which have lain dormant' for centuries. Every 'generation and every age' has had some 'fallow ground of Scripture ... some considerable passage ... that hath never been so generally understood ... as in the present

---

[164] Ibid. 296–97.
[165] Ibid. 298.
[166] Ibid. 297.
[167] Ibid. 298–99.
[168] Ibid. 301–303.
[169] Ibid. 303–304.
[170] Ibid. 306.

generation'. It is 'the proper work of the Spirit ... to take away the veil ... when he findeth some person whom he doth much delight in'.[171] The Spirit-filled believer not only puts the highest value on Scripture but also witnesses the miracle by which, through the Spirit's dynamic energy, its priceless words effect necessary, radical and perceptible changes in daily life.[172]

Under recurrent persecution, Dissenters are bound to experience 'tormenting fears'; 'armed' in their 'hearts by the fulness of the Spirit', they will not only 'have no cause to fear any danger for the future'[173] but will experience an abundance of 'joy and peace'. If rejected by hostile contemporaries, even by their own families, 'filled with the Spirit' they will enjoy 'a free and large communion with God'[174] even in the darkest times. For 'a man to have the ear of a king ... as oft as he should reasonably desire it' is 'a great piece of worldly felicity', and those who come to him dependently[175] have immediate and constant access to limitless resources.

This preoccupation with the command to be 'filled with the Spirit' might suggest that Nonconformists were characterized by spiritual insularity. Their faith was indeed essentially personal, but it was not remotely individualistic. Vilified by many of their contemporaries, they needed each other and did everything possible to enrich and deepen their corporate solidarity. We turn now to focus on their experience of the Spirit's ministry in enriching their worship, informing their minds, encouraging personal and corporate holiness, and expressing compassionate concern. Scripture promised that the Holy Spirit would inspire, teach, purify and use the local church. Here we see them adoring God, sharing truth, maintaining integrity and serving others.

---

[171] Ibid. 309.
[172] Ibid. 310.
[173] Ibid. 430.
[174] Ibid. 439.
[175] Ibid. 471.

Part IV

Partnership in Adversity

Chapter 6

Adoring God

Dissenters emphasized the importance of personal spirituality, but never at the expense of corporate devotion. The local congregation's 'praises of God' was its 'highest and holiest employment upon Earth' and 'if ever you should do anything with all your might and with a joyful ... frame of soul, it is this'.[1] 'Closet prayer' was a spiritual lifeline, but meeting together for worship was uniquely beneficial,[2] irreplaceable[3] and obligatory.[4] The Suffolk preacher Nicholas Bownd was not the only Puritan to liken 'the meetings of the godlie' to 'a great many ... firebrands layde together'. Retained heat was dependent on physical proximity, without which 'every one would dye of it selfe'. Although 'every man hath some grace of Gods spirit in himselfe, yet it is greatly increased by conference, as it were by borrowing the heate of others'.[5] In persecuting times, Bartholomew Ashwood urged his readers to prove their love to God by their 'valuation of His presence in His ordinances ... howsoever expensive it be on your dearest comforts'.[6]

Although Baxter reminded his people that they seldom read of God revealing himself 'in a throng',[7] he was the last person to marginalize corporate devotion. It was part of the Dissenters' rich Puritan heritage,[8] and the distinguishing feature of their testimony, forbidden as it was by parliamentary legislation. In this chapter we explore three important dimensions of the corporate spirituality of Dissent: public worship, the 'visible signs' of sacramental observance and family devotion.

---

[1] Baxter, *Christian Directory*, III, ch.IX, Direction 15, in *Works* (ed. Orme), V, 221.
[2] Baxter, *Works* (ed. Orme), V, 442: 'While you are doing this, you will feel your graces stir, and feel that comfort from the face of God, which you are not like to meet in any other way whatsoever.'
[3] Ibid. 443: nothing 'is more pleasing to God that the cheerful praises of his servants'.
[4] Ibid. 440, 438: it is 'the highest and noblest work' in any believer's life, and 'the highest service that the tongue of men or angels can perform'.
[5] Nicholas Bownd, *The Doctrine of the Sabbath Plainley layde forth* (1595), 219. For similar use of this illustration, cf. Robert Harris, *A Treatise of the New Covenant* (1632), II, 23; Clarkson, *Works*, III, 193.
[6] Ashwood, *Heavenly Trade*, 'Epistle to the Readers', [unpaginated].
[7] Baxter, *Rest*, 715.
[8] Horton Davies, *The Worship of the English Puritans* (1948); idem, *Worship and Theology in England*, II: *From Andrewes to Baxter and Fox, 1603–1690* (Princeton, NJ, 1975).

Corporate Worship

The nature and method of public worship divided Nonconformists from their conformist neighbours. In varying degrees, Dissenters were unhappy with the Anglican liturgy. Defying probability, many Presbyterians continued to hope that, with a more acceptable Prayer Book, some form of comprehension within the national church might yet be possible. Independents and Baptists looked for nothing more than toleration outside the Established Churches, with complete freedom to worship publicly, uninhibited by a compulsory liturgy. Totally committed to their distinctive 'silent' meetings, Quakers found no help in the worship patterns of their fellow Dissenters.

Although Nonconformists valued their differing practices in corporate worship, they were of one mind concerning its priority. The London Independent minister David Clarkson strenuously maintained that public worship takes precedence over personal devotion.[9] Given a believer's wholehearted spiritual commitment, 'Public worship is to be preferred before private'. The 'posterity of Jacob' would not 'neglect the worship of God in their families' but God's greatest delight is when he is 'publicly worshipped'.[10] If God sets the highest value on public worship, believers must give it priority, assured not only of God's preference for 'public ordinances' but also his guaranteed presence in them, 'more effectually, constantly and intimately' than anywhere else. 'Effectually', because after 'he had given instructions for public worship',[11] God told his people he would manifest himself among them and would not come 'empty-handed'; 'constantly', for 'after he had given order for the administration of public ordinances' (Mt. 28: 16–20), Jesus gave his worshipping followers the assurance that he would always be among them; and 'intimately', because he would not fail to honour his promise that '[w]here two or three are gathered together in my name, there am I in the midst of them' (Mt. 18: 20). Clarkson cites biblical examples and explores relevant pastoral issues, drawing some practical conclusions.

His biblical illustrations include Israel's leaders from the Old Testament, and the Patmos exile and Jesus himself from the New. Although David was a king, he derived his greatest pleasure not from his crown, throne, palace or kingdom, but from belonging to God's worshipping community: 'One thing have I desired ... the house of the Lord', in order to see God's beauty and seek God's will (Psa. 27: 4). Even in a desolate wilderness, David longed not for

---

[9] See Clarkson's exposition of Psa. 87: 2: 'The Lord loveth the gates of Zion more than all the dwellings of Jacob': *Works*, III (i), 187–209. Philip Henry shared this interpretation of Clarkson's text. On a February Sunday in 1663, there was 'no preaching at Chapel ... in the afternoone wee went to Whitch[urch]: for still ye gates of Sion are better than all ye dwellings of Jacob': *Diaries* (ed. Lee), 130.

[10] Clarkson, *Works*, III (i), 187.

[11] Exod. 20: 24: 'in all places where I record my name I will come unto thee, and I will bless thee.'

'outward refreshments' but for 'the public ordinances' because only within that context could he fully experience God's power and discern his glory'.[12] Other kings, such as Jehoshaphat, Hezekiah and Josiah, also came to value corporate worship more than private devotion, for where 'did their zeal more appear, but for the public worship of God?'[13] To John on Patmos the Lord was revealed 'in the midst of the churches' (Rev. 1: 10–20) so that throughout history Christians might know that rich 'discoveries of Christ are made in the assemblies of his people'. There can be no 'such clear' and 'effectual representations ... of the glory and majesty of Christ, as in the public ordinances'.[14] During Christ's earthly ministry, he 'did not think himself above ordinances ... You find him frequently in the synagogues ... in the temple, always at the passover', so that the words of the psalmist could be applied to him: 'The zeal of thy house hath eaten me up.'[15]

Following the biblical examples, Clarkson turns to pastoral experience. For a variety of reasons, some of his congregation had absented themselves from public worship, hardly surprising in a period of repression, but the pastor deals with their difficulties. Some members maintained that 'sometimes in private' they experienced 'more of God's presence, more assistance of his Spirit' and 'more joy' than in public worship. At meetings they sometimes felt a 'dullness of heart' and inhibiting 'straitness' that contrasted sharply with their exaltation in prayer at home. They found it virtually impossible to agree with their minister's conviction that 'public worship is preferred before private'. Clarkson insists that exultant feelings are not the best judge of spiritual values. Highly subjective emotional impulses are variable and vacillating. There might be a time when, 'in some extremity of cold', they 'find more refreshment from a fire than from the sun'. Will they always, therefore, 'prefer the fire, and judge it more beneficial to the world than the sun?' In Clarkson's day, when Nonconformists 'bewail the want of public liberties as an affliction', God may choose to visit them in private to compensate for their loss, but that does not mean that personal devotion is always preferable to corporate worship. 'So it was with David in his banishment'. He too was kept from communal worship but this did nothing to diminish his appreciation of 'public ordinances'. Was it not possible that their 'enjoyments in private' were 'the fruits' of earlier public devotion? They may be deriving more help corporately than they realize. 'It is not ... flashes of joy, stirrings of affections, that argue most of God's presence; there may be much of these when there is little of God.' Fleeting feelings are inadequate judges of spiritual values. Possibly, they have derived limited help from public worship because they had brought little to it. They must not come 'unprepared ... without due apprehensions, either of the Lord, or of

---

[12] Clarkson, *Works*, III (i), 191, quoting Psa. 63: 1–2.
[13] Ibid. 194–95, quoting, 2 Chron. 20: 3–4, 9; 29: 2–3; 34: 1 – 35: 27.
[14] Ibid. 191–92.
[15] Ibid. 195, quoting Psa. 69: 9, Jn 2: 17.

yourselves'.[16] In private devotion, believers may concentrate on familiar and comforting biblical passages, but attendance at public worship exposes them to a message over which they have had no personal control. Its truths may probe the depths of the human conscience, exposing undetected need, and areas of life possibly undisturbed in private prayer.

Other members of Clarkson's church may have heedlessly absented themselves from corporate worship. A 'little rain, a little cold' they 'take for a sufficient excuse to be absent'. In Old Testament times no such thing hindered Israel's eager pilgrims 'from coming to the gates of Zion at the appointed seasons', however distant their homes might be, and whatever the weather. Yet 'many amongst us make every sorry thing a lion in the way', preferring 'their sloth and ease before God's public worship'.[17]

Clarkson's practical conclusions concentrate on the importance of thoughtful preparation before worship, diligent attendance at meetings, and serious 'improvement' after them. God's promised blessing on corporate worship begins in thoughtful preparation at home. They should not come 'rashly', 'without due consideration' of the God they are to meet, or 'with guilt and pollution' upon their consciences, or with their busy minds still 'meddling with the world'. Once met for worship they should be present 'with hearts hungering after the enjoyment of Christ in his ordinances', and an appropriate sense of personal need. The 'conceitedness of our own abundance ... shuts up the treasury of heaven against us'. They are to shake off 'that slothful, indifferent, lukewarm temper, which is so odious to God'. 'Spiritual slothfulness is the ruin of souls' and 'Soul-poverty' will be its damaging consequence.[18] The enrichment promised in corporate worship extends far beyond the meeting time. Do they think their 'work done when the minister has done'? That is the moment its work should begin. Its blessings need to be 'improved', and put to excellent use as they resume their everyday activities. 'The ordinances are like grapes; it is not enough that they are given into your hands ... they must be pressed, that is your work in secret.' The 'negligence ... of men in not improving public ordinances in secret' causes God to 'withdraw himself, and his blessings in public'.[19]

Clarkson's exposition is dominated by two leading ideas, God's glory and human benefit. First, to marginalize corporate worship is to 'neglect the glory of God' where it is best promoted, and to 'slight the presence of God' where it is most evident.[20] Second, public worship benefits others as well as the individual worshipper. 'In private [devotion] you provide for your own good, but in public you do good both to yourselves and others'. When, whatever the

---

[16] Ibid. 197–200.
[17] Ibid. 202, recalling Prov. 22: 13.
[18] Ibid. 208–209.
[19] Ibid. 201.
[20] Ibid. 204, cf. 202.

cost, Dissenters resolutely take their places when opportunities are given public meetings, they 'stir up others' by their faithful example and 'quicken one another' as they 'join together in worshipping God'. The 'rejecting of public ordinances' might become the first step to apostasy.[21]

He insists that the crucial question is not, 'Where may I *receive* most good?' but 'where may I *do* most good?'[22] Furthermore, the evangelistic impact must not be forgotten. 'The saving of souls should be preferred before our comforts'. In corporate worship, lives may be transformed by 'conversion and regeneration', which 'come nearest to miracles', not ordinarily achieved in private prayer. The Lord has 'not confined himself to work these wonderful things only in public' worship, but 'his greatest works are wrought ordinarily by public ordinances, and not in private'.[23]

Clarkson's argument that corporate worship is superior to personal prayer is crowned with a reference to the believer's future. 'Public worship is the nearest resemblance of heaven'. The heavenly worshippers (Heb. 12: 22–3; Rev. 4: 10–11; 5: 6–14) are an adoring community, not isolated individuals. In heaven 'there is nothing done in private ... all the worship of that glorious company is public'.[24] Corporate worship anticipates the greater exultation of all God's redeemed people. Minimizing its importance devalues the promised glory.

'How can you long for the enjoyment of God in Heaven', asks Bartholomew Ashwod, 'who care not for his company on Earth?' Believers are reminded of life's limited opportunities for corporate worship. 'Your Glass runs ... walk in the light while you have it ... how glad would you be of enjoying time to hear the voice of peace when you are entering upon Eternity', you who seem 'not at leisure now to hear Divine precepts while in the possession of time'.[25] When believers gather together, they worship as travellers to another world.

Sacramental Observance: 'Visible Signs'

A second dimension of Nonconformist worship that must not be minimized is their doctrine, practice and experience of the sacraments. Although preaching was a Puritan and Dissenting priority, their finest expositors recognized that the most persuasive sermons had their limitations. In order to communicate his truth, God had given his people eyes to see as well as ears to hear.[26] One ejected minister said that in preaching 'we speak generally ... whereas in the Sacrament Christ is offered personally ... and is put, as it were (Sacramentally),

---

[21] Ibid. 192–93.
[22] Ibid. 202.
[23] Ibid. 202, 193–94.
[24] Ibid. 194.
[25] Ashwood, *Heavenly Trade*, 'Epistle to the Readers', [unpaginated].
[26] The sacraments are 'nothing but visible wordes and promises': Perkins, *A Reformed Catholicke*, in *Works*, I, 611.

into every ones hand'.[27] The 'Word speaks to all promiscuously, as inviting; the Sacraments to every one in particular, as obliging'. The preached word can be totally ignored, ruthlessly criticized, summarily dismissed or eagerly obeyed, but the sacraments give expression to a personal, immediate response. The 'Word universally propoundeth that which in the Seals is particularly applied'.[28]

Puritans were discontented with indiscriminate sacramental observance because godless people were treating the Lord's Supper much like hearing a sermon, physical presence at which was no guarantee of spiritual appropriation. The promiscuous use of the sacraments became a divisive issue in the Elizabethan church and marked the emergence of the Puritan ideal of personal and corporate holiness. In such thinking, verbal and visual were inseparable elements in spiritual communication; preaching and the sacraments were never meant to be rivals in the quest for prominence.

With the exception of the Quakers,[29] the Nonconformist ideal for corporate worship found rich expression in its sacramental life, though some of them preferred an alternative descriptive terminology.[30] Baptism was the visible sign of entrance into the redeemed community, while the Lord's Supper testified to the believers' privilege, desire and determination to stay within that community.[31] Within the thematic limitations of this study, an examination of Dissenting theology and practice regarding Baptism and the Lord's Supper cannot be remotely comprehensive. An exploration of their sacramental theology and practice in this context must be illustrative rather than extensive. We shall therefore limit it to the question of the relation of the sacraments to their experience of persecution: how did continuing adversity influence their interpretation of the sacraments?

---

[27] Thomas, *Preservative*, 24.

[28] Thomas Manton, 'How we ought to improve our Baptism', in *A Supplement to the Morning Exercise at Cripplegate* (1674), 147–48. Manton uses two Mosaic narratives to make the distinction. Preaching functioned in a similar manner to the command to look upon the brazen serpent: the plague victim need only hear the message and respond to its demands. The sacraments were typified at Israel's first Passover; the word had been heard but now it was visibly displayed and publicly obeyed.

[29] For the distinctive Quaker approach to the sacraments, see Barbour and Roberts (eds), *Early Quaker Writings*, 253, 256, 258; Hugh Barbour, *The Quakers in Puritan England* (New Haven, CT, 1964), 144–45; Barclay, *Apology*, Proposition 12.

[30] Many referred to them as 'ordinances'. The Elizabethan Separatist Henry Barrow was not alone in regarding the term 'sacrament' as 'that traditional word which engendreth strife rather than godly edifying': *A Brief Discoverie of the False Church* (1590), 116.

[31] Bury, *Help*, 5, cf. ibid. 32: '[t]he one for our Entrance into the Church, the other for our growth and nourishment'.

Baptism

The doctrine and practice of baptism was inevitably controversial in an ecclesiastical culture which was dominated by commitment to paedobaptism but which also saw many thousands of Dissenters coming to insist that baptism be restricted to believers only.[32] Baptists were widely regarded as divisive[33] and misguided intruders with a dubious, if not dangerous, ancestry.[34] With their non-sacramental pattern of worship, Quakers placed themselves outside this debate although, being on the left wing of Dissent, they were in several respects considerably closer to some Baptists than to Independents and Presbyterians.[35] A significant number of early Quakers were 'shattered Baptists', as Fox described them,[36] 'convinced' Friends originally belonging to Baptist churches who had come to regard external 'forms', including baptism, as redundant 'ceremonies' belonging to an unenlightened past. Many of the Quakers' public debates with Baptist leaders provided opportunities for both sides to defend their views vigorously.[37] Further verbal conflict took place between Baptists and paedobaptist Dissenters, and a voluminous,[38] often fractious,[39] pamphlet

---

[32] For the practice of infant baptism in the Restoration Church, see David Cressy, *Birth, Marriage, and Death: Ritual, Religion, and the Life-Cycle in Tudor and Stuart England* (Oxford, 1997), 181–94.

[33] Presenting a case for the introduction of confirmation for committed believers, Baxter said that the 'odium of Division, and unpeaceableness, hath so long laine upon' the Baptists 'that meethinks they should be willing to have it taken off ... by becoming Lovers and Promoters of Union, Communion and Peace among the Churches of Christ': *Confirmation and Restauration* (1658), 232.

[34] Widespread reference to them as 'Anabaptists' recalled the horrific Münster debacle of the previous century: G.H. Williams, *The Radical Reformation* (3rd rev.ed., Sixteenth Century Essays and Studies XV; Kirksville, MO, 1992), 553–88. It sounded ominous warnings of possible sedition and anarchy. In their apologetic literature, Baptists made strenuous efforts to dissociate themselves from 'the opinions and practices of those at Munster': William Kiffin et al., *Apology of some commonly called Anabaptist ...* (1660), 6–7; cf. Hercules Collins, *Believers Baptism from Heaven and of Divine Institution* (1691), 95–107; Henry Danvers, *A Treatise of Baptism* (1674), 322–28. Baxter knew many English Baptists who were 'not such as the Munster Anabaptist ... but godly men': *A Defence of the Principle of Love* (1671), 6–7.

[35] T.L. Underwood, *Primitivism, Radicalism, and the Lamb's War: The Baptist-Quaker Conflict in Seventeenth-Century England* (New York, 1997).

[36] Fox, *Journal* (ed. Smith), 26.

[37] Underwood, *Primitivism*, 68–77. For details of debates between Baptists and others in the period, see A.S. Langley, 'Seventeenth-Century Baptist Disputations', *TBHS* 6 (1919), 216–43. Although baptism was a prominent theme in discussion, debates covered a variety of controversial issues such as trinitarian theology, worship patterns, lay preaching, universal redemption, the nature of the church and the payment of tithes.

[38] The British Library's extensive Thomason Collection of tracts contains 125 items on the interrelated themes of baptism and discipline: Paul Lim, in J. Coffey and P.C.H. Lim, *The Cambridge Companion to Puritanism* (Cambridge, 2008), 233; *Catalogue of the Pamphlets ... Collected by George Thomason, 1640–1661* (1908).

exchange was sustained across many decades. Without minimizing the divisive nature of this issue, it needs to be recognized that in difficult times paedobaptists and Baptists treasured distinctive baptismal ideals, each being important in any interpretation of their personal and corporate spirituality. Both groups found aspects of their distinctive baptismal teaching particularly supportive in a period of repression. For both, baptisms were a public or semi-public act of forbidden corporate worship, involving an element of risk. In hazardous times, John Flavel travelled from Dartmouth to Totnes for an infant baptism disguised as a woman riding on horseback behind a man.[40] Believers' baptisms always exposed participants to the danger of arrest. In the following discussion of paedobaptist and Baptist theology and practice, we shall focus on four specific aspects of the teaching of each side, noting their particular relevance in a persecution context.

Infant Baptism

It is clear that paedobaptist Dissenters continued to derive immense comfort from a Reformed and Puritan baptismal theology.[41] Paedobaptist themes of particular significance in this period of recurrent adversity were infant baptism's covenant foundation, ecclesiological significance, pastoral importance and continuing efficacy.

Its Covenant Foundation

The divine initiative in baptism was deliberately affirmed. Baxter observed that throughout his ministry his friend Joseph Alleine had valued baptism and the Lord's Supper as specific occasions for every believer's 'Sacramental Covenanting'.[42] When infants were born into Dissenting families the grateful parents gave sacramental expression to a covenant theology which they found both inclusive and supportive in an era of political, social and ecclesiastical exclusion. This was also a period of doctrinal conflict in which the debate about election and predestination gained increasing prominence; baptismal practice

---

[39] E.g. the late seventeenth-century pamphlet exchange for and against paedobaptism between Giles Shute and Benjamin Keach. Keach expresses dissatisfaction regarding Shute's adversarial style, though Keach himself is hardly tactful in his response: e.g. *A Counter-Antidote to purge out the Malignant Effects of a Late Counterfeit, prepared by Mr. Giles Shute, an Unskillful Person in Polemical Cures* (1694), 3.

[40] E. Windeatt, 'John Flavel: A Notable Dartmouth Puritan and his Bibliography', *Transactions of the Devonshire Association for the Advancement of Science, Literature and Art* 43 (1911), 172–89, at 181.

[41] Ronald S. Wallace, *Calvin's Doctrine of the Word and Sacrament* (Edinburgh, 1953); E.B. Holifield, *The Covenant Sealed: The Development of Puritan Sacramental Theology in Old and New England, 1570–1720* (New Haven, CT, 1986).

[42] Richard Baxter, 'Introduction' to Alleine, *Life*, 14; cf. Bury, *Help*, 170: baptism offers 'a visible sign, and Seal of the Covenant of Grace whereby ... he confirmeth unto the Elect, the free promise of the Gospel; Christ and all his Benefits, and also bindeth them unto Obedience to his revealed Will'.

dependent on a covenant theology gave a measure of welcome assurance in a context of widespread spiritual uncertainty. At a time when sensitive souls were tortured as to whether they were genuinely converted and destined for a promised heaven, it brought reassurance to many objectively to affirm, as a personal declaration, not on the basis of any work or effort of their own, 'I am baptized'.[43] The faith, assurance, commitment, hope and prayers of their godly parents and the local believing community inspired and strengthened the conviction that they had belonged to God from their earliest days.[44] Infant baptism encouraged their sense of security. It expressed the spiritual confidence of parents and church and, in dark times, helped to buttress a highly vulnerable faith and commitment. Paedobaptist believers were convinced that the 'seal' of the covenant extended to their infants as well as themselves.

Baxter pointed out that loving and responsible parents frequently act on behalf of their children. It is their 'plain natural duty' to 'make covenants *in their behalf*':

> Who buyeth not Lands for himself and his Heirs? ... Do wee not make and Seal Deeds of Gift to infants ordinarily? and Testaments wherein we bequeath them Legacies? and put their names in sealed Leases, wherein we engage our selves to them?[45]

No greater provision could be made for a child's welfare than the spiritual

---

[43] Henry, *Diaries* (ed. Lee), 33: 'A Gentleman was wont to repell temptation with this word, *I am Baptiz'd*.'
[44] The congregation's responsibility was 'to pray that the child may be made partaker of Christ and his benefits': Thomas Cartwright, *A Treatise of the Christian Religion* (1616), 225.
[45] Richard Baxter, *Plain Scripture Proof of Infant Church Membership and Baptism* (1651), 113, 324. For the Puritan concept of parental faith on the child's behalf, see Perkins, *Golden Chaine*, in *Workes*, I, 74; cf. idem, *Cases of Conscience*, in *Works*, II, 75: '*I will be thy God and the God of thy seed*. By virtue of this promise, the parent layes hold on the covenant, for himself and for his child; and the child beleeves because the father believes ... by his faith, comes his child to be in the covenant and partaker of the benefits and priviledges thereof'. The vows at baptism were made by 'their sureties ... But when they come to age, themselves are bound to performe them': Richard Bernard, *The Common Catechisme. Expressed in the Common Prayer Booke, with a Commentarie thereupon* (11th ed.; 1640), C6 r–v. Cf. the Savoy Liturgy 'as it was presented to the Right Reverend Bishops by the Divines' [1661], in Peter Hall (ed.), *Reliquiae Liturgicae: Documents Connected with the Liturgy of the Church of England; Exhibiting the Substitutes that have been successively proposed for it at home* (5 vols, Bath, 1847), IV, 83: 'your faith, and consent, and dedication, will suffice for your children no longer till they come to age themselves, and then they must own their baptismal covenant, and personally renew it'. Dissenters believed with Cartwright 'that as God hath quickened' the father 'after his baptisme, so will hee his child': *Christian Religion*, 224.

commitment made in infant baptism. Convinced of their own participation in the covenant, the parents trusted that their totally dependable God would act mercifully in the life of the child they brought gratefully and dependently for baptism in the presence of the believing community.

Baptism offered this sustaining assurance but did not exonerate the baptized person from personal, declared and active involvement later in life. The sacrament 'doth represent and confirme our very ingrafting into Christ'[46] but it was a mutual commitment. It was 'a sealing both of God's promises to them and their believing response'.[47] According to Baxter, baptism, 'the mutual covenant between God and man', was like a marriage, in which both parties made precise vows to each other.[48]

Nehemiah Rogers and William Ames had expressed the believer's responsibility perfectly to the previous generation. Rogers said that as we 'covenant one by one at our Baptisme with him, to be obedient and faithfull, *So* also he with us, to be a God All-Sufficient unto us, and our God for ever'.[49] Ames also insisted on mutuality, claiming that the 'primary end of a Sacrament is to seale the covenant, and that not on God's part onely, but consequently also on ours'. It 'is, not onely the grace of God, and promises [that] are sealed to us, but also our thankfulnesse and obedience towards God'.[50] When a mature believer made the affirmation, 'I am baptized', it was a commitment to continuance as well as a declaration of privilege. It recognized that the 'life of a Christian is ... not a sitting or standing still'. Believers contented with their 'poore mediocrity' had not yet put their 'right foote forward in the way to the Kingdome of God'.[51] Bunyan's generation heard an identical exhortation to steadfast continuance. 'I beseech you ... that none of you do Run so lazily in the way to heaven'. There can be 'no dallying in this matter ... Run apace, and hold out to the end. And the Lord give thee a prosperous Journey.'[52]

Its Ecclesiological Significance

Baptism was also an outward 'seal' of the infant's public reception into the

---

[46] William Ames, *The Marrow of Sacred Divinity* (1642), 181.

[47] J. von Rohr, *The Covenant of Grace in Puritan Thought* (Atlanta, GA, 1986), 90. Perkins says that in baptism 'there is propounded and sealed a marveilous solemn covenant and contract: first of God with the baptized ... secondly of the baptized with God who promiseth to acknowledge, invocate, and worship none other God': *Golden Chaine*, in *Works*, I, 74. Cartwright taught that both sacraments 'seale also our promise to God ... that we will take him onely for our God ... whom alone by faith we rest upon, and [to] whom we bind ourselves to obey': *Christian Religion*, 214.

[48] Baxter, *Christian Directory*, in *Works* (ed. Orme), V, 44.

[49] Nehemiah Rogers, *True Convert ... Exposition upon the XV chapter of Luke* (1632), 160.

[50] Ames, *Marrow*, 165.

[51] Paul Baynes, *Commentarie upon the first and second chapters of Colossians ... Two Parts* (1634), II, 202.

[52] Bunyan, *Heavenly Foot-Man*, in *MW*, V, 176, 178.

visible church. During a period when, in some contexts, Dissenters were ostracized or marginalized in local society, the corporate aspects of faith were especially treasured. Others might criticize, malign, misrepresent or reject them but baptism was further testimony to the constantly replenished resources of the believing community. During persecution, meetings for Nonconformists were regularly held in ministers' and members' homes where, naturally, many infant baptisms took place;[53] but Dissenters insisted that these were not 'private' baptisms as such. This was a church ordinance, not a domestic observance.[54]

Although fearful that the local conforming minister might use the sign of the cross at the baptism of his son, Matthew, it was important to Philip Henry that it should not take place in the home but in the presence of the worshipping congregation.[55] William Bagshaw also 'thought it most proper to baptize in Publick', for the sake both of the infant and of those present to witness the sacrament. The child, 'who was by that Sacred Rite enter'd into the Church of Christ, might have the Prayers of the Congregation' and they in turn 'might be reminded of their own Baptismal Engagements'.[56]

Each infant baptism presented every baptized person present with a natural opportunity to reflect on the fact that they too had been baptized. One ejected minister, Walter Marshall, pointedly asked such worshippers:

> What good use do you make of your baptism? How often, or seldom, do you think upon it ... Though baptism be administered to us but once in our lives, yet we ought frequently to reflect upon it ... to put the question to ourselves, Unto what were we baptised? ... we must stir up and strengthen ourselves, by our baptism, to lay hold on the grace which it seals to us, and fulfil its engagements.[57]

Children baptised and publicly received were not thereby 'regenerated, yet [they] are in a more hopefull way of attayning regenerating grace' for they are 'under Church-watch' and, at appropriate times, will become subject 'to the reprehensions, admonitions' and even 'censures' of the local church. These

---

[53] In 1669 'one Mr. Vincent ... baptizeth Children, some privately some publickly in his Conventicle': GLT, I, 143; cf. 144. 'There was a Church Meeting at the house of brother Thomas Piel in [Low] Lorton' in October 1669 'upon the account of the baptizing of a child of his ... called Joseph': Cockermouth Independent Church Book, 49, cf. 51, 52, 60.

[54] There was considerable discussion in the Restoration Church concerning the increase in the practice of 'private' baptism, with its social as well as theological implications: Cressy, *Birth, Marriage and Death*, 188–94.

[55] Henry thought it necessary for baptisms to take place in his parish church, even though it exposed Puritan parents to the risk of unacceptable 'ceremonies'; cf. Henry, *Diaries* (ed. Lee), 118: 'Wee had no God-father ... but he signed him with the Cross, which I could not help. ipse viderit'.

[56] Ashe, *Life of William Bagshaw*, 16.

[57] Walter Marshall, *The Gospel Mystery of Sanctification* (Glasgow, 1764; first publ. 1692), 268–69.

instructive and corrective ministries will serve 'for their healing and amendment',[58] bringing them closer to fulness of faith.

Its Pastoral Context

'Death was a part of life' in seventeenth-century England, 'and was realistically treated as such.'[59] In a period of high infant mortality,[60] the early baptism of children conveyed a deep sense of security to Nonconformist households. Eight of Isaac Archer's children died before reaching their sixth birthday.[61] Only one of John Owen's eleven children lived beyond infancy or childhood. Few Dissenters seriously believed that unbaptized children were spiritually imperilled,[62] yet in bereaved homes it was an immense comfort to know that their children had been visibly welcomed into the believing community. Mary and Robert Franklin had already lost four infants in succession when their four-year-old daughter also died, and in tragic circumstances. The grieving mother said:

> But the Lord, I trust, hath taken her up to inherit everlasting glory, and the rest of them ... that died in their infancy. I have rejoiced, sometimes, when I have been

---

[58] 'Cambridge [New England] Platform' (1648), XII, 7, in Williston Walker, *The Creeds and Platforms of Congregationalism* (New York, 1991; first publ. 1893), 224.

[59] Lawrence Stone, *The Family, Sex and Marriage in England, 1500–1800* (abridged ed.; Harmondsworth, 1979), 66.

[60] Archbishop Tillotson claimed that where parents employed 'such Nurses as make a Trade of it', scarcely one child out of five reached its first birthday: John Tillotson, *Six Sermons ... of Stedfastness in Religion* (1694), 105–106 (Sermon III, 'Concerning the Education of Children'). Newborn infants were especially vulnerable, with an exceptionally high death rate for children in their first year. The birth of many infants who died within a few days was not even recorded. 18% of children died before their fifth birthday. The mortality rate was higher in urban areas but between one quarter and a third of all children, from whatever class, died before reaching the age of fifteen: Stone, *Family, Sex and Marriage*, 54–55.

[61] In addition to these losses, Isaac's wife, Anne, had a series of miscarriages: Storey (ed.), *Two Diaries*, 20. Isaac's parents had similar bereavements in their family. Of five children born during his father's first marriage, Isaac was the only one to survive.

[62] The English Reformers were at pains to dissociate themselves from the Roman Catholic view that unbaptized infants were without guarantee of eternal security: Thomas Becon, *A New Catechism set forth Dialogue-Wise ... between the Father and the Son* (Parker Society, 11; 1844), 214–17. Cf. Calvin, *Institutes* IV.15.20 (ed. Henry Beveridge [2 vols; 1953], II, 525): to those who fear that anyone 'sick may be deprived of the gift of regeneration if he decease without baptism', Calvin responds: 'By no means. Our children, before they are born, God declares that he adopts for his own when he promises that he will be a God to us and to our seed after us [Gen. 17: 7]. In this promise their salvation is included'. Concerning the salvation of infants, the Presbyterian *Directory* stated that 'outward Baptisme is not so necessary, that through the want thereof the Infant is in danger of Damnation, or the Parents guilty, if they doe not contemne or neglect the Ordinance of Christ when and where it may be had': *A Directory for the Publique Worship of God through these Three Kingdomes* (1646), 21.

thinking of them, that any of my children should be so advanced as to be made heirs and inheritors of God's kingdom; which I hope I have no reason to doubt of.

Convinced that they were 'children in the covenant', she could say that the Lord had enabled her 'truly to give them up to him in their baptism'.[63]

As previously mentioned, Katharine and Philip Henry lost their first child, John, in his sixth year. The day following his baptism, the child fell sick, and Henry wrote, 'little one not well ... I desire to sit loose from him, having given him to God ... & I am bid to expect to see him often at Deaths door'.[64] When the boy was taken, Henry was distraught, fearing he may have 'over-loved' the treasured child, 'my heart bleeds, lord have mercy.' On the funeral day, he found comfort in the assurance that his son belonged to God and was eternally secure: 'my dear child, now mine no longer ... not lost, but sown to bee raysd again a glorious body and I shall goe to him but hee shall not return to mee'.[65] A fortnight later, he wrote: 'If my dear child had liv'd to this day hee had been Six yeares of Age, but hee lives, I trust, a better life in the Armes of Jesus, accord[ing] to the termes of the Covenant of grace.' They had made plans for young John's birthday as 'a day of rejoycing, now of mourning, but the same God both gave & took away, blessed bee his name'.[66] The resignation was accompanied by the assurance that they would see their boy again, a consoling mercy beyond price.[67]

Its Continuing Efficacy

With the assurance that, both at home and in church, children were being instructed in the faith, parents could take heart that the efficacy of baptism would continue long after its administration. It was frequently maintained that 'the promises sacramentally sealed' in baptism could be 'extended throughout the course of the believer's life, so long as there is believing and repentance'.[68]

---

[63] 'The Experiences of Mary Franklin', 393. Similarly, four of Owen Stockton's children died in infancy and childhood, 'concerning whom he had much satisfaction as to their Eternal Salvation': Clarke, *Lives of Sundry Eminent Persons*, 196. When in 1675 the Archers suddenly lost a newborn child, they were disturbed that 'through an unavoidable necessity' the baby was unbaptized, but reassured concerning their son's eternal security. They did not 'question the child's happiness (whatever St. Austin thought)', and were sure that God, who is 'not tied to meanes, hath washed it's soul in Christ's blood': Storey (ed.), *Two Diaries*, 145, 150–51; cf. Diary of Sarah Savage, fols 2–3.
[64] Henry, *Diaries* (ed. Lee), 85–86.
[65] Ibid. 198, quoting 1 Cor. 15: 43–4; 2 Sam. 12: 23; cf. ibid. 199, 281, 287–88.
[66] Ibid. 199.
[67] 'My hope is, through the everlasting Covenant of mercy, that I shall meet him again with comfort, at the right hand of Jesus Christ at the last day': ibid. 205.
[68] von Rohr, *Covenant of Grace*, 177; cf. Isaac Ambrose: 'Sacraments were never intended by God to exert their vertue onely in, or during the administration, As in the Lord's Supper, Christians by their experiences can testifie, that the benefit is most-what

In John Ball's words, baptism was regarded as a 'great force to strengthen faith and ease the heart in distresse'. Whatever their age, regularly catechized people would acknowledge the seriousness of sin and begin to feel their need of forgiveness. When such disturbed sinners felt 'heavie laden', tempted 'to doubt or despaire' and 'deeply perplexed with feare of falling away: then the consideration and remembrance of what was promised and sealed in Baptisme, will serve to stay, support and comfort the soule'. The recollection of God's promise 'to wash away ... sinnes' and its ratification 'confirmed by seale' in the sign of baptism helped to free the troubled soul from despair.[69]

Presbyterians made it abundantly clear that 'the inward Grace and virtue of Baptisme is not tyed to that very moment of time wherein it is administred, and that the fruit and power thereof reacheth to the whole course of our life'.[70] When the question was asked, if 'a man falling into sinne, after he is baptised, may have any benefit of his Baptisme', Perkins, a Puritan minister of the Elizabethan Church of England, said affirmatively that he may, 'if he repent'. His 'Indentures and Evidences remaine whole in respect of God, and his name is not put out of the covenant'. This was of special value in times when the soul might be cast down or harassed by a sense of spiritual isolation or under the persistent assault of temptation. When 'a man is in danger of the shipwracke of his soul', baptism is 'a planke or boord to swimme upon', 'the sacrament of Repentance' with a continuing efficacy which has 'sealed unto him the pardon of all his sinnes, past, present and future'. Truly penitent, 'he is standing to the order of his baptisme, beleeving and repenting'.[71] The intended progression of baptismal commitment was largely dependent on three aspects of corporate spirituality: parental responsibility, catechetical instruction and public confirmation.

First, it is scarcely possible to exaggerate the importance of the family in the continuing efficacy of the child's baptism. In presenting their daughter or son for baptism, parents were making a public vow to do everything humanly possible to promote and further the child's spiritual life. Godly ministers grasped opportunities to encourage families in the spiritual development of those baptized in infancy, and parents prayed for their enlightenment and responsive obedience, the fulfilment of everything anticipated in a child's baptism. Thomas Jolly set aside one of his monthly days of private prayer to 'entreat' God that 'the blessing might be propagated from generation to

---

after the receiving of it, so in baptism it may be many years after the receiving of it': *War with Devils*, 18 (Book II, ch.1, section 4).

[69] John Ball, *A Treatise of Faith* (1632), 412–13. Puritans insisted that word and sacrament were inseparable. Sacraments are 'seales annexed to the letters patents of God's evangellical promises, which assure or conveigh nothing, but what is contained in the promise and upon the same condition': George Downame, *A Treatise of the Certainty of Perseverance* (1631), 395–96.

[70] *Directory for Publique Worship*, 21.

[71] Perkins, *Cases of Conscience*, in *Works*, II, 80.

generation' in his family, and that his 'eldest son now coming to years of discretion might lay hold of the lords covenant'. During the day he was given 'help and hope' that the parents' baptismal vows would come to fruition and, to that end, planned a series of sermons on the text, 'He is my God, and I will prepare him an habitation; my father's God, and I will exalt him' (Exod. 15: 2). It occurred to Jolly that it might be helpful if the sermons were 'transcribed and enlarged for the sake of posterity', that his children and others 'might be p[er]suaded to own god as theirs and prepare him an habitation'.[72]

Second, to the parents' intercessions on the child's behalf, and their consistent example, was added the daily responsibility of systematic teaching. Catechetical instruction was the established pedagogical pattern in homes, schools and churches. Stockton's practice was typical of Nonconformist parental responsibility throughout the period, especially among church leaders. 'Once a week usually he did Catechise both his Children and Servants. And once a fortnight ... he opened and explained some Principle of Religion in a Catechetical way, which his children and servants were to give him an account of the next Fortnight.'[73] Nonconformist parents treasured the hope that, given such regular teaching in a spiritually sensitive environment, their children would come to recognize the need of forgiveness and trust in the work of Christ, and 'confirm' their baptism by making an evident response in personal commitment to him.

Third, Baxter was convinced that participation in a public ceremony of confirmation represented the progression which had been anticipated in the spiritual experience of children from believing households. He was persuaded that parents, children, 'nominal' Christians, ministers, churches and the general public would all be helped by the provision of such services of public commitment. Such provision would encourage parents to recognize that 'the knowledge of the Letter' in family instruction was the usual 'way to the receiving of the Spirit'. They could look forward to the time when, responding to such teaching, their child might progress from being an interested seeker to a committed follower. Baxter and others were appalled by the indiscriminate use of the sacrament of initiation. As 'things go now, in most places, they may bring their Children to Baptism, without understanding what Baptism is', and their children could simply 'slide into the state of the Adult Christians ... without knowing whether Christ were a man or a woman, or who he is, or what business he came about into the world'. It is therefore 'no wonder if so many Heathens do sit among Christians' in the churches.

Believing children growing to maturity would grasp this opportunity to make an outward and public profession of their inward spiritual resolve. Confirmation would encourage wholehearted commitment to Christ far more than 'a secret sliding into the number of Adult Christians will do' for 'solemn

---

[72] Jolly, *Note Book* (ed. Fishwick), 32.
[73] Clarke, *Lives of Eminent Persons*, 196–97.

engagements and obligations, have some force upon Conscience to hold men to Christ and restraine them from sinne'. In Old Testament times, the Hebrew people expressed their dedication by participating in covenant renewal ceremonies. 'But with us, men feel no such bonds upon them. And many question whether they are bound at all, by their Parents promises for them in Baptism'. Those who had been baptized as infants but had not made such a personal and public response would be challenged by such services. At such times, they might consider the seriousness of the 'sinne and misery ... of that Condition which multitudes do now rest in; and so to waken them to look after a safer state, and to be what they must seem to be, if they will be taken to be Christians'. It was surely a massive act of deception 'to be currantly esteemed Christians, when they are not'. Human nature is such that 'men are very easily brought to think well of themselves, and hardly brought to confess their misery'. The person that 'thinks he is ... a true Christian already, will seek to be made what he takes himself already to be'.

Confirmation would certainly be of great help to ministers. Preaching would be more effective, for people 'would better understand and apply our Sermons, whereas now, they lose the benefit by misapplying them', thinking they are Christians simply because they were baptized in infancy. Pastors are required 'to labour all our lives (and with most, in vaine) to make unbelievers ... understand what they are'.

> [When] they all go together under the name of Christians, whatever comforts they hear offered to Believers, they take to themselves ... But if once we could but get men to stand in their own places ... how easily then would our message work? Methinks the Devil should not be able to keep one man of an hundred, in a state of ungodliness and condemnation if they knew that they are in such a state.

Ministers would also benefit in their pastoral work from the clear definition and distinction that confirmation would provide. Believers who had publicly registered their commitment by being confirmed were placing themselves at their minister's disposal for any work they might be able to do in the local church. The pastor would know they were available 'like a workmans tooles in his shop, that all are in their place, and so at hand when he should use them'.

Confirmation would distinguish them from those who, at present, are simply 'Hearers', not thinking to be used in the same way as confirmed believers, whereas in many situations unconverted people were offended if not allowed to participate actively in local church life. Such frustrated attenders are 'snatching at our fingers for the Childrens bread, that belongs not to them', and are even 'drawn to hate and raile at Ministers, for not fulfilling their desires.' The Lord's Supper would also be more appropriately reserved for the participation of committed believers, and 'not imbittered to us by the pollutions of Infidels'.

Local churches would benefit from confirmation because they would be able more carefully to observe 'those that are not yet fit for Adult-membership and

Priviledges' and encourage them to remain for a while 'in the place of Catechumens or Expectants'.

> If you teare them not out of the Church's wombe, till they are ready for the birth, they will prosper there, that else may perish. Your Corne will best prosper in the cold earth ... till the Springing time shall come. ... A boy in his ABC will learne better in his own place, among his fellows, then in a higher form, where he hath work set him which he is uncapable of doing.

Christian communities would also be better equipped for the necessary practice of church discipline when believers 'know what it was they were engaged to' when they declared themselves to be committed Christians. Publicly confirmed believers 'understandingly consent to live under such a Discipline', and acknowledge the necessity of honouring their vows.

Furthermore, the general public would benefit, as 'the Christian Religion will be more honourable in the eyes of the world, who judge by the members and professours lives, before they can judge of the thing as in it self'. They will be able to identify those who have outwardly acknowledged Christ in their confirmation, and distinguish them from those who, however genuine, are at this stage simply church attenders, 'hearers' or seekers.

Baxter was additionally persuaded that, if adopted by all the churches, confirmation would be a shared element of corporate spirituality, serving to draw Episcopalians, Presbyterians, Independents and Baptists, even, 'I may put it, the Papists themselves', closer together.[74]

Believers' Baptism

Throughout this period, as later, the concept of believers' baptism remained a minority conviction in an ecclesiastical milieu firmly dominated by paedobaptist doctrine and practice. In a period hardly noted for ecumenical co-operation, some paedobaptists and Baptists did meet together for worship, prayer and mutual support,[75] though Baptists were themselves fragmented.[76] Particular Baptists had 'closed' and 'open' membership churches, which often strained inter-congregational relationships. Closed membership churches restricted both membership and participation at the Lord's Table to those who

---

[74] Baxter, *Confirmation*, 194–206; cf. Cockermouth Independent Church Book, 1 September 1672, 9 July 1674, for examples of confirmation in an Independent congregation. For further advocacy of confirmation by a Presbyterian minister later ejected from Bishop's Tawton, Devon, see Jonathan Hanmer, *An Exercitation upon Confirmation ... so long buried ... to which are Annexed some Directions for the putting of it into practice* (1658).

[75] *Broadmead Records* (ed. Hayden), 147, 149, 150–52, 159–63, 179.

[76] Particular Baptists were Calvinist in their soteriology, whereas General Baptists were committed to an Arminian theology of 'General' redemption and the universal scope and efficacy of Christ's sacrifice for all mankind. Both traditions had further divisions within their own ranks.

had been baptized as believers on profession of faith.[77] 'Open' membership churches were a minority, and though equally committed to believer's baptism, refused to make it obligatory for membership and participation in the Lord's Supper. They preferred to welcome participants and members on the basis of 'faith in Christ and holines of life'.[78] The Broadmead church and Bunyan's church at Bedford belonged to this group,[79] and Bunyan himself became the most eloquent advocate of this more inclusive pattern of church membership.[80] General Baptists were also divided on a sacramental issue. Some churches insisted that the imposition of hands for the reception of the Holy Spirit must take place either at baptism or subsequently at reception into church membership. These churches viewed the practice as an essential element in their communion with other General Baptist churches, fracturing their relationships with churches which had never practised it or had declined to make it obligatory for church membership.[81] A further, relatively small, group of Baptist churches were committed to the 'Seventh Day' Sabbath,[82] with occasionally strained relationships with the wider body. Despite these divergent sacramental convictions, in the teaching and practice of Baptist congregations believer's baptism was widely regarded as an exemplary model, an authenticating seal, a distinguishing badge and a privileged token.

An exemplary model

Baptists were hardly the first to recognize that the baptism of Jesus was 'a good

---

[77] See, e.g., William Kiffin, *A Sober Discourse of Right to Church Communion ... proved ... no unbaptized person may be regularly admitted to the Lord's Supper* (1681). Kiffin says that the exclusion of unbaptized believers from the Lord's Supper is a matter of church order, not a criticism of their spirituality. He insists that they are not removed 'from our love' and 'we esteem them Christian Brethren and Saints', while praying for their further enlightenment.

[78] For the 'principle upon which' the Bedford church 'entered into fellowship one with another' from the ministry of John Gifford onwards, see *Bedford Minutes* (ed. Tibbutt), 17.

[79] Nuttall, *Visible Saints*, 119–20.

[80] 'I do not plead for a despising of Baptism, but a bearing with our Brother, that can not do it for want of Light': John Bunyan, *Differences in Judgment about Water-Baptism, No Bar to Communion* (1673), in *MW*, IV, 216; 'I have denied, that Baptism was ever ordained of God to be a wall of Division between ... the Holy that are, and the Holy that are not So baptized with Water as we': idem, *Peaceable Principles and True* (1674), in *MW*, IV, 269; cf. idem, *A Confession of my Faith, and a Reason of my Practice in Worship* (1672), in *MW*, IV, 131–87. For Bunyan's controversy with fellow Baptists, see Greaves, *Glimpses*, 271–77, 291–301.

[81] When Benjamin Keach left the General Baptists, he retained their baptismal practice of the 'Imposition of hands ... that so you may receive a further Measure of the Promised Spirit': *Gospel Mysteries Unveil'd*, Book III, 56.

[82] Bryan W. Ball, *The Seventh Day Men, Sabbatarians and Sabbatarianism in England and Wales, 1600–1800* (Oxford, 1994).

Pattern for Believers to follow'.[83] The Synoptic Gospels' narrative of Christ's baptism figured prominently in Baptist apologetic. Four distinctive features dominated their exemplarist interpretation. The submission of Jesus to John's baptism in the Jordan became a model of declared obedience, unique relationship, lifelong vocation and guaranteed resources.

John Norcott described the baptism of Jesus as 'an Act of Obedience' to his Father's 'glorious Will'. So 'is the Lord well pleased' when 'from the heart we obey the form of doctrine delivered to us' by being baptized.[84] Hercules Collins urged the unbaptized to consider that Christ was 'willing to be baptised in Blood for your Salvation, and will you not be baptised in water in obedience to his Commission?'[85] But this 'binding duty'[86] could be extremely costly in many of these persecuted communities. A Dissenter's commitment might not be widely known in the local community, especially when the conventicle was held outside the immediate area, but the public act of baptism in a nearby river was an event impossible to conceal. Within days, people would be fully aware of their neighbour's declaration of loyalty. The cost might prove greater than unpopularity alone;[87] work and home might also be at stake. One prospective baptismal candidate confessed that the ordinance presented difficulties for him because 'he hired a farm of Mr. Bendich, and if he should know that he was baptized he would turn him out'. His Fenstanton church leader reminded this anxious believer that 'the earth was the Lord's ... and wished him to trust God', who would prove 'a better landlord than Mr. Bendich'.[88]

As Jesus stood in the river Jordan, the voice from heaven publicly identified him as God's unique Son, and so 'Christ as Head was sealed' at his obedient baptism. In the baptism of believers God likewise 'seals the Sonship of his Members' and does so at that moment, 'in this very Act of Baptism'.[89] In a period when many genuine believers were haunted by a sense of uncertainty

---

[83] John Norcott, *Baptism discovered plainly and faithfully according to the Word of God* (1675), 24. In his baptism, 'Christ ... is our Pat[t]ern': John Griffith, *Gods Oracle and Christs Doctrine, or Six Principles of the Christian Religion* (1655), 30.

[84] Norcott, *Baptism*, 5–6.

[85] Collins, *Baptism*, 9.

[86] Griffith, *Gods Oracle*, 29.

[87] In 1659, the Oxford antiquary and historian Anthony Wood was present at a river baptism at High Bridge conducted by the Baptist leader Lawrence King, when the preacher was heckled by a noisy crowd: Kreitzer, *'Seditious Sectaryes'*, 117. River baptisms continued to attract ridicule: cf. A.G. Fuller (ed.), *The Complete Works of the Rev. Andrew Fuller* (1841), xix.

[88] *Records of the Churches of Christ gathered in Fenstanton, Warboys and Hexham 1644–1720* (ed. E.B. Underhill, 1854), 82.

[89] Norcott, *Baptism*, 6. Henry Jessey and others provided an eschatological dimension to their teaching about baptism as 'sealing', represented as 'signifying, representing and sealing up to them their union with Christ ... in his Death and Burial and Resurrection (as also their bodily Resurrection, that it shall be)': *Miscellanea Sacra or Diverse Necessary Truths* (1665), 128.

about their salvation, baptism offered committed people the opportunity publicly to declare their faith at a precise moment of time and, in the act of obedience, receive assurance of their acceptance with God. In the act of submitting themselves to the ordinance many became deeply convinced that they too were sons and daughters of God.

The baptism of Jesus marked the beginning of his public ministry, when he was designated not only as 'Son' but also Servant. The 'voice from Heaven', 'in whom I am well pleased', recalled the Isaianic Servant Song (Isa. 42: 1; Mt. 3: 17, Lk. 3: 22). In the Jordan Jesus was publicly committing himself to his work as God's unique Servant, and in their baptism these believers were likewise surrendering themselves to the lifelong service of Christ. In the households of nobility, 'a servant wears his Lord's livery, a Garment which demonstrates him to be a servant to such a Lord'.[90] So 'we by Baptism put on Christ'. In the sacrament 'we put on our Lord's livery', wearing 'his 'cloth[e]s from head to foot'.[91]

Baptists also recalled that in baptism Jesus was assured of the dynamic support of the Holy Spirit in exercise of his unique vocation. In the course of his London ministry, Norcott had observed that 'some of Christ's followers' have, similarly, 'found glorious openings of Heaven in Baptism'. The Spirit who descended on Jesus in the Jordan is 'the very same that is promised to Believers at their Baptism'. Norcott emphasised the trinitarian resources available to every Christian, for 'he who is baptized and doth sincerely believe' will discover that 'the whole Trinity, the Father, Son and Spirit is his portion' for 'that glorious Union of the Trinity' manifest in Christ's baptism 'is in every Believers Baptism commemorated'.[92]

An Authenticating Seal

Many Dissenters could sincerely affirm their personal faith, but could not honestly point to a particular date that marked the beginning of their relationship with Christ. They envied those who could speak persuasively of a 'Damascus Road' type of personal encounter that began at a definite moment. Some could recall a particular sermon that brought them to repentance and personal faith, while others who had benefited from hundreds of sermons could not point to a date when they were unmistakably 'converted'.[93]

---

[90] For earlier use of the 'livery' imagery in a baptismal context, cf. Edward Drapes [Draper], *Gospel Glory Proclaimed before the Sonnes, in the Visible and Invisible Worship of God* (1649), 111: 'wearing his livery, whereby he distinguishes his people in a speciall manner from the world'; John Gosnold, *Of the Doctrine of Baptisms* (1657), 37: 'As Servants are known by their Livery, and who is their Master, so we in Baptism: 'tis as it were our Livery, whereby we own Christ our Lord: therefore ... serve Him'.
[91] Norcott, *Baptism*, 18.
[92] Ibid 5–6.
[93] Ezekiel Culverwell knew of many who 'could never come to such certainty of their salvation'. He devoted 500 pages of his *A Treatise of Faith ... Applied especially unto*

In the opening decades of the seventeenth century, Puritan preachers developed a complicated morphology of conversion which sought to trace in detail the various stages[94] by which a penitent person might be brought to personal faith, each supported by a complex series of 'evidences', tests or signs by which authenticity and sincerity might be judged.[95] They actively encouraged 'the examination and tryall of that confidence and assurance we seeme to have of Gods favour, and our own salvation'.[96] Many, however, feared that their genuine quest for faith did not fit neatly into such a sharply defined schema. Bunyan was not the only tortured seeker.[97] As young men, Baxter and Kiffin experienced the same disturbing uncertainty. Baxter's 'inquisitive mind' was constantly 'wounded with uncertainties' and 'doubts' he 'was not able to resolve'.[98] Hearing of dramatic conversions, he became disturbed with 'Doubts of my own Salvation' and 'could not distinctly trace' such 'Workings of the Spirit' in his own life, 'nor knew the Time of my Conversion'.[99] He readily confessed: 'whether sincere Conversion began now, or before, or after, I was never able to this day to know'.[100] Kiffin's experience was much the same. In 'great perplexity of mind', sometimes trusting but often 'shut up in unbelief', he found little peace. Then he heard John Goodwin say that although there was but one gospel, with its clear call for repentance and faith, different people might come by a variety of routes. 'This was of great use to me', said Kiffin, 'so far as to satisfy me that God had not tied himself to any one way of converting a sinner but ... took several ways to bring a soul to Jesus

---

the use of the weakest Christians (1648), because 'very few attained to ... the assurance of their salvation': ibid., Ep. Ded., 'To all God's People', 1.

[94] In the quest for personal faith, Perkins, for example, identified two main divisions. The 'giving of the first grace' was then divided into ten 'severall actions', followed by the 'giving of the second grace', further subdivided: *Cases of Conscience*, in *Works*, II, 13–14.

[95] e.g. William Perkins, 'A Treatise Tending to a Declaration whether a man be in the estate of Damnation, or the estate of Grace' (1608), in *Works*, I, 356–420; cf. idem, 'Consolations for the troubled Consciences of weake Christians'; 'A Declaration of Certaine Spirituall Desertions, serving to terrifie all drowsie Protestants, and to comfort them that mourne for their sinnes'; 'A Case of Conscience ... how a man may know whether he be a childe of God or no', ibid. 421–28; William Ames, *Conscience with the Power and Cases thereof* (1643), Book II, 1–25.

[96] Arthur Hildersam, *Lectures upon the Fourth of John* (1629), 311.

[97] *Memoirs of Ambrose Barnes* (ed. W.H.D. Longstaffe, Surtees Society, 50; Durham, 1867), 134–38, cf. 137: 'to point out the time of the espousel, to show you, as I may tearm it, the wedding-ring ... truly I am not able'.

[98] Baxter, *Reasons*, 205.

[99] Sylvester (ed.), *Reliquiae*, I, i, §6, 1: 'Since then I understood that the soul is in too dark and passionate a plight at first, to be able to keep an exact account of its own Operations'. Few people would be 'able to give any true account of the just time when special Grace began'.

[100] Ibid., §3.

Christ.'[101] Baxter had such a keen analytical mind that it was natural for him later to want to know by what precise stages he had been brought to personal faith.[102] 'Doubts of my own Sincerity in Grace' troubled him for 'many years',[103] but he too found peace in the conviction that God deals differently with each individual.[104]

With this quest to itemize personal experience, and the awareness that some, like Baxter, could not point to a decisive moment of conversion, the act of believer's baptism brought assurance[105] and support to many people. Thousands of spiritually sensitive women and men, unable to recall a specific time of conversion, found in baptism a precise moment of public commitment and a specific act in which they might appropriate for themselves God's promise of forgiveness. Baptist writers frequently quoted Ananias's exhortation to Saul of Tarsus, '[a]rise, and be baptized, and wash away thy sins' (Acts 22: 16), though they were always at pains to insist that baptism could only confirm the believer's forgiveness, not effect it. Danvers described it as 'a Sign to the Believer of the Covenant on God's part of washing away his sins', but emphasized that if an unconverted person was baptized it was devoid of meaning.[106] Bunyan can scarcely be accused of exalting the ordinance[107] but even he held that baptism was an act in which a committed believer could experience the confirmation of the forgiveness of sins. The person baptized could 'know by that circumstance [baptism], that he hath received remission of sins; if his Faith be as true, as his being baptized is felt by him'.[108] Baptism was not intended 'to convey grace where it is not, but to confirm Grace, and strengthen it where it is'. It was always necessary that 'faith and repentance must needs precede baptism ... it [is] a seal of the new Covenant',[109] but in and

---

[101] Orme (ed.), *William Kiffin*, 4, 10–11.
[102] 'I never thought I understood any thing till I could anatomize it, and see the parts distinctly'; for Baxter, 'Definition and Distinction led the way': Sylvester (ed.), *Reliquiae*, I, i, §5.
[103] Ibid.
[104] Ibid., §6, 4.
[105] Some Puritan writers viewed robust Christian assurance with suspicion. 'And for one that Sathan hath overthrowne by desperation, there are twenty whom he hath overthrowne with ... false assurance ... it were better for a man to be vexed with continuall doubts and feares, than to be lulled asleepe with such [false] assurance', counsel which, however necessary, cannot have relieved many of their acute anxiety: Hildersam, *Lectures*, 311.
[106] Danvers, *Treatise of Baptism*, 18.
[107] Bunyan says of the unbaptized believer: 'all then that he wanteth, is but the sign, the shadow ... The best of Baptisms he hath; he is Baptized by that one spirit; he hath the heart of Water-baptism; he wanteth only the outward show, which if he had would not prove him a truly visible Saint': *Confession of my Faith*, *MW*, IV, 172.
[108] Ibid.
[109] Thomas Patient, *The Doctrine of Baptism and the distinction of covenants, or a plain treatise wherein the four essentials of baptism ... are deliberately handled* (1654), 152–53.

through this visible act of witness many people received, 'Sacramentally and Symbolically',[110] the deep assurance that they belonged to God.

A distinguishing badge

The Baptists' pattern of initiation thrust their distinctive act of Christian profession into the public arena. For those who insisted on baptism by immersion, local rivers, deep streams or nearby lakes were the only places where this visible act of witness could take place. Such outdoor services often attracted large crowds of observers, and not all were remotely sympathetic. These were occasions when Nonconformist worship was taking place in a church without walls, and candidates were taught to regard their baptism as an identity marker, the privileged adoption of their distinctive 'badge', the sign 'by which ... Disciples are known'.[111] In the context of persecution, mere attendance at such a conventicle was illegal, and to be identified at such as a baptized person was for many a costly act of Christian profession.[112]

When Bristol's open-membership church met for baptisms, crowds gathered at the riverside, whatever the weather. Four women and ten men were baptized in the Avon in the winter of 1667. Inclement conditions had led to repeated postponement but with the onset of fine warm weather, a new date was fixed. In the event, the weather changed yet again, 'ye like had not been all That winter before ... Exceeding high and sharp pierceing Wind, Frost, and Snow'. One of the female candidates, 'in goeing to ye place through ye Meadows, her Handkerchiefe received some wet, being about her Neck, was frozen'. Knowing this, the 'Maid that waited upon her' warned that 'if she went into ye Water she would not come forth alive'. Another candidate, Thomas Jennings, an ejected minister, had suffered severe toothache for a week, 'soe great, that his face was very much swelled' and 'bound up', and 'that day [he was] very ill with it'. Another, with a badly sprained leg, 'was carryed upon a horse to ye place', while yet another was so 'very weakly, thinn and Consumptive' that his family 'were very averse to ye Ordinance'. But the minister conducting the baptisms had travelled from South Wales to be present and because he 'was come so farr on purpose' the members believed it inappropriate to 'deferr it any longer'. The Bristol congregation longed that the Lord would 'worke a Miracle, to give a President [precedent] to others that should fear ye Coldnesse ... to doe his will', and their prayers were answered. The 'Lord Preserved them all; and not so much as one Ill, but rather better by it; and are alive to this day, being

---

[110] Collins, *Baptism*, 10. Collins warned against having a low view of the sacraments: 'Take heed you are not guilty of Contempt, looking upon Christ's Ordinances as mean, low and little things, for nothing is mean that hath Christ's Authority stamp'd upon it'.
[111] Gosnold, *Baptisms*, 37.
[112] Stevington Baptists sought to minimize the dangers of arrest as well as hostile crowds by conducting baptisms at night: H.G. Tibbutt (ed.), *Some Early Nonconformist Church Books* (Bedfordshire Historical Record Society, 51: 1972), 27, cf. 29, 35.

about 10 years since'.[113]

Such sturdy profession of Christian faith was unlikely to be admired by all the spectators. To some 'adversaryes', it was foolhardy and irresponsible, who 'Looked upon ye People as madd' to 'Adventure on such a worke' in wintry conditions.[114] But when elderly and physically frail people were baptized, and neighbours saw that they suffered no ill effects, it must have caused some at least to reflect on their sincerity of Christian commitment and the reality of their resources. Speldhurst villagers may well have felt like that when their eighty-four-year-old neighbour Matthew Calverly was baptized. Two members 'carried [him] in a chair' to and from the river but he was none the worse for the experience. Indeed, 'for several weeks after [he was] much better than for several years before and could walk about long'. His baptism was greatly to the 'wonder of some of his carnal friends' who, naturally concerned for the old man, had deliberately 'kept out of sight expecting he would dye in the Administration of the Ordinance'.[115]

A Privileged Token

Thomas Patient expounded a particular aspect of Baptist teaching that was both inspiring and supportive in contexts where persecution was particularly fierce. In describing the baptism of believers Patient drew on the use of baptismal imagery by Jesus to describe inevitable suffering (Lk. 12: 50): 'Dipping doth hold forth a conformity to Christ in his ... afflictions, as Christ saith, I have a Baptism'. He maintained that 'one end of Baptism is, to represent Christ's Sufferings, and our Sufferings with him, which is in a lively manner set out by dipping into water'. He observed that 'when the Saints ... express their afflictions' in Old Testament passages, 'they do set them forth by being in the depths, or in the deep waters'. David calls to God, 'Out of the depths ... meaning deep afflictions', and 'God saith ... When thou passest through the waters they shall not overflow thee, meaning affliction' (Psa. 130: 1; Isa. 43: 2). Therefore 'when a believer is ... dipped and plunged, all over into the River or water' it is specifically 'to hold forth' that 'now he must resolve to take up the Cross of Christ and suffer'. The undoubted cost is matched by assured resources; 'being raised ... out of the water again by the hands of the Minister, doth hold forth, that so shall such believing souls be saved ... from all their afflictions' (citing Psa. 34: 17). For Patient, baptism is an affirmation of submission and a guarantee of power. It is both 'to sign, and confirm signally our Sufferings and Afflictions with Christ' and our 'Deliverance from them

---

[113] See *Broadmead Records* (ed. Hayden), 123–24, cf. 125–26, 138, 142–44, 184–85, 202, 207, 212, 218–19, 225, 230, 269–70, for further river baptisms in Bristol, including that of another 'Antient Member of ye Congregation ... at last convinced of a long-neglected duty': ibid. 268.
[114] Ibid. 125.
[115] *A Transcription of the Church Book of Speldhurst and Pembury (later Tunbridge Wells)* (ed. Leonard J. Maguire; 1998), 7 (transcribed from BL, Add. MS 36709).

all'.[116] The believer's promised 'deliverance' is perpetually guaranteed by the fact of Christ's resurrection, for 'although he dyed and was buried, yet ... [he] was raised again'.

Patient was no detached theorist when he wrote about suffering, having experienced considerable hardship during his life in three different countries. The quest for religious freedom took him to New England in the 1630s, but newly adopted convictions about believer's baptism[117] brought him into conflict with fellow emigrants.[118] He realized that, because of his changed views, he would be 'generally dispised and slighted of all the godly in that Countrie' and denied 'Communion and Fellowship with them'. In a land where he had hoped for freedom, he 'must expect to suffer imprisonment, confiscation of goods and banishment at least'.[119] When he refused to have his child baptized, a warrant was issued for his arrest, but he was enabled to flee the country with his family. Back in London in 1643, he became a colleague of William Kiffin,[120] and later travelled to Ireland where he became instrumental in establishing its first Baptist meeting-house, in Swift's Alley, Dublin. Here again, he met with opposition when local people cursed and stoned Patient and his colleagues in the streets. It was recorded that these 'evil persons intended to destroy them by shooting at them'.[121]

Returning to England, he became an assistant pastor at the Pithay closed-membership church in Bristol but was arrested for his activities there and imprisoned.[122] Following his release in 1664, Patient went back to London where, once again, he assisted Kiffin, but his London ministry was cut short when he died in the summer of 1666, a victim of the plague.[123] No stranger to adversity, Patient was certainly qualified to encourage fellow Baptists to regard baptism as an act of voluntary initiation into suffering for Christ.

Patient was not the only Baptist preacher to relate his baptismal teaching to the Dissenters' experience of suffering. Edward Draper had earlier written: 'as Christ died, and was surrounded with miseries, so in this Ordinance, by faith,

---

[116] Patient, *Doctrine*, 12–13.

[117] Murray Tolmie, *The Triumph of the Saints: The Separate Churches of London 1616–1649* (Cambridge, 1977), 52.

[118] Twenty years later, John Clark and Obadiah Holm[e]s were arrested at a meeting in 1651 and imprisoned in Boston for preaching believers' baptism and for claiming that it was appropriate for non-ordained members to preach: J. Clark, *Ill newes from New England* (1652), which also contains a letter from the prisoners to London Particular Baptist leaders.

[119] B.R. White, 'Thomas Patient in England and Ireland', *Irish Baptist Historical Society Journal* 2 (1969–70), 36–48, at 37; idem., 'Isaac Backus and Baptist History', *Baptist History and Heritage* 1 (1970), 13–23.

[120] Patient's name appears alongside that of Kiffin in the Confession of Faith issued by seven London Particular Baptist churches in 1644.

[121] St John D. Seymour, *The Puritans in Ireland 1647–1661* (Oxford, 1969), 60.

[122] *Broadmead Records* (ed. Hayden), 33, 61, 70, 118.

[123] Wilson, *Dissenting Meeting Houses*, I, 431–43.

wee see our sufferings to be the dyings of Christ in us; and as we suffer with him, so are we planted into the likeness of his resurrection'.[124] John Gosnold focused on Christ's 'Baptism of Suffering' sayings (Mt. 10: 22–3; Mk 10: 38–9; Lk. 12: 50), describing contemporary 'Disciples' as 'partakers with him' in baptism 'of his Crosse, as well as his Crown' when they were 'Dipped and Plung'd into afflictions',[125] especially those who suffered for the gospel.

We turn now from paedobaptist and Baptist theology and practice of baptism to examine suffering as a context for the Nonconformist interpretation of the Lord's Supper.

The Lord's Supper

Committed Dissenters valued any opportunity to meet at the Lord's Table,[126] and it is possible that their desire for the Lord's Supper was greater than that of many worshippers in the parish churches.[127] At Earls Colne, with over a thousand parishioners, Ralph Josselin frequently had no more than twelve to fifteen regular communicants.[128] When a rural Bedfordshire vicar began his ministry at Caddington in 1691, he discovered that out of several hundred parishioners only ten came regularly to communion.[129] Yet in the same county a young member of Bunyan's congregation 'was begging of the Lord ... that he would please' to provide an opportunity for her to get to Gamlingay in order to be 'at his Table'. Many 'times before' it had 'beene A sweet seeling ordinance' to Agnes Beaumont. 'In those dayes', she said, 'I was Always laying up many A prayre in heaven Against I came to the Lords Table, where I often found a very plentifull returne'.[130] The contrast could hardly be greater. A young worshipper in her early twenties was eager to travel several miles in wintry

---

[124] Drapes, *Gospel Glory*, 110. Describing his baptism, a young apprentice, familiar with Old Testament narrative as well as New Testament teaching, also used the motif of burial and resurrection with Christ: Charles Doe, *A Collection of the Experience of the Work of Grace* ([1700]), 19.

[125] Gosnold, *Baptisms*, 38, citing Old Testament imagery of severe adversity from Psa. 42: 7; 69: 1–2; 88: 7; Ezek. 26: 19; cf. also [Powell], *Sufferer's Catechism*, 25.

[126] Stephen Mayor, *The Lord's Supper in Early English Dissent* (1972), 1972.

[127] John Spurr, 'Religion in Restoration England', in Lionel K.J. Glassey (ed.), *The Reigns of Charles II and James VII and II* (1992), 90–124, at 113–14; cf. Josselin's frequent comments on the poor attendance of Earls Colne communicants: *Diary* (ed. Macfarlane), 516, 546, 553, 574, 631. For further examples, see *CSPD* 1663–64, 64; Whiteman with Clapinson (eds), *Compton Census*, xxxviii n.12.

[128] Josselin, *Diary* (ed. Macfarlane), 533, 631.

[129] Arnold Hunt, 'The Lord's Supper in Early Modern England', *P&P* no. 161 (1998), 39–83, at 82, quoting Lambeth Palace Library, MS 933/9, Edward Bowerman (the vicar) to Archbishop Tenison, 17 December 1692. Hunt maintains that there is little evidence of lay demand for the sacrament in the period; cf. Spurr, *Restoration Church*, 360–6.

[130] *Narrative* (ed. Harrison), 11–12.

conditions to be at communion,[131] while scores of Caddington parishioners would scarcely cross the village for the sacrament. Moreover, once at the Gamlingay service, Agnes was not remotely disappointed:

> god made it a blessed meeting to my soul indeed. Oh it was a feast of ffatt things to me! My soul was filled w[i]th Consolation ... when I was at the Lords Table. I found such a returne of prayre that I was scarse able to beare up under it.[132]

A higher level of eucharistic commitment in Dissent is also suggested by the repeated publication of Thomas Doolittle's *A Treatise concerning the Lord's Supper,* one of the most popular expositions of Nonconformist corporate spirituality in sacramental context. First appearing in 1665, it reached fifteen editions by 1689. With its supplementary volume, *The Lord's Last Sufferings* (1682), also for sacramental use, it was highly regarded.[133]

A Kidderminster resident, young Doolittle had been brought to personal faith through Baxter's sermons (later published as *The Saints' Everlasting Rest*) and, encouraged and financially supported by the distinguished author, graduated from Cambridge and entered the ministry. Following ejectment from St Alphege, London Wall, he exercised an influential ministry as a leading London Presbyterian, at the Monkwell Street Meeting House,[134] developing ministerial contacts throughout the country. Repeatedly fined, sometimes excessively, for his preaching, he gave considerable time to writing as well as to sensitive pastoral care, a fact evident in his published works. He spent little time expounding abstruse or controversial theological concepts[135] but was always at pains to relate his teaching to the pressing issues of everyday life. For many years, Doolittle's home adjoined his meeting-house and, like his mentor, he devoted many hours each week to personal counselling of troubled believers as well as individuals without clear personal faith. A distinguished Nonconformist leader, his life had not been free from hardship. He experienced considerable persecution apart from fines, kept a boarding school to support his family, and was forced to move home on a number of occasions. From the day of his ejectment, Doolittle was convinced that his financial needs would be met. At that time he had three children and his wife was expecting a fourth, but at the close of his farewell sermon a member of his congregation pressed twenty

---

[131] Ibid. 18–19.
[132] Ibid. 17.
[133] Thomas Doolittle, *A Treatise concerning the Lords Supper* (1680). The book retained its popularity well into the early eighteenth century, its 26th edition appearing in 1718.
[134] Built some time after the Great Fire, it was licensed for Presbyterian worship in 1672. Described as a 'large substantial brick-building ... with three deep galleries', it was situated 'under a gate-way' and, 'invisible from the street ... admirably adapted' to a time of repression 'when their preaching was considered a crime, and imprisonment the consequence of a discovery': Wilson, *Dissenting Meeting Houses*, III, 186.
[135] Williams, *Christian Sincerity*, unpaginated conclusion.

pounds into his hand, urging his minister to regard it as a token of God's promised provision for his future.[136] As a pastor with experience of adversity,[137] including years of painful illness,[138] he had listened patiently to the trials of others, and so was well equipped to offer an exposition of sacramental theology with particular relevance to hard times. Doolittle covered a range of inter-related themes in his interpretation of the Lord's Supper; we shall focus on five that became particularly relevant in a context of repression and persecution.

Its Unifying Value

Although preaching and teaching dominated Puritan church life,[139] the Lord's Supper was accorded high priority in the development of every congregation's corporate life. Doolittle's exposition emphasized that when believers met at the Lord's Table it was always for 'the closer knitting' of their hearts 'in greater affection and love'. Participants were to use the occasion to examine themselves whether their love for one another was evident, sincere and given practical expression. At the table, they were reminded of Christ's love for them, and those were appropriate moments to reflect on the reality and value of their love for each other and to 'imitate the Lord Jesus in loving' others. Doolittle employed strong metaphors of cohesion, claiming that the 'ordinance ... should have *cemented* us in love and *soldered* our hearts together'.

In the ministry of preaching, one figure was dominant, and, however large the congregation, the remainder were at best attentive, hopefully responsive, hearers, but at the Lord's Supper every single person was of equal importance. Presbyterians, Independents and Baptists alike were sensitive to the qualifications necessary for appropriate administration of the Supper but Nonconformists entertained no notions of priestly precedence and were careful to emphasize that, at the table, every member was present as a grateful and equally needy participant. That sense of a cohesive local community was particularly necessary when, in many places, congregational life was seriously fractured or under imminent threat of dissolution. Congregations in many parts of the country witnessed the invasion of their premises, the frenzied destruction of pulpits and pews, the smashing of windows, and sometimes the total destruction of the meeting-house itself and the imprisonment of its minister. On

---

[136] Wilson, *Dissenting Meeting Houses*, III, 191–92.

[137] Williams, *Christian Sincerity*, unpaginated conclusion.

[138] Daniel Williams said that Doolittle preached 'in the midst of Weakness' and 'Pains must quite disable him' but 'they could not keep him out of the Pulpit'. Chronic gout made mobility difficult and his 'publick Usefulness was ... lessen'd ... by his unfitness to walk': ibid.

[139] Contrast Laud's conviction, expressed at his trial, 'that in all ages of the Church, the touchstone of religion was not to hear the word preached, but to communicate', yet 'at this day, many will come and hear sermons, who yet will not receive the communion together'. Laud called 'the holy table the greatest place of God's residence upon earth': *The Works of ... William Laud* (7 vols; 1847–60), IV, 284.

some occasions, all that was left was the vulnerable core of believing people that had enjoyed meeting on its now desolate premises.

This context of actual or threatened fragmentation meant that any spiritual exercise that expressed, engendered, encouraged or increased congregational solidarity was an emotional and spiritual priority. These believers emphasized that the Lord's Supper was designed for the believing community, not 'single Christians'. It was never intended for an ill-defined group 'meeting as a fluid company, like clouds uncertainly', but for 'fixed' and settled 'incorporated bodies',[140] local churches where fellow believers belonged and had committed themselves to each other in a shared faith, mutual love and practical support.

When they 'see' they are '*one bread*', knowing that they are 'redeemed by *one Lord*, and fed at *one Table* ... and enjoy the same privileges, and are here assured of the same inheritance and Glory', the occasion should 'engage' them 'to be of one heart' and 'to be kindly affectionate one to another'.[141] The sacrificial love of Christ was uninhibited and inclusive.

> As Christ shed his blood, and thereby manifested that he loved all his people; so when we partake of it in the Sacrament, we are ingaged to love one another, as he has loved us. ... Live in love with all that are partakers of the same benefits with you. Yea in this Ordinance you have an example of loving your very enemies as Christ did when he died for you; but a more special and particular love you are taught to have to all the Members of Christ's mystical Body, when you see in this Ordinance how Christ hath loved them all.[142]

Other Dissenters were equally convinced that it was 'Christs uniting ordinanc[e]'[143] in which the participants 'testify true unity with the Church: who are hereby shewed to be one Bread'.[144]

Its Ethical Importance

Discipline and the Lord's Supper were inseparable elements in Puritan

---

[140] Thomas Goodwin, *Exposition of ... Ephesians* (n.d.), in *Works*, II, 389.
[141] Doolittle, *Treatise*, 33.
[142] Ibid. 94–95 (quoting 1 Cor. 13; Eph. 2: 13–16); 129 (quoting Eph. 5: 2). The theme is prominent in Puritan sacramental theology. Perkins, for example, describes both sacraments as 'the bond of mutuall amitie betwixt the faithful': *Golden Chaine*, in *Works*, I, 72. In the Westminster Confession, the Lord's Supper is described as 'a bond, and pledge' of the believing participant's 'communion with him and with each other, as members of his mysticall body': XXIX, I.
[143] *The General Baptist Church in and about Canterbury: Church Book 1660 to 1695* (ed. John Creasey and Leonard J. Maguire; General Baptist Assembly Occasional Paper, 18; 1992), 14.
[144] Thomas Grantham, *St. Paul's Catechism; or a brief and plain Explication of the Six Principles* (1687), 57; cf. idem, *Christianismus Primitivus* (1678), II, 88: 'can anything be more effectually spoken to unite the Members of Christ'.

eucharistic doctrine and experience.[145] 'Fencing the Table' had a significant history and, disturbed by the inappropriate conduct of some national church worshippers,[146] as were their Puritan forefathers, Nonconformists were eager to preserve consistent standards of behaviour among professing believers. 'Drinking or eating unworthily' was both a Pauline prohibition and a subject for contemporary pastoral warning. Opportunity was invariably provided for meticulous self-examination prior to the sacrament. Preparation services became a regular feature of Nonconformist corporate spirituality[147] but with the passing of the years stringent spiritual expectation on the part of ministers caused some to neglect the sacrament, troubled lest they become unworthy recipients.[148] High standards isolated some of a congregation's most spiritually sensitive members and those responsible for the conduct of preparation services had to be aware of their potential dangers as well as their undoubted value.

Doolittle asserted the crucial role of self-examination, and made imaginative use of Old Testament and rabbinic sources for his emphasis on the necessity of purification. The necessary scrutiny was imperative for pastors as much as for other participants. According to the Chronicler's description of the officiating priesthood at the Passover in the time of Hezekiah, it was because the priestly officiants 'had not sanctified themselves sufficiently' that the festival had to be postponed. When it was held, numerous participants were unprepared and 'had not cleansed themselves', so 'prayed for the pardon of their imperfect preparation'. Doolittle reminded his readers that the Mosaic Law made provision for a delayed Passover in the case of those considered ceremonially 'unclean'. The vessels used must also be uncontaminated, and before partaking of the Supper believers must likewise 'cleanse' their 'hearts and lives from all known sin'. Participants must treasure the highest possible moral standards and only come to the Table 'with sins bewailed' and not one single sin 'allowed and

---

[145] Patrick Collinson, *The Elizabethan Puritan Movement* (1967), 346: 'No blemish of the Elizabethan Church was more prominent or more wounding to the puritan conscience than the general absence of discipline', which was 'properly congregational and which in the first instance ought to be exercised by the officers of the local church'.

[146] William Thomas wrote about those 'who had committed notorious sins, and not sufficiently testified to their repentance'. He quoted John Chrysostom, commenting on Matthew, that he would rather suffer his own blood to be shed then give up the most sacred Blood of Christ to an unworthy Receiver': *Preservative*, 27.

[147] Ministers' diaries and Church Books contain frequent references to preparation meetings in churches and homes: e.g. Heywood, *Autobiography* (ed. Turner), I, 277, 292, 294; II, 78, 108; III, 123, 125, 134; IV, 211; Henry, *Diaries* (ed. Lee), 97, 103; Newcome, *Diary* (ed. Heywood), 8, 209; Thoresby, *Diary* (ed. Hunter), I, 46; DWL, MS 201.11, Ipswich [Tacket Street] Independent Church Book, 1686–1791, fols 4–7: 'being preparation day'; *Broadmead Records* (ed. Hayden), 187, 189, 192.

[148] Particularly in the light of forcefully expressed teaching such as Arthur Hildersam, *CLII Lectures upon Psalm 51* (1635), 112, where he can 'confidently affirme it were a matter of lesse danger to you, to eate a morsell of Rats-bane, then to eat that Holy Bread; to drink a cup of poyson, then to drink that Blessed Cuppe, if you come to it in malice'.

approved of'. As the Passover participants searched every corner of their homes for undetected leaven, so they needed 'a closer searching' of their lives by 'lighting the Candle of Conscience at the fire of God's Word' to 'find out sin', not 'to forsake and kill it'. Believers must also recognize the likelihood of unconscious sin. 'Lord ... if there be any sin in me which is not severely dealt with, it is not because I love it, but because I could not find it.'[149]

Painful though it might be, they were to be precise and specific in the act of confession. It was no time to shelter behind a vague acknowledgement of the shortcomings common to humankind. The preparatory meetings and consequent pastoral conversations are as close as Dissenters came to both the rigours and relief of the confessional, an aspect of Catholicism of which, with predictable qualifications, even Perkins approved.[150] Doolittle urged potential confessors to 'watch most against that sin, that you have oftenest found prevailing against you' and that 'your heart is almost ready to yield unto, and your Conscience did most reproach you for'. They must not only be 'against all Sin', but 'chiefly against your chiefest Sin'. It is a mistake ever to 'smile' upon such transgression, for it was that which 'put to death your Lord, the Prince of Life'.[151] But while insisting on appropriate standards of consistent behaviour, Doolittle took care to avoid the dangers of unhealthy scrupulosity and the reluctant self-banishment of sensitive believers genuinely disturbed by spiritual unworthiness or moral rectitude.

Its Confirmatory Nature

As 'a sweet sealing ordinance',[152] the Lord's Supper was a visual and verbal confirmation of the truth that God had given himself in Christ to believers, and a treasured opportunity for Dissenters to declare their faith in him and renew their vows of love and fidelity. It was God's affirmation of ownership and their declaration of loyalty. Nonconformists would have identified wholeheartedly with John Preston's description of this mutuality of commitment at the Lord's Supper.

> As this is the Covenant, on God's part that is sealed to us in the Sacrament, so you must remember, that you put ... your seale likewise to confirme the condition of

---

[149] Doolittle, *Treatise*, 34–36, quoting 2 Chron. 30: 3, 18–19; Num. 9: 6–12.

[150] Perkins said that 'how ever we condemne Auricular confession ... as a rack to the consciences of poore Christians, yet we not only allowe, but call and cry for that confession, whereby a Christian voluntarily at all times may resort to his Pastor ... and disburden his conscience of such sins as disquiet him, and crave his godly assistance and holy prayers': *Of the Calling of the Ministerie, Two Treatises* (1606), in *Works*, III, 447.

[151] Doolittle, *Treatise*, 128.

[152] Heywood, *Autobiography* (ed. Turner), I, 232; cf. I, 183, 283; Asty, *Treatise of Rejoycing* (1683), 78: 'And this is the one end of that grand Ordinance ... to seal and ensure Believers ... wherein the Lord Jesus does come ... clearing up the soul's Interest in himself and telling of him what he hath done for him, and sealing all that hath *past* upon his Soul.'

the Covenant, on your part ... (for it is Reciprocall): for all Covenants must be mutuall.[153]

We have seen that in this period Nonconformist spirituality was hardly noted for its robust doctrine of assurance. Pastors spent long hours endeavouring to bring peace to troubled consciences; Baxter and his colleagues were frequently in the company of people who for many years had faithfully read Scripture, prayed earnestly in their families and attended Dissenting meetings in persecuting times, but who lacked any confidence that they were truly redeemed. Intimate journals and diaries frequently recorded the quest for confirming 'evidences', with precise dates when these hard-won ambitions were attained,[154] and illustrate the spiritual hesitancy of many Nonconformists possessed of genuine personal piety. Doctrines such as predestination and election dominated religious discussion in many devout homes, as tortured souls sought proof that they truly belonged to God and might enjoy eternal security.

The Lord's Supper provided such hesitant believers with regular occasions for confirmatory support. Here was a 'seal' of God's unchanging commitment to them on the basis of a totally reliable covenant relationship. This visible 'seal of the Covenant of grace' was instituted by God to 'convey to believers an assurance of the blessings of the Covenant Promise'.[155] Trusting this unwavering declaration of divine fidelity, those who came to the Table as grateful participants humbly claimed that they had 'a right to him', and to the rich 'priviledges' which Christ had 'purchased by his death, and will seal' unto them 'in this Sacrament'. At 'this Ordinance' the dependent believer could confidently declare that here 'I may be assured of my pardon'.[156]

> When I saw the bread broken and heard the Minister say ... *broken for you* and saw him pour out the wine, and heard him say, *This was the blood of Christ shed for you* ... I did take ... I did believe that God was really though invisibly, dealing forth his Son, and all his benefits to me, as well as to others and I was enabled to apply him particularly to myself, and take him as my own.

The believing participant could testify: 'then oh then my heart was warmed with love and filled with joy'.[157]

In an insecure environment, the lives of many godly people were clouded

---

[153] John Preston, *The New Covenant, or the Saints Portion* (1629), I, 180 (Sermon 6).
[154] *Some Remarkable Passages in the Holy Life and Death of Gervase Disney* (1692), 102: 'I kept a constant Diary or Journal recording my Carriage towards God, towards others, and my self'. Typical 'Evidences' are followed by comments such as: 'G.D.'s Heart answers Aff[irmative], Dec. 7, [16]85'. For Disney on the importance of 'Evidences', see ibid. 127.
[155] Doolittle, *Treatise*, 39.
[156] Ibid. 70–71.
[157] Ibid. 175.

with despair but the sacrament consistently offered them an occasion for renewed confidence. Participants were visually confronted with the commemorative bread and wine on the table. In the sacrament 'you do not only see that you are redeemed but also that you are sealed unto the day of redemption', not merely informed of its power but assured of its permanence.[158]

Its Strengthening Potential

Congregations were frequently reminded that the table was set in the presence of their enemies.[159] On many occasions, the physical context of their observance reminded them that they lived in dangerous times. We have seen that, like other London congregations in the 1680s, Doolittle's meeting was frequently raided and its minister and members heavily fined. In the same period, Axminster Independents met 'for the celebration of that sacred ordinance of the Lord's Supper in a lonesome place near a great wood where a great number of people from divers parts were assembled together'. The secret location and the visiting preacher were visible reminders of threatening adversity. The 'violence of persecution' had forced Henry Butler, an ejected minister,[160] to leave his home and congregation, and finding refuge that Sunday morning among his Axminster friends he preached on the psalmist's prayer, 'Hide me under the shadow of thy wings'. The occasion was one of evident blessing, 'touching, affecting, melting, warming and enlivening the hearts of

---

[158] Ibid. 127. Other writers also pointed out the complementary truth that the Lord's Supper provided believers with a regular opportunity to renew their own commitment to Christ. Baxter says that a believer's personal covenant with Christ 'should be actually renewed ... And the Lord's supper is an ordinance instituted to this end': *Christian Directory*, in *Works* (ed. Orme), V, 47–48. Cf. also his *Reformed Pastor*, which reminds ministers that at 'the Supper of the Lord' they have repeatedly 'called men to renew their Covenant': *Gildas Salvianus*, 35 (ch.1, section XIV). Thomas Wadsworth said it was 'an outward sign to Ratifie this Covenant betwixt God and you ... you do not think it enough in marriage to take one anothers word, but you compleat it by a solemn vow in the presence of witnesses ... Christ hath not thought it enough to take your word, but he will have it confirmed solemnly by this Ordinance'. It must be 'often repeated, for he knows ... our proneness to backsliding, which by this Supper he would prevent'. The Lord 'will beget faith by the preaching of the word ... and yet may reserve the confirmation of your faith and establishment of your love to him, to be wrought by ... the Lord's Supper': in *Supplement to the Morning Exercise*, 255–56.

[159] In 1683, Stephen Towgood, the Axminster pastor, preached on this text in Psa. 23: 5, when their church went 'to celebrate that blessed ordinance of the Lord's *supper* ... in a solitary wood' at a time when 'several soldiers and informers were abroad, hunting for their prey ... to break this assembly, as they had several others': *Ecclestiastica* (ed. Howard), 82–83.

[160] No stranger to adversity, Henry Butler had been nurtured in a Puritan family that under pressure of earlier persecution had emigrated to New England. He became a Harvard graduate and served as a schoolmaster before returning to England. He was vicar of Yeovil when ejected, and was fined and imprisoned on several occasions for holding conventicles in the area.

many'. They planned to resume their worship an hour or two later when their own minister, Bartholomew Ashwood, was appointed to preach, but the people soon found themselves surrounded by soldiers 'raging abroad like ravening wolves ... riding furiously by the place', scattering the people and carrying several away. Others managed to reach home, while some hid themselves and their families 'in the wood and secretly in corners to escape the hands of the enemy'. A few hours later, without planning it, a large group, including pastor and visiting preacher, came together in the wood. They 'resolved to spend the night' together in prayer at a safe house two miles away, especially to intercede for those who had been arrested. Their urgent prayers were answered, for the soldiers, admiring 'the courage and undauntedness of their prisoners', suddenly released them and 'in the morning [they] came to their brethren who had been wrestling with the Lord for them' throughout the long night. It had been a remarkable sacrament day for the Axminster people.[161]

On a later occasion they met in a remote house 'for the breaking of bread and prayers together' but 'when the pastor and people were sat down together at the table, an officer with an informer' began knocking angrily at the door. When the people did not answer, the two men left in order to return with more soldiers, but the intervening time gave the congregation opportunity to disperse, 'carrying the elements of bread and wine with them. So escaping into a wood about two or three miles distant ... they sat down together with much peace and safety' at 'the administration of that sacred ordinance'.[162]

In 1685 this congregation was especially encouraged by the 'very great number of people' who met for 'that sacred Ordinance of the Supper' in 'such an evil and distressing' time. They viewed it as 'a cordial to strengthen them for greater troubles',[163] resources they certainly needed, for within months the Duke of Monmouth had landed nearby at Lyme Regis. This congregation and others entertained hopes 'that this man might be a deliverer for the nation' but such dreams were speedily shattered, to the great personal cost of many local Dissenters.[164] In the 'dismal time' following Monmouth's disastrous rebellion, this church met at night for the Lord's Supper in a 'desert place', despite 'all the dangers and dreadful calamities of the day'. Although 'bands of rude soldiers were ... round about them ... the Lord made this a feasting season to them'. That night a new member was added to their church. 'Thus the Lord was still building them up in the most troublesome time.'[165]

Even when Dissenters met in members' houses, they were not free from harassment. Once, when Baxter was 'preaching in a Private House, where we

---

[161] *Ecclesiastica* (ed. Howard), 21–22.
[162] Ibid. 86–87.
[163] Cf. Heywood's experience at the Lord's Table, when he had a 'strong apprehension it was preparatory to some more than ordinary sufferings': *Autobiography,* I, 232.
[164] *Ecclesiastica* (ed. Howard), 92–93,
[165] Ibid. 105–106.

received the Lord's Supper, a Bullet came in at the Window'.[166] In such circumstances, believers were frequently reminded that their Lord's Last Supper in Jerusalem was set in a persecution context, and those who meet with Christ at his table must be prepared, as he was, to face enmity with courage and heroism. 'When you have been commemorating Christ's death, you must come away purposing to imitate his life ... Christ in his sufferings hath left us an example how we ought to suffer.' Believers can be said to 'walk sutably to that Ordinance, which is a Commemoration of Christ's death', when they 'tread in his steps'.[167] As they recall 'how Christ hath suffered' for them, 'even unto death', they will not count their life 'too dear to lay down for Christ'.[168] Remembering Christ's unique sacrifice and receiving the elements will encourage them to be 'more resolved to suffer, and to dye for Christ', and be infinitely 'more eminent' in their 'active' obedience, and 'more patient' in their 'passive obedience' than previously.[169]

They were convinced that costly demands would be matched with sufficient resources. Doolittle said that believers always knew when they had been enriched by the ordinance, for they are 'more strengthened and emboldned to undergo the loss of all things for Jesus sake'.[170] When Thomas Hardcastle was catechizing his people in Bristol, he also urged them to 'Receive that you may be strengthened', for the Lord's Supper is 'a strengthning ordinance'.[171] All are in need, and it is only the one who 'comes to this holy table without a sense of his wants' who 'is most likely to go away without refreshment'.[172] The sacrament is for 'babes in Christ for strengthning' and for 'poore weak penitent doubting believers ... that know not whether they may receive or not'. Hardcastle asserts that it is for all believers for, 'though never soe young and weake here's food provided for you'.[173] Jesus Christ will be here himselfe at this supper', and he always 'comes in to see that they want nothing'.

> [He] saith friends ... call for what you want, doest thou want peace of Conscience, why here it is, call for it, doe you want strength against temptation, here it is, call for it, doe you want support under outward afflictions, here is enough for all

---

[166] Sylvester (ed.), *Reliquiae*, I, ii, §440. There are frequent references to congregational meetings for the Lord's Supper in members' homes: Lowe, *Diary* (ed. Sachse), 78; 90–91; Henry, *Diaries* (ed. Lee), 272; *Life of Trosse* (ed. Brink), 174; Heywood, *Autobiography* (ed. Turner), I, 195; *CSPD* 1663–64, 64.
[167] Doolittle, *Treatise*, 126, quoting 1 Pet. 2: 21; 1 Jn 2: 6 (incorrectly as Jn 6: 2).
[168] Ibid. 122.
[169] Ibid. 129.
[170] Ibid. 122.
[171] Bristol Baptist College, MS, Thomas Hardcastle, 'Expositions' [1671–72], fol.149.
[172] Grantham, *Christianismus*, II, 92.
[173] Hardcastle, 'Expositions', fol.149.

whatever you want, here it is in this supper ... here's that that is sutable for every condition.[174]

Its Eschatological Declaration

This sacramental meal would not be served for ever. It was a highly meaningful but temporary act of corporate thanksgiving 'until he come'. When believers met for communion they were nearer to heaven than at the best of other times. Then, the believer's 'desires after full enjoyment of God and Christ in glory are more enlarged. Here you feel the workings of his Spirit, that makes you long to behold his face in his glorious Kingdom'. The 'little tast[e] you have of Gods manifested love unto your Soul' at the Supper 'makes you almost impatient till God shall take you to himself'.[175] Agnes Beaumont felt exactly like that, and was so deeply moved at the Lord's Table that she wished that, there and then, she might have been transported to Heaven.

> Oh, I had such a sight of Jesus Christ ... Oh, how I longed that day to bee w[i]th Jesus Christ; how faine would I have dyed in the place, yt I might have gone the next way to him, my blessed Saviour. A sence of my sinns, and of his dying love, made me love him, and long to be with him.[176]

At the Lord's Supper Dissenters knew that they could be firmly 'assured of Heaven and eternal Life', for 'every participating believer is 'a person that in the Sacrament hath had the seal of the Covenant of grace' with its perpetual guarantee of 'life and glory'.[177]

When, in the menacing autumn of 1685, Stephen Towgood's Axminster congregation met in a local cave to prepare for the Lord's Supper, he told them that 'though you be, as to your outward state and condition, in the wilderness, your souls may be in heaven, and heaven in your souls'. This 'Ordinance may become ... a heaven before heaven. O you may see Christ here by an eye of faith: here you may enjoy Him ... be dandled upon His knee' and 'have an earnest of the blessed inheritance ... Therefore now, souls, long for His coming.'[178]

Family Devotion

Severe prohibitions regarding the public worship of Dissenters gave them 'more enlarged opportunities' than they 'had formerly, to teach and instruct' their 'own housholds'.[179] This emphasized the value of, and increased their

---

[174] Ibid., fol.153.
[175] Doolittle, *Treatise*, 122.
[176] *Narrative* (ed. Harrison), 17–18.
[177] Doolittle, *Treatise*, 127.
[178] *Ecclesiastica* (ed. Howard), 110.
[179] Cheare, *Words in Season*, 226.

appreciation of, family devotion, a prominent feature in the teaching and example of their Puritan forefathers.[180] Before leaving our examination of Nonconformist worship patterns, we need to glance at this important dimension of their home and family life.

Family worship was part of Puritanism's heritage from those continental and English reformers who stressed the householder's responsibility for religious instruction in the home.[181] The Geneva Bible, the first to have numbered verses, continued to have an honoured place in many Nonconformist homes, even after the appearance of the Authorized [King James] Version. One of its marginal notes encouraged 'masters in their houses' to be devoted 'preachers to their families that from ye hiest to ye lowest they may obey the wil[l] of God'.[182]

Baxter echoed Perkins's description of the Christian family as 'a little church',[183] and Richard Greenham was persuaded that if 'we would have the Church of God to continue among us, we must bring it into our households and nourish it in our families'.[184] Puritan preachers and their Nonconformist successors not only did everything possible to promote family worship but also made sure that godly homes were provided with good books to support and enrich the exercise.[185]

The crucial importance of family religion was highlighted in the farewell sermons of many ejected ministers. They could no longer preach and pray with their people, but they urged that Nonconformist homes become centres of

---

[180] For 'the Puritan family ... Divine worship is, not incidentally but primarily, family worship': Levin L. Schucking, *The Puritan Family: A Social Study from the Literary Sources* (1969), 56.

[181] The 'master of the house should teach his household to commend themselves to God both night and morning': Luther's *Short Catechism* (1529), in B.J. Kidd (ed.), *Documents Illustrative of the Continental Reformation* (Oxford, 1911), 218. William Tyndale maintained that 'every man ought to preach in word and deed unto his household': *Expositions and Notes on Sundry Portions of the Holy Scriptures* (Parker Society; Cambridge, 1849), 36. Schucking believes that, knowing better than anyone else the composition of his 'congregation', the 'head of the family was 'better fitted for this task than the clergyman': *Puritan Family*, 57.

[182] Geneva Bible (1560 ed.), marginal note to Gen. 17: 23.

[183] William Perkins, *True Gaine ... A Warning against the Idolatry of the Last Times*, in *Works*, I, 714; John Geree, *The Character of an old English Puritane, or Non-Conformist* (1646), 5: 'his family hee endeavoured to make a Church'; Baxter, *Works* (ed. Orme), IV, 75; Thomas Taylor, 'The Jaylor's Conversion' (n.d.), in *Works* (1653), 190: 'Let every Master of a Family ... make his house a little Church'; cf. the reference of John Bruen's biographer to the 'Church in his house': Hinde, *John Bruen*, 55.

[184] Greenham, *Workes* (1612), 799, cf. R. Cawdrey, *A Godlie Forme of Household Government*, amended and augmented by John Dod and Robert Cleaver (1612), sig. A2v–A3.

[185] For example, Baxter's *Christian Directory* (1673), *The Poor Man's Family Book* (1674) and *A Paraphrase of the New Testament* (1685) were written specifically for this purpose.

devout worship[186] and that householders maximize their potential for the effective promotion of Puritan ideals.[187] The household consisted not only of family members but servants, apprentices, visitors and (frequently) neighbours. Until legal limits were placed on the number of people allowed to be present, a substantial congregation could be found sitting around the dining room table in the average Nonconformist home.[188] Even after the prohibition, many risked fines, loss of goods and even imprisonment in order to extend family worship to include others from the immediate locality. Nonconformists (and many of their Puritan colleagues in the national churches) portrayed the ideal family as a mini-community at worship: disciplined, learning, praying and caring.

If worship in the home was to be enriching in persecuting times, it had to be a disciplined exercise, and must be carefully organized on a daily basis. On any day, in any household, said Baxter, sins are committed, blessings are received and needs arise;[189] therefore, family devotion must match the reality of daily experience and not take place occasionally or spasmodically. Baxter and most of his like-minded contemporaries encouraged families to meet twice daily for Bible reading, catechizing and prayer.[190] Additional time might be allocated to the exercise on Saturdays, preparing the family for the spiritual opportunities of the following day.

Philip Henry devoted these Saturday occasions to 'children and servants', encouraging them to give him 'an account of what they could remember of the chapters he had expounded all the week before', thus 'helping one another's memories by the recollection of it'. If there were issues they had not fully understood, they were encouraged to talk about them during a session which was generally profitable because 'managed by him with so much prudence and sweetness'. Young Matthew Henry kept a small notebook in which he had

---

[186] For example, in *Compleat Collection*, sermons by Thomas Jacombe, Thomas Lye, Matthew Newcomen, John Crodacot, Daniel Bull and G[eorge]. N[ewton]. all make a plea for family worship.

[187] Family worship was 'the way to preserve religion alive, now that the public ordinary means are ceased': John Flavel, *Antipharmacum Saluberrimum: A Serious and Seasonable Caveat to all the Saints in this Hour of Temptation* (n.d.), in *Works*, IV, 537.

[188] Baxter held that the legal restriction (on the number of people allowed to be present in addition to family members) seriously disadvantaged 'those many thousand families' totally without literacy, who had been pleased to meet in their neighbours' homes: 'Preface to the Reader' in Thomas Young, *The Lord's Day ... Lately translated out of the Latine* (1672), sig. A4.

[189] Baxter, *Works* (ed. Orme), IV, 87.

[190] Ibid.; cf. Howe, 'Obligations to Family Religion and Worship', in *Works* (ed. Hunt), V, 412–21, at 415–18. Philip Henry said the family ought to let 'prayer be the key of the morning, and the bolt of the night': W. Urwick, *Historical Sketches of Nonconformity in the County Palatine of Chester* (1864), 110. For Thomas Paget, morning and evening was the most 'convenient opportunity' because 'in other parts of the day their affaires may call them' to be in different places and 'severed one from another': *A Demonstration of Family Duties* (1643), 58–59.

preserved 'Questions of Conference' that they had discussed as a family.[191] Further meetings in the home might be arranged to coincide with the visit of an itinerant preacher such as Oliver Heywood, such a visit providing a reason for swelling the family numbers with local friends to make the best spiritual use of a special occasion.[192]

The effectiveness of the daily exercise depended largely on the commitment and initiative of the householder.[193] Ideally, he should rise before the rest of the family in order to prepare for it, and then call his 'family' together. John Bruen set a good example to later generations, waking well before 4 a.m. in the summer, and an hour later in the winter, so that he might have 'an houre or two' for his personal devotions 'before he rung the bell, to awaken the rest of the family'.[194]

The second ideal was that of a learning family in which each believing household became a 'Schoole of God'.[195] Central to the family's worship was the methodical and systematic reading of Scripture,[196] with comment on the passage either by the householder or by reading from published helps such as Baxter's *Christian Directory*,[197] his *Paraphrase of the New Testament*[198] or the earlier Westminster Assembly's *Annotations*.

---

[191] Henry, *Life*, 80, 359–60. Conference topics included such questions as: 'How far may a man go towards heaven, and yet fall short?', 'What are the common hindrances of men's salvation?', and 'How are we to express love to our neighbour?' In *The Poor Man's Family Book*, Baxter offers suitable material for 'Conference Days', largely set in the form of a serious conversation between P[aul]., a pastor, and S[aul]., 'an ignorant sinner': *Works* (ed. Orme), XIX, 298–564. Abraham Cheare included 'gracious Conference' alongside 'Instruction [and] reading the Scriptures' in his description of 'Family Worship', which was a time when Nonconformist 'houses may become as so many Churches of Christ': *Words in Season*, 226.

[192] The practice of additional meetings also had good Puritan precedent. Paget said it was 'lawful', 'expedient', 'useful' and 'necessary' for the head of the family to arrange 'extraordinary occasions ... and opportunities' for 'the company and assistance of some godly brethren and christian neighbours' to meet with the family for worship: *Family Duties*, 82.

[193] Owen Stockton, *A Treatise of Family Instruction* (1672), Ep. Ded; cf. Bunyan, *Mr. Badman* (ed. Forrest and Sharrock), 38, where Badman's master, 'a very devout person', took care to provide for 'the Worship of God in his Family'.

[194] Hinde, *John Bruen*, 66–67.

[195] Perkins, *Reformed Catholicke*, in *Works*, I, 586: 'God's grace may as well be exercised in the family as in the Cloyster'.

[196] Philip Henry ensured the family heard systematic exposition from a biblical book, a chapter a day. Many of the small notebooks containing neat outlines of his daily expositions, with precise dates, are in DWL, New College Collection, L4/7/1–26.

[197] Baxter, Introductory 'Advertisement' to *Christian Directory*, in *Works* (ed. Orme), II, ix. Baxter hoped the book would prove useful 'to the more judicious masters of families, who may choose to read such parcels to their families, as at any time the case requireth'.

[198] Baxter's Preface to his *Paraphrase* expressed the hope that the book might be used 'when they Read the New Testament daily in their Houses making Use of such Exposition and Doctrinal Notes, as they find most suitable'.

In this didactic enterprise, more was expected of the assembled group than an attentive ear. Participation was of the utmost importance. Questions were asked, opinions sought, and discussion encouraged. Intelligent 'Conference' was a noble ideal, inherited from the Reformers and Puritans,[199] but may not always have been successfully achieved; drowsy attenders in the morning and weary ones in the evening may not have proved the most promising audience for biblical exposition and spiritual discussion. Involvement was encouraged by the use of catechisms,[200] sometimes by allocating a specific day of the week for using this important teaching device. On Thursday evenings, instead of his usual Bible reading and exposition, Philip Henry catechized his children and servants, normally using the Westminster Assembly's Catechism,[201] introducing variety into the teaching with 'a little Catechism concerning the matter of prayer'[202] or even an occasional anti-Catholic polemic.[203] It was expected that even the youngest children in these families would be acquainted with the catechism.[204] For example, Mary Franklin said: 'As for the time of my conversion, I cannot give account'; personal faith came gradually and imperceptibly, 'being from my childhood instructed by my parents in the concerns of my soul. They took great care of ... their children, teaching us catechisms and the holy Scriptures'.[205] The imprisoned Joseph Alleine urged his Taunton members to ensure that 'weekly Catechising' took place 'in every one of your Families'.[206] Gentle interrogation and invitation to expand on memorized catechetical responses were often used to aid the discussion

---

[199] The Edwardian reformer Thomas Becon maintained that children should read a chapter of either the OT or NT at the meal table, which should then be discussed by the family: *A New Catechism* (Parker Society; 1844), 351. Parents and children should be equally free to contribute. '[L]et the husband with the wife, let the father with the *childe talke* together of these matters, and both to and fro let them enquire and give their judgments': Immanuel Bourne, *The True Way of a Christian* (1622), quoted in Millar Maclure, *The Paul's Cross Sermons 1534–1642* (Toronto, 1958), 238.

[200] The Laudians urged households to send their children and servants to church for catechetical instruction (Laud, *Works*, V, 446) but Puritans believed the exercise might prove more effective if undertaken at home.

[201] Henry, *Life*, 79; cf. Heywood, *Autobiography* (ed. Turner), I, 34, for Heywood's use of family catechetical instruction; and Clarke, *Lives of Sundry Eminent Persons*, Part II, 196–7, for Stockton's weekly catechesis in his home.

[202] Henry, *Life*, 79.

[203] Ibid. 80; cf. Matthew Poole, *A Dialogue between a Popish Priest and an English Protestant* (1667).

[204] Edward Bowles of York produced 'A plain short Catechism for Young Children' that Calamy held to be 'as good an one for children as most I have seen': *Continuation*, II, 934; *Account*, 778–83. Bowles's catechism (8th impression, 1676) is reproduced in *Continuation*, II, 933–39, without his name. Thomas Becon's popular *New Catechism* (1560) took the form of a discussion between a father and his six-year-old son.

[205] 'The Experiences of Mary Franklin', 388.

[206] Alleine, *Letters* (1673), 41 (14 October 1663).

process.²⁰⁷

The third ideal was that of a praying family. A specific aim in these daily exercises was for the householder 'to pray with them and for them'.²⁰⁸ Always kneeling, Philip Henry prayed extempore, relating the prayers to the psalm they had sung and the biblical passage he had earlier read and explained. He was not opposed to 'prescribed forms' of prayer but, like many of his Puritan forefathers,²⁰⁹ regarded them as 'crutches' for the 'lame' and not to be encouraged for regular or continuing use.²¹⁰ In addition to special prayers for each of his children, especially on their birthdays, he took care to pray specifically for visitors and servants, remembering their particular needs. Matthew Henry recalled these times with gratitude, especially how well his father conducted 'his daily family-worship', making it 'a pleasure and not a task … for he was seldom long and never tedious'.²¹¹ Elsewhere, these devout occasions were not always free from being misused, and were exposed to three predictable perils: resentment, boredom and inconsistency.

Attendance was far from voluntary, and any member of the company out of sympathy with the exercise may have found it an irksome duty rather than a spiritual delight. Nonconformist households were not exempt from the pain of errant family members and experience of this aspect of domestic life in their earlier years may not have helped. Matthew Henry recognized that the family worship of other Dissenters might not always have been as beneficial as his experience at Broad Oak. He feared that 'many of those prejudices, which young persons are apt to conceive against religion' might have had their beginning in a daily spiritual discipline that had gradually become 'a toil and a terror to them'.²¹² Many, as we have noted, might have found concentration difficult early in the morning or towards the end of the day, especially when the prayers became boringly repetitive or wearisomely extended. Some Puritans had warned that tediously long prayers at family worship could be counter-productive.²¹³ A more serious problem was inconsistent conduct on the part of

---

²⁰⁷ Extensive material for this exercise was provided by Baxter in *The Catechising of Families: A Teacher of Householders* (1683), in *Works* (ed. Orme), XIX, 3–292, with questions on the Creed and Decalogue: ibid. 298–655.
²⁰⁸ Taylor, *Works*, 190; idem, *Peter his Repentance*, 46 [in the same volume but separately paginated]: the 'Master by his godly example, should be as a light to his Family'.
²⁰⁹ Perkins said that a Christian 'may lawfully use a set forme of prayer, as a man that hath … a lame legge, may leane upon a crutch'. He pointed out that the Psalms are 'used and read in a set forme of words' and 'most of them are prayers': *Cases of Conscience*, in *Works*, II, 67.
²¹⁰ Henry, *Life*, 76–77. Baxter provided prayers for use in the home in *The Poor Mans Family Book*; cf. *Works* (ed. Orme), XIX, 602–45, and frequently elsewhere.
²¹¹ Henry, *Life*, 78–79.
²¹² Ibid. 79.
²¹³ Prayers were published for use in Puritan families, and they could be inordinately lengthy for household use. A pocket-book edition of Michael Sparke, *The Crums of*

those leading worship. It was crippling for servants if a householder prayed unctuously and expansively but was a mean or unjust master. Bunyan was acquainted with 'some poor Servants' who told him they had often experienced 'more fairness of dealing' and were far better treated 'in some carnal families' than 'among Professors' of religion. Such employers made 'Religion stink', he said, and inflicted untold damage on the Christian cause. Servants should always 'learn something of the kindness of Christ' in a believing household. Christian masters must remember that their employees 'are goers as well as comers', and should 'take heed' that they 'give them no occasion to scandal the Gospel when they are gone' to alternative employment.[214]

Finally, Dissenters maintained that worship in the home ought to stimulate the generosity of a caring family. Puritan handbooks of devotion, and similar publications by their Nonconformist successors, insisted that worship was more than words. Adequate provision for the poor was an important dimension of Puritan social concern and, although occasionally marred by self-regarding motivation, it met the urgent needs of many deprived families. William Gouge included this benevolent obligation in his detailed exposition of Puritan family responsibilities, maintaining that husband and wife were jointly responsible for such neighbourly social care. The husband may 'better know those that are abroad out of the family'. Tied to the home, his wife may not be quite so familiar with local need but, aware 'of what things there is greatest store' in her larder, she knows 'the things that are fittest to be given away'. Some husbands are 'hard-hearted ... never giving anything' and some wives 'covetously hoord up all they can get' and even 'suffer victuals to perish in the house', ignoring the needs of 'the poore that have wanted'. Joint generosity is the marriage partners' Christian obligation, for 'unmercifulness to the poore' is an offence to the God they profess to honour.[215]

In some localities, there may have been times when unrelenting persecution encouraged a degree of insularity but in the main these families knew that there were untold needs in every community that must not be ignored by the servants of Christ. Poverty was a serious seventeenth-century problem, not easily relieved when 'the poor of England ... daily perish in the streets, fields and ditches', according to one pamphleteer, 'defrauded of larger provisions' made

---

Comfort ... with godly prayers (1628), contains prayers for each day of the week, morning and evening. It also includes a Thanksgiving Prayer ('to be used of godly Christians in their families') which extends to 25 pages, undoubtedly 'hard on the knees and the attention': H.C. White, *English Devotional Literature, Prose, 1600–1640* (University of Wisconsin Studies in Language and Literature; Madison, WI, 1965), 174.
[214] Bunyan, *Christian Behaviour*, in *MW*, III, 32. Pepys grieved that his wife's 'indiscretion' with a dismissed servant would become a topic for domestic gossip at the maid's next place of employment: *Diary* (ed. Latham and Matthews), VI, 28–31.
[215] William Gouge, *Of Domesticall Duties* (1634), 267–68.

for impoverished people in other countries.[216]

Philip Henry's house at Broad Oak was close to the roadside and, as they grew up, his children saw for themselves his concern for 'strangers, and such as were any way distressed' in their travels, 'though his charity and candour were often imposed upon by cheats and pretenders'. Gullibility was preferable to remorse. When chided over indiscriminate giving, he frequently adapted a biblical quotation, 'Thou knowest *not* the heart of a stranger',[217] to remind his family that, unlike Israel's slaves, they had little experience of deprivation. It was the heart of the needy woman or man Henry longed to reach. Only love could do that.

---

[216] John Jones, *The New Returna Brevium, or the Law returned from Westminster* (1650), 48–49. In this tract, addressed to Cromwell, the passionate author expresses the longing that his fellow-citizens might no longer witness their poor neighbours' 'empty ... mouths and hungrie' bodies, begging 'crums of some Alms-houses to prolong their daies'.

[217] Henry, *Life*, 120, cf. Exod. 23: 9.

Chapter 7

Sharing Truth

Much as they valued the teaching role of ministers and pastors, Dissenters generally stressed the need for mutual edification in local church life. There were times when Independents, Baptists and Quakers may have been more insistent on the local congregation's didactic responsibility than Presbyterians, who were at pains to emphasize the distinctive teaching responsibilities of the ordained ministry. Throughout the Restoration period, large numbers of Presbyterians continued to treasure the possibility of comprehension within the Established Church, where the primacy of the clerical office was scarcely in doubt. But in an era of continued repression and recurrent persecution, denied the leadership of gifted teachers, many groups of believers encouraged one another with the biblical assurance that the Holy Spirit was the primary distributor of pastoral gifts and, in difficult times especially, non-ministerial members might be equipped to impart encouraging truths to the local church. Earlier Puritans had encouraged such mutual edification in the 'ordinance' of 'conference'. If a group of eager learners kept themselves 'within the compass of Gods word', they would often grasp truths 'which not onely none of them had before', but which none of them 'could have by himselfe alone attained unto'.[1] Two specifical didactic opportunities warrant special attention – first (briefly) catechetical instruction, and second (more fully) repetition of sermons.

Teaching by Catechism

The use of catechisms in church, school and home[2] had a rich precedent in Reformed[3] and Puritan[4] teaching and practice, but its use extended beyond

---

[1] Bownd, *Doctrine of the Sabbath*, 219.
[2] I.M. Green, *The Christian's ABC: Catechisms and Catechising in England, c.1530–1740* (Oxford, 1996), 93–169 (in church), 170–229 (in school and at home).
[3] Luther produced a *Larger Catechism* for the use of Christian teachers, and a *Shorter Catechism* for the young, based on the Decalogue, Creed, Lord's Prayer and the sacraments: cf. Kidd, *Documents*, 205–22. Calvin said: 'I wish we could retain the custom, which ... existed in the early Church,' of 'catechising ... briefly explaining the substance of almost all the heads of our religion': *Institutes* IV.19.13 (ed. Beveridge, II, 632). For the Edwardian reformers, see Thomas Becon, *A New Catechism ... Familiar Talk between the Father and the Son* (Parker Society, Cambridge; 1844; first publ. [1560]).

theological boundaries. No lover of Puritans, the Arminian Archbishop Laud commanded that parents send their servants and apprentices to church for catechetical instruction, as well as their children.[5] Disturbed by the 'growing increase of the prevailing sects', Archbishop Sheldon urged his clergy 'to enjoin the use and exercise of our said catechism',[6] an activity which was ideally suited to Sunday afternoons in the parishes.[7] Such regular methodical instruction might counteract the teaching of Dissenters who were influencing unenlightened worshippers in the Established Church.[8] We have seen that Dissenters were accustomed to maximizing this valuable teaching opportunity in the family,[9] and influential leaders such as John Owen,[10] Richard Baxter,[11] Joseph Alleine,[12] Owen Stockton,[13] Thomas Doolittle,[14] John Bunyan,[15] George

---

[4] John More and Edward Dering, *A Short Catechism for Householders, or a Brief and Necessarie Catechism* (1580); Bownd, *Doctrine of the Sabbath*, 210–22, 235–40, 378–79; cf. Patrick Collinson, *A Mirror of Elizabethan Puritanism: The Life and Letters of 'Godly Master Dering'* (Friends of the Dr Williams's Library Lecture, 1963; 1964), 9–10.

[5] Diocese of Canterbury Visitation Articles (1637), in Laud, *Works*, V, 446.

[6] Edward Cardwell (ed.), *Documentary Annals of the Reformed Church of England* (Oxford, 1839), II, 286–87; the catechism referred to by Sheldon was probably Alexander Nowell, *A Catechisme; or, First Introduction and Learning of the Christian Religion* (1570).

[7] *JHC*, IX, 259 (27 February 1672); for the Restoration Church's increasing recognition of the importance of catechizing, see Anne Whiteman, 'The Re-Establishment of the Church of England, 1660–1663', *TRHS* 5th ser. 5 (1955), 111–31, at 127.

[8] Gabriel Towerson, *An Explication of the Catechism of the Church of England* (4 vols, 1678–88), I, B2v. Towerson believed that the 'large spreading of heresies in the late licentious times' was largely due to inadequate or non-existent catechizing. Richard Sherlock was convinced that it was 'the most fickle and giddy people' in parishes who were drawn away by Nonconformist preachers because they are not 'first well Catechiz'd', their 'minds like a Ship without ballast' unable to 'keep a steddy course': *The Principles of the Holy Christian Religion* (11th ed., 1673), sig. A3v; cf. Bunyan, *MW*, VIII, xxx–xliii.

[9] Bunyan's *bête noire*, Edward Fowler, urged the practice of catechizing in the homes of Established Church worshippers: Preface to John Worthington, *A Form of Sound Words: or a Scripture-Catechism* (1673), sig. A7v.

[10] John Owen, *The Principles of the Doctrine of Christ: Unfolded in Two Short Catechismes* (1684). Owen's brief 'Lesser' Catechism was for the young, the 'Greater' for adults.

[11] Baxter, *The Catechising of Families* (1683); *The Poor Man's Family Book* (1674), both in *Works* (ed. Orme), XIX.

[12] Joseph Alleine, *A Most Familiar Explanation of the Assemblies Shorter Catechisms* (1674).

[13] Owen Stockton, *A Scriptural Catechism* (1672), in which the answers to the catechetical questions were given in scriptural quotations.

[14] Thomas Doolittle, *Catechism made Practical* (1688); idem, *A Plain Method of Catechizing* (1699).

[15] Bunyan, *Instruction for the Ignorant* (1675), in *MW*, VIII, 7–44.

Fox,[16] Hercules Collins[17] and Thomas Grantham[18] produced catechisms of varying range and length for the use of Dissenting families and churches.

Nonconformist ministers often used a favourite catechism as a basic structure for systematic preaching, thus reminding their people of central biblical themes,[19] but the home was considered to be the most appropriate venue for regular catechetical teaching, where doctrine could be adapted to the intellectual capacities of the smaller group.[20] Prior to the Restoration, it had been the foundation of Baxter's highly effective ministry in Kidderminster homes, and he was not alone in commending its rich evangelistic potential.[21] He and a junior colleague had devoted two half-days each week to 'Personal Conference with every Family apart ... Catechizing and Instructing them'.[22] Baxter also devoted Thursday evenings to a 'lecture' at his home for those desiring additional spiritual help. A sermon from the previous Sunday was 'repeated', so that anyone could raise questions either about its content, anything unclear, 'what Doubts any of them had ... or any other Case of Conscience'. Weekly ministry to young people gave 'the younger sort who were not fit to pray in so great an Assembly' an opportunity to pray audibly with a smaller group of their peers. That they frequently 'spent three Hours in prayer together' suggests it was a mutually supportive enterprise.[23]

Baxter said that these midweek meetings in the ministers' or parishioners' homes 'were a marvellous help' in promoting, enriching and sustaining holiness of life in Kidderminster. 'Truths' they heard on Sundays, but had 'slipt away', were often 'recalled' and 'good desires cherished'. Such meetings were of inestimable value to the pastor for, if anyone was deeply 'touched and awakened in publick' worship, it was likely to surface in more informal

---

[16] G[eorge]. F[ox]., *A Catechisme for Children* (2nd ed.; 1660).
[17] Hercules Collins, *An Orthodox Catechism* (1680), includes an Appendix affirming the value of congregational singing.
[18] Grantham, *St. Paul's Catechism* (1687).
[19] John Billingsley, Thomas Doolittle, Daniel Wilcox and John Ratcliffe were among the London ministers who preached regularly on the catechism: Wilson, *Dissenting Meeting Houses*, I, 79; III, 195–96, 204; IV, 355–56.
[20] Cf. *Life of Angier*, 97, 77, for Angier's pastoral concern for individual young people during catechetical instruction.
[21] Stockton, *Scriptural Catechism*, Title Page and 'To the Reader'. Bunyan presented his *Instruction for the Ignorant* 'to all those unconverted, old and young, who have been at any time under my preaching, and yet remain in their sins', urging such readers to 'receive it as a token of my love for their immortal Souls', that it may be used 'to the awakening of many sinners': Bunyan, *MW*, VIII, 7.
[22] Sylvester (ed.), *Reliquiae*, I, i, §137 (24). These two men catechized fourteen different families every week. Each session began by reciting the catechism to the minister, no visitors or non-family members being present, 'lest Bashfulness should make it burthensom, or any should talk of the Weaknesses of others'. Baxter then 'helpt them to understand it', enquiring 'modestly into the State of their Souls', devoting about an hour to each visit: ibid., §135.1.
[23] Ibid., §135.

sessions for teaching and prayer. He could then spend time, on a more personal basis, 'answering their Doubts' and helping them to make progress in spiritual maturity.[24]

Catechisms also featured as part of the personal and corporate preparation for the Lord's Supper.[25] Philip Henry made use of such material on the 'admission of young people out of the rank of catechumens into that of communicants'. He gathered together those who appeared to be personally committed to Christian faith and life and, when he had a sizeable group, spent a number of Sundays in further catechetical instruction 'touching the Lords' Supper ... and their baptismal covenant'. In the 'ordinance they were to take' the covenant 'upon themselves' and, making it 'their own act and deed', 'bind themselves faster to it'. At a special preparation day during the week preceding communion, he prayed publicly for them as individuals, and preached an appropriate sermon. When the appointed day came, 'they were all received together' at the Lord's Supper, and Henry looked upon this 'as the right confirmation, or transition into ... adult church-membership'.[26]

Repressive legislation robbed Dissenters of their freedom to meet unhindered, imposing severe limits on midweek teaching and other opportunities for mutual encouragement and corporate prayer. But patterns of catechetical instruction such as those adopted by Baxter and Henry were not abandoned. Baxter admired 'the true Episcopacy of a silenced Minister' in the life of his friend Thomas Gouge, 'voluntarily Catechising the Christ's Church boys when he might not preach'.[27] Believers continued to use their homes for mutual encouragement and support, whatever the cost, and Baxter urged his contemporaries to grasp these opportunities for catechetical instruction within families. Although the legislation was daunting, '[n]one forbiddeth Ministers to catechise those that are under sixteen years of age, or to teach them by preaching, or to pray with them'. There was nothing on the statute book forbidding 'people to catechise and teach their families, and read good books to them'. Opportunities to provide instruction and example in the home were as

---

[24] Ibid., §137 (9).
[25] Green, *The Christian's ABC*, 34–38, 549–53; cf., for example, John Owen, *Two Short Catechisms ... proper for all persons to learn before they be admitted to the Lord's Supper* (1645), in *Works*, I, 463–94. Ministers sometimes prepared their own catechisms for use in preparation for the Lord's Supper, e.g. Thomas Trescot's manuscript, 'A Catechism by way of preparation to ye worthy receiving of ye Sacrament of the Lords Supper': Taunton, Somerset Archaeological and Natural History Society archives, Manuscript volume of 17th-century sermons, fols 21–44.
[26] Henry, *Life*, 195–96. Henry's eldest daughter, Sarah Savage, wrote about a visit to her former home at Broad Oak, witnessing the catechizing of 'the young people ... .shortly to be admitted to the Lord's Supper ... all the company, as well as dear father, were much affected': ibid. 195n, diary entry for 11 March 1687/8.
[27] Sylvester (ed.), *Reliquiae*, III, §73, 190–91.

rich as ever, '[a]nd yet how much is this neglected'.[28]

Learning by Repetition

We turn to an activity that became an increasingly effective teaching aid in Nonconformist homes: the 'repetition' of a sermon preached on an earlier occasion. It was a highly effective exercise in a time of repression, providing small groups with a valuable learning opportunity and not dependent on the presence of an ordained minister.[29] Here they could recall previous teaching, reflect on complementary biblical passages and illustrations, discuss problematic issues raised by the sermon's content, identify the practical application of the message, and talk about how its teaching had been (or might yet be) implemented. It was one of the simplest and most convenient of teaching methods among Dissenters. In the case of Presbyterians, the sermon repeated might have been preached by a local conforming minister in the parish church, or by one of the Nonconformist ministers in their locality. Among Independents, it may have been heard at a recent conventicle or house meeting. Understandably, Quakers, with their insistence on the Spirit's direct illumination, gave little place to the repetition of truths spoken earlier under the immediacy of the Spirit's inspiration. Baptists were often favoured with unordained church members who might always be ready to convey an artless biblical message and therefore did not practice the repetition of earlier preaching material to the same extent as their fellow Dissenters.[30] Repetitions played such an important role in the edification of Nonconformists generally that some consideration must be given to the nature, purpose, practice and value of this activity.

Widespread among Puritans,[31] and not distinctively Nonconformist in origin, the practice involved the discipline of taking detailed notes during a sermon with the express purpose of making its message available to others. It was hoped that the sermon might in this way be preached again, as fully as possible, to a group, whether or not those present had already heard it. It was a well-established tradition. When Bristol Independents first met together in 1640, 'those whose hearts God had touched would gett together and praye' and 'repeate their sermon-notes ... For which they were branded with ye name of Puritans', a 'common tearme of Derision'.[32]

---

[28] Baxter, *Of Obedient Patience in Particular Cases* (1683), in *Works* (ed. Orme), XI, 422.
[29] After their regular meeting was broken up in 1670, Dissenters in Rye met 'in several *parcels* ... praying together, & repeating a Sermon': *Diary of Samuel Jeake* (ed. Hunter and Gregory), 148.
[30] Among Baptists it was often practised as a corporate exercise for younger members: Orme (ed.), *William Kiffin*, 11–12; cf. *Broadmead Records* (ed. Hayden), 191–92.
[31] Collinson, *Elizabethan Puritan Movement*, 373–82.
[32] *Broadmead Records* (ed. Hayden), 82–83.

The Elizabethan preacher John Udall had recognized that during public worship, all preaching encountered two hazards: the hearer's limited concentration (the 'corruption of our nature') and the devil's diversionary tactics, suggesting 'other cogitations into our minds ... that hee may bereave us of the benefite of Gods heavenly word'. Preachers also feared that any good might be speedily lost for, when people left the church, 'they think their dutie to God fully performed, and so goe in all hast[e], to dice, cards, bowling, tipling', and into company 'wherein they want neither cursing, swearing, nor blasphemy, to the great dishonor of God'. Udall said that his contemporaries had much to learn from Bethlehem's shepherds. When these men 'heard the message of God', 'they conferre[d]' together about it, determined not to 'forget the thinges that they had heard, and talked about 'how they may be further edified'. Like them, when 'the Sermon is done, we ought at our coming home, to meet together & say to one another: come, wee have all beene where wee have heard Gods woord taught, let us conferre about it ... that we may have the benefit of the labors of others'. Repetitions were an expression of mutual pastoral responsibility, 'that we bee the meanes to stir ... up' our fellow-Christians 'and further them in the duties of Christianity'. Few hearers imbibed at one sitting the entire contents of an expansive Puritan sermon, so 'if one have missed the observation of this or that point, another hath marked it, so that among them they may bring away the whole, and so be edified by one another'. Some objected that preaching (and, therefore, repetition) was the minister's work, not theirs, and even he ought not do it in people's homes. He should not teach 'unless he bee in the pulpit' and 'hedged in with a peece of wood on each side'. Despite such criticism, Udall insisted that it is 'the dutie ... of all men privately, to instruct those that be ignorant'. Neither was it appropriate 'to cavill at that man that dooth it' or to criticize 'the place where it is done: but in reverence ... receive it, as from the Lord'. Household leaders, in particular, should pay close attention to public preaching, because their children and servants are 'often carelesse, in attending unto the word of God'.[33]

Repetitions quickly became an established part of Puritan family life. Samuel Fairclough's 'Forenoon Sermon was usually repeated by one of his Children after Dinner. In the Evening he repeated it himself. After Repetition, he examin'd his whole Family, not only what they remembred of the Sermons, but what good they had gained by the worship of that day'.[34]

At an early age, children were expected to give some reasonable account of what they had heard in church.[35] Lucy Hutchinson may have been slightly

---

[33] First Sermon in 'Two Sermons of Obedience to the Gospell', in John Udall, *Certaine sermons taken out of Severall places of Scripture* (1596), sig. Ii ijv–iiijv.
[34] Clarke, *Lives of Sundry Eminent Persons*, Part I, 181.
[35] In 1688–89, Philip Henry's married daughter Sarah Savage continued to read notes of sermons preached by her father: Diary of Sarah Savage, fols 5–6.

precocious in her ability to repeat sermons at the age of four,[36] but she was certainly not an isolated instance of infant mental concentration.[37] Many Nonconformist householders, other than ministers, developed similar patterns of devotion in their homes.[38]

Whatever its Puritan prototype, Dissenters had to be assured that the practice had firm biblical authority. The Somerset ejected minister William Thomas believed it could be found in the ministry of Jeremiah, who directed Baruch 'to write, then to read' what the prophet had preached. It had further precedent in the Pauline injunction to Christians in both Colossae and Laodicea regarding their exchange of letters.[39] Hesitant about accepting Jeremiah as good biblical authority for repetitions, some suggested that the prophet's use of Baruch as an amanuensis may have been 'a special case, because Jeremy was shut up … therefore it is not to be drawn to common use'. Thomas made the point that the Jeremiah illustration could hardly be more appropriate. The experience of Nonconformist ministers was almost identical to that of the prophet in that, given the restrictions on their liberties after 1662, nobody 'knows how soon Ministers' in this country 'may be shut up (as Jeremy here was)', so that 'they cannot speak to their ordinary hearers'. Moreover, those who listen to Nonconformist sermons 'know not how soon they [too] may be shut up, either by sickness or restraint'. They should 'make use', therefore, of their 'present liberty' for 'if the old Sermons be forgotten, and new Sermons cannot be gotten, Christians are likely to be at a sad loss'. Believers must not merely compile books of sermons to treasure as a household's devotional resource 'and there leave them', but should put them to maximum use as they 'repeat and communicate them to others'.[40]

In addition to suggesting appropriate biblical evidence for the practice, William Thomas claimed strong historical support for the 'godly Family Exercise' of repetition.[41] John Chrysostom had urged fourth-century Antiochenes to repeat the sermon in their families. On arriving back home, believers were 'to take our Bibles into our hands, and call our wife and children

---

[36] Lucy Hutchinson, *Memoirs of the Life of Colonel Hutchinson* (ed. Neil H. Keeble; 1995), 14.

[37] Owen Stockton's first child 'had been so instructed by her Father that before she was eight years old, she understood the Method of a Sermon and, if preached by her Father, would give him an account of the most considerable Heads and Passages therein, and before she was full nine years old, she would write a Sermon after him without missing the Heads': Clarke, *Lives of Sundry Eminent Persons*, 196.

[38] Margaret Corbet took careful notes during sermons that she then used in 'Catechizing, and instructing her servants … She used to examine them of the Sermons they heard, and she customarily read over those Sermon Notes to them which she had taken at Church.' The servants were later expected to 'give an account thereof to her Husband': Samuel Clarke, *A Collection of the Lives of Ten Eminent Divines* (1662), 506.

[39] Thomas, *Preservative*, 182–87, quoting Jer. 36; Col. 4: 16.

[40] Ibid. 185–86.

[41] Ibid. 191.

to join us in putting together what we have heard'. They would derive much spiritual benefit if they could 'give up this one day of the week entire to hearing and to recollection of the things we have heard'. To his patristic precedent, Thomas added, in a marginal reference, the support of Calvin, citing the reformer's comments on Jeremiah 36: 2 as illustrating the value of the written sermon.[42]

The first step was to enlist a church member equipped to take careful notes during the sermon, often in shorthand. It was not always easy to secure the services of such a volunteer as some regarded note-taking as a task for social inferiors, 'being a thing which some will look upon, as too low for higher and more considerable Persons'. The preservation and circulation of sermons in written form was likely to be important for Thomas feared that the days ahead would be increasingly difficult for Dissenters. Listening to the sermon was 'for present use' but if 'accompanied with writing' it 'may be read and reviewed a month, or twelve-months after' – even 'many years after we are dead'. Thomas recognized that this was a time-consuming undertaking, for what was 'written for [the] present hastily' would need to be 'written out legibly' later, and this was difficult to do for 'whole Sermons', which might have taken an hour or more to deliver. If the writer did not have the time to set whole sermons down in writing, the next best thing might be to 'cull out, and write out fair the choicest passages'.[43] Better to have an abbreviated sermon than none at all.

It was said of John Angier's note-taking that 'he constantly writ Sermons, when others preached'. He believed it to be especially beneficial, and did so to encourage the practice, as an 'example to others', and as a means of keeping his own mind sharply focused on what the preacher was saying, so as to 'prevent diversions'.[44] Philip Henry took copious notes of every sermon, either in the parish church or the Nonconformist meeting, many of which survive in his minuscule handwriting, preserved in small notebooks.[45] When 'silenced', Henry Newcome regarded it as a continuing pastoral opportunity; by this means he could spread the biblical message in writing if not by preaching. A few weeks after 'Black Bartholomew', he 'read over p[ar]t of ye notes transcribed for M[ist]ris Holland', and just over a week later, 'I wrot[e] out my sermon for M[ist]ris Haworths maid on 2 Tim. 4: 7.'[46]

Dissenters, other than ministers, became proficient in the art of preserving the main outlines and sub-divisions of sermons, with their innumerable biblical references. Isaac Archer began the exercise at boarding school, when he spent time 'looking over my notes of the sermon I was to repeat to my master'.[47] During his undergraduate years in Cambridge he continued the practice.

---

[42] Ibid. 184.
[43] Ibid. 183–84.
[44] *Life of Angier*, 79.
[45] e.g. DWL, New College Collection, MS L4/9/3.
[46] Newcome, *Diary* (ed. Heywood), 125, 128.
[47] Storey (ed.), *Two Diaries*, 51.

Hearing William Shelton in Jesus College chapel, he 'diligently wrote his sermons, and read them by my selfe, chiefly about the worth of the soule, the great danger of loosing it, the little profit, and the irrecoverable losse ... also ... of making sure of that enduring substance'.[48]

Several books on the art of speed-writing were in popular circulation,[49] helpful not only to the earnest Dissenter who wished to retain good sermon material for spiritual encouragement, but also to the alert entrepreneur who could turn note-taking into a lucrative sideline. Baxter knew of enterprising 'Scribes' who took down sermons, such as the farewell expositions of ejected ministers, some very reliably, 'word by word', though only to pass the manuscript on to 'covetous Booksellers'. At the hands of a careless, ignorant or inattentive note-taker, many a sermon had suffered in transmission. What was advertised as Baxter's 'Farewel Sermon' was so 'mangled' in 'both Matter and Style' that he 'could not own it'. Things some of these preachers had never said were quickly in print, and Baxter was not the only minister to be 'much abused by it'.[50]

When Ralph Thoresby was in his early twenties, he always took notes at Nonconformist meetings. On visits to London he was often frustrated that the meeting-places where he could hear well-known Dissenters were so crowded that it was difficult to hear them distinctly, let alone take notes. 'Dr. [John] Owen preached very well of the power of Christ; but [it] was sore thronged, that I could neither write nor hear very well.'[51]

Writing sermons was a popular Sunday occupation for young Dissenters.[52] Roger Lowe supplemented his meagre income as an apprentice shopkeeper by taking notes of sermons on behalf of people unable to do it themselves: 'Widow

---

[48] Ibid. 63, quoting Mt. 16: 26; Heb. 10: 34; cf. ibid. 64, where Archer says he continued writing out Shelton's sermons, 'for a farther perusall'. When Archer became the (albeit hesitant) conforming minister at Chippenham, Cambridgeshire, he took notes during the preaching at the archdeacon's visitation, adding the comment in his diary that local gentry, specifically addressed in the sermon, were not present. Yet such people 'had their notaries to write sermons, chiefly such things as they did not like', and so, although not present, they would certainly 'come to heare of' the 'railing sermon' preached on that occasion by the vicar of Fordham: ibid. 90.

[49] Job Everardt, *An Epitome of Stenographie* (1658), for example, outlined skills in the 'art of short, swift, and secret writing ... methods and kindes of abreviation, and contraction of words, clauses and sentences'; cf. also Henry Dix, *The Art of brachygraphy, or short-writing* (1641); T. Shelton, *Tachy-graphy* (1668); T. Metcalfe, *Short-Writing* (1660); John Farthing, *Short-writing shotned* [sic] (1684); William Addy, *Stenographia, or the art of short-writing* (1695). These manuals clearly had the sermon note-taker particularly in mind, suggesting a wide range of useful abbreviations for biblical books, names, doctrines and themes.

[50] Sylvester (ed.), *Reliquiae*, II, ii, §168.

[51] Thoresby, *Diary* (ed. Hunter), I, 4, cf. 9: 'Dr. [William] Bates preached at the Glasshouse, of the New-birth; but I could scarcely hear anything. Rest of the day writing part of a Sermon'; cf. ibid. I: 53, 135.

[52] Lowe, *Diary* (ed. Sachse), 58: 'Lord's day. I began to write sermon this morning'.

Low came and gave me 1 s[hilling] for sermon writeinge'.[53] Young Roger became especially proficient at the art and often repeated sermons in the company of his friends. He was encouraged by the continuing pastoral care of their ejected minister, James Woods, in whose home he frequently repeated sermons to local Dissenters,[54] sometimes when Woods was away from home.[55] After Woods moved to another area, Roger continued his unofficial ministry of repeating sermons, even doing so outdoors. On the Sunday after Woods's departure, '[a]tt noone Thomas Smith and severall young women we assembled togather in [the] feilds, and I repeated sermon.' It says much for the young Dissenter's commitment that he was eager to do this, despite feeling 'somewhat pensive' that day due to a natural grievance that his avaricious 'Master' had taken £3 from him, money he had earned from 'writing' for others.[56]

Young Nonconformists in different parts of the country grasped opportunities to meet for repetitions. As a young Baptist, William Kiffin met with a group of like-minded friends in the early hours of Sunday mornings. They regularly attended a 6 a.m. lecture but made it their practice to gather an hour before that, 'to spend it in prayer ... communicating to each other what experience we had received from the Lord; or else to repeat some sermon which we had heard before'.[57] Baxter's Kidderminster congregation also had many 'of the younger sort' who met in homes on Saturday evenings 'to repeat the Sermon of the last Lord's Day, and pray and prepare themselves for the following Day'.[58]

Meetings specifically for repetitions became a regular feature in the corporate life of Dissenters. Homes were a favourite rendezvous, where families, especially those of ministers, encouraged others to join them for the devotional exercise.[59] When John Angier began his ministry at Ringley, Lancashire, such large numbers attended the repetition of sermons in his 'little house' that they could not be accommodated and the company was divided into two meetings.[60] It was of such importance to John Machin that, following the

---

[53] Ibid. 51; cf. Thoresby, *Diary* (ed. Hunter), I, 43: 'very happily lighted upon a Sermon of worthy Mr Sharp's, that I had writ for cousin Eliz. Idle, repeated it with joy'.

[54] Lowe, *Diary* (ed. Sachse), 16: 'after evening prayer there was a few went to Mr. Woods' to spend the remaineing part of the day. I repeated sermon and stayd [for] prayer, and then came our way'.

[55] Ibid. 51: 'Tho. Smith and I went to Mr. Woods' and ware all night. Mr. Woods was gone to the funeralle of his wife's mother, soe I repeated sermon. There was foure young folkes presant on purpose to hear repetition'.

[56] Ibid. 20; cf. 19. Woods left for Cheshire in April 1663.

[57] Orme (ed.), *William Kiffin*, 11–12.

[58] Sylvester (ed.), *Reliquiae*, I, i, §135.

[59] It became a regular Sunday evening activity in the Newcome household: Newcome, *Diary* (ed. Heywood), 6, 122.

[60] *Life of Angier*, 56. When the ejected minister Nathaniel Baxter was chaplain at Beauchief Abbey he was required to preach there each Sunday, but 'returning Home at Night ... he usually repeated his Sermons to a Room full of People, in his own House',

morning service, he 'would often choose rather to repeat the Sermon to the people at Noon, than go to his Dinner'. Although sympathetic to his conviction regarding the priority of spiritual food (his biographer cites John 4: 33–4), the postponement of the midday meal was 'more than his body or the peoples convenience could well bear'. But 'as it was sincerely meant by him, so it was generally well taken by them', despite their weekly hunger.[61] When ejected ministers met together on weekdays, they frequently encouraged each other by repeating sermons they had found particularly helpful.[62]

The sermons repeated were not restricted to those preached by Dissenters. Presbyterians frequently repeated sermons they had heard on Sundays in their parish churches. One Sunday in 1665, the curate preached twice at Roger Lowe's parish church at Ashton-in-Makerfield, and that evening Lowe went with a friend 'to old John Robinson's and there repeated both sermons'. The following Friday he wrote: 'Ann Barrow sent for me. She lived with her sister … on Edg Greene, and there I repeated Mr. Henmar's sermons.'[63]

Henry Newcome made a regular practice of repeating the sermons of his local conformist minister and usually enjoyed doing so,[64] especially when it provided him with a natural opportunity to supplement the teaching with ideas of his own.[65] Adam Martindale also made the most of the opportunities provided by repetitions, not only to share his own insights along with the original message, but to repeat the message with possibly greater enthusiasm than the original preacher. He recalled: 'it was my custom … to heare my successor constantly, and to recite his sermons … at home to an housefull of parishioners … adding a discourse of mine owne'. His hearers would say 'that they liked his sermons better in the repetition then in the preaching'. The conforming minister had good material but 'in delivering [it] seemed to freeze in his mouth'.[66]

Repetitions were appreciated when a local clergyman had preached a sermon

---

and did so for seventeen years. On the death of his patron, his son 'desir'd him to desist, not out of Disrespect to him, but out of Fear, because of the Severities that were then used with the nonconformists': *Continuation*, I, 570–71.

[61] [Newcome], *Life of Machin*, 74.

[62] Henry, *Diaries* (ed. Lee), 130: 'I met Mr. [Richard] Steel[e] at Wm Benets where hee repeated sermons & pray'd, blessed bee God'; Newcome, *Diary* (ed. Heywood), 163: 'Mr. [Nathaniel] Baxter repeated Mr Angeirs Sermon last L[or]d's day about fervency in prayer.'

[63] Lowe, *Diary* (ed. Sachse), 87–88.

[64] Newcome, *Diary* (ed. Heywood), 157: earlier that day, 'Mr. Weston preached on John 3: 16. I was at ye Sacram[en]t ys day … Mr. Mosely preached in ye afternoone about pardon of sin on Psa. 25: 11 … Yn after supp[er] I repeated ye sermons'. Cf. ibid. 131, 133: '[Saturday] Wee had repetition on 2 Tim. 3: 5. [Sunday] Mr. Mosely preached both ends of ye day on Mt. 5: 6, very well … I repeated to my family before supp[er] & prayed. [The following Saturday] 'at night prepared to repeat on 2 Tim. 3: 5'.

[65] Ibid. 133.

[66] Martindale, *Life* (ed. Parkinson), 173.

hardly worth repeating. When Newcome heard 'a learned' but, 'to ye generality of ye people', largely 'unprofitable' exposition, it was a relief to come home and hear a friend repeat a sermon preached earlier at Denton by Angier. On a subsequent Sunday, when they had again endured a poor sermon at church, the same visiting friend again 'repeated Mr. Angeir's sermon' at the close of the day, to their great profit.[67] Inevitably, there were occasions when the exercise made these men wistful that they had been denied the freedom to preach publicly to their former congregations.[68]

Nonconformist ministers frequently repeated their own sermons, and sometimes found that the coveted inspiration, disappointingly lacking at the first preaching, descended at its repetition. Just prior to the ejectment, Newcome regretted that, for a particular Sunday, he had given insufficient time to the composition of his sermon. Consequently he 'had not yt freedome & assistance' that might have been his experience had he 'taken more heed to preparation'. Returning home, his midday diary entry expressed the hope that 'comfort may come in at repetition', not only for him, but also for others that 'may partake of it' at the end of the day, later adding with relief, 'wee had sweet repetition'.[69]

Oliver Heywood described a typical Sunday at the Denton home of his father-in-law, John Angier, whose sermons were always repeated the day they were delivered. It was an undeviating routine, and typically exacting. After 'private devotions in their closets', the family met together for prayer at about 8 a.m. when 'a Chapter was read, a Psalm sung' and Angier led in prayer. An hour later, they went together to 'the Chappel, which was but a few steps from his door'. At noon, 'immediately after Dinner' one member of the family 'repeats the Forenoons Sermon in his house' and 'at the same time another [person] was repeating [it] in the Chappel to many people who stayed there, singing Psalms both before and after'. This continued until the commencement of the next service. When the family returned home 'shortly after, Mr Angier sung a Psalm, and went to prayer, then to Supper'. Later, another 'Psalm was sung', and another member of the family then 'repeated the Afternoon Sermon, and another Psalm being sung all was finished with a short prayer, and so the Family, was dismissed to their apartments'.[70]

Barely a month after the ejectment, local authorities in some areas were beginning to look unfavourably at the practice of repetitions in the homes of ejected ministers. It was a delicate issue. These men were simply repeating sermons preached in their parish churches, and the Conventicle Act, controlling the numbers at house meetings, was yet to come onto the statute book.

---

[67] Newcome, *Diary* (ed. Heywood), 138–39, 141.
[68] Ibid. 133: 'Mr. Johnson [preached] all ys day ... on Rev. 3: 20. After eveninge sermon I conceived someth[ing] of ye text, and after supp[er] repeated it, & that w[i]th it', but 'w[ha]t a sad th[ing] is it yt wee may not do w[ha]t good wee can'.
[69] Ibid. 83.
[70] *Life of Angier*, 85.

Newcome and his local Presbyterian colleagues feared that more stringent restrictions were on the horizon. In September 1662, he wrote: 'I also heard today how our poore repetitions are eyed & begin to be enquired after'. The following day, 'I was ascited [summoned] to Chester as my deare Bre[thre]n Mr [John] Harrison, [John] Walker, [Thomas] Holland [and Peter] Leigh. Mine [offence] it seems for repeateinge in my family. Blessed be God it is for no unrighteousness or iniquity yt is in my hands'. Refusing to be threatened by the proceedings, they 'had repetition to a few after all'.[71]

The practice of writing and repeating sermons was especially helpful to Dissenters when local restrictions made meetings difficult. When Obadiah Grew was ejected from St. Michael's, Coventry, he remained in the city as long as possible, but when in 1682 local persecution intensified, he was imprisoned, with an additional burden, 'his Eyesight being gone'.[72] On release, he was compelled to move home. Undaunted, he was determined to continue his expository ministry to the Coventry people. Calamy records that 'he kept an Amanuensis, and dictated to him a new Sermon every Week' and then 'sent it to be read, to four or more Writers in short Hand, every Saturday Night' or even as late as the 'Lords Day Morning'. Each of these men 'read it to four new Men who transcrib'd it also'. By this means, 'it was afterwards read at twenty several Meetings', and though 'many could not safely get together at once', the blind preacher had reached a large congregation gathering in small groups in different parts of the city. 'This practice he continued till the Revolution.'[73]

Repetition was not sufficient in itself, however: William Thomas told his Somerset friends that their dedicated writing and repeating of sermons was of marginal worth if their message was not applied and practised in the lives of the hearers, quoting a saying of John Preston, that 'as Kine and Sheep return not to their owners, grass and hay, but, milk, and fleece and flesh; so Sermons are not to be returned and represented only by reading notes'. Christians were to repeat them, not just vocally, but 'in their lives ... growing in grace and godly in all their carriage'.[74] The effectiveness of the sermon was best proved by the transformation of the hearer.

---

[71] Newcome, *Diary* (ed. Heywood), 126. A footnote describes a primary source available to Heywood, in which Newcome recorded his conversation at this time with his accusers: 'I told them I had desisted from preaching & did not think repeating had been any offence. But the Justice told me it was.' When the ministers appeared at Chester, however, they were all discharged.

[72] The 'blind old Gentleman ... endur'd six Months imprisonment in a nasty Chamber tho' the best that Goal afforded. He lik'd his Goal the better, because Mr. Glover, Mr. Sanders and others had lain in it, and perfum'd it in the days of Queen Mary': *Account*, 737–38.

[73] Ibid. 738.

[74] Thomas, *Preservative*, 'The Epistle to the Christian Reader', [unpaginated].

Chapter 8

Maintaining Integrity

Recognizing that they lived for Christ in an alien and frequently hostile environment,[1] Dissenters acknowledged the need for high moral standards and exemplary conduct in the community. It was for this reason that they covenanted together to 'watch over one another in love'. They must not set themselves up as carping critics of others, but neither must they turn a blind eye to inconsistent behaviour within the local church. It was a finely balanced responsibility. Inappropriate lifestyles would react badly on their distinctive witness and alert critics were in plentiful supply.[2] Therefore Dissenters such as those at Yarmouth made not only a general verbal commitment to each other but itemized their pastoral responsibilities, with precise obligations to their fellow believers. They promised: 'we will, in all love, improve our communion as brethren, by watching over one another, and as need shall be, counsel, admonish, reprove, comfort, relieve, assist, and bear with one another'.[3] The Covenant obligation to care was at the heart of what Milton described as 'the sacred and dreadfull works of holy Discipline, to be exercised with 'milde severity' and 'melting compassion'.[4]

Neglect

In many churches, however, it was a missing element. When Baxter began his work at Kidderminster, he was concerned about 'the promiscuous giving of the Lord's Supper to all Drunkards, Swearers, Fornicators', even to 'Scorners at Godliness'.[5] But, once such issues were firmly yet lovingly addressed, he discovered that 'the Exercise of Church-Discipline was no small furtherance of

---

[1] Jean Gailhard condemned the 'Prophaneness' and 'Immorality' that 'bare and brazen-faced walk in our Streets': *The Blasphemous Socinian Heresie Disproved and Confuted* (1697), A3.
[2] Bunyan's pastoral experience in Bedford convinced him that a 'loose Professor in Church, does more mischief to Religion, than ten can do to it that are in the World': *Good News*, in *MW*, XI, 83.
[3] John Browne, *History of Congregationalism and Memorials of the Churches in Norfolk and Suffolk*, (1877), 211.
[4] John Milton, 'Of Reformation touching Church Discipline in England', in J.M. Patrick (ed.), *The Prose of John Milton*, Stuart Editions (New York, 1968), 75.
[5] Sylvester (ed.), *Reliquiae*, I, I, §19.

the Peoples Good'. Some acceptable pattern of church discipline was not only necessary in cases of blatant immorality, but also when otherwise devout people found themselves at variance. 'I found plainly that without it I could not have kept the Religious sort from Separations and Divisions.'[6]

Prior to the Restoration, discipline was one of the functions of Baxter's Worcestershire Association. The participating ministers agreed to help each other with such issues. It was especially necessary if a local church found it impossible to convince offenders of their errors, or when an accused person thought it only 'the Opinion of the Pastor of the Place' and alleged that the disciplinary procedures had been prescribed 'out of ill Will or Partiality'. Wrongdoers were required to meet the Association's representatives at their monthly meeting in the hope that colleagues might be more successful.[7]

Considering how many 'volumes they have written for it' and 'how zealously they have contended for it', Baxter was bewildered that many 'will do little or nothing in the exercise of it'.[8] It was one of the reasons he and his colleagues were unhappy with the contemporary episcopate. He wrote in 1681 that he never heard of 'one man or woman called openly to repentance' by the bishops, whatever the sin, nor anyone 'publickely confess or lament' any offence. 'Nor [of] one that was excommunicate' in any county where he had travelled, 'except the nonconformists'.[9] He 'never yet knew one Prelatist well perform' the pastoral ministry of 'Over-Sight ... and few of them meddle with it at all'.[10] In England it was regarded 'as a thing impossible to be done'. Each diocese had but 'one Court or Consistory', and rural deans, although responsible for such matters, contributed little to the disciplinary process. Such men 'are themselves scarce known', and in the parishes 'the Pastor and Churchwardens do nothing but present Men to the Courts', eager to pass all responsibility on to others.[11] Baxter was convinced that loose-living people in any community were 'all for Prelacy' because they 'found by experience, that under their Government they might sin quietly', and they 'make this the great shelter for their disobedience and unreformed lives'.[12]

Baxter's disciplinary ideals were similar to those widely practised in Independency.[13] But he had little sympathy for that tradition.[14] He feared that

---

[6] Sylvester (ed.), *Reliquiae*, I, I, §137, 25.

[7] Ibid., I, ii, §31. Baxter also refers to the Association's disciplinary function in *Christian Concord, or the Agreement of the Associated Pastors and Churches of Worcestershire* (1653), A3v–B2; *A Treatise of Episcopacy* (1681), Part II, 185–86. For the need of discipline and its general neglect, see idem, *Gildas Salvianus*, 213–34.

[8] Baxter, *Gildas Salvianus*, 213–14 (ch.IV, section VII).

[9] Baxter, *Treatise of Episcopacy*, II, 184.

[10] Sylvester (ed.), *Reliquiae*, III, I, §8, 1.

[11] Ibid., I, ii, § 329, 4.

[12] Baxter, *Gildas Salvianus*, 197–98.

[13] *Savoy Declaration* (ed. Matthews), 9, 124–25, 'The Savoy Declaration of the Institution of Churches and the Order Appointed in them by Jesus Christ', XVIII–XXII

whilst the conformists were slack, many 'separatists' were over-zealous in the exercise of discipline.

> And to the Congregational Brethren I may boldly say ... be not Righteous overmuch: Remember how tender Christ is of his little ones ... and will not break the bruised Reed. If he carry the Lambs in his armes ... it beseemes not us to turn them out of the fold.[15]

He urged his conformist friends not to be 'blinde under pretence of Charity, nor to let in known swine, for feare of keeping out the sheep'.[16] If accused of being too strict, he says that at the coming judgement 'some will find Christ more severe, and be less able to endure his Censure than mine, when he shall call some men to account'.[17]

Baxter was too experienced a pastor to imagine that in every disciplinary issue it was easy to apportion blame and discern the best course of action, especially in the delicate sphere of human relationships. Leaders must remember that 'when the case is doubtfull and difficult', so that one 'cannot make a separation without a danger of pulling up the wheate with the tares, it's better to let both alone till harvest'. The importance of truth and purity must never be downplayed, but love must also have a voice in the matter. All Christians are 'of so much sinne and unworthyness, our selves, as should provoke us to deale more tenderly and compassionately with others'. If, in the concern for compassion, they sometimes make mistakes and err on the side of leniency, then they must remember that, although in his holiness God both expects and honours purity, in his sovereignty he is free to use anybody, holy or not. Some inedible fish may well slip through the net. If godly people are genuinely worried about that, 'we may yet believe, that God hath much service', even 'for Hypocrites in his Church',[18] and such issues are best left in better and higher hands than theirs.

(regarding church censures, admonition and excommunication). For an example of a local church's commitment to the disciplinary ideals of the Declaration, see Cockermouth Independent Church Book, 4: 'That for the faith and judgment of this Church as to discipline &c, it is the same with that drawn up by the Elders and Messengers of the Churches, met at the Savoy in London, October 14, 1658, in which meeting they had their Pastor, George Larkham ... that confession of faith and the expressed judgments of the meeting touching order is owned by this particular Church. It was read amongst us at Thornthwaite Chapel in Crosthwaite parish and assented to.'

[14] Philip Henry was equally critical of 'the Independent way' but commended them in this, 'That they keep up discipline among them': *Diaries* (ed. Lee), 277.
[15] Baxter, *Confirmation*, 224–25.
[16] Ibid. 226.
[17] Richard Baxter, *The English Nonconformity* (1690), 151.
[18] Baxter, *Confirmation*, 226–27.

Priorities

Disciplinary procedures in Dissenting congregations were controlled by three sets of criteria: biblical, social and spiritual. First, motives, decisions and actions taken must have precise scriptural authority. Second, procedures must be 'public' in the sense that the corrective action must be decided not by an autocratic individual but by the church members or their representatives, and, hopefully, seen by the local community to have been implemented. Third, whatever the *modus operandi*, everything must be done in love, with the ultimate aim of reclaiming the offender.

Biblical Authority

In providing biblical authority for their pattern of church discipline, Nonconformists made frequent reference to key New Testament texts[19] and also appealed to a number of Old Testament passages. Bristol Dissenters, for example, made elaborate typological use of the 'leprosy' contamination laws in Leviticus 13: 1–46, persuaded that they enshrined 'a rule shewing ... how a Church should proceed to deale with offending Members'.[20] This description of priestly custom provided them with an unusual model for the congregation's detailed disciplinary procedure. Application of this Levitical provision does not appear to have been widespread among Dissenters, but Old Testament narratives were certainly significant for the promotion and application of discipline. In describing the motivation for such procedures, a greater number referred to the Achan narrative in Joshua 7, persuaded that one person's unacknowledged and unconfessed sin seriously impaired the congregation's relationship with God.[21] The corporate solidarity of these congregations was such that, in times of moral failure, members were distressed not only by the poor witness of guilty members but also at the possibility that God's severe displeasure might affect the wellbeing of the believing community to which they belonged.[22]

Many Dissenters feared that, like a highly infectious disease, the offence might somehow communicate itself to the rest of the congregation, and Old

---

[19] Mt. 18: 15–20; 1 Cor. 5: 1–5. Deptford General Baptists also cited 2 Thess. 3: 6 and 1 Cor. 5: 11 as 'dyrection given by paull': DWL, MS OD, 15, Deptford General Baptist Church Book, 1674–1719, 5 January 1679.

[20] *Broadmead Records* (ed. Hayden), 195–96.

[21] Cf. *Ecclesiastica* (ed. Howard), 53: the church met concerning a member accused of theft, who had compounded the offence by lying after proof that he was guilty, 'the offending brother being present'. Their minister 'preached from that scripture, Josh. 7: 25', saying that, as with Achan, 'the scandalous sins of professors do draw much trouble' upon the local church.

[22] Disciplinary procedures were necessary that 'ye Church might bee cleansed, and not bee partakers of sinn and wickedness to provoke ye Lord': *Broadmead Records* (ed. Hayden), 214.

Testament authority was cited for such a damaging eventuality. A pastoral letter to the Kettering Independents from their exiled pastor specifically mentioned a number of Old Testament characters to illustrate the truth that, in one way or another, personal sin seriously affected the lives of others. It was enough for John Maidwell merely to mention the names 'of Jonah, David and Hezekiah', proof that such narratives were thoroughly familiar to these biblically literate people. The 'sin of any one ... may provoke him [God] against every one'.[23] Moreover, ignoring the offence was a profound disservice to the offender. In the case of these characters, each one was confronted with their sin as an essential preliminary to reconciliation with God.

Bunyan utilizes a different typology when he likens the disciplinary responsibility of the local congregation to the 'Snuffers' used to 'Trim the Lamps and Candles' in Solomon's temple, 'that their Lights may shine the brighter'. They are 'those righteous reproofs, rebukes and admonitions, which Christ has ordained to be in his house for good', but such admonitions 'must be used wisely'. ''Tis not for every fool to handle Snuffers ... lest perhaps, instead of mending the light, they put the Candle out.' In accordance with the Pauline exhortation (2 Cor. 13: 1), the rebuke must be given with a view 'to edification, and not for destruction'.[24] Bunyan says that the letters to the seven churches (Rev. 2–3) illustrate the necessity of 'snuffers'. Christ stood in the midst of those 'Candlesticks' in Asia Minor. The 'Candles' they held were in serious need of the 'rebukes he gave those Churches ... that their lights might shine brighter'. But, like Baxter, Bunyan insists that, in the exercise of discipline the local church needs love, sensitivity and 'caution', that the light 'might not be impaired'. It must never be done out of 'private revenge, but of a design to nourish grace and gifts in Churches'. The people disciplined are cherished. 'As many as I love, I rebuke and chasten' (Rev. 3: 19).

Social Responsibility

In addition to providing biblical authority for mutual correction, Nonconformists were also aware of the social importance of congregational discipline. A cursory reading of their church books might create the impression that these congregations were concerned with little other than the moral welfare of their members, but Dissenters would have been exposed to serious local criticism if they had not taken action when one of their members was guilty of an offence which was known about in the community. They were not alone in endeavouring to deal with moral failure. Parish churches and local society were similarly concerned about the damaging effects of inappropriate behaviour.

Conforming Anglicans had longstanding disciplinary structures, though at times parishes may have been lax in their application. Those who offended by

---

[23] Anon., 'Letters of Maidwell', 369.
[24] Bunyan, *MW*, VII, 66–68.

immorality, sexual misconduct or drunkenness, for example, could be included in churchwardens' presentments.[25] Diocesan 'visitation articles' detailed specific offences that must be reported. In addition to persistent absentees, people guilty of unbecoming conduct in church, and those accused of 'swearing, adultery, fornication, incest ... drunkenness, ribauldry, slander, contention, sowing of discord betweene neighbours', as well as non-attending Dissenters, were all liable for prosecution, as were the churchwardens who failed to report them.[26] But, when such presentments were required, churchwardens often baulked at the prospect of disciplinary proceedings. Knowing that once an accusation had been committed to writing, they still had to live alongside their delinquent neighbours, many chose to silence the twice-yearly enquiry with a brief but effective *omnia bene*, 'all well'.[27]

Nevertheless, in addition to the provision made by ecclesiastical authorities, local communities had their own mechanisms for dealing with offenders,[28] so it is a mistake to regard Nonconformist congregations as repressive enclaves, out

---

[25] In 1662 churchwardens' presentments in Buckinghamshire included a man for 'not standing up att the readinge of the creede'; a woman 'for keeping her child unbaptised a yeare'; a vicar 'for frequentinge of alehouses and keepinge diso[r]derly companie', being 'an encourager of gam[ing] and settinge neighbours att variance'; another man 'for not causing his sonne and daughter ... to be baptised'; a couple 'for living together as man and wife and having a child borne between them not being married, so farr as we know': *Episcopal Visitation Book for the Archdeaconry of Buckingham, 1662* (ed. E.R.C. Brinkworth, Buckinghamshire Record Society, 7; Aylesbury, 1947), 3, 10, 17, 50. During 1664–66, Sussex presentments included items such as 'enterteyning youthes to tiple in his howse in time of divine service'; 'refusing to come to church to make her publicke thanksgiving after delivery in childbirth'; 'for having a baseborne childe and the reputed father thereof is ...'; 'for having a bastard child, by one whom we did not know': H. Johnstone (ed.), *Churchwardens' Presentments (Seventeenth Century) Part I, Archdeaconry of Chichester* (Sussex Record Society, 49; Lewes, 1947–48), 128, 130, 134, 139.

[26] Kenneth Fincham (ed.), *Visitation Articles and Injunctions of the Early Stuart Church* (2 vols, Church of England Record Society; Woodbridge, 1994), I, 122–35; F.S. Hockaday, 'The Consistory Court of the Diocese of Gloucester', *Transactions of the Bristol and Gloucestershire Archaeological Society* 46 (1924), 195–287; cf. Johnstone (ed.), *Chichester Churchwardens' Presentments*, 49; Barry Till, *The Church Courts 1660–1720: The Revival of Procedure* (Borthwick Paper 109; York, 2006).

[27] Donald A. Spaeth, *The Church in an Age of Danger: Parsons and Parishioners, 1660–1740* (Cambridge, 2000), 66–67, 165, for the diocese of Salisbury; cf. the honest response of the Sarratt (Herts) churchwardens in 1681: 'no parish if they will write truth can say omnia bene to this querie for some go to church and some to other meetings': Spufford, *Rural Dissenters*, 12. For further examples of the frequency of *omnia bene* responses, see Pruett, *Parish Clergy*, 119; for qualification in respect of south-eastern Cambridgeshire, see Eric Carlson, 'The Origins, Function and Status of the Office of Churchwarden, with particular reference to the Diocese of Ely', in Spufford, *Rural Dissenters*, 164–207, at 175–79.

[28] Barry Reay (ed.), *Popular Culture in Seventeenth-Century England* (1985), 13–14; Harris, *London Crowds*, 80.

of touch with the moral norms of their contemporaries.[29] Local society itself plainly disapproved of disruptive, offensive or objectionable conduct and developed its own means of expressing dissatisfaction by measures such as public exposure, social exclusion, coordinated derision[30] and, in some cases, withholding the parish's financial support.[31]

With the exception of issues such as 'marrying out', most of the behaviour considered unfitting by Nonconformists would have been deemed equally reprehensible in wider society; to have ignored their own offenders would have seriously damaged the reputation of Dissenting worshippers. Local communities strongly disapproved of the unmarried pregnant woman, for example; she would soon become an additional burden on her neighbours through an increased poor rate. In a period of economic stringency, the local drunkard might be happy to spend his money in the alehouse rather than support for his wife and children, but the family would soon be compelled to seek parish help, its cost shouldered by the community. Occasional inebriation would be overlooked but the habitual drunkard was despised. A dishonest tradesman or a gossiping member of a Dissenting congregation was a damaging advertisement. It had to be seen that Nonconformists expected a high standard of moral conduct from their members. To ignore such offences would be to condone sin and disregard the agreed moral and spiritual standards of the congregation. Dissenters insisted that these transgressions had to be dealt with because they were an offence to God, a denial of their message, a discredit to the church, a bad example to fellow members and a serious danger to their corporate spiritual life.

Spiritual Ideals

Convinced of biblical authority for church discipline, and aware of the need of it in local society, Dissenters recognized that their greatest challenge was to

---

[29] John Spurr, *The Post-Reformation: Religion, Politics and Society in Britain 1603–1714* (Harlow, 2006), 262–65; cf. A. Fletcher, *Reform in the Provinces: The Government of Stuart England* (New Haven, CT, 1986), 277–81.

[30] For the use of 'processional ridings' and of mocking rhymes as a form of popular public rebuke, see Martin Ingram, 'Ridings, Rough Music and Mocking Rhymes in Early Modern England', in Reay (ed.), *Popular Culture*, 166–97.

[31] For examples of community 'discipline', cf. Reay (ed.), *Popular Culture*, 14: '[s]ections of the people took part in the regulation of sexuality and marriage ... control was not ... simply imposed from above'. In 1664 a Sussex man was accused of keeping 'Thomas Cheesman as a servant in his hows, although there hath bene an aggravacion many times declared and published in the church' against the servant: Johnstone (ed.), *Chichester Churchwardens' Presentments*, 132. For early Stuart examples of public rebuke in church by local clergy, see R.C. Richardson, *Puritanism in North-West England: A Regional Study of the Diocese of Chester to 1642* (Manchester, 1972), 48. The saintly John Angier was not beyond publicly rebuking an offender if they failed to respond to his private admonitions, *Life of Angier*, 77.

exercise such ministry in love. When a Cambridgeshire Independent congregation renewed their church covenant they acknowledged that the responsibility of 'Restoring the fallen' must be exercised 'in tenderness & meekness'.[32] Its effectiveness could be seriously marred by unworthy motives, and offenders and churches damaged by inaccurate reporting, premature accusations, malicious judgements, careless speech, misapplied zeal or unforgiving activity on the part of the disciplinary community. John Owen insisted that, in the process of church discipline, members must long for the offender's reconciliation, with all 'readiness for the restoration of love in all the fruits of it'. Efforts to reclaim the wrongdoer must be 'corrective, not vindictive; for healing, not destruction'.[33] Milton believed that, although a church ban was a harsh judgement, there was 'no act in all the errand of Gods Ministers to mankind' in which there was a more 'loverlike contestation' between Christ and the disciplined believer than 'before, and in, and after the sentence of Excommunication'. By 'Fatherly admonishment and Christian rebuke' the soul is cast into 'godly sorrow', but the intended 'end is joy'.[34]

The 'loverlike contestation' was best expressed in the church's continuing patience. Whilst it was important not to ignore inappropriate conduct, the church must not act hastily or fail to give time for offenders to reflect on the seriousness of their behaviour. The Bedford Independent church first sought an explanation for continuing absence from one member, Robert Nelson, in 1661, and asked Bunyan to visit him to ascertain why he had 'withdrawne' himself.[35] Repeated attempts to secure a meeting with the absentee were not successful; he had no intention of returning, having been 'openly bishopt'. But it was almost nine years, when he had 'bene long under the admonition of the Church ... refusing to heare it', before he was 'cut ... off from, and cast out' of their congregation.[36] They could hardly be accused of precipitate action. Canterbury Baptists displayed similar patience with a member who 'made not good her place ... as formerlye'. They sent 'to admonish her ... and shee pretended shee was not able to come to the Church'. The congregation 'longe waited upon her' and 'sent to her severall times ... But shee would not herken ... The Church after many admonitions with patience & very longe forbear[a]nce perceivinge her to be past recovery ... w[i]th[drew] there communion from her'.[37]

---

[32] Anon., 'Congregationalism in the Fen Country', *TCHS* 7 (1916–18), 3–15, at 8.
[33] John Owen, *The True Nature of a Gospel Church and its Government*, in *Works* (ed. Goold), XVI, 171.
[34] John Milton, 'Of Reformation touching Church Discipline in England', in *The Prose of John Milton* (ed. Patrick), 85.
[35] The church's request was made when Bunyan had been a prisoner for ten months, further indication that he was occasionally allowed to leave jail: *Bedford Minutes* (ed. Tibbutt), 37.
[36] Ibid. 37, 39, 40, 41, 54, 63, 64.
[37] *Canterbury General Baptist Church Book* (ed. Creasey and Maguire), 4. The church's 'forbearance' is frequently illustrated in its church book entries, e.g. ibid. 5–6.

Practice

The disciplinary practice of Dissenting churches was conditioned by Christ's words in Matthew 18: 15–17, with their insistence that any correction must first be expressed at a personal level. 'By good company erring Saints have been recovered', said George Swinnock. 'Holy David lay sleeping in his sin till his good friend Nathan jogged and awakened him. Many a one hath been aroused out of his spiritual Lethargy by private admonition'.[38] Amersham Baptists were charged never to bring an accusation against a fellow member without having first endeavoured to settle the matter privately. 'Let them keepe it in there own brest tell ye have An opertunity to doe ther duty Acording to Gods word that soe as James saith we may gaine a sole and hide a Multitude of sin.'[39] A Norwich Dissenter accused of 'scandallous walking' was 'dealt withall first more privatly', enabling him to 'make a solome acknowlidgment of his sin' when he came before the church, 'with a great deale of seeming brokennesse of hearte'. After prayer, the offender was given a solemn admonition by the pastor and restored to fellowship.[40]

Members must choose the right time for private 'correction', never dealing with offenders 'when they are in a passion, or drunk, or in publick, where they will take it for a disgrace'. If a person is sick, 'Physick' is given 'in season', for 'the Remedy must not only be fitted to the disease, but also to the strength of the Patient'; 'learners and young beginners must not be dealt with as open Professors'. Choose the best moment. 'When the earth is soft, the Plow will enter'. Wisdom is also necessary, 'in suiting yr Exhortation to the quality and temper' of the disciplined member. 'All meats are not for all stomachs ... All cannot bear that rough dealing as some can'. A sensitive approach, made with 'Love and Plainness, and Seriousness', will be received by most people, 'but the words of terror some can scarce bear'.[41]

When it was reluctantly decided that an Independent or Baptist church member must be excommunicated, the proceedings were conducted with great seriousness, the offender sometimes being present.[42] As the church's admonition was read, one Bristol congregation made it their practice for the members to stand, when 'all ye Brethren Putt off their Hatts, ye sisters not to sitt but stand up'.[43]

Concerned not to be misrepresented in the local community, churches kept

---

[38] Swinnock, *Calling*, III, 245.
[39] *Ford and Amersham Church Books* (ed. Whitley), 203, quoting James 5: 20.
[40] Norwich Old Meeting Church Book, fol.47.
[41] Baxter, *Rest*, 511–12.
[42] As at Cockermouth, when a member who had committed a 'foul sin ... by which he had brought general reproach on the ways of God', was present at his excommunication, the pastor preaching on Ezek. 9: 4: 'Go through the midst of the city ... and set a mark upon the foreheads of the men that sigh and that cry for all the abominations that be done in the midst thereof': Cockermouth Independent Church Book, 144–45.
[43] *Broadmead Records* (ed. Hayden), 188.

careful records of their dealings with members under discipline, whether fruitful or not. When unable to make personal contact with an offender, copies were made of correspondence sent by the church, some being entered into church books. Although such letters were composed by a church leader, it was required that they be read to the members and approval obtained before despatch.[44] Church books also preserved details of the church's decisions regarding disciplinary action. Recognizing that such information was on permanent record, offenders sometimes requested that matters concerning them remain unrecorded,[45] or that members agree that some previous indiscretion be erased from the book.[46]

Offences

Nonconformist church books record a wide range of typical misdemeanours: moral, social, financial, domestic and spiritual. Their variety cannot be our major concern here, as discussion must be restricted to those offences that were the direct effect of repressive legislation and the consequent persecution.

One particularly interesting case of such disciplinary action concerns the Bristol, Broadmead, congregation's determination to take seriously Christ's command to 'love your enemies' and the injunction not to speak evil of anyone, not even ruthless persecutors (Mt. 5: 44; Titus 3: 2). Of all Nonconformist churches in the West of England, Broadmead had perhaps suffered most, yet it was determined to maintain high standards of spirituality in exceptionally difficult times. Although Bristol's bishop, Guy Carleton, had been fiercely hostile towards the city's Dissenters, the Broadmead congregation was grieved to hear that one of their members had spoken inappropriately of him in public. A onetime officer in Charles I's army and chaplain to his exiled son, the resolute bishop was determined to root out the city's numerous Nonconformists. Several of his clergy were enlisted to work as informers, their activities initiating a harsh period of persecution during the late 1670s. Accompanied by several clergymen, magistrates and military personnel, the bishop went to John Thompson's Independent meeting, personally supervising the arrest of its minister. During imprisonment, Thompson became seriously

---

[44] See *Speldhurst Church Book* (ed. Maguire), 21–23, for examples of letters preserved by Speldhurst Baptists in 1686–7. For similar admonitory letters sent by Friends, see *The Minute Book of the Monthly Meeting of the Society of Friends for the Upperside of Buckinghamshire 1669–1690* (ed. Beatrice S. Snell, Records: Buckinghamshire Archaeological Society, 1; High Wycombe, 1937), 7–8, 27–28, 194–95.

[45] A member of Thomas Jolly's congregation who 'quarrelled with some doctrine the Pastor delivered' asked that the matter 'might not be recorded in the Church Book, and desired his dismission. His letter was fully answered': 'Altham and Wymondhouses Church Book', in Jolly, *Note Book* (ed. Fishwick), 134.

[46] For example, *Canterbury General Baptist Church Book* (ed. Creasey and Maguire), 10, 12–13, 14–19, where many entries were crossed out on the offender's restoration.

unwell, and a local physician urged that he be removed from the foul conditions of the common gaol to prison accommodation more suitable for a desperately sick man. The bishop adamantly refused, threatening the sheriff if his strict orders were not obeyed. Within days, Thompson died, and news of his death in grim circumstances caused a major stir in Bristol,[47] and did little to endear Dissenters to the prelate. But it was still considered unfitting for a member of the Broadmead congregation to use vulgar terms to describe him. The church dealt with their offending member, who, having had too much to drink, had said 'hee would dash out ye Bishop's teeth'. The church reminded him that 'we are commanded to speak Evill of noe man', concerned that because of his unguarded words, the 'wayes of ye Lord' had been 'Evill spoken of' in Bristol. Rebuked and disciplined by the congregation, and urged to repent, the offender left the congregation, never to return.[48]

Absenteeism was a more common problem. When local persecution was intense, otherwise devout members sometimes baulked at regular attendance. Some of their close friends may have become seriously impoverished, losing hard-earned money to pay heavy fines simply for being present at a conventicle. Others known to them may have seen their furniture, clothing and food distrained, loaded on to carts, never to be seen again and, more seriously, wage earners led off to prison. It was hardly surprising that some could not face the prospect of repeated suffering.

Non-attendance might be the first step to defection, and defectors were almost inevitable, so what was to be done concerning church discipline in respect of such absentees? For Dissenters, attendance at the weekly meeting was not optional. Their physical presence alongside other suffering members was a visible sign of personal commitment and a token of corporate solidarity. Writing from prison in 1663,[49] Bunyan urged his fellow Dissenters not to miss their regular meetings, 'yeelding active obedience to that under which we ought to suffer', whatever the cost. Members as well as preachers must be willing, indeed eager, to serve God actively and not sit safely in their undisturbed homes.[50] In the winter of 1664-5 some Bristol Dissenters had been 'remisse in their duty of Assembling ... by reason of these troubles'. A few months later it was requested that their leading elder 'should Ingrosse all ye Members' names in Parchment' so that, reading the names at the Lord's Supper, it would be possible to 'see who doth omitt their duty'. Some had stayed away 'through fear' but absentees were greatly missed.[51]

---

[47] It led to a brittle pamphlet exchange in *The Bristol Narrative* (1675) and the Dissenters' *A Reply to the Bristol Narrative, or a more Just Account of the Imprisonment and Death of Mr. John Thompson* (1675).
[48] *Broadmead Records* (ed. Hayden), 144–45, 150, 194–96.
[49] The title page of Bunyan's *Christian Behaviour* (2nd ed.; 1663), in *MW*, III, 5, describes its author as a 'Prisoner of Hope'.
[50] Ibid. 19: 'To be at plow in the field when I should be hearing the Word is not good.'
[51] *Broadmead Records* (ed. Hayden), 121.

The church's pastoral responsibility towards absent members was that they be visited, instructed, entreated and if necessary disciplined. They must first be visited in their homes. Broadmead members 'sent [three] Messengers to some that had not been with us of late in ye fields', an intervention with a happy outcome, for a week later the absentees joined fellow members at a day of prayer.[52] Many visits were not so fruitful. Humphrey Merrill had been a longstanding member of the Bedford congregation when Bunyan and a colleague were asked to meet him in 1668 regarding his attendance at the parish church. Although his visitors' 'words and carriage were … winning', Merrill demonstrated some apparently typical 'impatiency', charging the church with a selective use of Scripture and refusing to meet his fellow church members, 'bidding them do their worst'. Bunyan and a different leader were instructed to visit Merrill again, but they only succeeded in hearing further accusations against his former friends such as that 'they had their hands in the blood of the king … were disobedient to government, and that they were not a [true] church'. Merrill was eventually removed from membership but a full fifteen months had elapsed since their first approach to him. They were hardly guilty of the offender's 'impatiency'.[53]

With appropriate teaching, absentees must be reminded of the serious implications of their disloyalty. While Hercules Collins was in prison he shared his thinking about defection with his London congregation. His exhortation, a model of sensitive and realistic pastoral concern, explains that a Dissenter's fear of attending meetings in adverse circumstances has seven damaging consequences. It undermines the local fellowship, reflects badly on the absentee's doctrinal convictions, undermines the authority of Scripture, and is an insult to God himself. It betrays an alarming ignorance of spiritual resources, encourages the church's opponents, and is a tragic evangelistic deterrent.

First, continuing absenteeism in persecution discourages other believers. Collins knows how 'uncomfortable it is' to imprisoned pastors, to have 'such News brought to us, in our Bonds', especially when specific individuals are mentioned. 'Such a tall Cedar is fallen, such a Star is fallen from Heaven'. Such defections 'sadden the Hearts of the Lord's sufferers'.[54]

Absentees must also consider the theological implications of their withdrawal. 'To Depart from God in a Trying Day Reflects upon his Being and Attributes'. With pastoral sensitivity, Collins echoes the plea of the young Jeremiah to his spiritually disloyal contemporaries: 'What iniquity, said God …

---

[52] Ibid. 252.

[53] *Bedford Minutes* (ed. Tibbutt), 40–42.

[54] General Baptists in Kent were also aware of the discouraging effect of absenteeism in a congregation. Among several offences which caused a Bessels Green member to be 'withdrawn from', one was that fear had made him 'an instrument of Satan in labouring to make our knees feeble … and to hide our light under a bushel by creeping into corners': *The Early Records of the General Baptist Church, meeting in or about Bessels Green, Kent* (ed. Leonard J. Maguire; 2001), 2.

have your Fathers found in me, that they are gone far from me? Am I not the same as ever? Are not my Promises the same? Have I fail'd in any one thing?'[55]

Absenteeism also suggests that the offender no longer treasures biblical truth. Defectors 'preach aloud, That ... Promises ... are vain and empty Complements', that Scriptural 'Threatnings ... are nothing but Scare-Crows'. Disloyalty arrogantly dismisses biblical 'Precepts' as 'the most unreasonable Laws in the world'.[56]

Spiritual desertion is an affront to God, reflecting 'Dishonour upon the Author of all good, God himself'. It is either an act of silent atheism, saying 'that there is no God', or a denial of eternity, when he will call the offender to 'Account for such an Action'. It is a defamation of his person, says Collins, that God 'is not worth Suffering for', discrediting his character, 'as if he could be out-done in his Wisdom, or were weak in his Power, or ... Unfaithful to his poor Troubled People, and would forsake them in their time of Distress ... What cause hath any thus to Reproach the Living God by Revolting from him?'[57]

Moreover, defectors must have forgotten their priorities and the available spiritual resources. Illustrating his message from Reformation history, Collins says that when Luther 'had great Offers made to him to Return to the Church of Rome', he answered, 'Can you give me Christ ... and Eternal Life?' The Reformers took 'great care ... not to lose the Crown' and 'so it should be ours'.[58] The 'forsaking of a good way in Troublesom times' indicates 'great Ignorance in the Understanding, or else they would never prefer Temporal before Spiritual things, and present Pleasure before future Glory'. The spiritually 'ignorant' believer 'will comply with his and God's Enemies on any termes, to preserve ... his greatest Happiness ... [and] their Chief supream good': undisturbed comfort.[59]

Zealous persecutors are delighted when frightened Dissenters turn their backs on their convictions. Defection 'hardens Gods Enemies, and makes them bold in sin'. Success in one act of oppression will encourage them to continue, even intensify, their destructive activities in the lives of other believers and in different localities.[60]

Finally, disloyalty in times of persecution has a devastating effect on local evangelism. It 'stumbles the poor seeking Soul'.[61] The defection of a greatly admired believer might be the very thing that turns an almost Christian into a reluctant atheist. When the Nonconformist abandons his convictions, it shouts to the unbeliever that the things once declared to be of the utmost consequence

---

[55] Collins, *Voice*, 14.
[56] Ibid. 20.
[57] Ibid.
[58] Ibid. 14–15.
[59] Ibid. 17.
[60] Ibid. 21.
[61] Ibid.

are of merely marginal significance.

But, from Newgate, Collins is not satisfied simply to marshal his facts and present his case. His aim is not to win an argument but to reclaim a soul. The faithful teacher is a compassionate pastor. Whilst he warns, he pleads. Foremost amongst his entreaties is the plea to return to a former commitment while there is time. Drawing on Old Testament imagery, he appeals: 'return ... to the Church again ... get into the Refuge City before the Pursuer overtake thee', to Christ, 'the best Refuge before that day come'. Moreover, the defector should return whilst the persecution continues, 'before this day of Trouble be over', for to delay the return 'till the Storm be over' might incite 'a great ground of fear thou art not sincere'.[62]

The defector must return whilst his conscience prompts him to do so. Like countless preachers of the period, Collins reminds the disloyal believer of Francis Spira, who 'did what he did to save his Estate ... but lost his peace'. Spira opposed 'the Spirits striving when he Confest with Anguish afterwards ... I have sinned against the Spirit, for when I was about to sign my Recantation, the Spirit said don't write Spira ... and yet I did it; there is no mercy for me.' Collins warns the defector by exposing the danger of impaired judgment and its possible mistiming. 'Is it not great folly, for a man to save his Glove, and lose his Hand? ... What a case such a Soul will be in, if God should take away his Soul that very day he backslides, and give him no time for Repentance.'[63] Albeit with a bruised conscience, the defector can return confidently, not on the grounds of his eloquent penitence but because God is uniquely compassionate. The biblical preacher can contradict Spira's anguished cry that his sin was greater than God's mercy. 'O what a gracious, merciful God is this that ... inviteth such to come to him which have committed Spiritual Adultery! ... the Lord hath proclaimed he will not let his Anger fall upon you.'[64]

Some absentees, however, would remain deaf to such entreaties, maintaining their dogged resolve to leave the Nonconformist community. The local church could only respond to this resolute defection by disciplining the member concerned. When the persecution increased in the early 1680s, Axminster Independents grieved that there were such evident 'decays ... among many professors'. It was a 'heart breaking sight ... to behold many that had stood firm ... for many years past', only now to 'let go their profession'. In these circumstances, overlooking defection would infer that loyalty was of little consequence, which would have a demoralizing effect on the congregation's corporate commitment.[65]

After appropriate pastoral appeals for the absentee to return, appointed visitors would begin by warning the offender of disciplinary action beginning

---

[62] Ibid. 27–28.
[63] Ibid. 24.
[64] Ibid. 25–26.
[65] *Ecclesiastica* (ed. Howard), 80.

with admonition which, if ineffective, would be followed by suspension from the Lord's Supper for a given period, then separation, and eventually excommunication.

Cost

Compassionate exercise of church discipline made inevitable demands, both on the minister and local members. People were averse to having their faults exposed, even privately.[66] It wounded their pride, 'the most radicated [rooted] and natural of all sins'.[67] The initial intervention of a caring pastor was not always appreciated. About to embark on such an exercise, Joseph Alleine said: 'I am going about that which is like to make a very dear and obliging Friend, to become an Enemy: But ... it cannot be omitted', adding, 'it is better to lose man's favour, than GOD's'.[68] Lancashire ministers such as Isaac Ambrose, Adam Martindale and Thomas Jolly appreciated the warm hospitality of the distinguished Houghton family at Ho[u]ghton Tower, near Leyland.[69] Prior to the Restoration, Lady Margaret Houghton had 'for a long time' opened her spacious home for 'two days of prayer' each month. It became a haven for the ejected ministers, especially in the hostile context of the mid 1660s. When he was not in prison, Jolly was often present on such occasions. Another family member particularly valued the ministry there of the newly ordained John Bayley, but, exercising faithful discipline, he paid a high price for his pastoral care. Jolly wrote: 'For admonishing Lady [Sarah?] Houghton for leaving her husband he lost a friend.'[70]

It was also costly for sensitive congregations. Church members felt themselves personally involved in any known transgression, invariably considering that they were not dealing with the isolated sin of a particular individual but the failure of a believing community. Early in 1670, Yarmouth Independents met to discipline three members, one for 'disowning the Church and for other misdemeenors', another for 'separating himself from his wife and for evill wordes spoken by him of the Church', and yet another for 'evill Miscarages'. The burdened members set a day aside 'to humble' themselves not simply for the public failures of three fellow members, but 'for all our

---

[66] Baxter said that at Kidderminster, 'of about 3,000 persons, 1,800 or more of which were at age to be Communicants' refused to do any more than hear him preach (for fear of discipline) except about 600 or a few more': *Treatise of Episcopacy*, II, 185.
[67] Baxter, *Plain Scripture Proof*, d4v, preface, 'The True History of this Treatise'.
[68] [Alleine], *Life*, 46.
[69] Halley, *Lancashire Puritanism and Nonconformity*, 383–5. For the Ho[u]ghton family, see also J.T. Cliffe, *The Puritan Gentry Besieged, 1650–1700* (1993).
[70] 'Altham and Wymondhouses Church Book', in Jolly, *Note Book* (ed. Fishwick), 133–34. G.C. Miller, *Hoghton Tower* (rev. ed.; Preston, 1954), 147, says that Lady Sarah 'was twice married'.

miscarriages'.[71]

The Broadmead congregation were relieved when a disciplinary issue seemed to be resolved, but it was the 'cause of great lamentation' among them. In reproving and offering considerable practical support to the offending member, they had done their utmost 'to regaine ye Glory they had lost', but were grieved that 'Christ should be soe wounded afresh by us'.[72] Their reaction illustrates not only the distress experienced at the moral failure of a member and their acute sense of corporate guilt but also, and more seriously, their conviction that, because of the wrongdoing, the Lord of the whole church was suffering also.

A church was particularly wounded if required to discipline a leader. When the Bedworth Independent congregation excommunicated a deacon, guilty of 'lascivious carriage', it 'spent the night in prayer' and never before 'saw such a time'. Aware of their own failings, a sense of awe fell upon the congregation, 'an awefull terrible Resemblance of the great day of Judgment',[73] with 'not one dry eye in the place'.[74]

Restoration

Hercules Collins was not alone in raising a problem regarding the absentee: if a defector genuinely desired to return to his Nonconformist meeting, what kind of reception might he reasonably expect? Those who had suffered intense hardships while he had been comfortably at home or securely worshipping at his parish church might be hesitant, even grudging, in their welcome. Collins urged the faithful to be grateful for the offender's return. 'Rejoice not in thy Brothers fall. But ye which are Spiritual, Restore [Gal. 6: 1] such an one in the Spirit of meekness'. The imprisoned pastor informed his people that Paul's verb 'restore', '*katartizesthe* ... is borrowed from the Chirurgeons' vocabulary. When the surgeon deals 'with a broken joint [he] handles the same very Tenderly. The original word signifieth to set a Bone broken or out of joint into its right place', so the welcoming church should deal with 'one overtaken in a

---

[71] DWL, MS 76.2, Great Yarmouth Church Book, fol.125.
[72] *Broadmead Records* (ed. Hayden), 216. The concept that Christ is 'wounded afresh' by the transgressions of believers (possibly suggested by Heb. 6: 6) is not unusual in Nonconformist teaching about holiness.
[73] The eschatological dimension of excommunication features in Owen's teaching about church discipline. 'It is to be accompanied with a due sense of the future judgment of Christ': *Nature of a Gospel Church*, in *Works*, XVI, 170. Here he cites the Latin text of Tertullian's *Apologeticus* 39.4: 'There is, besides, exhortation in our gatherings, rebuke, divine censure. For judgment is passed, ... and it is a notable forestaste of judgment to come, if any man has so sinned as to be banished from all share in our prayer, our assembly, and all holy intercourse' (transl. T.R. Glover, Loeb Classical Library; 1931), 175.
[74] Bedworth Independent Church Book, 10 December 1689.

Fault' and 'seek to bring him into his right place', within the security of a forgiving community.[75]

Occasionally, the restoration of an absentee member tested the compassion of the welcoming community. A Cockermouth member stayed well away from their meetings 'in time of danger and difficulty' but with the 1672 Indulgence made her way back. She had not supported her fellow members in harrowing times, but when she applied for readmission they spoke 'very savourily' in the meeting and she was happily restored.[76] Owen insisted that whenever a believer was disciplined, immense demands were made upon the congregation, particularly if the member had been excommunicated or 'cut off'. In addition to the pastor's admonition, there must be special prayer for the individual concerned, 'compassion in his distressed' state, and even greater love and concern if the offender should prove indifferent to the church's action. It challenged all the members to exercise 'forbearance', and refrain from judgemental attitudes.[77]

The prospect of restoration brought a measure of relief to congregations troubled by disciplinary action. They were cheered that some disciplined believers realized that the fellowship of their church was too rich to abandon and, in a spirit of genuine penitence, made their way back to the warmth and welcome of the local Christian community.[78] Some entries in the Canterbury General Baptist Church Book are typical of many. One member 'was withdrawn from by reason of Sinn But uppon Repentance is received [in] to communion again'. Another 'acknowledged [his] evell in w[i]th drawing from C[omm]union w[i]th the congregation [and offers] the right hand of fellow[ship] and [is] received into communion a[gain]'.[79] Even congregations that disapproved of 'marrying out'[80] were pleased when the disciplined offender was restored. The unequally yoked believer had ignored the local church's conventions but its disappointed members did not wish to lose such people from their fellowship.[81]

Sometimes Dissenters returned to the church many years after they had been excluded. An excommunicated Yarmouth member, 'cast out ... for the scandalous sin of uncleanness' seventeen years earlier, desired the church 'to forgive him and receive him againe'. They welcomed him back, although it is apparent from their records that during his absence he had caused them

---

[75] Collins, *Voice*, 28–29.
[76] Cockermouth Independent Church Book, 82, 90.
[77] Owen, *Works*, XVI, 171.
[78] *Ecclesiastica* (ed. Howard), 31–32.
[79] *Canterbury General Baptist Church Book* (ed. Creasey and Maguire), 3, 4.
[80] It was an offence in some Nonconformist congregations (especially General Baptist) for a member to marry a person not in membership of the local church or the local association of churches to which it belonged. Quakers discouraged marriage to non-Quakers.
[81] E.g. ibid. 17, where details of the offence are crossed out.

considerable pain. He was willingly restored, although, knowing his vulnerability, with some precise conditions, including the requirement that he publicly renew 'his Covenant with God and with his Church'.[82] A Bury St Edmunds member, 'having stood off fro[m] ye Comunion of ye Church some years, expressed her sorrow and engaged afresh to walk with ye Church, as her distance of place allow[ed] her'. Another member who had absented himself from the same congregation for over twenty years, returned 'w[i]th much Contrition of Spirit' and was restored to his place among them. He provided the church with a written account of his many sins committed 'ag[ain]st Light and Love', his 'Departures, backslidings, turning aside ... from ye path of life'. His 'large paper' indicated that his long absence was entirely due to his unwillingness to suffer persecution, that he might not 'come under ye Crosse', but he was warmly restored.[83]

Disciplined members seeking restoration were sometimes asked to say what they had learnt during exclusion. A Bristol Dissenter declared 'to ye Church how ye Lord turned him to leave his sinn of Drunkenness'.[84] A disciplined member of the Fenstanton General Baptist congregation made it clear on her return how much she had appreciated the church's resolute action. She regarded it as proof of their 'care over her' as a fellowship of believers 'in sending ... to reprove her for her faults', and she 'did bless the Lord for it'; it was a token of God's love as well as theirs.[85]

These unsophisticated Christian communities believed that to ignore the serious faults of fellow believers was to fail them in love. A healthy concern for the moral and spiritual wellbeing of their Christian friends was of greater importance than any other form of compassionate service. It concerned not simply physical comfort and material needs, but the spiritual welfare and eternal destiny of those who belonged to the same family of faith.

---

[82] Great Yarmouth Independent Church Book, fols 139–41.

[83] Bury St Edmunds Congregational Church Book, fols 63–64. Part of the returned member's 'large paper' is recorded.

[84] *Broadmead Records* (ed. Hayden), 203.

[85] *Records of Churches of Christ* (ed. Underhill), 20. The church book quotes Psa. 141: 5: 'Let the righteous smite me, it shall be a kindness ... it shall be an excellent oil that will not break my head', adding, 'Because the Lord loveth thee, therefore he sendest his prophets to reprove thee.'

Chapter 9

Serving Others

Most Dissenters treasured the idea of the Church as a separated people, a concept repeatedly expressed in their doctrinal statements and corporate covenants.[1] The church at Gamlingay to which Agnes Beaumont belonged described themselves as 'visible saints ... separated from the wicked world'.[2] A founding member of the Broadmead church 'practized that truth ... (which was then hated and Odious), namely, Separation'. For some twenty years prior to the formation of her local church, she had belonged to a group of believers in Bristol determined 'to Separate from ye World ... Sensible of ye Sins and Snares of their day'.[3] Many of these churches referred to themselves as an 'enclosed garden', a separationist ideal expressed later in a hymn by one of their most gifted members:

We are a Garden wall'd around,
Chosen and made peculiar Ground;
A little Spot, inclosed by Grace,
Out of the World's wide Wilderness.[4]

Separation was part of their ecclesiology, but political pressures intensified their experience of detachment. Repression and persecution drew members of Dissenting congregations closer together, yet in this vulnerable context their churches were in danger of developing an insular and withdrawn mentality. Influenced by the judgements of unsympathetic contemporaries, social historians have frequently regarded Nonconformist churches as isolationist ghettos,[5] taking at face value the claims that these were composed largely of 'inferior',[6] 'meane',[7] 'poore',[8] 'and vulgar'[9] people 'of ordinary Ranke',[10] who

---

[1] For an exposition of this idea in the teaching of English Independent churches, see Nuttall, *Visible Saints*, 43–69.
[2] Gamlingay Baptist Church archives, The [first] Gamlingay Baptist Church Book, fol.4.
[3] *Broadmead Records* (ed. Hayden), 85.
[4] Isaac Watts, 'The Church, the Garden of Christ', in *Hymns and Spiritual Songs* (19th ed.; 1755), Book I, 68, no. LXXIV (cf. Song of Sol. 4: 12).
[5] A view earlier expressed by Margaret Spufford in *Contrasting Communities: English Villages in the Sixteenth and Seventeenth Centuries* (Cambridge, 1979), 344–50, but since revised: eadem, *Rural Dissenters*, 18–23.
[6] GLT, I, 28, 39, 40, 70.

would have had little to contribute to the structures of local society. Recent research has demonstrated that some revision is necessary regarding both the social composition of these churches[11] and the integration of their members into the local community.[12]

A detailed study of their life and work in three counties indicates that members of Dissenting congregations 'were not confined to any particular rank or sub-group' and that they ranged from 'lowly servants and labourers, to humble craftsmen and husbandmen, small retailers, prosperous wholesalers, yeomen, professionals and gentlemen'.[13] This conclusion is substantiated by others,[14] and much the same can be said about their integration into the social life of their local communities. In many localities, Dissenters did not withdraw from local society but recognized the importance of contributing creatively to its life and wellbeing. Any intentional detachment was expressed in two specific contexts, first (for all) ethical and second (for some) ecclesiastical. First, to be 'separate' was to 'keep oneself unspotted from the world' (James 1: 27) in a distinctly moral sense, avoiding contamination by corrupt values. Additionally, for some Dissenters, notably most Independents and Baptists and all Quakers, 'separation' further referred to withdrawal from the national church. But these interpretations were not intended to encourage social isolation. When George Hughes expounded Genesis to his Plymouth congregation, the account of Joseph's employment in Potiphar's household provided an opportunity to insist that 'Church-separation from the world keeps not from civill society with them of the world'.[15] John Owen also insisted that separation must never be 'in respect of natural affections ... nor yet in offices

---

[7] Ibid. 14, 17, 19, 28, 29, 34, 35, 38, 39.
[8] Ibid. 30, 31, 41, 104, 116.
[9] Ibid. 44, 67, 102.
[10] Ibid. 119.
[11] Bill Stevenson, 'The Social and Economic Status of post-Restoration Dissenters', in Spufford, *Rural Dissenters*, 332–59.
[12] Bill Stevenson, 'The Social Integration of post-Restoration Dissenters', in Spufford, *Rural Dissenters*, 360–87.
[13] W. Stevenson, 'The Economic and Social Status of Protestant Sectaries in Huntingdonshire, Cambridgeshire and Bedfordshire (1650–1725)' (Ph.D. thesis, University of Cambridge, 1990), 343–44, partially quoted in Spufford, *Rural Dissenters*, 19.
[14] K. Wrightson and D. Levine, *Poverty and Piety in an English Village: Terling 1525–1700* (New York, 1979), 168; Kreitzer, *'Seditious Sectaryes'*, 318–19; David Scott, *Quakerism in York, 1650–1720* (Borthwick Paper, 80, York, 1991), 5–6, 24, 28–29; W.J. Sheils, 'Oliver Heywood and his Congregation', in idem and Diana Wood (eds), *Voluntary Religion* (SCH, 23; Cambridge, 1986), 261–77, at 272–77; Brian Watkins, *Taming the Phoenix: Cirencester and the Quakers 1642–1686* (York, 1998), 218. Adrian Davies demonstrates that the relationship between Quakers and the 'world' was not remotely static, with significant changes occurring from the mid 1670s: *The Quakers in English Society 1655–1725* (Oxford, 2000), 210–15.
[15] Hughes, *Genesis*, 515.

of love and civil converse ... much less in not seeking their good and prosperity ... or not communicating good things unto them ... or not living profitably or peaceably with them'.[16] Dissenters wished to make a positive impact on their immediate neighbourhoods, and endeavoured to do so in four areas of life: as contributors, educators, messengers and carers.

Contributors

We begin with Quakers. With their distinctive social conventions, speech and dress, they were the group most susceptible to social isolation, and so they have been frequently portrayed.[17] Initially, Friends were warned about the dangers of moral contamination in society,[18] but within a decade or two earlier restrictions were relaxed. At most periods and in many communities they were positive contributors. Later writings of Quaker leaders encouraged involvement in the needs of the community. William Penn asserted: 'True godliness does not turn men out of the world, but enables them to be better in it, and ... mend it.'[19] Friends were generous not only to impoverished members of their own societies but also to funds for the parish poor, making significant bequests for their future care.[20] They were widely trusted and used as local midwives,[21] for

---

[16] Owen, *Works*, XIII, 68. Owen cites Pauline texts in support of each of these qualities.

[17] Clive Holmes, *Seventeenth-Century Lincolnshire* (History of Lincolnshire, 7; Lincoln, 1980), 44, described Quakers, for example, as a group '[d]ifferentiated from the larger society and seeking to minimize contact with it'.

[18] Quakers were to shun 'vicious and lewd men, of bad and naughty conversations; we should contemne them ... we should withdraw from them and show our dislike of their wayes, and reprove them': [Anon], *The Querers and Quakers cause at the second hearing* (1653), 19; cf. [James Parnell], *The Shield of the Truth* (1655), 38: 'purity and impurity cannot agree together, and it is our desires to keep ourselves unspotted of the world ... and from that we are separated'.

[19] Penn, *No Cross* (1682), ch.V, section 12.

[20] For example, loaves were generously distributed in Witham, Essex, on the day of a Quaker's funeral, and 5% of Friends made bequests to non-Quaker poor: Davies, *Quakers*, 203. Cf. also *Posthuma Christiana, or a Collection of some Papers of William Crouch* (1712), 16. Other Dissenters also made bequests to the poor in their community, cf. Stevenson, 'Social Integration', 375–76.

[21] Elizabeth Hewlings, a widowed Quaker, was a greatly appreciated midwife in the Ampney villages near Cirencester, and particularly valued by several moneyed families. When imprisoned in 1658–59, Lady Dunch went personally to secure her release. Besse records details of a Quaker meeting in 1670 when an irate local justice and two aggressive thugs threw several Friends down the stairs, including this elderly midwife who suffered a dislocated shoulder and died a few days later: *Sufferings*, I, 216–17; cf. Anon., 'At a Meeting of the Midwives in Barbadoes', *JFHS* 37 (1940), 22–24; Phyllis Mack, *Visionary Women: Ecstatic Prophecy in Seventeenth-Century England* (Berkeley and Los Angeles, CA, 1992), 345–46. Friends employed non-Quaker midwives, and welcomed non-Quakers into their homes as apprentices and servants: Stevenson, 'Social Integration', 384–85.

example, despite their refusal to baptize infants. Some Quakers were alehouse keepers,[22] an occupation hardly consistent with detachment from society. Many served as parish 'overseers of the poor', involving not only fund distribution but the less popular responsibilities of collecting the poor rate, making difficult decisions regarding eligibility for benefit, and negotiating when parishioners stubbornly withheld the obligatory payment. In some cases, Friends subsidized these funds to meet essential needs.[23] Quakers sometimes gave a home to an impoverished local inhabitant in return for modest payment from local funds.[24] Parish apprentices were regularly placed with Quakers, some indication of social integration and local confidence.[25] Other Friends became highway surveyors, vestrymen, vermin destroyers and parish constables.[26] A Huntingdonshire draper, John Peacock, was parish constable in 1661–2;[27] in 1670 a Chatteris Friend also served as parish constable, but some of his cattle were distrained when he refused to serve a distress warrant on another Quaker.[28]

Another indication of involvement in local society is that many Dissenters used their writing skills for the benefit of neighbours, such as Roger Lowe, whom we have already met. Lowe had many friends in the Ashton-in-Makerfield district and regularly came to their aid by writing letters, drawing up bonds, preparing accounts, indentures and wills, as well as giving essential literary help to his local parish constable.[29] Edmund Mayle [Maile], a longstanding member of the General Baptist church at Fenstanton, was another

---

[22] See Davies, *Quakers*, 202 n.54, for one Friend in Colchester and three in the village of Terling who were alehouse keepers.

[23] Ibid. 204–205. Henry Haslum, a Quaker overseer of the poor, made payments from his own pocket to sick and lame people in the parish of Southminster, Essex. He also paid widows and nurses for local services, met the cost of clothing the needy, and the expenses involved in the death of poor parishioners. However, for evidence that some Quakers strenuously resisted parish office, see ibid. 215.

[24] Ibid. 206. A Great Coggeshall Quaker agreed with local overseers that a poor woman be kept in his home for two shillings a week, and other Friends provided homes for pauper children.

[25] Ibid. 211.

[26] Ibid. 204. For similar involvement elsewhere in the country, see Watkins, *Taming*, 218, for twenty-four Cirencester Quakers who held public office during this period, including sixteen overseers of the poor, six supervisors of the highways, and a constable.

[27] Huntingdon Monthly Meeting Sufferings Book 1656–1739, quoted in Stevenson, 'Social Integration', 369. Peacock was formally excommunicated in the parish church for not paying church-rate, and parishioners told they should not 'buy or sell' with him. Monthly Meeting records say that following his excommunication Peacock's business 'was better than Ever it had bene formerly'.

[28] Besse, *Sufferings*, I, 94. This Quaker constable, Richard Cope, had goods distrained in the year prior to his appointment as constable, but that did nothing to prevent his appointment to office. For further examples of Friends and other Dissenters who served as parish constables, see Stevenson, 'Social Integration', 369–71.

[29] Stevenson, Social Integration', 376–78.

literate Dissenter ready to help his neighbours, witnessing far more wills than anyone else in the area. Most of these were for people other than Baptists, and he was asked to be scribe for the majority of the wills he witnessed. Many people who witnessed local wills only did so once; for Mayle to have been asked to do so on twenty-one occasions indicates that, like Lowe, he must have been regarded as a reliable person throughout the area.[30]

Several parish 'overseers of the poor' were leading members of the Baptist congregation in Oxford, notably its minister, Richard Tidmarsh, a master tanner, and his colleague, Lawrence King, a master glover. Tidmarsh was also briefly a city 'chamberlain', later a collector of war taxes, and all at a time when some parish officials were planning his excommunication.[31] Other Oxford Baptists such as the horticulturalist author Ralph Austen, the cordwainers Edward Wyans senior and junior,[32] and Captain Abraham Davies[33] served for a time either as overseers of the poor or parish constables. Others such as Thomas Tisdale were trustees of local charities.[34] While serving in such capacities, these men and their wives continued to be harassed by ecclesiastical authorities for not being at church, and by the secular establishment for attending conventicles. In 1669 a Bridgwater Nonconformist stood as a candidate for the office of mayor, and in a disputed election a third of his colleagues voted in his favour, a further indication of the social integration of some Dissenters and their involvement in the life of the local community.[35]

A detailed study of Nonconformists in the Essex village of Terling reveals that between 1662 and 1688, eleven served as local churchwardens, seven as sessions jurymen, six as constables, eight as overseers of the poor, and four as vestrymen. During that period over one third of Terling's churchwardens were convinced Dissenters, for all had been prosecuted at some time or other for their Nonconformity.[36]

Educators

Not more than a hundred of the ejected ministers were men of private means, so

---

[30] Ibid. 378–83. Stevenson also cites Friends who served in a similar capacity for non-Quakers, further examples of local confidence in Dissenters.

[31] Kreitzer, 'Seditious Sectaryes', 313–9, 116, 219, 240, especially 317–19. Tidmarsh and others would have served longer in office but for their conviction that it was unbiblical to take oaths. On several occasions Lawrence King and Ralph Austen also served as tax assessors for Oxford parishes.

[32] Ibid. 61, 66.

[33] Ibid. 130.

[34] Ibid. 88–98.

[35] JHC, IX, 118–19. At least some of the candidate's supporters appear to have shared his convictions, 'being Persons holding Conventicles in their Houses ... refusing to conform or resort to the Service of the Church, or receive the Sacrament, as the Act does enjoin'.

[36] Wrightson and Levine, Poverty and Piety, 168.

a dominant concern for the majority was the urgent necessity of alternative employment. Some received spontaneous support from local Nonconformists[37] but these sums would rarely have been sufficient to maintain a family[38] and their continuance could not be guaranteed. It was necessary to supplement any modest income from a local conventicle or itinerancy. Generous amounts were donated by prosperous Dissenters, sympathetic nobility and gentry,[39] and were distributed to the most needy ministers, but a regular income was essential. Nonconformists were legally prohibited from entering the leading professions of law, medicine and education, but the restrictions were not rigidly enforced. Some, such as Baxter, had become proficient in basic forms of 'Physick' and brought physical as well as spiritual help to their people.[40] Many with the means to do so endeavoured to refine their medical skills at university level, some ministers acquiring exceptional skills.[41] A minority turned to trade, others took up farming, and a significant number, including over a hundred ejected ministers, kept either schools or academies for young adults, some receiving ministerial training there. A.G. Matthews observes:

> some of these callings were by no means exclusive of one another. A country minister, if he were a man of parts and enterprise, might doctor his neighbour's ailments, school some of their children, and keep a small farm into the bargain, provided the local justices were not hostile, and they were not always so.[42]

---

[37] Many conventiclers admired the resolute commitment of ministers and made considerable efforts to support them. When 'they lay in Prison for preaching the Gospel, both they, and their Wives and Children, were like to find more pity and relief, than if they should forsake their People and their Work': Sylvester (ed.), *Reliquiae*, III, §12.

[38] Thomas Tarrey [Terrey] 'was reduc'd so low, that his Wife made Band-strings (much in Fashion in those Days) for a Livelihood': *Continuation*, II, 641; cf. *CSPD* 1663–64, 65, for the poverty of some ejected ministers.

[39] For such benefactions, cf. *CR*, lvi.

[40] Sylvester (ed.), *Reliquiae*, I, I, §137, 17. Baxter held that his 'Practice of Physick' among the people of Kidderminster was a 'very great advantage' to his ministry. People 'that cared not for their Souls did love their Lives, and care for their Bodies', and 'doing it for nothing so obliged them, that they would readily hear me'.

[41] Almost sixty ejected ministers served as physicians, some attaining distinction in their profession. Edward Hulse and Richard Morton became Fellows of the College of Physicians and served royalty.

[42] *CR*, lvi. Cf. *Continuation*, II, 955, for the Cambridge graduate Thomas Wait, known in his Yorkshire parish as 'Burn Roast' because 'he commonly held them so long in his Preaching'. Wait remained in Wetwang 'after his Ejectment, and his Wife taught Scholars, and he assisted her ... two Lessons a Day. He kept three or four Cows, and look'd after them himself in the Winter Season. He also hir'd the tilling of ... Land which he had purchas'd, the Crop of which he us'd himself to thrash out in Winter ... He kept also about forty or fifty Sheep, which he look'd after in Winter, and fodder'd Evening and Morning, commonly in his own Yard ... After he was ejected, he continu'd preaching in his own House, and would have all his Scholars resort thither twice every Lord's Day, and open'd his Doors, and preach'd without Fear, tho' he was sometimes

In addition to the ejected ministers, a considerable number of Nonconformists who were not of their number supported their families by teaching and exercised an equally beneficial influence on the younger generation. Many of these teachers were highly qualified graduates, many with fine academic distinctions.[43]

When they could afford to do so, Nonconformist ministers sent their sons to such schools,[44] and people of more considerable means were glad to commit their children's education to the care of men of principle who were also gifted scholars. Many parents may not have shared the teachers' convictions but trusted them to enrich the lives of their children intellectually, morally and spiritually.[45]

The range of teaching varied enormously. Some had modest opportunities, such as Thomas Taylor (not to be confused with the Independent minister of the same name), whose family of nine children was maintained by his heroic wife 'teaching Children to read' in a school which continued in Salisbury under two bishops. Everything changed under Seth Ward's episcopate when Taylor was condemned for the activity by an ecclesiastical court and excommunicated.[46] Despite legal prohibitions, some ministers obtained employment in established schools,[47] some becoming head teachers, but the majority taught children in

---

disturb'd by the Constable of the Town'.

[43] The Sussex minister Thomas Jackson, for example, was 'Very well skill'd in the Oriental Languages': *Continuation*, II, 821. Samuel Winney, who taught a school in Bristol, was 'held in high repute as a 'Grammarian ... reckon'd to excell most in the West of England': ibid. 754.

[44] Oliver Heywood, Henry Newcome and Christopher Richardson, for example, all sent their sons as boarders to Henry Hickman's school near Bromsgrove: *CR, s.n.* 'Henry Hickman'; Heywood, *Autobiography* (ed. Turner), I, 204. Cf. ibid. 296, 'where he [Eliezer] and his brother are trained up with Mr. Hickman in university-learning'.

[45] Edmund Thorpe remained in the parish from which he had been ejected, and taught. 'Many Gentlemen in Kent and Sussex sent their Children to him, and even three Conforming Ministers trusted him with the Education of their Sons'; Titus Oates was among his more notorious pupils: *Account*, 679. John Seaton 'taught School at Islip [Northants], where several of the Neighbouring Gentlemen committed their Children to his Care and Instruction': *Continuation*, II, 646. Another Northamptonshire minister, Thomas Tarrey, had 'a flourishing School, and many Gentlemen sending their Sons to him for Instruction, he grew rich': ibid. 641.

[46] *Continuation*, II, 866. The ejected Presbyterian Thomas Palke was another minister who was 'Harras'd by the Spiritual-Court for teaching School and forc'd to desist ... Excommunicated for his Nonconformity, and dy'd under it': *Account*, 256.

[47] For example, Samuel Shaw, Master at Ashby-de-la-Zouch Grammar School: ibid. 426–36; Edward Sherman, Master of Dedham School, Essex: ibid. 645–46; Thomas Singleton, Master of Reading School: Charles Coates, *The History and Antiquities of Reading* (1802), 341–42; William Angel, Master of Houndsditch Grammar School, Middlesex: *Continuation*, II, 815; Thomas Powell (?1656–1716): Gordon, *Freedom after Ejection*, 335.

their own homes, often boarding their pupils.[48] Some had ten,[49] twenty or thirty scholars,[50] while Thomas Singleton, onetime master at Eton, ran a school at Clerkenwell for 300 boys.[51]

Life was often difficult for these teachers. There were many like the Leicestershire minister John Bennet, who 'taught some Boys in his House, and preach'd up and down occasionally in the darkest Times, but met with many Troubles several Ways'.[52] Whereas some authorities turned a blind eye to the necessary licence regulations demanding religious conformity,[53] in other localities they were rigorously pursued and schools closed. Richard Woolley was excommunicated in 1673 for 'teaching school without a licence, and not teaching scholars the Church Catechism, as ordered by the bishop'.[54] A Middlesex minister, Philip Taverner, 'was sentenc'd to Newgate-Gaol, for Teaching a few Children at Brainford, but paying his Fine, prevented it'.[55]

The accolade for the most altruistic and enterprising Nonconformist teaching must surely be awarded to those imprisoned Somerset Quakers who in 1662 were allowed to open a free school in Ilchester. Crowded prison conditions meant that some were accommodated in The Friary, a 'great house' nearby, and the less restricted conditions encouraged three well educated Quaker prisoners to provide daily education for local children. Within a month they were teaching seventy boys, all non-Quakers, to read, write and master basic

---

[48] The Oxford graduate Nathaniel Webb (Presbyterian), ejected from Yatesbury, 'liv'd in his own House, kept a School, and had Boarders. He sometimes preached at Caln[e] and other Places as Opportunity offer'd': *Continuation*, II, 875. For further examples of these small 'boarding schools', see *Account*, 696 (Richard Turner); *Continuation*, II, 821 (Thomas Jackson).

[49] Thomas Gardiner had a school at Wokingham 'where he boarded eight or nine Youths at a Time, and taught them Grammar-Learning ... He was a great Grammarian, and Master in Critical and all School-Learning; and a very excellent Preacher and Liver'. Three other ejected ministers shared his home together with the brother of one of them: *Continuation*, I, 142.

[50] The ejected ministers John Goldwire and his son (also John) had a school in Hampshire with about 35 pupils: *CR, s.n.* 'John Goldwire'.

[51] In his later years, when Singleton was in difficult financial circumstances, he was greatly helped by one of his former pupils, Richard Mead, who became a leading physician. Mead was the son of a leading Independent minister, Matthew Mead of Stepney: Coates, *History of Reading*, 341–42.

[52] *Account*, 420.

[53] Some Nonconformist teachers were helped locally by having a sympathetic conforming minister. William Westmacot, an Independent, taught at Pershore but the vicar was in trouble with the ecclesiastical authorities for allowing him to do so: *CR, s.n.* 'William Westmacot', citing the Worcester Diocese Act Book for 3 March 1669/70.

[54] Ibid.

[55] Sylvester (ed.), *Reliquiae*, III, §83. William Wilson had a school at Billingshurst, Sussex, where he had been vicar, but his 'two greatest Enemies were a neighbouring Justice and the Parson that succeeded him' and he was forced to close it: *Continuation*, II, 823–27.

arithmetic, and continued their work until compelled to stop at the insistence of a local clergyman.[56] Local authorities naturally feared indoctrination, especially when they heard of men like Thomas Walton of Bethnal Green who 'carryes his Schollars to Conventicles';[57] the historian Calamy had been one of his pupils.[58]

With freedom to develop a syllabus that met contemporary needs, these men also served as pioneers, publishing important works on educational methods, one example being the Independent minister Hezekiah Woodward, whose 'significance as an educationalist has not been sufficiently recognised'.[59] Other Nonconformist teachers ventured into innovative projects such as providing girls with educational opportunities.[60] A certain 'Mrs Davies yt teaches younge women'[61] in Oxford was mentioned in a 1670 Privy Council letter, 'being one in ye former Conventicles'. The Privy Council ordered the University Vice-Chancellor 'to pull down her Schoole', forbidding her to teach until she had a licence from the bishop which, of course, could only be obtained if she abandoned her Nonconformity.[62] The command to destroy her premises suggests that the authorities were as disturbed about her unacceptable teaching programme as her deviant church loyalties.[63]

---

[56] The full account in manuscript, 'originally belonging to Bristol and Somerset Quarterly Meeting', written by local Friends, and now deposited at the Somerset County Record Office, Taunton, is meticulously transcribed in Anon., 'A School in Ilchester Jail, 1662', *JFHS* 8 (1911), 16–18.

[57] *CR, s.n.* 'Thomas Walton'.

[58] Calamy, *Life*, I, 130.

[59] *ODNB, s.n.* 'Woodward, Hezekiah'.

[60] Girls were certainly welcome at some Quaker schools in the period, e.g. the school Fox established in 1668 at Waltham Abbey where Margaret Rous (granddaughter of Margaret Fox) was a pupil in 1680: Fox, *Journal* (Bicentenary ed.), II, 119; cf. ibid. 422; Braithwaite, *Second Period*, 526; A.N. Brayshaw, *The Personality of George Fox* (1933), 113–14.

[61] Larry Kreitzer thinks it likely that she was the wife of Captain Abraham Davies, 'identified as a ringleader of Dissent' in an earlier Privy Council letter, having been accused by the parish church authorities in 1663 of non-attendance at St Aldate's. He was ordered 'to receive the holy Sacram[en]t from the hands of his Minister upon or before Whitsunday next', and later charged with not having an infant baptized. Davies claimed that the child had been baptized 'by a Minister Episcopally ordained', without revealing the identity of the minister. When ordered to have his child rebaptized in the presence of the St Aldate's congregation, Davies produced an authentic baptismal certificate, revealing the officiating minister's identity, but he was again ordered to attend his parish church regularly: '*Seditious Sectaryes*', 129–30.

[62] For the education of women in the Restoration period, see Antonia Fraser, *The Weaker Vessel: Women's Lot in the Seventeenth Century* (1985), 132–57; Sara Mendelson and Patricia Crawford, *Women in Early Modern England 1550–1720* (Oxford, 1998), 321–27.

[63] A bishop's licence was necessary in order to teach. Elizabeth Loveman was presented to the ecclesiastical authorities in 1665, 'not licensed and Excommunicate': GLT II, 1168.

When the English universities were closed to Dissenters, a number of their ministers became concerned about the church's leadership in the next generation. Some Presbyterian and Independent ministers with evident teaching gifts, such as Philip Henry, John Angier and John Flavel, opened their homes to promising young men as boarders, not simply to receive a biblical and theological education but also to gain practical experience of a minister's life and work.[64]

Other Dissenting ministers taught young adults in newly formed academies which not only provided specialist theological training for prospective ministers but also a general education of a high standard for men who would one day enter the professions or work in a family business. Academy tutors were equally subject to harassment, and several were compelled to change their location on more than one occasion. The ejected minister Richard Frankland was a gifted Cambridge graduate whose academy, 'Christ's College', initially located at Rathmell (near Settle in Yorkshire), was compelled to move four times. Frankland twice suffered excommunication. His teaching ministry was highly influential and during the academy's thirty-year life its total number of students exceeded three hundred,[65] the majority becoming Nonconformist ministers, mainly in the North of England. Other Nonconformist academies were established,[66] serving a constituency not remotely confined to Dissenters, and making a rich contribution to further education in England.[67]

Nonconformist education was also promoted by the published work of several ministers who recognized the importance of providing basic teaching materials for children.[68] Henry Jessey,[69] Abraham Cheare,[70] John Bunyan and

---

[64] When the young Heywood first discerned a call to the ministry, he planned 'to go live a while with some godly ancient minister in the country, and make approaches to that weighty calling by degrees'; a 'way was made' for him to live 'in Mr. Angiers house': Heywood, *Autobiography* (ed. Turner), I, 162–63. At Dartmouth, Flavel trained 'four young men for the ministry, one of whom he maintained entirely at his own expense': *Works*, I, 8. The use of the home for the residential training of ministers had good Puritan precedent, e.g. William Ames in Holland: Beeke, *Puritan Reformed Spirituality*, 128.

[65] See F.Nicholson and E. Axon, *The Older Nonconformity in Kendal* (Kendal, 1913), 113–98, 532–634 for Frankland's ministry and biographical details of his pupils; also Heywood, *Autobiography* (ed. Turner), II, 9–16, for another list of 'Mr. Frankland's pupils'; and ibid., IV, 306–21, for 'Notes respecting Mr. Frankland's pupils, with details of family, ordination, pastorates, and death of the minister'.

[66] See 'Early Nonconformist Academies', *TCHS* 3 (1907–1908), 272–90, for academies formed by ejected ministers Theophilus Gale, Charles Morton, Ralph Button, Thomas Doolittle and Edward Veal.

[67] For Nonconformist academies, see Isabel Rivers and David L. Wykes, eds, *A History of the Dissenting Academies in the British Isles, 1660–1860* (Cambridge, forthcoming) and its projected databases of archival sources, academies, tutors and students.

[68] These writers recognized with Benjamin Keach that one of 'the Advantages of early Age' was that 'religion now is most likely to make the deepest Impression … A plant set

Benjamin Keach all wrote popular books for children. Bunyan's *A Book for Boys and Girls* contained introductory alphabets, specific help regarding vowels and consonants, spelling guides, and teaching about Arabic and roman numerals, followed by seventy-four poems, part of this country's 'emblem' literature.[71] Not remotely uniform in quality, the poems have been described as 'lively, direct, effective and multileveled, but never labored or tediously lengthy',[72] expressing 'his gentleness' and his 'excited observation' of the natural world.[73] Though primarily for children, its author believed that readers of all ages, even 'Boys with Beards, and Girls that be Big as old women, wanting Gravity',[74] could benefit from his unsophisticated poetic reflections.[75]

Keach's first publication was a book for children.[76] It cost him a fortnight in prison and two hours in the pillory at Aylesbury and Winslow. What was his 'seditious and venomous' offence? Two deeply held convictions: that baptism was for believers rather than infants, and that an unordained ministry might be blessed by God. Fifteen hundred copies had been printed, but it was ordered that every copy be recalled and burnt, a task accomplished with such severity that not a single copy remains, and the only clues to its 'factious, Schismatical, heretical matter' are the quotations found in his accusation.[77] On moving to London, Keach rewrote from memory the material in his first book, though with modifications due to his new allegiance to Calvinist theology. He wrote further books for young readers, *The Child's Delight*, a reading primer, and his fuller, best-selling, *Instructions for Children*.[78] His friend Hanserd Knollys claimed that, having taught children throughout his life, he could commend the latter wholeheartedly to teachers and parents alike.[79] Dissenters believed that the writing and publication of such literature made an invaluable contribution to the spiritual welfare of countless children.

---

but the last Year, is sooner plucked up than an old Tree': *Gospel Mysteries Unveil'd*, Book II, 225 (Sermon XXXIX, 'The Householder').

[69] Henry Jessey, *A Looking Glass for Children* (1672).

[70] For Cheare's poems, see ibid. 21–96. For his evangelistic concern for children, see his *Words in Season*, 221–30.

[71] Rosemary Freeman, *English Emblem Books* (1948), 204–28. Emblem books were a popular teaching aid in the seventeenth century. Images and emblems were accompanied by explanatory text on both religious and non-religious themes.

[72] Kathleen M. Swaim, *Pilgrim's Progress, Puritan Progress: Discourses and Contexts* (Urbana, IL, 1993), 243.

[73] Graham Midgley, in Bunyan, *MW*, VI, lvii.

[74] Bunyan, *MW*, VI, 190.

[75] Greaves, *Glimpses*, 538–48.

[76] [Keach], *Child's Instructor*.

[77] Walker, *Keach*, 63–72, 147; cf. *CSPD* 1663–1664, 595.

[78] Walker, *Keach*, 151–60.

[79] Benjamin Keach, *Instructions for Children* (1704), Preface.

Messengers

Most Dissenters were eager to share their message among people with no clear faith. Heywood said that his 'first undertaking' in ministry was 'to bring soules home to god by conversion'.[80] Baxter could 'truly say that a fervent desire of winning souls to God' was his main 'motive'.[81] Newcome wrote of John Machin's 'large desire after soules', not only for the salvation of 'his friends and kindred, but of all his neighbours'.[82] Paying tribute to the life and work of Joseph Alleine, Baxter said that the secret of his relatively short but effective ministry in Taunton was 'his Zeal and Thirst for the peoples Conversion'. If a preacher 'long not for mens Conversion, he is seldom the means of Converting many'. Baxter grieved that in 1662 gifted men with such genuine evangelistic zeal had 'been silenc't in England', when their 'holy Skill and Conscience, Fidelity and Zeal' might have changed the direction of many lives.[83]

Many preachers maintained that rather than inhibit evangelism, persecution might even serve to promote it.[84] Writing from prison, Collins said that 'as a Tree is known by its Fruit, so is a Christian by a Patient wearing of Christs Cross'; this had often 'Convinced an Adversary, when a bare Profession will not'.[85] As persecution intensified and an increasing number of Quakers were imprisoned, Oliver Sansom felt compelled to take his 'Part and Lot with the Sufferers ... Thus were the Bonds and Sufferings of Faithful Friends made a Means to confirm and embolden me to Profess the Truth.'[86] These repressed people shared the good news with their contemporaries by preaching, testimony, books and correspondence.

Preaching

Public proclamation of the Christian message continued to be their most effective means of evangelism. Despite prohibitive legislation, meetings were

---

[80] Heywood, *Autobiography* (ed. Turner), I, 205.

[81] Baxter, *Plain Scripture Proof*, b3, 'The true history ...'; cf. Sylvester (ed.), *Reliquiae*, I, §213, 23: 'There being no Employment in the World so desirable in my Eye, as to labour for the winning of such miserable Souls: which maketh me greatly honour Mr. John Eliot, the Apostle of the Indians in New England, and whoever else have laboured in such work'. John Gifford, Bunyan's pastor, 'was made through grace a father to some through the Gospell ... sister Cooper ... was converted by the first sermon he preached in publicke': *Bedford Minutes* (ed. Tibbutt), 16.

[82] [Newcome], *Life of Machin*, 15.

[83] [Alleine], *Life*, 8–9, 15–16.

[84] Polhill, *Armatura Dei*, 136: 'Pious sufferers do propagate and multiply the Church ... The more the Children of Israel were afflicted in Egypt, the more they multiplied and grew [Exod. 1: 11]. As the ground that is most harrowed, is most fruitful'.

[85] Collins, *Voice*; cf. another imprisoned minister, Nathanael Vincent, *Covert*, 35, who hoped that some, witnessing Dissenters' 'constancy ... may be brought to make tryal of your Lord, and so to the liking and loving of him'.

[86] Sansom, *Remarkable Passages*, 11.

still held, for much depended on the attitudes of local magistrates, constables and parish clergy, and the activities of local informers. At times local opposition may have been minimal, and some authorities consistently turned a 'blind eye' to the Nonconformity of their neighbours.[87] In such areas, Dissenters met without serious disturbance, whilst in other parts of the country meetings had to be in secret. Wherever the location, conventicles continued to be held and many of their preachers were gifted evangelists.[88] Charles Doe described Bunyan as 'a second Paul', knowing large numbers of people converted under his ministry.[89]

A Bedfordshire congregation well known to Bunyan encouraged one of their number in his ministry of preaching, despite contemporary prohibitions.[90] Its records preserve an unsophisticated account of the importance assigned to preaching by a Dissenting congregation, the preacher concerned having suffered for his faith. Itemizing their convictions, they were persuaded that the brother concerned was uniquely equipped, God having 'competently fitted him for that work'. In view of the 1662 ejectment, there was evident need of such men, 'many off the Lord's servants being thrust out of his vineyard'. There were parishes where, sadly, such men had been replaced by 'idoll shepherds' and, in consequence, 'many poor soules were in great danger of miscar[ry]ing for lack of vision'. Here was a meaningful contribution this little church could make to the needs of other congregations in the locality, and they thought it their 'duty out of our poverty to afford them the best assistance' they could. Other church leaders had requested this form of help, and their 'earnest and importunate calls ... did not a little prevaile' with them. This preacher's ministry had already brought enrichment to local people and 'God's eminent owning off him whilst he exercised his guift more privately' should not 'be overlookt nor sleighted'. He was offering more than well-chosen words, for his message had been validated at cost by 'the sufferings which he had endured for Christ's sake and the gospell's and his ready willingness to encounter all difficultyes on Christ's behalf' at a time 'when very many once eminent have given back for fear off danger'. In the light of these factors, it was their duty to

---

[87] Philip Henry maintained the regular public worship he had commenced in 1672 'which had continued about three years'. Following the withdrawal of licences, 'there was such a general connivance of authority, that the meetings grew again as full as ever ... the neighbouring magistrates at Flintshire being very civil': *Life*, 135.

[88] See Eamon Duffy, 'The Long Reformation: Catholicism, Protestantism and the Multitude', in Nicholas Tyacke (ed.), *England's Long Reformation, 1500–1700* (1998), 33–70, at 52–6, for the suggestion that the effect of restrictive legislation in many parishes was to prioritize church attendance and liturgical conformity at the expense of imaginative evangelism, which became a Nonconformist enterprise.

[89] C[harles]. D[oe]., 'The Struggler', [unpaginated], at the close of *The Works of That Eminent Servant of Christ Mr. John Bunyan ... containing Ten of his Excellent Manuscripts ... never before printed* (ed. Charles Doe, 3 vols; 1692), also in Bunyan, *MW*, XII, 453–60.

[90] Tibbutt (ed.), *Nonconformist Church Books*, 20–21.

give their 'utmost to the encouraging and strengthening off him in soe good a work'.[91]

Recognizing the primacy of preaching in evangelism, Bury St Edmunds Independents frequently placed on record the biblical texts expounded when one of their number had made a significant commitment. Benjamin Carter, a young man in his early twenties, regularly walked ten miles from Rattlesden, and was 'first awakened with ye sermon upon 2 Cor. 2: 14-15, and encouraged to pray by Job. 33: 26 and to take hold upon C[hris]t and [appropriate] God's Strength by some Sermons upon Isa. 27: 4-5'. When a Bury grocer requested church membership, their congregation was told that 'ye Scripture in Job. 15: 15-16 preacht' was 'yt w[hi]ch seemed to be the means of his Co[n]version'. A widow 'was converted' in her early sixties 'by yt Sermon upon Isa. 27: 4-5 which work was carried on by her [continuing] attendance on ye Ministry' of the church. Sometimes, it was through a preacher's exposition of Scripture's 'uncomfortable words' that a hearer was brought to faith. Mary Burland, 'ye Daughter of strangers to God's Cov[enan]t', lived in the village of Barrow but made the six-mile journey to the same church and, 'coming under the ministry' of the Matthean warning about 'speaking a word ... against the Holy Ghost', began the quest for personal faith. This initial work of grace 'was gradually carried on' until she became a convinced believer.[92]

Such people walked considerable distances in variable weather to listen to these expositors. It speaks well for their tenacity that they did so, but some credit must also go to the preachers, who had prayed that their message might be conveyed with firm conviction and evident love. Philip Henry took advantage of the relatively brief period of liberty in 1672–3 to preach throughout Shropshire, Cheshire and Denbighshire, 'laying out himself exceedingly for the good of souls'. Of 'that time it was said, that this and that man was born again, then and there', and 'savingly brought home to Jesus Christ'.[93]

Baxter knew of eloquent preachers of fine intellectual stature, with commendable material and rich vocabularies, whose sermons 'did but play with holy things'. Their ministry contrasted sharply with that of 'the plain and pressing, downright Preacher', speaking 'with life, and light, and weight',[94]

---

[91] Keysoe, Brook End, Church Book [no longer extant], 2 May 1664, from the transcript by Joseph Rix in DWL, repr. in Tibbutt (ed.), *Nonconformist Church Books*, 20–21.
[92] Bury St Edmunds Congregational Church Book, fols 55, 54, 55–56, 54.
[93] Henry, *Life*, 131. Preaching Hercules Collins's funeral sermon in Wapping church, John Piggott said it could be said of 'this Man and that Woman, they were born here'. His pulpit ministry was 'a constant Flame', and 'no man could preach with more affectionate Regard for the Salvation of souls': 'Funeral Sermon for Hercules Collins' [1702], in John Piggott, *Eleven Sermons preached upon special occasions* (1714), 236.
[94] Baxter, *A Treatise of Conversion* (1657), a3, 'To the Reader'. Hanmer's ejected minister, Richard Steele, complained that too many preachers filled their sermons with 'sapless niceties, impertinent quotations, cholerick reflections, or with that unquiet

never merely to present an argument but to reach the soul. Francis Holcroft, Fellow of Clare College, Cambridge, was such a man, and 'the lord o[w]ned him much in [the] co[n]verchon of souls'. Richard Conder senior's family was transformed by his preaching, and his son loved to tell how Holcroft's itinerant ministry began. With execrable spelling, Conder junior recorded the story in his 'shoort ... account of the Relashion of God's servant mist[er] Holldcroft'. On Sunday mornings, from his window over the college gate, the devout Holcroft had often seen a horse waiting for a 'druncken scoller', the appointed preacher for the village of Littlington, near Royston. Most Sundays, the horse stood unwanted. The appointed preacher's hangover meant that he did not stir from his bed, and 'no soply' was sent to the village congregation. One Sunday, 'hafing a sence of the woorth of preshous solls', Holcroft mounted the horse, 'not knoing at all the way'. But the horse knew and took him 'into the contri about nine or ten miles' from Cambridge to a congregation waiting hopefully in the village church. For some time, Holcroft had been praying that God would 'lead him into som[e] dark place', possibly overseas, 'to preach the gospell', but that Sunday he realized that, denied a resident godly minister, Littlington and its surrounding villages were equally in the 'darck', urgently needing faithful preachers. Following ejectment from his college fellowship, Holcroft joined like-minded colleagues in exercising an itinerant ministry, establishing village congregations that became an integral part of 'the Church of Christ in Cambridgeshire'.[95]

Although these preachers had a large following of appreciative hearers, they were far from being pulpit prima donnas intent on gratifying an admiring audience. Men such as Francis Holcroft, John Bunyan, Henry Maurice, William Mitchell and Oliver Heywood exercised their itinerancy with a compassionate concern for individual people in their congregations.[96]

---

controversial Divinity (especially about points less momentous) which hardly ever produce any effect, save exasperation': *The Husbandman's Calling, being the substance of twelve sermons to a country congregation* (1670), Ep. Ded.

[95] For the members of this church in 1675, and their village locations, see Bodl, MS Rawlinson D.1480, 'Church of Jesus Christ in Cambridgeshire', fols 123r–126v. See Tibbutt, 'Holcroft', for a transcript of Richard Conder's 'Account' from pages loosely inserted in the First Church Book of the Great Gransden [Strict] Baptist Church [Hunts], originally the associate of the Croydon-cum-Clopton [Cambs] Independent Church; cf. also Margaret Spufford, 'A Note on the Conder Family', *TCHS* 21 (1971–2), 77–79.

[96] The pastoral importance of conversations with individual worshippers featured prominently in a paper by John Howe written towards the close of the Protectorate. Howe thought it 'might prove a great furtherance to the success of the gospel, if they who are appointed to the work of public preaching, did also ... use other more private endeavours with their hearers ... instructing them in the things of God they are ignorant of; pressing upon them what they know; inquiring into the state of their souls; and applying themselves to them accordingly'. By this means, 'many inattentive hearers (who regard not often what is spoken to them from the pulpit ...) would yet be obliged' to give attention to the message. Ministers should therefore give some time each week

Young Mary Churchman was an unlikely candidate for an invitation to a conventicle. In young life, she had repeatedly tormented a Dissenter, urging her angry dog to attack the woman as she walked to her Sunday meeting. But, in her late teens, Mary became seriously unwell and, because the same neighbour had been especially kind to her, she responded to an invitation to hear 'that great man of God Mr. Holcroft' for herself. His sermon touched on eternal issues and, overwhelmed by what she had heard, she 'looked upon Christ' as her 'terrible judge and enemy. This trouble I vented in floods of tears, and many wishes that ... I had never came there ... I seemed now to like their persons worse than ever'. But Holcroft had noticed her in the meeting; 'the minister came to me, and asked where I lived? Who was I? and whether I knew any thing of the Lord Jesus'. He was not content simply to preach to this awe-struck young woman attending her first conventicle, but made personal contact at the close of the meeting. It marked the beginning of her devoted Christian life. The preacher cared, and his compassionate concern spoke as effectively as his memorable sermon.[97]

Moreover, these preachers grasped opportunities to preach outside conventicles. The Bristol ministers Andrew Gifford, George Fownes, John Weeks and John Thompson all preached to the colliers at Kingswood,[98] and men of this calibre could not be silenced, even by imprisonment. The Somerset ejected minister John Norman preached to outsiders through his Ilchester prison window,[99] as did George Fox at Lancaster.[100] When Thomas Palmer at Nottingham did so, some of his hearers were beaten and imprisoned for listening to him.[101] Thomas Ewins, Francis Bampfield, John Bunyan and John Quick[102] were among those who preached regularly in their gaols,[103] and unordained church members were encouraged to devote some time to prison

---

'for visiting of families ... to instruct, warn, exhort, or comfort them, as the case shall require': letter of John Howe among the Baxter MSS, partly reproduced in Rogers, *Howe* (1863), 67–68.

[97] James, *Abstract*, 68–69.

[98] *Broadmead Records* (ed. Hayden), 70.

[99] Norman (ejected from Bridgwater) was imprisoned for eighteen months at Ilchester; his sermons were reproduced in John Norman, *Christ Confessed: written by a Preacher of the Gospel, and now a Prisoner* (1665). For extracts, see Charles Stanford, *Joseph Alleine: His Companions and Times* [1861], 255–70.

[100] Fox, *Journal* (ed. Smith), 286.

[101] Hutchinson, *Colonel Hutchinson* (ed. Keeble), 296. Palmer, an Independent minister, preached from 'a grated window ... almost even with the ground'. Far from deterring the outdoor congregation, 'a thousand came in armed to the town, and marched to the prison window to hear the prisoner preach'. Palmer lived only a few months after this.

[102] Bishop Ward of Exeter took legal action against Quick for prison preaching but he was acquitted: *Continuation*, I, 332.

[103] '[It was] desired that brother Burton would spend one hour in a weeke, in exhorting [pris]oners, in the County Goale, and he consented to enter upon that work': *Bedford Minutes* (ed. Tibbutt), 23.

evangelism.

Matthew Mead urged his colleagues to consider new patterns of ministry, less public but possibly more rewarding. Those who had not moved far from their former parishes could 'go to their Houses, and ... converse with them ... it may be more effectual than all your former labours were'. If the Five Mile Act had compelled them to change location and 'tis amon[g]st Strangers you are cast, yet acquaint your selves with them'. They too needed to hear the message.

> Do you think that's only whilst you stand on a high place in the midst of an Assembly? Did not Christ preach the Gospel to a Woman alone, and Philip to the Eunuch? In some respects ... personal discourse hath much advantage of publick Preaching ... What moved you to Preach to your people before? ... was it a desire to save the Souls of your people ... Why then do not you continue it?[104]

Evangelistic enterprise, either public or personal, was not uniformly successful. Settled ministries, itinerancy and personal work each had their discouragements. Heywood suffered a full year's incarceration in York Castle, but maintained that it was infinitely preferable to the pain of unsuccessful evangelism. Preaching a few months after his release, he said:

> ... it is a great burden to labour for souls when they are not converted. You think it hard, when for preaching God's Word we are imprisoned with thieves and rogues ... but we have greater trials than these when we labour to do good to souls and see no good effects.[105]

In 1687 Thomas Jolly made strenuous efforts to go into the 'blind corners' of unevangelized Lancashire during the 'present liberty', but local people were not always there to hear him. On busy Sundays, he was happy enough to 'travell 4 miles betwixt the exercises upon the Lord's day' but, without hearers, 'I was sometimes more left to myself to humble and mortify me'.[106]

Testimony

The Dissenters' message was communicated by grateful hearers as well as gifted ministers. 'Man is a communicative Creature', said Baxter, and people love to talk about that which matters most to them.[107] The personal experience shared by a London Dissenter with William Davenport marked the beginning of

---

[104] M[atthew]. M[ead]., *Solomon's Prescription for the Removal of the Pestilence* (1665), 74–75.

[105] Richard Slate (ed.), *Select Nonconformists' Remains* (1814), 156 (sermon preached on 29 April 1686). Heywood was imprisoned from 26 January to 19 December 1685.

[106] Jolly, *Note Book* (ed. Fishwick), 82–83.

[107] Baxter, *Reasons*, A3, 'To the Christian Reader'; cf. Baxter, *Calendar* (ed. Nuttall and Keeble), II, 53 (Letter 734): 'Quod cogitamus, loquimur: That which is most and deepest in my thoughts, is aptest to break forth to others'.

his journey to faith: 'I began to see something of an Excellency' in Christ 'which I never saw before'.[108] It was exactly as Thomas Goodwin had said: 'That God pardon'd such a man in such a Condition, is often brought home unto another Man in the same Condition ... that so he may do to me.'[109] One did not have to be ordained to be the herald of good news. During Holcroft's imprisonment, members in his Cambridgeshire church filled the gap, speaking at conventicles 'simply by way of ex[h]ortation', and people were converted.[110]

When public meetings were forbidden, a Dissenter's home could still be used to gather a few friends together. Sansom's neighbours told him that 'if ever there should be a meeting' at his Boxworth home at which an itinerant Quaker evangelist was to speak, 'if they had notice of it they would come to it'. Not long after, a 'Ministring Friend' arrived in the village and such a meeting took place. Angered by this intrusion into parochial life, the local clergyman 'sent immediately for the Tythingman ... to come away forthwith, and break up the meeting. But neither he, nor the Constable was at home', wrote Sansom, 'for they were both of them at my House, peaceably assembled with many others in the Meeting'. While the parish minister was attempting to despatch local officials to break up an innocent meeting, he was at home with his 'Card-Players'.[111] The entertaining narrative illustrates a Berkshire Quaker's evangelistic zeal, and further demonstrates that in many communities Nonconformists were far from being ostracized by local society.

The 'three or four poor women' Bunyan met in Bedford were ordinary members of John Gifford's congregation, but played a major part in the gradual, if harrowing, process of Bunyan's conversion,[112] and in his minister's home he was able to 'confer with others about the dealings of God with the Soul', and move one step further on his journey of faith.[113] These people realized that sharing the Christian message was every member's privileged

---

[108] Charles Doe, *A Collection of Experience of the Work of Grace* ([1700]), 4.
[109] Thomas Goodwin, *Works* (5 vols; 1681–1704), V, xii.
[110] Tibbutt, 'Holcroft', 299: 'the meetings were ceept up in the absence of God's servants, and the worck of God went forward in the confershon of soolls and the church was edefied'.
[111] Sansom, *Remarkable Passages*, 39–40.
[112] Bunyan, *GA*, §§36–41, 45–46, 77. Although Bunyan knew of sudden, dramatic conversions (and portrayed such, e.g. *Pilgrim's Progress*, 38) he was also aware that in most lives it was a more gradual process. 'For the Spirit, as I may so say, sitteth and broodeth upon the Powers of the Soul, as the Hen doth on cold Eggs, till they wax warm and receive life. The Spirit then warmeth us ... (for so 'tis before Conversion) ... and this is the beginning of the work of the Spirit by which the Soul is made capable of understanding what God and himself is': *The Water of Life ... The Richness and Glory of the Grace and Spirit of the Gospel* (1688), in *MW*, VII, 204.
[113] Topics discussed in Gifford's home may be reflected in the conversations between Christian and Hopeful in *Pilgrim's Progress*, 136–48. Note especially the searching questions: 'Did you think ... ask ... And what did you do then ... And how was he revealed to you?'

responsibility. 'O let's think before their Passing-bell do startle us, whether we have done our utmost for the saving of the man or woman that is now sailing for Eternity.'[114]

Their conduct must be as eloquent as their verbal confession, 'examples which ... beckon to the yet unconverted', for it is by such 'Lights upon a Hill' that the godless will discern that 'there is a People otherwise-minded'.[115] Every departing Christian should bequeath the legacy of an attractive testimony, and, 'earnestly desire to go out of the world as a Perfume, and not as a Snuff'.[116] Consistent behaviour was the persuasive verification of verbal confession.

Literature

'Sermons preached ... pass away with many like wind ... soon ... buried in the grave of Oblivion!' But 'sermons printed' live when the preachers 'are dead, and become an image of eternity'.[117] 'Silenced ministers' acknowledged the importance and vitality of the printed word. When 'I might not speak by Voice to any single Congregation, he enabled me to speak by Writings to many', wrote Baxter.[118] He was one among many to realize and utilize the power of the book.

Many of them, or their parents, had been brought to faith by reading. Baxter was indebted to a copy of 'Bunny's *Resolution*' that a 'poor Day-Labourer' had passed on to his father, and 'it pleased God' to use the badly torn book 'to awaken' his soul.[119] Works by leading Puritans Sibbes and Perkins became additional heralds of grace.[120] Bunyan's pastor, John Gifford, once a heavy drinker and compulsive gambler, was converted while 'looking into one of Mr. Bolton's bookes'.[121] The two books which Bunyan's first wife brought as the only dowry to their marriage spoke powerfully to him,[122] a classic commentary

---

[114] Steele, *Husbandman's Calling*, Ep. Ded.
[115] Bunyan, *Christian Behaviour*, in *MW*, III, 15–16.
[116] Powell, *Bird*, 73.
[117] Swinnock, *Calling*, I, 42.
[118] Baxter, *Dying Thoughts*, 225.
[119] In 1584 Edward Bunny (1540–1618) published this distinctly Protestant version of *A Book of Resolution*, written initially for English Catholics by the Jesuit missionary Robert Persons [Parsons]. Bunny hoped that by this unorthodox means he might reach Catholic readers but his work became highly popular among Protestants, being frequently reprinted during the seventeenth century.
[120] Sylvester (ed.), *Reliquiae*, I, i, §3.
[121] *Bedford Minutes* (ed. Tibbutt), 15–16; cf. *Mr. [Robert] Boltons last and learned worke of the foure last things* (1633). Gifford was in a fiercely angry mood that day, having lost £15, 'with many desperate thoughtes against God, but 'something therein tooke hold upon him and brought him into a great sense of sin'.
[122] Bunyan, *GA*, §15–16; Arthur Dent, *The Plaine Man's Pathway to Heaven* (1605); Lewis Bayly, *The Practice of Piety: directing a Christian how to walk that he may please God* (1648).

on Galatians made an unforgettable impact, and his own books were used to bring life and light to thousands. A London apprentice said that when 'it pleased God to cast' one of Bunyan's books into his hands, just one of its penetrating sayings turned his mind to eternal issues.[123]

Knowing the popularity and wide circulation of chap-books,[124] other Nonconformist writers besides Bunyan[125] produced evangelistic literature to meet the spiritual need of people unlikely to make their way to a conventicle. Two sermons preached by John Howe in a Suffolk house were published as an evangelistic booklet with the hope that it would 'contribute to the saving of men's souls'.[126] First issued three years after its author's death, Joseph Alleine's *Alarm to the Unconverted* was deeply serious but immensely popular. Edmund Calamy claimed that 20,000 copies were sold under the title *Call* or *Alarm*, and a later edition entitled *A Sure Guide to Heaven* sold a further 50,000 copies, 30,000 at one impression.[127] Matthew Mead's *The Almost Christian Discovered* also enjoyed wide circulation and was greatly used, especially among those with a merely nominal Christian allegiance.[128] Other titles were intended to reach the half-hearted believer. Searching for a comfortable Christianity, young Oliver Sansom was tempted to 'fly the Cross' until he read Isaac Penington's *The Way of Life and Death made Manifest*. The book's message made him willing 'to indure the Cross', recognizing that it must 'be taken up by all, that would walk in the Way of Life'.[129]

Good books had to be written, read and valued by sympathetic readers but they must also find their way into the lives of people ignorant of the author but needing his Lord. Baxter's friends made strenuous efforts to place his books in places with a potentially receptive readership. A native of Shropshire, Baxter

---

[123] Doe, *Collection of Experience*, 11. The title was Bunyan's *A Few Sighs from Hell, or the Groans of a Damned Soul* (1658). Later published as *Sighs from Hell*, it reached seven editions in less than three decades.

[124] These were cheap pamphlets containing stories, ballads and religious teaching, sold by travelling chapmen. Baxter's copy of Sibbes's *Bruised Reed* was bought by his father when 'a poor Pedlar came to the Door that had ballads and some good books': Sylvester (ed.), *Reliquiae*, I, i, §3; cf. Margaret Spufford, *Small Books and Pleasant Histories: Popular Fiction and its Readership in Seventeenth-Century England* (1981), 111–28, also 194–218 on the appeal of 'small godly books'.

[125] Six editions of Bunyan's popular *Come, and Welcome, to Jesus Christ* (1678) appeared in a decade. An exposition of Jn 6: 37, its skilled pastoral treatment of the doctrine of election was helpful to as many attending conventicles as those outside. *The Water of Life* ([1688]), with its biblical exposition (Rev. 22: 17), telling illustrations and shafts of humour, is another fine example of Bunyan's evangelistic preaching and writing: *MW*, VII, 179–219.

[126] R.F. Horton, *John Howe* (1895), 165. The sermons, 'Yield yourselves unto God', were printed as an evangelistic pamphlet in 1688: Howe, *Works* (ed. Hunt), I, 499–527.

[127] *Account*, 577.

[128] The book began its life as a series of seven sermons, preached by Mead in 1662 on the response of King Agrippa to Paul's preaching (Acts 26: 28).

[129] Sansom, *Remarkable Passages*, 9–10.

had a natural concern for Wales[130] and gave copies of the Welsh translation of his *Call to the Unconverted* 'to be distributed freely ... Ex dono Authoris', on condition that the recipient read it through twice and be willing to lend his copy to others. Baxter knew of 'almost whole Households converted by this small Book which I set so light by'.[131] Philip Henry passed copies on to colleagues in North Wales who made them available to serious readers.[132] The book inspired a Newent believer to meet the cost of making it available in prisons in three counties. Impressed by '*Saints Rest* & some other' of Baxter's 'most awakening books', he wanted them placed in prisons on '2 or 3 shelves' with chaines running on from barres (as in Libraryes) for their preservation'. The cost would not be excessive, for 'the Press Chaines & about a dozen of small practicall Treatises *with a Bible*' would cost little more than £4. Fear was expressed that few prisoners would read the books but the correspondent argued that it would be infinitely worthwhile if only a few prisoners took advantage of their availability and were converted in gaol.[133]

Content to be 'a Pen in God's hand',[134] Baxter was known to respond quickly to pastoral and evangelistic needs.[135] Living in London, he realized the vulnerability of its many apprentices and, while writing a book especially for them, made sure that there were additional chapters for students of medicine, law and divinity, as well as the sons of magistrates and wealthy citizens.[136]

Letters

Innumerable Dissenters with no pretensions to authorship used personal letters to share their faith. Hester Johnson, the wife of a young ejected minister, wrote

---

[130] G.F. Nuttall et al., *The Beginnings of Nonconformity: The Hibbert Lectures* (1964), 25–32; cf. Eifion Evans, 'Richard Baxter's Influence in Wales', *National Library of Wales Journal* 33 (2003), 141–67; *EB* I, 75–77, for the Welsh Trust (1672–81), its distribution of literature, support of eighty schools, and the work of Thomas Gouge.
[131] Sylvester (ed.), *Reliquiae*, I, I, §174.
[132] Henry, *Diaries* (ed. Lee), 193.
[133] Baxter, *Calendar* (ed. Nuttall and Keeble), II, 132–33, 134–35 (Letters 886, 890); J.I. Packer, *The Redemption and Restoration of Man in the Thought of Richard Baxter* (Carlisle, 2003), 313, who quotes DWL, MS 59, vi, fol.7., 24 July 1672, 'I do resolve by Gods assistance, that the prisons in ye 3 adjacent counties, shall not want such a book as your Call to the unconverted whilest I live tho I am att the Charge of renewing them every yeare', an extract from Letter 890 not quoted in the *Calendar*.
[134] William Bates, *Funeral Sermon for ... Richard Baxter* (1692), 125: 'and what praise is due to a Pen?'
[135] 'Some sudden occasions or other extorted almost all my Writings from me: and ... Usefulness or Necessity prevailed against all other Motives': Sylvester (ed.), *Reliquiae*, I, I, §212.
[136] Baxter, *Compassionate Counsel*.

to her brother, John Strype,[137] shortly after the death of their mother, enquiring 'what evidences we have for heaven': 'deare brother what ever ye neglect, don't neglect the salvation of your soule'.[138] John Machin was a zealous evangelist, 'always aflame', especially 'where the power of the gospel had scarce ever come before', not only distributing Baxter's *Call* among 'Kindred and Servants' but also writing individual and personal '*Dialogues* ... suitable to the Souls Estate'.[139]

Alleine's letters from Ilchester prison were not confined to the believers who missed his public ministry but were also addressed more widely to 'the beloved people ... inhabitants ... of Taunton', urging them to respond to his message. If they repeatedly ignored his appeal, 'I shall account all my letters but wasted paper'.[140] The weekly pastoral letters sent by the exiled Samuel Wells to his church at Banbury gave expression to his deep concern, the first four letters being essentially evangelistic in motive, aim, content and appeal.[141]

During long hours of imprisonment, Abraham Cheare thought of colleagues in the ministry, sending copies of Jessey's *Instructions for Children* for each household and enclosing a letter for parents. In uncertain times he was conscious of how suddenly they 'may be hurried, pluck'd, and separated from' their children 'not only by death, which climbeth up at the windows in most Families ... but by ... violence' through persecution. The many trials for Dissenters included 'dangers ... designed to spoyl and destroy both Infants and Youth, not only [intellectually,] in respect of their Schooling', but morally, 'through the looseness of the times'.[142]

Authors frequently received letters from appreciative, anxious, or enquiring readers, and their replies provided natural, sometimes continuing, opportunities to develop and extend their pastoral and evangelistic ministry. Public meetings

---

[137] Strype (1643–1734) later became a notable ecclesiastical historian. See *CR*, 299, for Hester Johnson's husband, John.

[138] Cambridge, Cambridge University Library, Add. MS 4, Baumgartner Papers: Strype Correspondence, III, pt I, fol.18, Hester Johnson to John Strype, 2 November 1665: 'git god to be y[ou]r portion & then ye have promisis for this life & that w[hi]ch is to com[e]'.

[139] [Newcome], *Life of Machin*, 73; cf. ibid. 7–8, for letters urging his family to 'look after their soules and to minde the things of Eternity ... so that he was an instrument to convert all his three Sisters early unto God, and to prevaile very hopefully with his Parents ... as appeared afterwards'; ibid. 72–73, for a 'serious Discourse to his Son on 1 Chron. 28: 9' and another which he called 'A Word to my Mearly Natural Friends on Isa. 55: 7'.

[140] Alleine, *Letters*, 55 (14 November 1663); cf. ibid. 15 (4 July 1663), for another letter to Taunton residents: 'These eight years have I been calling ... and alas ... how few souls have I gained to Christ by sound conversion.' For further letters addressed to the town rather than to the congregation, see ibid. 51–54 (28 August 1663), 111–21 (undated).

[141] Wells, *Spiritual Remembrancer*, 24–63.

[142] Cheare, *Words*, 221–30; quotations at 223–24.

were prohibited but there was no embargo on letter-writing. In correspondence with Baxter, John Hollingworth, a businessman, confessed he had 'bissied' himself far 'too much in the world' but, having read the author's *A Sermon of Judgment* (1655) and *A Call to the Unconverted* (1658), sought further help. His 'long Custome in sin' made him feel like a prisoner, 'shackled and manackled', and he desperately wanted to know by what means he might 'gett out [of] being ... dead in trespasses'.[143]

Carers

Dissenters realized that seekers like Hollingworth might be won by eloquent deeds as well as persuasive words. One of Alleine's prison letters exposed the risk that his members might become so preoccupied with their personal spirituality that they ignored others: 'Think it not enough to look to your own souls, but watch for others ... Pray for them' and 'warn them'. Further, they must remember that the message is expressed in actions as well as words: 'be kind to them, study to oblige them, that by any means you may win them, and gain their souls'.[144] Alleine's friend Baxter also promoted the evangelistic value of practical kindness: 'Do as much good as you are able to men's bodies, in order to the greater good of souls.'[145] Preaching about the gifts Joseph sent from Egypt to his father, Jacob (Gen. 45: 21–3), George Hughes said that compassionate 'works' were often 'better props to faith with men, than words'.[146] Few Dissenters wished to emulate Bunyan's Talkative, who held 'that hearing and saying' alone 'will make a good Christian',[147] and most gave considerable thought to meeting the needs of vulnerable members of society.

Practical concern for the financially impoverished in church and community was uppermost in their minds. Just as the regular collection of the poor-rate was a parish necessity, so provision for fellow believers' care became an obligatory feature of Nonconformist corporate life, repeatedly expressed both in national confessions of faith[148] and the covenants of individual congregations.[149] The

---

[143] Baxter, *Calendar* (ed. Nuttall and Keeble), II, 62 (Letter 754).
[144] Alleine, *Letters*, 90 (7 July 1666).
[145] Richard Baxter, *How to do good to many, or the Public Good is the Christian's Life*, in *Works* (ed. Orme), XVII, 303. Baxter wrote this book when he felt that his 'pulpit work' was 'at an end': ibid. 289.
[146] Hughes, *Genesis*, 551.
[147] Bunyan, *Pilgrim's Progress*, 79.
[148] For such references in Baptist covenants, see, e.g., 'The Faith and Practice of Thirty [Midland General Baptist] Congregations' (1651), item 57; the Particular Baptist London Confession (1677), ch.XXVII; the Somerset [Particular Baptist] Confession (1656), Article XXV; and the Standard [London General Baptist] Confession (1660), Article XIX: W. Lumpkin (ed.), *Baptist Confessions of Faith* (Chicago, IL, 1959), 184, 290, 210, 230–31 respectively.

first charge on them was the fellow members of their local church, but it was impossible to ignore the needs of the wider community. Economic deprivation was one of the most pressing contemporary social problems and Nonconformists usually responded to its challenge with well organized generosity.

Among Dissenters it is scarcely possible to surpass the benevolence of Quakers.[150] From their earliest days, their leaders inveighed against the evils of poverty, and did more than speak and write.[151] Poverty was seen as an offence against human equality, dignity and charity. William Penn wrote that in their early history, following 'the Example of the Primitive Saints', a 'Holy Care fell upon some of the Elders' among Quakers 'to supply the Necessities of the Poor'.[152] With typical practical concern, George Fox pressed for the introduction of homes for the elderly, and other large houses, 'where an Hundred may have Rooms to Work in, and Shops of all sorts of things to Sell, and where Widows and young Women might work and live'.[153] The early Quakers' social action had a firm biblical foundation: 'we was taught to do good unto all but especially to the household of faith'.[154]

More was necessary than the occasional loan or monetary gift for, in many homes, especially in times of sickness, compassionate physical support was an ongoing need. In Dissenting congregations, many ordinary members performed unpretentious but much appreciated pastoral functions. Living alone, the young Roger Lowe might well have been lonely, but numerous diary entries describe the generous hospitality of fellow Nonconformists,[155] and Roger was not slow to return the kindness by serving others. A keen book-lover,[156] he offered considerable help to people who were unwell, more than willing to beguile their long hours by reading to sick neighbours if requested to do so. During the

---

[149] In their covenant, members of the Woodbridge Independent church committed themselves to 'pleasing our Neighbours in Him ... that we may give no offence': Records of the Woodbridge Congregational Church, fol.2.

[150] 'The Society of Friends has achieved results wholly out of proportion to their numbers. No religious order can point to services rendered to humanity more unsullied by selfishness, or nobler in far-seeing wisdom': B.F. Westcott, *Social Aspects of Christianity* (1887), 130.

[151] London's Quaker women organized regular help for people in need and never limited their generosity to Friends. Their accounts include frequent payments 'for cloth for poors shifts', and other entries such as help for a 'prisoners wife', another 'to discharge severall debts', and money for 'cloth[e]s and passage to Barbadoos': London, Library of the Society of Friends, London Women's [Box] Meeting Accounts 1681–1750, fols 5, 7, 9, 11.

[152] William Penn, *A Brief Account of the Rise and Progress of the People called Quakers* (1694), 69.

[153] Fox, *Epistles*, 287 (Letter 264 [1669]).

[154] Fox, *Journal* (ed. Smith), 283, quoting Gal. 6: 10.

[155] Lowe, *Diary* (ed. Sachse), 16, 60, 65, 90.

[156] Ibid. 15, 25, 54, 99, 101.

winter of 1666, a local woman with a terminal illness found great peace as he read to her from Lewis Bayly's *Practice of Piety* until the moment she quietly passed away.[157] Henry Newcome must have longed for people of that calibre, willing to go into sick people's homes, whatever their social status. Visiting a lonely widow in her illness, he feared that fellow members had failed her badly, simply because they were unhappy about entering the home of an impoverished neighbour.[158]

Not content merely to alleviate immediate distress, Dissenters sometimes applied their best minds to the cause and solution of the problem. Quakers such as the Westmorland schoolmaster Thomas Lawson and the young London cloth merchant John Bellers were among those who wrote about the social and economic dimensions, making practical suggestions as to how inequality might be relieved if not removed. Lawson's suggestion of a 'Poor mans Office' anticipated the employment exchange, a forum for the regular meeting of employers and potential employees, youths desiring apprenticeships and servants looking for household placements.[159] As early as his mid twenties, Bellers became treasurer of an employment fund of £100 established by London Quakers in the late 1670s to buy flax for poor Friends at home to weave into cloth.[160] The simple experiment led him to think of ways in which the lives of poor people could be more radically improved, and later to make imaginative practical suggestions in a series of modest publications.[161]

Baptists in Bristol and Independents in Yarmouth endeavoured to meet these and other pastoral demands by instituting the office of deaconess.[162] Supported by the local church, such women devoted themselves to the care of those who

---

[157] Ibid. 109.

[158] Newcome, *Autobiography* (ed. Parkinson), I, 182–83: 'I called of [on] poor Mrs. Wollen. I was ashamed to hear her say that nothing but poverty makes any one contemptible, as if her low condition made her so little visited in her weakness.'

[159] Thomas Lawson, *An Appeal to the Parliament concerning the Poor that there may not be a beggar in England* (1660), 2. Lawson was disturbed that there were 'such multitudes of Beggars in this fruitful Kingdom': ibid. 3.

[160] In addition to the Bellers initiative, see also London Women's Meeting Accounts, fol.5: 'for a stock for spinning'. In 1670 Buckinghamshire Quakers also collected ten shillings 'to lay out in Hemp or flaxe to imploy' a local Friend: *Upperside Monthly Meeting* (ed. Snell), 5.

[161] A. Ruth Fry, *John Bellers 1654–1725, Quaker, Economist and Social Reformer* (1935), reproduces several of Bellers's tracts and pamphlets on social issues; cf. also Braithwaite, *Second Period*, 571–94; Charles R. Simpson, 'John Bellers in Official Minutes', *JFHS* 12 (1915), 120–27, 165–71; Joshua Rowntree, *Social Service: Its Place in the Society of Friends* (Swarthmore Lecture; n.pl., 1913).

[162] Great Yarmouth Independent Church Book, fols 137–38: 'This day [8 June 1680] was set apart for the set[t]ling of [three] widows for the service of the Church'. The Yarmouth Independents appointed 'widows' to this pastoral office as early as 1650: Browne, *Norfolk and Suffolk*, 227. It was generally held that deaconesses were to be widows over the age of sixty who agreed not to remarry, in accordance with 1 Tim. 5: 9–11.

were unwell by regular sick-visiting, dealing with such physical, material and spiritual needs as were apparent, and reporting frequently to the church's leaders concerning 'all ye Sick Members of ye Congregation'. These women were to be alert and proactive, having 'Eye and Ear open to hearken and enquire who is sick', visiting 'ye sick sisters in an Especiall manner', without neglecting the 'sick Brethren alsoe'. Whenever possible, they were to attend to women and men alike, 'that theire wants may be supplyed', being sure to 'speake a word to their soules ... for support or consolation'.[163]

The welfare of destitute children became a high priority. Friends from various Buckinghamshire meetings gave generously for the 'diet & cure of ... a poor Orphan' known to them, a boy 'in danger of losing his limbs'.[164] On a Spring day in 1674, Cockermouth Independents 'took into their care Stephen, the son of Joseph Wilson of Eaglesfield, deceased, who otherwise must have gone on the country for a living'. It was hard enough that the lad was without a godly father; their generous provision would spare him the additional loss of friends, local church support and familiar surroundings.[165]

Fox said that God sometimes entrusts the care of 'Christ's Chickens, Doves, Lambs, Babes and little Children' to other believers, for 'the Lord hath many adopted Sons'.[166] Quakers frequently raised necessary financial support for a destitute child's board and lodging or for apprenticing a lad from a poor Quaker home.[167] Fox enjoined them to be 'careful how you set your feet amongst the tender plants ... lest ye ... hurt, bruise, or crush them in God's vineyard'.[168] They were urged to facilitate apprenticeships for the children of poor widows, a spiritual opportunity for the young as well as relief for an anxious parent.[169]

Dissenters were especially urged to meet the needs of persecuted sufferers, whether known to them personally or not. Twenty-four Friends imprisoned in Gloucester's Northgate jail for over a year, 'the greater part women, some with suckling children', included 'several poor tradesmen in a strait prison, first committed for their religious meetings, then the oath of allegiance put to them and to the women also'.[170] When York Quakers heard of their trouble, they

---

[163] *Broadmead Records* (ed. Hayden), 208, cf. 51, 117, 142.
[164] *Upperside Monthly Meeting* (ed. Snell), 74; cf. 59, when local Quakers gave fifteen shillings 'for 6 weeks dyet for a grandchild' of a needy Friend.
[165] Cockermouth Independent Church Book, 111. .
[166] George Fox, *Gospel-Truth Demonstrated* (1706), 876, 875.
[167] London Women's Meeting Accounts, fol.9.
[168] Fox, *Journal* (Bi-centenary ed.), I, 391.
[169] Fox, *Epistles*, 286 (Letter 264 [1669]); cf. the Buckinghamshire meetings' provision for 'an honest poor Friend's son Apprentice at London': *Upperside Monthly Meeting* (ed. Snell), 201, 203, 205; and, for Bristol Quakers' generosity to apprentices: *Minute Book of the Men's Meeting of the Society of Friends in Bristol 1667–86* (ed. Russell Mortimer, Publications of the Bristol Record Society, 26; Bristol, 1971), 2, 60, 80, 84.
[170] *CSPD* 1683, January–June, 133.

immediately sent £20 towards the cost of everyday needs.[171] Two Baptist ministers in Ilchester gaol acknowledged with gratitude the monetary 'tokens of love' sent to them by Somerset churches.[172] Andrew Gifford, minister of the Pithay Particular Baptist Church in Bristol, often preached in Wiltshire towns and villages and helped in the establishment of new congregations. During his imprisonment, members of the Trowbridge church sent a gift to him in Gloucester Castle with words of personal encouragement by their appointed representative.[173]

A benevolent exercise such as conveying gifts and offering pastoral support to prisoners could prove hazardous. A former clergyman, recently turned Dissenter, went to see George Fownes, the Broadmead minister, during his imprisonment in Gloucester gaol. The visitor was recognized by an inveterate informer who happened to be in the prison, and 'charged with preaching at a Conventicle in ye fields' at some time during the previous two years, an accusation he could not refute. The charges were so vague and imprecise that he ought never to have been brought to court, but the visitor had no wish to deny that he too had preached among Dissenters. An innocent pastoral visit robbed him of freedom for the next eighteen months.[174]

The grim physical conditions of imprisonment were difficult enough to bear when in good health, but in sickness life became intolerable. Friends took practical steps to help incarcerated Quakers during illness, such as paying for better prison accommodation,[175] or renting a nearby house with heating and nursing care, where sick and elderly prisoners were permitted to live in less crowded conditions.[176] They did their utmost for the welfare of isolated Friends in London gaols whose families lived in the provinces.[177]

The care of depressed or 'melancholic' people was another concern,

---

[171] London, Library of the Society of Friends, Minutes of the Meeting for Sufferings, London Yearly Meeting, II, 193 (16 March 1683). For this reference, I am indebted to Watkins, *Taming*, 246, 261.

[172] 'Letter from Ministers in Ilchester gaol in 1663', *Baptist Annual Register*, 4 vols (1790–1802), IV, 1022–1029, at 1029.

[173] See Ivimey, *English Baptists*, I, 414–15, for Gifford's grateful acknowledgement (14 April 1684).

[174] *Broadmead Records* (ed. Hayden), 251, 264.

[175] In 1678 London Quakers met the cost of 'providing 'a chamber for the supply of prisoners, if any should be ill': London, Library of the Society of Friends, Minutes of the London Six Weeks Meeting, II, 44, 46.

[176] London Quakers rented a house close to Newgate in 1684 where imprisoned Friends were allowed to stay, providing, for instance, '2 chaldron of coals for the prisoners there'. They also met the cost of provisions for prisoners that 'shall be sick' and 'ye necessarys for ye poore &c which ye nurses who are said to dwell in ye said house': ibid.

[177] In 1683 two Friends were appointed to meet with the 'warden of the Fleet [prison] to discuss payment for 'a room or rooms for ye accommodation of prisoners sent out of ye country thither, that they may not be exposed to ye common ward': ibid. 25.

especially in a society with an innate fear of mental illness. Fox was particularly attentive to the needs of the 'distempered' in mind, suggesting that residential homes be provided for them.[178] In 1673 London Quakers responded by renting a property, arranging for the care of a number of 'discomposed persons', taking responsibility for their medical needs and for their financial affairs as necessary.[179]

In 1673 the needs of John Fry, an unmarried member severely afflicted with a period of mental illness,[180] brought the best out of Bristol's Broadmead congregation. The unexpectedly detailed narrative in the church book invites reflection on the nature of this local church's prayerful response to an urgent pastoral need. The congregation recognized the delicate interaction between physical, mental and spiritual elements in sickness; in this particular instance, the symptoms appear to have originated in the member's insecurity concerning his relationship with God. Both men and women from the congregation personally visited this occasionally violent, blaspheming member in his own home, despite a measure of potential physical danger. The narrative makes no reference to any other resident family member, suggesting that this bachelor may have lived alone, in which case the presence on several occasions of compassionate, non-judgemental, praying people must have been warmly supportive. They discussed whether he should 'be Carryed into ye Country for help', demonstrating that his fellow members were eager to make any form of practical assistance available, including 'Outward means' ('Bloodying, Purgeing and Leeching'), however unscientific we might consider these measures to be. They refused to draw a sharp distinction between 'medical' assistance and supernatural help, believing that either might be used for the patient's restoration. Their appointment of full days for fasting and prayer was a sacrificial corporate decision, involving loss of income, at least for some. This congregation clearly believed it necessary to practise some basic form of exorcism, identifying specific destructive 'spirits' while they prayed together. These compassionate church members were especially helpful during the recovered patient's predictable remorse, when, 'filled with such shame', he felt unable to pray himself, and shared in mutual rejoicing when he was so

---

[178] Fox, *Epistles*, 287 (Letter 264 [1669]).

[179] Braithwaite, *Second Period*, 571 n.1; cf. *George Fox's 'Book of Miracles'* (ed. Cadbury), 69–71.

[180] *Broadmead Records* (ed. Hayden), 139–41. For the seventeenth-century diagnosis and treatment of such illnesses, and the differing perceptions of Anglicans and Dissenters, see David Harley, 'Mental Illness, Magical Medicines and the Devil in Northern England, 1650–1700', in R. French and A. Wear (eds), *The Medical Revolution of the Seventeenth Century* (Cambridge, 1989), 114–44; cf. also Michael Macdonald, *Mystical Bedlam: Madness, Anxiety and Healing in Seventeenth-Century England* (Cambridge, 1981), 150–60; and especially his 'Religion, Social Change, and Psychological Healing in England, 1600–1800', in S.J. Mews (ed.), *The Church and Healing* (SCH, 19, Oxford, 1982), 101–25, with specific reference to Fry's treatment.

evidently restored. Whatever the nature of his illness, the sensitive support of the local church must have played a significant part in his recovery.

The fact that these circumstances were related in such detail illustrates not only the congregation's prayerful dependence on God but also a desire that later generations might benefit from its experience in dealing with a distressing form of mental illness. Recording this particular narrative reminded the Bristol scribe of a similar instance of a day of prayer for a mentally sick child similarly 'Betwitched, (as termed)' twenty years earlier, 'when Br. Jessey was here', and of the congregation's gratitude for a similar answer to their prayers.[181]

Travellers were frequently in danger, especially those going overseas. Friends in ports were glad to offer practical assistance to deprived people hoping for a better life in another country, and the generosity was not restricted to Quaker emigrants. Bristol Friends helped those leaving for America[182] and Ireland.[183] Victims of piracy were always in serious danger,[184] particularly those held as captives by Barbary pirates[185] who demanded large sums of ransom money.[186] Their plight touched the hearts of many generous Dissenters, though Friends urged that Quaker merchants should not put themselves and crews at risk by dangerous overseas trading, and the spontaneous help of meetings was more forthcoming when innocent captives were seeking a new life in Virginia or the West Indies.[187]

The material needs of Protestant refugees were evident not only in the

---

[181] *Broadmead Records* (ed. Hayden), 141–42. For an example of the devoted pastoral care of Quakers in 1687 for a seriously depressed Friend 'driven to the brink of despair', including visitation and 'their offer of assisting him if he would put himself into ye hands of some skilfull Physician', see *Upperside Monthly Meeting* (ed. Snell), 187–89, 190, 197–201.

[182] *Minute Book of the Men's Meeting of the Society of Friends in Bristol 1686–1704* (ed. Russell Mortimer, Publications of the Bristol Record Society, 30; Bristol, 1977), 137.

[183] In 1673 a group of Bristol Quakers were asked to take £5 and 'ride downe to the Pill', the pilot station in the Bristol Channel, 'to vissitt the passingers bound for Ireland … that hath related to us their present destress': *Bristol 1667–86* (ed. Mortimer), 79–80; cf. ibid. 121, for financial help given to a married couple, 'streingers in this citty being poore & intending to travell to Ireland', including 'ten shillings to pay their passage when they shall be ready [to] sayle'.

[184] *Upperside Monthly Meeting* (ed. Snell), 75 and note, 79–80, 142, 144, 153, 'for ye Redemption of Friends yt are Captives in Algiers'.

[185] G.N. Clark, 'The Barbary Corsairs in the Seventeenth Century', *Cambridge Historical Journal* 8 (1944), 22–35.

[186] E.H.W. Meyerstein's transcript of a seaman's [later Quaker] journal, *Adventures by Sea of Edward Coxere* (Oxford, 1945), describes typical hazards in this period, including enslavement by pirates. Coxere's personal experience of this barbaric treatment (some 'under this bondage five years, some ten; one old man had been there thirty–two years, as was reckoned': ibid. 67), explains why compassionate Friends were so eager to secure their release.

[187] Arnold Lloyd, *Quaker Social History* (1950), 38–39.

capital but in other parts of the country and, as we have seen, at different times national appeals for house to house collections were made by the king.[188] Over the years, Bristol Quakers had endured intense hardship and were particularly sensitive to the needs of sufferers. In the spring of 1688, they saw for themselves Huguenot families 'in destress within this citty'. They gave a fortnight's notice that 'a collection shal be made for them publickly' at 'the dores to receive what friends are free to give' for the 'said destressed protestants' among them, generously raising over twenty-one pounds.[189]

Quakers in another English port lacked the numerical strength of Bristol Friends but in 1664 were given an opportunity to care for a sizeable group of visiting seamen arrested at the close of their Yarmouth meeting and imprisoned.[190] Cruelly treated, they were placed in a room at the top of a building, given water but not allowed visitors. Food was available but its cost totally beyond their means.[191] One night, the ingenious prisoners discovered how to pick two locks (later re-locking them) by which they gained access to another room where there was 'a little square hole in the wall ... about a span square, and ... about ten yards from the ground ... over a back alley'. Local Friends went to this secluded alley every night when, by means of a sailor's line 'out of the hole', food could be hauled up to the prisoners.

> When done, we locked the two doors again, and quietly filled our bellies, and slept very comfortably, for the Lord's presence was with us day and night, who enabled us beyond what our adversaries could see.

> Though the bailies and the jailor were deceived by us, in that we picked their locks, yet we were honest, in that it was for life and not for liberty, for we never offered to meddle with the outward door, which opened to the street.

---

[188] W.A. Bewes, *Church Briefs* (1896), 207–19; cf. *Consistory Minutes* (ed. Gwynn), 171n, 243n, 254n, 256, 348.

[189] *Bristol 1686–1704* (ed. Mortimer), 18–19, cf. 32; cf. William Tanner, *Three Lectures on the Early History of the Society of Friends in Bristol & Somersetshire* (1858), 82–83.

[190] Besse, *Sufferings*, I, 491–2. The seamen 'had come to the Town to take in Red-Herrings for the Straits'.

[191] The jailor demanded that they 'eat such vituals as he would provide for us' at 'one shilling a meal apiece, besides what else' [i.e. other charges]. The average labourer's wage in this period was five shillings a week. One prisoner (Edward Coxere) contrasted this treatment unfavourably with the barbaric conditions he endured when captive 'under the hands of Turks ... yet they gave me my bellyful of bread to eat with my water, but here ... gave me not the privilege as they gave their dogs': *Edward Coxere* (ed. Meyerstein) 100–101. For a further example of excessive charges for prison meals, see *A Journal of the Life, Labours, Travels and Sufferings ... of ... John Banks* (1712), 12–13, partly reproduced in Barbour and Roberts (eds), *Early Quaker Writings*, 187: four Quakers were imprisoned in Carlisle, 'without either bread or water', because they 'could not ... satisfy' the jailer's 'covetous desire ... of ... 8 pence a meal'. He ensured that no food was brought to them; 'neither would he suffer any of our Friends to bring us any bedding, not so much as a little straw'.

None of those prisoners were local residents but testified that Yarmouth 'Friends were very careful' of them 'and kind', providing food every night for seven weeks, though there were few Quakers in the local meeting.[192] Love was not confined to the persecuted Dissenters themselves. Many neighbours gave practical support to their families, willingly paying fines, refusing to buy 'distrained' goods,[193] offering shelter when homes were plundered,[194] or enabling escape from their oppressors.[195]

It has to be acknowledged, however, that the quality of love freely expressed within a congregation was not always evident in the local church's relationships with neighbouring congregations. Sharply defined denominational boundaries were yet to be drawn but Nonconformist witness in a particular locality was occasionally marred by disagreements among congregations with divergent views. They were not always good at handling differences. The verbal tirades of some of their finest leaders illustrate the difficulty. Baxter and Bunyan occasionally share the same paragraph in this book, but the two very different men are not likely to have met and, if they had, would have been distinctly uncomfortable in each other's company.[196] Bunyan regarded Baxter's theology as far too accommodating to ideas he would have fiercely dismissed as rank 'Arminianism'. Baxter was distinctly unhappy about some aspects of Bunyan's theology,[197] 'separatist' churchmanship, encouragement of 'unordained' preachers and especially the fact that despite baptism in infancy Bunyan had been publicly baptized as a committed believer: 'Anabaptism' indeed. Whatever their differences, Baxter and Bunyan shared an implacable hostility to Quakerism, and both were derided by Edward Burrough, the young Friend with a 'ready Tongue'.[198] Divisiveness was an all too common feature in late

---

[192] *Edward Coxere* (ed. Meyerstein), 100–102.
[193] *CSPD* 1670, 243, 417; Besse, *Sufferings*, II, 17.
[194] *A True and Impartial Narrative of some Illegal and Arbitrary Proceedings ... against several innocent and peaceable nonconformists ... Bedford* (1670), 7. When most of a Bedfordshire widow's goods were seized, she borrowed 'sheets of her Neighbours to lie in, being not willing to lodge out of her own house, though invited by her friendly Neighbours'.
[195] *Broadmead Records* (ed. Hayden), 155, 246.
[196] F.J. Powicke, *The Reverend Richard Baxter under the Cross (1662–1691)* (1927), 57–59.
[197] Baxter said that Bunyan's covenant theology 'ignorantly subverteth the Gospel of Christ': *Calendar* (ed. Nuttall and Keeble), II, Letter 1025; cf. Richard Baxter, *The Scripture Gospel Defended* (1690), Pt II, 49, where, although identifying Bunyan with 'men of sincere Holiness', he regarded the Bedford preacher as 'an unlearned Antinomian', although 'Bunnian's last preachings gave me hope that he repented of his Errors'.
[198] *Life of Thomas Ellwood* (ed. Graveson), 19. Bunyan had described Burrough as one of the 'false prophets who ... make merchandise of souls': *A Vindication of some Gospel Truths Opened* (1657), in *MW*, I, 84. In his reply, *Truth (the Strongest of all) witness'd ... against all deceit ... particularly by one John Bunion (one of Gog's Army)* (1657), Burrough arraigned Bunyan as a purveyor of 'abominable doctrine' and 'a

seventeenth-century Dissent. Baxter confessed there were few that did 'not over-vilifie and wrong those from whom they differ'.[199]

But the undoubted differences can be exaggerated. Local church records provide occasional evidence of cooperation between Nonconformists with differing views on baptism, church government, lay preaching, 'open' or 'closed' membership, or qualifications for participation in the Lord's Supper. Independent, Baptist and Presbyterian congregations in Bristol responded to fierce persecution and the imprisonment of their ministers by appointing representatives to meet regularly to master legal complexities, share news and discuss strategies, as well as pray regularly together.[200] Unless a Leicestershire incumbent was misinformed, the 'Presbyterian, Independent & Anabaptisticall Conventicle' in his Sibbeston parish was 'usually held together' in 1669, meeting on both 'Sundayes and week dayes attended by about '40 meeters'.[201] Similar cooperative ventures took place elsewhere, although Dissenting groups normally prized their distinctive local identity. At Theobalds, near Cheshunt, Presbyterians and Baptists worshipped together with two ministers, Thomas Wadsworth and Joseph Maisters respectively, preaching on alternate Sundays. Maisters requested that at his funeral Baptist, Presbyterian and Independent ministers should be pallbearers; his funeral sermon was preached by a paedobaptist friend, Jeremiah Hunt.[202] Funerals provided a public opportunity to defy public worship restrictions, openly declare Nonconformist values and demonstrate their corporate solidarity.[203] Presbyterians and Independents had

---

Hypocrite and Dissembler': *The Memorable Works of a Son of Thunder and Consolation ... Edward Burroughs* (1672), 284, 288, 309. See also Burrough's *Many Strong Reasons Confounded ... sent into the World by Richard Baxter, a Frequent Contender against the Wayes of God* (1657), accusing Baxter of 'a malicious heart' and 'lying Scribbles': in *Memorable Works*, 311, 313.

[199] Baxter, *Scripture Gospel*, Pt II, 49; cf. *Continuation*, II, 583, of Matthew Clarke: 'His Judgment was Congregational; But nothing of Party could alienate his Affection from true Piety, in whomsoever he beheld it.'

[200] *Broadmead Records* (ed. Hayden), 147, 149, 150–52.

[201] Evans, 'Leicestershire, 1669', 128. Presbyterians and Independents appear to have met together in other parts of Leicestershire, e.g. at Market Harborough: ibid. 130.

[202] W. Urwick, *Nonconformity in Herts* (1884), 507–509; cf. also M. Clapinson (ed.), *Bishop Fell and Nonconformity: Visitation Documents from the Oxford Diocese, 1682–3* (Oxfordshire Record Society, 52; Oxford, 1980), 44, 42, though it is difficult to think that the Kingston Blount incumbent was correctly informed in 1683 when he reported the 'mixt' meeting of local 'Presbyterians, Independents, Quakers & Sabbatarians'.

[203] An intercepted letter from the ejected minister William Hooke to John Davenport in New England described the funeral of a London Friend in 1663 'who died lately in prison and his corpse was ... accompanied to the grave by 1500 or 2000' Quakers: A.G. Matthews, 'A Censored Letter: William Hooke in England to John Davenport in New England, 1663', *TCHS* 9 (1924–26), 262–83, at 277. At Thomas Ewins's interment, he was 'Accompanied with many hundreds to ye Grave, ye like funeral not seen long before in Bristoll': *Broadmead Records* (ed. Hayden), 127. Roger Morrice wrote that in 1687 there was 'a great company' at the funeral of Thomas Jacombe, 'its thought a

their differences although, with paedobaptism and much else to unite them, strenuous efforts were made in some parts of the country to establish closer relationships.[204]

In preaching and writing, many leaders did everything possible to promote unity and emphasized the primacy of love, for conformist opponents as well as fellow Dissenters. The Coventry Presbyterian John Bryan urged Nonconformists to 'leave off ... reviling the Government Ecclesiastical and the Ministers that conform', urging them 'not to be stiff in your own Opinions or perswasions ... if you be in the truth, Love them not the less, that err from it ... believe they may be godly Men for all that'.[205] Hercules Collins held that because Christians 'agree in the Fundamental Doctrine ... there is sufficient ground to lay aside all bitterness and prejudice, and labour to maintain a spirit of love each to [the] other, knowing we shall never see all alike here'.[206] Thomas Ewins claimed that he did not 'love any man the more or less for his judgements sake, whether he be Presbyterian, Independent, Baptized, &c. But wherever I see the Image of Christ appear (which is love and holiness) there I desire to love and honour'.[207] All three had spent time in prison and valued the things that matter most. When tempted to criticize their fellow believers, of other traditions or their own, Dissenters were sometimes reminded that it was folly to expect perfection this side of heaven; they should 'look not for that in the Saints, which is alone in Christ'.[208]

---

hundred Nonconformist Ministers': *EB*, IV, 5 [Q87]; cf. also Sharon Achinstein, *Literature and Dissent in Milton's England* (Cambridge, 2003), 27–37.

[204] Michael R. Watts, *The Dissenters: From the Reformation to the French Revolution* (Oxford, 1978), 289–90.
[205] John Bryan, *Dwelling with God* (1670), 314, 327.
[206] Collins, *Orthodox Catechism*, Preface, A4.
[207] Thomas Ewins, in [Purnell], *Church of Christ in Bristol*, 68 [misprinted as 60].
[208] Baxter, *Rest*, 81.

Postscript

With the passing of the years, Nonconformists began to realize that the legislation's punitive measures had not proved as seriously detrimental to congregational life as they might have feared. Though severely disruptive for ministers, many of them acknowledged that the repression was not bereft of benefits. When Oliver Heywood was ejected, close friends advised him not to fret but 'silently wait til the lord open a doore for me [in] other ways'.[1] We have seen that, like many others, Heywood found his new opportunity in strenuous itinerancy lasting over thirty years. Looking back over a full year of freedom following an eleven-month imprisonment, he gratefully recorded the miles he had travelled and the number of occasions he had preached throughout a wide area.[2] Scattered congregations in the northern counties were sustained by his regular visits and ongoing care, and his vigorous peripatetic ministry was far from unique. Other ejected ministers may not have travelled so widely but, compelled by adverse legislation, most of them were obliged to move their homes to fresh territory at least five miles from the localities where they had served. There is considerable evidence that new Dissenters' meetings rarely drew their numbers from their ejected ministers' former parishes.[3] Over the years, despite the hazards, some disenchanted worshippers from local parish churches found their way to forbidden conventicles, but there is little evidence of direct sheep-stealing. Ministry in unfamiliar local contexts demanded imaginative enterprise on the part of displaced ministers; ministers with vision found new ways of gathering people from a different community to hear their message.

Even imprisonment did not deter men of robust spirit; change of location rarely silenced the messenger. The Seventh-Day Baptist minister Francis Bampfield was in Dorchester gaol for nine years and a sizeable congregation of prisoners and visitors gathered regularly to hear him and his colleagues, including 'People of the Town who came to them, every day once, and on the Lord's Day twice', until a compliant jailer was ordered to bring their meetings to an end.[4] Fellow prisoners who would never have darkened the doors of a Nonconformist conventicle heard what these men were eager to share with

---

[1] Heywood, *Autobiography* (ed. Turner), I, 181–82.
[2] cf. ibid., III, 224. In 1686 he travelled about a thousand miles, 'preacht 132 times on weekdays, besides Lords days, kept 37 fasts, 15 days of thankfulness'.
[3] David L. Wykes, 'Early Religious Dissent in Surrey after the Restoration', *Southern History* 33 (2011), 54–77, at 56–57; idem, 'The Bishop of Gloucester's Letter about Nonconformist Conventicles, August 1669', *Transactions of the Bristol and Gloucestershire Archaeological Society* 114 (1996), 97–104, at 102.
[4] Sylvester (ed.), *Reliquiae*, I, ii, §423.

others.

The writing of books, pamphlets, and collections of letters for distribution in printed form extended the ministry of those who had preached earlier at the cost of their freedom but were now 'silenced' prisoners. New forms of communication opened up to them. In 'chains to preach to them in chains', Bunyan longed to share freely what he 'smartingly did feel',[5] but he could not possibly have imagined such a vast, varied and continuing audience as Pilgrim's story reached into countless homes and began its worldwide journey, to say nothing of his many other books, sending their message to places where his voice could never have been heard. Outside prisons as well as in them, eloquent preachers became gifted authors. Restricted preaching opportunities caused men as different as Thomas Goodwin, John Owen, Richard Baxter, Thomas Manton, Thomas Brooks, Benjamin Keach, Stephen Charnock, George Fox, William Penn, David Clarkson and a host of others to devote hours of their time to writing, developing skills that took their expositions way beyond the confines of a local conventicle. In addition to doctrinal treatises, most of them explored pastoral issues, such as the believer's response to suffering, themes that in more congenial contexts might well have been ignored. Theirs was the richest contribution to the century's Nonconformist life and thought.

Although plagued by occasional informers and vindictive magistrates, many Dissenting congregations acknowledged the possibility that even the heavy punishments inflicted might come to have a refining effect within a local Nonconformist community. Intimidating hardship at least distinguished casual attenders (like Bunyan's Timorous and Mistrust, frightened by lions)[6] or those of an 'Unstable Weathercock Spirit'[7] from committed believers who, for all their failings, provided Dissenting churches with a more robust and dependable membership. If these churches were to survive in such a hostile context, they were in need of sturdy people, determined to 'go against against Wind and Tide' and 'own Religion in his Rags, as well as in his Silver Slippers'.[8]

When the Five Mile Act robbed these congregations of their ministers, members came to value the essential contribution of devoted lay leaders,[9] men who, in more favourable conditions, might never have developed so many gifts. When a minister was compelled to leave an area, it was his unordained colleagues who made arrangements for the discreet gathering of a continuing congregation and became examples of steadfast loyalty. These leaders often provided a meeting place either in their own homes or business premises,[10] or in the barns and outhouses of sympathetic farmers. It was their responsibility to organize financial help for visiting ministers and practical support for members

---

[5] Bunyan, *GA*, §276–77.
[6] Bunyan, *Pilgrim's Progress*, 43.
[7] Bunyan, *Doctrine of Justification*, in *MW*, IV, 83.
[8] Bunyan, *Pilgrim's Progress*, 100.
[9] For strategic lay leadership in this period, see Wykes, 'Surrey', 54–77.
[10] For the use of lay leaders' business premises in Surrey, see ibid. 69-70.

in need, which included the care of families when householders were in prison. Lay leaders who had little pretension to any preaching gift, discovered that, with full notes available, they or a delegated colleague might repeat a recent sermon for the benefit of those who had not heard it, or who would like to hear it again to reflect further on its teaching. Some lay leaders had the additional opportunity of encouraging other vulnerable churches as well as their own. Men with business interests in other towns and cities often formed close links with Dissenting congregations in those localities.

Enoch Prosser was a 'Gifted Br[other]' who belonged to Benjamin Keach's Particular Baptist church in Horsleydown, Southwark. His work took him to Bristol and it was as he shared in Broadmead's Sunday worship that he was arrested, along with another visiting businessman, Samuel Crisp. Both men were in the city for its annual fair; goods were removed from their stalls and sold well below their value in lieu of fines. The Broadmead members valued their partnership in adversity: 'Thus they suffered for being at that Meeting'.[11] Samuel Buttall's sugar trading business demanded regular visits to Plymouth and Bristol. He was another London Baptist leader who visited the Broadmead church whenever he could and sometimes preached for them. In the spring of 1681, when local hostility forced the church meet to outdoors, 'near 1000 people' gathered to hear him on two consecutive Sunday mornings.[12]

These leaders were the usual recipients of letters written by imprisoned or exiled ministers, with messages that they shared with their people at the first opportunity. Dissenters who regularly met in conventicles without the support of a preacher would also have appreciated the many published works available for reading to a congregation, not least printed sermons aimed specifically at 'conventiclers'. When Thomas Wadsworth had to leave his Newington people in 1660 on the return of the sequestered rector, he published his final message, sharing his 'whole Heart in Print, that it may speak to you when I am absent'.[13] That his *Serious Exhortation to an Holy Life* reached three editions in its first two years and (with further editions in 1680 and 1687) continued to be circulated after the author's death, testifies to the popularity as well as didactic value of this kind of literature in Nonconformist life and work. Such publications could easily be read publicly by lay leaders when either a large conventicle or modest house-meeting found itself without a preacher.

Threatening punishments were not effective in keeping Dissenters away from proscribed meetings. In many localities conventicles continued to attract substantial numbers, gathering significantly more people than in the local parish churches where, legally, attendance was compulsory. Larger homes, such as that of a Southwark widow, could accommodate a hundred, a Presbyterian congregation composed mainly of London tradesmen; at another

---

[11] *Broadmead Records* (ed. Hayden), 236–37.
[12] Ibid. 240.
[13] Thomas Wadsworth, *A Serious Exhortation to an Holy Life* (1660), [A3r].

location in the same district, about a thousand Baptists were said to meet in purpose-built premises in Shad Thames; yet another, meeting in the same Southwark parish, regularly attracted between 500 and 600 Presbyterians.[14] In some areas, primarily urban, local authorities turned a blind eye to Nonconformist audacity as larger congregations built their own meeting-houses at a time when their meetings were illegal.[15] Nonconformity was not lacking in numerical strength, particularly in towns and cities. Life was more difficult for Dissenters in rural areas where they may have met more surreptitiously, particularly sensitive to local opposition. Yet, even in rural communities, with imaginative organization larger numbers did meet in remote locations such as at North Bradley, near the Wiltshire-Somerset border, when about 1,500 Dissenters came together for outdoor worship in Brokerswood in the autumn of 1670, only months after the renewed Conventicle Act had increased the penalties. A fortnight later, numbers at this 'unlawfull Meeting and Conventicle' rose to nearer 2,000 as Dissenters came from a wider area for mutual support, encouragement and witness.[16]

Smaller congregations relied on the courageous hospitality of members with reasonably spacious housing and, as we have seen, larger companies of Dissenters were often compelled, for safety reasons, to divide into smaller groups or 'parcels'. The regular use of members' homes must have greatly helped the integration of a congregation and would have enriched its corporate life immeasurably as members from a variety of different social backgrounds met frequently together.

The continuing vigour of Restoration Dissent owed an immense amount to the daily worship of the Nonconformist family. These 'little churches' were the nucleus of many a small Dissenting community. We have seen that the seventeenth century 'family' consisted not only of members and domestic servants, but visitors and, on many occasions, day labourers and neighbours.[17] Eager to encourage their fellow church members, many householders refused to limit attendance at family prayers to the restricted number of permissible guests. It was worth risking a fine if local church members could be edified and enriched. Homes were carefully watched; local opponents knew only too well the importance and influence of these informal meetings. To such occasions, nobody was more welcome than Nonconformist guests from other parts of the

---

[14] GLT, I, 143–44.
[15] Wykes, 'Surrey', 68. In Southwark, four of the eleven Nonconformist meetings reported in 1669 met in 'a house built on purpose': GLT, I, 143–44.
[16] Wiltshire Record Office, Quarter Sessions Roll, 12 and 27 September, 1670, cited in Richard D. Land, 'Doctrinal Controversies of the English Particular Baptists (1644-1691) as illustrated by the career and writings of Thomas Collier' (D.Phil. thesis, University of Oxford, 1980), 65.
[17] Cf. H.D. Roberts, *Matthew Henry and his Chapel 1662–1900* (Liverpool, [1901]), 20, for young Matthew Henry's recollections of the 'extended family' at Broad Oak's daily worship.

country, sharing news of work and witness in more distant towns and villages, providing a meaningful sense of corporate solidarity when local witness might have seemed weak or fractured by oppression. A minister among the family's visitors could participate in worship by sharing its teaching opportunity, a different voice bringing fresh insights to a familiar biblical passage. Ministers' homes especially were convenient meeting places for fellow ministers scattered over a larger area, and such networks of supportive relationships gave additional strength to otherwise isolated leaders.

On the bleak day when Oliver Heywood left his people at Coley, a heartening possibility lifted his spirits: '[W]ho knows what effects this providence may produce'; it might even 'help to the improvement of ordinances'. Surely, in God's 'due time he wil arise and have mercy upon Zion, when the set time is come'. Heywood dared to believe that 'this eclipse of the gospel may tend to the furtherance of the gospel'.[18] Despite the anguish, in most places it did.

---

[18] Heywood, *Autobiography* (ed. Turner), I, 182.

Select Bibliography

Primary Sources

Manuscripts

Angus Library, Regent's Park College, Oxford
Porton (with Broughton) Baptist Church Book, 1657–87.

Bodleian Library, Oxford
Carte MS 45, fol.151, Archbishop Sheldon to the Duke of Ormonde, 1663.
MS Add. c.302, fol.71r, William [Nicholson], bishop of Gloucester, to Archbishop Sheldon, 22 September 1666.
MS Add. c.305, fol.142, Bishop Seth Ward to Archbishop Sheldon, 19 December 1663.
MS Rawlinson D.1480, fols 123r–126v, 'Church of Jesus Christ in Cambridgeshire', 1675 (photocopy in Dr Williams's Library, London).
MS Tanner 45, fols 278, 288, Bishop John Hacket to Archbishop Sheldon.

Bristol Baptist College Library
Thomas Hardcastle, 'Expositions', [1671–2].

British Library, London
Add. MS 11342, fols 15–16, 'Information and depositions' laid against John Howe for preaching rebellion, 1660.
Add. MS 19526, H. Gregory, 'Travels of King Charles II, 1640–60', I.
Add. MS 34508, Mackintosh Collections: Political Correspondence 1685–88, fol.133.
Add. MS 34769, fol.70, Archbishop Sheldon to Compton, bishop of London, 8 June 1669; Compton's copy to his fellow bishops, 10 June 1669.
Add. MS 53728, Bulstrode Whitelocke, 'Lectures upon Particular Occasions by a Father to his family', 1667.
Stowe MS 209, Essex Papers, January–June 1676, fol.237v, 13 May 1676.

Cambridge University Library
MS 7338, Philip Henry, Sermon notes on Genesis, 1658–9.
Add. MS 4, Baumgartner Papers: Strype Correspondence, III, pt I, fol.18, Hester Johnson to John Strype, 2 November 1665.

Congregational Library, London
MS I.f.34, Thomas Browning, Autobiography [c.1683–5].
MS I.i.4, 'Earliest Records of Protestant Nonconformity in and about Cockermouth, 1651–1706' [Cockermouth Independent Church Book], transcribed by P.H. Davison, 1848.

Dr Williams's Library, London
Baxter Letters, 6.56, Richard Hollingworth to Henry Vaughan, 1 December 1661.
MS 12.63 (22), John Maidwell to Robert and Elizabeth Gidley, 6 July 1685.

MS 24.7, Owen Stockton, 'Observations and experiences of gods dealing with my soul and other memorable passages of his providence taken and recorded since April 1st 1665, by Owen Stockton; continued to 24 August 1680', 1665–80.
MS 28.4.30, Elias Pledger junr, Diary, 1665–1725.
MS 28.31.3, Owen Stockton, Notes of Sermon on Gen. 32: 1, 27 June 1675.
MS 38.34–35, John Quick, 'Icones Sacrae Anglicanae, or Lives and Deaths of Several Eminent Divines', 1694–1702, II, undated transcript.
Harmer MS 76.1, 'The Church Book belonging to the Society of Christians who assemble for divine Worship at the Old Meeting, Norwich', 1643–1839, transcribed by Joseph Davey, 1848.
Harmer MS 76.2, Great Yarmouth Independent Church Book, 1642–1813, transcribed 1848.
Harmer MS 76.4, Whiting Street Congregational Church, Bury St Edmunds, Church Book, 1646–1801, transcribed 1849.
Harmer MS 76.15, Wattisfield Church Book, 1678–1847, transcribed 1849.
Harmer MS 76.5, Records of the Congregational Church worshipping at the Quay Meeting, Woodbridge, Suffolk, 1651–1851, undated transcript.
MS 90.10, Diary of Sarah Savage, 1688–95, copied 1812.
MS 201.11, Ipswich [Tacket Street] Independent Church Book, 1686–1791.
MS OD, 15, Deptford General Baptist Church Book, 1674–1719.
New College Collection, MSS L4/7/1–26 and L4/9/3, Notebooks of Philip Henry, 1659–83.

Essex County Record Office, Chelmsford
MS D/NC//35/1, Clavering Church Book, 'The Covenant first entred into at Woodhall the 22th day of the twelfth month, 1682/3'.

Gamlingay Baptist Church
The [first] Gamlingay (Bedfordshire) Baptist Church Book.

Library of the Society of Friends, London
MS 10/10, 'Some Account of the Birth, Education and Religious Exercises and Visitations of God to Josiah Langdale', 1673–1725.
London Women's ['Box'] Meeting Accounts 1681–1750 (includes some notes from 1669 onwards).
Minutes of the Meeting for Sufferings, London Yearly Meeting, II.
Minutes of the London Six Weeks' Meeting, II, 1682–92/3.

Shrewsbury School Library
MS James XXVIII, Diary of Philip Henry, 1673.

Somerset Archaeological and Natural History Society, Taunton
Manuscript volume of 17th-century sermons, including Thomas Trescot, 'A Catechism by way of preparation to ye worthy receiving of ye Sacrament of the Lords Supper', n.d.

Warwickshire County Record Office, Warwick
MS CR 802, Bedworth Independent (Old Meeting) Church Book [also known as Julius Saunders, Diary], 1687–1815.

Yorkshire Archaeological Society, Leeds
MS 21, 'Diary of Ralph Thoresby', September 1677 – 31 May 1683.

In private hands
Transcript of Philip Henry's 1662 Diary, possibly by Thomas Stedman, in the possession of Mr John Warburton Lee, Broad Oak, Whitchurch, Shropshire.

Books and Articles

(Place of publication: London, unless otherwise stated)
Addy, William, *Stenographia, or the art of short-writing*, 1695.
Alleine, Joseph, *A Call to Archippus, or an Humble and Earnest Motion to some ejected Ministers ... to take heed to their Ministry, That they fulfil it*, 1664.
— *Christian Letters*, 1671.
— *A Most Familiar Explanation of the Assemblies Shorter Catechisms*, 1674.
— *Remaines of that excellent Minister ...* , 1674.
Alleine, Richard, *The Godly Man's Portion and Sanctuary Opened, being the Second Part of Vindiciae Pietatis*, 1663.
— *Heaven Opened*, 1665.
[Alleine, Theodosia], *The Life and Death of ... Joseph Alleine*, 1671 (includes his *Christian Letters*).
Ambrose, Isaac, *Compleat Works*, 1674.
— *Prima, Media and Ultima* (4 parts), 1654.
— *War with Devils*, 1674.
Ames, William, *The Marrow of Sacred Divinity*, 1642.
Anon., *Axminster Ecclesiastica 1660–1698* (ed. K.W.H. Howard), Sheffield, 1976.
— *The Bristol Narrative*, 1675.
— *The Calendar of State Papers, Domestic Series, in the Reign of Charles II* (28 vols), 1860–1939.
— *The Calendar of State Papers, Domestic Series, in the Reign of James II* (3 vols), 1960–72.
— *The Church Books of Ford or Cuddington and Amersham Baptist Churches* (ed. W.T. Whitley), 1912.
— *A Collection of the Farewell Sermons of Divers London and Country Ministers in Three Volumns*, 1663.
— *A Compleat Collection of Farewel Sermons, Preached by Mr. Calamy, Dr. Manton etc ...* , 1663.
— *The Confession of Faith and the Larger and Shorter Cathechisme ... Assembly of Divines at Westminster*, 1651.
— 'Congregationalism in the Fen Country', *TCHS* 7 (1916–18), 3–15.
— *A Declaration of the present sufferings of above 140 Persons... (Who are now in Prison,) called Quakers, with a briefe accompt of about 1900 more, being but a part of many more that have suffered within these six years last past ... Together with the number of 21 Persons who were imprisoned and persecuted until Death*, 1659.
— *A Declaration from the Harmless and Innocent People of God called Quakers, against all Plotters and Fighters in the World*, 1661.
— *A Directory for the Publique Worship of God through these Three Kingdomes*, 1646.
— *The Early Records of the General Baptist Church, meeting in or about Bessels Green, Kent* (ed. Leonard J. Maguire), 2001.

— *England's Joy, or a Relation of the most remarkable Passages, from his Majesty's arrival at Dover, to his entrance at Whitehall,* 1660, in *Stuart Tracts, 1603–1693* (ed. C.H. Firth), 1903.
— *England's Remembrancer, Being a Collection of Farewel Sermons Preached by Divers nonconformists in the Country*, 1663.
— *Episcopal Visitation Book for the Archdeaconry of Buckingham, 1662* (ed. E.R.C. Brinkworth), Buckinghamshire Record Society, 7; Aylesbury, 1947.
— *An Exact Collection of Farewel Sermons preached by the Late London-Ministers*, 1662.
— 'The Experiences of Mary Franklin', *TCHS* 2 (1905–6), 387–401.
— *The General Baptist Church in and about Canterbury: Church Book 1660 to 1695* (ed. John Creasey and Leonard J. Maguire), General Baptist Assembly Occasional Paper, 18; 1992.
— *The Journals of the House of Commons*, IX, *from Oct. 10, 1667 to April 28, 1687*, 1802.
— *The Lamentable Sufferings of the Church of God in Dorsetshire, and the persecution there*, 1659.
— *The Life of George Trosse* (ed. A.W. Brink), Montreal, 1974 (first publ. 1714).
— *The London-Ministers Legacy to their several congregations, being a Collection of Farewel Sermons*, 1662.
— 'Manuscript Volume in the Handwriting of Thomas Thompson (1631–1704) of Skipsea, Yorks', *JFHS* 28 (1931), 50.
— 'At a Meeting of the Midwives in Barbadoes', *JFHS* 37 (1940), 22–4.
— *Minute Book of the Men's Meeting of the Society of Friends in Bristol 1667–86* (ed. Russell Mortimer), Publications of the Bristol Record Society, 26; Bristol, 1971.
— *Minute Book of the Men's Meeting of the Society of Friends in Bristol 1686–1704* (ed. Russell Mortimer), Publications of the Bristol Record Society, 30; Bristol, 1977.
— *The Minute Book of the Monthly Meeting of the Society of Friends for the Upperside of Buckinghamshire 1669–1690* (ed. Beatrice Snell), Records Branch of the Buckinghamshire Archaeological Society, 1; High Wycombe, 1937.
— *Minutes of the Consistory of the French Church of London, Threadneedle Street, 1679–1692* (ed. Robin D. Gwynn), Huguenot Society of Great Britain and Ireland Quarto Series, 58; 1994.
— *The Minutes of the First Independent Church [now Bunyan Meeting] at Bedford 1656–1766* (ed. H.G. Tibbutt), Bedfordshire Historical Record Society, 55; Bedford, 1976.
— *Morning Exercise at Cripplegate* (ed. James Nicholls, 6 vols), 1844 (first publ. 1674).
— 'The Prison Correspondence of an Ejected Minister', *TCHS* 1 (1901–4), 345–52.
— 'The Prison Letters of Thomas [John] Maidwell', *TCHS* 3 (1907–8), 367–78.
— *The Querers and Quakers cause at the second hearing*, 1653.
— *The Records of a Church of Christ ... Broadmead, Bristol 1640–1687* (ed. E.B. Underhill), Hanserd Knollys Society; 1847.
— *The Records of a Church of Christ in Bristol, 1640–1687* (ed. Roger Hayden), Bristol Record Society, 27; Bristol, 1974.
— *A Reply to the Bristol Narrative, or a more Just Account of the Imprisonment and Death of Mr. John Thompson*, 1675.
— *The Savoy Declaration of Faith and Order, 1658* (ed. A.G. Matthews), 1959.
— 'A School in Ilchester Jail, 1662', *JFHS* 8 (1911), 16–18.
— *The Second and Last Collection of the Late London Ministers' Farewell Sermons*, 1663.

Bibliography

— *Statutes of the Realm*, IV, Part II, and V, 1819.
— *The Third Volumn of Farewel Sermons, preached by some London and Country Ministers*, 1663.
— *A Transcription of the Church Book of Speldhurst and Pembury (later Tunbridge Wells)* (ed. Leonard J. Maguire), 1998.
— *A True and Impartial Narrative of some Illegal and Arbitrary Proceedings by certain Justices of the Peace and others: against several innocent and peaceable Nonconformists in and near the town of Bedford ...*, 1670.
— *The Western Martyrology*, 1687.
Ashe, John, *A Short Account of the Life of the Rev. Mr. William Bagshaw*, 1704.
Ashwood, Bartholomew, *The Best Treasure, or The Way to be truly Rich*, 1681.
— *The Heavenly Trade, or the Best Merchandizing*, 1679.
Asty, John (ed.), 'Memoirs', in *A Complete Collection of the Sermons of ... John Owen*, 1721.
Asty, Robert, *A Treatise of Rejoycing in the Lord Jesus*, 1683.
Austen, Ralph, *The Spiritual Use of an Orchard* [with *A Treatise of Fruit Trees*], 1653.
Bagshaw, Edward, *The Life and Death of Mr. Vavasor Powell*, 1671.
Banks, John, *A Journal of the Life, Labours, Travels and Sufferings ... of ... John Banks*, 1712.
Barbour, Hugh, and Arthur O. Roberts (eds), *Early Quaker Writings 1650–1700*, Grand Rapids, MI, 1973.
Barnes, Ambrose, *Memoirs of Ambrose Barnes* (ed. W.H.D. Longstaffe), Surtees Society, 50; Durham, 1867.
B[artlet]., J[ohn]., *The Practical Christian*, 1670.
Bates, William, *The Great Duty of Resignation to the Divine Will in Afflictions enforced from the Example of our Suffering Saviour*, 1684.
— *Funeral Sermon for ... Richard Baxter*, 1692.
Baxter, Richard, *An Account of the Reasons*, published with *Catholick Communion Defended against both Extreams*, 1684.
— *An Apology for the nonconformists Ministry*, 1681.
— *A Breviate of the Life of Margaret ... Charlton*, 1681.
— *Calendar of the Correspondence of Richard Baxter* (ed. G.F. Nuttall and N.H. Keeble, 2 vols), Oxford, 1991.
— *Compassionate Counsel to all Young Men ... especially I, London Apprentices, II, Students of Divinity, Physic and Law, III, The Sons of Magistrates and Rich Men*, 1681.
— *Confirmation and Restauration the necessary means of Reformation and Reconciliation*, 1658.
— *A Defence of the Principle of Love*, 1671.
— *Dying Thoughts*, 1683.
— *The English Nonconformity*, 1690.
— Farewell Sermon [on Jn 16:22], in *The Practical Works of Richard Baxter* (4 vols; 1707), IV, 931–44.
— *Gildas Salvianus, or the Reformed Pastor*, 1656.
— *How far Holinesse is the Design of Christianity ... referring to Mr. Fowlers Treatise on this subject*, 1671.
— *The Last Work of a Believer*, 1682.
— *The Mischiefs of Self-Ignorance*, 1662.
— *A Paraphrase of the New Testament*, 1685.
— *Plain Scripture Proof of Infant Church Membership and Baptism*, 1651.
— *The Poor Man's Family Book*, 1674.

— *The Practical Works of the Rev. Richard Baxter* (ed. W. Orme, 23 vols), 1830.
— *The Reasons of the Christian Religion*, 1667.
— *The Saints Everlasting Rest*, 1669.
— *A Treatise of Episcopacy*, 1681.
— *Richard Baxter's Penitent Confession and his Necessary Vindication*, 1691.
Bayly, Lewis, *The Practice of Piety: directing a Christian how to walk that he may please God*, 1648.
Beaumont, Agnes, *The Narrative of the Persecution of Agnes Beaumont in 1674* (ed. G.B. Harrison), n.d.
Besse, Joseph, *A Collection of the Sufferings of the People called Quakers* (2 vols), 1753.
Birdwood, James, *Hearts-Ease in Heart Trouble*, 1690.
Bolde, Samuel, *A Sermon against Persecution*, 1682.
Bolton, Robert, *Mr. [Robert] Boltons last and learned worke of the foure last things*, 1633.
Bradstreet, Ann, 'Meditations Divine and Morall', in *The Complete Works of Anne Bradstreet* (ed. J.R. McElrath and Allan P. Robb; Boston, MA, 1981), 195–209.
Bridge, William, *A Lifting up for the Downcast*, 1961 (first publ. [1648?]).
— *Seasonable Truths in Evil Times*, 1668.
Brooks, Thomas, *Works* (6 vols), Edinburgh, 1980.
Browning, Andrew (ed.), *English Historical Documents*, VIII, *1660–1714*, 1966.
Bruce, Thomas [Earl of Aylesbury], *Memoirs of Thomas, Earl of Ailesbury* (2 vols), 1890.
Bryan, John, *Dwelling with God*, 1670.
Bunyan, John, *Grace Abounding to the Chief of Sinners, with 'A Relation of my Imprisonment'* (ed. Roger Sharrock), Oxford, 1962.
— *Life and Death of Mr. Badman* (ed. James F. Forrest and Roger Sharrock), Oxford, 1988.
— *Miscellaneous Works of John Bunyan* (gen. ed. Roger Sharrock; 13 vols), Oxford, 1976–94.
— *The Pilgrim's Progress*, Part II (ed. J.B. Wharey, rev. Roger Sharrock), Oxford, 1960.
Burroughs, Edward, *The Memorable Works of a Son of Thunder and Consolation ... Edward Burroughs*, 1672.
Burton, Robert, *The Anatomy of Melancholy*, 1628.
Bury, Edward, *A Help to Holy Walking, or a Guide to Glory, containing Directions how to worship God, and to walk with him in the whole course of our Lives*, 1675.
Byfield, Nicholas, *Directions for the Private Reading of the Scriptures*, 1618.
Calamy, Edmund [1600–1666], *The Godly Man's Ark, or City of Refuge in the Day of his Distress*, 6th ed. 1669.
— *The Art of Divine Meditation ... several Sermons on GEN. 24.63*, 1686.
Calamy, Edmund [1671–1732], *An Account of the Ministers ... who were Ejected or Silenced after the Restoration in 1660* (2nd ed.), 1713.
— *A Continuation of the Account of the Ministers ... Ejected* (2 vols), 1727.
— *An Historical Account of my own Life* (ed. J.T. Rutt, 2 vols), 1829.
— 'The Life of John Howe', in *The Works of John Howe* (ed. Edmund Calamy, 2 vols; 1724), I, 1–88.
Charnock, Stephen, *A Discourse of Divine Providence*, in *The Complete Works of Stephen Charnock* (ed. James M'Cosh; Edinburgh, 1864), I, 10–120.
Cheare, Abraham, *Words in Season*, 1668.
Clapinson, M. (ed.), *Bishop Fell and Nonconformity: Visitation Documents from the*

Oxford Diocese, 1682–3, Oxfordshire Record Society, 52; Oxford, 1980.
Clarke, J., *Ill newes from New England*, 1652.
Clarke, Samuel, *A Collection of the Lives of Ten Eminent Divines*, 1662.
— *A General Martyrologie*, 1677.
— *The Lives of Sundry Eminent Persons in this Later Age*, 1683.
Clarkson, David, *Practical Works* (3 vols), Edinburgh, 1864–5.
[Claude, Jean], *An Account of the persecutions and oppressions of the Protestants in France*, 1686.
Coale, Joseph, *Some Account of the Life, Service, and Sufferings of ... Joseph Coale*, 1706.
Coale, Josiah, 'Testimony', in *The Memorable Works of a Son of Thunder and Consolation ... Edward Burroughs*, 1672, [unpaginated].
Collinges, John, *Several Discourses concerning the Actual Providence of God*, 1678.
Collins, Hercules, *Believers Baptism from Heaven and of Divine Institution*, 1691.
— *An Orthodox Catechism*, 1680.
— *Counsel for the Living ... A Discourse ... Arising from the Deaths of Mr. Fran[cis] Bampfield and Mr. Zach[ary] Ralphson*, 1684.
— *Mountains of Brass*, in Three Books, 1696.
— *The Scribe instructed ... Kingdom of Heaven*, in Three Books, 1696.
— *Some Reasons for Separation from the Communion of the Church of England and the Unreasonableness of Persecution upon that Account*, 1682.
— *A Voice from the Prison or Meditations on Revelations III.XI*, 1684.
Corbet, John, *The Remains of ... John Corbet ... from his own Manuscripts*, 1684.
— *Self-Imployment in Secret*, 1681.
Cosin, John, *Correspondence of John Cosin, Bishop of Durham*, Surtees Society, 55, pt II; Durham, 1870.
Coxere, Edward, *Adventures by Sea of Edward Coxere* (ed. E.H.W. Meyerstein), Oxford, 1945.
Crofton, Zachary, *The Hard Way to Heaven*, 1662.
Crook, John, *The Design of Christianity, with other Books, Epistles and Manuscripts of ... John Crook*, 1701.
Crosby, Thomas, *The History of the English Baptists* (4 vols), 1738–40.
Crouch, William, *Posthuma Christiana, or a Collection of some Papers of William Crouch*, 1712.
Danvers, Henry, *A Treatise of Baptism*, 1674.
Dent, Arthur, *The Plaine Man's Pathway to Heaven*, 1605.
Dewsbury, William, *A Discovery of the Ground from whence Persecution did arise, and the Proceedings of those that were Actors in it, in Northamptonshire*, 1665.
D[ewsbury]., W[illiam]., *This for dear Friends in London, and them that are Aboard Ship, in order to Transportation; or else where all abroad*, 1664.
Disney, Gervase, *Some Remarkable Passages in the Holy Life and Death of Gervase Disney*, 1692.
Dix, Henry, *The Art of brachygraphy, or short-writing*, 1641.
Doe, Charles, *A Collection of the Experience of the Work of Grace*, [1700].
— 'The Struggler', in *The Works of That Eminent Servant of Christ Mr. John Bunyan ... containing Ten of his Excellent Manuscripts ... never before printed* (ed. Charles Doe, 3 vols), 1692 [unpaginated conclusion]; also in Bunyan, *MW*, XII, 453–60.
Doolittle, Thomas, *The Lord's Last Sufferings showed in the Lords-Supper*, 1682.
— *A Treatise concerning the Lords Supper*, 1680.
— *Catechism made Practical*, 1688.
— *A Plain Method of Catechizing*, 1699.

Downame, George, *A Treatise of the Certainty of Perseverance*, 1631.
Drapes [Draper], Edward, *Gospel Glory Proclaimed before the Sonnes, in the Visible and Invisible Worship of God*, 1649.
Dyer, William, *A Cabinet of Jewels*, 1663.
— *Christ's Famous Titles*, 1675.
— *Christ's Voice to London*, 1670.
Ellis, Henry, *Original Letters illustrative of English History*, First Series, III, 1969.
— *Original Letters illustrative of English History,* Second Series, IV, 1969.
Ellwood, Thomas, *The History of the Life of Thomas Ellwood* ... (ed. S. Graveson), 1906.
Evans, A[rise]., *An Echo to the voice from heaven. Or a Narration of the Life, and Manner of the Special Calling and Visions of Arise Evans*, 1652.
Everardt, Job, *An Epitome of Stenographie*, 1658.
Farthing, John, *Short-writing shotned* [sic], 1684.
Fell, Leonard, and William Addamson, *The Persecution of them People, they call Quakers, in several places in Lancashire*, 1656.
Fell, Margaret, *A Brief Collection of Remarkable Passages ... relating to ... Margaret Fell*, 1710.
Fincham, Kenneth (ed.), *Visitation Articles and Injunctions of the Early Stuart Church* (2 vols, Church of England Record Society; Woodbridge, 1994), I.
Flavel, John, *Works* (6 vols), 1968 (first publ. 1820).
Fowler, Edward, *The Design of Christianity*, 1671.
Fox, George, *A Collection of the ... Epistles of George Fox*, 1698.
— *George Fox's 'Book of Miracles'* (ed. H.J. Cadbury), Cambridge, 1948.
— *Gospel-Truth Demonstrated*, 1706.
— *A Journal, or Historical Account of the life, travels, sufferings, Christian experiences and labour of love in the work of the ministry of ... George Fox* (ed. Thomas Ellwood, 2 vols), 1694–8.
— *The Journal* (Bicentenary ed., 2 vols), 1891.
— *Journal of George Fox* (ed. John L. Nickalls), Cambridge, 1975.
— *George Fox: The Journal* (ed. Nigel Smith), Harmondsworth, 1998.
— *The Narrative Papers of George Fox* (ed. H.J. Cadbury), Richmond, IN, 1972.
F[ox]. G[eorge]., *A Catechisme for Children* (2nd ed.), 1660.
Foxe, John, *Acts and Monuments* (ed. J. Pratt, 8 vols), [1877].
Froysell, Thomas, *Sermons concerning Grace and Temptation*, 1678.
Gailhard, Jean, *The Blasphemous Socinian Heresie Disproved and Confuted*, 1697.
— *The Controversie between Episcopacy and Presbytery Stated and Discussed*, 1660.
Gale, Theophilus, *The Court of the Gentiles* (4 parts), 1669–78.
— *The Life and Death of Thomas Tregoss*, 1671.
G[askin]., J., *A Just Defence*, 1660.
Geree, John, *The Character of an old English Puritane, or Non-Conformist*, 1646.
Gilling, Isaac, *The Life of Mr. George Trosse*, 1715.
Goodwin, John, *ΠΛΗΡΩΜΑ ΤΟ ΠΝΕΥΜΑΤΙΚΟΝ or A Being Filled with the Holy Spirit*, 1670 (repr. Edinburgh, 1867).
Goodwin, Thomas, *The Vanity of Thoughts Discovered, with their Danger and Cure*, 1643.
— *Patience and its Perfect Work under Sudden and Sore Tryals*, 1667, in *Works* (12 vols; Edinburgh, 1861), II, 429–67.
— *Works* (5 vols), 1681–1704.
Gosnold, John, *Of the Doctrine of Baptisms*, 1657.

Gouge, Thomas, *Christian Directions*, 1675.
— *Joshua's Resolution, or the Private Christian's Duty in Time of Publick Corruption*, 1663.
— *The Surest and Safest Way of Thriving*, 1676, in *The Works of Thomas Gouge* (1706), 76–174.
— *The Young Man's Guide thro' the Wilderness of this World to the Heavenly Canaan*, 1672.
Gouge, William, *Of Domesticall Duties*, 1634.
Grantham, Thomas, *Christianismus Primitivus*, 1678.
— *St. Paul's Catechism; or a brief and plain Explication of the Six Principles*, 1687.
Graveson, S., 'In the year of the Great Fire', *Friends' Quarterly Examiner* 78 (1944), 243–5.
Greenham, Richard, *Grave Counsels and Godly Observations*, in *The Workes of ... Richard Greenham* (3rd ed.), 1601.
Griffith, John, *Gods Oracle and Christs Doctrine, or Six Principles of the Christian Religion*, 1655.
— *Some Prison Meditations and Experiences*, 1663.
Hall, Joseph, *Works* (10 vols), 1863.
— *Meditations and Vowes, Divine and Morall*, 1605.
— *Arte of Divine Meditation*, 1607.
— *Holy Observations*, 1607.
— *Occasional Meditations*, 1630.
— *The Remedy of Prophanenesse, or the True Sight and Feare of the Almighty*, 1637.
— *The Breathings of the Devout Soul and Select Thoughts ... A Century of Divine Breathings for a ravished Soule*, 1648.
— *Susurrium cum Deo: or Holy Self-Conferences of the Devout Soul*, 1651.
— *Holy Raptures*, 1654.
Hanmer, Jonathan, *An Exercitation upon Confirmation ... so long buried ... to which are Annexed some Directions for the putting of it into practice*, 1658.
Harris, William, 'Memoirs of the Life and Character of Thomas Manton', in Thomas Manton, *Works* (1870; repr. Edinburgh, 1993), I, vii–xxxii.
Henry, Philip, *Diaries and Letters of Philip Henry 1631–1696* (ed. M.H. Lee), 1882.
Heywood, Oliver, *Closet Prayer, a Christian Duty*, 1671.
— *Heart-Treasure*, 1667.
— *Oliver Heywood, His Autobiography, Diaries, Anecdotes and Event Books* (ed. J. Horsfall Turner, 4 vols), Brighouse and Bingley, 1882–5.
— *Oliver Heywood's Life of John Angier of Denton*, Chetham Society, n.s. 97; Manchester, 1937.
Hickes, George, *The True Notion of Persecution Stated*, 1681.
[Hickes, John], *A True and Faithful Narrative of the Unjust and Illegal Sufferings of Many Christians, injuriously and injudiciously call'd FANATICKS ... in the County of Devon since the 10th of May, 1670*, 1671.
Hickes, John, *A Discourse of the Excellency of the Heavenly Substance*, 1673.
Hinde, William, *A Faithfull Remonstrance of the Holy Life and Happy Death of John Bruen Esquire of Bruen Stapleford in the County of Chester*, 1641.
Hoby, Margaret, *Diary of Lady Margaret Hoby, 1599–1605* (ed. D.M. Meads), 1930.
H[olcroft]., F[rancis]., *A Word to the Saints from the Watch Tower*, 1668.
Howe, John, *The Whole Works of John Howe* (ed. John Hunt, 8 vols), 1810–22.
H[owgill]., F[rancis]., *A Testimony concerning the Life, Death, Trials, Travels and Labours of Edward Burroughs ... who Dyed a Prisoner in 1662*, 1663.
Hughes, George, *An Analytical Exposition of Genesis ... Exodus*, 1672.

— *Dry Rod Blooming and Fruit-Bearing*, 1644.
Hutchinson, Lucy, *Memoirs of the Life of Colonel Hutchinson*, ed. Neil H. Keeble, 1995.
Isham, Gyles (ed.), *The Correspondence of Bishop Brian Duppa and Sir Justinian Isham, 1650–1660*, Northamptonshire Record Society, 17; Northampton, [1954].
James, Samuel, *An Abstract of the Gracious Dealings of God with some Eminent Christians* (4th ed.), 1774.
Jeake, Samuel, *An Astrological Diary of the Seventeenth Century: Samuel Jeake of Rye 1652–1699*, Oxford (ed. Michael Hunter and Annabel Gregory), 1988.
Jenkyn, William, *The Burning yet unconsumed Bush ... Two Farewell Sermons*, 1662.
Jessey, Henry, *The Lord's Loud Call to England*, 1660.
— *Miscellanea Sacra or Diverse Necessary Truths*, 1665.
— *A Looking Glass for Children*, 1672.
Johnstone, H. (ed.), *Churchwardens' Presentments (Seventeenth Century) Part I. Archdeaconry of Chichester*, Sussex Record Society, 49; Lewes, 1947–8.
Jolly, Thomas, *The Note Book of the Rev. Thomas Jolly 1671–1693* (ed. H. Fishwick), Chetham Society, n.s. 33; Manchester, 1895.
Josselin, Ralph, *The Diary of Ralph Josselin 1616–1683* (ed. Alan Macfarlane), Oxford, 1976.
Keach, Benjamin, *AntiChrist Stormed: or, Mystery Babylon the great Whore ... the present Church of Rome*, 1689.
[—] *The Child's Instructor; or a New and Easy Primmer*, 1664.
— *A Counter-Antidote to purge out the Malignant Effects of a Late Counterfeit, prepared by Mr. Giles Shute, an Unskillful Person in Polemical Cures*, 1694.
— *The Everlasting Covenant: A Sweet Cordial for a Drooping Soul, A Sermon preached at the Funeral of Henry Forty ... Abingdon ... wherein the Arguments used to prove the Covenant of Redemption a distinct Covenant from the Covenant of Grace, are Examined, Weighed and found Wanting*, 1693.
— *Instructions for Children*, 1704.
K[each]., B[enjamin]., *The Travels of True Godliness ... shewing the Troubles, Oppositions, Reproaches, and Persecutions he hath met with in every Age, together with the Danger he seems to be in at this present Time ...* (3rd ed.), 1684.
Keiser, R.M., and Rosemary Moore (eds), *Knowing the Mystery of Life Within: Selected Writings of Isaac Penington in their Historical and Theological Context*, 2005.
Kenyon, J.P. (ed.), *The Stuart Constitution 1603–1688: Documents and Commentary* (2nd ed.), Cambridge, 1986.
Kiffin, William, et al., *Apology of some commonly called Anabaptist ...*, 1660.
— *A Sober Discourse of Right to Church Communion ... proved ... no unbaptized person may be regularly admitted to the Lord's Supper*, 1681.
Knollys, Hanserd, *The Life and Death of that old disciple of Jesus Christ ... Mr. Hanserd Knollys, who died in the 93rd year of his age, written with his own hand to the year 1672, and continued in general with an epistle by Mr. William Kiffin*, 1692.
Lamb, Philip, *The Royal Presence, or God's Tabernacle with Men*, 1662.
Lawson, Thomas, *An Appeal to the Parliament concerning the Poor that there may not be a beggar in England*, 1660.
Lowe, Roger, *The Diary of Roger Lowe, of Ashton-in-Makerfield, Lancs 1663–1674* (ed. W.L. Sachse), 1938.
Lumpkin, W. (ed.), *Baptist Confessions of Faith*, Chicago, IL, 1959.
Luther, Martin, *A Commentarie of M. Doctor Martin Luther upon the Epistle of S. Paul to the Galathians*, 1575.
Lye, Thomas, *The Fixed Saint, held forth in a Farewell Sermon ... All Hallows, Lumbard Street*, 1662.

[Mall, Thomas], *A True account of What was done by a Church of Christ in Exon (whereof Mr. Lewis Stucley is Pastor) ... when two members thereof were Excommunicated*, [1658].
Marshall, Walter, *The Gospel Mystery of Sanctification*, Glasgow, 1764.
Martindale, Adam, *The Life of Adam Martindale* (ed. R. Parkinson), Chetham Society, 4; Manchester, 1845.
Matthews, A.G., 'A Censored Letter: William Hooke in England to John Davenport in New England, 1663', *TCHS* 9 (1924–6), 262–83.
Maurice, Matthias, *Monuments of Mercy*, 1729.
Mead, Matthew, *The Almost Christian Discovered, or the False Professors Tried and Cast*, 1662.
— *The Pastors Valediction*, 1662.
— *The Vision of the Wheels*, 1689.
M[ead]., M[atthew]., *Solomon's Prescription for the Removal of the Pestilence*, 1665.
Metcalfe, T., *Short-Writing*, 1660.
Milton, John, 'Of Reformation touching Church Discipline in England', in J.M. Patrick (ed.), *The Prose of John Milton* (Stuart Editions; New York, 1968), 41–92.
— *Areopagitica*, in *The Complete Prose Works of John Milton*, II, *1643–1648* (New Haven, CT, [1959]), 480–570.
Milward, John, *The Diary of John Milward* (ed. C. Robbins), Cambridge, 1938.
Morrice, Roger, *The Entring Book of Roger Morrice, 1677–1691* (ed. Mark Goldie et al., 7 vols), Woodbridge, 2007–9.
Newcome, Henry, *Autobiography of Henry Newcome* (ed. Richard Parkinson, 2 vols), Chetham Society, 26–27; Manchester, 1852.
[—], *A Faithful Narrative of the Life and Death of ... John Machin*, 1671.
— *Diary of Henry Newcome, 1661–1663* (ed. T. Heywood), Chetham Society, 18; Manchester, 1849.
Newton, George, *A Sermon preached at the Funeral of Mr. Joseph Alleine*, 1672.
Norcott, John, *Baptism discovered plainly and faithfully according to the Word of God*, 1675
Norman, John, *Christ Confessed: written by a Preacher of the Gospel, and now a Prisoner*, 1665.
Orme, William (ed.), *Remarkable Passages in the Life of William Kiffin*, 1823.
Owen, John, *The Works of John Owen* (ed. W.H. Goold; 24 vols), Edinburgh, 1862.
Parnell, James, *The Shield of the Truth*, 1655
Patient, Thomas, *The Doctrine of Baptism and the distinction of covenants, or a plain treatise wherein the four essentials of baptism ... are deliberately handled*, 1654.
Pearse, Edward, *The Conformist's Fourth Plea for the nonconformists*, 1683.
Penington, Isaac, *The Works of Isaac Penington*, 1681.
Penn, William, *No Cross, No Crown*, 1669 and 1682 eds.
— *A Brief Account of the Rise and Progress of the People called Quakers*, 1694.
— *A Collection of the Works of William Penn* (ed. Joseph Besse), 2 vols; 1726.
Penney, Norman (ed.), *Extracts from State Papers relating to Friends 1654–1672*, 1913.
— (ed.), *The First Publishers of Truth*, 1907.
Pepys, Samuel, *The Diary of Samuel Pepys* (ed. R. Latham and W. Matthews, 11 vols), 1971–83.
Perkins, William, *Of the Calling of the Ministerie, Two Treatises*, 1606.
— *Works* (3 vols), 1616.
Perrot, John, *To the Suffering Seed of Royalty*, 1661.
— *A Narrative of the Sufferings of J[ohn] P[errot] in the City of Rome*, 1661.

Philoeusebias Misonebulonides, *A Letter to Hilton, the Grand Informer: In Answer to his Several Late Printed Libels*, 1682.
Piggott, John, 'A sermon preached at the funeral of Rev. Mr. Hercules Collins', in *Eleven Sermons preached upon special occasions*, 1714.
Polhill, Edward, *Armatura Dei ... Preparation for Suffering in an Evil Day*, 1682.
Powell, Vavasor, *The Bird in the Cage chirping Four Distinct Notes to his Consorts Abroad* (2nd ed. corrected and enlarged), 1662.
[—] *The Sufferer's Catechism*, 1664.
Preston, John, *The New Covenant, or the Saints Portion*, 1629
— *The New Creature, or a Treatise of Sanctification*, published with *The Saints Qualification*, 1634.
P[urnell]., R[obert]., *The Church of Christ in Bristol*, 1657.
Ranew, Nathanael, *Solitude Improved by Divine Meditation*, 1670.
Reresby, John, *Memoirs of Sir John Reresby* (ed. Andrew Browning), Glasgow, 1936.
Reeve, John, ΜΕΤΑΣΧΗΜΑΤΙΣΜΟΣ, *or a Sermon preached ... Funeral of Thomas Brooks*, 1680.
Rigge, Ambrose, *Constancy in the Truth Commended ... True Account of the Life and Sufferings ... of Ambrose Rigge*, 1710.
Roberts, Daniel, *Some Memoirs of the Life of John Roberts*, Exeter, 1746.
Rogers, John, *Ohel or Bethshemesh ... An Idea of Church Discipline*, 1653.
Rogers, Richard, *Seaven Treatises*, 1610.
Rutherford, Samuel, *Letters of Samuel Rutherford* (ed. Andrew Bonar), Edinburgh, 1891.
— *Joshua Redivivus, or Mr. Rutherfoord's Letters*, [Edinburgh], 1664.
Ryther, John, *Sea-Dangers and Deliverances Improved*, published with *James Janeway's Legacy to his Friends*, 1675.
Samm, John, *A Salutation to the Little Flock ... And an exhortation*, 1663.
Sancroft, William, *Lex Ignea, or The School of Righteousness, A sermon preached before the King on October 10, 1666, at the Solemn Fast appointed for the late fire in London*, 1666.
Sansom, Oliver, *An Account of many Remarkable Passages in the life of ... Oliver Sansom*, 1710.
S[haw]., S[amuel]., *The Voice of one Crying in the Wilderness*, 1674.
Shelton, T., *Tachy-graphy*, 1668.
Shower, John, *Serious Reflections on Time and Eternity*, 1689.
Sibbes, Richard, *A Fountain Sealed, or the Duty of the Sealed to the Spirit*, 1637.
— *The Christian Work* [1639], in *The Complete Works of Richard Sibbes* (ed. A.B. Grosart, 7 vols; Edinburgh, 1862–4), V, 1–34.
— *The Excellencie of the Gospell above the Law*, 1639.
Slate, Richard (ed.), *Select Nonconformists' Remains*, 1814.
Sparke, Michael, *The Crums of Comfort ... with godly prayers*, 1628.
Spurstow, William, *The Spiritual Chymist, or Six Decads of Divine Meditations*, 1666.
Steele, Richard, *The Husbandman's Calling, being the substance of twelve sermons to a country congregation*, 1670.
Stockton, Owen, *Consolation in Life and Death*, 1681.
— *A Treatise of Family Instruction*, 1672.
— *A Scriptural Catechism*, 1672.
Stouppe, Jean-Baptiste, *A Collection or Narative sent to ... the Lord Protector ... concerning ... Massacres ... in the Valleys of Piedmont*, 1655.
Storey, Matthew (ed.), *Two East Anglian Diaries: Isaac Archer and William Coe*, Suffolk Records Society, 36; Woodbridge, 1994.

Swinnock, George, *The Christian-Man's Calling; or a Treatise of making Religion Ones Business*, 3 parts, 1668, 1663, 1665.
— *The Pastors Farewell and Wish of Welfare for His People*, 1662.
Sylvester, Matthew (ed.), *Reliquiae Baxterianae*, 1696.
Taylor, Nathaniel, *A Funeral Sermon occasioned by the sudden death of Nathanael Vincent*, 1697.
Thomas, William, *A Preservative of Piety*, 1662.
Thoresby, Ralph, *The Diary of Ralph Thoresby* (ed. Joseph Hunter, 2 vols), 1830.
Thorne, George, *The Saints Great Duty in Times of Dangerous Afflictions, Persecutions and Oppressions*, 1664.
Tibbutt, H.G. (ed.), *Some Early Nonconformist Church Books*, Bedfordshire Historical Record Society, 51; Bedford, 1972.
Tillotson, John, *Six Sermons ... of Stedfastness in Religion*, 1694.
Tomlyns, Samuel, *The Great Duty of Christians ... Go forth without the Camp*, 1682.
Tong, W., *Some Memoirs of the Life and Death of ... John Shower*, 1716.
Turner, G. Lyon (ed.), *Original Records of Early Nonconformity under Persecution and Indulgence* (3 vols), 1911.
[Tutchin, John], *A New Martyrology*, 1693.
Udall, John, *Certaine sermons taken out of Severall places of Scripture*, 1596.
Underhill, E.B. (ed.), *Confessions of Faith, and other Public Documents, illustrative of the History of the Baptist Churches of England in the Seventeenth Century*, 1854.
— (ed.), *Records of the Churches of Christ gathered in Fenstanton, Warboys and Hexham 1644–1720*, 1854.
Ussher, James, *A Method for Meditation*, 1651.
Vincent, Nathanael, *A Covert from the Storm, or The Fearful Encouraged in Times of Suffering*, 1671.
— *The Cure of Distractions in attending upon God in several sermons preached from 1 Cor. 7: 35*, 1695.
Vincent, Thomas, *The Foundation of God standeth sure: or, a defence of those fundamental ... doctrines, the Trinity of Persons in the Unity of the Divine Essence; the Satisfaction of Christ; ... the Justification of the Ungodly by the imputed righteousness of Christ, against the cavils of W[illiam] P[enn] J[unior], in his pamphlet entituled, The Sandy Foundation shaken, etc.*, 1668.
V[incent]., T[homas]., *God's Terrible Voice in the City ... in the History of the two late dreadful Judgments of Plague and Fire in London*, 1667.
Wadsworth, Thomas, *Supplement to the Morning Exercise at Cripplegate*, 1674.
Walker, Williston (ed.), *The Creeds and Platforms of Congregationalism*, New York, 1991; first publ. 1893.
Watson, Thomas, *A Body of Practical Divinity ... Sermons on the Lesser Catechism*, 1692.
— *A Christian on the Mount, or a Treatise concerning Meditation* (2nd ed., 1659), in *Three Treatises* (6th ed., 1660), 331–431.
— *The Fight of Faith Crowned ... preached at the Funeral of Mr. Henry Stub[b]s*, 1678.
— *Heaven taken by Storm*, 1669.
— *Light in Darkness, or Deliverance proclaimed unto the Church ... in all despondencies and discouragements*, 1679.
— *A Pastors Love ... in a Farewel Sermon*, 1662.
Wells, Samuel, *A Spiritual Remembrancer ... with 32 Epistolary Discourses ... by their Absent Pastor week after week*, 1676.
White, B.R. (ed.), *Association Records of the Particular Baptists of England, Wales and*

Ireland to 1660, Part II, *The West Country and Ireland*, n.d.
Whitehead, George, *The Christian Progress of ... George Whitehead*, 1725.
Whiteman, Anne, with Mary Clapinson (eds), *The Compton Census of 1676: A Critical Edition*, Oxford, 1986.
Whitelocke, Bulstrode, *The Diary of Bulstrode Whitelocke* (ed. Ruth Spalding), Records of Social and Economic History, n.s. 13; Oxford, 1990.
Whiting, J., *Persecution Exposed*, 1791.
Williams, Daniel, *Christian Sincerity... Funeral Sermon ... Thomas Doolittle*, 1707.
Wilkins, D., *Concilia Magnae Britanniae et Hiberniae* (4 vols), 1737.
Wood, Anthony, *The Life and Times of Anthony Wood, Antiquary, of Oxford 1635–1695 described by Himself* (ed. Andrew Clarke, 5 vols), Oxford, 1894.

Broadsheets

Alleine, Joseph, *Directions for Covenanting with God*, 1674
— *Old Mr. Dod's Sayings*, 1671.
— *Old Mr. Edmund Calamy's Former and Latter Sayings upon Several Occasions*, 1674.
— *Mr. Jenkin's Dying Thoughts*, 1685.

Newspapers

Domestick Intelligence, or News from both City and Country, nos 14 (22 August 1679), 16 (29 August 1679).
Mercurius Politicus, no. 563 (21–28 April 1659).
Mercurius Publicus, no. 1 (3–10 January 1661).
The Kingdome's Intelligencer, no. 14 (1–8 April 1661).

Secondary Sources

Books

Achinstein, Sharon, *Literature and Dissent in Milton's England*, Cambridge, 2003.
Appleby, David, *Black Bartholomew's Day: Preaching, Polemic and Restoration Nonconformity*, Manchester, 2007.
Ball, Bryan W., *The Seventh Day Men, Sabbatarians and Sabbatarianism in England and Wales, 1600–1800*, Oxford, 1994.
Barbour, Hugh, *The Quakers in Puritan England*, New Haven, CT, 1964.
Bate, Frank, *The Declaration of Indulgence, 1672: A Study in the Rise of Organised Dissent*, Liverpool, 1908.
Beeke, Joel R., *Puritan Reformed Spirituality*, Grand Rapids, MI, 2004.
Bewes, W.A., *Church Briefs*, 1896.
Bosher, R.S., *The Making of the Restoration Settlement*, 1951.
Bozeman, T.D., *To Live Ancient Lives: The Primitivist Dimension in Puritanism*, Chapel Hill, NC, 1988.
Braithwaite, W.C., *The Beginnings of Quakerism*, York, 1970.
— *The Second Period of Quakerism*, 1919.
Brayshaw, A.N., *The Personality of George Fox*, 1933.

Brentnall, J.M., *William Bagshawe: The Apostle of the Peak*, 1970.
Browne, John, *History of Congregationalism and Memorials of the Churches in Norfolk and Suffolk*, 1877.
Carpenter, Edward, *The Protestant Bishop: Being the Life of Henry Compton, 1632–1713, Bishop of London*, 1956.
Cliffe, J.T., *The Puritan Gentry Besieged, 1650–1700*, 1993.
Clifton, R., *The Last Popular Rebellion: The Western Rising of 1685*, 1984.
Coffey, John, *John Goodwin and the Puritan Revolution*, Woodbridge, 2006.
— *Politics, Religion and the British Revolutions: The Mind of Samuel Rutherford*, Cambridge, 1997.
— and P.C.H. Lim (eds), *The Cambridge Companion to Puritanism*, Cambridge, 2008.
Coleby, Andrew M., *Central Government and the Localities: Hampshire, 1649–1689*, Cambridge, 1987.
Collinson, Patrick, *From Cranmer to Sancroft*, 2006.
— *The Elizabethan Puritan Movement*, 1967.
— *A Mirror of Elizabethan Puritanism: The Life and Letters of 'Godly Master Dering'*, Friends of the Dr Williams's Library Lecture, 1963; 1964.
Cox, Janice V. (ed.), *The People of God: Shrewsbury Dissenters, 1660–1699* (2 vols), Shropshire Record Series, 9–10; Keele, 2006–7.
Cragg, Gerald R., *Puritanism in the Period of the Great Persecution 1660–1688*, Cambridge, 1957.
Cressy, David, *Birth, Marriage, and Death: Ritual, Religion, and the Life-Cycle in Tudor and Stuart England*, Oxford, 1997.
Davies, Adrian, *The Quakers in English Society 1655–1725*, Oxford, 2000.
Davies, Horton, *The Worship of the English Puritans*, 1948.
Davies, Horton, *Worship and Theology in England*, II: *From Andrewes to Baxter and Fox, 1603–1690*, Princeton, NJ, 1975.
Davies, Horton and Marie-Hélène, *French Huguenots in English-Speaking Lands*, New York and Washington, DC, 2000.
Earle, Peter, *Monmouth's Rebels: The Road to Sedgemoor, 1685*, 1977.
Flew, R. Newton, *The Idea of Perfection in Christian Theology*, Oxford, 1934.
Fry, A. Ruth, *John Bellers 1654–1725, Quaker, Economist and Social Reformer*, 1935.
Glass, Norman, *The Early History of the Independent Church at Rothwell*, 1871.
Goldie, Mark, *A Darker Shade of Pepys: The Entring Book of Roger Morrice*, Friends of the Dr Williams's Library Lecture, 2007; 2009.
Gordon, Alexander (ed.), *Freedom after Ejection: A Review (1690–92) of Presbyterian and Congregational Nonconformity in England and Wales*, Manchester, 1917.
Greaves, Richard L., *Deliver us from Evil: The Radical Underground in Britain 1660–63*, Oxford, 1986.
— *Glimpses of Glory: John Bunyan and English Dissent*, Stanford, CA, 2002.
— *John Bunyan and English Nonconformity*, 1992.
— *Saints and Rebels: Seven Nonconformists in Stuart England*, Macon, GA, 1985.
— and R. Zaller (eds), *Biographical Dictionary of British Radicals in the Seventeenth Century* (3 vols), Brighton, 1982–4.
Green, I.M., *The Re-establishment of the Church of England*, Oxford, 1978.
— *The Christian's ABC: Catechisms and Catechising in England, c.1530–1740*, Oxford, 1996.
Grell, O.P., J. Israel and N. Tyacke (eds), *From Persecution to Toleration: The Glorious Revolution and Religion in England*, Oxford, 1991.
Gwynn, Robin, *Huguenot Heritage: The History and Contribution of the Huguenots in Britain* (2nd rev. ed.), Brighton, 2001.

— *The Huguenots of London*, Brighton, 1998.
Halley, Robert, *Lancashire: Its Puritanism and Nonconformity* (2nd ed.), Manchester, 1872.
Harris, Tim, *London Crowds in the Reign of Charles II: Propaganda and Politics from the Restoration until the Exclusion Crisis*, Cambridge, 1987.
— *Restoration: Charles II and his Kingdom, 1660–1685*, 2005.
— *Revolution: The Great Crisis of the British Monarchy*, 2006.
Hart, A.Tindal, *The Life and Times of John Sharp, Archbishop of York*, 1949.
Hilton, J.A., *Catholic Lancashire: From Reformation to Renewal 1559–1991*, Chichester, 1994.
Historical Manuscripts Commission, *Calendar of the Manuscripts of the Marquess of Ormonde*, n.s., III, VII, RCHM, 36, 1904, 1912.
Historical Manuscripts Commission, *XIIth Report, Appendix VII, The Manuscripts of S.H. Le Fleming*, RCHM, 25, 1890.
Historical Manuscripts Commission, *Fourteenth Report, Vol. III, Appendix II, The Manuscripts of His Grace the Duke of Portland*, RCHM, 29, 1894.
Historical Manuscripts Commission, *XVth Report, Appendix VIII, The Manuscripts of His Grace the Duke of Buccleuch, and Queensberry*, RCHM, 44, 1897.
Holifield, E.B., *The Covenant Sealed: The Development of Puritan Sacramental Theology in Old and New England, 1570–1720*, New Haven, CT, 1986.
Holmes, Clive, *Seventeenth-Century Lincolnshire*, History of Lincolnshire, 7; Lincoln, 1980.
Horton, R.F., *John Howe*, 1895.
Hughes, Philip Edgcumbe, *The Theology of the English Reformers*, 1965.
Huntley, F.J., *Bishop Joseph Hall 1574–1656: A Biographical and Critical Study*, Cambridge, 1979.
Hutton, Ronald, *The Restoration: A Political and Religious History of England and Wales, 1658–1667*, Oxford, 1985.
Ivimey, Joseph, *A History of the English Baptists* (4 vols), 1811–30.
Kaufmann, U. Milo, *The Pilgrim's Progress and Traditions in Puritan Meditation*, New Haven, CT, 1966.
Keeble, N.H. (ed.), *John Bunyan: Reading Dissenting Writing*, Bern, 2002.
— *The Literary Culture of Nonconformity in Later Seventeenth-Century England*, Leicester, 1987.
— *The Restoration: England in the 1660s*, Oxford, 2002.
— *Richard Baxter, Puritan Man of Letters*, Oxford, 1982.
Kenyon, J.P., *The Popish Plot*, 1972.
Knott, John R., *Discourses of Martyrdom, 1561–1694*, Cambridge, 1993.
Kreitzer, Larry J., *'Seditious Sectaryes': The Baptist Conventiclers of Oxford 1641–1691*, Bletchley, 2006.
Lacey, D.R., *Dissent and Parliamentary Politics in England, 1661–1689*, New Brunswick, NJ, 1969.
Lewis, Peter, *The Genius of Puritanism*, Haywards Heath, [1975].
Lloyd, Arnold, *Quaker Social History*, 1950.
McCabe, Richard A., *Joseph Hall: A Study in Satire and Meditation*, Oxford, 1982.
Macdonald, Michael, *Mystical Bedlam: Madness, Anxiety and Healing in Seventeenth-Century England*, Cambridge, 1981.
McElligott, J. (ed.), *Fear, Exclusion and Revolution: Roger Morrice and Britain in the 1680s* (Burlington, VT, and Aldershot, 2006), 189–203.
Macfarlane, Alan, *The Family Life of the Rev. Ralph Josselin: An Essay in Historical Anthropology*, Cambridge, 1970.

McGee, J. Sears, *The Godly Man in Stuart England 1629–1670*, New Haven, CT, 1976.
Mackay, John A., *A Preface to Christian Theology*, 1942.
Mascuch, Michael, *The Origins of the Individualist Self: Autobiography and Self-Identity in England*, Cambridge, 1997.
Matthews, A.G., *Calamy Revised, being a revision of Edmund Calamy's Account of the Ministers and others Ejected and Silenced, 1660–2*, Oxford, 1934.
Mayor, Stephen, *The Lord's Supper in Early English Dissent*, 1972.
Miller, John, *After the Civil Wars: English Politics and Government in the Reign of Charles II*, Harlow, 1999.
— *Charles II*, 1991.
— *James II: A Study in Kingship*, 1989.
— *Popery and Politics in England 1660–1688*, Cambridge, 1973.
Mullett, Michael, *Catholics in Britain and Ireland, 1558–1829*, Basingstoke, 1989.
—, (ed.), *Early Lancaster Friends*, Occasional Paper, University of Lancaster Centre for North West Regional Studies; Lancaster, 1978.
Nuttall, Geoffrey F., *The Holy Spirit in Puritan Faith and Experience*, Oxford, 1947.
— *Visible Saints: The Congregational Way 1640–1660*, Oxford, 1957.
— *The Welsh Saints, 1640–1660*, Cardiff, 1957.
— and Owen Chadwick, *From Uniformity to Unity 1662–1962*, 1962.
— et al., *The Beginnings of Nonconformity: The Hibbert Lectures*, 1964.
Orchard, Stephen, *Nonconformity in Derbyshire: A Study of Dissent, 1600–1800*, Milton Keynes, 2009.
Packer, J.I., *The Redemption and Restoration of Man in the Thought of Richard Baxter*, Carlisle, 2003.
Powicke, F.J., *Richard Baxter under the Cross*, 1927.
Pruett, J.H., *The Parish Clergy under the Later Stuarts: The Leicestershire Experience*, Urbana, IL, 1978.
Reay, Barry (ed.), *Popular Culture in Seventeenth-Century England*, 1985.
Richardson, R.C., *Puritanism in North-West England: A Regional Study of the Diocese of Chester to 1642*, Manchester, 1972.
Rogers, Henry, *The Life and Character of John Howe*, 1863.
Rohr, J. von, *The Covenant of Grace in Puritan Thought*, Atlanta, GA, 1986.
Rowntree, Joshua, *Social Service: Its Place in the Society of Friends*, Swarthmore Lecture; n.pl., 1913.
Schucking, Levin L., *The Puritan Family: A Social Study from the Literary Sources*, 1969.
Scott, David, *Quakerism in York, 1650–1720*, Borthwick Paper, 80; York, 1991.
Seaward, Paul, *The Cavalier Parliament and the Reconstruction of the Old Regime, 1661–1667*, Cambridge, 1989.
— *The Restoration, 1660–1688*, Basingstoke, 1991.
Sharp, T., *The Life of John Sharp, Lord Archbishop of York* (2 vols), 1825.
Smith, David L., *A History of the Modern British Isles, 1603–1707*, Oxford, 1998.
Spaeth, Donald A., *The Church in an Age of Danger: Parsons and Parishioners, 1660–1740*, Cambridge, 2000.
Spalding, Ruth, *The Improbable Puritan: A Life of Bulstrode Whitlocke 1605–1675*, 1975.
Spencer, Carole Dale, *Holiness: The Soul of Quakerism. An Historical Analysis of the Theology of Holiness in the Quaker Tradition*, Milton Keynes, 2007.
Spufford, Margaret, *Contrasting Communities: English Villages in the Sixteenth and Seventeenth Centuries*, Cambridge, 1979.
— *Small Books and Pleasant Histories: Popular Fiction and its Readership in*

Seventeenth-Century England, 1981.
— (ed.), *The World of Rural Dissenters 1520–1725*, Cambridge, 1995.
Spurr, John, *England in the 1670s: 'This masquerading age'*, Oxford, 2000.
— *English Puritanism 1603–1689*, Basingstoke, 1998.
— *The Post-Reformation: Religion, Politics and Society in Britain, 1603–1714*, Harlow, 2006.
— *The Restoration Church of England, 1646–1689*, New Haven, CT, 1991.
Stanford, Charles, *Joseph Alleine: His Companions and Times*, [1861].
Sutherland, Martin, *Peace, Toleration and Decay: The Ecclesiology of Later Stuart Dissent*, Carlisle, 2003.
Swaim, Kathleen M., *Pilgrim's Progress, Puritan Progress: Discourses and Contexts*, Urbana, IL, 1993.
Swatland, A., *The House of Lords in the Reign of Charles II*, Cambridge, 1996.
Sykes, Norman, *From Sheldon to Secker: Aspects of English Church History 1660–1768*, Cambridge, 1959.
Tanner, William, *Three Lectures on the Early History of the Society of Friends in Bristol and Somersetshire*, 1858.
Taylor, Edgar, *The Suffolk Bartholomeans*, 1840.
Till, Barry, *The Church Courts 1660–1720: The Revival of Procedure*, Borthwick Paper, 109; York, 2006.
Tolmie, Murray, *The Triumph of the Saints: The Separate Churches of London 1616–1649*, Cambridge, 1977.
Toon, Peter, *God's Statesman: The Life and Work of John Owen*, Exeter, 1971.
Underwood, T.L., *Primitivism, Radicalism, and the Lamb's War: The Baptist-Quaker Conflict in Seventeenth-Century England*, New York, 1997.
Urwick, W., *Historical Sketches of Nonconformity in the County Palatine of Chester*, 1864.
Wakefield, Gordon S., *Puritan Devotion: Its Place in the Development of Christian Piety*, 1957.
— *Bunyan the Christian*, 1992.
Walker, Austin, *The Excellent Benjamin Keach*, Dundas, ON, 2004.
Wallace, Dewey D., junr, *The Spirituality of the Later English Puritans*, Macon, GA, 1987.
Wallace, Ronald S., *Calvin's Doctrine of the Word and Sacrament*, Edinburgh, 1953.
Walsham, Alexandra, *Providence in Early Modern England*, Oxford, 1999.
Watkins, Brian, *Taming the Phoenix: Cirencester and the Quakers 1642–1686*, York, 1998.
Watkins, Owen C., *The Puritan Experience*, 1972.
Watts, Michael R., *The Dissenters: From the Reformation to the French Revolution*, Oxford, 1978.
Wesley, John, *The Works of John Wesley, 22, Journals and Diaries, Vol. V (1765–1775)* (ed. W.R. Ward and R.P. Heitzenrater), Nashville, TN, 1993.
Westcott, B.F., *Social Aspects of Christianity*, 1887.
White, B.R., *The English Baptists of the Seventeenth Century*, 1983.
— *The English Separatist Tradition*, Oxford, 1971.
Whiting, C.E., *Studies in English Puritanism from the Restoration to the Revolution 1660–1688*, 1931.
Williams, J.B. (ed.), *The Lives of Philip and Matthew Henry*, Edinburgh, 1974.
Wilson, Walter, *The History and Antiquities of Dissenting Churches and Meeting Houses in London* (4 vols), 1808–14.
Wrightson, K., and D. Levine, *Poverty and Piety in an English Village: Terling 1525–*

1700, New York, 1979.
Wykes, David L. *'To Revive the Memory of some Excellent Men': Edmund Calamy and the Early Historians of Nonconformity*, Friends of Dr Williams's Library Lecture; 1997.
Yuille, J. Stephen, *Puritan Spirituality: The Fear of God in the Affective Theology of George Swinnock*, Milton Keynes, 2007.

Articles and Chapters

Anon., 'Baptists in East Kent', *BQ* 2 (1924–5), 90–2, 137–41, 180–8.
— 'Early Nonconformist Academies', *TCHS* 3 (1907–8), 272–90.
Bauman, R., 'Aspects of Seventeenth Century Quaker Rhetoric', *Quarterly Journal of Speech* 56 (1970), 67–74.
Beddard, R.A., 'James II and the Catholic Challenge', in Nicholas Tyacke (ed.), *The History of the University of Oxford*, IV, *Seventeenth-Century Oxford* (Oxford, 1997), 907–54.
— 'The Protestant Succession', in idem (ed.), *The Revolutions of 1688* (Oxford, 1991), 1–10.
— 'The Restoration Church', in J.R. Jones (ed.), *The Restored Monarchy* (1979), 155–75.
— 'Sheldon and Anglican Recovery', *HistJ* 19 (1976), 1005–17.
— 'Vincent Alsop and the Emancipation of Restoration Dissent', *JEH* 24 (1973), 161–84.
Bitterman, M.G.F., 'The Early Quaker Literature of Defence', *ChH* 42 (1973), 203–28.
Blackwood, B.G., 'Agrarian Unrest and Early Lancashire Quakers', *JFHS* 51 (1966), 72–6.
Braithwaite, A.W., 'Early Tithe Prosecutions: Friends as Outlaws', *JFHS* 49 (1960), 153–5.
Brown, Raymond, 'Baptist *Relating and Resourcing* in Difficult Times: A Historical Perspective', in P.J. Lalleman (ed.), *Challenging to Change – Dialogues with a Radical Baptist Theologian: Essays presented to Nigel G. Wright* (2009), 11–24.
— 'Bedfordshire Nonconformist Devotion: Another Look at the Agnes Beaumont Story (1674), *BQ* 35 (1994), 310–23.
Chadwick, S.J., 'The Farnley Wood Plot', in *Miscellanea*, Thoresby Society Publications, 15 (1905–9), 122–6.
Clark, G.N., 'The Barbary Corsairs in the Seventeenth Century', *Cambridge Historical Journal* 8 (1944), 22–35.
Clark, R., 'Why was Re-Establishment of the Church of England Possible? Derbyshire: A Provincial Perspective', *Midland History* 8 (1983), 86–105.
Clarke, P. 'Migration in England during the late Seventeenth and early Eighteenth Centuries', *P&P* no. 83 (1979), 57–90.
Cottle, B., and M.J. Crossley Evans, 'A Nonconformist Missionary Journey to Lancashire and Cheshire in July, 1672', *Transactions of the Historical Society of Lancashire and Cheshire* 137 (1987), 77–91.
Evans, Eifion, 'Richard Baxter's Influence in Wales', *National Library of Wales Journal* 33 (2003), 141–67.
Evans, R.H., 'Nonconformists in Leicestershire in 1669', *Transactions of the Leicestershire Archaeological Society* 25 (1949), 98–143.
Findlay, Elspeth, 'Ralph Thoresby the Diarist: The Late Seventeenth-Century Pious Diary and its Demise', *The Seventeenth Century* 17 (2002), 108–30.

Fletcher, Anthony, 'The Enforcement of the Conventicle Acts, 1664–1679', in W.J. Sheils (ed.), *Persecution and Toleration* (SCH, 21; Oxford, 1984), 235–46.

Freeman, Thomas S., 'A Library in Three Volumes: Foxe's 'Book of Martyrs' in the Writings of John Bunyan', *Bunyan Studies* 5 (Autumn 1994), 47–57.

Furley, O.W., 'The Pope-Burning Processions of the Late Seventeenth Century', *History* 44 (1959), 16–23.

Gee, H., 'The Derwentdale Plot, 1663', *TRHS* 3rd ser. 11 (1917), 125–42.

—— 'A Durham and Newcastle Plot', *Archaeologia Aeliana* 3rd ser. 14 (1917), 145–56.

Goldie, Mark, 'The Hilton Gang and the Purge of London in the 1680s', in *Politics and the Political Imagination in Later Stuart Britain: Essays presented to Lois Green Schwoerer* (ed. Howard Nenner; Rochester, NY, 1997, 43–74.

—— 'The Search for Religious Liberty, 1640–1690', in J. Morrill (ed.), *The Oxford Illustrated History of Tudor and Stuart Britain* (Oxford, 1996), 293–309.

—— and John Spurr, 'Politics and the Restoration Parish: Edward Fowler and the Struggle for St. Giles, Cripplegate', *English Historical Review* 103 (1994), 572–96.

Goring, Jeremy, 'Some Neglected Aspects of the Great Ejection of 1662', *Transactions of the Unitarian Historical Society* 13 (1963), 3–6.

Harley, David, 'Mental Illness, Magical Medicines and the Devil in Northern England, 1650–1700', in R. French and A. Wear (eds), *The Medical Revolution of the Seventeenth Century* (Cambridge, 1989), 114–44.

Hockaday, F.S., 'The Consistory Court of the Diocese of Gloucester', *Transactions of the Bristol and Gloucestershire Archaeological Society* 46 (1924), 195–287.

Hopper, A., 'The Farnley Wood Plot and the Memory of the Civil Wars in Yorkshire', *HistJ* 45 (2002), 281–303.

Hunt, Arnold, 'The Lord's Supper in Early Modern England', *P&P* no. 161 (1998), 39–83.

Jones, R. Tudur, 'The Sufferings of Vavasor', in Mansel John (ed.), *Welsh Baptist Studies* (Cardiff, 1976), 77–91.

Kendall, J., 'The Development of a Distinctive Form of Quaker Dress', *Costume* 19 (1985), 58–61.

Langley, A.S., 'Seventeenth-Century Baptist Disputations', *TBHS* 6 (1919), 216–43.

MacDonald, Michael, 'Religion, Social Change, and Psychological Healing in England, 1600–1800', in S.J. Mews (ed.), *The Church and Healing* (SCH, 19; Oxford, 1982), 101–25.

Macintyre, A., 'The College, King James II, and the Revolution, 1687–1688', in L. Brockliss, G. Harris and A. Macintyre (eds), *Magdalen College and the Crown: Essays for the Tercentenary of the Restoration of the College, 1688* (Oxford, 1988), 31–82.

Miller, John, ' "A Suffering People": English Quakers and their Neighbours, c.1650 – c.1700', *P&P* no. 188 (2005), 71–103.

More, E., 'John Goodwin and the Origins of the New Arminianism', *Journal of British Studies* 22 (1982–3), 50–70.

Morgan, N.J., 'Lancashire Quakers and the Oath, 1660–1722', *JFHS* 54 (1980), 235–54.

Nicholson, F., 'The Kaber Rigg Plot', *Transactions of the Cumberland and Westmorland Antiquarian and Archaeological Society* n.s. 11 (1911), 212–13.

Norrey, P.J., 'The Restoration Regime in Action: The Relationship between Central and Local Government in Dorset, Somerset and Wiltshire 1660–1678', *HistJ* 31 (1988), 789–812.

Nuttall, Geoffrey F., 'The Beginnings of Old Meeting, Bedworth', *TCHS* 20 (1965–70), 255–64.

— 'John Horne of Lynn', in *Christian Spirituality: Essays in Honour of Gordon Rupp* (ed. Peter Brooks; 1975), 231–47.
— 'Nothing else would do: Early Friends and the Bible', *Friends Quarterly* 22 (1982), 651–9; reprinted in idem, *Early Quaker Studies and the Divine Presence* (Weston Rhyn, 2003), 13–24.
— 'The Nurture of Nonconformity: Philip Henry's Diaries', *Transactions of the Honourable Society of Cymmrodorion 1997* n.s. 4 (1998), 5–27.
— 'A Puritan Prayer-Journal 1651–1663', in *Der Pietismus in Gestalten und Wirkungen: Martin Schmidt zum 65. Geburtstag* (ed. H. Bornkamm, F. Heyer and A. Schindler; Arbeiten zur Geschichte des Pietismus, 14; Bielefeld, 1975), 343–54.
— *Studies in English Dissent*, Weston Rhyn, 2002.
Pollock, F., and W.S. Holdsworth, 'Sir Matthew Hale on Hobbes: An Unpublished MS', *Law Quarterly Review* 37 (1921), 274–303.
Reay, Barry, 'Popular Hostility towards Quakers in Mid-Seventeenth-Century England', *Social History* 5 (1980), 387–407.
— 'Quaker Opposition to Tithes, 1652–1660', *P&P* no. 86 (1980), 98–120.
Rivers, Isabel, 'Grace, Holiness, and the Pursuit of Happiness: Bunyan and Restoration Latitudinarianism', in N.H. Keeble (ed.), *John Bunyan: Conventicle and Parnassus, Tercentenary Essays* (Oxford, 1988), 45–69.
Robbins, Caroline, 'The Oxford Session of the Long Parliament of Charles II', *Bulletin of the Institute of Historical Research* 21 (1948), 214–24.
Seaward, Paul, 'Gilbert Sheldon, the London Vestries, and the Defence of the Church', in Tim Harris, Paul Seaward and Mark Goldie (eds), *The Politics of Religion in Restoration England* (Oxford, 1990), 49–73.
Sheils, W.J., 'Oliver Heywood and his Congregation', in idem and Diana Wood (eds), *Voluntary Religion* (SCH, 23; Oxford, 1986), 261–77.
Simmons, J., 'Some Letters from Bishop Ward of Exeter, 1663–1667', *Devon and Cornwall Notes and Queries* 21 (1940–1), 359–61.
Simon, W.G., 'Comprehension in the Age of Charles II', *ChH* 31 (1962), 440–8.
Simpson, Charles R., 'John Bellers in Official Minutes', *JFHS* 12 (1915), 120–7, 165–71.
Spufford, Margaret, 'A Note on the Conder Family', *TCHS* 21 (1971–2), 77–9.
Spufford, Peter, 'Population Mobility in Pre-Industrial England', *Genealogists' Magazine* 17 (1973–4), 420–9, 475–81.
Spurr, John, 'Religion in Restoration England', in Lionel K.J. Glassey (ed.), *The Reigns of Charles II and James VII and II* (1992), 90–124.
Thomas, Roger, 'The Seven Bishops and their Petition, 18 May, 1688', *JEH* 12 (1961), 56–70.
Tibbutt, H.G., 'Francis Holcroft', *TCHS* 20 (1965–70), 295–301.
Vaughan, F.J., 'Bishop Leyburn and his Confirmation Register of 1687', *Northern Catholic History* 12 (1980), 14–18.
Wadsworth, K.W., 'A Tercentenary – Elizabeth Gaunt', *JURCHS* 3 (1986), 316–20.
Walker, J., 'The Yorkshire Plot, 1663', *Yorkshire Archaeological Journal* 31 (1932–4), 348–59.
Webster, Tom, 'Writing to Redundancy: Approaches to Spiritual Journals and Early Modern Spirituality', *HistJ* 39 (1996), 1–34.
White, B.R., 'Isaac Backus and Baptist History', *Baptist History and Heritage* 1 (1970), 13–23.
— 'Thomas Patient in England and Ireland', *Irish Baptist Historical Society Journal* 2 (1969–70), 36–48.

Whiteman, Anne, 'The Re-Establishment of the Church of England, 1660–1663', *TRHS* 5th ser. 5 (1955), 111–31.
Whiting, C.E., 'The Great Plot of 1663', *Durham University Journal* 22 (1920), 155–67.
[Whitley, W.T.], 'Church Covenants', *BQ* 7 (1934–5), 227–34.
Wigfield, W.M., '*Ecclesiastica*, The Book of Remembrance', *Somerset Archaeology and Natural History* 119 (1975), 51–5.
— 'Recusancy and Nonconformity in Bedfordshire, Illustrated by Select Documents 1622–1842', *Publications of the Bedfordshire Historical Record Society* 20 (1938), 145–229.
Williams, J.A., 'English Catholicism under Charles II: The Legal Position', *Recusant History* 7 (1963–4), 123–43.
Williams, Sheila, 'The Pope-Burning Processions of 1679, 1680 and 1681', *Journal of the Warburg and Courtauld Institutes* 21 (1958), 104–18.
Windeatt, E., 'John Flavel: A Notable Dartmouth Puritan and his Bibliography', *Transactions of the Devonshire Association for the Advancement of Science, Literature and Art* 43 (1911), 172–89.
Wykes, David L., 'The 1669 Return of the Nonconformist Conventicles', in K.M. Thompson (ed.), *Short Guides to Records: Second Series, Guides 25–48*; 1994 (Guide 33).
— 'The Bishop of Gloucester's Letter about Nonconformist Conventicles, August 1669', *Transactions of the Bristol and Gloucestershire Archaeological Society* 114 (1996), 97–104.
— 'The Church and Early Dissent: The 1669 Return of the Nonconformist Conventicles for the Archdeaconry of Northampton', *Northamptonshire Past and Present* 8 (1991–2), 197–209.
— 'Early Religious Dissent in Surrey after the Restoration', *Southern History* 33 (2011), 54–77.
— ' "The Sabbaths ... spent before in Idleness and the neglect of the word": the Godly and the Use of Time in their daily Religion', in R.N. Swanson (ed.), *The Use and Abuse of Time in Christian History* (SCH, 37; Woodbridge, 2002), 211–22.
— 'They "assemble in greater numbers and [with] more dareing then formerly": The Bishop of Gloucester and Nonconformity in the late 1660s', *Southern History* 17 (1995), 24–39.

Theses

Black, J.W., 'Richard Baxter and the Ideal of the Reformed Pastor', Ph.D., Cambridge University, 2000.
Brouwer, J.F., 'Richard Baxter's *Christian Directory*: Context and Content', Ph.D., Cambridge University, 2005.
Dowley, Timothy E., 'The History of the English Baptists during the Great Persecution', Ph.D., University of Manchester, 1976.
Field, David P., '"Rigid Calvinisme in a Softer Dresse": The Moderate Presbyterianism of John Howe (1630–1703)', Ph.D., Cambridge University, 1993.
Land, Richard D, 'Doctrinal Controversies of the English Particular Baptists (1644–1691) as illustrated by the career and writings of Thomas Collier', D.Phil., Oxford University, 1980.
Schildt, Jeremy M., ' "Eying and applying and meditating on the promises": Reading the Bible in Seventeenth-Century England', Ph.D., Royal Holloway College, University of London, 2009.

Stevenson, W., 'The Economic and Social Status of Protestant Sectaries in Huntingdonshire, Cambridgeshire and Bedfordshire (1650–1725)', Ph.D., Cambridge University, 1990.

GENERAL INDEX

absenteeism during persecution, 293-7; restoration of offenders, 298-300
academies, 310
Achinstein, Sharon, 333
Acts,
    35 Elizabeth, 4
    for Settling Ministers (1660) 4
    Corporation (1661) 6, 7, 41, 44
    Quaker (1662), 7
    of Uniformity (1662), 8, 14
    Conventicle (1664), 11, 12, 14, 20, 22, 153, 281
    Five Mile (1665), 18-19, 25, 31, 81, 125, 317, 335
    Second Conventicle (1670), 22-24, 337
    Test (1673), 30, 39, 41, 44
Acts and Monuments, 6, 37, 51, 52, 100, 108, 111-12, 130, 152; see also Foxe, John,
Adamson, William, 112
Addy, William, 278
Alleine, Joseph, 59, 69, 78, 79, 80, 81, 85, 102, 109, 117, 118, 119, 120, 121, 123, 127, 128, 145, 146, 147, 148, 155, 156, 158, 163, 164, 165, 169, 170, 172, 178. 181, 200, 234, 266, 271, 297, 312, 316, 320, 322, 323
Alleine, Richard, 55, 56, 148, 149, 155
Alleine, Theodosia, 59
Alsop, Vincent, 28, 41
Ambrose, Isaac, 50, 51, 53, 60, 97, 145, 146, 163, 164, 165, 166, 167, 173, 203, 206, 213, 239, 297
Ambrose, of Milan, 202
Ames, William, 236, 247, 310
Angel, William, 307

Angier, John, 124, 132, 133, 134, 207, 272, 277, 279, 280, 281, 289, 310
Angier, Samuel, 194
Annesley, Samuel, 26, 28, 33
anti-Catholic activity, 6, 30, 40
antinomianism, 161-62. 332
aphorisms, 48, 49, 66, 143
Appleby, David, 10, 154
apprentices, 192, 194, 264, 271, 278, 304, 319, 321, 325, 326
Archer, Isaac, 36, 119, 127, 131, 137, 138, 200, 238, 239, 277-78
Arlington, Lord, 18
Arran, Earl of, 35
Ashe, John, 131, 237
Ashe, Simeon, 124-25
Ashurst, Henry, 137
Ashwood, Bartholomew, 24, 63, 88, 145, 200, 216, 217, 227, 231, 260
Asty, John, 196
Asty, Robert, 86, 145, 147, 167, 257
Augustine, of Hippo, 61, 200, 201, 202, 204
Austen, Ralph, 210-11, 213, 305
Axon, E, 310

Backus, Isaac, 251
Bagshaw, Edward, 50, 211
Bagshaw[e], William, 19, 127, 129, 131, 237
Baker, Daniel, 3
Ball, Bryan W, 244
Ball, John, 240
Bampfield, Francis, 73, 316, 334
Banks, John, 330
baptism, 233-34
    of believers, 243-52, 331
    of infants, 16, 234-43, 309, 331
Barbour, Hugh, 47, 232, 330
Barclay, Robert, 177, 232
Barnes, Ambrose, 247
Barret, John, 55, 158
Barrow, Henry, 232

Index

Bartlet, John, 94, 101, 102, 103, 104, 105
Bate, Frank, 20
Bates, William, 3, 20, 28, 41, 42, 56, 63, 87, 157, 278, 321
Baxter, Nathaniel, 279, 280
Baxter, Richard, 3, 4, 20, 28, 38, 41, 48, 49, 54, 62, 68, 73, 79, 81, 82, 86, 87, 90, 94, 95, 97, 98, 100, 104, 113, 114, 118, 123, 128, 129, 130, 138, 140, 141, 155, 158, 161-62, 172, 178, 182, 183, 194, 195, 199, 202, 203, 204, 205, 206, 208, 209, 210, 211, 227, 233, 234, 235, 236, 241-43, 247, 248, 258, 259, 260, 263, 264, 265, 267, 271, 272, 273, 274, 278, 279, 283, 284, 285, 291, 297, 306, 312, 314, 317, 319, 320, 321, 322-23, 331, 332, 333, 335
Bayley, John, 297
Bayly, Charles, 8
Bayly, Lewis, 319, 325
Baynes, Paul, 236
Beard, Thomas, 104
Beaumont, Agnes, 93, 116, 191, 197-98, 252, 253, 262, 301
Becon, Thomas, 238, 266, 270
Beddard, R.A., 15, 19, 28, 39, 40
Beeke, Joel R., 204, 310
Beerman, William, 79, 169
Bellers, John, 325
Bennet, John, 308
Bernard, of Clairvaux, 162, 201, 204
Bernard, Richard, 235
Besse, Joseph, 3, 4, 7, 8, 13, 25, 26, 79, 303, 304, 330, 331
Best, Paul, 190
Bewes, W.A., 330
Biddle, Esther, 182
Biddle, John, 190
Billingsley, John, 272
Birch, Robert, 102
Birch, Samuel, 54, 135-36, 193

Birdwood, James, 49, 53, 60, 158, 164, 178, 196
bishops, the Seven, trial of, 42
Boersma, Hans, 162
Bolde, Samuel, 185
Bolton, Robert, 319
Book of Common Prayer, delay in distribution of, 8-9
books, for children, 310-11
Booth, Lady, 102
Bourne, Immanuel, 266
Bowerman, Edward, 252
Bowles, Edward, 3, 266
Bownd, Nicholas, 227, 270
Boyle, Robert, 215
Bradford, John, 50, 54, 130
Bradshaigh, Sir Roger, 13
Bradstreet, Anne, 195, 213
Braithwaite, William C., 8, 13, 174, 175, 309, 328
Brayshaw, A.N., 309
Breda, Declaration of, 3
Brentnall, J.M. 129
Bridge, William, 20, 64, 108
Brinkworth, E.R.C., 288
Broadhead, Caleb, 104
Brooks, Thomas, 55, 57, 60, 65, 68, 71, 72, 73, 79, 86, 87, 104, 107, 164, 168, 335
Brown, Raymond, 17
Browne, John, 283, 325
Browning, Thomas, 34, 70, 96, 197
Bruce, Thomas, Earl of Ailesbury, 183
Bruen, John, 194, 263, 265
Bryan, John, 333
Buccleuch and Queensberry, Duke of, 37
Bull, Daniel, 10, 79, 264
Bunny, Edmund, 319
Bunyan, John, 4, 5, 24, 35, 47, 51, 52, 53, 56, 65, 66, 67, 70, 74, 75, 76, 77, 80, 81, 85, 86, 88, 89, 90, 93, 98, 99, 101, 106, 107, 108, 109, 110, 112, 113, 114, 116, 117, 122, 123, 126, 127, 128,

129, 130, 131, 132, 135, 137, 140, 146, 150, 151, 159-61, 166, 169, 170-72, 174, 176, 179, 180, 182, 191, 193, 195, 196, 197, 198, 199, 212, 213, 236, 244, 247, 248, 252, 265, 268, 271, 272, 283, 287, 290, 293, 294, 310, 311, 313, 315, 316, 318, 319, 320, 323, 331, 335
Burnet, Gilbert, Bishop, 9
Burrough[s], Edward, 7, 8, 182, 331, 332
Burton, Robert, 140
Burton, Thomas, 8
Bury, Edward, 193, 199, 205, 232, 234
Butler, Henry, 259
Buttall, Samuel, 336
Button, Ralph, 310
Byfield, Nicholas, 200

Calamy, Edmund (1600-1666), 3, 50, 52, 54, 55, 56, 67, 70, 125, 157, 196, 197, 207
Calamy, Edmund (1634-85), 33
Calamy, Edmund (1671-1732), 5, 33, 36, 42, 69, 124, 125, 282, 309, 320
Calvin, John, 85, 130, 234, 238, 270, 277
Campbell, Archibald, Earl of Argyll, 36
Capp, B.S., 5
Cardwell, Edward, 40, 271
Carlson, Eric, 288
Carleton, Guy, Bishop, 155, 292
Carpenter, Edward, 40, 186
Cartwright, Thomas, 235, 236
Caryl, Joseph, 57, 60, 181
Case, Thomas, 63, 102
catechisms, 95, 151, 266, 270-74, 308
Catholic Confirmations, 41
Cawdrey, R., 263
Chadwick, S.J., 11

Charnock, Stephen, 48, 60, 64, 65, 71, 96, 190, 335
Cheare, Abraham, 49, 61, 70, 72, 76, 106, 262, 265, 310, 311, 322
children,
    books for, see Books for children
    destitute, care of, 326
Christ Church, Oxford, deanery of, 39, 42
Chrysostom, John, 123, 199, 201, 256, 276
Churchman, Mary, 100, 101, 104, 316
Clapinson, Mary, 31, 252, 332
Clark, G.N., 329
Clark, John, 251
Clark, R., 4
Clarke, Matthew, 17, 18, 19, 332
Clarke, Samuel, 18, 49, 52, 72, 79, 82, 112, 178, 194, 239, 241, 266, 276
Clarkson, David, 57, 59, 61, 74, 86, 87, 88, 89, 93, 149, 168, 227-31, 335
Claude, Jean, 187, 188
Cleaver, Robert, 263
Cliffe, J.T., 297
Clifton, R., 37
Coale, Joseph, 106
Coale, Josiah, 182
Coates, Charles, 307, 308
Coffey, John, 145, 218
Coleby, Andrew M., 34
Collier, Thomas, 17, 337
Collinges, John, 102
Collins, Hercules, 56, 57, 62, 63, 64, 65, 73, 76, 85, 86, 93, 97, 98, 108, 114, 150, 181, 233, 245, 249, 272, 294-96, 298, 312, 314, 333
Collins, Robert, 52, 56, 65, 78, 79
Collinson, Patrick, 47, 83, 256, 271, 274
Compton Census, 31, 252

Index 365

Compton, Henry, Bishop, 22, 31, 40, 186
Conder, Richard, 111, 116, 315
Condren, C., 14
Confessions of Faith, 323
   Baptist, 32, 323
   Independent, Savoy, 32, 98, 284, 285
   Presbyterian, Westminster, 32, 154, 255
confirmation, public, 241-43
Constantine, Emperor, 136
conventicles,
   numbers present at, 12, 20, 21, 23, 26, 49, 78, 260, 336, 337
Cook, William, 10, 186
Corbet, John, 53, 89, 94, 118, 119, 182
Corbet, Margaret, 276
Cosin, John, Bishop, 5, 23
Cottle, B., 128, 142
court, Royal, conduct at, 13-14
Cousins, A.D., 14
covenants, 98
   personal, 155-57, 273
   corporate, 151-55, 323
Cox, Janice V., 4
Coxere, Edward, 330-31
Cradock, Walter, 129, 210
Crawford, Patricia, 309
Cressy, David, 233, 237
Cripplegate, see *Morning Exercise at*,
Crisp, Samuel, 336
Crodacot, John, 264
Croese, G., 77
Crofton, Zachary, 49-50
Cromwell, Oliver, 4, 5, 14, 63, 104, 269
Crook, John, 78, 174, 180
Crosby, Thomas, 71, 173
Crosley, David, 17
Cross, William, 65, 74
Crouch, William, 303
Culverwell, Ezekiel, 246
Cyprian, of Carthage, 123, 202

d'Adda, Ferdinand, Papal Agent, 41
Danvers, Henry, 233, 248
Davenport, John, 104, 332
Davenport William, 317
Davies, Captain Abraham, 305, 309
Davies, Adrian, 302, 303
Davies, Horton, 129, 183, 187, 227
Davies, Marie-Helene, 183, 187
deaconesses, 325-26
de Krey, Gary S., 34, 35
Delamere, Lord, 207
Dell, William, 122
Dent, Arthur, 319
depression, 140-41, 327-29
Dering, Edward, 271
Dering, Sir Edward, M.P., 21
Dewsbury, William, 112, 181
diaries, journals, keeping of, 104, 105, 116, 119, 143, 182, 197, 207, 211, 256, 258
Diocletian, Emperor, 110
Directions to Preachers (James II), see preachers
discipline, 283-300
Disney, Gervase, 119, 258
Dix, Henry, 278
Dod, John, 95, 263
Doe, Charles, 252, 313, 318, 320
'Dons and Ducklings', 28
Doolittle, Thomas, 155, 183-89, 211, 253, 254, 255, 257-62, 271, 272, 310
Downame, George, 240
Downame, John, 202, 240
Draper [Drapes], Edward, 246, 251, 252
Drowry, Thomas, 108
Duffy, Eamon, 313
Dunch, Lady, 303
Dunton, John, 37
Dyer, William, 49, 58, 69, 119, 145, 157, 158, 159, 178, 192, 193

Earle, Peter, 37
elderly, Quaker homes for the, 324
Eliot, John, 312
Ellis, Henry, 18, 37, 40, 42
Ellwood, Thomas, 7, 331
Erasmus, 177
Eulalia, Spanish martyr, 108
Evans, Arise, 193
Evans, Eifion, 321
Evans, John (Wrexham), 195
Evans, M.J. Crossley, 128, 142
Evans, R.H., 17, 18, 22, 332
Everardt, Job, 278
Ewins, Thomas, 12, 25, 219, 316, 332, 333
Exclusion Crisis, 30-31, 32, 33

Fairclough, Samuel, 194, 275
Fairfax, John, 71
family, spiritual care of, 262-69, 337-8
    worship, see worship,
Fanshaw, Lord, 15
Farthing, John, 278
Federal Theology, see Covenant
Fell, Leonard, 112
Fell, Margaret, 6, 10, 309
Fifth Monarchism, 5, 154
Fincham, Kenneth, 288
Fire, Great (1666), 23, 55, 82, 253
Flavel, John, 47, 57, 58, 79, 80, 99, 101, 103, 104, 105, 108, 109, 115, 148, 162, 163, 167, 234, 264, 310
Fletcher, Anthony, 17, 289
Flew, R. Newton, 177
Fowler, Edward, Bishop, 160, 271
Fownes, George, 38, 316, 327
Fox, George, 3, 6, 13, 34, 76, 77, 78, 82, 86, 111, 112, 118, 124, 128, 129, 159, 170, 181, 188, 233, 272, 309, 316, 324, 326, 328, 335
Foxe, John, 6, 16, 100, 108; see also *Acts and Monuments*

Frankland, Richard, 310
Franklin, Mary, 37, 38, 54, 68, 69, 134, 159, 238-9, 266
Franklin, Robert, 37, 68, 69, 134, 159, 238
Fraser, Antonia, 309
Freeman, Rosemary, 311
Freeman, Thomas S., 52
French Protestants, see Huguenots
Froysell, Thomas, 48, 199, 200
Fry, A. Ruth, 325
Fry, John, 328-29
Fuller, Andrew, 245
Furley, O.W., 30

Gailhard, Jean, 3, 5, 283
Gale, Theophilus, 111, 178, 310
Galpin, John, 18, 65,
Gardiner, Thomas, 308
Gardner, William, 124
Gaunt, Elizabeth, 21
Gee, H., 11
Geree, John, 263
Gifford, Andrew, 316, 327
Gifford, John, 195, 244, 312, 318, 319
Gilling, Isaac, 113
Glass, Norman, 96
Goldie, Mark, 17, 69, 162, 183, 186
Goldwire, John, father and son, 308
Goodwin, John, 151, 190, 218-24, 247
Goodwin, Thomas, 69, 82, 83-85, 115, 132, 134, 135, 136, 137, 151, 213, 215-16, 217, 255, 318, 335
Gordon, Alexander, 19, 82-83, 307
Goring, Jeremy, 7
Gosnold, John, 246, 252
Gouge, Thomas, 49, 58, 59, 98, 104, 209, 273, 321
Gouge, William, 133, 268

Index 367

Grantham, Thomas, 17, 255, 261, 272
Granville, Denis, 30
Graveson, S., 23
Greaves, Richard L., 5, 42, 52, 66, 113, 140, 161, 244, 311
Green, I.M., 4, 15, 270, 273
Greenham, Richard, 203, 263
Greenhill, William, 63, 72, 85
Gregory, H., 4
Grew, Obadiah, 149, 282
Grey, A., 88
Griffith, George, 42
Griffith, John, 30, 60, 245
Grindal, Edmund, Archbishop, 152
Grovier, Kelly, 12
Gwynn, Robin, 186, 187, 330

Hacket, John, Bishop, 14
Hale, Sir Matthew, 39, 104
Hall, Joseph, Bishop, 55, 200, 213, 214
Halley, Robert, 102, 297
Halyburton, Thomas, 211
Hanmer, Jonathan, 243
Hardcastle, Thomas, 51, 56, 57, 59, 67, 69, 71, 81, 97, 150, 155, 179, 261
Harley, David, 328
Harris, Robert, 227
Harris, Tim, 13, 16, 21, 30, 66, 288
Harris, William, 25
Harrison, John, 282
Harrison, Thomas, 5
Hart, A. Tindal, 40
Hartupp, Sir John, 196
Hartus, George, 4
Hatton, Viscount, 36
Henchman, Humphrey, Bishop, 18
Henning, B.G., 15
Henry, John, 239
Henry, Katharine, 212, 239
Henry, Matthew, 28, 38, 44, 145, 195, 237, 239, 264, 267, 337
Henry, Philip, 9, 10, 11, 17, 18, 23, 24, 26-27, 29, 35, 38, 44, 96,
101, 109, 110, 111, 114, 116, 120, 123, 127, 129, 137, 145, 146, 157, 162, 181, 185, 195, 199, 207, 211, 212, 228, 235, 237, 256, 261, 264, 265, 266, 267, 269, 273, 275, 277, 280, 285, 310, 313, 314, 321
Hewson, Thomas, 194
Heywood, Oliver, 3, 17, 20, 24-25, 26, 27, 29, 33, 34, 38, 54, 56, 71, 79, 87, 115, 116, 119, 122, 124, 132, 135, 137, 142, 143, 156, 193, 208, 256, 257, 260, 261, 265, 266, 279, 281, 282, 307, 310, 312, 315, 317, 334, 338
Hickes, George, 185
Hickes, John, 26
Hickman, Henry, 307
Hieron, John, 154
Hildersam, Arthur, 247, 256
Hilton, J.A., 41
Hilton Gang, 66, 68, 183, 184
Hinde, William, 194, 265
Hoby, Lady Margaret, 115
Hockaday, F.S., 288
Holcroft, Francis, 17, 21, 56, 98, 101, 111, 116, 145, 152, 315, 316, 318
Holdsworth, W.S., 39
Holifield, E.B., 234
Holland, Thomas, 282
Hollingworth, John, 323
Hollingworth, Richard, 95
Hollinworth, Richard, Lancashire Presbyterian, 114
Holmes, Clive, 303
Holmes, Geoffrey S., 83
Holmes, Obadiah, 251
Hooke, William, 332
Hopper, A., 11
Horne, John, 219
Horton, R.F., 320
Houghton, Lady Margaret, 297
Houghton, Lady Sarah, 297
Howard, Sir Robert, 39

Howe, John, 4, 5, 9, 20, 33, 41, 42, 89, 90, 117, 118, 123, 163, 217-18, 264, 315-6, 320
Howgill, Francis, 6, 8, 182
Hughes, George, 61, 70, 81, 82, 96, 97, 105, 106, 107, 109, 302, 323
Hughes, Obadiah, 70
Hughes, Philip Edgcumbe, 51
Huguenots, 27, 36, 39, 40, 66, 103, 104, 174, 183-8, 330
Hulse, Edward, 306
Hunt, Arnold, 252
Hunt, Jeremiah, 332
Hunter, Joseph, 169
Hutchinson, Colonel John, 316
Hutchinson, Lucy, 275-76
Hutton, Ronald, 11, 13, 15

Imitation of Christ, 203
imposition of hands, 244
Ince, Peter, 111, 124
Indulgence, Declaration of
   Charles II (1672), 27-29, 191
   James II, first (1687), 41
   second, 42
infant mortality, 47, 238, 239
informers, 12, 19, 24, 25, 26, 30, 35, 58, 66, 69, 112
Ingram, Martin, 289
intercession, 133-34
Ironsides, Gilbert, Bishop, 25
itinerancy, 17-18, 19, 20, 87, 128, 208, 315, 317
Ivimey, Joseph, 32, 57, 106, 327

Jackson, Arthur, 196
Jackson, Thomas, 307, 308
Jacombe, Thomas, 20, 61, 65, 73, 264, 332
James, Samuel, 70, 99, 101, 105, 116, 128, 316
Janeway, James, 28, 102
Jeake, Samuel, 37, 115-16, 274
Jeffreys, Judge George, 37, 38, 111

Jenkyn, William, 62, 69, 109, 123, 173
Jennings, Thomas, 249
Jerome, 177, 201
Jessey, Henry, 245, 310, 322, 329
Johnson, Hester, 321-22
Johnson, John, 321-22
Johnstone, H., 288, 289
Jolly, Thomas, 33, 34, 43, 111, 125, 126, 127, 133, 157, 240, 241, 292, 297, 317
Jones, John, 269
Jones, R. Tudur, 50
Josselin, Ralph, 111, 119, 130, 185, 252
judgments on oppressors, 110-13

Kaufmann, U. Milo, 215
Keach, Benjamin, 21, 66, 71, 99, 151, 152, 173, 234, 244, 311, 335, 336
Keach, Elias, 152
Keach, Jane, 173
Keeble, N.H., 6, 118, 161, 316
Keeling, Sir John, Justice, 130
Kenyon, John, 32
Kidd, B.J., 263, 270
Kidder, Richard, Bishop, 9
Kiffin, William, 71, 211, 233, 244, 247, 248, 251, 274, 279
King, Lawrence, 245, 305
Knollys, Hanserd, 71, 152, 311
Knott, John R., 52
Knowles, John, 190
Kreitzer, Larry J., 211, 245, 302, 305, 309

Lacey, D.R., 14
Lamb, Philip, 52, 55, 67, 79, 124, 149, 150
Land, Richard D., 337
Langdale, Josiah, 128, 193
Langley, A.S., 233
Larkham, George, 19, 285
Laud, William, 254, 266, 271

Index 369

Laudian oppression, 100, 214
Lawson, Thomas, 325
legislation, repression, not disastrous, 334-38
Leigh, Peter, 282
L'Estrange, Roger, 38
letters, pastoral importance of, 321-3
Levine, D., 302, 305
Leyburn, John, Catholic Bishop, 41
Lim, Paul C.H., 233
Liu, Tai, 218
Lloyd, Arnold, 329
Loe, Thomas, 174
Lord's Supper, 147, 154, 155, 157, 172, 182, 183, 184, 201, 232, 234, 243, 244, 252-62, 273, 283, 297, 309, 332
Love, Christopher, 63
Love, Harold, 14
Lowe, Roger, 101, 128, 192, 208, 261, 278-79, 280, 304, 305, 324
Loveman, Elizabeth, 309
Luther, Martin, 124, 164, 171, 177, 263, 270, 295
Luttrell, N., 32, 40, 42, 113
Lye, Thomas, 79, 143, 169, 180, 264

Macdonald, Michael, 140, 328
Machin, John, 211, 279, 280, 312, 322
Macintyre, A., 39
Mack, Phyllis, 303
Maclure, Millar, 266
Magdalene College, Oxford, presidency of, 39-40, 42
Maidwell, John, 70, 126, 134, 287
Maisters, Joseph, 332
Mall, Thomas, 154
Manton, Thomas, 3, 25, 28, 61, 63, 85, 86, 232, 335
Marsden, Jeremiah see Ralphson, Zachary [alias],
Marshall, Walter, 237

Martindale, Adam, 5, 103, 280, 297
Marvell, Andrew, 23
Mather, Increase, 104
Matthews, A.G., 12, 98, 306
Matthews, Daniel, 212
Maurice, Henry, 17, 128, 142, 315
Maurice, Matthias, 70, 96
Mayle [Maile], Edmund, 304, 305
Mayor, Stephen, 252
McGee, J. Sears, 160
Mclachlan, H.J., 190
Mead, Matthew, 18, 43, 65, 79, 119, 308, 317, 320
Mead, Richard, 308
meditation,
  occasional, 209-15
  outdoors, 208
  preparing the mind for, 208-209
  Puritan doctrine of, 204
meeting-houses,
  building of, 253, 337
  plundering of, 12, 26, 33, 57, 254
  raiding of, 183, 259
melancholy, see Depression
Melanchthon, Philip, 54
Mendelson, Sara, 309
Metcalfe, T., 278
Meyerstein, E.H.W., 329, 331
Midgley, Graham, 311
Miller, G.C., 297
Miller, John, 3, 9, 35, 36, 39, 41
Milton, John, 16, 17, 196, 201, 215, 218, 283, 290
Milward, John, 15
Mitchell, William, 17, 315
Monmouth Rebellion, 35-38, 105, 111, 260
Moore, Joseph, 3, 50, 51, 88
More, E., 218-19
More, John, 271
Morning Exercise at Cripplegate, 10, 157, 232, 259

Morrice, Roger, 32, 34, 36, 37, 38, 39, 40, 41, 42, 43, 44, 52, 71, 82, 162, 185, 187, 332
Mortimer, Russell, 326, 329, 330
Morton, Charles, 310
Morton, Richard, 306
Mullett, Michael, 6, 41

Nantes, Edict of, 36
Nero, Emperor, 136
Newcome, Henry, 11, 20, 29, 102, 104, 121, 127, 132, 138, 204, 205, 207, 211, 277, 279, 280, 281, 282, 307, 312, 322, 325
Newcomen, Matthew, 31, 264
Newton, George, 123, 124, 264
Nicholson, F., 11, 310
Nicholson, William, Bishop, 22, 23
Norcott, John, 245, 246
Norman, John, 316
Nowell, Alexander, 271
Nuttall, Geoffrey F., 21, 54, 77, 113, 122, 136, 150, 152, 156, 190, 194, 210, 219, 244, 301, 321

Oates, Titus, 32, 37, 307
occasional meditation, see meditation
Ormonde, Duke of, 5, 12, 35
Overton, J.H., 42
Owen, John, 17, 68, 73, 98, 103, 114, 130, 145, 152-3, 154, 158, 190, 195, 196, 199, 216, 218, 238, 271, 273, 278, 290, 298, 299, 302, 303, 335

Packer, J.I., 321
Paget, Thomas, 264, 265
Palke, Thomas, 307
Palmer, Thomas, 316
Parisian massacre, 103, 104
Parnell, James, 303
Pasfield, Robert, 194
Patient, Thomas, 248, 250-51

Patrick, Symon [Simon], Bishop, 4
Peacock, John, 304
Pearse, Edward, 34
Penington, Isaac, 181, 320
Penn, William, 124, 174-78, 303, 324, 335
Penney, Norman, 6, 7, 13, 182
Pepys, Samuel, 4, 5, 11, 21, 268
Perkins, William, 94, 95, 231, 235, 236, 240, 247, 255, 257, 263, 265, 267, 319
Perrot, John, 8, 93, 106
Persons [Parsons], Robert, 319
Philpot, John, 130
Piggott, John, 314
Plague, Great (1665), 18, 55, 58, 71, 97, 125, 205, 251
plots
   Northern, 11
   Popish, 30, 32, 154
   Rye House, 34, 35, 66
Polhill, Edward, 47, 50, 51, 106, 107, 312
Pollock, F., 39
Poole, Matthew, 20, 266
poor, practical help for, 23, 268, 303, 323-26
Popple, William, 23
Porter, Joseph, 155
Porter, Robert, 72
Powell, Thomas, 307
Powell, Vavasor, 47, 50, 53, 57, 58, 61, 64, 67, 81, 89, 95, 96, 129, 167, 252, 319
Powicke, F.J., 162, 331
Powys, Earl of, 38,
prayer,
   corporate, 134, 260, 272
   delayed answers to, 136
   difficulties regarding, 135-44
   outdoors, 127, 128
   personal, 115-44
   unanswered, 135-38
preachers, directions to (James II), 40

Preston, John, 99, 125, 202, 257, 258, 282
Pringle, Walter, 211
prison,
   conditions in, 6, 7, 8, 10, 12, 13, 49, 106, 182
   preaching, in and from, 316, 334
   school in, 308-309
prisoners, care of, 306, 326-27
   literature for, 321
   substitutes for, 7-8
   visiting of, dangerous, 327
Prosser, Enoch, 336
Pruett, J.H., 4, 11, 288
Punchard, William, 106
Purnell, Robert, 219, 333

Quick, John, 9, 316

Rainbow, Edward, Bishop, 23
Ralphson, Zachary [alias of Jeremiah Marsden], 73
Ranew, Nathanael, 201, 205, 206, 208
Ratcliffe, John, 272
Reay, Barry, 3, 288, 289
recreation, importance of, 202
Reeve, John, 168
repetitions, 10, 11, 207, 274-82
Reresby, Sir John, 14, 29, 42
Reynolds, Edward, Bishop, 3, 23
Richards, R.D., 75
Richards, Thomas, 29
Richardson, Christopher, 307
Richardson, R.C., 289
Richardson, Thomas, 13
Rigge, Ambrose, 8, 52, 65, 180
Rivers, Isabel, 161, 310
Robbins, Caroline, 19
Roberts, A.O., 47, 232, 330
Roberts, H.D., 337
Rogers, Henry, 9, 33, 183, 316
Rogers, John, 151, 207
Rogers, Nehemiah, 236
Rogers, P.G., 5

Rogers, Richard, 202, 203
Rogers, Thomas, 203
Rogerson, Joseph, 155
Root, Timothy, 25, 26
Rous, Margaret, 309
Rowntree, Joshua, 325
Rumbold, Richard, 34, 35
Runyon, David, 47
Rutherford, Samuel, 47, 68, 145, 146
Ryther, John, 102, 103

sacraments, 231-62
Sagar, Charles, 33
Saltmarsh, John, 129
Samm, John, 78
Sancroft, William, Archbishop, 42, 55, 183
Sansom, Oliver, 193, 312, 318, 320
Saturday, preparation for public worship, 264
Saunders, Julius, 53
Savage, Sarah, 119, 213, 273, 275
schools, 305-309
Schuking, Levin L., 263
Scott, David, 302
Seaton, John, 307
Seaward, Paul, 12, 15, 34, 39
Seddon, Robert, 73
self-examination, 115-122, 200
sermons,
   taking notes of, 207
   farewell, ejected ministers, 10, 54, 73, 124, 163, 192, 200, 253, 263, 278
Seymour, St. John D., 251
Sharp, John, Archbishop, 40
Sharp, Thomas (son), biographer, 40
Sharp, Thomas, Leeds minister, 50, 169
Shaw, Samuel, 97, 125, 307
Sheils, W.J., 302
Sheldon, Gilbert, Archbishop, 12, 14, 18, 19, 21, 22, 23, 31, 271
Sheldon, Sir Joseph, 31

Shelton, T., 278
Shelton, W., 278
Sherlock, Richard, 271
Sherman, Edward, 307
Shower, John, 33, 126
Shute, Giles, 234
Shuttlewood, John, 18
Sibbes, Richard, 113, 122, 128, 145, 209, 217, 319, 320
Simmons, J., 20
Simon, W.G., 28
Simpson, Charles R., 325
Singleton, Thomas, 307, 308
Slate, Richard, 317
Slater, Samuel jr., 190
Sleigh, Anthony, 19
Smith, Joseph, 7, 47
Smythies, William, 186
Snell, Beatrice S., 292, 325, 326, 329
Solemn League and Covenant, 6, 7, 8
Spaeth, Donald A., 288
Spalding, Ruth, 74
Sparke, Michael, 267
Spooner, Lawrence, 70, 128
Spufford, Margaret, 47, 288, 301, 302, 315, 320
Spurr, John, 14, 28, 161, 162, 252, 289
Spurstowe, William, 214
Stanford, Charles, 316
Steele, Richard, 48, 110, 120, 280, 314-15, 319
Stevenson, W., 302, 303, 304, 305
Stockton, Owen, 18, 30, 58, 71, 116, 117, 157, 167, 168, 239, 241, 265, 266, 271, 272, 276
Stone, Lawrence, 238
Stoupe, Jean-Baptiste, 188
Strype, John, 322
Stubbs, Henry, 168
Stucley, Lewis, 154
Sutch, Victor D., 19
Sutherland, Martin, 5

Swaim, Kathleen M., 311
Swatland, A., 14
Swift, Jonathan, 215
Swinnock, George, 48, 49, 50, 53, 55, 58, 59, 60, 62, 65, 68, 71, 77, 97, 106, 122, 133, 143, 157, 203, 291, 319

Tanner, William, 330
Tarrey [Terrey], Thomas, 306, 307
Taverner, Philip, 308
Taylor, Edgar, 71,
Taylor, Jeremy, Bishop, 160
Taylor, Nathaniel, 193
Taylor, Thomas [1576-1632], 211, 263, 267
Taylor, Thomas, ejected minister, 307
Tenison, Thomas, 252
Tertullian, 79
thanksgiving, importance of, 132-33, 135
Thomas, Roger, 28, 42
Thomas, William, 130, 199, 200, 201, 232, 256, 276, 277, 282
Thompson, John, 292-93, 316
Thompson, Thomas, 78
Thoresby, Ralph, 33, 36, 43, 52, 169, 190, 208, 256, 278, 279
Thorne, George, 158
Thorpe, Edmund, 307
Tibbutt, H.G., 111, 116, 318
Tidmarsh, Richard, 305
Till, Barry, 288
Tillotson, John, Archbishop, 238
Tisdale, Thomas, 305
Toland, John, 218
Tolmie, Murray, 251
Tomlyns, Samuel, 48, 159, 173
Tong, W., 33
Towerson, Gabriel, 271
Towgood, Stephen, 259, 262
transportation, 13, 181
travellers, practical help for, 329-31

Index 373

Trescot, Thomas, 151, 273
Trosse, George, 113, 131, 261
Turner, G. Lyon, 82
Turner, Richard, 308
Turner, William, 104
Tutchin, John, 26, 37
Tyndale, William, 177, 263

Udall, John, 275
Underwood, T.L., 233
Urwick, W., 264, 332
Ussher, James, Archbishop, 115, 124, 207

Vaughan, F.J., 41
Vaughan Henry, 95
Veal, Edward, 310
Venner, Thomas, 5, 6, 106
Venning, Ralph, 219
Vernon, George, 17
Vincent, Nathaniel, 27, 47, 50, 64, 71, 72, 76, 97, 138-42, 149, 153, 157, 164, 168, 193, 201, 312
Vincent, Thomas, 27, 125, 175, 194
von Rohr, J., 236, 239

Wadsworth, Thomas, 259, 332, 336
Wait, Thomas, 306
Walker, Austin, 66, 173, 311
Walker, J., 11
Walker, John, 282
Walker Obadiah, 39
Walker, Williston, 238
Wallace, Ronald S., 234
Walsham, Alexandra, 112
Walter, Lucy, 35
Walton, Thomas, 309
Ward, Seth, Bishop, 20, 23, 307, 316
Watkins, B., 302, 304, 327
Watson, Thomas, 10, 26, 28, 49, 60, 67, 73, 94, 97, 109, 110, 111, 113, 114, 116, 119, 121, 151, 168
Watts, Isaac, 301
Watts, Michael, 333
Webb, Nathaniel, 308
Webster, Tom, 119
Weeks, John, 316
Wells, Samuel, 117, 121, 322
Wesley, John, 16
Westcott, B.F., 324
Westmacot, William, 308
Whitaker, William, 26
White, B.R., 32, 127, 128, 152, 251
White H.C., 268
Whitehead, George, 7
Whitelocke, Bulstrode, 10, 54, 73, 74
Whiteman, Anne, 31, 252, 271
Whiting, C.E., 11
Whitley, W.T., 152
Whitlock, John, 56
Wigfield, W.M., 37
Wilcox, Daniel, 272
Wilkins, D., 21, 22, 31
Wilkins, John, Bishop, 23
Williams, Daniel, 155, 211, 253, 254
Williams, G.H., 233
Williams, J.A., 39
Williams, J.B., 38, 195
Williams, Sheila, 30
Williamson, Sir Joseph, 28
Windeatt, E., 234
Wilson, John F., 154
Wilson, Joseph, 326
Wilson, Walter, 190, 251, 253, 254, 272
Wilson, William, 308
Winney, Samuel, 307
Wishart, George, 124
withdrawal, of God, seeming, 142-43
Wood, Anthony, 36, 43, 245
Woods, James, 279
Woodward, Hezekiah, 309

Woolley, Richard, 308
worship,
    family, 38, 262-9
    public, 228-31
Worthington, John, 271
Wren, Matthew, Bishop, 100
Wrightson, Keith, 302, 305

Wyans, Edward, 305
Wycliffe, John, 51, 52
Wykes, David L., 21, 22, 169, 185, 310, 334, 335, 337

Young, Thomas, 264
Yuille, J. Stephen, 203

www.ingramcontent.com/pod-product-compliance
Lightning Source LLC
Chambersburg PA
CBHW071438300426
44114CB00013B/1482